The Nassi/Levy SPANISH THREE YEARS WORKBOOK

Stephen L. Levy

Head, Foreign Language Department
Roslyn (New York) Public Schools

Robert J. Nassi

Former Teacher of Spanish
Los Angeles Valley Junior College
Los Angeles, California

Please visit our Web site at:

www.amscopub.com

When ordering this book, please specify either **R 470 W** or
the NASSI/LEVY SPANISH THREE YEARS, Workbook Edition

AMSCO SCHOOL PUBLICATIONS, INC.
315 Hudson Street / New York, N.Y. 10013

With grateful acknowledgment to the coauthors,
Bernard Bernstein
Theodore F. Nuzzi

A la memoria de mis queridos padres por su inspiración, su apoyo y su amor.

S.L.L.

Please visit our Web site at:

www.amscopub.com

Cover photograph of Medellín, Colombia by H. Kanus/Shostal Associates.

Preface

The NASSI/LEVY SPANISH THREE YEARS is designed to give students a comprehensive review and thorough understanding of the elements of the Spanish language and the highlights of Hispanic culture. Abundant and varied exercises help students master each phase of the work.

ORGANIZATION

For ease of study and reference, the book is divided into seven Parts. Parts One to Four are organized around related grammatical topics. Part Five covers the culture of Spain and Part Six the culture of Spanish America. Both cultural parts treat language, geography, history, life-style, science, literature, music, art, and architecture. Part Seven provides materials for comprehensive practice and testing of the speaking, listening, reading, and writing skills.

GRAMMAR

Each grammatical chapter deals fully with one major grammatical topic or several closely related ones. Explanations of structure are brief and clear. All points of grammar are illustrated by many examples, in which the key elements are typographically highlighted.

A book intended for third-level review of Spanish assumes that students have completed a basic sequence. Care has been taken, however, especially in the critical *Part One: Verbs*, to avoid the use of complex structural elements that are treated in other parts of the book. To enable students to concentrate on the structural practice, the vocabulary has been carefully controlled and systematically "recycled" throughout the grammatical chapters.

In order to enrich the scope of the book, a number of grammatical elements not usually found in books of this type are included. Among these elements are common expressions with verbs (Chapter 16), common expressions with prepositions (in Chapter 20), common adverbial expressions (Chapter 21), and fractions (in Chapter 23).

EXERCISES

For maximum efficiency in learning, the exercises directly follow the points of grammar to which they apply. Carefully graded, the exercises proceed from simple assimilation to more challenging manipulation of elements and communication. To provide functional continuity of a grammatical topic, the exercises are set in contexts. Many are also personalized to stimulate student response.

While the contents of the exercises afford extensive audiolingual practice, the book's format also encourages reinforcement through written student responses, including English to Spanish exercises intended to sharpen composition skills. The grammatical chapters conclude with Mastery Exercises, in which all grammatical aspects in the chapter are again practiced in recombinations of previously covered elements. All directions to exercises are in Spanish.

FLEXIBILITY

The topical organization and the integrated completeness of each chapter permit the teacher to follow any sequence suitable to the objectives of the course and the needs of the students. This flexibility is facilitated by the detailed table of contents at the front of the book and the comprehensive grammatical index at the back. Teachers as well as students will also find the book useful as a reference source.

CULTURE

The cultural chapters in Parts Five and Six are entirely in Spanish. Every effort was made to keep the narratives clear and readable. In addition to their wealth of cultural information, these narratives provide extensive reinforcement of structural and syntactical elements reviewed in Parts One through Four. To encourage students to read for comprehension with minimal interference from footnote referencing, footnoted meanings have been limited to unusual words and idioms. These footnotes are keyed by number to the text line in which the footnoted element occurs. Each cultural chapter includes exercises designed to test comprehension.

OTHER FEATURES

The Appendix features complete model verb tables and the principal parts of common irregular verbs, along with basic rules of Spanish punctuation and syllabication. Spanish-English and English-Spanish vocabularies and a comprehensive Index complete the book.

The NASSI/LEVY SPANISH THREE YEARS is a thoroughly revised and updated edition. With its comprehensive coverage of the elements of Spanish, clear and concise explanations, extensive practice materials, functional vocabulary, and readable cultural narratives, the book will help students strengthen their skills in the Spanish language. As students pursue proficiency, they will also gain valuable insights into the cultures of the Hispanic world.

Thanks are due to our consultants who reviewed substantial parts of the manuscript and made valuable suggestions: Dr. Linda L. Lesack, George Washington High School, Philadelphia, PA; Dr. Marta E.B. Perez, Farmingdale (NY) High School; Mr. Albert R. Turner, Glenbrook South High School, Glenview, IL; and Dr. Alan D. Weiner, Beverly Hills (CA) High School.

PART TWO
Nouns; Pronouns; Prepositions

PART THREE
Adjectives; Adverbs; Numbers

PART FOUR
Other Structures

PART FIVE
Civilization: Spain

PART SIX
Civilization: Spanish America

PART   SEVEN
Comprehensive Testing:
Speaking, Listening, Reading, Writing   *484*

PART

ONE

VERBS

Present Tense

1. Regular Verbs

The present tense of regular verbs is formed by dropping the infinitive ending (**-ar**, **-er**, **-ir**), and adding the following endings:

cantar:	**cant**	*-o, -as, -a, -amos, -áis, -an*
vender:	**vend**	*-o, -es, -e, -emos, -éis, -en*
recibir:	**recib**	*-o, -es, -e, -imos, -ís, -en*

Ejercicio A

La familia Gómez cuenta lo que hace cuando es el cumpleaños de alguien en México: Escriba lo que ellos dicen:

EJEMPLO: Ellos / tocar un disco
Ellos tocan un disco.

1. Yo / comprar una tarjeta _____

2. Los tíos / mandar flores _____

3. La madre / preparar un pastel _____

4. Nosotros / buscar un regalo _____

5. Tú / cantar las Mañanitas _____

6. Los amigos / llamar por teléfono _____

7. La abuela / organizar una cena _____

Ejercicio B

Los niños hablan de lo que hacen en la escuela. Escriba lo que dicen. Siga el ejemplo del Ejercicio A:

1. yo / abrir las ventanas _____

2. María / no correr en el patio _____

3. Los alumnos / comer en la cafetería _____

4. Tú / recibir buenos informes _____

5. Nosotros / aprender la lección _____

6. La maestra y yo / vivir cerca de la escuela _____

7. Ellos / escribir la tarea _____

Ejercicio C

En su casa todos ayudan con los quehaceres. Escriba lo que hace cada persona, usando las sugerencias:

SUGERENCIAS: pasar la aspiradora, lavar las ventanas, sacudir los muebles, barrer el piso, usar el lavaplatos, arreglar las camas, sacar la basura

1. Mi madre _____

2. Mi padre _____

3. Mis abuelos _____

4. Mi hermana _____

5. Yo _____

6. Mis hermanos y yo _____

2. Verbs Irregular in the Present Tense

The following verbs are irregular only in the first person singular of the present tense:

caber (*to fit, to be room for*): *quepo*, **cabes, cabe, cabemos, cabéis, caben**

caer (*to fall*): *caigo*, **caes, cae, caemos, caéis, caen**

conocer (*to know, to be acquainted with*): *conozco*, **conoces, conoce, conocemos, conocéis, conocen**

Like **conocer:**

aborrecer *to hate, to loathe*
agradecer *to thank*
aparecer *to appear*
carecer *to lack*
crecer *to grow*
desaparecer *to disappear*

desconocer *to be ignorant of*
establecer *to establish*
estremecerse *to shudder*
merecer *to deserve*
nacer *to be born*
obedecer *to obey*

ofrecer *to offer*
parecer *to seem*
permanecer *to remain*
pertenecer *to belong*
reconocer *to recognize*

dar (*to give*): *doy*, **das, da, damos, dais, dan**

hacer (*to make, to do*): *hago*, **haces, hace, hacemos, hacéis, hacen**

Like **hacer: deshacer** (*to undo*); **satisfacer** (*to satisfy*)

poner (*to put, to set*): *pongo*, **pones, pone, ponemos, ponéis, ponen**

Like **poner:**

componer *to compose*
disponer *to dispose*
exponer *to expose*

imponer *to impose*
oponer(se) *to oppose*
proponer *to propose*

saber (*to know*): *sé*, **sabes, sabe, sabemos, sabéis, saben**

salir (*to go out*): *salgo*, **sales, sale, salimos, salís, salen**

traducir (*to translate*): *traduzco*, **traduces, traduce, traducimos, traducís, traducen**

   Like **traducir: conducir** (*to conduct, to lead*); **producir** (*to produce*); **reducir** (*to reduce*)

traer (*to bring*): *traigo*, **traes, trae, traemos, traéis, traen**

   Like **traer: atraer** (*to attract*)

valer (*to be worth*): *valgo*, **vales, vale, valemos, valéis, valen**

ver (*to see*): *veo*, **ves, ve, vemos, veis, ven**

   NOTE: Most verbs ending in **-cer** or **-cir** and having a vowel directly before the **c,** change the **c** to **zc** in the first person singular (see **conocer** and **traducir**).

   EXCEPTIONS: **decir** (*digo*), **hacer** (*hago*), **cocer** (*cuezo*)

   IMPORTANT: Irregular verbs that change **c** to **zc** are identified in the vocabulary lists by **zc** in parentheses after the verb: **conocer (zc).**

Ejercicio D

Usted trata de recordar lo que oyó en unos diálogos breves. En cada diálogo, complete las frases, usando la forma correcta del verbo de la primera frase:

EJEMPLO: —Yo **voy** al cine.
   —¿_____**Va**_____ Alicia al cine contigo?
   —Sí, ¿_____**vas**_____ tú también?

1. —¿**Traen** Concha y Federico sus discos?

    —Sí, y yo _____ mis discos también.

    —Tú siempre _____ los mismos discos.

2. —¿Qué **hacen** Uds. esta noche?

    —Yo no _____ nada, pero Alicia _____ la tarea.

    —¡Tú nunca _____ nada!

3. —¿Dónde **ponemos** las maletas?

    —Yo siempre las _____ en la alcoba.

    —Enrique las _____ cerca de la puerta.

4. —¿Dónde **establecen** Uds. su casa?

    —Yo _____ mi casa en Los Angeles.

    —Y nosotros _____ la nuestra en Chicago.

5. —¿**Sabe** Ud. a qué hora termina la película?

    —Yo no _____ a qué hora termina.

    —Entonces nosotros no _____ si debemos entrar.

6. —¿**Da** Ud. una propina al mozo?

    —Yo siempre le _____ una propina.

    —Casi todos nosotros le _____ propinas.

7. —¿**Conoces** tú a ese chico?

    —No, yo no lo _____.

    —Nosotros no lo _____ tampoco.

8. —¿Quién **propone** esta fiesta?

    —El que la _____, necesita dinero.

    —Pues, yo no _____ nada.

9. —Nosotros **obedecemos** las leyes siempre.

    —¡Ja! Tú nunca _____ las leyes.

    —Antes no, pero ahora sí, yo las _____.

10. —¿Cuánta gente **cabe** en tu carro?

    —Creo que _____ seis personas.

    —Si no van dos personas, entonces _____ yo.

Ejercicio E

Ud. recibió esta carta de un amigo que está estudiando en Chile. Complete la carta con la forma correcta de los verbos dados en paréntesis:

Querido amigo/Querida amiga,

Yo _____ mucho tu carta. Aquí te cuento algunas noticias mías. Ahora yo
    1 (agradecer)

_____ a un club deportivo. Varios amigos míos _____
    2 (pertenecer)   **3 (pertenecer)**

al mismo club también y me _____ que voy a divertirme mucho. El club
                                 4 (parecer)

_____ muchas actividades y _____ abierto hasta
    5 (ofrecer)   **6 (permanecer)**

muy tarde todos los días. Yo _____ de las escuela a las dos y media y voy
                                 7 (salir)

al club. Yo me _____ la ropa deportiva y _____
             8 (poner)   **9 (hacer)**

muchos ejercicios. Ya _____ a muchos jóvenes y ahora nosotros
                             10 (conocer)

_____ planes para ir a Viña del Mar. Cuando regreso a casa yo
    11 (hacer)

_____ las tareas. Yo _____ que te gustaría esta vida.
    12 (hacer)   **13 (saber)**

No _____ de nada y yo me _____ cuando
    14 (carecer)   **15 (estremecer)**

recuerdo mi apatía antes de hacer el viaje. Es una experiencia que _____
                                                              16 (valer)

la pena. Hasta pronto y saludos.

3. Other Verbs With Irregular Forms in the Present Tense

decir (*to say, to tell*): *digo, dices, dice*, decimos, decís, *dicen*

estar (*to be*): *estoy, estás, está,* estamos, estáis, *están*

haber (*to have*): *he, has, ha,* hemos, **habéis,** *han*

ir (*to go*): *voy, vas, va,* vamos, vais, van

oír (*to hear*): *oigo, oyes, oye,* **oímos, oís,** *oyen*

ser (*to be*): *soy, eres, es,* somos, sois, son

tener (*to have*): *tengo, tienes, tiene,* tenemos, tenéis, *tienen*

> Like **tener:**
>
> | | |
> |---|---|
> | **contener** *to contain* | **mantener** *to maintain* |
> | **detener** *to detain* | **obtener** *to obtain* |
> | **entretener** *to entertain* | **sostener** *to sustain* |

venir (*to come*): *vengo, vienes, viene,* venimos, venís, *vienen*

Ejercicio F

Después de ver una película policíaca, Ud. y varios amigos creen que oyen ruidos. Escriba lo que dicen:

> EJEMPLO: Tú / oír gritos
> **Tú dices** que **oyes** gritos.

1.   Sarita / oír disparos _____

2.   Carlos y yo / oír pasos _____

3.   Los hermanos / oír voces _____

4.   Yo / oír suspiros _____

5.   Tú / oír música _____

6.   Elena y Clara / oír una sirena _____

Ejercicio G

Escriba lo que estas personas dicen que tienen y lo que van a hacer:

> EJEMPLO: Pedro / tener hambre / ir a comer
> **Pedro tiene** hambre y **va** a comer.

1.   Claudia / tener sed / ir a tomar un refresco

_____

2.   Ellos / tener sueño / ir a dormir

_____

3.   Tú / tener dolor de cabeza / ir a tomar una aspirina

_____

4.   Mi hermano y yo / tener calor / ir a nadar

_____

5.   Yo / tener suerte / ir a jugar la lotería

_____

Ejercicio H

Ud. regresa de un viaje a la América del Sur y le ayuda al agente de inmigración en el aeropuerto. Ud. le dice de dónde son los turistas que llegan. Escriba de dónde son estas personas:

EJEMPLO: Este señor / ser de Colombia.
Este señor es de Colombia.

1.   Yo / ser de los Estados Unidos

_____

2.   Estos niños / ser de Chile

_____

3.   Esta señora / ser de Bolivia

_____

4.   El joven / ser de México

_____

5.   Esta muchacha y yo / ser de los Estados Unidos

_____

Ejercicio I

Hay una fiesta en el gimnasio de la escuela. Escriba a qué hora viene cada persona al gimnasio:

EJEMPLO: Silvia / 6:30
Silvia *viene* a las seis y media.

1.   Pablo / 8:00 _____

2.   Tú / 7:15 _____

3.   Carmen y Ana / 7:45 _____

4.   Yo / 6:00 _____

5.   Roberto y yo / 6:25 _____

6.   Ustedes / 8:10 _____

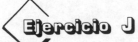

Ejercicio J

Escriba dónde están sus amigos durante el verano:

> EJEMPLO: Alfredo / en el campo
> **Alfredo está** en el campo.

1.   Ricardo / en España _____

2.   Yo / en la ciudad _____

3.   Tú / en el mar _____

4.   Paula y Esteban / en la escuela _____

5.   Los hermanos López / en la granja _____

Ejercicio K

Ud. cuida a dos niños mientras sus padres salen. Usando las sugerencias, escriba cinco frases para describir lo que pasa:

> SUGERENCIAS: Yo   oír los gritos de los niños
> Los niños   venir a las once
> Sus padres   no tener sueño
> Los vecinos   estar en la sala
> La niña   ser bueno(a)
> Los niños y yo   ir a mirar la televisión

1.   _____

2.   _____

3.   _____

4.   _____

5.   _____

Ejercicio L

Ud. habla con un alumno extranjero en la escuela. Conteste las preguntas que él le hace:

1.   ¿Adónde van tú y tus amigos los fines de semana?

_____

2.   ¿Qué tienes ganas de hacer esta noche?

_____

3.   ¿Qué haces cuando estás aburrido?

_____

4.   ¿Por qué dices que tus amigos son simpáticos?

_____

5.   ¿Cuál es el primer ruido que oyes por la mañana?

_____

6.   ¿A qué hora vienen tus amigos?

_____

7.   ¿Dónde están ellos ahora?

_____

4. Uses of the Present Tense

a. The present tense may have the following meanings in English:

Pablo *sale.*	*Paul leaves (is leaving).*
Van **a casa.**	*They go (are going) home.*
¿Estudia **Ud. español?**	*Do you study Spanish?*
No *hablo* **español.**	*I do not speak Spanish.*

b. The present tense is often used instead of the future to ask for instructions or to refer to an action that will take place in the immediate future:

¿Lo *pongo* **aquí?**	*Shall I put it here?*
¿Qué *hacemos* **ahora?**	*What shall we do now?*
Llamo **más tarde.**	*I'll call later.*
Después *comemos.*	*We'll eat afterwards.*

c. The construction **hace** + an expression of time + **que** + the present tense is used to express an action or event that began in the past and continues in the present. In such situations, the question is expressed by **¿Cuánto tiempo hace que** ...? + the present tense or **¿Hace cuánto tiempo que** ...? + the present tense:

Hace un año que *vivo* **aquí.**	*I have been living here for a year.*
Hace una hora que *esperamos.*	*We have been waiting for an hour.*
¿Cuánto tiempo hace que Ud. *trabaja*?	*How long have you been working?*

NOTE: The present tense + **desde hace** + an expression of time is also used to express a past action or event that continues in the present. In such situations, the question is expressed by **¿Desde cuándo** ...? + the present tense:

Vivo **aquí desde hace un año.**	*I have been living here for a year.*
¿Desde cuándo *trabaja* **Ud.?**	*How long have you been working?*

Ejercicio M

Ud. le cuenta a un amigo desde cuándo Ud. hace o no hace varias cosas. Escriba las frases según los ejemplos:

EJEMPLOS: montar a caballo (seis años)
Hace seis años que monto a caballo.
Monto a caballo **desde hace seis años.**

no ir a un museo (dos meses)
No voy a un museo **desde hace dos meses.**
Hace dos meses que no voy a un museo.

1.   estudiar el español (cuatro años)

_____

_____

2.   aprender a conducir (tres meses)

_____

_____

3.   no jugar con el equipo de béisbol (dos años)

_____

_____

4.   no pasar la Navidad en Puerto Rico (cinco años)

_____

_____

5.   vivir en esta casa (diez años)

_____

_____

6.   no comer un helado (una hora)

_____

_____

7.   salir con esos amigos (dos semanas)

_____

_____

Ejercicio N

A Ud. no le gusta hacer las cosas en el momento. Escriba cuándo va a hacer estas cosas, usando las expresiones siguientes:

hoy por la tarde (noche, mañana)	más tarde
esta noche (tarde, mañana)	después
	mañana

EJEMPLO: ir a la biblioteca
Voy a la biblioteca **más tarde.**

1.   arreglar el cuarto _____

2.   preparar la tarea _____

3.   ayudar a su hermano _____

4.   leer una novela _____

5.   estudiar para el examen _____

6.   devolver los libros a la biblioteca _____

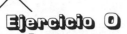 **Ejercicio O**

Ud. pasa el verano en un campamento y acaba de conocer a unos jóvenes. Escriba las preguntas que Ud. les hace para saber desde cuándo hacen ellos estas cosas:

>   EJEMPLO: venir a este campamento
>   **¿Cuánto tiempo hace que** Uds. **vienen** a este campamento?
>   **¿Desde cuándo vienen** Uds. a este campamento?

1. saber remar _____

_____

2. pescar _____

_____

3. practicar el esquí acuático _____

_____

4. conocer a estas muchachas _____

_____

5. salir juntos _____

_____

6. ser amigos _____

_____

7. hacer excursiones _____

_____

◆ MASTERY EXERCISES ◆

Ejercicio P

Conteste las preguntas que le hace un primo acerca de la escuela:

1. ¿Saludan Uds. al profesor al entrar en la clase?

_____

2. ¿Dónde pones tus libros en la escuela?

_____

3. ¿Debes estudiar mucho?

_____

4. ¿A qué hora salen Uds. de la escuela?

_____

5. ¿Pasas mucho tiempo charlando con tus amigos?

_____

6. ¿Tienes que trabajar después de las clases?

_____

7. ¿Eres un buen alumno (una buena alumna)?

_____

8. ¿Qué haces el día antes de un examen?

_____

9. ¿Cuánto tiempo hace que no preparas una tarea?

_____

10. ¿Qué hacen Uds. cuando el profesor está ausente?

_____

Ejercicio Q

Ud. está en una fiesta y ve que un amigo suyo está agitado porque la persona que él invitó a la fiesta no le hace caso. Escriba las preguntas que Ud. hace, según las respuestas dadas:

EJEMPLO: **¿Cuánto tiempo hace que sales con ella?**
Hace diez días que salgo con ella.

1. _____

Están juntos desde hace dos horas.

2. _____

Hace una hora y media que bailan juntos.

3. _____

Yo la conozco desde hace un mes.

4. _____

Hace dos días que él tiene interés en conocerla.

5. _____

Estoy agitado desde hace una hora más o menos.

Ejercicio R

Escriba lo que Ud. le dice a un amigo cuando bajan del autobús escolar:

EJEMPLO: I'll see you later.
Te veo después.

1. Will you help me with the assignment?

_____

2. I'll be in your house at 7:00 P.M.

_____

3. I'll bring my textbooks.

   _____

4. Will you have the new magazine at home?

   _____

5. Will we listen to the Julio Iglesias record tonight?

   _____

6. We'll study later.

   _____

7. I'll call you in fifteen minutes

   _____

Ejercicio S

Hace una hora que Ud. espera a un amigo que no llega. Escriba una nota que Ud. le deja en la puerta, en la cual le dice lo siguiente:

you are furious because you have been waiting for him/her for an hour;
you do not understand why he/she is not here;
he/she always arrives on time;
you do not deserve this;
will he/she call you to explain;
you will not be at home until 8:00 P.M.

_____

_____

_____

_____

_____

_____

_____

_____

_____

_____

Present Tense of Stem-Changing Verbs

1. Stem-Changing Verbs Ending in *-ar* and *-er*

Stem-changing verbs ending in **-ar** or **-er** change the stem vowel in the present tense as follows:

e to **ie**	in all forms except for those for
o to **ue**	**nosotros** and **vosotros**

pensar (*to think*): **pienso, piensas, piensa, pensamos, pensáis, piensan**

querer (*to want, to love, to wish*): **quiero, quieres, quiere, queremos, queréis, quieren**

mostrar (*to show*): **muestro, muestras, muestra, mostramos, mostráis, muestran**

volver (*to return, to come or go back*): **vuelvo, vuelves, vuelve, volvemos, volvéis, vuelven**

Like **pensar:**

acertar *to hit the mark, to guess right*
apretar *to tighten, to squeeze; to be tight*
atravesar *to cross*
cerrar *to close*
comenzar *to begin, to commence*
confesar *to confess*
despertar(se) *to awaken; (to wake up)*
empezar *to begin*

encerrar *to lock in; to contain*
gobernar *to govern*
helar *to freeze*
nevar *to snow*
quebrar *to break*
remendar *to patch, to mend*
sentar(se) *to seat, (to sit down)*

Like **querer:**

ascender *to ascend; to promote*
defender *to defend*
descender *to descend*

encender *to light; to ignite*
entender *to understand*
perder *to lose*

Like **mostrar:**

acordarse (de) *to remember*
acostar(se) *to put to bed, (to go to bed)*
almorzar *to eat lunch*
contar *to count; to tell*
costar *to cost*
encontrar *to find, to meet*

jugar (u to ue) *to play (games, sports)* *
recordar *to remember*
renovar *to remodel, to renew*
tronar *to thunder*
volar *to fly*

Like **volver:**

conmover *to move (emotionally)*
devolver *to return, to give back*
doler *to pain, to ache*
llover *to rain*
mover *to move*

oler (o to hue) *to smell*
poder *to be able*
resolver *to solve; to resolve*
soler *to be in the habit of, to be accustomed to*

---

*The verb **jugar** is conjugated as follows: **juego, juegas, juega, jugamos, jugáis, juegan.**

Ejercicio A

¿Qué hace su familia? Escriba lo que hace cada persona:

EJEMPLO: Mi mamá / despertar a mi papá
Mi mamá despierta a mi papá.

1. Mi papá / leer el periódico

   _____

2. Mis hermanos / cerrar las puertas

   _____

3. Yo / empezar a estudiar

   _____

4. Mi abuelo / contar su dinero

   _____

5. Nosotros / descender al comedor

   _____

6. Tú / contar un chiste

   _____

Ejercicio B

¿Qué hacen estas personas? Escriba lo que hace cada persona:

EJEMPLO: Raúl / atravesar la calle
Raúl atraviesa la calle.

1. El jefe / ascender a los empleados _____
2. La mamá / remendar los calcetines _____
3. Los jóvenes / almorzar en la cafetería _____
4. Tú y yo / resolver el problema _____
5. Sarita / encontrar una novela buena _____
6. Tú / devolver el regalo _____
7. Juan y Eduardo / contar el dinero _____
8. Rafael y yo / defender a los niños _____
9. Yo / comenzar a trabajar _____
10. Los actores / conmover al público _____

Ejercicio C

Ud. llama al Cine Real para obtener información. Complete las frases con la forma correcta del verbo:

Señorita: Buenas tardes, Cine Real. ¿En qué _____ ayudarle?
1 (poder)

Usted: Buenas tardes. ¿ _____ Ud. darme alguna información, por favor?
2 (poder)

Señorita: Sí, cómo no. ¿Qué _____ Ud. saber?
3 (querer)

Usted: ¿A qué hora _____ la función?
4 (comenzar)

Señorita: La función _____ a las 5:10, las 7:30 y las 9:50.
5 (empezar)

Usted: ¿Y cuánto _____ las entradas?
6 (costar)

Señorita: Cada entrada _____ cuatro pesos.
7 (costar)

Usted: ¿Y a qué hora _____ la taquilla?
8 (cerrar)

Señorita: Las taquillas _____ quince minutos después de la última función.
9 (cerrar)

Usted: Debemos apresurarnos. Nosotros _____ llegar tarde.
10 (soler)

Señorita: Sí, deben apresurarse. Es una lástima si Uds. se _____ esta película.
11 (perder)

Mucha gente _____ verla y a veces la cola _____ a
12 (querer)   13 (comenzar)

formarse una hora antes. Pero Uds. _____ comprar las entradas para
14 (poder)

cualquier función.

Usted: Gracias, señorita. Yo _____ su consejo muy útil.
15 (encontrar)

Señorita: De nada. Adiós.

Ejercicio D

Conteste las preguntas que le hace un joven chileno que visita su escuela:

1. ¿Atraviesas varias calles para llegar a la escuela?

_____

2. ¿Juegan Uds. al ajedrez?

_____

3. ¿A qué hora te despiertas los sábados?

_____

4. ¿Dónde almuerzan tú y tus amigos todos los días?

_____

5. ¿Suelen Uds. ir al cine?

_____

6. ¿Entiendes el francés?

_____

7. ¿Recuerdas mi número de teléfono?

_____

8. ¿Dónde te encuentro el sábado?

_____

2. Stem-Changing Verbs Ending in -ir

Stem-changing verbs ending in **-ir** change the stem vowel in the present tense as follows:

e to **ie**	
o to **ue**	in all forms except those for **nosotros** and **vosotros**
e to **i**	

consentir (_to consent_): **consiento, consientes, consiente, consentimos, consentís, consienten**

dormir (_to sleep_): **duermo, duermes, duerme, dormimos, dormís, duermen**

pedir (_to ask for, to request_): **pido, pides, pide, pedimos, pedís, piden**

Like **consentir:**

advertir _to notify, to warn_
convertir _to convert_
divertirse _to enjoy oneself, to have a good time_
hervir _to boil_
mentir _to lie_

preferir _to prefer_
referir _to recount; to refer_
sentir _to regret, to feel sorry_
sentirse _to feel (well, ill)_

Like **dormir:**

dormirse _to fall asleep_

morir(se) _to die_

Like **pedir:**

despedirse (de) _to take leave (of), to say goodbye (to)_
gemir _to groan, to moan_
impedir _to prevent_
medir _to measure_
reír(se) _to laugh_

reñir _to quarrel, to scold_
repetir _to repeat_
servir _to serve_
sonreír(se) _to smile_
vestir(se) _to dress (oneself)_

NOTE:

1. The verb **adquirir** (_to acquire_) is like **consentir: adquiero, adquieres, adquiere, adquirimos, adquirís, adquieren.**

2. The verb **reír** (and **sonreír**) has an accent mark over the letter **i** in all forms: **río, ríes, ríe, reímos, reís, ríen.**

 **Ejercicio E**

Escriba el pasatiempo que prefiere cada persona:

EJEMPLO: Manuel / el béisbol
Manuel **prefiere** el béisbol.

1.   Sofía / el tenis _____

2.   Tú / el fútbol _____

3.   Eduardo y Carlos / el volibol _____

4.   Yo / la natación _____

5.   Luz y yo / las damas _____

6.   Ricardo / el ajedrez _____

7.   Mi padre / el dominó _____

Ejercicio F

¿Dónde duermen estas personas? Escriba dónde duerme cada persona:

EJEMPLO: Yo / en casa de mi amigo
Yo **duermo** en casa de mi amigo.

1.   Mi madre / en el sofá _____

2.   Lola / en la hamaca _____

3.   Mi abuelo / en el sofá _____

4.   Los niños / en el coche _____

5.   Yo / en la sala _____

6.   Tú / en el comedor _____

7.   Rafael y yo / en el patio _____

Ejercicio G

Escriba a quién riñe cada persona:

EJEMPLO: Los padres / a sus hijos
Los padres riñen a sus hijos.

1.   Yo / a mi hermanito _____

2.   La profesora / a los alumnos _____

3.   El jefe / a los trabajadores _____

4.   Tú / a tu perro _____

5.   Nosotros / a nuestros amigos _____

6.   Clara y Luis / a su gato _____

Ejercicio H

¿Cómo reaccionan estas personas? Escriba lo que hacen, usando la forma correcta del verbo indicado:

EJEMPLO: Pablo y Lourdes no entienden la tarea. (pedir ayuda al profesor)
Por eso Pablo y Lourdes **piden** ayuda al profesor.

1. María quiere comprar tela para hacer cortinas nuevas. (medir las ventanas)

_____

2. Yo preparo té para mi mamá. (hervir el agua)

_____

3. Los señores están en México y necesitan pesos, pero sólo traen dólares. (convertir los dólares en pesos)

_____

4. La policía está en la esquina porque hay un accidente automovilístico. (impedir el paso)

_____

5. Carlos habla con su abuelo pero él no oye bien. (repetir las frases)

_____

6. Tú preparas la cena y toda tu familia está en la mesa. (servir la cena)

_____

7. Tú quieres usar el coche pero tus padres dicen que no. (reñir con ellos)

_____

8. Todo el mundo escucha un chiste que Rafael cuenta. (reír a carcajadas)

_____

9. Encontramos un ladrón en casa. (advertir a la policía)

_____

10. Alfonso quiere pasar la noche en casa de un amigo. (pedir permiso a sus padres)

_____

11. El payaso es muy bueno. (divertir mucho a los niños)

_____

12. El señor lee el termómetro. La temperatura está en 20°F. (sentir frío)

_____

13. La fiesta termina y los jóvenes se van a casa. (decir adiós)

_____

14. Mi padre está muy cansado y hay un programa aburrido en la televisión. (dormir en el sillón)

_____

15. La madre mira el reloj y cree que van a llegar tarde. (vestir a su hijito rápidamente)

_____

3. Verbs Ending in *-uir*

In verbs ending in **-uir** (except **-guir**),* a **y** is inserted after the **u** in all forms except those for **nosotros** and **vosotros**:

huir (*to flee*): **huyo, huyes, huye, huimos, huís, huyen**

Like **huir**:

concluir *to conclude, to end*   **distribuir** *to distribute*
construir *to construct*   **incluir** *to include*
contribuir *to contribute*   **influir** *to influence, to have influence*
destruir *to destroy*   **sustituir** *to substitute*

Ejercicio 1

Escriba lo que pasa en cada dibujo. Use los verbos **concluir, construir, contribuir, distribuir, destruir:**

EJEMPLO:

Carlos construye una casa de muñecas.

1.

Los obreros _____
_____

3.

La señora _____
_____

2.

La película _____
_____

4.

Carmen _____
_____

*See Chapter 3, page 26.

5.

Elías _____

_____

6.

El niño _____

_____

Ejercicio J

¿Qué hacen estas personas al ver un tigre en la calle? Escriba lo que hacen:

EJEMPLO: Pedro
Pedro huye al ver un tigre.

1. Los niños _____

2. Carolina _____

3. Yo _____

4. Roberto y yo _____

5. Tú _____

6. El señor _____

7. Todo el mundo _____

Ejercicio K

La emisora WABO pide contribuciones para los pobres. Escriba las respuestas que da el locutor en una entrevista:

1. ¿Qué contribuye Ud.?

    _____

2. ¿Qué contribuye el público?

    _____

3. ¿Quién distribuye las cosas?

    _____

4. ¿Sobre quiénes influyen Uds.?

    _____

5. ¿Cuándo concluye este proyecto?

    _____

4. Verbs Ending in *-iar* and *-uar*

Some verbs ending in **-iar** or **-uar** stress the **i** or the **u** (**í, ú**) in all forms except those for **nosotros** and **vosotros**. In the **vosotros** form the **a** takes an accent mark.

enviar (*to send*): **envío, envías, envía, enviamos, enviáis, envían**

continuar (*to continue*): **continúo, continúas, continúa, continuamos, continuáis, continúan**

Like **enviar:**

confiar (en) *to rely (on), to confide (in)*   **guiar** *to guide*
espiar *to spy*   **resfriarse** *to catch cold*
fiarse (de) *to trust*   **variar** *to vary*

Like **continuar:**

actuar *to act*   **graduarse** *to graduate*

NOTE: All stem-changing verbs are identified in the vocabulary lists by the type of change (**ie, ue, i, y, í, ú**) after the verb: **pensar (ie).**

Ejercicio L

En una reunión familiar, las tías hablan de sus hijos. Escriba lo que ellas dicen:

EJEMPLO: Roberto / graduarse de la secundaria
Roberto se gradúa de la secundaria.

1.   Clarisa / graduarse de la primaria

_____

2.   Los gemelos / graduarse de la universidad

_____

3.   Pilar / graduarse de la preparatoria

_____

4.   Elena /graduarse de la escuela de belleza

_____

5.   Jorge y Javier / graduarse de la Facultad de Leyes

_____

Ejercicio M

En el consultorio del médico, Ud. responde a las preguntas que le hace el médico:

1.   ¿En qué estación se resfría Ud. más fácilmente? (en el invierno)

_____

2.   ¿De qué tipo de medicina se fía Ud.? (las aspirinas)

_____

3.   ¿Cuándo varía Ud. su dieta? (los fines de semana)

_____

4.   ¿Adónde envía Ud. estas formas? (a la compañía de seguros)

_____

5.   ¿En quién confía Ud.? (en los buenos amigos)

_____

◆ MASTERY EXERCISES ◆

Ejercicio N

Usted va a presentar este anuncio en una emisora. Complete las frases con la forma correcta de los verbos:

¿_____ Ud. una comida sabrosa que no _____ mucho? Si Ud.
    1 (querer)   **2** (costar)

_____ al Restaurante Dos Caminos, Ud. y sus invitados _____
    3 (venir)   **4** (encontrar)

todo lo mejor. Una comida completa _____ sólo ciento cincuenta pesos e
                                    5 (costar)

_____ el café y la propina. En el Restaurante Dos Caminos nosotros
    6 (incluir)

_____ la comida desde la una y media y la cocina no _____
    7 (servir)   **8** (cerrar)

hasta las cinco todos los días. Ud. no _____ encontrar un lugar mejor. Nuestros
                                      9 (poder)

meseros _____ a los clientes con cortesía y _____ la comida
          10 (atender)   **11** (servir)

rápidamente. Uds. _____ bien cuando _____ al Restaurante
               12 (acertar)   **13** (venir)

Dos Caminos que _____ en la esquina de la calle Dolores y la Avenida Juárez.
          14 (encontrarse)

Uds. no _____ reservación.
       15 (requerir)

Ejercicio O

Usted está en una zapatería y se prueba zapatos. Conteste las preguntas que le hace el dependiente:

Dependiente: ¿Le puedo mostrar algo?

Ud: (*Tell him that you want to try on these black shoes.*)

_____

Dependiente: ¿Qué número calza Ud.?

Ud: (*Tell him to measure your foot.*)

_____

Dependiente: ¿Cómo los siente?

Ud: (*Tell him that they are tight.*)

_____

Dependiente: ¿Le muestro otro par de zapatos?

Ud: (*Ask him to show you the blue pair.*)

_____

Dependiente: ¿Se refiere Ud. a éstos?

Ud: (*Tell him that yes, you want to try those on.*)

_____

Dependiente: ¿Cuál de los dos prefiere Ud.?

Ud: (*Tell him which pair you prefer.*)

_____

Dependiente: ¿Quiere Ud. otra cosa?

Ud: (*Ask him the price.*)

_____

Dependiente: Cincuenta y cinco dólares.

Ud: (*Tell him that you prefer a less expensive pair.*)

_____

Dependiente: Lo siento. Ahora no tenemos nada más barato.

Ud: (*Thank him and tell him that you will return next week.*)

_____

Ejercicio P

En una carta que Ud. escribe a un amigo por correspondencia que vive en Costa Rica, Ud. le explica cómo es el invierno en el norte de los Estados Unidos. Escriba las frases en español:

1. In the winter it snows a lot and the lakes freeze over.

_____

2. It also rains often and the rain freezes too.

_____

3. The trees are very pretty because they are dressed in white.

_____

4. The weather influences the things people do.

_____

5. The children play in the snow and they cross the streets on sleighs.

_____

6. My father lights a fire in the fireplace, and we sit in front of it when we return home from school.

_____

_____

7. Many people prefer to stay at home if they are unable to go out in their car.

_____

8. In reality, they lock themselves in their houses.

_____

9. Many people flee from the cold and travel south.

_____

10. My grandparents prefer the warm weather, and they usually go to Arizona.

_____

_____

11. When it snows a lot and the snow measures 6 or 8 inches, they close the schools.

_____

_____

12. I will graduate from high school next year and I want to live in a warm climate.

_____

_____

13. What place do you recommend?

_____

14. We return to school tomorrow.

_____

15. When do they close the schools in Costa Rica?

_____

Spelling Changes in the Present Tense

Verbs with changes in spelling are not truly irregular. The spelling change occurs before certain letters in order to preserve the original sound in accordance with the rules for Spanish pronunciation.

1. Verbs Ending in *-cer* or *-cir*

In verbs ending in **-cer** or **-cir**, **c** changes to **z** before **o** or **a**:

vencer (*to conquer, to overcome*): **ven*z*o, vences, vence, vencemos, vencéis, vencen**

> Like **vencer: convencer** *to convince*
> **ejercer** *to exert, to exercise, to practice (a profession)*

2. Verbs Ending in *-ger* or *-gir*

In verbs ending in **-ger or -gir**, **g** changes to **j** before **o** or **a**:

dirigir (*to direct*): **diri*j*o, diriges, dirige, dirigimos, dirigís, dirigen**

> Like **dirigir:**
>
> | | |
> |---|---|
> | **afligir** *to afflict, to grieve* | **fingir** *to pretend* |
> | **coger** *to seize, to grasp, to catch* | **proteger** *to protect* |
> | **escoger** *to choose, to select* | **recoger** *to gather, to pick up* |
> | **exigir** *to demand, to require* | |

3. Verbs Ending in *-guir*

In verbs ending in **-guir, gu** changes to **g** before **o** or **a**:

distinguir (*to distinguish*): **distin*g*o, distingues, distingue, distinguimos, distinguís, distinguen**

> Like **distinguir: extinguir** *to extinguish*

NOTE:
1. Some verbs with spelling changes also have stem changes. (See Chapter 2, pages 14 and 17.) Some verbs of this type are:

cocer (*to cook*): *cuezo, cueces, cuece,* **cocemos, cocéis,** *cuecen*

> Like **cocer: torcer** *to twist, to turn*

corregir (*to correct*): *corrijo, corriges, corrige,* **corregimos, corregís,** *corrigen*

> Like **corregir: elegir** *to elect, to choose*

seguir (*to follow, to continue*): *sigo, sigues, sigue,* **seguimos, seguís,** *siguen*

Like **seguir:** **conseguir** *to get, to obtain, to succeed in*
perseguir *to pursue, to persecute*
proseguir *to continue, to proceed*

2. Verbs ending in **-car**, **-gar**, and **-zar** have no spelling changes in the present tense. Changes occur only in the preterite (see Chapter 4), in commands (see Chapter 16), and in the present subjunctive (see Chapter 13).

3. Verbs with spelling changes are identified in the vocabulary lists by the type of change (**z, j, g**) in parentheses after the verb: **vencer (z).**

Ejercicio A

Usando las sugerencias, escriba a quién convencen estas personas:

SUGERENCIAS: a los niños   a mis padres
a su jefe   al juez
al enfermo   a tu hermano
a los alumnos   a nuestros amigos

EJEMPLO: El médico
El médico **convence a los enfermos.**

1. El abogado _____

2. Yo _____

3. Los padres _____

4. Roberto y yo _____

5. El maestro _____

6. Tú _____

Ejercicio B

Escriba la profesión que ejercen estas personas, usando las sugerencias:

SUGERENCIAS: salvavidas / abogado / dentista / profesor / carpintero / dependiente / enfermera

EJEMPLO: María cuida a los enfermos en el hospital.
María ejerce la profesión de enfermera.

1. Yo trabajo en un almacén y vendo ropa de niños.

Yo _____

2. Mi padre enseña a los alumnos.

Mi padre _____

3.   Elena defiende a los criminales en la corte.

     Elena _____

4.   Mi tío arregla los dientes de muchas personas.

     Mi tío _____

5.   Pablo y yo cuidamos a los nadadores en la playa.

     Pablo y yo _____

6.   Tú construyes muchas cosas de madera.

     Tú _____

Ejercicio C

Unos amigos están en una tienda de deportes. Mire cada dibujo y escriba lo que escogen las personas:

EJEMPLO:

Pilar escoge un guante de béisbol.

1.

Alberto _____

_____

3.

Elena y Ana _____

_____

2.

Tú _____

_____

4.

Yo _____

_____

5.

Sarita y yo _____

_____

Ejercicio D

¿Qué hacen las personas cuando no quieren hacer algo? Escriba lo que fingen estas personas en cada situación:

> EJEMPLO: David no quiere sacar la basura. (estar ocupado)
> **David finge estar ocupado.**

1. Luis no quiere ir a la escuela hoy. (estar enfermo)
   Luis _____

2. Yo no quiero bailar con esa persona. (estar cansado)
   Yo _____

3. La niña no quiere cantar para los invitados. (tener dolor de garganta)
   La niña _____

4. Tú no quieres ayudar a tu papá a las ocho de la mañana. (estar dormido)
   Tú _____

5. Mi abuelo no me contesta cuando le pido dinero. (ser sordo)
   Mi abuelo _____

6. Lisa y yo no contestamos cuando nuestros amigos nos llaman. (estar distraídos)
   Lisa y yo _____

Ejercicio E

*¿Es todo igual? En cada frase escriba la forma correcta de **distinguir** para mostrar si todo es igual o no:*

1. Rafael le habla de «tú» a la profesora de español.

   Él no _____ entre «tú» y «Ud.».

2. ¿Ves bien cuando no hay luz?

   No, en la oscuridad yo no _____ nada.

3. ¿Es éste un suéter verde o marrón?

   Nosotros no _____ los colores.

4. En ese cine el precio de las entradas es igual para todo el mundo.

   Ellos no _____ entre los adultos y los niños.

5. Mis hermanitos son gemelos.

   Nadie _____ quién es Ramón y quién es Raúl.

Ejercicio F

Le entrevistan a Ud. sobre sus impresiones de su escuela para un artículo en el periódico escolar. Conteste las preguntas que le hacen:

1. ¿Quién corrige las faltas en su clase de español?

   _____

2. ¿Quién convence a los estudiantes para que estudien más?

   _____

3. ¿Distinguen los profesores entre los alumnos preparados y los que no están preparados?

   _____

4. ¿Eliges tú los cursos que sigues?

   _____

5. ¿Cómo consiguen Uds. sacar buenas notas?

   _____

6. ¿Exigen los profesores mucho a sus alumnos?

   _____

7. ¿Finges tú estar distraído cuando no quieres contestar en una clase?

   _____

8. ¿Escogen Uds. a sus profesores?

   _____

9. ¿Quién protege los derechos de los estudiantes?

   _____

10. ¿Quién dirige esta escuela?

   _____

◆ MASTERY EXERCISES ◆

Ejercicio G

*En la clase de cocina, Silvia siempre quiere hacer lo mismo que hacen los otros alumnos.
Escriba lo que ella dice:*

EJEMPLO: Tú cueces legumbres hoy.
Yo cuezo legumbres también.

1. Javier recoge las habas.

   _____

2. Elena extingue el fuego.

   _____

3. Uds. siguen las instrucciones.

   _____

4. Nosotros corregimos la receta.

   _____

5. Carolina y Luis consiguen platos limpios.

   _____

6. Arturo escoge otra receta.

_____

7. La profesora exige mucho cuidado en la cocina.

_____

Ejercicio H

Exprese en español lo que dicen los candidatos en la campaña para elegir al alcalde del pueblo:

1. The firemen put out all fires.

_____

2. The politicians don't choose their friends for jobs.

_____

3. The police protect the people.

_____

4. I do not protect the criminals.

_____

5. I demand a lot from my employees.

_____

6. The police pursue criminals.

_____

7. The garbage collectors pick up the garbage according to the official schedule.

_____

8. I do not pretend to hear your complaints.

_____

9. We follow your advice.

_____

10. I distinguish between good and bad.

_____

11. You elect the best candidate.

_____

12. We don't twist your arm.

_____

13. We demand support from the people.

_____

Preterite Tense

1. Regular Verbs

The preterite tense of regular verbs is formed by dropping the infinitive ending (**-ar, -er, -ir**), and adding the following endings:

invitar:	invit	*-é, -aste, -ó, -amos, -asteis, -aron*
correr:	corr	⎱
admitir:	admit	⎰ *-í, -iste, -ió, -imos, -isteis, -ieron*

 **Ejercicio A**

Escriba esta descripción de una llamada telefónica que hizo Amelia:

EJEMPLO: Yo / llamar por teléfono a Clara
Yo llamé por teléfono a Clara.

1. Clara / contestar el teléfono

   _____

2. Yo / saludar a Clara

   _____

3. Nosotros / hablar de la fiesta del sábado pasado

   _____

4. Enrique y Carlos / invitar a muchas personas

   _____

5. Sus padres / preparar muchas cosas para comer

   _____

6. Todo el mundo / pasar un buen rato allí

   _____

7. Tú / cantar y bailar mucho

   _____

8. Yo / regresar a casa tarde

   _____

 **Ejercicio B**

Describa cómo pasó el sábado cada persona, usando las sugerencias:

SUGERENCIAS: lavar el carro   limpiar la casa
prepara una cena especial   visitar un museo
trabajar en el jardín   estudiar en la biblioteca
mirar la televisión   contestar unas cartas
guardar la ropa de verano

EJEMPLO: **Sarita visitó un museo.**

1. Mi hermana _____

2. Mi abuela _____

3. Yo _____

4. Mis hermanitos _____

5. Mi madre _____

6. Mi padre _____

7. Mis hermanos y yo _____

8. Tú _____

Ejercicio C

Jorge le cuenta a Carlos sobre el lugar donde Eduardo y él trabajaron durante el verano. Conteste las preguntas que Carlos le hace a Jorge:

1. ¿Dónde trabajaron Uds.? (en el supermercado)

_____

2. ¿Cuánto tiempo pasaron Uds. trabajando allí? (yo/20 horas a la semana; Eduardo/15 horas)

_____

3. ¿Cuánto dinero ganaste tú? (80 dólares)

_____

4. ¿Qué compraste con el dinero? (una bicicleta)

_____

5. ¿Y qué compró Eduardo con su dinero? (una raqueta de tenis)

_____

6. ¿Quién más trabajó allí contigo? (Raquel)

_____

7. ¿A qué hora regresaron Uds. a casa la última noche? (10:00 P.M.)

_____

8. ¿Les gustó el trabajo? (sí)

_____

 **Ejercicio D**

Escriba lo que dicen que pasó el sábado pasado:

EJEMPLO: Claudia / aprender un baile nuevo
Claudia aprendió un baile nuevo.

1. Manuel y Pablo / no asistir a la fiesta

_____

2. Rosita / recibir un carro de sus padres

_____

3. Tú / salir con tus primos

_____

4. Mis padres / vender el automóvil

_____

5. Llover / todo el día

_____

6. Yo / conocer a la novia de mi hermano

_____

7. Mis abuelos / volver de Europa

_____

8. Rocío y yo / correr en una carrera

_____

9. Usted / comer paella por primera vez

_____

10. Juan y Pedro / cumplir dieciséis años

_____

Ejercicio E

Complete la carta que escribe Rogelio sobre su amigo Víctor:

Querido Alberto,

Cuando mi amigo Víctor _____ a pasar el verano en la playa, él
                                    1 (salir)

_____ invitarme a pasar unos días allí con él. Víctor _____ de
2 (prometer)   **3** (decidir)

repente ir a la playa por dos meses. Él _____ su motocicleta para tener dinero
4 (vender)

con qué vivir. Unos amigos suyos le _____ alojamiento con ellos. Víctor
5 (prometer)

_____ a estos amigos el año pasado cuando él _____ a una
6 (conocer)   **7 (asistir)**

reunión de motociclistas. Víctor me _____ una carta y cuando yo la
8 (escribir)

_____ , _____ en seguida. Víctor _____ con
9 (recibir)   **10 (responder)**   **11 (cumplir)**

su palabra. Yo no _____ tiempo. _____ mi ropa en una maleta
12 (perder)   **13 (meter)**

y _____ en seguida. _____ sólo una vez durante mi visita y
14 (salir)   **15 (llover)**

_____ a muchas personas. También yo _____ por toda
16 (conocer)   **17 (correr)**

la playa. Entonces yo _____ por qué le gusta a Víctor la vida de
18 (comprender)

la playa.

Tu amigo,

Rogelio

Ejercicio F

Conteste las preguntas que le hace un amigo sobre su accidente:

1. ¿Cuándo ocurrió el accidente? (hace tres días)

   _____

2. ¿Dónde sucedió? (cerca del estadio)

   _____

3. ¿Qué perdiste en el accidente? (la bicicleta)

   _____

4. ¿Cuándo saliste del hospital? (ayer)

   _____

5. ¿Sufriste mucho después del accidente? (un poco)

   _____

6. ¿Vendieron tus padres tu bicicleta? (Sí)

   _____

7. ¿Cuánto recibieron por ella? (5 dólares)

   _____

8. ¿Prometiste no volver a hacer lo mismo? (Sí)

   _____

Ejercicio G

¿Conoce Ud. a alguna persona que hace muchísimas cosas en un día? Escriba lo que hizo esa persona ayer, usando los verbos indicados:

EJEMPLO: despertar
Mi mamá *despertó* a la familia a las cinco de la mañana.

1. preparar *Mi hermano preparó suyo comida*
2. limpiar *Sophia limpió la cocina despues la sena*
3. trabajar *Fred trabajó in mi officina para dies horas.*
4. salir *Marcos salió de compras las cosas para deseyuno.*
5. asistir *Tu asististe con tu mama in la casa.*
6. volver *Olivia volvió los libros a la biblioteca*
7. escribir *Juan y Julio escribieron una carta a Sammy.*
8. meter *Patty y yo metimos las flores en el florero*
9. mirar *Mi padre miró mi sobrino juega el soccar.*
10. cerrar *Mes hermanas cerraron las puertos con llaves.*

Ejercicio H

Conteste las preguntas que le hace un amigo acerca de una fiesta de sorpresa a la que Ud. asistió:

1. ¿A qué hora llegaste a la fiesta?
    Yo llegué a las siete.

2. ¿Quiénes entraron después?
    Lucy entró despues

3. ¿Cuántos años cumplió tu amigo?
    Roberto cumplió vente-cinco años.

4. ¿Qué regalos recibió?
    El recibió dos CD's y un sombrero

5. ¿Asistieron muchas personas a la fiesta?
    Si, treinte personas asistieron.

6. ¿Quién preparó la comida?
    Maria preparó muchas cosas y Felix preparó las bebides

7. ¿Qué comiste?
    Yo comí birria y ensalada verde

8. ¿Conociste a todos los invitados?
    No, yo conoci Lucy, Maria, Felix y Roberto.

9. ¿Cuándo regresaste a casa?

   Yo regressé a dos horas en la manaña,

10. ¿Llamaste para dar las gracias?

   Sí, yo llamé hoy.

2. Verbs that Change *i* to *y* in the Preterite

Verbs ending in **-er** or **-ir**, and containing a vowel immediately before the ending, change in the third person singular from **-ió** to **yó** and in the third person plural from **-ieron** to **-yeron**. The **i** has an accent mark in all the other forms:

caer:	ca ~) *fall*
creer:	cre } *believe*
leer:	le *read* } -í, -íste, -yó, -ímos, -ísteis, -yeron
oír:	o *hear*
poseer:	pose } *own*

NOTE:
1. Exceptions: **traer, atraer,** and all verbs ending in **-guir**.

2. Verbs that end in **-uir** (**construir, contribuir, distribuir, huir, incluir,** and others) also belong in this group, but no accent appears in the endings **-uiste, -uimos,** and **-uisteis**.

Ejercicio 1

Escriba lo que Ud. ve en estos dibujos, usando los verbos **construir, distribuir, huir, incluir, leer** *y* **oír** *en el pretérito:*

EJEMPLO:

El niño **se cayó** de la bicicleta.

1.

Carmen _leyó una libro_

2.

Los jóvenes _poseyeron una un barco de vela_

3.

El ladrón _huyó de federales_

5.

Los señores _oyeron el avión_

4.

El hombre rico _distribuyo los pesos a los niños_

6.

La cuenta _estuvo muy caro pero no incluyo el vino._

Ejercicio J

Escriba las preguntas que Ud. haría en una entrevista con un científico famoso que acaba de recibir un premio. Use los verbos **concluir, contribuir, creer, influir, leer** *y* **oír:**

EJEMPLO: **¿Dónde *oyó* Ud. la noticia?**

1. ¿ Que contribuyo-ud. al entendimento de esta tema?
2. ¿ Que leyo-ud. in el universidad?
3. ¿ Que persona influyo su trabajo?
4. ¿ Creyo-ud.lo quando ud. oyo el anuncio?
5. ¿ Quando concluyo-isd sus investigaciones?

3. Verbs Ending in *-car, -gar,* and *-zar*

Verbs ending in **-car, -gar, and -zar** change in the first person singular of the preterite as follows:

c changes to **qu**
g changes to **gu**
z changes to **c**

atacar (*to attack*): **ataqué, atacaste, atacó, atacamos, atacasteis, atacaron**

Like **atacar**:

acercarse *to approach*
aplicar *to apply*
arrancar *to root out, to pull out*
buscar *to look for, to seek*
colocar *to place, to put*
comunicar *to communicate*
dedicar *to dedicate, to devote*
educar *to educate*
embarcarse *to embark*
equivocarse *to be mistaken*
explicar *to explain*
fabricar *to make, to manufacture*

indicar *to indicate*
marcar *to designate, to mark*
masticar *to chew*
pescar *to fish*
publicar *to publish*
replicar *to reply; to contradict (argue)*
sacar *to take out*
sacrificar *to sacrifice*
significar *to mean*
suplicar *to beg, to implore*
tocar *to touch, to play (music)*

pagar (*to pay [for]*): **pagué, pagaste, pagó, pagamos, pagasteis, pagaron**

Like **pagar**:

agregar *to add*
ahogarse *to drown*
apagar *to put out, to extinguish*
cargar *to load*
castigar *to punish*
colgar *to hang*
encargar *to put in charge;*
    to entrust; to order (goods)

entregar *to deliver, to hand over*
jugar *to play (games, sports)*
llegar *to arrive*
madrugar *to rise early*
negar *to deny*
obligar *to obligate, to compel*
pegar *to stick, to beat*
rogar *to ask, to beg*

cruzar (*to cross*): **crucé, cruzaste, cruzó, cruzamos, cruzasteis, cruzaron**

Like **cruzar**:

abrazar *to embrace, to hug*
alcanzar *to reach, to overtake*
almorzar *to eat lunch*
amenazar *to threaten*
avanzar *to advance*
comenzar *to begin, to commence*
deslizarse *to slip, to glide*

empezar *to begin*
gozar *to enjoy*
lanzar *to throw*
realizar *to fulfill*
rezar *to pray*
tropezar *to stumble*

Ejercicio K

Escriba lo que estas personas dicen que hicieron anoche: they did last night

EJEMPLO: Yo / pescar en el río
          Yo pesqué en el río.

1. Yo / colocar mi ropa en el armario

     *Yo coloqué mi ropa en el armario*

2.   Yo / buscar *look for* mis zapatos rojos

Yo busqué

3.   Yo / tocar la guitarra

Yo toqué

4.   Yo / comunicar la noticia a mis padres

Yo comuniqué

5.   Yo / fabricar un avión de plástico

Yo fabriqué

6.   Yo / explicar una película a mi hermanito

Yo expliqué

7.   Yo / sacar *empty* la basura

Yo saqué

Ejercicio L

Su hermana busca unos discos en la casa. Conteste las preguntas que le hace:

1.   ¿Dónde colocaste los discos? (en el estante)

Yo coloqué en el estante

2.   ¿Los buscaste allí? (Sí)

Sí, yo busquélos. allí.

3.   ¿Quién los tocó? (yo)

Yo toquélos ayer. los

4.   ¿Cuándo los sacaste del album? (anoche)

Yo saqué el anoche.

5.   ¿Indicaste qué discos perdiste? (no)

No, yo no indiqué.

6.   ¿Cuánto tiempo dedicaste a buscarlos? (toda la mañana)

Yo busquélos toda la mañana.

7.   ¿Los marcaste con tu nombre? (no)

No, yo no marquélos.

Ejercicio M

Esteban explica cómo pasó el día de ayer. Escriba lo que dice:

EJEMPLO: madrugar ayer
Yo madrugué ayer.

1. colgar mi ropa del día anterior

    Yo colgué (hang up)

2. llegar a la escuela temprano

    Yo llegué (arrived)

3. cargar muchos libros

    Yo cargué (loaded)

4. entregar el trabajo en la clase de inglés

    Yo entregué (turned in)

5. encargar a Rosa de la reunión del comité

    Yo encargué jo

6. jugar tenis

    Yo no jugué

7. castigar a mi perro

    Yo castigué

8. apagar la luz a las nueve

    Yo apagué

Ejercicio N

Conteste las preguntas que le hace un amigo acerca de una excursión en que él no participó:

1. ¿A qué hora llegaste a la escuela? (7:30 A.M.)

    Yo llegué a las 7:30

2. ¿Quién se encargó de la excursión? (Roberto)

    Roberto encargó

3. ¿Quiénes cargaron la comida en el autobús? (nosotros)

    Nosotros cargamos

4. ¿A quién le entregaste el boleto? (al chofer)

    Yo entreguélo al chofer

5. ¿Dónde colgaste tu saco? (en el autobús)

    Yo colguélo en el autobús

6. ¿Qué jugaron Uds. en el camino? (las damas)

    Nosotros jugamos las damas

7. ¿Se ahogó alguien en el lago? (nadie)

    No, nadie ahogóse.

8. ¿Te castigaron? (no)

    No, mi castigaron

9. ¿Cuánto pagaste por la excursión? ($25)

   Yo pagué 25

10. ¿Quién se negó a pagar? (tú)

    Si. Tuno pagaste

Ejercicio O

Amelia siempre dice que ella hace lo mismo que sus amigas. Escriba lo que Amelia dice:

EJEMPLO: Claudia empezó una clase de yoga.
Yo también **empecé** una clase de yoga.

1. Sarita abrazó a su abuelo al verlo.

2. Patricia se deslizó en el hielo.

3. Carlota e Inés almorzaron en el restaurante nuevo.

4. Carmen realizó su sueño en el viaje.

5. Lourdes avanzó mucho en el curso.

6. Pilar y tú alcanzaron a nadar cien metros.

7. Yo empecé a leer una novela muy interesante.

8. Mis primas gozaron de la visita.

Ejercicio P

David quiere conocer mejor a un amigo nuevo de Venezuela. Conteste las preguntas:

1. ¿A quién abrazaste antes de salir de Caracas?

2. ¿Con quién almorzaste ayer?

3. ¿Qué clases comenzaste a tomar?

_____

4. ¿Avanzaste mucho en el estudio del inglés?

_____

5. ¿Realizaste un sueño al venir aquí?

_____

6. ¿Gozaste de la ceremonia en la escuela ayer?

_____

7. ¿Empezaste a acostumbrarte a nuestro modo de vivir?

_____

Ejercicio Q

Escriba los verbos que faltan en esta carta que Javier les escribió a sus padres del campamento de verano:

Queridos padres,

No comprendo por qué Uds. me ___obligaron___ a venir a este campamento. Yo
1 (obligar)

___rogué___ mucho pero Uds. no me ___oyeron___ . El consejero que
2 (rogar)   **3** (oír)

___se encargó___ de mi grupo es muy antipático. Cuando yo ___coloqué___ mis
4 (encargarse)   **5** (colocar)

cosas junto a mi cama, él me ___castigó___ . Cuando yo ___colgué___ mi ropa,
6 (castigar)   **7** (colgar)

él la ___sacó___ .
8 (sacar)

Mis compañeros son más o menos simpáticos. Pero ellos ya ___empezaron___ a aburrirme. _(bore me ?)_
9 (empezar)

Ayer Juan y yo ___jugamos___ volibol y ___él perdió___ el partido. El domingo
10 (jugar)   **11** (perder)

pasado unos compañeros y yo ___almorzamos___ en una cafetería cerca del campamento.
12 (almorzar)

Entre los pocos pasatiempos a que ___yo me dediqué___ , me ___gusta___ más la
13 (dedicarse)   **14** (gustar)

pesca. Anteayer Rafael y yo ___pescamos___ en el lago y él ___pescó___ tres
15 (pescar)   **16** (pescar)

peces grandes. Yo sólo ___pesqué___ uno chiquito.
17 (pescar)

Yo sé que Uds. ___realizaron___ un sueño y ___se sacrificaron___ mucho al mandarme
18 (realizar)   **19** (sacrificarse)

aquí. Sin embargo, yo ___me equivoqué___ cuando ___yo escogí___ este lugar. Tengo
20 (equivocarse)   **21** (escoger)

(Nevertheless)

que despedirme porque el consejero ya ___apagó___ las luces.
      22 (apagar)

Su hijo,

Javier

4. Stem-Changing Verbs Ending in -ir

Verbs ending in **-ir** that have a stem change in the present tense also have a stem change in the preterite. In the preterite tense, the stem vowel changes in the third person singular and plural, from **e** to **i** or from **o** to **u**:

> **convertir** (*to convert*): **convertí, convertiste, convirtió, convertimos, convertisteis, convirtieron**
> **servir** (*to serve*): **serví, serviste, sirvió, servimos, servisteis, sirvieron**
> **dormir** (*to sleep*): **dormí, dormiste, durmió, dormimos, dormisteis, durmieron**

NOTE:

1. The verbs **reír** and **sonreír** are conjugated in the preterite as follows:

> **reí, reíste, rió, reímos, reísteis, rieron**
> **sonreí, sonreíste, sonrió, sonreímos, sonreísteis, sonrieron**

2. Verbs ending in **-ir** that have **ñ** directly before the ending (**ceñir, gruñir, reñir**) drop the **i** of the ending in the third person singular and plural (**riñó, riñeron**). Note that, because of the **ñ**, the sound of the ending is still regular.

Ejercicio R

¿Qué hicieron ellos cuando oyeron la noticia? Escriba lo que hizo cada persona cuando oyó la noticia:

> EJEMPLO: María / sonreír
> María **sonrió**.

1. los padres / reñir a los hijos

_____riñeron_____ (scolded)

2. Gabriel / mentir a su madre

_____minió_____

3. Susana / repetir la noticia

_____repitió_____

4. Tú / preferir no estar allí

_____preferiste_____

5. Yo / sentirse mal

_____me sentí_____

6. Beto y Raúl / servir la cena

_____sirvieron_____

7. Juan y yo / vestirse rápidamente

_____ se vistieron _____

8. El abuelo / gruñir

_____ gruñó _____

9. Mi tío / dormirse en el sofá

_____ se durmió _____

10. Uds. / advertir a los demás

_____ advirtieron _____ (they warned everyone)

Ejercicio S

(relatives)

Escriba cuál de sus parientes hizo una de estas cosas ayer durante una reunión en su casa. Use estas sugerencias:

SUGERENCIAS: divertirse mucho (enjoy)
servir los refrescos (serve)
reñir a los nietos (scold)
despedirse de nosotros (to leave)
reírse mucho (laugh)
medir la terraza (to measure)
sonreír dos veces (to smile)
dormirse en la hamaca

1. Mi madre _____ sirvió los refrescos _____
2. Mis padres _____ riñeron a los nietos _____
3. Mi tía _____ sonrió dos veces _____
4. Mis abuelos _____ divirtieron mucho _____
5. Mi primo _____ midió la terraza _____
6. Yo _____ me dormí en la hamaca _____
7. Mis primos _____ se rieron mucho _____
8. Todos mis parientes _____ se despidieron de nosotros _____

5. Verbs Irregular in the Preterite

a. The following verbs have an irregular stem in the preterite. The endings for these verbs are:
-e, -iste, -o, -imos, -isteis, -ieron (-eron if **j** precedes the ending):

walk **andar:** *anduve, anduviste, anduvo, anduvimos, anduvisteis, anduvieron*
to fit into **caber:** *cupe, cupiste, cupo, cupimos, cupisteis, cupieron*
to be **estar:** *estuve, estuviste, estuvo, estuvimos, estuvisteis, estuvieron*
to have **haber:** *hube, hubiste, hubo, hubimos, hubisteis, hubieron*
to do **hacer:** *hice, hiciste, hizo, hicimos, hicisteis, hicieron*
to be able **poder:** *pude, pudiste, pudo, pudimos, pudisteis, pudieron*

to put	poner: *puse, pusiste, puso, pusimos, pusisteis, pusieron*
to want	querer: *quise, quisiste, quiso, quisimos, quisisteis, quisieron*
to know	saber: *supe, supiste, supo, supimos, supisteis, supieron*
to hold	tener: *tuve, tuviste, tuvo, tuvimos, tuvisteis, tuvieron*
to come	venir: *vine, viniste, vino, vinimos, vinisteis, vinieron*

to says, tell

to produce

to bring

decir:	*dije, dijiste, dijo, dijimos, dijisteis, dijeron*
producir:	*produje, produjiste, produjo, produjimos, produjisteis, produjeron*
traer:	*traje, trajiste, trajo, trajimos, trajisteis, trajeron*

b. The verbs **dar**, **ser**, and **ir** are also irregular in the preterite. **Dar** takes the endings of regular -**er**, -**ir** verbs; **ser** and **ir** have the same forms in the preterite:

to give

dar: *di, diste, dio, dimos, disteis, dieron*

to be

to go

ser ⎫
ir ⎬ *fui, fuiste, fue, fuimos, fuisteis, fueron*

NOTE:

1. The third person singular of **hacer** is spelled **hizo.** The **c** changes to **z** to avoid the **k** sound.

2. All compounds of **poner** (**proponer**, etc.), **tener** (**detener**, etc.), **hacer** (**satisfacer**, etc.), **venir** (**convenir**, etc.), and **traer** (**atraer**, etc.) are conjugated in the same manner as the basic verb.

3. All verbs ending in -**ducir** are conjugated like **producir:**

> **conducir** (*to lead, to drive*): *conduje, -iste, -o, -imos, -isteis, -eron*
> **traducir** (*to translate*): *traduje, -iste, -o, -imos, -isteis, -eron*

4. The accent mark is omitted in the preterite forms of **dar, ver, ser,** and **ir.**

Ejercicio T

Después de tener un día libre durante una excursión a Madrid, los compañeros de excursión cuentan cómo pasaron el día. Escriba lo que dijeron:

> EJEMPLO: Yo / andar por El Retiro
> **Yo anduve** por El Retiro.

1. Los señores Castro / ir a una corrida de toros

   _____fueron_____

2. Graciela / hacer una excursión a Toledo

   _____hizo_____

3. Los parientes de Ana / venir a visitarla

   _____vinieron_____

4. Yo / estar en la Plaza Mayor

   _____estuve_____

5. Micaela y yo / ir de compras

   fuimos

6. Tú / querer visitar El Prado

   quisiste

7. Nosotros / poder ver una tuna

   pudimos

8. Gerardo y Pablo / estar en el estadio

   estuvieron

9. Yo / querer conocer el metro

   quise

10. La señorita Álvarez / andar por la Gran Vía

    anduve

11. Ellos / ver una zarzuela

    vieron (operetta)

12. Sofía / poder conseguir boletos para el teatro

    pudo

13. Tú / ir a una tertulia

    fuiste (gathering, salon)

14. Elena / querer ir al Valle de los Caídos

    quiso

15. El guía / ponerse a descansar

    me puse (se puso) put me to sleep

Ejercicio U

You have just returned

Ud. acaba de volver a casa después de pasar el fin de semana en casa de un amigo que vive en otra ciudad. Escriba diez frases, usando las sugerencias, que describan sus actividades durante el fin de semana:

SUGERENCIAS:　ir al cine (teatro, circo, etc.)
　　　　　　　　hacer empanadas
　　　　　　　　andar por la ciudad
　　　　　　　　estar en el centro
　　　　　　　　poner tarjetas postales
　　　　　　　　poder ver un desfile
　　　　　　　　dar una fiesta
　　　　　　　　tener (ganas) de ver una película (tener gana – to feel like)
　　　　　　　　conducir un carro

1. _____

2. _____

3. _____
4. _____
5. _____
6. _____
7. _____
8. _____
9. _____
10. _____

6. Uses of the Preterite Tense

The preterite tense expresses a particular single action or event completed at a specific time in the past:

Comenzó a leer el libro **ayer**.	He began to read the book yesterday.
Cesó de llover **a las cuatro**.	It stopped raining at 4 o'clock.
Carlos me *visitó* **el mes pasado**.	Charles visited me last month.

NOTE: The verbs **conocer** (*to know, to be acquainted with*), **saber** (*to know*), **tener** (*to have*), **querer** (*to want*), and **poder** (*to be able*) often have a different meaning in the preterite:

Le **conocí** en México.	I met him in Mexico. (began to know)
¿Cuándo **supieron** la verdad?	When did they find out (learn) the truth? (began to know)
Tuve carta de él esta mañana.	I received a letter from him this morning. (it came into my possession)
No **quiso** hacerlo.	He refused to do it. (final decision)
Pude convencerle.	I managed to convince him. (finally was able)

Ejercicio V

Un político de su pueblo (ciudad) acaba de regresar de un viaje al espacio. Ud. lo entrevista para un artículo en el periódico de su escuela. Escriba las diez preguntas que Ud. va a hacerle. Use las sugerencias siguientes:

SUGERENCIAS: Cuándo, Quién(es), (De) Dónde, Adónde, Por qué, Cuánto(s)

ir, hacer, pasar, visitar, conocer, andar, saber, estar, poder, poner, querer, venir, tener, empezar

EJEMPLOS: **¿Cuánto tiempo pasó Ud. en el espacio?**
¿Quiénes fueron con Ud.?

1. _____
2. _____
3. _____
4. _____
5. _____
6. _____
7. _____
8. _____
9. _____
10. _____

Ejercicio W

Imagínese que Ud. es ese político y conteste las preguntas del Ejercicio V:

EJEMPLOS: **Yo pasé una semana en el espacio.**
Varios astronautas fueron conmigo.

1. _____
2. _____
3. _____
4. _____
5. _____
6. _____
7. _____
8. _____
9. _____
10. _____

♦ MASTERY EXERCISES ♦

Ejercicio X

Cuando Ud. llega de la escuela su mamá no está en la casa. Encuentra una lista en la que ella escribió lo que tenía que hacer ese día. Escriba lo que ella hizo:

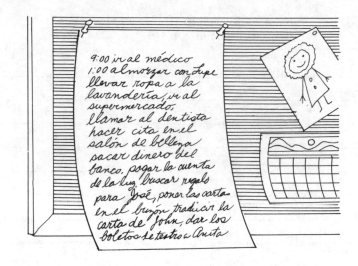

1. _____
2. _____
3. _____
4. _____
5. _____
6. _____
7. _____
8. _____
9. _____
10. _____
11. _____
12. _____

Ejercicio Y

Sus abuelos acaban de regresar de un viaje al extranjero. Conteste las preguntas que le hace un amigo:

1. ¿Cuánto tiempo estuvieron ellos fuera?

_____

2. ¿Te trajeron muchos regalos?

_____

3. ¿Qué ciudad les impresionó más, Roma o París?

_____

4. ¿Hicieron el viaje solos?

_____

5. ¿Tuviste que ir al aeropuerto cuando llegaron?

_____

6. ¿Cómo supiste que el avión se demoró?

_____

7. ¿Llegaste al aeropuerto a tiempo?

_____

8. ¿Quién fue contigo al aeropuerto?

_____

9. ¿Condujiste tú el carro?

_____

10. ¿Cuándo empezaste a conducir en la ciudad?

_____

11. ¿Pudiste estacionar el carro cerca de la terminal?

_____

12. ¿Tuvieron ellos alguna dificultad en la aduana?

_____

13. ¿Quién los vio cuando salieron de la aduana?

_____

14. ¿Les dio gusto verte?

_____

15. ¿Cargaste tú las maletas al carro?

_____

16. ¿A qué hora se despidieron Uds. de ellos?

_____

 **Ejercicio Z**

Exprese estas frases en español para explicar el problema que Ud. tiene con un juguete que compró:

1. Last week I bought a toy for my nephew.

_____

2. It didn't work when I returned home.

_____

3. I tried to return it to the store in which I bought it.

_____

4.   They told me that I broke it.

_____

5.   I paid $36 for the toy.

_____

6.   It was the last toy they sold.

_____

7.   I worked hard to earn the money.

_____

8.   I didn't give my nephew a birthday gift.

_____

9.   I was unable to fix it.

_____

10.   My friend tried to fix it but it broke again.

_____

11.   The store denied its responsibility and didn't want to exchange it.

_____

12.   I sent a copy of my letter to the manager of the store.

_____

C•H•A•P•T•E•R

5

Imperfect Tense

1. Regular Verbs

The imperfect tense of regular verbs is formed by dropping the infinitive ending (**-ar, -er, -ir**), and adding the following endings:

tomar:	tom	**-aba, -abas, -aba, -ábamos, -abais, -aban**
leer:	le ⎰	
subir:	sub ⎱	**-ía, -ías, -ía, -íamos, -íais, -ían**

Ejercicio A

Héctor habla de la vida de su pueblo. Escriba lo que dice:

EJEMPLO: Nosotros / cenar a las diez.
Nosotros cenábamos a las diez.

1. Yo / comprar un helado por cinco centavos

    compraba

2. Todo el mundo / bañarse en el lago

    se bañaban

3. Nosotros / almorzar a las dos (had lunch)

    almorzabamos

4. Los niños / cantar villancicos en la calle   carols

    cantaban

5. Las personas / celebrar todas las fiestas

    celebraban

6. Mis amigos y yo / jugar fútbol en la calle

    jugabamos

7. Mis padres / andar por el parque todos los domingos

    andaban

8. El circo / llegar a mi pueblo en abril

    llegaba

9. Los muchachos y las muchachas / no caminar juntos (together)

    no caminaban

10. Tú / comprar todo en el mercado

comprabas

Ejercicio B

Unos jóvenes recuerdan cosas que ellos o sus parientes hacían. Escriba lo que dicen:

EJEMPLO: Yo / dormir hasta las dos de la tarde.
Yo dormía hasta las dos de la tarde.

1. Mis amigos y yo / subir a los árboles   (climb up the trees)

subíamos

2. Carmen / escribir poemas románticos

escribía

3. Elías / vestirse de gaucho

se vestía

4. Mi hermanito / repetir lo que todos / decir

repetía   decían

5. Tú / seguir a tu hermana mayor

seguías

6. Yo / compartir todo lo que yo / tener   [share]

compartía   tenía

7. Uds. / construir castillos de arena

construían

8. Beto / volver con la cara sucia   [return]

volvía

9. Yo / beber la leche con una pajita

bebía

10. Sarita / tener miedo de la oscuridad   [fear of the dark]

tenía

Ejercicio C

Escriba seis frases en que Ud. cuenta lo que Ud. u otra persona hacía antes. Use las sugerencias:

SUGERENCIAS: jugar   comer   vivir
               trabajar   perder   dormir(se)
               arreglar   poner   abrir

EJEMPLO: **Yo ponía la mesa todos los días.**

1. _Yo jugaba miento mi tia cocinaba_
2. _Mi padre trabajaba hasta las cinco._
3. _Maria perdia las llaves todos los dios_
4. _Jose queria la receta para hacer una margarita_
5. _Felix arreglaba las ventanas antes llovia._
6. _Mi madre cria que dinero crece en los arbos._

Ejercicio D

Conteste estas preguntas que Ud. le hace a su abuela:

1. ¿Dónde vivías de niña?
   Yo vivia in Begota.

2. ¿Con quién jugabas?
   Yo jugba con mi hermana y mi prima

3. ¿Tenías muchos novios?
   No, tenia solemente Jaime.

2. 4. Ustedes ¿Trabajaban tú y tus hermanos por la tarde?
   No, trabábamos de los ochos en la mañana de los cinco en la tarde.

5. ¿Te castigaban mucho tus padres?
   No. Era una angel.

6. ¿Qué hacías los sábados?
   Yo iba a la biblioteca todos los sabados.

7. ¿Leías novelas románticas?
   No, yo estudia el historia.

8. ¿Asistían tú y tus amigas a muchas fiestas?
   Si, Asistabamos la fiesta de la Virgin de Guadaloupe y el Cinco de Mayo

9. ¿Cosías tu propia ropa?
   No, yo compraba los al mercado de Saks!

10. ¿Querían Uds. viajar a otros países?
   Si. Me padres y yo queriamos ir al España.

2. Verbs Irregular in the Imperfect Tense

There are three verbs that are irregular in the imperfect tense. They are:

ir:	*iba, ibas, iba, íbamos, ibais, iban*
ser:	*era, eras, era, éramos, erais, eran*
ver:	*veía, veías, veía, veíamos, veíais, veían*

Ejercicio E

Escriba adónde iban estas personas los domingos:

EJEMPLO: Carlos / al estadio
Carlos iba al estadio.

1. Las hermanas / al cine

_____iban_____

2. Yo / a la iglesia

_____iba_____

3. Rafael y Juan / a la corrida de toros

_____iban_____

4. Tú / al parque

_____ibas_____

5. Elena y yo / a la piscina

_____ibamos_____

6. Ud. / a casa de sus abuelos

_____iba_____

Ejercicio F

Escriba de qué país eran estas personas que se conocieron en una fiesta:

EJEMPLO: Ud. / de Colombia
Ud. era de Colombia

1. Yo / de España

_____era_____

2. Pedro / de Puerto Rico

_____era_____

3. Las señoritas / de México

_____eran_____

4. Nosotros / de Costa Rica

_____eramos_____

5. Tú / de Guatemala

_____eras_____

6. Nilda / de Bolivia

_____era_____

Ejercicio G

Escriba dónde dicen estas muchachas que veían a un señor todos los días. Use las sugerencias:

SUGERENCIAS: en la parada del autobús   en la entrada de su oficina
en la estación del metro   en la esquina de su casa
en el ascensor   en un taxi
en la cafetería

EJEMPLO: María
María lo veía en un taxi todos los días.

1. Carlota _veía lo en la parada del autobús_
2. Ana y Pilar _veían lo en la estación del metro_
3. Yo _veían lo en el ascensor_
4. Mi jefa _veía lo en el entrada de su oficina_
5. Alicia y yo _veíamos lo en la esquina de nuestros casa_
6. Tú _veías lo en la cafetería_

Ejercicio H

¿Quién hacía estas cosas? Escriba quién las hacía:

lavar el carro los sábados   ver a los amigos los viernes por la noche
ir al supermercado todos los días   ir al campamento cada verano
visitar a los abuelos los domingos   ponerse furioso cuando los padres salían
jugar béisbol los sábados por la mañana   ver una película los sábados

1. Mis padres _visitaban la los abuelos todos los días_
2. Mi hermanito _jugaba béisbol los sábados por la mañana_
3. Mis amigos _visitaban_
4. Mi hermano _se ponía furioso cuando los padres salían_
5. Mi abuela _veía una película los sábados_
6. Mi padre _iba al campamento cada verano_
7. Yo _lavaba el carro los sábados_
8. Mis hermanos y yo _íbamos al supermercado todos los días_

3. Uses of the Imperfect Tense

The imperfect tense expresses continuous or repeated past actions, events, or situations. It is also used to describe the circumstances surrounding a past action or event.

a. The imperfect is used to describe what was happening, used to happen, or happened repeatedly in the past:

Los pájaros **cantaban.**	The birds *were* singing.
Vivíamos en esta calle.	We *used to live* on this street.
Tomás *llegaba* tarde **a menudo.**	Thomas *would arrive* (*arrived*) often late.

b. The imperfect is used to describe persons or things in the past:

Pedro *era* rubio y *tenía* los ojos azules.	Peter *was* blond and had blue eyes.
La sala *estaba* llena de gente.	The living room *was* full of people.

c. The imperfect expresses a state of mind in the past with the verbs **creer, pensar, querer,** and **saber:**

Creían (Pensaban, Sabían) que era importante.	They *believed* (*thought, knew*) that it *was* important.
Queríamos comprar un coche nuevo.	We *wanted* to buy a new car.

d. The imperfect expresses the time of day in the past:

Eran las ocho.	It *was* eight o'clock.

e. The imperfect is used to describe a situation that was going on in the past when another past single action or event expressed in the preterite occurred:

Comíamos cuando nos llamó.	We *were eating* when he called us.

Ejercicio 1

Ud. habla de las fiestas de su juventud. Conteste las preguntas que le hace un amigo:

1. ¿Dónde eran las fiestas? (en casa de Raquel)
   Las fiestas iban en casa de Raquel.

2. ¿Quiénes estaban allí? (todo el mundo)
   Todo el mundo iban allí.

3. ¿Quién servía los refrescos? (Raquel)
   Raquel servía

4. ¿Qué clase de vestido llevaba ella puesto? (un vestido de fiesta)
   Ella llevaba puesto un vestido de fiesta

5. ¿Qué clase de aretes usaba ella? (de oro)
   Ella usaba los aretes de oro

6. ¿Dónde estaba ella mientras llegaban los invitados? (en la puerta)
   Ella estaba en la puerta

7. ¿Qué clase de música tocaban? (música latina)
   Estaba música latina

8. ¿Sabías tú que Elena iba siempre allí? (No)
   No, Elena no iba siempre.

9. Al verla ¿bailabas siempre con ella? (Sí)

Sí, yo bailaba con ella.

10. ¿A qué hora empezaba a irse la gente? (a las doce)

Empezaban irse a las doce.

Ejercicio J

Ud. acaba de visitar una casa modelo. Conteste las preguntas para describir la casa:

1. ¿De cuántos pisos era la casa?

Eran

2. ¿Cuántos cuartos tenía?

Tenían   (tenía)

3. ¿Había muebles bonitos?

Sí, había

4. ¿De qué color era la alfombra?

Era azul

5. ¿De qué color estaban pintadas las paredes?

Estaban pintadas terra cotta

6. ¿Cuántos dormitorios había?

Habían trés quartos   (Había)

7. ¿Era grande la cocina?

Sí, la cosina era grande

8. ¿Qué clase de muebles tenía?

Tenía las muebles Mexicana

9. ¿Había muchas flores en el jardín?

Sí, habían —

10. ¿Cobraban por entrar?

No cobraban

Ejercicio K

Imagínese que Ud. presenció un robo y ahora Ud. describe al ladrón. Escriba la descripción:

EJEMPLO: Eran las seis de la tarde. Era un joven alto. Medía seis pies y pesaba unas doscientas libras.

_____

_____

_____

_____

_____

_____

_____

Ejercicio L

Escriba lo que hacían estas personas cuando se apagó la luz. Use estas sugerencias:

SUGERENCIAS: preparar la cena   hacer las tareas
bañar a los niños   hablar por teléfono
dormir la siesta   comer el almuerzo
escribir una carta   jugar naipes *card game*

1. Ernesto *jugaba naipes*
2. Los padres *bañaban los niños*
3. Yo *dormía la siesta*
4. Enrique y tú *comían el almuerzo*
5. Sarita y yo *hacíamos las tareas*
6. Mi abuelo *preparaba la cena*
7. La tía Lourdes *escribía una carta*
8. Don Álvaro *hablaba por teléfono*

4. *Hacía* + Time Expression + *que* + the Imperfect Tense

The construction **hacía** + an expression of time + **que** + the imperfect tense is used to describe an action or event that began in the past and continued in the past. In such situations the question is expressed by **¿Cuánto tiempo hacía que...?** + the imperfect tense or **¿Hacía cuánto tiempo que...?** + the imperfect tense:

    Hacía un mes que *viajaban*.   *They had been traveling for a month.*
    ¿Cuánto tiempo hacía que *dormían*?   *How long had they been sleeping?*

NOTE: The imperfect tense + **desde hace** + an expression of time is also used to describe an action or event that began in the past and continued in the past. In such situations, the question is expressed by **¿Desde cuándo...?** + the imperfect tense:

    ***Viajaban* desde hacía un mes.**   *They had been traveling for a month.*
    ¿Desde cuándo *dormían*?   *How long had they been sleeping?*

Ejercicio M

A Pedro le gusta saber desde cuándo sus amigos hacían ciertas cosas. Escriba las preguntas que hace Pedro, usando las expresiones ¿Cuánto tiempo hacía que...? y ¿Desde cuándo...?:

EJEMPLO: María / tocar el violín
¿Cuánto tiempo hacía que María **tocaba** el violín?
¿Desde cuándo tocaba María el violín?

1. Jorge / trabajar en el banco

   Cuánto tiempo hacía que Jorge trabajaba en el banco?
   Desde cuando trabajaba en el branco?

2. Esteban / tener su propio carro

   Cuando tiempo hacía que Esteban tenía su propio carro?
   Desde cuando tenía Esteban su propio carro?

3. Anita y Carmen / viajar juntas

   Cuando tiempo hacía que Anita y Carmen viajaban juntas?
   Desde cuando viajaban Maria y Carmen juntas?

4. Tú / correr en las carreras

   Cuando tiempo hacía que tu corrias en las carreras?
   Desde cuando corrias-tu en las carreras?

5. Nosotros / ser amigos

   Cuando tiempo hacía que nostros eramos amigos?
   Desde cuando eramos amigos?

6. Alicia / vivir con sus abuelos

   Cuando tiempo hacía que Alicia vivia con sus abuelos?
   Desde cuando viria Alicia con sus abuelos?

7. Uds. / no ir a trabajar los sábados

   Cuando tiempo hacía que ustedes no iban a trabajar los sábados
   Desde cuando no iran a trabajar los sábados?

Ejercicio N

Escriba las respuestas a las preguntas del ejercicio M, usando la información dada:

EJEMPLO: (cinco años)
Hacía cinco años que María **tocaba** el violín.
María **tocaba** el violín **desde hacía cinco años.**

1. (tres meses) Hacía tres meses que Jorge trabajaba en el banco.
   Jorge trabajaba desde hacía tres meses

2.   (una semana) _Hacía una semana que Esteban tenía su propia carro._
Esteban tenía su propia carro desde hacía una semana.

3.   (un año) _Hacía cuando Un año que Anita y Carmen viajaban juntas._
Anita y Carmen viajaban juntas desde hacía un año.

4.   (dos años) _Hacía cuando dos años que tú corrías las carreras._
Tú corrías las carreras desde hacía dos años.

5.   (15 años) _Hacía 15 años nos. éramos amigos_
Nos. éramos los amigos desde hacía 15 años.

6.   (un mes) _Hacía un mes que Alicia vivía con sus abuelos_
Alicia vivía con sus abuelos desde hacía un mes.

7.   (4 semanas) _Hacía 4 semanas que ustedes no trabajaban los sábados_
Uds. no trabajaban los sábados desde hacía 4 semanas.

♦ MASTERY EXERCISES ♦

Ejercicio O

Usando las expresiones dadas, describa los dibujos para expresar lo que hacían estas personas:

EXPRESIONES: todos los días   todas las noches   a menudo
(cada) fin de semana   cada sábado   *often*
every

EJEMPLO:

Arturo y Juan
**Arturo y Juan jugaban tenis
cada fin de semana.**

1.

El señor Ramos _pescaba_
a menudo al sábado

2.

Sarita y María _eran al_
película cada domingo

3.

Roberto _practicaba el piano todos los dias_

5.

Los niños _eran al museo a menudo_

4.

Los hermanos García _llavaban el carro cada Sabado_

6.

Mi madre _era al supermercado cada fin de semana_

Ejercicio P

Conteste las preguntas que le hace un periodista a un escritor célebre:

1. ¿Qué edad tenía Ud. al llegar a este país?

   _____

2. ¿En qué ciudad quería vivir Ud.?

   _____

3. ¿Con quién vivía Ud.?

   _____

4. ¿Sabía Ud. hablar inglés al llegar a este país?

   _____

5. ¿Estudiaba Ud. mucho?

   _____

6. ¿Era Ud. un alumno listo?

   _____

7. ¿Iba Ud. al museo a menudo?

   _____

8. ¿Desde cuándo soñaba con ser escritor?

_____

9. ¿Qué escribía Ud. cuando era niño?

_____

10. ¿Buscaba Ud. la ayuda de sus profesores?

_____

11. ¿De dónde sacaba Ud. los temas de sus cuentos?

_____

12. ¿Cuánto tiempo hacía que Ud. no regresaba a su país?

_____

13. ¿Ahorraba Ud. el dinero que ganaba?

_____

14. ¿Visitaba Ud. las ciudades que describía en sus novelas?

_____

15. ¿Pasaba Ud. mucho tiempo en esas ciudades?

_____

16. ¿Desde cuándo trabajaba Ud. en su primera novela?

_____

 **Ejercicio Q**

Exprese en español esta carta que Emilio recibió de un amigo que estaba estudiando en Madrid:

Dear Emilio,

(1) Last week the sun was shining every day. (2) It was cool and I was able to walk around the city. (3) Every day I followed the same routine. (4) I got up very early because I liked to see the sunrise. (5) Then I got dressed and I ran in El Retiro. (6) Nothing could be heard except the birds that were singing. (7) Upon returning home, I bathed and went out in order to have breakfast. (8) I ate breakfast in a small café that was close to El Prado. (9) Each day I ate the same breakfast, churros and hot chocolate. (10) Then I used to go to my classes. (11) My classmates and I ate lunch every day in the cafeteria of the university. (12) In the afternoon, I went to the library because I had to write a paper. (13) In the evenings we always went out. (14) Sometimes we went to the theater, or to the movies, or we used to sit at a table in a café. (15) While I was in the café, I used to count the number of people that passed on the street. (16) I wanted to learn well the numbers in Spanish! (17) I used to return home about 8:30 P.M. and had dinner with the family with whom I was living.

Regards,
Federico

1. La semana pasado el sol brillaba todo los dias.

2. Hacia fresco y yo andaba alrededor de la cuidad

3. Todos los dias yo seguia la mismo routra.

4. Yo me leventaba muy temprano porque yo me gustaba la salida del sol.

5. Entonces yo me vestia y corria en El Retiro

6. Nada escuchaba excepto los aves que cantado.

7. Quando yo regressaba a mi casa, yo me banaba y salia por desayuno. (salia haber desayuno)?

8. Yo comia me desayuno en una cafe picena circa de El Prado.

9. Todo los dios yo comia lo mismo desayuno: los churros y chocolate caliente.

10. Entonces yo iba a mes classes.

11. Mes condicipulos y yo almozabamos cada los dias en el cafeteria del universidad.

12. En la tarde, yo iba al biblioteca porque necesitaba escribir un ensayo.

13. En la noche siempre saliamos.

14. A veces iriamos al teatro ou al pelicula, ou nos sentabamos a el mesa en un ...

15. Quando yo era en el cafe, yo contaba los gentes pasaban en la calle.

16. Yo queria aprender bueno los numeros en Espanol

17. Yo regresaba a mi casa a las 9:30, y comia la sena con la familia con yo vivia.

Salud!

Preterite and Imperfect Tenses Compared

The uses of the preterite and imperfect tenses are summarized in the chart below:

PRETERITE	IMPERFECT
1. Expresses specific actions or events completed in the past: ***Estuvieron* contentos de verlo.** *They were glad to see him.*	**1.** Describes ongoing or continuous actions or events in the past: ***Estaban* contentos con su casa.** *They were content with their house.*
2. Expresses a specific action or event at a specific point in time: ***Hoy llegó* a casa temprano.** *Today he arrived home early.* **El sol *salió a las cinco de la mañana.*** *The sun came out at 5 A.M*	**2.** Describes habitual or repeated actions or events in the past: ***Llegaba* temprano *muy a menudo.*** *He arrived early very often.* **El sol *brillaba por las mañanas.*** *The sun shone in the mornings.*
3. States a particular action: ***Tuvo* un accidente.** *He had an accident.*	**3.** Describes the circumstances or conditions surrounding an action: **La carretera *era* peligrosa.** *The road was dangerous.*
	4. Describes persons, things, or a state of mind: ***Era* muy alto.** *He was very tall.* **El cielo *estaba* azul.** *The sky was blue.* ***Quería* estudiar música.** *He wanted to study music.*

 **Ejercicio A**

En cada trozo aparecen las formas del pretérito y del imperfecto de los verbos. Escoja las formas que deben usarse:

1. Yo (nacía, nací) en Santiago en 1960. En aquel entonces mi padre (tenía, tuvo) unos cuarenta años. En su temprana juventud (iba, fue) a la América Hispana de arquitecto. De la Argentina (pasaba, pasó) a Chile, donde (conocía, conoció) a una chilena. Allí (se casaba, se casó) y allí (veía, vio) nacer a sus tres hijos. Al llegar a Nueva York, mi familia (tenía, tuvo) largos años de lucha contra la miseria. Durante esa época, sólo (soñábamos, soñamos) con mejorar nuestra fortuna y (esperábamos, esperamos) días mejores.

2. Esta mañana (abría, abrió) los ojos y (saltaba, saltó) de la cama. (Se vestía, Se vistió) y (salía, salió). La mañana (era, fue) hermosa. En los árboles las aves (cantaban, cantaron) alegremente. Los niños que (jugaban, jugaron) en el patio (parecían, parecieron) más risueños que nunca. Toda la naturaleza (llevaba, llevó) un aspecto más joven, más verde, más vivo. Suspirando de placer, Luisita (volvía, volvió) a pensar en el baile de la noche anterior.

3. (Eran, Fueron) ya las cuatro de la tarde. Ramón y Elena (estaban, estuvieron) sentados en la sala. De las otras habitaciones (se oía, se oyó) el lejano rumor de voces, de gente que (hablaba, habló) en tono animado. Elena (se levantaba, se levantó) y (se acercaba, se acercó) a la ventana. (Miraba, Miró) afuera y (veía, vio) que todavía (caía, cayó) la lluvia. (Experimentaba, Experimentó) una sensación de tristeza.

Ejercicio B

Escriba la forma correcta del pretérito o del imperfecto de los verbos entre paréntesis:

1. Alrededor de la mesa la familia _____ (cenar), chicos y mayores comiendo, riendo

y hablando a la vez. De repente _____ (sonar) la campana del pueblo. ¡Fuego!

Todos _____ (dejar) la mesa y _____ (echarse) a correr hacia la plaza. Allí

_____ (ver) una escena horrible. _____ (arder) la casa de un vecino.

Por todas partes _____ (encontrarse) gente que _____ (gritar) y

_____ (hacer) esfuerzos inútiles para extinguir el fuego. De pronto

_____ (aparecer) en una ventana la figura de una mujer.

2. Él _____ (ir) camino de la estación cuando _____ (tropezar) con un amigo

que le _____ (detener) para charlar un momento. Al llegar a la estación,

_____ (notar) que el tren ya _____ (estar) allí. _____ (darse)

prisa pero _____ (llegar) tarde. _____ (comenzar) a pasearse por el andén,

impaciente, lleno de enojo. _____ (mirar) el reloj. Las nueve menos veinte. Le

_____ (quedar) solamente veinte minutos para llegar a la oficina y seguramente no

llegaría a tiempo.

3. Hernán Cortés _____ el conquistador de México. Cuando
   (ser)

   _____ los españoles, los indios nunca habían visto caballos y
   (llegar)

   _____ que hombre y caballo _____ una sola persona.
   (creer)   (ser)

   También _____ que Cortés mismo _____ su antiguo dios,
   (creer)   (ser)

   que _____ para gobernarlos. Con solamente 400 soldados, y con la ayuda de
   (volver)

   Marina, una india que _____ de guía e intérprete, Cortés
   (hacer)

   _____ conquistar la capital azteca, Tenochtitlán (que es hoy la Ciudad de
   (poder)

   México).

Ejercicio C

Ud. está muy desilusionado(a) porque nadie fue a una fiesta que Ud. organizó. Conteste las preguntas que le hace un primo:

1. ¿A cuántas personas invitaste?

   _____

2. ¿Les dijiste la fecha correcta?

   _____

3. ¿Sabían tu dirección y número de teléfono?

   _____

4. ¿Por qué dabas la fiesta?

   _____

5. ¿Esperabas recibir regalos?

   _____

6. ¿Qué hiciste al ver que nadie llegaba?

   _____

7. ¿Qué descubriste?

   _____

Ejercicio D

Conteste las preguntas que le hace su padre sobre una ventana rota en casa de un vecino:

1. ¿Dónde estabas tú esta tarde?

   _____

2.   ¿Con quién jugabas?

_____

3.   ¿A qué jugaban?

_____

4.   ¿Viste cuando la pelota pasó por la ventana?

_____

5.   ¿Qué hicieron Uds. entonces?

_____

6.   ¿Por qué no me dijiste nada cuando yo llegué a casa?

_____

7.   ¿Quién rompió la ventana?

_____

8.   ¿De quién era la pelota?

_____

Ejercicio E

Diez años después de graduarse de la escuela secundaria, Ud. va a una reunión. Escriba
lo que Ud. hizo durante esos diez años:

EJEMPLO: Cuando me gradué de la escuela, me matriculé en la universidad.
           Quería llegar a ser ingeniero.

_____

_____

_____

_____

_____

_____

_____

_____

_____

_____

_____

_____

_____

Ejercicio F

Exprese estas frases en español para contarle este cuento a un amigo que sólo habla español:

1. Richard never thought it was possible to win first prize in the lottery.

   _____

   _____

2. Nevertheless, every week he bought a lottery ticket.

   _____

   _____

3. He knew that, although he didn't win, the money was used to support education.

   _____

   _____

4. One day while he was waiting for the bus, he saw an old woman selling lottery tickets in the street.

   _____

   _____

5. Although the line for the bus was very long, he left it and approached the old woman.

   _____

   _____

6. He bought a lottery ticket from her.

   _____

   _____

7. When he returned to the bus stop there was no room on the bus.

   _____

   _____

8. He had to wait for another bus but he felt very lucky.

   _____

   _____

9. That night he waited anxiously for the announcement of the winning number.

   _____

   _____

10. When he heard the number he could not believe it.

    _____

    _____

11. He jumped up and down with joy and called all his friends.

    _____

12. On the following day he returned to the street where he bought the ticket.

13. He looked for the old woman but he could not find her.

14. He asked all the shopkeepers if they knew her.

15. He wanted to share the prize with her.

Ejercicio G

Escriba cinco frases en español con las que Ud. termina el cuento del ejercicio anterior:

1.

2.

3.

4.

5.

C•H•A•P•T•E•R
7

Future Tense and Conditional

1. Future Tense of Regular Verbs

The future tense of regular verbs is formed by adding the following endings to the infinitive:

> **ayudar**
> **aprender** } -é, -ás, -á, -emos, -éis, -án
> **escribir**

NOTE:

1. All future endings except **-emos** have an accent mark.

2. Verbs that have an accent mark in the infinitive (**oír, reír,** etc.) drop that accent in the future (**oiré, reiremos,** etc.).

Ejercicio A

Escriba lo que estas personas van a hacer mañana:

EJEMPLO: Luz / asistir a una conferencia
Luz asistirá a una conferencia.

1. Pedro / trabajar en el taller

   _____

2. Mi madre / ir de compras

   _____

3. Petra / visitar a sus amigas

   _____

4. Los amigos / jugar tenis

   _____

5. Yo / descansar todo el día

   _____

6. Tú / comer en el centro

_____

7. Eduardo y yo / defender el título del equipo de fútbol

_____

8. Raquel y María / aprender otra canción española

_____

9. Mi abuelo / cortar la hierba

_____

10. Los niños / vender limonada en la esquina

_____

Escriba cuándo Ud. va a hacer estas cosas. Use las sugerencias:

SUGERENCIAS:	graduarse de la escuela	en dos años
	viajar al extranjero	el año que viene
	trabajar en una oficina	el verano próximo
	casarse	mañana
	comprar su propio carro	en diez años
	subir una montaña	en seis meses

EJEMPLO: **Yo viajaré al extranjero el verano próximo.**

1. _____

2. _____

3. _____

4. _____

5. _____

6. _____

2. Verbs with Irregular Future

_a._ Verbs like **poder** drop the **e** of the infinitive and then add the endings of the future tense:

poder: _podr_ **-é, -ás, -á, -emos, -éis, -án**

Like **poder: caber, haber, querer, saber**

b. In verbs like **poner**, the **e** (or **i**) of the infinitive is replaced by a **d** and the endings of the future tense are added:

> **poner:** *pondr* **-é, -ás, -á, -emos, -éis, -án**

> > Like **poner: salir, tener, valer, venir**

c. The verbs **decir** and **hacer** are irregular in the future tense:

> **decir:** *dir* **-é, -ás, -á, -emos, -éis, -án**

> **hacer:** *har* **-é, -ás, -á, -emos, -éis, -án**

> NOTE:　Compounds of the irregular verbs are also irregular:

> > **disponer,** *dispondré*; **contener,** *contendrán*; **convenir,** *convendrá*; **satisfacer,** *satisfaremos*; **contradecir,** *contradirá*; and others.

Ejercicio C

Exprese la forma correcta del futuro de los verbos en esta carta que Enrique escribe a unos amigos que lo visitarán:

Queridos amigos,

Yo _____ ir a la estación por ustedes. Sé que todos ustedes _____
　　　1 (poder)　　　　　　　　　　　　　　　　　　　　　　　　　　　　　　　　　**2** (querer)

ir juntos en mi carro, pero todo el mundo no _____ a la vez. Yo
　　　　　　　　　　　　　　　　　　　　　　　　3 (caber)

_____ que hacer dos viajes a la estación. Mientras tanto, los demás
　　4 (tener)

_____ esperar en un café cerca de la estación. Yo _____ todo lo
　　5 (poder)　　　　　　　　　　　　　　　　　　　　　　　　　**6** (hacer)

posible por llevarlos a la fiesta rápidamente. Yo _____ de mi casa temprano.
　　　　　　　　　　　　　　　　　　　　　　　　　　　　7 (salir)

Según el horario, ustedes _____ en el tren de las 7:35. Creo que todas las
　　　　　　　　　　　　　　8 (venir)

maletas _____ en el carro también. Si no, Roberto y yo _____
　　　　9 (caber)　　　　　　　　　　　　　　　　　　　　　　　　　**10** (poder)

volver a la estación por ellas. _____ muchas personas en la fiesta. Creo que su
　　　　　　　　　　　　　　11 (haber)

viaje _____ la pena. Sé que Elena _____ mucho gusto de
　　12 (valer)　　　　　　　　　　　　　　**13** (tener)

verlos y tanto ella como yo _____ todo lo posible para que se diviertan.
　　　　　　　　　　　　　　14 (hacer)

Después Uds. nos _____ cómo les fue.
　　　　　　　　　15 (decir)

Saludos,
Enrique

Ejercicio D

Imagínese que Ud. y varios amigos van a vender cosas en el mercado de las pulgas el sábado próximo. Escriba lo que hará cada persona, usando las sugerencias:

SUGERENCIAS:

Yo	tener que estar allí temprano
Mis amigos y yo	hacer los carteles
Usted	poner los precios
Ellos	poner todo en orden
Ustedes	querer ser el cajero
Tú	decir los precios
Todos nosotros	querer vender
	salir al mediodía
	poder atender a los clientes
	querer irse temprano

1. _____
2. _____
3. _____
4. _____
5. _____
6. _____
7. _____
8. _____
9. _____
10. _____

Ejercicio E

Conteste las preguntas que le hace un(a) amigo(a) sobre una cita que Ud. tendrá con un(a) joven desconocido(a):

1. ¿Dónde se encontrarán el viernes por la noche?

   _____

2. ¿A qué hora estará él (ella) allí?

   _____

3. ¿Adónde irán Uds.?

   _____

4. ¿Qué clase de ropa tendrás que llevar?

   _____

5. ¿Qué harán Uds. después?

   _____

6.   ¿Podrás invitarlo(la) a la fiesta de Javier?

_____

7.   ¿Me dirás cómo te fue?

_____

3. Uses of the Future Tense

a. The future tense is used in Spanish, as in English, to express future time:

Vendremos mañana.	*We will come tomorrow.*
¿Cuándo **irán Uds.?**	*When will you go?*

b. The future is used to express wonderment or probability at the present time and is often equivalent to English *I wonder, probably, must be, can:*

¿Cuántos años *tendrá?*	*I wonder how old he is. (How old can he be?)*
¿Qué hora *será?*	*I wonder what time it is. (What time can it be?)*
Serán **las dos.**	*It is probably (It must be) two o'clock.*
Estará **cansado.**	*He must be (He is probably) tired.*

NOTE: The expression **deber de** followed by an infinitive may also be used to express probability at the present time:

Deben de estar cansados.	*They must be tired.*
Debe de ser la una.	*It is probably one o'clock.*

Ejercicio F

Escriba cuándo estas personas harán las cosas:

EJEMPLO: Ramón / aprender a esquiar / el año próximo
Ramón aprenderá a esquiar el año próximo.

1.   Carmen / sacar la basura / más tarde

_____

2.   Elena y yo / visitar a los abuelos / la semana que viene

_____

3.   Tú / poder hablar español / después del verano

_____

4.   Lina / tener que trabajar / los fines de semana

_____

5.   Uds. / venir a comer / por la noche

_____

Ejercicio G

Conteste las preguntas que le hace un compañero de viaje en una excursión en autobús por la ciudad de Wáshington:

1. ¿Qué edificio será ése? (el Capitolio)

   _____

2. ¿Dónde estarán todos los políticos hoy? (en casa; es sábado)

   _____

3. ¿A qué hora comeremos? (a las doce)

   _____

4. ¿Qué hora será ahora? (las diez y media)

   _____

5. ¿Cuántas paradas haremos en esta excursión? (tres)

   _____

6. ¿Cuál será la próxima parada? (la Casa Blanca)

   _____

7. ¿Le gustará al guía hacer la misma excursión todos los días? (Sí)

   _____

8. ¿Qué clase de regalos venderán en la tienda de recuerdos? (vasos y camisetas)

   _____

9. ¿Cuántas personas habrá en este autobús? (cuarenta y siete)

   _____

10. ¿Cuándo podremos dormir la siesta? (por la tarde)

    _____

♦ MASTERY EXERCISES — FUTURE TENSE ♦

Ejercicio H

¿Cómo será el mundo cuando Ud. tenga 35 años? Conteste estas preguntas:

1. ¿En qué año tendrá Ud. 35 años?

   _____

2. ¿Dónde vivirá Ud.?

   _____

3. ¿Cómo se ganará Ud. la vida?

   _____

4. ¿Estarán los miembros de su familia en la misma ciudad?

_____

5. ¿Habrá paz en el mundo?

_____

6. ¿Vendrán personas de otros planetas a la tierra?

_____

7. ¿Qué clase de música estará de moda?

_____

8. ¿Qué usarán Uds. para pagar las cuentas?

_____

9. ¿Cabrá todo el mundo en el país?

_____

10. ¿Qué clase de edificios se construirán?

_____

Ejercicio I

Exprese estas frases en español, para ayudarle a una amiga que hará un viaje a México para visitar a unos primos:

1. I will leave Chicago on Monday morning at 8:00 A.M.

_____

2. My parents will take me to the airport.

_____

3. The plane will probably arrive late.

_____

4. Will you be at the airport to meet me?

_____

5. I will have three suitcases.

_____

6. How will we go from the airport to your house?

_____

7. Will the suitcases fit in your car?

_____

8. Will all of my cousins be at the airport?

_____

9. I will stay in Mexico for one month.

    _____

10. Will it be possible to visit Acapulco?

    _____

11. I will bring my Spanish dictionary.

    _____

12. I know that you and I will have a good time together.

    _____

4. Conditional of Regular Verbs

The conditional of regular verbs is formed in the same way as the future tense. The following endings are added to the infinitive:

ayudar   **aprender**   *-ía, -ías, -ía, -íamos, -íais, -ían*   **escribir**

NOTE: Verbs that have an accent mark in the infinitive (**oír, reír,** etc.) drop that accent in the conditional (**oiría, reiríamos,** etc.).

Ejercicio J

Unas amigas quieren hacer un viaje al extranjero durante el verano. Escriba lo que ellas harían en el viaje:

> EJEMPLO: Elena / visitar las iglesias
> **Elena visitaría** las iglesias.

1. Gabriela / comer tapas en España

    _____

2. Josefina y Graciela / ir a acampar

    _____

3. Beatriz y yo / ir de compras todos los días

    _____

4. Tú / tomar todas las excursiones

    _____

5. Yo / conocer a muchos jóvenes

    _____

6.   Clara y Anita / encontrar las discotecas

_____

Ejercicio K

Ud. no sabe el pronóstico del tiempo para mañana. Escriba las cosas que haría o no haría en las circunstancias dadas. Use las sugerencias:

SUGERENCIAS: mirar la televisión   dar un paseo por el parque
ir al cine   jugar tenis
ir a la playa   estudiar para un examen
limpiar su cuarto   nadar en la piscina
leer una revista   dormir hasta el mediodía
montar en bicicleta   jugar baloncesto

1. Si hace buen tiempo, **yo no iría al cine. Yo nadaría en la piscina.**

_____

_____

_____

_____

_____

2. Si hace mal tiempo, **yo no montaría en bicicleta. Yo limpiaría mi cuarto.**

_____

_____

_____

_____

_____

5. Verbs Irregular in the Conditional

a. Verbs like **poder** drop the **e** of the infinitive and then add the endings of the conditional:

poder: *podr* -ía, -ías, -ía, -íamos, -íais, -ían

Like **poder:** caber, haber, querer, saber

b. In verbs like **poner**, the **e** (or **i**) of the infinitive is dropped and replaced by a **d** and the endings of the conditional are added:

poner: *pondr* -ía, -ías, -ía, -íamos, -íais, -ían

Like **poner:** salir, tener, valer, venir

C. The verbs **decir** and **hacer** are irregular in the conditional:

decir: *dir* ⎫
hacer: *har* ⎭ -ía, -ías, -ía, -íamos, -íais, -ían

NOTE: Compounds of the irregular verbs are also irregular:

disponer, *dispondría*; **contener**, *contendría*; **satisfacer**, *satisfaríamos*, and others.

Ejercicio L

Varios compañeros de clase no comprendieron lo que dijo el profesor. Escriba lo que cada alumno cree que dijo el profesor:

EJEMPLO: él / poner los ejemplos en la pizarra
El pondría los ejemplos en la pizarra.

1. no haber clases el viernes

   _____

2. los alumnos / poder salir temprano

   _____

3. unos alumnos / tener que esperar hasta las cuatro

   _____

4. el director / venir a la clase el viernes

   _____

5. Ricardo y yo / no decir nada

   _____

6. tú / salir en una excursión el viernes

   _____

7. valer la pena estudiar mucho

   _____

8. la clase / querer una fiesta el viernes

   _____

9. yo / hacer los tacos para la fiesta

   _____

10. todo el mundo / no caber en el autobús

    _____

11. nadie / saber la respuesta a las preguntas

    _____

12. mis compañeros y yo / poner los libros debajo de las sillas

    _____

Ejercicio M

Escriba lo que Ud. haría con un millón de dólares. Puede usar las sugerencias o pensar en otras:

SUGERENCIAS: ponerlo en el banco, hacer donaciones, salir al extranjero, poder comprar una casa, querer compartirlo con sus parientes, tener que ayudar a sus . . .

1. _____
2. _____
3. _____
4. _____
5. _____
6. _____

Ejercicio N

Escriba lo que Ud. haría en estas circunstancias:

EJEMPLO: Tu mamá espera invitados a cenar y necesita ayuda.
(poner la mesa) **Yo pondría** la mesa.

1.   Tu amigo te presenta a una prima suya que acaba de llegar de Caracas.

   (decirle mucho gusto) _____

2.   Tienes planes para salir con unos amigos pero hace mal tiempo.

   (no salir con ellos) _____

3.   Tu abuela no puede hacer las compras porque está enferma hoy.

   (hacer las compras por ella) _____

4.   Tus padres te dicen que debes venir a la casa antes de las diez.

   (venir a la casa temprano) _____

5.   Tus padres van a una boda y no quieren dejar a tu hermanita sola.

   (tener que cuidarla) _____

6. Uses of the Conditional

a. The conditional is generally used as in English:

Ana no lo **pondría** allí.	*Anna would not put it there.*
Me gustaría verlo.	*I would like to see it.*
¿Podría Ud. mostrármelo?	*Would you be able to (Could you) show it to me?*

NOTE:

1. When *would* has the sense of *used to*, the imperfect tense is used in Spanish:

Arturo nos **visitaba a menudo.**   *Arthur would often (used to) visit us.*

2. When *would* has the sense of *to be willing (to want)*, the preterite tense of **querer** is used in Spanish:

No **quiso** pagar la cuenta.   *He wouldn't (wasn't willing to, refused to) pay the bill.*

b. The conditional is used to express wonderment or probability in past time and is often equivalent to English *I wonder, probably, must have, could,* etc.:

¿Qué hora sería cuando salió?   *I wonder what time it was when he went out. (What time could it have been when he went out?)*

Serían las dos.   *It was probably (It must have been) two o'clock.*

NOTE: The expression **deber de** in the imperfect followed by an infinitive may also be used to express probability in past time:

Debían de estar cansados.   *They must have been tired.*
Ella debía de tener veinte años.   *She must have been twenty years old.*

 **Ejercicio O**

Varios amigos leen el periódico para buscar trabajo para el verano. Escriba qué clase de trabajo harían estas personas según los anuncios:

EJEMPLO:

> Se busca
> vendedor de ropa de niños.
> Preséntese en Galerías Gómez,
> Calle Mayor, 3.

Yo vendería ropa de niños.

1.
> Se busca
> persona para tomar
> recados telefónicos.
> Llame al 625-15-55.

2.
> Familia busca
> persona responsable
> para cuidar tres niños
> durante la mañana
> Sra. Flores, 516-59-18

Elena _____

Roberto _____

3.

> Se necesita
> joven responsable
> para entregar flores a domicilio.
> Florería Naturaleza,
> Calle del Jardín, 18.

Jorge _____

_____

4.

> Se buscan
> dos señoritas para cajeras
> en la taquilla del cine Roble.
> Preséntese en persona,
> Lunes de 9 a 11.

Dolores y María _____

_____

5.

> Se buscan
> jóvenes fuertes y corteses
> para servir mesas.
> Restaurante de Oro,
> Calle Principal, 104.

Javier y Octavio _____

_____

Ejercicio P

Conteste las preguntas que le hace un agente de viajes:

1. ¿Adónde le gustaría ir a Ud.?

   _____

2. ¿Cuándo podría salir la familia?

   _____

3. ¿Y en qué fecha volverían Uds.?

   _____

4. ¿Cuántos días pasaría la familia allí?

   _____

5. ¿Haría Ud. el viaje solo(a)?

   _____

6. ¿Cuánto dinero querría Ud. gastar en el viaje?

   _____

7. ¿Harían Uds. excursiones allí?

   _____

8. ¿Tendría Ud. que alquilar un coche allí?

_____

9. ¿Preferiría la familia quedarse en un hotel o en una casa de huéspedes?

_____

10. ¿Cómo pagaría Ud. la cuenta, al contado o con tarjeta de crédito?

_____

◆ MASTERY EXERCISES — CONDITIONAL ◆

Ejercicio Q

_**Complete esta carta que Raquel le escribió a una amiga. Escriba los verbos entre parén-
tesis en el modo potencial:**_

Querida Amelia,

León me escribió que _____ a visitarme. Dijo que me _____
                          1 (venir)   **2** (llamar)

antes de venir. Le aseguré que _____ en casa y le prometí que no _____
                                    3 (estar)   **4** (hacer)

otra cosa. A eso de las cuatro de la tarde él llamó para decirme que no _____
                                                                              5 (poder)

venir. Él _____ que posponer la visita a otra fecha y le _____
              6 (tener)   **7** (gustar)

venir el domingo próximo. Quería saber si yo _____ libre ese día porque
                                                  8 (estar)

_____ invitarme al cine. Nosotros _____ a ver el último estreno
      9 (querer)   **10** (ir)

en el Cine Azteca.

Ejercicio R

_**El año escolar acaba de terminar. Escriba cinco cosas que Ud. haría de manera diferente
el año que viene:**_

EJEMPLO: **Me levantaría más temprano todos los días.**

1. _____

2. _____

3. _____

4. _____

5. _____

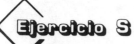

Ejercicio S

Ud. y un amigo quieren pasar el verano estudiando en España. Exprese en español estas frases que Ud. le escribe al director de un programa.

1. A friend and I would like to take a trip to Spain.

   _____

2. We would not like to travel alone.

   _____

3. We would enroll in a summer program.

   _____

4. We would be able to spend two months in Spain.

   _____

5. We would also want to travel within Spain.

   _____

6. Where would we live? We would prefer to live with a Spanish family.

   _____

7. Could you recommend a family to us?

   _____

8. What would we need to travel to Spain?

   _____

9. How much would the trip cost?

   _____

10. Would we receive credit for the summer program?

    _____

Gerundio; Progressive Tenses

The **gerundio** is generally equivalent to the English present participle.

1. *Gerundios* of Regular Verbs

The **gerundio** of regular verbs is formed by dropping the infinitive endings (**-ar, -er, -ir**) and adding **-ando, -iendo**:

cantar:	**cant*ando***	*singing*
comer:	**com*iendo***	*eating*
abrir:	**abr*iendo***	*opening*

2. *Gerundios* Ending in *-yendo*

The **gerundio** of **-er** and **-ir** verbs with stems ending in a vowel is formed by adding **-yendo**:

caer:	**ca*yendo***
creer:	**cre*yendo***
leer:	**le*yendo***
oír:	**o*yendo***
traer:	**tra*yendo***

3. Irregular *Gerundios*

a. In the **gerundio**, stem-changing **-ir** verbs change the stem vowel from **e** to **i** and from **o** to **u**:

decir:	*diciendo*	**pedir:**	*pidiendo*
dormir:	*durmiendo*	**sentir:**	*sintiendo*
morir:	*muriendo*	**venir:**	*viniendo*

b. Other irregular **gerundios**

ir:	*yendo*	**poder:**	*pudiendo*

NOTE: In reflexive verbs, the reflexive pronoun is usually added to the **gerundio** and a written accent is required: **vestirse:** *vistiéndose;* **reírse:** *riéndome;* **bañarse:** *bañándonos;* and so on.

4. *Gerundio* in Progressive Tenses

The **gerundio** is used with forms of the verbs **estar, seguir, continuar,** and with verbs of motion, to stress that an event is (or was or will be) in progress or is continuing at the moment indicated. These tenses are called progressive tenses:

Los niños están jugando.	*The children are playing.*
Salió llorando.	*He went out crying.*
Los tiempos van cambiando.	*Times are changing.*
Siga Ud. leyendo.	*Keep on reading.*
Continuarán estudiando.	*They will continue studying.*
	(They will continue to study.)
Venían corriendo.	*They came running.*

NOTE: The **gerundios** of **estar, ir,** and **venir** are not used to form the progressive tenses of these verbs. Instead, the simple tenses are used:

Ella viene aquí.	*She is coming here.*
Rosa iba al parque.	*Rose was going to the park.*

5. Other Uses of the *Gerundio*

The **gerundio** is often the equivalent of *by* + an English present participle:

Viajando, se aprende mucho.	*By traveling, one learns much.*
Estudiando, saldrás bien en los exámenes.	*By studying, you will pass the examinations.*

Escriba lo que están haciendo las personas en los dibujos:

EJEMPLO:

Arturo y Homero están jugando tenis.

1.

Pepe _____

_____

2.

Elena y Esteban _____

_____

3.

La señora _____

_____

4.

Los señores Cabal _____

_____

5.

Sarita _____

_____

6.

Carlos _____

_____

7.

El niño _____

_____

8.

Las muchachas _____

_____

Ud. está en la cola para entrar en el cine. Escriba cómo salieron del cine estas personas:

EJEMPLO: María / bailar
María salió bailando.

1. Los niños / temblar _____

2. Eduardo / reír _____

3. La señora Tomás / llorar _____

4. Tú / pensar _____

5. Daniel y Fernando / correr _____

6. Leonardo / gritar _____

Ejercicio C

Describa lo que Ud. vio cuando entró en su casa el sábado por la tarde:

EJEMPLO: Cuando entré en la casa, mi mamá **estaba cosiendo** un vestido nuevo. Mi hermana **estaba tocando** el piano y el perro **estaba cantando**. Mi padre **estaba tratando de dormir** la siesta.

_____

_____

_____

_____

_____

_____

_____

_____

_____

Ejercicio D

Ud. va a pasar las vacaciones en el pueblo donde viven sus abuelos. Escriba lo que su abuelo le cuenta de las personas del pueblo. Use el verbo **estar** o **seguir** o **continuar**, *según el caso:*

EJEMPLO: El señor Vargas / vender trigo
El señor Vargas **sigue vendiendo** trigo.

1. Don José / cultivar naranjas _____

2. Doña Petra / morirse _____

3. Los hermanos Pinto / estudiar _____

4. El señor Rangel / cortar leña _____

5. Don Arturo / ser el banquero _____

6. Rosita / cuidar a sus hermanitos _____

7. El hermano de Pedro / decir mentiras _____

8. El pobre anciano / pedir limosna _____

9. Tu abuelita / oír ruidos _____

10. El tío Octavio / perder las llaves _____

Ejercicio E

Es el Año Nuevo y Ud. está trabajando en una emisora. Ud. está describiendo cómo las personas están pasando la noche en un restaurante popular. Complete las frases siguientes, usando el gerundio de uno de los verbos dados (cada verbo debe usarse solamente una vez):

comenzar	divertirse
caer	tirar
tocar	comer
celebrar	cantar
besar	bailar

1. La orquesta está _____ muchas canciones populares.

2. En una mesa un grupo de diez personas está _____ la cena tradicional.

3. Varias personas están _____ el Año Nuevo con champaña.

4. Los jóvenes continúan _____ .

5. Ahora los globos están _____ del techo.

6. La gente está _____ la canción tradicional.

7. Todo el mundo está _____ a comer las doce uvas.

8. Todos los esposos están _____ a sus esposas.

9. Muchas personas siguen _____ serpentinas.

10. Parece que todo el mundo está_____ .

Ejercicio F

Ud. y su familia acaban de comer la cena. Escriba lo que está haciendo cada persona de su familia. Use el verbo **estar** *o* seguir *o* continuar *con gerundios:*

EJEMPLO: **Mi abuelo está mirando la televisión.**

1. Mi madre _____

2. Mi padre _____

3. Mi hermano _____

4. Mi hermana _____

5. Yo _____

Ejercicio G

Exprese en español lo que una profesora les dijo a sus estudiantes al terminar las clases:

1. By studying every day, you can receive good grades.

   _____

2. By traveling, you will see many interesting things.

   _____

3. By working in the summer, you can earn enough money.

   _____

4. By reading a lot, you can increase your vocabulary.

   _____

5. By helping others, you can feel satisfaction.

   _____

6. By following the rules, you do not make mistakes.

   _____

♦ MASTERY EXERCISES ♦

Ejercicio H

Escriba lo que el médico aconseja a los enfermos, usando los verbos beber, comer, dormir, fumar, hacer *y* tomar *(cada verbo debe usarse solamente una vez):*

1. Continúe _____ ocho horas cada noche.

2. Siga _____ la misma medicina.

3. Siga _____ mucha fruta fresca.

4. Siga _____ mucho ejercicio.

5. Continúe _____ cinco vasos de agua al día.

6. Siga_____ menos.

Ejercicio I

Exprese en español los preparativos que Ud. está haciendo para celebrar las bodas de oro de sus abuelos:

1. We will be celebrating the anniversary for two days.

    _____

2. The guests will continue arriving in the afternoon.

    _____

3. The orchestra will be playing in the living room while we eat.

    _____

4. The waiters will keep on serving food in the tent in the garden until late.

    _____

5. The children will be happy playing in the garden.

    _____

6. My grandparents will be standing at the door, greeting everyone.

    _____

7. Everyone will be having a good time, eating well and dancing.

    _____

Ejercicio J

Describa lo que Ud. estará haciendo en el año 2000 (su trabajo, su familia, sus pasatiempos, etc.):

_____

_____

_____

_____

_____

_____

_____

_____

Past Participle; Compound Tenses

1. Past Participles

a. Past participles of regular verbs

The past participle of regular verbs is formed by dropping the infinitive ending and adding **-ado** or **-ido:**

tomar:	**tom***ado*	taken
comer:	**com***ido*	eaten
sufrir:	**sufr***ido*	suffered

b. Past participles ending in **-ído**

The past participles of **-er** and **-ir** verbs with stems ending in a vowel have an accent mark:

caer:	**ca***ído*	**oír:**	**o***ído*
creer:	**cre***ído*	**reír:**	**re***ído*
leer:	**le***ído*	**traer:**	**tra***ído*

c. Irregular past participles

The following verbs and compounds of these verbs have irregular past participles:

abrir: *abierto* opened	**morir:** *muerto* died
cubrir: *cubierto* covered	**poner:** *puesto* put
decir: *dicho* said	**resolver:** *resuelto* resolved, solved
escribir: *escrito* written	**romper:** *roto* broken
hacer: *hecho* done	**ver:** *visto* seen
imprimir: *impreso* printed	**volver:** *vuelto* returned

Also, **descubrir (***descubierto***), deshacer (***deshecho***), imponer (***impuesto***), devolver (***devuelto***),** and others.

Ejercicio A

Complete esta carta que Sofía le escribió a Clara, usando los participios pasados de los verbos indicados:

Querida Clara,

¿No has _____ mis dos últimas cartas? ¿Por qué no me has _____ ?
1 (recibir)   **2** (escribir)

He _____ de llamarte por teléfono, pero nadie ha _____ . Ya he
    3 (tratar)   **4** (contestar)

_____ de mi viaje y también te he _____ varias tarjetas
    5 (regresar)   **6** (mandar)

postales de las ciudades que he _____ .
                                        7 (visitar)

¡Ya han _____ las vacaciones! ¡Qué lástima! Pero Rafael y yo hemos
        8 (terminar)

_____ de un viaje estupendo. Ya hemos _____ al trabajo,
    9 (disfrutar)   **10** (volver)

pero no hemos _____ los días que hemos _____ en
                11 (olvidar)   **12** (pasar)

la Costa del Sol. Tú nunca has _____ allí, ¿verdad? Desde que hemos
                                13 (estar)

_____ a casa, hemos _____ ese viaje a todos nuestros amigos.
    14 (llegar)   **15** (recomendar)

Rafael y yo hemos _____ que jamás hemos _____ playas más
                    16 (decir)   **17** (ver)

bonitas. Y todo el mundo ha _____ tan simpático. Ya hemos
                            18 (ser)

_____ en hacer otro viaje allí pronto.
    19 (pensar)

Me sorprendió no haber _____ noticias tuyas. Sé que has _____
                        20 (tener)   **21** (ir)

a casa de tu hermana y que has _____ cuidando a tus sobrinos mientras que tu
                                22 (estar)

hermana ha _____ un viaje a París. ¿Se han _____ bien los
            23 (hacer)   **24** (portar)

niños? Ha _____ mucho trabajo, ¿verdad?
        25 (ser)

Hasta pronto,

Sofía

2. Compound Tenses

The past participle is used with the various tenses of the verb **haber** (*to have*) to form the compound tenses.

a. Present perfect tense

The present perfect tense is used to describe an action that began in the past and continues up to the present or an action that took place in the past but is connected with the present. It is formed with the present tense of **haber** and the past participle:

I have entered (eaten, lived) here lately.

he		hemos	
has	**entrado (comido, vivido)**	**habéis**	**entrado (comido, vivido)**
ha	aquí últimamente.	**han**	aquí últimamente.

b. Pluperfect (past perfect) tense

The pluperfect tense is used to describe an action that was completed in the past before another action took place. It is formed with the imperfect tense of **haber** and the past participle:

I had entered (eaten, lived) here before.

había	⎫		**habíamos**	⎫
habías	⎬ **entrado (comido, vivido)**		**habíais**	⎬ **entrado (comido, vivido)**
había	⎭ aquí antes.		**habían**	⎭ aquí antes.

c. Preterite perfect tense

The preterite perfect tense is used mainly in literary style to indicate that the action or event had just ended. It usually follows such expressions as **cuando** (*when*); **apenas** (*scarcely, hardly*); **después (de) que** (*after*); **luego que, en cuanto, así que, tan pronto como** (*as soon as*). In conversation and informal writing, the preterite perfect is replaced by the preterite or the pluperfect tense. The preterite perfect is formed with the preterite tense of **haber** and the past participle:

I had entered (eaten, lived)

hube	⎫		**hubimos**	⎫
hubiste	⎬ **entrado (comido, vivido)**		**hubisteis**	⎬ **entrado (comido, vivido)**
hubo	⎭		**hubieron**	⎭

LITERARY: **Apenas hube llegado** cuando me llamó.　⎱ *I had scarcely arrived when*
INFORMAL: **Apenas había llegado** cuando me llamó.　⎰ *he called me.*

LITERARY: **En cuanto hubo entrado,** todos se
　　　　　levantaron.　　　　　　　　　⎱ *As soon as he had entered,*
INFORMAL: **En cuanto entró,** todos se levantaron.　⎰ *everyone got up.*

d. Future perfect tense

The future perfect tense is used to describe an action or event that will have been completed in the future. It is formed with the future tense of **haber** and the past participle:

I shall (will) have entered (eaten, lived), etc.

habré	⎫		**habremos**	⎫
habrás	⎬ **entrado (comido, vivido)**		**habréis**	⎬ **entrado (comido, vivido)**
habrá	⎭		**habrán**	⎭

NOTE:
1. The future perfect may be used to express probability in past time:

¿Lo **habrá terminado?**	*I wonder if he has finished it.* (*Can he have finished it?*)
Habrán perdido las llaves.	*They (have) probably lost the keys.* (*They must have lost the keys.*)

2. The expression **deber de** followed by the perfect infinitive may be substituted for the future perfect in expressing probability in past time:

Deben de haber perdido las llaves.	*They must have lost the keys.*
Debe de haber tomado el libro.	*He must have taken the book.*

e. Conditional perfect tense

The conditional perfect tense is used to describe an action or event that would have been completed in the past. It is formed with the conditional tense of **haber** and the past participle:

I would have entered (eaten, lived), etc.

habría ⎫		habríamos ⎫	
habrías ⎬ entrado (comido, vivido)		habríais ⎬ entrado (comido, vivido)	
habría ⎭		habrían ⎭	

NOTE: The conditional perfect is used to express probability in past time:

¿Lo **habría terminado?** *I wonder if he had finished it. (Could he have finished it?)*

Habrían perdido las llaves. *They had probably lost the keys.*

f. Perfect infinitive

The perfect infinitive is formed with the infinitive of **haber** and the past participle:

haber entrado (comido, vivido) *to have entered (eaten, lived)*

g. Perfect participle

The perfect participle is formed with the **gerundio** of **haber** and the past participle:

habiendo entrado (comido, vivido) *having entered (eaten, lived)*

 **Ejercicio B**

Escriba lo que han hecho estas personas para un picnic en el parque.

EJEMPLO: Arturo / comprar el pan
Arturo ha comprado el pan.

1. Graciela / preparar la ensalada

_____

2. Tú / traer una manta

_____

3. Elena y Roberto / sacar fotos

_____

4. Javier / encender el fuego

_____

5. Yo / cocinar las salchichas

_____

6. Sarita / poner la mesa

_____

7. Jorge y yo / llevar una canasta de fruta

_____

8. Ricardo / buscar dónde comprar los refrescos

_____

9. Beatriz / organizar unos juegos

   _____

10. Todo el mundo / contribuir dinero

    _____

Ejercicio C

Es sábado y Ud. ha dormido hasta el mediodía. Escriba lo que los otros miembros de su familia han hecho mientras Ud. dormía. Use las sugerencias o piense en otras:

SUGERENCIAS: limpiar la sala   sacar al perro
               lavar el carro   cortar la hierba del jardín
               ir de compras   hacer los ejercicios físicos
               arreglar el cuarto

1. Mi padre _____

2. Mi madre _____

3. Mi hermana _____

4. Mis hermanos _____

5. _____

6. _____

Ejercicio D

Conteste las preguntas que le hace un joven colombiano:

1. ¿Ha visto Ud. muchos partidos de béisbol?

   _____

2. ¿Han terminado ya las clases para este año?

   _____

3. ¿Ha decidido Ud. cómo va a pasar las vacaciones?

   _____

4. ¿Ha ido Ud. a los conciertos al aire libre durante el verano?

   _____

5. ¿Le han gustado esos conciertos?

   _____

6. ¿Ha buscado Ud. trabajo?

7. ¿Ha visitado Ud. Colombia?

8. ¿Han hecho Ud. y sus amigos algún viaje al extranjero?

9. ¿Ha escuchado Ud. las noticias del día?

10. ¿Ha jugado Ud. dominó alguna vez?

Ejercicio E

Escriba lo que estas personas habían hecho antes de la llegada de los invitados a la fiesta:

EJEMPLO: Anita / decorar el cuarto
            Anita había decorado el cuarto.

1. Raúl / traer los refrescos

2. Gabriel y Alfonso / poner las mesas

3. Marta / cortar la carne

4. Yo / comprar los platos de papel

5. Tú / preparar los refrescos

6. Carlos / arreglar las sillas

7. Mi madre / cocinar una paella

8. David y yo / escoger los discos

9. Mi papá / bajar el tocadiscos

10. Gloria / apagar el televisor

Ejercicio F

Escriba qué comodidades encontró la señora Cajal en su último viaje:

> EJEMPLO: Cuando llegamos al cuarto del hotel,
> el botones / subir las maletas
> **el botones ya había subido** las maletas.

1. Cuando llegamos al cuarto del hotel,
   a. la camarera / limpiar el cuarto

   _____

   b. el gerente / poner flores frescas

   _____

   c. el guía / mandar una botella de vino al cuarto

   _____

2. Cuando íbamos a los restaurantes,
   a. el guía / hacer la reservación

   _____

   b. el mesero / poner pan y mantequilla en la mesa

   _____

   c. el capitán / pedir agua mineral

   _____

3. Cuando visitábamos los museos,
   a. el guía / conseguir las entradas

   _____

   b. el chofer / estacionar cerca de la puerta de salida

   _____

Ejercicio G

Es el último día de su clase de español. Escriba cinco cosas que Ud. no había hecho hasta este año. Use las sugerencias o piense en otras:

> SUGERENCIAS: declamar un poema en español   hacer un viaje a España
> comer en un restaurante español   preparar una piñata
> escribir una carta comercial   leer una obra de teatro

1. _____

2. _____

3. _____

4. _____

5. _____

Ejercicio H

Escriba quién(es) habrá(n) hecho estas travesuras durante una excursión al parque:

> EJEMPLO: Jaime / quitar las flores
> **Jaime habrá quitado** las flores.

1. Ramón / romper la ventana _____

2. Tú / dejar la basura en el suelo _____

3. Mi hermanito / perder el guante de béisbol _____

4. Rosa / caerse al lago _____

5. Los niños / esconder la comida _____

6. Nosotros / llenar los globos de agua _____

7. Uds. / chocarse con otros barcos en el lago _____

Ejercicio I

Escriba lo que habrán pensado sus padres cuando Ud. salió con unos amigos por un fin de semana:

> EJEMPLO: llevar un suéter
> **¿Habrá llevado** un suéter?

1. llevar un paraguas

    _____

2. tener bastante dinero

    _____

3. comer bien

    _____

4. comprar el boleto de vuelta

    _____

5. nadar en la piscina

    _____

6. jugar tenis

    _____

7. conocer a muchos jóvenes

    _____

8. darles propina a los meseros

    _____

9. gastar todo el dinero

_____

10. olvidar llamarnos por teléfono

_____

Ejercicio J

Escriba lo que Ud. habría hecho en estas circunstancias:

      EJEMPLO: Dos carros chocaron en la esquina. (llamar a la policía)
                  Yo habría llamado a la policía.

1. Un anciano se cayó en la calle. (ayudarle a levantarse)

_____

2. Se le olvidó a su madre comprar leche. (ir a la tienda a comprarla)

_____

3. Un amigo estuvo en el hospital por cinco días. (visitarlo en el hospital)

_____

4. Su padre no quería hablar con alguien por teléfono. (decir que no estaba en casa)

_____

5. Su hermanito tenía mucha hambre. (prepararle un sandwich)

_____

6. Ayer fue el cumpleaños de una amiga suya. (darle flores)

_____

7. Un amigo suyo no tenía dinero para ir al cine con Ud. (prestarle 5 dólares)

_____

Ejercicio K

Escriba lo que Ud. habría hecho en estas circunstancias:

1. No pudo cerrar la llave del baño.

_____

2. Oyó ruidos extraños en la casa por la noche.

_____

3. Olió gas en la cocina.

_____

4. Perdió todo su dinero y no pudo subir al autobús.

_____

5. Ud. rompió un florero valioso de su mamá.

_____

6. Su perro mordió a un niño en la calle.

_____

Ejercicio L

Escriba lo que hicieron estas personas habiendo terminado estas cosas:

EJEMPLO: Carlos escribió una carta. (ponerla en un sobre)
Habiendo escrito la carta, **Carlos la puso** en un sobre.

1. María acostó a su hijito. (apagar la luz)

_____

2. Ellos comieron la merienda. (lavar los platos)

_____

3. Lourdes y yo salimos del cine. (volver a casa)

_____

4. Mi hermana lavó la ropa. (ponerla en la secadora)

_____

5. Los amigos jugaron una partida de ajedrez. (tomar un refresco)

_____

6. Tú compraste ropa nueva. (guardarla en el armario)

_____

7. Yo cerré el libro. (dejarlo en la mesa)

_____

Ejercicio M

El director de su escuela va a presentar unos premios a unos estudiantes de intercambio de países hispanos. Ayúdele a expresar lo siguiente en español:

EJEMPLO: For having studied hard.
Por haber estudiado mucho.

1. For having won many races.

_____

2. For having drawn the best poster.

_____

3. For having written the best poem.

_____

4. For having helped others.

_____

5. For having built the best train.

_____

6. For having learned the most English.

_____

7. For having prepared the best skits.

_____

♦ MASTERY EXERCISES ♦

Ejercicio N

Describa lo que Ud. y un amigo han hecho antes de salir de viaje al extranjero. Use las sugerencias o piense en otras:

SUGERENCIAS: sacar el pasaporte   hacer la maleta
                comprar el boleto   lavar la ropa
                hacer la reservación   leer las guías turísticas
                escribir a los hoteles   visitar la oficina de turismo
                cambiar dinero   hablar con otras personas
                confirmar la reservación del vuelo   sacar dinero del banco

1. _____

2. _____

3. _____

4. _____

5. _____

6. _____

7. _____

8. _____

9. _____

10. _____

Ejercicio O

Exprese en español sus planes para la universidad:

1. You have thought about several universities.

_____

2. You have written requesting their catalogues.

_____

3. Your parents have asked how much it will cost.

_____

4. The four years will have cost more than ten thousand dollars.

_____

5. Your parents have thought that was a lot of money.

_____

6. Your sister's friend had recommended another university to you.

_____

7. He had told you that many of his cousins had studied there.

_____

8. Having sent your application early, you should have heard from them already.

_____

9. To have been accepted at this university is an honor.

_____

10. In four years you will have completed your studies.

_____

Ser and Estar

1. Uses of *ser*

Ser is used:

a. to express an inherent quality or characteristic of the subject:

> **Este vino *es de España*.**
> **La casa *es de madera*.**
> **Felipe *es bueno*.**

b. to describe or identify the subject:

> **María *es alta (joven)*.**
> **Mi hermano *es médico (fuerte)*.**
> **El coche *es nuevo (blanco)*.**
> **Juana *es rica (feliz)*.**
> **¿Quién *es*? *Soy* yo (*es* él).**

c. to express time, dates, and where an event takes place:

> **¿Qué *hora es*? *Son las dos*.**
> **¿*Dónde es* el concierto? El concierto *es en el parque*.**
> **Hoy *es treinta de enero*.**

d. with impersonal expressions:

> **Es necesario estudiar.**
> **Es importante llegar a tiempo.**

e. to express a passive action with the past participle (see Chapter 12, page 131):

> **Las ventanas *fueron cerradas* por el profesor.**
> **La puerta *fue abierta* por el niño.**

> NOTE: The forms of **ser** are summarized in the section on irregular verbs in the Appendix, page 509.

 **Ejercicio A**

Conteste las preguntas que le hace un amigo nuevo:

1. ¿Quién es usted?

_____

2. ¿De dónde es usted?

_____

3. ¿Cuál es su nacionalidad?

   _____

4. ¿Cómo es usted?

   _____

5. ¿De qué es su casa?

   _____

6. ¿De qué color es su casa?

   _____

7. ¿Es usted un estudiante aplicado?

   _____

8. ¿Quién es el hijo mayor de su familia? ¿el hijo menor?

   _____

9. ¿Son simpáticos sus hermanos?

   _____

10. ¿Cómo es su cuarto?

    _____

11. ¿Cuáles son sus pasatiempos favoritos?

    _____

12. ¿Quién es su mejor amigo(a)?

    _____

13. Es importante estudiar, ¿verdad?

    _____

14. ¿Cuál es la fecha de hoy?

    _____

15. ¿Qué hora es?

    _____

Ejercicio B

Ud. acaba de recibir una carta de una nueva amiga que vive en México. Complete las frases con la forma apropiada del verbo **ser**:

Querido amigo/Querida amiga,

Yo _____ Gloria Carballo. Ahora vivo en México pero no _____
      1   2

mexicana. _____ de España y vivimos en México porque mi padre
          3

_____ el cónsul de España y le toca trabajar en México por dos años.
                  4

Nosotros _____ una familia grande y unida. Mis dos hermanos, Jorge y
                         5

Víctor, _____ mayores y mi hermana Pilar _____ menor que
                 6   7

yo. Mi mamá no trabaja pero como _____ la esposa de un diplomático,
                                                     8

_____ importante que ella vaya a muchas funciones del gobierno con mi padre.
            9

Yo creo que mis hermanos _____ guapos. También _____
                                          10   11

muy enérgicos y _____ buenos futbolistas. Ellos _____
                            12   13

estudiantes de la universidad.

La casa en que vivimos _____ muy grande. _____ de ladrillo.
                                       14   15

Las casas de México no _____ de madera porque _____ más
                                       16   17

frescas cuando hace calor si _____ de piedra. Esta casa _____
                                         18   19

de un señor rico. Hay muchos cuartos. Mi dormitorio _____ pequeño pero lindo.
                                                                    20

Da al jardín y _____ agradable sentarme allí por la tarde. Mi hermana
                        21

_____ celosa y siempre me dice: «Oye, tú _____ la preferida
            22   23

de esta familia porque tu cuarto _____ el más bonito.» Mis amigos
                                              24

_____ de muchas partes del mundo pero la mayoría de ellos
            25

_____ mexicanos. Sus fiestas _____ muy
            26   27

animadas y _____ bonito escuchar la música de los mariachis. Todos mis amigos
                    28

_____ simpáticos, pero Rocío Pérez _____ mi mejor amiga.
            29   30

También mi hermana y yo _____ buenas amigas.
                                         31

Ahora _____ las cuatro y media de la tarde y debo despedirme de ti porque
               32

_____ la hora de mi clase de piano. Tocar un instrumento musical
            33

_____ lindo, ¿verdad? En tu carta cuéntame de tus amigos y dime cuáles
            34

_____ tus pasatiempos preferidos. _____ muy interesante
            35   36

tener amistades de otros países, ¿verdad?

                                                        Hasta pronto.

2. Uses of *estar*

Estar is used

a. to express the location, position, or situation of the subject:

> **Madrid** *está en España.*
> *¿Dónde está* **la casa?**
> **Felipe** *está delante de la biblioteca.*

b. to indicate a state or condition of the subject:

> **María** *está cansada (sentada).*
> **El coche** *está lleno (sucio).*
> **Ellos** *están alegres (tristes).*
> **Luis** *está enfermo (bien).*
> **La puerta** *está abierta (cerrada).*
> **El gato** *está vivo (muerto).*

c. to form the progressive tenses (with the **gerundio**):

> **Están cantando.**
> **Estaban jugando.**

NOTE:

1. A condition may be a phase: **Juan está enfermo (triste);** a temporary state: **Está cansado (sentado);** or the result of an action: **La puerta está cerrada.** Note that a condition does not identify, describe, or express a characteristic.

2. The forms of **estar** are summarized in the section on irregular verbs in the Appendix, page 508.

d. in certain common expressions:

estar a punto de + infinitive *to be just about to*
estar para + infinitive *to be about to*
estar por *to be in favor of*
estar por + infinitive *to be inclined to*
estar conforme, estar de acuerdo (con) *to be in agreement (with), to agree*
estar de vuelta *to be back*

Espérame, *estoy a punto de* **terminar.**	*Wait for me, I'm just about to finish.*
Estoy para **salir.**	*I'm about to leave.*
Estoy por **el nuevo candidato.**	*I am in favor of the new candidate.*
Estoy por **ir de compras.**	*I am inclined to go shopping.*
No *está de acuerdo* **conmigo.**	*He doesn't agree with me.*
No *estoy conforme* **con su opinión.**	*I am not in agreement with your opinion.*

Ejercicio C

Usted presenció un accidente. Conteste las preguntas que le hace un policía:

1. ¿Dónde estaba Ud. cuando los vehículos chocaron? (en la esquina)

2.   ¿Estaban sentados o de pie los pasajeros del autobús? (sentados y de pie)

_____

3.   ¿Estaba lleno el autobús? (Sí)

_____

4.   ¿Dónde estaba el autobús? (parado en el semáforo)

_____

5.   ¿Dónde estaba el coche? (detrás del autobús)

_____

6.   ¿Cómo estaba la puerta del autobús? (abierta)

_____

7.   ¿Estaban bajándose algunos pasajeros del autobús? (Sí, tres personas)

_____

8.   ¿Quién estaba conduciendo el coche? (un señor)

_____

9.   ¿Qué estaban haciendo los pasajeros del coche? (hablando)

_____

10.   ¿Quién estaba sentado detrás del chofer del coche? (un niño)

_____

11.   ¿Qué estaba haciendo este niño? (jugando)

_____

12.   En su opinión, ¿cómo estaba el señor del coche? (distraído)

_____

Ejercicio D

David no se siente bien y va a la oficina de la enfermera de la escuela. Habla con ella.
Complete este diálogo con las formas apropiadas de **estar:**

David: Buenas tardes.

Enfermera: Buenas tardes, David. ¿Cómo _____ tú hoy?
                                              1

David: Yo no _____ bien. _____ enfermo. Me duele todo
                            2   3

                el cuerpo.

Enfermera: Sí, tú _____ muy pálido. ¿Desde cuándo _____ tú
                            4   5

                así?

David: Hoy por la mañana yo _____ bien. Luego, cuando yo
6

_____ en la clase de inglés, me dio tos.
7

Enfermera: ¿_____ tus padres en casa ahora?
8

David: No. Mi padre _____ trabajando y mi madre _____
9   10

visitando a mis abuelos porque mi abuelo _____ en el hospital. Ella
11

no _____ de vuelta hasta las cinco.
12

Enfermera: ¿_____ tu padre en su oficina ahora?
13

David: No lo creo. Él debe _____ en la oficina de uno de sus clientes. Él
14

_____ a punto de salir para allá cuando yo llamé.
15

Enfermera: ¿Dónde _____ tus hermanos?
16

David: Uno _____ estudiando en la universidad y los otros dos
17

_____ trabajando. Ellos _____ lejos de aquí.
18   19

Enfermera: ¿Dónde _____ situada la oficina de tu médico?
20

David: Su oficina _____ en la Calle Madero, pero él no va a
21

_____ allí hasta las seis.
22

Enfermera: Aquí hace frío porque las ventanas _____ abiertas. Tú deberías
23

_____ en casa.
24

David: Yo _____ de acuerdo. Mis tíos _____ en casa
25   26

ahora y su casa _____ cerca de la escuela.
27

Enfermera: Voy a llamarlos. Si ellos no _____ ocupados, tú puedes ir a su casa.
28

3. Adjectives Used with *ser* or *estar*

a. Some adjectives may be used with either **ser** or **estar,** but the meaning of an adjective used with
ser will differ from its meaning when used with **estar:**

Julio *es bueno (malo).*   *Julio is good (bad).*   (characteristic)
La sopa *está buena (mala).*   *The soup is good (bad).*   (condition)

Es listo.	*He is clever (smart).*	(characteristic)
Está listo.	*He is ready.*	(condition)
Es pálido.	*He is pale-complexioned.*	(characteristic)
Está pálido.	*He is pale.*	(condition)
Es seguro.	*It is safe (reliable).*	(description/characteristic)
Está seguro.	*He is sure.*	(condition/state of mind)
Él es vivo.	*He is sharp (quick).*	(characteristic)
Él está vivo.	*He is alive.*	(state/phase)
Es viejo (joven).	*He is old (young).*	(description)
Está viejo (joven).	*He looks old (young).*	(condition)
Él es aburrido.	*He is boring.*	(characteristic)
Él está aburrido.	*He is bored.*	(condition/state)

b. Adjectives used with **ser** and **estar** agree with the subject in gender and number:

> **Alicia está ocupada.**   *Alicia is busy.*
> **Eran pobres.**   *They were poor.*

Ejercicio E

Complete esta descripción que hace Arturo de un domingo de primavera, con las formas apropiadas de **ser** *o* **estar**:

Hoy _____ domingo. _____ el dos de mayo y empieza a hacer
            1   2

buen tiempo, porque nosotros _____ en primavera. _____ las
                                      3   4

ocho de la mañana cuando me levanto. Las ventanas de mi cuarto _____ abiertas
                                                                        5

y el aire que entra _____ fresco.
                             6

_____ un buen día para _____ en el parque. Mis amigos
        7   8

_____ de acuerdo, pero ellos _____ trabajando y no pueden
        9   10

acompañarme. No me gusta _____ solo, pero la única persona que
                                 11

_____ dispuesta a pasar el día conmigo _____ mi hermano
        12   13

menor. Mi hermana mayor _____ lista e interesante, pero hoy ella
                                14

_____ muy preocupada. No le gusta su trabajo. Ella _____
        15   16

buscando un trabajo nuevo y va a _____ ocupada hoy porque
                                         17

_____ 18 _____ escribiendo cartas a varias compañías. Yo _____ 19 _____ seguro

de que mis padres van a _____ 20 _____ furiosos si no quiero llevar a mi hermano menor.

_____ 21 _____ cansado de salir con él porque siempre me _____ 22 _____

haciendo muchas preguntas. Él _____ 23 _____ un chico bueno, pero él nunca

_____ 24 _____ satisfecho. Le gusta _____ 25 _____ sentado delante de la casa y

hablar con las personas que _____ 26 _____ caminando por la calle. No quiero

_____ 27 _____ malo, pero voy a decirles a mis padres que hoy yo voy a

_____ 28 _____ fuera hasta muy tarde. Entonces no tendré que

_____ 29 _____ cuidando a mi hermano menor. Yo _____ 30 _____ muy listo,

¿verdad?

Ejercicio F

Teresa le cuenta a su madre sobre su viaje a España y las personas que conoció. Complete las frases con las formas correctas de ser _o_ estar:

1. Elena _____ cubana pero ahora ella y su familia _____ viviendo en España.

2. Lionel _____ muy listo en la escuela pero nunca _____ listo para salir a tiempo.

3. Su padre _____ médico pero él _____ en el hospital porque _____ enfermo.

4. El museo _____ enfrente de la casa en que vivía.

5. El señor Vargas _____ ingeniero. Sus hijos siempre _____ jugando en el patio.

6. Los vestidos de la señora Vargas _____ de colores muy vivos y siempre _____ limpios.

7. El señor Vargas les dice a sus hijos que _____ importante honrar a sus padres.

8. Las ventanas _____ abiertas y los muebles _____ llenos de polvo.

9. Comíamos en un restaurante que _____ cerca de la casa, pero la sopa nunca _____ caliente.

10. Mamá, tú todavía _____ pálida de la sorpresa.

Ejercicio G

Usted ha conocido a alguien por medio de una carta. Conteste las preguntas que le hizo a Ud. en la carta:

1. ¿De dónde es Ud.?

    _____

2. ¿Dónde está Ud. ahora?

    _____

3. ¿Cómo está Ud. hoy?

    _____

4. ¿Quién está al lado de Ud.?

    _____

5. ¿Qué está Ud. haciendo ahora?

    _____

6. ¿Qué quiere Ud. ser algún día?

    _____

7. ¿Cómo es Ud.: alto/alta o bajo/baja; rubio/rubia o moreno/morena; gordo/gorda o delgado/delgada?

    _____

8. ¿Es Ud. un amigo/una amiga fiel?

    _____

9. ¿Dónde está situada su casa?

    _____

10. ¿Es su casa de piedra, de madera o de ladrillos?

    _____

11. ¿Está rodeada de árboles su escuela?

    _____

12. ¿Está Ud. atento/atenta cuando hablan sus profesores?

    _____

13. ¿Está Ud. de acuerdo con lo que dicen?

    _____

14. ¿Quién fue elegido presidente de los Estados Unidos?

    _____

15. ¿Está Ud. conforme con las ideas del nuevo presidente?

    _____

16. ¿Por quién estuvo Ud.?

    _____

17. ¿Estaba Ud. ocupado/ocupada ayer?

_____

18. ¿Qué estaba Ud. haciendo?

_____

19. ¿Es Ud. un estudiante ejemplar?

_____

20. ¿Dónde están sus amigos/amigas ahora?

_____

21. ¿Qué hace Ud. cuando está cansado/cansada?

_____

22. ¿Es Ud. una persona perezosa?

_____

23. ¿Por qué está Ud. alegre hoy?

_____

24. ¿A qué hora está Ud. de vuelta en su casa por las tardes?

_____

♦ MASTERY EXERCISES ♦

 **Ejercicio H**

Escoja la forma correcta del verbo ser *o* estar *para completar los trozos siguientes:*

1. (Estaban, Eran) las tres de la tarde. (Estaba, Era) un día hermoso de agosto. Los árboles (estaban, eran) cargados de frutas que más tarde (estarían, serían) recogidas por niños y mayores. El aire (estaba, era) lleno del rumor de pájaros e insectos que se aprovechaban de la luz del sol. En los campos de trigo y de maíz, los agricultores (estaban, eran) trabajando entre gritos y risas. El cielo (estaba, era) completamente libre de nubes. (Estaba, Era) una escena de belleza ideal. «Esto (está, es) vivir»pensaba el turista, respirando fuerte. La tristeza que había sentido antes iba cambiando. Ahora (estaba, era) alegre.

2. Luisito (está, es) un muchacho de trece años. (Está, Es) alto y rubio y tiene una sonrisa de ángel. (Está, Es) bueno, listo y simpático, pero bastante pícaro y atrevido. Ayer se subió a un manzano y comió un par de manzanas verdes. Ahora (está, es) enfermo, con fiebre, y tiene que (estar, ser) en cama todo el día. Le visité esta mañana y (estaba, era) pálido. Le pregunté:«¿Cómo (estás, eres)?» Me contestó con voz muy débil:«(Estoy, Soy) muy mal hoy.» El médico dice que la enfermedad no (está, es) grave, y que dentro de dos o tres días Luisito (estará, será) tan bien como antes.

3. Los aztecas (estaban, eran) dueños del Valle de México. Su capital (estaba, era) Tenochtitlán (que hoy día (está, es) la Ciudad de México). (Estaba, Era) situada en un lago y (estaba, era) comple-

tamente rodeada de agua. Para llegar allí, (estaba, era) necesario cruzar por medio de uno de los numerosos puentes. En el centro de la ciudad (estaba, era) el palacio del emperador. (Estaban, Eran) una raza bárbara y militar y se habían hecho propietarios de mucho terreno ajeno. Cuando llegó Cortés, muchas naciones (estaban, eran) sujetas al poder de los aztecas. Su gobierno (estaba, era) severo y cruel, y practicaban el culto del sacrificio humano en los altares de sus templos.

4. El director de la expedición (estuvo, fue) el Sr. Suárez. (Estaba, Era) un hombre de mucha experiencia, de origen gallego, que había (estado, sido) navegante y que había (estado, sido) en muchos puertos. (Estaba, Era) martes, el treinta de enero, cuando salimos y nos dirigimos al África, donde, según él, (estaba, era) el tesoro. El mar (estaba, era) tranquilo. Una noche (estábamos, éramos) sentados en el salón, cuando uno de los compañeros de la empresa le preguntó si (estaba, era) seguro de que el mapa (estaba, era) genuino. Lleno de risa, se levantó de su asiento.

5. El Sr. Torres (estaba, era) de España. (Estaba, Era) español de nacimiento. Había venido a Buenos Aires para (estar, ser) administrador del negocio de su padre, en la industria de la lana. (Estaba, Era) viudo y vivía con sus hijas y sus nietos. Su trabajo (estaba, era) fácil, y tenía muchas horas libres. Su casa (estaba, era) situada en la avenida principal de la ciudad y (estaba, era) de buena construcción, de ladrillos. Tenía una biblioteca que también (estaba, era) despacho, con gran número de libros, cuadros y curiosidades. (Estaba, Era) muy aficionado a la lectura y prefería obras de historia. La puerta siempre (estaba, era) abierta para los amigos y conocidos.

Ejercicio I

Lea este cuento sobre un viaje que hicieron Roberto y Luis. Complete cada frase con la forma correcta de ser o estar:

Roberto y Luis _____ viajando en automóvil. _____ de noche.
                        1   2

El cielo _____ muy oscuro y _____ lleno de nubes. Los jóvenes
                3   4

_____ para atravesar un puente. El puente parecía _____ muy
        5   6

viejo. Ellos querían _____ seguros de que el puente _____ muy
                            7   8

seguro. Roberto _____ manejando el coche. El coche _____
                        9   10

detenido delante de la entrada al puente. Luis _____ leyendo un letrero que
                                                        11

decía: «El puente _____ inspeccionado por las autoridades hace un mes.» Los
                        12

jóvenes _____ decididos a llegar a su destino antes del amanecer. Roberto
                13

_____ preocupado, pero Luis le dijo que no debía _____
        14   15

preocupado porque el puente _____ seguro.
                                    16

Ejercicio J

Exprese en español este diálogo que tiene lugar en casa de Alicia:

Juan: Who is it?

_____

Señor: It is I, Mr. Rivera. Is Alicia at home?

_____

Juan: She is in the living room. She is speaking on the telephone.

_____

_____

Señor: Will she be busy for a long time?

_____

Juan: I doubt it. She was about to hang up. Here she is now.

_____

_____

Señor: Hello, Alicia. Are you ready for your violin lesson?

_____

Alicia: I'm ready but I am worried because I have not been practicing every day.

_____

_____

Señor: You are a smart girl. You know that it is important to practice every day.

_____

_____

Alicia: I agree with you but I have been very busy.

_____

Señor: This work was written by a famous composer. He was German.

_____

_____

Alicia: It is very beautiful.

_____

Señor: What time is it?

_____

Alicia: It is five-thirty. My parents will be back soon.

_____

_____

Señor: Today I have been running from one side of the city to the other and I am very tired.

_____

_____

Alicia: At what time will you be here next week?

_____

_____

Señor: I'll be here at the same time. This has been a good lesson today.

_____

_____

Alicia: So long.

_____

Señor: And remember that it is very important to practice every day. Good-bye.

_____

_____

Reflexive Verbs

1. Reflexive Constructions in Simple and Compound Tenses

The reflexive pronouns (**me, te, se, nos, os, se**) generally precede the verb in the simple and compound tenses:

PRESENT TENSE

(yo) *me* **lavo**	(nosotros, -as) *nos* **lavamos**
(tú) *te* **lavas**	(vosotros, -as) *os* **laváis**
(Ud., él, ella) *se* **lava**	(Uds., ellos, -as) *se* **lavan**

PRETERITE
me lavé, te lavaste, etc.

IMPERFECT
me lavaba, te lavabas, etc.

FUTURE
me lavaré, te lavarás, etc.

CONDITIONAL
me lavaría, te lavarías, etc.

PRESENT PERFECT TENSE

(yo) *me* **he lavado**	(nosotros, -as) *nos* **hemos lavado**
(tú) *te* **has lavado**	(vosotros, -as) *os* **habéis lavado**
(Ud., él, ella) *se* **ha lavado**	(Uds., ellos, -as) *se* **han lavado**

PLUPERFECT
me había lavado, te habías lavado, etc.

FUTURE PERFECT
me habré lavado, te habrás lavado, etc.

CONDITIONAL PERFECT
me habría lavado, te habrías lavado, etc.

NOTE: The reflexive pronoun is another form of object pronoun, either direct or indirect. It indicates that the subject and the object of the verb are the same person or thing:

Nosotros levantamos el baúl.	*We lift the trunk.*
Nosotros *nos* levantamos.	*We stand up. (We lift ourselves.)*

119

Pongo el sombrero en la mesa.
Me pongo el sombrero.

I put the hat on the table.
I put on my hat. (I put the hat on myself).

Ejercicio A

Escriba quién hace estas cosas por la mañana en su casa:

Yo	bañarse rápidamente	poinarse por quince minutos
Mi madre	afeitarse	despertarse solo
Mi padre	cepillarse los dientes	no desayunarse
Mi hermano	vestirse de prisa	levantarse con dificultad
Mi hermana	despedirse con un beso	
Mis hermanos		

EJEMPLO: **Yo me visto de prisa.**

1. _____
2. _____
3. _____
4. _____
5. _____
6. _____
7. _____
8. _____

Ejercicio B

Ud. es consejero/consejera de un grupo de niños en un campamento de verano. Escriba cuál de los niños ha hecho estas cosas:

EJEMPLO: Roberto / encerrarse en el baño
Roberto se ha encerrado en el baño.

1.   Clara y Sarita / dormirse en el cine

_____

2.   Javier / acostarse debajo de un árbol

_____

3.   Los gemelos / quedarse en la piscina

_____

4. Eduardo / esconderse en el bosque

_____

5. Carlos / irse sin permiso

_____

6. Gabriel y Raúl / negarse a comer

_____

7. Otro consejero y yo / enfadarse

_____

8. Yo / ponerse nervioso(a)

_____

Ejercicio C

Escriba lo que pasó en estas circunstancias. Use las sugerencias o piense en otras:

SUGERENCIAS:

quedarse	enfadarse	resfriarse
casarse	escaparse	pararse
quejarse	pasearse	mojarse
enojarse	desmayarse	ahogarse
despertarse	esconderse	bañarse
asustarse	irse	

EJEMPLO: Nevó ayer y yo **me quedé en casa.**

1. Llovió ayer y los jugadores de béisbol _____ .

2. Carlos esperó a Anita por una hora y ella no llegó. Carlos _____ .

3. Mi papá no oyó el despertador por la mañana y él _____ .

4. Las niñas vieron un ratoncito y ellas _____ .

5. Pedro y Graciela fueron novios por un año. Ayer en la iglesia ellos _____ .

6. Yo conducía el carro cuando vi la luz roja del semáforo. Entonces yo _____ .

7. Tú usaste mi blusa nueva. Yo _____ .

8. El médico le puso una inyección a mi hermanito. Él _____ .

9. El niño no quería tomar la medicina. Él _____ .

10. Elena y yo fuimos al parque donde nosotros _____ .

11. Yo atrapé una rana pero la rana _____ de la caja en que la tenía.

12. La señora Pérez oyó malas noticias y ella _____ .

13. El perro no pudo nadar en el río y _____ .

14. No me gustó la película que daban en el cine y yo _____ .

15. Roberto se cayó en la calle. Cuando llegó a casa él _____ .

2. Reflexive Commands

The reflexive pronouns in affirmative commands follow the verb and are attached to it. In a negative command, the reflexive pronoun precedes the verb:

¡láve*se* Ud.!   ¡láven*se* Uds.!
¡láva*te* tú!   ¡lava*os* vosotros!

¡no *se* lave Ud.!   ¡no *se* laven Uds.!
¡no *te* laves tú!   ¡no *os* lavéis vosotros!

NOTE: When the reflexive pronoun is attached to the affirmative command, there is an accent mark on the stressed vowel of the verb of the **tú, Ud.** and **Uds.** forms.

Escriba cinco órdenes que sus padres le dan a Ud. por la mañana. Use las sugerencias o piense en otras:

SUGERENCIAS: despertarse ahora   levantarse rápidamente
                 bañarse primero   cepillarse los dientes
                 lavarse el pelo   vestirse ahora mismo
                 desayunarse bien   peinarse antes de salir

EJEMPLO: **¡Despiértate ahora!**

1. _____
2. _____
3. _____
4. _____
5. _____

Alfredo y su hermano nunca hacen lo que su madre quiere. Escriba las órdenes que ella les da:

EJEMPLO: quedarse en la cama
¡No se queden en la cama!

1. tardarse en el baño _____

2. quejarse del desayuno _____

3. irse sin despedirse _____

4. cepillarse el pelo en la sala _____

5. olvidarse de preparar la tarea _____

6. acostarse en el sofá _____

7. quitarse los zapatos _____

Ejercicio F

Usando la sugerencia dada en paréntesis, escriba la orden que Ud. daría en cada caso:

EJEMPLO: Tu hermano va a salir de la casa con tu raqueta de tenis. (irse)
¡No te vayas con mi raqueta de tenis!

1. Ud. está cuidando a dos niños y ellos ya tienen mucho sueño. (acostarse)

    _____

2. Tú y tu hermana están sentados en la sala cuando suena el teléfono. Tú no quieres contestar el teléfono. (levantarse)

    _____

3. Una amiga de su mamá llama a la puerta. Ud. la invita a entrar en la sala para esperar a su mamá. (sentarse)

    _____

4. Su amigo acaba de arreglar su bicicleta y Uds. van a comer. (lavarse las manos)

    _____

5. Ud. y un amigo van a luchar. Su amigo lleva gafas. (quitarse las gafas)

    _____

6. Su madre no le permite a un amigo acompañarle a Ud. al centro. (enfadarse)

    _____

7. Ud. no salió bien en un examen y va a decírselo a sus padres. (ponerse furiosos)

    _____

8. Ud. está en el parque de diversiones y va a subir a la montaña rusa con un amigo miedoso. (asustarse)

    _____

3. Reflexive Constructions with Infinitives and the *Gerundio*

When used with an infinitive or a **gerundio,** the reflexive pronoun may follow the verb and be attached to it or it may precede the conjugated form of the verb:

INFINITIVE: Voy a **peinar*me*** ahora.   *Me* **voy** a **peinar** ahora.
           Acabamos de **desayunar*nos*.**   *Nos* **acabamos** de **desayunar.**

GERUNDIO: María **está lavándo*se*** la cara.   María *se* **está lavando** la cara.
         Tú **estabas lavándo*te*** el pelo.   Tú *te* **estabas lavando** el pelo.

NOTE: With the **gerundio,** an accent mark is placed on the stressed vowel of the verb if the reflexive pronoun is attached to it:

Estamos **lavándonos.**   Estaba **desayunándome.**

Ejercicio G

Complete, con la forma apropiada de los verbos dados, este diálogo telefónico entre Carmen y Luz sobre una fiesta que tendrá lugar el sábado:

Carmen: ¿Piensas _____ en la fiesta de Rosa?
         1 (divertirse)

Luz: Claro que sí. Y quiero _____ allí hasta muy tarde.
         2 (quedarse)

Carmen: Hasta qué hora te dejarán tus padres _____ en la fiesta?
         3 (quedarse)

Luz: Hasta medianoche. Si llego después, ellos van a _____ .
         4 (enfadarse)

Carmen: ¿Qué piensas _____ ?
         5 (ponerse)

Luz: Todas las chicas van a _____ blusa y falda. Pero yo prefiero
         6 (ponerse)

_____ un vestido nuevo que acabo de comprar.
         7 (ponerse)

Carmen: ¿Podré _____ en tu casa? Trabajo el sábado y tendré que
         8 (vestirse)

_____ para llegar a la fiesta a tiempo. Si debo volver a casa a
         9 (apresurarse)

_____ antes de ir a la fiesta, no llegaré nunca. También
         10 (cambiarse)

así podrás ayudarme a _____ .
         11 (peinarse)

Luz: ¡Por supuesto que puedes _____ aquí! Así tendremos tiempo
         12 (vestirse)

para decidir en quiénes debemos _____ en la fiesta.
         13 (fijarse)

Carmen: Bueno, debo _____ ahora porque tengo mucho que hacer. Y
         14 (irse)

gracias, porque ahora podré _____ .

15 (tranquilizarse)

Luz: De nada. Hasta el sábado.

Carmen: Adiós.

◇ **Ejercicio H**

Usando los verbos dados a continuación, escriba una frase para explicar por qué ciertas personas a quienes Ud. conoce, van a, deben, pueden, quieren, o prefieren hacer la acción del verbo.

EJEMPLO: acostarse
Cuando mi padre tiene sueño, prefiere acostarse enseguida.

1. quejarse _____

2. preocuparse _____

3. lavarse _____

4. enojarse _____

5. apresurarse _____

6. resfriarse _____

7. afligirse _____

8. alegrarse _____

9. fijarse _____

10. despertarse _____

4. Summary of the Position of Reflexive Pronouns

SIMPLE TENSE	*Se* **lava.**	*He washes himself.*
COMPOUND TENSE	*Nos* **hemos lavado.**	*We have washed ourselves.*
INFINITIVE	**Quiero lavar***me***.** or ***Me*** **quiero lavar.**	*I want to wash myself.*
GERUNDIO	**Estamos lavándo***nos***.** or *Nos* **estamos lavando.**	*We are washing ourselves.*
COMMANDS	**Lávense Uds.** (affirmative) but **No** *se* **laven Uds.** (negative)	*Wash yourselves.* *Don't wash yourselves.*

5. Uses of Reflexive Verbs

a. Some verbs have special meanings when used reflexively:

BASIC MEANING	REFLEXIVE MEANING
aburrir *to bore*	**aburrirse** *(to bore oneself) to become bored*
acostar *to put to bed*	**acostarse** *(to put oneself to bed) to go to bed*
bañar *to bathe (someone)*	**bañarse** *(to bathe oneself) to take a bath*
cansar *to tire*	**cansarse** *(to tire oneself) to become tired*
colocar *to place (some-thing)*	**colocarse** *to place oneself; to get a job*
engañar *to deceive*	**engañarse** *to deceive oneself; to be mistaken*
esconder *to hide (some-thing)*	**esconderse** *to hide (oneself)*
parar *to stop (something)*	**pararse** *to stop oneself, to stop*
poner *to put (something)*	**ponerse** *to place oneself; to put (something) on; to be-come*
sentar *to seat*	**sentarse** *(to seat oneself) to sit down*

b. Some verbs are always used reflexively in Spanish but not usually in English:

acordarse (de) *to remember*
apoderarse (de) *to take possession (of)*
apresurarse (a) *to hurry*
aprovecharse (de) *to avail oneself (of); to profit (by); to take unfair advantage (of)*
arrepentirse (de) *to repent, to regret*
atreverse (a) *to dare (to)*
burlarse (de) *to make fun (of)*
desayunarse *to have breakfast*
desmayarse *to faint*
empeñarse (en) *to insist (on)*
enterarse (de) *to find out about*

escaparse (de) *to escape (from)*
fiarse (de) *to trust*
figurarse *to imagine*
fijarse (en) *to stare (at), to notice*
irse *to go away*
negarse (a) *to refuse (to)*
olvidarse (de) *to forget*
parecerse (a) *to resemble*
pasearse *to stroll*
quejarse (de) *to complain*
reírse (de) *to laugh (at), to make fun (of)*
tratarse (de) *to concern, to be a question (of)*

c. Reflexive verbs express reciprocal action corresponding to English *each other, one another:*

Nos escribimos.	*We write to each other.*
Pepe y Elena **se aman.**	*Joe and Helen love one another.*

NOTE: **Uno a otro (Una a otra)** or **el uno al otro (la una a la otra)** may be added to clarify or reinforce the meaning of the reflexive pronoun:

Las muchachas **se miran.**	*The girls look at each other (or look at themselves).*
Las muchachas se miran *una a otra* (*la una a la otra*).	*The girls look at each other.*
Pepe y Elena se aman *uno a otro* (*el uno al otro*).	*Joe and Helen love each other.*

d. Reflexive verbs are often used to express a passive action when the subject is a thing (not a person) and when the agent (doer) is not indicated (see page 134).

Aquí *se habla* **español.**	*Spanish is spoken here.*
Estos libros *se venderán* **hoy.**	*These books will be sold today.*

Ejercicio I

Manolo y sus amigos hablan de un concierto al que asistieron. Escriba las frases siguientes, usando el pretérito de los verbos dados:

EJEMPLO: La policía / colocar / barricadas en la entrada
La policía colocó barricadas en la entrada.

1. Los policías / colocarse delante de ellas

    _____

2. Unos muchachos / sentar / a la gente

    _____

3. Ellos / sentarse / en los pasillos

    _____

4. Roberto / esconder / una grabadora en su mochila

    _____

5. Él / esconderse / cerca del foro

    _____

6. Tres personas / desmayarse

    _____

7. La primera parte del concierto / cansar al público

    _____

8. En la segunda parte / el público / no cansarse de aplaudir

    _____

9. Nadie / apresurarse / a salir

    _____

10. Los policías / empeñarse / en mantener el orden

    _____

11. Muchas personas / quejarse / del calor

    _____

12. Varios policías / parar / un disgusto entre dos aficionados

    _____

13. Yo / pararse / para ver la escena

    _____

14. Nosotros / acordarse / del primer concierto de este grupo

    _____

15. Los comerciantes / aprovecharse / del público

    _____

Ejercicio J

Conteste estas preguntas que le hace Rafael a Carmen sobre su novio:

EJEMPLO: ¿Desde cuándo lo conoces? (hace 2 años)
Nosotros nos conocemos desde hace dos años.

1.   ¿Dónde lo conociste? (en una fiesta)

_____

2.   ¿Con qué frecuencia le escribes? (cada semana)

_____

3.   ¿Cuándo hablas con él por teléfono? (todos los domingos)

_____

4.   ¿Cuándo lo ves? (durante las vacaciones)

_____

5.   ¿Lo amas mucho? (Sí)

_____

Ejercicio K

Ricardo está preparando los carteles para una fiesta que el Círculo Español va a ofrecer el sábado. Ayúdele a escribir los carteles:

EJEMPLO: entrar / por aquí
Se entra por aquí.

1. Aquí / cambiar / dinero

_____

2. Aquí / sacar / fotos

_____

3. Aquí / comprar / las entradas

_____

4. Vender / refrescos / aquí

_____

5. Jugar / dominó / aquí

_____

6. Vender / helado / aquí

_____

7. Prohibir / entrar / por aquí

_____

8. Salir / por aquí

_____

9. Leer / horóscopos

_____

10. Oír / discos allí

_____

♦ MASTERY EXERCISES ♦

Ejercicio L

Conteste estas preguntas que le hace un alumno de intercambio en su escuela:

1. ¿Se ponen Uds. tristes cuando terminan las vacaciones?

_____

2. ¿Se quejan Uds. cuando el profesor les da muchas tareas?

_____

3. ¿Por qué se enfada el profesor a veces con Ud.?

_____

4. ¿Se entrega Ud. a su trabajo con entusiasmo?

_____

5. ¿Se callan los alumnos mientras está hablando el profesor?

_____

6. ¿Admite Ud. su error cuando se equivoca?

_____

7. ¿Se apresura Ud. a regresar a casa después de las clases?

_____

8. ¿Se enfadan sus padres cuando Ud. llega a casa tarde?

_____

9. ¿Cuándo se graduará Ud. de esta escuela?

_____

10. ¿En qué universidad se matriculará Ud.?

_____

11. ¿Qué quiere Ud. hacerse?

_____

12. ¿Cómo se divierte Ud. cuando está con sus amigos?

_____

Ejercicio M

Claudio le explica a un amigo lo que hace en el campamento durante el verano. Ayúdele a expresarlo en español:

1. They wake us at 6:00 A.M.

2. I never get up immediately.

3. Then we bathe ourselves and go to the dining room to have breakfast.

4. On Mondays we wash our clothes.

5. When I don't feel well, I stay in bed all day.

6. If I don't like the food, I refuse to eat.

7. The other guys hurry to participate in all the activities.

8. I become bored if I have to participate in everything.

9. In the afternoons we put on our bathing suits and swim in the lake.

10. One year I tried to escape from the camp.

11. I wouldn't dare to try it again.

12. I always forget to bring my baseball glove.

13. We get dressed every night for dinner.

14. We try to behave ourselves.

15. My friends and I write to each other twice a week.

16. I usually enjoy myself in camp.

Passive Constructions

In the active voice, the subject generally performs some action. In the passive voice, the subject is acted upon:

ACTIVE: **El alumno *compró* el libro.**   *The student bought the book.*

PASSIVE: **El libro *fue comprado por* el alumno.**   *The book was bought by the student.*

1. Formation and Use of the Passive

If the agent (doer) is mentioned or implied, the passive construction in Spanish is similar to English: subject + form of **ser** + past participle + **por** + agent (doer):

Estas carreteras *fueron construidas por* el gobierno.   *These highways were built by the government.*

Todos mis amigos *han sido invitados por* Carlos.   *All my friends have been invited by Charles.*

La fiesta *será celebrada por* los habitantes.   *The festival will be celebrated by the inhabitants.*

Colón salió de España el 3 de agosto; **América *fue descubierta* el 12 de octubre.** (doer, Columbus, implied)   *Columbus left Spain on August 3; on October 12, America was discovered.*

NOTE:

1. In the passive, the past participle is used like an adjective and agrees with the subject in gender and number.

2. The agent is preceded by **por.** If the past participle expresses feeling or emotion, rather than action, **por** may be replaced by **de:**

Es amado (respetado, admirado) *de* todos.   *He is loved (respected, admired) by all.*

Era temido (odiado, envidiado) *de* la gente.   *He was feared (hated, envied) by the people.*

Ejercicio A

Hilda está muy orgullosa del papel que desempeñó su familia en el desarrollo de la ciu-dad. Escriba lo que le muestra Hilda a una amiga nueva durante un paseo por la ciudad. Use los verbos construir, dedicar, pagar, plantar, regalar, terminar:

EJEMPLO:

Este rascacielos fue construido por mi abuelo.

1.

_____

_____

5.

_____

_____

2.

_____

_____

6.

_____

_____

3.

_____

_____

7.

_____

_____

4.

_____

_____

8.

_____

_____

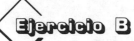 **Ejercicio B**

En una fiesta, Gabriela cuenta quién preparó cada cosa. Escriba lo que dijo:

EJEMPLO: Manolo compró los refrescos.
Los refrescos fueron comprados por Manolo.

1. Estela preparó el pastel.

    _____

2. Javier y Eduardo cocinaron la carne.

    _____

3. Vicente colgó los adornos.

    _____

4. Isabel puso la mesa.

    _____

5. Sergio consiguió las tortillas.

    _____

6. Yo invité a los amigos.

    _____

7. Taco Rico entregó los tacos.

    _____

8. Luis escogió los discos.

    _____

9. Raquel y yo hicimos los preparativos.

    _____

10. Mi mamá pagó las cuentas.

    _____

Ejercicio C

Leonardo está leyendo en el periódico sobre la tormenta de anoche y quiere explicárselo a Jorge en español. Exprese lo siguiente en español:

1. The city was surprised by a storm last night.

    _____

2. Many trees were destroyed by the rains.

    _____

3. The lights were put out by a bolt of lightning.

_____

4. The streets were flooded by the river.

_____

5. The schools were closed by the authorities.

_____

2. Substitute Constructions for the Passive

a. If the agent (doer) is not mentioned or implied and the subject is a thing, the reflexive construction is preferred in Spanish. In such constructions, the subject usually follows the verb:

Aquí *se habla* español.	Spanish is spoken here.
Aquí *se hablan* español y francés.	Spanish and French are spoken here.
¿A qué hora *se cierran* las tiendas?	At what time are the stores closed?
Se publicó el libro.	The book was published.
Se perdieron los documentos.	The documents were lost.
Desde aquí *se pueden* ver los monumentos.	From here the monuments can be seen.

Ejercicio D

El Círculo Español está preparando una cena. Escriba en qué tienda(s) se vende o se compra lo que van a necesitar:

carne molida	tortillas	queso
tomates	lechuga	rábanos
aceite	vinagre	cebollas
crema	servilletas	platos de papel
tenedores	cuchillos	

EJEMPLO: **En la lechería se vende crema.**
En la lechería se venden crema y queso.

_____

_____

_____

_____

_____

Ejercicio E

Es su primer día de trabajo en una oficina. Escriba lo que le dice su jefe:

EJEMPLO: llegar temprano a la oficina
Se llega temprano a la oficina.

1. contestar el teléfono en seguida

   _____

2. recibir el correo por la mañana

   _____

3. leer las cartas con cuidado

   _____

4. escribir las cartas a máquina

   _____

5. tomar una hora de almuerzo

   _____

6. llevar las cartas al correo

   _____

7. comprar sellos en el correo

   _____

8. archivar la correspondencia a diario

   _____

9. poner los recados en los escritorios

   _____

10. salir de la oficina a las cinco

    _____

Ejercicio F

Conteste las preguntas que le hace un primo que está de visita en su casa:

1. ¿A qué hora se cerrarán las tiendas el sábado?

   _____

2. ¿Cuándo se estrenará otra película en el cine?

   _____

3. ¿Hasta qué hora se servirá la comida en el restaurante?

_____

4. ¿Dónde se podrá encontrar una raqueta de tenis?

_____

5. ¿Cuándo se oirá el pronóstico del tiempo para mañana?

_____

6. ¿Dónde se comprarán regalos baratos?

_____

7. ¿Qué se venderá en la tienda de la esquina?

_____

8. ¿En qué tienda se regalarán tarjetas postales?

_____

9. ¿Dónde se podrá recibir el mejor tipo de cambio?

_____

10. ¿Cuánto se cobrará por entrar en el parque de diversiones?

_____

b. The pronoun **se** may also be used as an indefinite subject. In such constructions, **se** is not reflexive and is used only with the third person singular of the verb:

se dice:	*it is said, one says, people say, they say, you say*
se cree:	*it is believed, one believes, people believe, they believe, you believe*
se sabe:	*it is known, one knows, people know, they know, you know*

The forms **dicen** (*they say*), **creen** (*they believe*), and **saben** (*they know*) are used without **se**:

Se dice⎫
Dicen ⎭ que es muy rico.   *It is said*⎫
                                      They say⎭ *that he is very rich.*

c. The indefinite **se** may be used to express the passive when the doer is indefinite (not mentioned or implied) and a person is acted upon:

*Se **mató** al hombre.*	*The man was killed.* [Someone killed the man.]
*Se le **mató**.*	*He was killed.* [Someone killed him.]
*Se **mató** a los hombres.*	*The men were killed.* [Someone killed the men.]
*Se les **mató**.*	*They were killed.* [Someone killed them.]
*Se **castigará** a la niña.*	*The child will be punished.* [Someone will punish the child.]

Se la castigará.	She *will be punished.* [Someone will punish her.]
Se castigará *a las niñas.*	The *children will be punished.* [Someone will punish the children.]
Se las castigará.	They *will be punished.* [Someone will punish them.]

NOTE: Although the person acted upon is a direct object, the forms **le** and **les** (instead of **lo** and **los**) are used for the masculine.

d. Instead of the indefinite **se** construction, the active third person plural is often preferred:

Mataron al hombre (a los hombres).	They *killed the man (the men).* [indefinite]
Lo (los) mataron.	They *killed him (them).* [indefinite]
Castigarán a la niña (a las niñas).	They *will punish the child (the children).* [indefinite]
La (las) castigarán.	They *will punish her (them).* [indefinite]

3. Summary of Passive and Substitute Constructions

	AGENT (DOER) EXPRESSED	AGENT (DOER) NOT EXPRESSED
	PASSIVE CONSTRUCTION SIMILAR TO ENGLISH	REFLEXIVE
THING	**Las camisas *serán vendidas por* el dependiente.**	*Se venderán* **las camisas.**
		INDEFINITE
PERSON	**El alcalde *fue elegido por* el pueblo.**	*Se eligió* **al alcalde. (*Se le* eligió.)** *Eligieron* **al alcalde. (*Lo eligieron*.)**

Ejercicio G

Una madre da una lección a su hijo. Complete las frases con la forma necesaria del verbo apropiado. Escríbalas de dos maneras:

EJEMPLO: _____ gracias.
            Se dice gracias. **Dicen** gracias.

VERBOS: atravesar   saber   pagar
           comer   subir   aprender
           pasar   necesitar   decir
           entrar   poner

1. _____ por la escalera. _____ por la escalera.

2. _____ estudiando. _____ estudiando.

3. _____ la calle en la esquina. _____ la calle en la esquina.

4. _____ la mesa antes de comer. _____ la mesa antes de comer.

5. _____ por la puerta. _____ por la puerta.

6. _____ por favor. _____ por favor.

7. _____ que para comprar algo _____ dinero.

    _____ que para comprar algo _____ dinero.

8. _____ en el comedor. _____ en el comedor.

9. _____ el río por medio del puente. _____ el río por medio del puente.

10. En el autobús _____ al entrar. En el autobús _____ al entrar.

Ejercicio H

Paco es un niño que siempre repite lo que dicen todos. Escriba lo que él repitió cuando su mamá hablaba por teléfono:

EJEMPLO: Nombraron de jefe al Sr. Gómez.
            Se nombró de jefe al Sr. Gómez.
            Se le nombró de jefe.

1. Cogieron al hombre que robó la plata.

    _____

2. Acusaron al hombre del crimen.

    _____

3. Encerraron al ladrón en la cárcel.

    _____

4. Castigaron al ladrón.

    _____

5. Condenarán mañana al acusado.

    _____

♦ MASTERY EXERCISES ♦

Ejercicio 1

El hermanito de Felipe hace muchas preguntas. Conteste las preguntas que él le hace mientras Ud. espera a su hermano:

1. ¿Cómo se dice «railroad» en español?

   _____

2. ¿A qué hora se cena en su casa?

   _____

3. ¿Qué se lee en un periódico?

   _____

4. ¿En dónde se compran medicinas?

   _____

5. ¿A quiénes se cura en un hospital?

   _____

6. ¿En dónde se encierra a los criminales?

   _____

7. ¿En qué países se habla portugués?

   _____

8. ¿Por quién fue descubierto el Nuevo Mundo?

   _____

9. ¿Se venden guantes en una panadería?

   _____

10. ¿Es respetado el presidente de la gente?

    _____

11. ¿Por qué se castigará a los niños?

    _____

12. ¿Se sabe si hay civilización en la luna?

    _____

13. ¿Qué se dice cuando uno recibe un regalo?

    _____

14. ¿Por quién fue firmada la Declaración de Independencia?

    _____

15. ¿Por quién fue construido este puente?

    _____

Ejercicio J

Escriba una carta a un(a) amigo(a) que vive en Lima, en la que Ud. describe una fiesta local que se celebra en su ciudad (pueblo, barrio). Piense en estas cosas:

cuándo se celebra; cómo se celebra; si se cierran los negocios o no;
qué actividades se ofrecen; por quién(es) es organizada la celebración; etc.

_____

_____

_____

_____

_____

_____

_____

_____

_____

_____

_____

_____

_____

_____

_____

_____

Ejercicio K

Describa una fiesta a la que Ud. asistió. Use formas de la voz pasiva donde sea posible:

EJEMPLO: La fiesta fue dada por mi amiga Alba. Se celebraba el cumpleaños de su novio, Jaime. Se invitó a todos los amigos de Jaime y de Alba. Se comenzó la celebración a las dos de la tarde....

_____

_____

_____

_____

Subjunctive

1. Subjunctive in Spanish

Chapters 1 through 12 in this book deal with verb constructions in the indicative mood. The term *mood* describes the form of the verb showing the subject's attitude. In this and the next chapter, you will see how the subjunctive mood enables speakers of Spanish to express a variety of attitudes through different verb forms and constructions.

a. The indicative and the subjunctive

The indicative mood states facts and expresses certainty or reality. The subjunctive mood expresses uncertainty, doubt, wishes, desires, conjecture, supposition, and conditions that are unreal or contrary to fact. The subjunctive occurs much more frequently in Spanish than in English.

b. Use of the subjunctive

In Spanish, the subjunctive normally occurs in dependent clauses introduced by a conjunction or a relative pronoun.

2. Forms of the Subjunctive

a. Present subjunctive of regular verbs

The present subjunctive of most verbs is formed by dropping the ending **-o** of the first person singular (**yo** form) of the present indicative and adding the following endings:

-ar verbs: *-e, -es, -e, -emos, -éis, -en*

-er
-ir } verbs: *-a, -as, -a, -amos, -áis, -an*

INFINITIVE	PRESENT INDICATIVE YO FORM	PRESENT SUBJUNCTIVE
tomar	**tomo**	tome, tomes, tome, tomemos, toméis, tomen
comer	**como**	coma, comas, coma, comamos, comáis, coman
escribir	**escribo**	escriba, escribas, escriba, escribamos, escribáis, escriban

caber	quep*o*	quep*a*, -*as*, -*a*, etc.
coger	coj*o*	coj*a*, -*as*, -*a*, etc.
conocer	conozc*o*	conozc*a*, -*as*, -*a*, etc.
destruir	destruy*o*	destruy*a*, -*as*, -*a*, etc.
distinguir	doting*o*	doting*a*, -*as*, -*a*, etc.
salir	salg*o*	salg*a*, -*as*, -*a*, etc.

b. Spelling changes in the present subjunctive

In the present subjunctive of verbs ending in **-car**, **-gar**, and **-zar**, **c** changes to **qu**, **g** to **gu**, and **z** to **c**. These spelling changes are the same as those that occur in the **yo** form of the preterite (see page 38).

INFINITIVE	PRETERITE **YO** FORM	PRESENT SUBJUNCTIVE
buscar	**bus***qué*	**bus***que*, -*es*, -*e*, etc.
pagar	**pa***gué*	**pa***gue*, -*es*, -*e*, etc.
alzar	**al***cé*	**al***ce*, -*es*, -*e*, etc.

NOTE: In the verb **averiguar**, the **u** changes to **ü** before an **e** in order to keep the sound of the **u**, which otherwise would be silent:

PRETERITE: **averigüé**

PRESENT SUBJUNCTIVE: **averigüe**

c. Stem-changing verbs in the present subjunctive

(1) Stem-changing **-ar** and **-er** verbs have the same stem changes in the present subjunctive as in the present indicative (**e** to **ie**, **o** to **ue**):

   cerrar: c*ie*rre, c*ie*rres, c*ie*rre, cerremos, cerréis, c*ie*rren

   volver: v*ue*lva, v*ue*lvas, v*ue*lva, volvamos, volváis, v*ue*lvan

(2) Stem-changing **-ir** verbs have the same stem changes in the present subjunctive as in the present indicative (**e** to **ie**, **o** to **ue**, **e** to **i**). In the **nosotros** and **vosotros** forms, the stem vowel **e** changes to **i** and the stem vowel **o** changes to **u**:

   sentir: s*ie*nta, s*ie*ntas, s*ie*nta, s*i*ntamos, s*i*ntáis, s*ie*ntan

   dormir: d*ue*rma, d*ue*rmas, d*ue*rma, d*u*rmamos, d*u*rmáis, d*ue*rman

   pedir: p*i*da, p*i*das, p*i*da, p*i*damos, p*i*dáis, p*i*dan

(3) Some verbs ending in **-iar** or **-uar** have an accent mark on the **i** or the **u** (**í**, **ú**) in all forms except those for **nosotros** and **vosotros**.

   enviar: env*í*e, env*í*es, env*í*e, enviemos, enviéis, env*í*en

   continuar: contin*ú*e, contin*ú*es, contin*ú*e, continuemos, continuéis, contin*ú*en

d. Present subjunctive of irregular verbs

The following verbs have irregular forms in the present subjunctive:

  dar: *dé*, des, *dé*, demos, deis, den

  estar: *esté, estés, esté,* estemos, estéis, *estén*

haber: *haya, hayas, haya, hayamos, hayáis, hayan*

ir: *vaya, vayas, vaya, vayamos, vayáis, vayan*

saber: *sepa, sepas, sepa, sepamos, sepáis, sepan*

ser: *sea, seas, sea, seamos, seáis, sean*

NOTE: The subjunctive form **vaya** is used colloquially to express *what a:*

¡*Vaya* **lío en que estoy metido!**
What a mess I am involved in!

¡*Vaya* **memoria la suya!** Sabe todas las fechas históricas.
What a memory he has! He knows all the historical dates.

e. Imperfect subjunctive

The imperfect subjunctive of all verbs is formed by dropping the **-ron** ending of the third person plural of the preterite tense and adding either the **-ra** or **-se** endings:

-ra, -ras, -ra, '-ramos, -rais, -ran
-se, -ses, -se, '-semos, -seis, -sen

INFINITIVE	PRETERITE THIRD PLURAL	IMPERFECT SUBJUNCTIVE
llegar	**llegaron**	**llegara, llegaras, llegara, llegáramos, llegarais, llegaran** *or* **llegase, llegases, llegase, llegásemos, llegaseis, llegasen**
vender	**vendieron**	**vendiera, vendieras, vendiera, vendiéramos, vendierais, vendieran** *or* **vendiese, vendieses, vendiese, vendiésemos, vendieseis, vendiesen**
dormir	**durmieron**	**durmiera, durmieras**, etc., or **durmiese, durmieses**, etc.
pedir	**pidieron**	**pidiera**, etc., or **pidiese**, etc.
decir	**dijeron**	**dijera**, etc., or **dijese**, etc.
ir, ser	**fueron**	**fuera**, etc., or **fuese**, etc.
creer	**creyeron**	**creyera**, etc., or **creyese**, etc.

NOTE: The **nosotros** form of the imperfect subjunctive is the only form that has an accent mark (on the vowel immediately before the ending).

f. Perfect subjunctive and pluperfect subjunctive

(1) The perfect subjunctive consists of the present subjunctive of **haber** plus a past participle:

haya ⎫
hayas ⎬ **entrado**
haya ⎭

hayamos ⎫
hayáis ⎬ **entrado**
hayan ⎭

(2) The pluperfect subjunctive consists of the imperfect subjunctive of **haber** plus a past participle:

hubiera (hubiese)   hubiéramos (hubiésemos)
hubieras (hubieses) } **dicho**   hubierais (hubieseis) } **dicho**
hubiera (hubiese)   hubieran (hubiesen)

3. Uses of the Subjunctive

The subjunctive in dependent clauses is introduced by the conjunction **que**.

a. The subjunctive is used after verbs and expressions of advice, command, demand, desire, hope, permission, preference, prohibition, request, suggestion:

aconsejar *to advise*	**insistir (en)** *to insist (on)*	**preferir** *to prefer*
decir *to tell (to order)*	**mandar** *to command, to order*	**prohibir** *to forbid, to*
dejar *to let, to allow*	**¡Ojalá (que)**...! *I wish (hope)*	*prohibit*
desear *to wish, to want*	*that* ...! *If only*...!	**querer** *to wish, to want*
esperar *to hope*	**pedir** *to request, to ask for*	**rogar** *to beg, to request*
exigir *to require, to demand*	**permitir** *to permit, to allow*	**sugerir** *to suggest*
hacer *to make, to cause*		**suplicar** *to beg, to plead*

Le aconsejaron que *saliera* en seguida.	*They advised him to leave at once.*
Les digo que *entren*.	*I tell them to enter (that they should enter).*
Quieren que *lleguemos* temprano.	*They want us to arrive early.*
¡Ojalá que Uds. no *se enfermen*!	*I hope (that) you don't become ill!*
Espero que *se queden* aquí.	*I hope (that) they remain here.*
El profesor no permite que los alumnos *hablen* en la clase.	*The teacher does not permit the pupils to speak in class.*
Mis padres prefieren que yo no *mire* ese programa de televisión.	*My parents prefer that I do not watch that television program.*
Te ruego que *vengas*.	*I beg you to come.*

NOTE:

1. In all of the examples above, the verb in the main clause and the verb in the dependent clause have different subjects. If the subjects in both clauses are the same, **que** is omitted and the infinitive is used instead of the subjunctive:

Ellos quieren *ir* a la fiesta.	*They wish to go to the party.*
Mis hermanos prefieren *ver* esa película.	*My brothers prefer to see that movie.*

2. The verbs **dejar, hacer, mandar, permitir,** and **prohibir** may be followed by either the subjunctive or the infinitive:

Me manda que *salga*. } **Me manda** *salir*. }	*He orders me to leave.*
Déjele que *hable*. } **Déjele** *hablar*. }	*Let him speak.*

 **Ejercicio A**

Escriba el comentario que hace Roberto sobre estas personas:

Mi madre	aconsejar	yo	pintar el cuarto
Mi padre	decir	mi hermano(a)	lavar el coche
Mis padres	desear	mis hermanos	estudiar más
El profesor	esperar	mis hermanos y yo	acostarse temprano
Mi tío	exigir	tú	no salir por la noche
Tú	hacer		buscar trabajo
Yo	insistir (en)		descansar después de cenar
	pedir		ir de compras
	preferir		llegar temprano
	rogar		quedarse en casa

EJEMPLO: **Mi padre** *insiste* **en que mi hermana no** *salga* **por la noche.**

1. _____

2. _____

3. _____

4. _____

5. _____

6. _____

7. _____

8. _____

9. _____

10. _____

b. The subjunctive is used after verbs and expressions of feeling or emotion, such as fear, joy, sorrow, regret, surprise:

alegrarse (de) *to be glad*	**temer** *to fear*
sentir *to be sorry, to regret*	**tener miedo (de)** *to fear, to be afraid*
sorprenderse (de) *to be surprised*	

Temían que no *volviera*.	They were afraid that he would not return.
Me alegro de que Uds. lo *hayan visto*.	I am glad that you have seen it.
Sentimos que ellos no *puedan* **hacer el viaje con nosotros.**	We regret (We are sorry) that they cannot make the trip with us.
¿Se sorprenden Uds. de que *haya* **examen hoy?**	Are you surprised that there is an examination today?

 **Ejercicio B**

Unos parientes de Rosa acaban de llegar de Quito. Escriba lo que dice Rosa:

EJEMPLO: yo / sorprenderse / ellos / saber hablar inglés
Yo me sorprendo de que ellos sepan hablar inglés.

1.   yo / alegrarse / ellos / haber venido

_____

2.   yo / alegrarse / ellos / quedarse aquí por un mes

_____

3.   yo / temer / ellos / no tener bastante dinero

_____

4.   yo / tener miedo / ellos / ir a aburrirse

_____

5.   yo / sentir / ellos / no poder quedarse aquí por más tiempo

_____

6.   yo / lamentar / nosotros / no haberlos conocido hasta ahora

_____

Escriba la reacción de estas personas en cada circunstancia. Use los verbos dados entre paréntesis:

EJEMPLO: Adolfo acaba de recibir una carta de sus primos en que dicen que aceptan su invitación. (alegrarse)
Adolfo se alegra de que sus primos hayan aceptado su invitación.

1.   Los jardineros cortaron el árbol favorito de la señora Leña. Ella está muy triste. (sentir)

_____

2.   Robaron la casa de mi abuela. Ahora ella está muy asustada. (lamentar)

_____

3.   Al salir del examen final, Rafael le cuenta a un amigo que el examen fue muy fácil. (alegrarse)

_____

4.   Los padres de Rocío le regalaron un coche. Ella no puede creerlo. (sorprenderse)

_____

Escriba lo que sienten estas personas al saber lo siguiente:

Todo el mundo   alegrarse
Mi padre   sorprenderse

Los trabajadores	temer
Los dueños	tener miedo de
Yo	sentir
Mis amigos y yo	

EJEMPLO: Cancelan muchos vuelos a causa de la neblina.
Todo el mundo tiene miedo de que cancelen muchos vuelos a causa de la neblina.

1. El gobierno ha aumentado los impuestos.

_____

2. Ahora hay más trabajos.

_____

3. Se han acabado las huelgas.

_____

4. Cada empleado recibirá un aguinaldo bueno.

_____

5. Van a mejorar el servicio de correos.

_____

6. Habrá escasez de agua potable en las ciudades del norte.

_____

7. Las universidades rechazan mil solicitudes de estudiantes.

_____

8. Un cantante popular dará un concierto especial.

_____

9. Los «Azules» han ganado el campeonato mundial.

_____

10. Los campesinos no producen bastante trigo.

_____

Ejercicio E

Ud. acaba de cambiar de escuela. Escriba cinco frases en las que Ud. describe sus emociones al entrar en la nueva escuela. Use uno de los verbos siguientes en cada frase: **alegrarse (de), sentir, sorprenderse (de), temer** *o* **tener miedo (de):**

EJEMPLO: **Yo temo que nadie me hable.**

1. _____

2. _____

3. _____

4. _____

5. _____

Ejercicio F

Cambie las frases que Ud. escribió en el ejercicio E al pasado del subjuntivo:

EJEMPLO: Yo **temía** que nadie me **hablara (hablase).**

1. _____

2. _____

3. _____

4. _____

5. _____

C. The subjunctive is used after verbs and expressions of doubt, disbelief, denial:

dudar to doubt	**no creer** not to believe	**negar** to deny

Dudamos que lo _sepan._   We doubt that they know it.
No creo que Pedro lo _halle._   I don't believe that Peter will find it.
Niegan que esto _sea_ importante.   They deny that this is important.

NOTE:
1. The verb **creer,** when used interrogatively, indicates uncertainty and is usually followed by the subjunctive:

   ¿Cree Ud. que _vengan?_   Do you believe that they are coming?

2. **Creer, no dudar,** and **no negar** indicate belief or certainty and are usually followed by the indicative:

   Creo (No dudo, No niego) que Pedro lo   I believe (I don't doubt, I don't deny)
       hallará.   that Peter will find it.

Ejercicio G

Su hermanito nunca cree lo que Ud. le cuenta. Escriba lo que dice su hermanito, usando **no creo** _o_ **dudo:**

EJEMPLO: Yo conozco a Michael Jackson.
                Dudo que tú conozcas a Michael Jackson.

1. Nosotros te regalaremos una bicicleta.

_____

2. Eduardo juega tenis todos los días.

_____

3. Mi maestro hará un viaje a la luna.

_____

4. Este anillo vale más de mil dólares.

_____

5. Hay un programa interesante en la televisión.

_____

6. Unos marcianos llegan hoy.

_____

7. Tú y yo prepararemos la cena hoy.

_____

8. Estela tiene dieciséis años.

_____

9. Yo salgo con mis amigos esta noche.

_____

10. Mis padres te van a castigar.

_____

Ejercicio H

Escriba quién duda o no cree lo siguiente (yo, tú, mis amigos, mis padres, mi profesor):

1. Rafael se graduará con su clase.

_____

2. Yo saco buenas notas en los exámenes.

_____

3. Mis hermanos y yo nos acostamos temprano hoy.

_____

4. Sofía busca otro trabajo.

_____

5. Nosotros vamos a la playa el sábado.

_____

6. Tú me prestas tu carro nuevo.

_____

7. Carlos trae sus discos favoritos a la fiesta.

_____

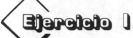 **Ejercicio I**

Escriba quién niega estas cosas:

EJEMPLO: La casa está terminada. (el ingeniero)
El ingeniero niega que la casa esté terminada.

1.   Los impuestos son altos. (el presidente)

   _____

2.   Yo trabajo bien aquí. (mi jefe)

   _____

3.   El examen es difícil. (la profesora)

   _____

4.   Los niños pueden romper la ventana. (la madre)

   _____

5.   Roberto hace muchas llamadas personales. (la telefonista)

   _____

 **Ejercicio J**

Escriba lo que piensa Carlos mientras escucha el pronóstico del tiempo.
Use **dudar, no creer** *o* **negar** *en cada frase.*

EJEMPLO: La tormenta puede causar muchos daños.
Dudo que la tormenta pueda causar muchos daños.

1.   La tormenta comenzará a eso de las siete.

   _____

2.   Los vientos serán muy fuertes.

   _____

3.   Uds. no deben salir de su casa.

   _____

4.   Habrá muchos relámpagos y truenos.

   _____

5.   Las autoridades ayudarán a las personas.

   _____

6.   Las lluvias inundarán las calles.

   _____

7.   Habrá muchos heridos.

   _____

8. Perderemos el servicio de teléfonos.

_____

9. El desastre durará varias horas.

_____

10. Se apagará la luz.

_____

11. Nosotros debemos tomar todas las precauciones posibles.

_____

12. Es un aviso importante para todos los ciudadanos.

_____

_d._ The subjunctive is used after impersonal expressions of possibility, doubt, uncertainty, necessity, emotion, and the like. If the impersonal expression indicates certainty, the indicative is used:

es dudoso _it is doubtful_	**es menester** ⎫
es importante _it is important_	**es necesario** ⎬ _it is necessary_
es imposible _it is impossible_	**es preciso** ⎭
es lástima _it is a pity_	**es posible** _it is possible_
es mejor ⎫ _it is better_	**es probable** _it is probable_
más vale ⎭	**es importante** _it is important_

Es preciso que yo lo _compre._
It is necessary that I buy (for me to buy) it.

Era importante que lo _viéramos._
It was important that we see (for us to see) it.

Más vale que _llegues_ temprano.
It is better for you to arrive early.

Es probable que _vayan._
It is probable that they will go.

Es posible que Juan _esté_ enfermo.
It is possible that John is sick.

But:

Es cierto que _irán._
It is certain that they will go.

Es evidente que él no lo _sabe._
It is evident that he does not know it.

Es verdad que Juan _está_ enfermo.
It is true that John is sick.

◇ **Ejercicio K**

Ud. y un amigo hablan de una fiesta que Ud. va a dar en su casa. Escriba lo que Uds. dicen:

EJEMPLO: Es probable / Rodolfo / no querer cantar
Es probable que Rodolfo no quiera cantar.

1. Es preciso / mi mamá / ir al supermercado

_____

2. Es dudoso / Elena / traer su tocadiscos

_____

3. Es importante / tú / estar aquí temprano

_____

4. Es posible / yo / hablar con Tomás más tarde

_____

5. Es mejor / los hermanos Soto / no venir

_____

6. Es imposible / Sarita / tener otro compromiso

_____

7. Es probable / Beto / llegar del aeropuerto a tiempo

_____

8. Es necesario / nosotros / preparar comida para veinte personas

_____

9. Es menester / yo / ayudarle a mi mamá

_____

10. Más vale / todo el mundo / divertirse

_____

Ejercicio L

Juan trabaja de aeromozo y habla con los pasajeros. Escriba lo que dice:

Es necesario	el capitán	hacer un anuncio
Es importante	los pasajeros	seguir las instrucciones de seguridad
Es dudoso	los niños	obedecer la señal de no fumar
Es mejor	todo el mundo	tomar su asiento en seguida
Es posible	nosotros	permanecer sentado(s)
	yo	poner sus cosas debajo del asiento
		llegar a tiempo
		ayudar a los otros pasajeros
		prestar mucha atención

EJEMPLO: **Es probable que nosotros evitemos una tempestad.**

1. _____

2. _____

3. _____

4. _____

5. _____

6. _____

7. _____

8. _____

9. _____

10. _____

Ejercicio M

Escriba siete cosas que Ud. cree necesarias o importantes para mejorar las condiciones de la ciudad en que Ud. vive. Use una expresión impersonal en cada frase:

EJEMPLOS: Es importante que los ciudadanos obedezcan las leyes.
Es menester que los parques estén limpios.

1. _____

2. _____

3. _____

4. _____

5. _____

6. _____

7. _____

Ejercicio N

Mientras Ud. estaba de vacaciones un vecino cuidó sus plantas. Usando la expresión impersonal dada en cada frase, escriba su respuesta al comentario de su vecino:

EJEMPLO: Es menester que esta planta tenga sombra. (Es claro)
Es claro que esta planta tiene sombra.

1.   Es evidente que yo he regado las plantas. (Es dudoso)

_____

2.   Es necesario que las plantas estén al sol. (Es verdad)

_____

3.   Es posible que yo haya cortado esta planta. (Es claro)

_____

4.   Es lástima que esta planta haya muerto. (Es cierto)

_____

5.   Es dudoso que yo haya dañado las plantas. (No cabe duda)

_____

4. Sequence of Tenses

The tense of the subjunctive depends on the form of the main verb:

VERB IN MAIN CLAUSE	VERB IN DEPENDENT CLAUSE
Present Indicative Present Perfect Future Command	Present Subjunctive or Perfect Subjunctive
Imperfect Preterite Conditional Pluperfect	Imperfect Subjunctive or Pluperfect Subjunctive

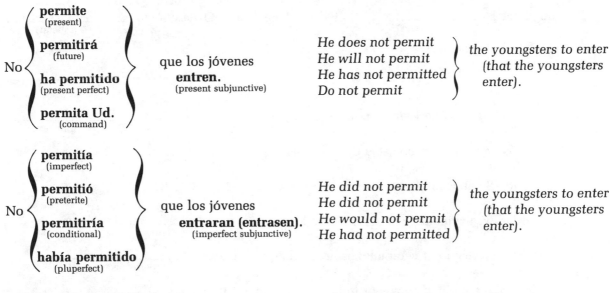

No {
permite (present)
permitirá (future)
ha permitido (present perfect)
permita Ud. (command)
} que los jóvenes **entren.** (present subjunctive)

He does not permit
He will not permit
He has not permitted
Do not permit
} the youngsters to enter (that the youngsters enter).

No {
permitía (imperfect)
permitió (preterite)
permitiría (conditional)
había permitido (pluperfect)
} que los jóvenes **entraran (entrasen).** (imperfect subjunctive)

He did not permit
He did not permit
He would not permit
He had not permitted
} the youngsters to enter (that the youngsters enter).

Dudo que lo ***hayan visto.***
(present)   (perfect subjunctive)

I doubt that they have seen it.

Dudaba que lo ***hubieran (hubiesen) visto.***
(imperfect)   (pluperfect subjunctive)

I doubted that they had seen it.

Ejercicio O

Complete estos cuentecitos con la forma correcta de los verbos dados en paréntesis:

1. La madre de Juan espera visita esta noche. Ella desea que Juan le _____. Le
    1 (ayudar)

    dice a Juan que _____ la mesa primero. Después es necesario que Juan
    2 (poner)

    _____ al mercado. Juan quiere _____ su bicicleta pero
    3 (ir)   **4** (usar)

    su madre le prohibió que _____ allí en bicicleta. Es lástima que Juan no
    5 (ir)

_____ ir en bicicleta porque su madre quiere _____ todo
     6 (poder)   **7** (tener)

listo y los invitados llegan en quince minutos.

2. Hoy es un día horrible para Rafael. Sus padres mandaron que él _____
            1 (ir)

a la peluquería. No cabe duda de que Rafael _____ porque si no, sus padres
         2 (cumplir)

no van a permitir que él _____ a sus amigos al campo el domingo. ¡Pobre
     3 (acompañar)

Rafael! Él no creía que la peluquería _____ cerrada aquel día. No buscó otra
         4 (estar)

porque temía que otro peluquero le _____ mal el pelo. Ahora es probable
         5 (cortar)

que Rafael _____ todo el día en casa. ¡Ojalá que no _____
      6 (pasar)   **7** (esperar)

tanto la próxima vez!

3. Ayer pasé un día interesante en la corte. El juez prohibió que el preso _____
            1 (protestar)

contra el castigo. Pero no cabía duda de que el preso _____
         2 (creerse)

inocente. Su abogado le había aconsejado que _____
         3 (decir)

la verdad. Era evidente que el jurado no le _____ cuando dio su
         4 (creer)

declaración. Según el veredicto, es necesario que el preso _____
         5 (permanecer)

en la cárcel por cinco años, por lo menos. Es dudoso que _____
         6 (haber)

otro juicio porque el abogado teme que _____ a otros testigos.
         7 (llamar)

4. Es posible que el primer día de clases no le _____ a Luis. Este año hicieron
         1 (agradar)

que él _____ unas materias muy difíciles. El año pasado el profesor exigió
     2 (tomar)

que sus estudiantes _____ muchos trabajos y era difícil que muchos
         3 (hacer)

alumnos _____ una buena nota. Sus amigos le aconsejaron que no
         4 (sacar)

_____ nunca a la clase porque el profesor no aprueba que los alumnos
     5 (faltar)

_____ su clase. Es seguro que Luis _____ que
      6 (perder)   **7** (tener)

estudiar mucho este año.

5. Esperaban que la nieve _____ los montes con un manto blanco. Los amigos
   1 (cubrir)

   deseaban _____ a esquiar y para hacerlo, era preciso que
   2 (ir)

   _____ mucho. Joaquín pidió que su padre le _____ cien
   3 (nevar)   **4 (prestar)**

   dólares para la excursión. Su padre sabía que era dudoso que Joaquín le _____
                                                                            5 (devolver)

   el dinero, pero quería que su hijo _____. Sólo le suplicó que
                                       6 (divertirse)

   _____ cuidado porque era probable que los montes _____
   7 (tener)   **8 (estar)**

   cubiertos de hielo por la lluvia del otro día. Al despedirse de los jóvenes el padre murmuró:

   «¡Ojalá que yo _____ ir a esquiar también! Es evidente que estos jóvenes
                   9 (poder)

   _____ divertirse».
   10 (saber)

Ejercicio P

Escriba la forma correcta de los verbos entre paréntesis para completar los comentarios de un profesor a sus alumnos en un examen:

1. ¿Es posible que Ud. _____ decir otra cosa? (querer)
2. Exijo que tú _____ más. (estudiar)
3. Prefiero que no lo _____ de esta manera. (decir)
4. Me sorprendí de que Ud. _____ eso. (pensar)
5. Es lástima que Ud. no lo _____ aún. (aprender)
6. Dudo que alguien te _____. (comprender)
7. Me alegré de que tú _____ el final del cuento. (adivinar)
8. Pide que yo te lo _____ otra vez. (explicar)
9. Es verdad que tú _____ muy claramente. (escribir)
10. Sería mejor que tú _____ después de la clase para recibir ayuda especial. (venir)

◆ MASTERY EXERCISES ◆

Ejercicio Q

Usando las expresiones dadas, escriba ocho frases que formarán una carta en la que Ud. acepta la invitación de un(a) amigo(a):

1. Me alegré de _____
   _____

2. No creía _____

_____

3. Insisto en _____

_____

4. Es dudoso _____

_____

5. Sentí _____

_____

6. Quería _____

_____

7. Será necesario _____

_____

8. Espero _____

_____

Ejercicio R

Exprese en español estos anuncios de protesta que los alumnos van a publicar en una edición especial del periódico escolar:

1. It will be necessary that we elect a new president.

_____

_____

2. We feared that they would raise the price of the tickets.

_____

_____

3. It's a pity that she has not maintained her enthusiasm.

_____

_____

4. I doubt that there is much danger.

_____

5. They do not allow me to begin my projects.

_____

6. They tell me that I should stay with them.

_____

7. If only a catastrophe does not occur!

_____

8. We fear that he will not act carefully.

_____

9. It was a pity that we could not be there.

_____

10. I don't doubt that he is courageous.

_____

11. They wanted to divide the amount into three equal parts.

_____

_____

12. They preferred to keep the secret.

_____

13. They begged us not to complain.

_____

14. It is better that they have lost.

_____

15. Do you believe that we are right?

_____

C•H•A•P•T•E•R 14

Subjunctive (Continued)

1. Subjunctive in Dependent Adverb Clauses

Adverb clauses are introduced by certain conjunctions and answer questions that state or imply *when?*, *where?*, *how?*, *why?*, and similar question words.

a. The subjunctive is used in dependent clauses that express uncertainty, doubt, purpose, anticipation, or proviso. Such clauses are usually introduced by the following conjunctions:

a fin de que } *in order that, so that*	**con tal que** *provided that*
para que }	**en caso de que** *in case (that)*
a menos que *unless*	**sin que** *without*
antes (de) que *before*	

Terminaré el trabajo **antes de que** ellos *vuelvan.*
I will finish the work before they return [whenever that may be].

Leyó el artículo despacio **para que** *pudiéramos* entenderlo.
He read the article slowly so that we could understand it. [We may or may not have understood it.]

Salió **sin que** yo lo *supiera.*
He left without my knowing it [in such a way that I would not know it].

Ejercicio A

Conteste las preguntas que le hace a una amiga a quien no le gusta hacer nada sin Ud.:

EJEMPLO: ¿Deseas ir a la fiesta?
Iré a la fiesta con tal que tú vayas también.

1.   ¿Deseas jugar tenis?

_____

2.   ¿Deseas ir de compras?

_____

3.   ¿Deseas asistir a la reunión?

_____

4.   ¿Deseas visitar a María?

_____

5.   ¿Deseas ver una película?

_____

 **Ejercicio B**

Conteste las preguntas que Ud. le hace a una hermana menor que no hace nada sola:

> EJEMPLO: ¿Vas a comer?
> **No comeré a menos que tú comas también.**

1.   ¿Vas a almorzar? _____

2.   ¿Vas a dormir la siesta? _____

3.   ¿Vas a arreglar tu cuarto? _____

4.   ¿Vas a ayudarle a mamá? _____

5.   ¿Vas a dar un paseo? _____

Ejercicio C

Conteste las preguntas que le hace un amigo, usando la expresión **sin que:**

> EJEMPLO: ¿Viste a Tomás?
> **No, él se fue sin que yo lo viera.**

1.   ¿Hablaste con Carlos?

_____

2.   ¿Le diste el dinero a Jaime?

_____

3.   ¿Le mostraste la foto a Pedro?

_____

4.   ¿Le leíste la carta a Alfonso?

_____

5.   ¿Invitaste a Gloria?

_____

Ejercicio D

Conteste las preguntas que su tía le hace a su mamá mientras esperan la visita de unos primos:

> EJEMPLO: ¿Llegan mañana? (antes de que)
> **Sí, te llamaré antes de que lleguen.**

1.   ¿Vienen mañana? (antes de que)

_____

2.   ¿Vuelven hoy? (con tal que)

_____

3.   ¿Se van esta tarde? (en caso de que)

_____

4.   ¿Se marchan esta mañana? (a menos que)

_____

5.   ¿Saldrán por la noche? (con tal que)

_____

Ejercicio E

Escriba una pregunta como respuesta a las preguntas que le hace un amigo con quien Ud. va a salir el domingo:

EJEMPLO: ¿Va a nevar?
¿Qué haremos en caso de que nieve?

1.   ¿Va a llover?

_____

2.   ¿Va a hacer frío?

_____

3.   ¿Va a costar mucho?

_____

4.   ¿Vas a llegar tarde?

_____

5.   ¿Vas a tener que trabajar?

_____

Ejercicio F

Ud. va a viajar por España con un pariente que visita a España por primera vez. Escriba lo que Uds. van a hacer:

EJEMPLO: Alquilaremos un carro / para que / tú / conocer los pueblos
Alquilaremos un carro **para que tú conozcas** los pueblos.

1.   Iremos a la Costa del Sol / con tal que / no costar mucho

_____

2.   Mandaré tarjetas postales / antes de que / yo / gastar todo el dinero

_____

3.   Llevaré mi cámara / en caso de que / no vender fotos

_____

4.   No iré a Barcelona / a menos que / tú / acompañarme

_____

5.   Visitaremos El Prado / a menos que / tú / aburrirse

_____

6.   Pasaremos tiempo en El Retiro / para que / tú / remar en el lago

_____

7.   Te llevaré al Palacio Real / a fin de que / nosotros / ver los tesoros

_____

8.   Nos quedaremos en Granada / con tal que / no hacer mucho calor

_____

Ejercicio G

Escriba por qué un millonario ha comprado las cosas indicadas. Use una expresión diferente en cada frase: **para que, a fin de que, a menos que, antes (de) que, con tal que, en caso de que,** *o* **sin que:**

EJEMPLO: un avión
Compró un avión para que su mujer pudiera viajar más fácilmente.

1.   un televisor

_____

2.   tres entradas para el partido de fútbol

_____

3.   una casa grande

_____

4.   un carro lujoso

_____

5.   un reloj de oro

_____

6.   una casa en la playa

_____

7.   una grabadora de video

_____

b. The following conjunctions require the subjunctive if uncertainty, doubt, anticipation, or indefiniteness is implied. Otherwise, the indicative is used:

aunque *although, even though, even if* **cuando** *when* **de manera que** ⎫ **de modo que** ⎬ *so that* **después (de) que** *after*	**en cuanto** ⎫ **luego que** ⎪ **tan pronto como** ⎬ *as soon as* **así que** ⎪ **hasta que** *until* **mientras** *while*

SUBJUNCTIVE

Aunque cueste **mucho dinero, lo compraré.**
Although it may cost a lot of money, I'll buy it. [I don't know how much it costs.]

Espere Ud. *hasta que* **ellos** *vengan.*
Wait until they come [whenever that may be].

Te llamaré *cuando llegue* **a casa.**
I will call you when I arrive home [whenever that may be].

Leyó despacio, *de modo que* **ellos** *pudieran* **entender.**
He read slowly, so that they would be able to understand. [It's not known if they understood.]

Dijo que lo haría *así que le pagáramos.*
He said he would do it as soon as we paid him.

INDICATIVE

Aunque costó **mucho dinero, lo compré.**
Although it cost a lot of money, I bought it. [It did cost a lot of money.]

Esperó *hasta que* **ellos** *vinieron.*
He waited until they came. [They did arrive.]

Siempre me llama *cuando llega* **a casa.**
He always calls me when he arrives home [his normal custom].

Leyó despacio, *de modo que* **ellos** *pudieron* **entender.**
He read slowly, so that they were able to understand. [They understood.]

Lo hizo *así que le pagamos.*
He did it as soon as we paid him.

NOTE: If the subjects of the main and the dependent clauses are the same, **que** is usually omitted and the infinitive is used:

Terminaré el trabajo *antes de volver.*

I will finish the work before I return (before returning).

Espere Ud. *hasta volver* **a casa.**

Wait until you return home (until returning home).

Leyó el artículo despacio *para entenderlo.*

He read the article slowly in order to understand it.

Salió *sin decir* **adiós.**

He left without saying good-bye.

Ejercicio H

Escriba lo que Miguel dice que no va a hacer ahora que no habla con su hermano:

EJEMPLO: cuidarlo / tener tiempo
No voy a cuidarlo aunque yo tenga tiempo.

1. ayudarle / necesitar ayuda

   _____

2. comprarle un regalo / ser su cumpleaños

   _____

3. prestarle el guante de béisbol / querer usarlo

   _____

4. darle de comer / tener hambre

   _____

5. devolverle la cámara / ser suya

   _____

Ejercicio I

Escriba lo que cuenta Adela de cómo ayuda a unas amigas:

EJEMPLO: Prometen avisarme / cuando / ellas / estar listas
Prometen avisarme **cuando ellas estén** listas.

1. Sé que les gustará el apartamento / luego que / ellas / verlo

   _____

2. Revisan los muebles / de modo que / el dueño / no enojarse

   _____

3. Deciden mudarse / en cuanto / ellas / firmar el contrato

   _____

4. No les entregará el apartamento / hasta que / ellas / pagar el alquiler

   _____

5. Tomarán el apartamento / aunque / no ser muy grande

   _____

Ejercicio J

Escriba las frases del Ejercicio I, cambiándolas al pasado:

EJEMPLO: Prometieron avisarme / cuando / ellas / estar listas
Prometieron avisarme **cuando estuvieran** listas.

1.   Sabía que les gustaría el apartamento / luego que / ellas / verlo

_____

2.   Revisaron los muebles / de modo que / el dueño / no enojarse

_____

3.   Decidieron mudarse / en cuanto / ellas / firmar el contrato

_____

4.   No les entregaba el apartamento / hasta que / ellas / pagar el alquiler

_____

5.   Tomaban el apartamento / aunque / no ser muy grande

_____

Ejercicio K

Lola es la directora de un teatro de aficionados. Conteste las preguntas que le hace un miembro del grupo:

EJEMPLO: ¿Cuándo se cerrará la puerta? (después de que / todos / llegar)
La puerta se cerrará después de que lleguen todos.

1.   ¿Cuándo se quitarán el abrigo los señores? (así que/ ellos/ entrar en / el teatro)

_____

2.   ¿Se callará el público? (en cuanto / alzarse el telón)

_____

3.   ¿Cómo arreglaremos los asientos? (de modo que / el público / poder ver la función)

_____

4.   ¿Cuándo se apagarán las luces? (tan pronto como / el locutor / aparecer en el escenario)

_____

5.   ¿Se presentará la función si no hay público? (aunque / haber sólo dos personas)

_____

6.   ¿Cuándo se limpiará el escenario? (después de que / la gente / salir del teatro)

_____

C. The subjunctive is used after compounds of **-quiera** and similar indefinite expressions:

dondequiera	*wherever*
cualquier(a) (pl. **cualesquiera**)	*whatever, any*
quienquiera (pl. **quienesquiera**)	*whoever*
cuandoquiera	*whenever*
por + adj. or adv. + **que**	*however, no matter how*

No se lo daré, *quienquiera que sea.*   I will not give it to him, *whoever he may be.*

Aceptaré *cualquier* puesto que *Ud. me ofrezca.*   I will accept any job (that) you offer me.

Por difícil que sea, lo haré.   However (No matter how) difficult it may be, I will do it.

Ejercicio L

Conteste las preguntas que alguien le hace a Ud. sobre otro amigo:

EJEMPLOS: ¿Cuándo irá?
Cuandoquiera que vaya, no importa.

¿Quién será?
Quienquiera que sea, podrá entrar.

¿Es interesante?
Por interesante que sea, no lo invitaré.

1. ¿Dónde viajará él?

_____ , hará nuevos amigos.

2. ¿Es largo el viaje?

_____ , él lo aguantará.

3. ¿Cuándo llegará?

_____ , será bien recibido.

4. ¿Quién lo verá?

_____ , se asombrará.

5. ¿Es valiente Vicente?

_____ , tendrá que acostumbrarse.

6. ¿Qué hotel escogerá?

_____ , le parecerá caro.

7. ¿Dónde vivirá?

_____ , se quejará.

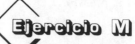 **Ejercicio M**

Después de leer las dos frases, combínelas en una sola, usando cuandoquiera, donde-quiera, quien(es)quiera, cual(es)quiera *o* por . . . que:

EJEMPLO: No sé quién lo hará. Todo el mundo puede hacerlo bien.
Quienquiera que lo haga, lo hará bien.

1.   No sé a qué hora ellos vendrán. Los esperamos de todos modos.

_____

2.   No sabemos cuánto pesa la mesa. Sólo sabemos que necesitarán cuatro hombres para moverla.

_____

3.   No sé qué blusa vas a escoger. Todas te quedarán bien.

_____

4.   No sé por qué trabajas tanto. Recibirás el mismo sueldo.

_____

5.   No sabemos quién comprará este televisor. Será una verdadera ganga.

_____

2. Subjunctive in Relative Clauses

The subjunctive is used in relative clauses if the person or thing in the main clause is indefinite, nonexistent, or desired but not yet attained:

SUBJUNCTIVE

Busca un apartamento que *sea* **cómodo y barato.**
She is looking for an apartment that is comfortable and cheap. [She may never find one.]

¿Conoce Ud. a alguien que *quiera* **trabajar?**
Do you know anyone who wants to work? [indefinite]

No encuentro a nadie que *pueda* **ayudarme.**
I can't find anyone who can help me. [nonexistent]

INDICATIVE

Tiene un apartamento que *es* **cómodo y barato.**
She has an apartment that is comfortable and cheap. [She has one.]

Conoce a alguien que *quiere* **trabajar.**
He knows someone who wants to work [definite person].

Encontré a un hombre que *puede* **ayudarme.**
I found a man who can help me. [There is such a person.]

Escriba lo que buscaban varias vecinas en las casas que compraron:

EJEMPLO: tres baños
Buscábamos una casa que tuviera tres baños.

1.   un comedor grande

    _____

2.   una piscina

    _____

3.   un jardín amplio

    _____

4.   un techo de barro

    _____

5.   cinco dormitorios

    _____

6.   un sistema de seguridad

    _____

Tomás está dirigiendo una campaña política. Escriba lo que él dice que van a hacer sus compañeros:

EJEMPLO: Claudia / un señor / sacar fotos
Claudia busca un señor que saque fotos.

1.   Fernando / alguien / hablar español

    _____

2.   Javier / varios jóvenes / llenar sobres

    _____

3.   Graciela / personas / repartir folletos

    _____

4.   Tú / una muchacha / escribir bien a máquina

    _____

5.   Yo / alguien / poder hacer llamadas teléfonicas

    _____

6.   María y Pablo / dos jóvenes / saber conducir bien

_____

Escriba lo que contesta el señor Lobos cuando sus amigos le recuerdan lo que dijo antes de hacer un viaje al extranjero:

EJEMPLO: Querías encontrar un cochero que condujera bien.
No encontré ningún cochero que condujera bien.

1.   Buscabas un guía que conociera bien la ciudad.

_____

2.   Deseabas encontrar un restaurante barato donde sirvieran buenas comidas.

_____

3.   Querías hablar con alguien que hubiera hecho el mismo viaje.

_____

4.   Buscabas un guía turístico que tuviera un plano claro de la ciudad.

_____

5.   Querías encontrar gente que quisiera hacer una excursión a la costa.

_____

3. Conditional Sentences

A conditional sentence consists of a condition (**si** clause) and a result (result clause). There are two basic types of conditions, "real" conditions and "unreal" or "contrary-to-fact" conditions.

4. Real Conditions

Real conditions describe situations that are likely, certain, or factual. The indicative is used in both the **si** clause and the result clause to express a real condition:

**Si estudias** más, *sacarás* mejores **notas.**	_If you study more, you will receive_ _better grades._ [You will almost certainly receive them.]
**Si me telefoneó** ayer, no *estaba* en **casa.**	_If he called me yesterday, I was not at_ _home._ [He did call, and I was out.]

5. Contrary-to-Fact Conditions

a. The imperfect and pluperfect subjunctives are used in contrary-to-fact conditions, as follows:

	SI-CLAUSE	RESULT CLAUSE
PRESENT TIME	Imperfect Subjunctive, **-se** or **-ra** form	Conditional (preferred in simple tenses) or Imperfect Subjunctive, **-ra** form only
PAST TIME	Pluperfect Subjunctive, **-se** or **-ra** form	Conditional Perfect or Pluperfect Subjunctive, **-ra** form only

Si tú *estudiases (estudiaras)* más, *sacarías (sacaras)* mejores notas.

If you studied more, you would receive better grades. [You don't receive good grades.]

Si tú *hubieses (hubieras) estudiado* más, *habrías (hubieras) sacado* mejores notas.

If you had studied more, you would have received better grades. [You didn't receive good grades.]

NOTE: The present subjunctive is never used in a **si** clause.

Lea las frases en que Eduardo dice lo que hará. Luego cámbielas para decir lo que él haría en esas circunstancias:

EJEMPLO: Si necesito dinero, se lo pediré a mi padre.
Si **necesitase (necesitara)** dinero, se lo **pediría** a mi padre.

1. Si nos levantamos tarde, no llegaremos a tiempo.

_____

2. Si me ofrecen un puesto, lo aceptaré.

_____

3. Si trabajo allí, ganaré mucho dinero.

_____

4. Si me das el dinero, lo compraré.

_____

5. Si vienen tarde, no los esperaré.

_____

6. Si hace mal tiempo, nos quedaremos en casa.

_____

7. Si vemos a Jorge, se lo contaremos.

_____

 Escriba qué haría Ud. en estas circunstancias:

        Ejemplo: ir de compras
                     Si fuera de compras, compraría un regalo para mis padres.

1. visitar un museo

_____

2. hacer un viaje

_____

3. gastar mucho dinero

_____

4. escribir una novela

_____

5. conocer a un actor (una actriz)

_____

6. construir una casa

_____

7. ganar la lotería

_____

8. ser médico

_____

 Escriba lo que su abuelo dice que hubiera hecho de manera diferente y cuál hubiera (habría) sido el resultado:

        Ejemplo: vivir en la ciudad
                     Si hubiera vivido en la ciudad, habría (hubiera) ido al teatro a menudo.

1. ahorrar dinero

   _____

2. practicar un deporte

   _____

3. tener su propio negocio

   _____

4. seguir un curso en la universidad

   _____

5. no vender la casa

   _____

6. aprender a pintar

   _____

7. viajar al extranjero

   _____

b. The imperfect and pluperfect subjunctives are also used after **como si** (*as if*):

Ud. le trata **como si** *fuera* un niño.	*You treat him as if he were a child [but he isn't].*
Me miró **como si** yo **hubiera cometido** un crimen.	*He looked at me as if I had committed a crime [but I didn't].*

Ejercicio T

*Escriba los comentarios que hace un dependiente sobre los clientes que entran en el almacén, usando **como si**:*

EJEMPLO: Ese señor / hablar / ser el dueño
Ese señor habla **como si fuera** el dueño.

1. Esa señora / hablar / nosotros / vender cosas defectuosas

   _____

2. Aquel joven / comprar / ser millonario

   _____

3. Esos niños / gritar / estar en su propia casa

   _____

4. Aquella señora / mirarme / yo / poner los precios

   _____

5.   Este hombre / quejarse / ser un niño

———

6.   Esas ancianas / vestirse / ser jóvenes

———

7.   Este muchacho / hacer preguntas / no saber nada

———

C. The **-ra** forms of the imperfect subjunctive of **querer, poder,** and **deber** may be used instead of the conditional of these verbs to express a polite request or statement:

Quisiera comprarlo.	*I would like to buy it.*
¿Pudiera Ud. hacerlo hoy?	*Could you do it today?*
Debiéramos verlo.	*We should (ought to) see it.*

Ejercicio U

Escriba la forma correcta de los verbos dados entre paréntesis en esta carta que Carolina le escribe a su amiga Lola:

Querida Lola,

Yo ———————————— invitarlas a ti y a tu hermana a una fiesta. Tú ————————————
      1 (querer)   **2** (deber)

pensarlo bien porque Raúl va a asistir. Tú y Gloria ———————————— tomar el autobús que
                                                                         3 (poder)

llega aquí a las seis y media. Mi mamá y yo ———————————— ir a esperarlas en la terminal,
                                                         4 (querer)

pero estaremos muy ocupadas. Voy a hablarle a José para ver si él ———————————— ir a la
                                                                                        5 (poder)

terminal. Mientras tanto, Uds. ———————————— decidir si vendrán o no.
                                        6 (deber)

¿ ———————————— tú llamarme por teléfono en cuanto recibas esta carta? Gracias.
      7 (poder)

Saludos de

Carolina

Ejercicio V

Teresa y Norma van a ir de compras. Ensayan lo que le van a decir al dependiente. Complete las frases con la forma correcta de **querer, poder** *o* **deber,** *según el caso:*

1.   Buenas tardes. Nosotras ———————————— comprar unos regalos.

2. ¿_____ Ud. mostrarnos un anillo?

3. No _____ ser muy caro.

4. Yo _____ ver algo más económico y no _____ tener piedras.

5. ¿_____ (nosotras) ver esos aretes?

6. ¿_____ Ud. envolverlos como regalo? Gracias.

♦ **MASTERY EXERCISES** ♦

Ejercicio W

Escriba la forma correcta de los verbos dados entre paréntesis en los cuentecitos que siguen:

1. Quería _____ un regalo especial que le _____ a su esposa.
                   1 (encontrar)   2 (gustar)

   Pasó días buscándolo en las tiendas. Por fin vio un alfiler precioso con cadena de oro. Era

   muy caro. «Por mucho que _____ , lo compraré» dijo. «Ahora es necesario
                                     3 (costar)

   que lo _____ para que ella no lo _____ , porque no quiero
              4 (esconder)   5 (ver)

   que _____ nada de esto antes de la Navidad». Entró en casa con cara
           6 (saber)

   risueña y buscó un lugar que _____ seguro, pero sin éxito. Su esposa
                             7 (ser)

   lo miraba con expresión extraña.

   —¿Por qué me miras como si _____ un criminal?—gritó él, con enojo.
                                8 (ser)

   —_____ que no me _____ —contestó ella.
         9 (querer)   10 (gritar)

2. El médico le aconsejó que _____ cama porque tenía un catarro. No quería
                             1 (guardar)

   _____ todo el día en casa; no obstante, su madre insistió en que lo
          2 (pasar)

   _____ . Pasó un día desagradable. Sintió no _____ ver a
         3 (hacer)   4 (poder)

   sus amigos. A la mañana siguiente, apenas se despertó, le dijo a su madre que

   _____ bien y que tenía el propósito fijo de salir.
         5 (estar)

Pero ella le prohibió que _____ hasta que no _____ el
6 (salir)   7 (llegar)

médico.

—¡Ojalá que _____ pronto! Porque si no _____, saldré aún
8 (venir)   9 (venir)

sin su permiso—dijo.

—No creo que _____ eso—le contestó su madre con calma, pero en tono
10 (hacer)

firme.

3. Colón negaba que el mundo _____ llano. Pidió a su majestad la reina
1 (ser)

Isabel que le _____ a realizar su sueño:
2 (ayudar)

—Si yo _____ unas naves, _____ encontrar una nueva
3 (tener)   4 (poder)

ruta occidental que me _____ a las Indias.
5 (conducir)

Además de las naves, buscó unos navegantes que no _____ miedo de
6 (tener)

_____ al mar infinito. Pero no había nadie que _____ a
7 (salir)   8 (atreverse)

confiarse a la furia y violencia de los elementos. Sin embargo, Colón no se resignó al

fracaso total de su proyecto. Tenía el espíritu firme.

«Aunque _____ que buscarlos en las cárceles, los encontraré» se dijo «y
9 (tener)

cuando los _____, podremos embarcarnos».
10 (encontrar)

4. Si _____ español, iré a España. Quienquiera que _____
1 (aprender)   2 (haber)

hecho tal viaje dice que es un país encantador. No dudo que _____ razón.
3 (tener)

Es probable que _____ en la primavera. Espero _____ un
4 (ir)   5 (hacer)

viaje directo, en avión, con tal que _____ bastante dinero.
6 (tener)

Así que _____ allí, trataré de ver las diversas cosas que tiene la España
7 (llegar)

actual. Después de unos días en Madrid, recorreré el país de un extremo a otro sin

descanso. Adondequiera que _____, estoy seguro de
8 (ir)

_____ sacar muchas fotos para mostrárselas más tarde a mis amigos
9 (poder)

íntimos. Es lástima que ellos no _____ acompañarme.
10 (poder)

5. Antes de que _____ el sol, ya corrían a través de los campos. Importaba que
1 (salir)

_____ a su destino, un pueblo cercano, a una distancia de diez millas de
2 (llegar)

allí, de modo que _____ reunirse con los otros.
  3 (poder)

—Luego que _____, podremos descansar—dijo el jefe.
  4 (llegar)

—Por rápidamente que _____ nuestros caballos—dijo un soldado con
  5 (correr)

amargura—es imposible que _____ allí a tiempo.
  6 (estar)

—En todo caso—dijo el jefe con ira—es necesario _____ en un milagro,
  7 (creer)

hacer esfuerzos como si _____ posible. Hay que andar sin tardanza, sin que
  8 (ser)

el enemigo _____ cuenta.
  9 (darse)

Cuando _____, vieron con emoción a sus compañeros esperando debajo de
  10 (llegar)

los árboles.

Ejercicio X

Exprese en español lo que un guía le dice a un turista que viaja en una excursión:

1. As soon as we reach the inn, we will be able to rest.

   _____

   _____

2. I would like to ask for your help.

   _____

3. If someone wastes time, we will never arrive at our destination.

   _____

   _____

4. They can have a cup of coffee provided that they return in ten minutes.

   _____

   _____

5. It is evident that they are hungry and thirsty.

   _____

6. No matter how firm I try to be, they always get their way.

   _____

   _____

7. Could you please hurry?

   _____

8. If we had departed earlier, we would not have had to rush now.

     _____

     _____

9. Whoever wants coffee should have it now.

     _____

10. As soon as they return, we will leave.

     _____

11. They are looking for a store that sells souvenirs.

     _____

     _____

12. I don't know any store that doesn't accept traveler's checks.

     _____

     _____

13. Yesterday one man left a store without getting his change.

     _____

     _____

14. We will wait here until the last person comes out of the store.

     _____

     _____

15. If I had finished my studies, I would not have become a travel guide.

     _____

     _____

Commands

1. Formal Commands

Formal commands with **Ud.** and **Uds.**, both affirmative and negative, are always expressed by the present subjunctive (see the Appendix, page 502).

tomar		*tome Ud.*		*tomen Uds.*		take
volver		*vuelva Ud.*		*vuelvan Uds.*		return
venir	**(no)**	*venga Ud.*	**(no)**	*vengan Uds.*	(don't)	come
ir		*vaya Ud.*		*vayan Uds.*		go
dar		*dé Ud.*		*den Uds.*		give

NOTE: With reflexive verbs, the reflexive pronoun is attached to the affirmative command and there is an accent mark on the next-to-last syllable of the verb. If the verb has only one syllable, it does not carry an accent mark: **dese**. In negative commands, the reflexive pronoun precedes the verb:

lavarse	*lávese Ud.*	*lávense Uds.*
	no se lave Ud.	*no se laven Uds.*
despedirse	*despídase Ud.*	*despídanse Uds.*
	no se despida Ud.	*no se despidan Uds.*

 Ejercicio A

Escriba las instrucciones para hacer una llamada de un teléfono público en México:

EJEMPLO: descolgar el auricular
Descuelgue Ud. el auricular.

1. escuchar el tono de marcar

   _____

2. poner la moneda

   _____

3. marcar el número

   _____

4. esperar hasta que alguien conteste

_____

5. oprimir el botón de la moneda

_____

6. hablar con la persona

_____

7. colgar el auricular

_____

8. comunicarse con la telefonista si hay algún problema

_____

Ejercicio B

Escriba lo que deben hacer los buenos ciudadanos:

EJEMPLO: leer el periódico todos los días
Lean Uds. el periódico todos los días.

1. escuchar las noticias todos los días

_____

2. no dejar de votar en las elecciones

_____

3. participar en las actividades de su comunidad

_____

4. ofrecer ayuda a los menos afortunados

_____

5. contribuir a las obras de caridad

_____

6. conocer a sus vecinos

_____

7. respetar los derechos de otros

_____

8. ser honrados

_____

9. escribir cartas al gobierno

_____

10. elegir a sus representantes

_____

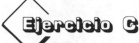

Escriba lo que la señora Perales les dice a sus hijos cuando los deja con una niñera:

EJEMPLOS: portarse bien   no pelearse
            Pórtense bien.   **No se peleen.**

1. no salir a la calle

_____

2. no acercarse a la piscina

_____

3. bañarse a las ocioto

_____

4. no olvidarse de cepillarse los dientes

_____

5. ponerse la bata después de bañarse

_____

6. no quedarse en la sala

_____

7. acostarse temprano

_____

8. dormirse rápidamente

_____

9. no levantarse de la cama

_____

10. no aprovecharse de la niñera

_____

2. Indirect Commands

a. Indirect commands are also expressed by the present subjunctive and are usually introduced by **que**:

Que hable él (ella).	Let (Have) him (her) speak.
Que oigan la verdad.	Let (Have) them hear the truth.
Que sean felices.	May they be happy.
Que lo haga Juana.	Let (Have) Jane do it.

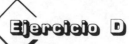 **Ejercicio D**

Ud. es el (la) director(a) de una obra de teatro en su escuela. Escriba lo que debe hacer todo el mundo:

EJEMPLO: Enrique / pintar el decorado
Que Enrique pinte el decorado.

1. Sarita / hacer el vestuario

_____

2. Jorge y Arturo / arreglar las luces

_____

3. Carlos / hacer el papel del payaso

_____

4. Clara / ser la locutora

_____

5. ellos / poner las sillas

_____

6. Pepe / bajar y alzar el telón

_____

7. Laura e Inés / recoger los boletos

_____

8. Miguel / tocar el piano

_____

 **Ejercicio E**

Beto es un niño a quien no le gusta hacer nada. Escriba quién debe hacer estas cosas, según él:

EJEMPLO: No quiero sacar al perro. (mi hermano)
Que lo saque mi hermano.

1. No quiero ir a la tienda. (Conchita)

_____

2. No quiero hacer la tarea. (la maestra)

_____

3. No quiero comer los guisantes. (los perros)

_____

4. No quiero poner la mesa. (mi mamá)

_____

5. No quiero ayudarte. (tus amigos)

_____

b. Let us (Let's)

    (1) The first person plural of the present subjunctive is used to express *Let us:*

        ***Esperemos* un momento.**   Let us *wait a moment.*
        ***Salgamos* ahora.**   Let us *leave now.*

    (2) *Let us go* is expressed by **vamos.** In the negative, the regular subjunctive form **vayamos** is used:

        ***Vamos* al teatro hoy.**   Let us *go to the theater today.*
        *No **vayamos* al teatro hoy.**   Let us *not go to the theater today.*

    (3) **Vamos a** + infinitive may also be used to express *Let us:*

        ***Vamos a* cantar** (or **Cantemos**).   Let us *sing.*
        ***Vamos a* aprender** (or **Aprendamos**) **la**   Let us *learn the lesson for tomorrow.*
        lección para mañana.

    (4) In expressing the affirmative *Let us* with reflexive verbs, the final **-s** of the verb ending is dropped before adding the reflexive pronoun **nos.** An accent is placed on the stressed syllable:

        Sentémonos (= **Sentemos** + **nos**).   Let's *sit down.*
        Vámonos (= **Vamos** + **nos**).   Let's *go (away).*

Ejercicio F

Escriba cómo Ud. y un amigo/una amiga piensan celebrar el cuatro de julio. Su amigo(a) está de acuerdo con sus sugerencias:

        EJEMPLO: dar una fiesta
                       Demos una fiesta.
                       Sí, vamos a dar una fiesta.

1. levantarse temprano_____

_____

2. ir al centro_____

_____

3. marchar en el desfile_____

_____

4. comprar cohetes_____

_____

5. reunirse con otros amigos_____

   _____

6. inflar muchos globos_____

   _____

7. colgar la bandera_____

   _____

8. divertirse mucho_____

   _____

Ejercicio G

Su amigo es muy indeciso. Escriba lo que dice cuando Ud. le sugiere algo durante un viaje al centro:

EJEMPLO: ¿Nos paramos en las tiendas?
           Sí, parémonos en las tiendas, pero no nos paremos ahora.

1. ¿Nos sentamos en el parque?

   _____

   _____

2. ¿Nos desayunamos en ese restaurante?

   _____

   _____

3. ¿Nos quejamos del servicio?

   _____

   _____

4. ¿Nos acercamos al parque zoológico?

   _____

   _____

5. ¿Nos vamos pronto?

   _____

   _____

3. Familiar Commands

a. Regular verbs

(1) The singular (**tú**) form of the familiar affirmative command is the same as the third person singular of the present indicative.

(2) The plural (**vosotros**) form of the familiar affirmative command is formed by changing the **-r** ending of the infinitive to **-d**.

(3) The negative familiar command forms are all expressed by the present subjunctive.

	AFFIRMATIVE	NEGATIVE
mirar	*mira* **tú** *mirad* **vosotros**	*no mires* **tú** *no miréis* **vosotros**
correr	*corre* **tú** *corred* **vosotros**	*no corras* **tú** *no corráis* **vosotros**
dormir	*duerme* **tú** *dormid* **vosotros**	*no duermas* **tú** *no durmáis* **vosotros**

NOTE: The familiar plural forms (**vosotros, -as**) are rarely used in Latin America. Formal plural commands (**ustedes**) are used instead.

Ejercicio H

Escriba lo que la maestra les dice a los alumnos:

EJEMPLO: (hablar) Niños, _____**hablad**_____ español en la clase; no ____**habléis**____ inglés.

1. (terminar) Alumnos, _____ la tarea; no _____ la práctica.

2. (continuar) Niños, _____ la lectura; no _____ la conversación.

3. (empezar) Niños, _____ el examen; no _____ la tarea.

4. (dibujar) Alumnos, _____ un castillo; no _____ una granja.

5. (escribir) Alumnos, _____ un cuento; no _____ una novela.

Ejercicio I

La señora Peña tiene problemas con sus hijos. Escriba lo que dijo el señor Peña al enterarse de estos problemas:

EJEMPLO: Carlos no se sienta a la mesa.
Carlos, **siéntate** a la mesa; **no te sientes** en el escritorio.

1. Inés no se lava la cara.

Inés, _____ la cara; no _____ el pelo.

2. Jorge no se despierta temprano.

Jorge, _____ temprano; no _____ al mediodía.

3.   Juan no se acerca a los libros.

Juan, _____ a los libros; no _____ al refrigerador.

4.   Pablo no se viste en seguida.

Pablo, _____ en seguida; no _____ tan despacio.

5.   Alicia no se pasea cuando hace sol.

Alicia, _____ cuando hace sol; no _____ cuando llueve.

Ejercicio J

Su hermanito cree que es muy listo. Escriba lo que él les aconsejó a unos amigos:

EJEMPLO: José no lee su libro.
José, **lee** tu libro; **no leas** la revista.

1.   Rosa no obedece a su madre.

Rosa, _____ a tu madre; no _____ a tu amiga.

2.   Pedro no cierra la boca.

Pedro, _____ la boca; no _____ los ojos.

3.   Alfredo no busca a su gato.

Alfredo, _____ a tu gato; no _____ al perro.

4.   Carolina no vuelve a su asiento.

Carolina, _____ a tu asiento; no _____ a la pizarra.

5.   Alberto no trae su cámara.

Alberto, _____ tu cámara; no _____ tu tocadiscos.

b. Irregular verbs

The only irregular commands occur in the affirmative singular (**tú**). All other familiar commands are regular:

decir	*di* tú	decid vosotros	no digas tú	no digáis vosotros
hacer	*haz* tú	haced vosotros	no hagas tú	no hagáis vosotros
ir	*ve* tú	id vosotros	no vayas tú	no vayáis vosotros
poner	*pon* tú	poned vosotros	no pongas tú	no pongáis vosotros
salir	*sal* tú	salid vosotros	no salgas tú	no salgáis vosotros
ser	*sé* tú	sed vosotros	no seas tú	no seáis vosotros
tener	*ten* tú	tened vosotros	no tengas tú	no tengáis vosotros
valer	*val* tú	valed vosotros	no valgas tú	no valgáis vosotros
venir	*ven* tú	venid vosotros	no vengas tú	no vengáis vosotros

Ejercicio K

Antes de participar en una competencia, la madre de Micaela le dice lo que debe hacer. Escriba la forma correcta de los verbos dados entre paréntesis:

EJEMPLO: (tener)   ¡No ___**tengas**___ prisa!
            (ir)   ¡___**Ve**___ con Dios!

1. (hacer)   ¡_____ lo mejor que puedas!
2. (decir)   ¡No _____ tonterías!
3. (tener)   ¡_____ paciencia!
4. (decir)   ¡_____ la verdad!
5. (ser)   ¡No _____ perezosa!
6. (poner)   ¡_____ mucha atención a las reglas!
7. (tener)   ¡_____ cuidado!
8. (ser)   ¡_____ buena!
9. (salir)   ¡_____ en seguida!
10. (ir)   ¡No _____ a llegar tarde!
11. (venir)   ¡_____ a casa en cuanto termines!
12. (hacer)   ¡No _____ caso a tus amigas!
13. (tener)   ¡No _____ miedo!
14. (ser)   ¡_____ muy lista!
15. (hacer)   ¡_____ muchas preguntas!

Ejercicio L

Escriba lo que dirían estas personas en las circunstancias siguientes:

EJEMPLO: Anita: Ya son la once y media y tengo una cita a las doce.
            Su amiga: (no tener prisa) ¡**No tengas prisa!**

1. Roberto: Mira, tu perro anda en el otro jardín.

    Tú: (venir acá) _____

2. Carlos: Yo no rompí la lámpara. Ésta no es mi pelota.

    Su madre: (no decir mentiras) _____

3. Sarita: ¡Ay! Hay un ratoncito allí.

    Su amigo: (no tener miedo) _____

4. Pilar: No sé si debo ir al baile con Ernesto.

      Luz: (no ser tonta / ir con él) _____

_____

5. Pablo: ¿Dónde debo poner el dinero?

      Papá: (poner el dinero en la mesa) _____

4. Object Pronouns With Commands

a. Object pronouns (including reflexive pronouns) are attached to affirmative commands. An accent mark is required if the original stress was on the next-to-last syllable. In negative commands, object pronouns precede the verb:

Ayúde*le* Ud.	No *le* ayude Ud.
Tráigan*lo* Uds.	No *lo* traigan Uds.
Hagámos*lo*.	No *lo* hagamos.
Levánta*te* tú.	No *te* levantes.
Aprended*lo* vosotros.	No *lo* aprendáis vosotros.
Di*les* el secreto.	No *les* digas el secreto.

b. With indirect commands introduced by **que**, the object pronoun always precedes the verb:

Que *lo* haga Juana.	Que no *lo* haga Juana.
Que *se* vayan en seguida.	Que no *se* vayan en seguida.

c. In the affirmative **vosotros** form of reflexive verbs, the final **-d** is dropped before adding the reflexive pronoun **os**:

Sentaos (= **Sentad** + **os**).	*Sit down.*
Divertíos (= **Divertid** + **os**).	*Enjoy yourselves.*
Exception:	
Idos	*Go away*

Ejercicio M

Escriba lo que este padre les dijo a sus hijos:

    EJEMPLO: Los niños no se divierten mucho.

                Niños, ***divertíos*** un poco; no ***os divirtáis*** demasiado.

1. Los niños no se portan bien.

    Niños, _____ bien; no _____ mal.

2. Sus hijos no se ríen de tonterías.

    Hijos, _____ de tonterías; no _____ de la verdad.

3. Las chicas no se reúnen en el salón.

   Chicas, _____ en el salón; no _____ en el jardín.

4. Pablo e Inés nunca se ponen serios.

   Pablo e Inés, _____ serios, pero no _____ tristes.

5. Sus hijos no se dedican a la caridad.

   Hijos, _____ a la caridad; no _____ a los placeres.

Ejercicio N

Conchita es una hermanita celosa. Escriba lo que ella y su hermana Elsa dicen cuando su madre quiere hacer algo por Elsa:

EJEMPLO: ¿Quieres que te prepare el desayuno?
Elsa: **Sí, prepáramelo, mamá.**
Conchita: **No se lo prepares.**

1. ¿Quieres que te envuelva el regalo?

   Elsa: _____

   Conchita: _____

2. ¿Prefieres que yo lave tu ropa hoy?

   Elsa: _____

   Conchita: _____

3. ¿Deseas que yo cambie el programa?

   Elsa: _____

   Conchita: _____

4. ¿Necesitas que yo te ayude?

   Elsa: _____

   Conchita: _____

5. ¿Quieres que tú y yo busquemos el vestido hoy?

   Elsa: _____

   Conchita: _____

6. ¿Prefieres que yo compre los refrescos?

   Elsa: _____

   Conchita: _____

7. ¿Deseas que tu papá y yo te acompañemos?

   Elsa: _____

   Conchita: _____

◆ MASTERY EXERCISES ◆

Escriba las reglas que deben seguirse en caso de un huracán:

> EJEMPLO: tener cuidado y no estar nerviosos
> **Tengan Uds.** cuidado y **no estén** nerviosos.

1. comprar bastante comida para una semana

   _____

2. conservar una linterna a la mano

   _____

3. preparar un aparato de radio portátil

   _____

4. poner cinta o tablas en las ventanas

   _____

5. quedarse dentro de la casa

   _____

6. cerrar todas las ventanas

   _____

7. correr las cortinas

   _____

8. no acercarse a las ventanas durante la tormenta

   _____

9. llenar la bañera de agua

   _____

10. hervir el agua antes de tomarla

    _____

11. no abrir el refrigerador a menudo

    _____

12. escuchar las noticias

    _____

13. no congestionar las líneas telefónicas

    _____

14. no dejar nada en la terraza ni en el patio

    _____

15. no salir hasta que la tormenta haya pasado

    _____

Ejercicio P

Escriba las instrucciones que Juan le da a un amigo para llegar a la playa:

EJEMPLO: tomar el Camino Real
Toma el Camino Real.

1. ir hacia el norte

_____

2. seguir de frente

_____

3. en el quinto semáforo, dar vuelta a la derecha

_____

4. atravesar el puente

_____

5. mantenerse en el carril izquierdo

_____

6. pararse en el semáforo

_____

7. doblar a la izquierda

_____

8. continuar derecho

_____

9. empezar a buscar dónde estacionar el carro

_____

10. caminar una cuadra

_____

Ejercicio Q

A Susana le gusta encargarse de todo. Exprese en español lo que dijo al encontrarse con su amiga Rosita:

1. Rosita, tell me what happened.

_____

2. Don't worry; everything will be all right.

_____

3. Let them wait until noon.

_____

4. Let's have coffee now.

_____

5. Waiter, bring us two cups of coffee, please.

_____

6. Don't forget the milk and the sugar.

_____

7. Don't become angry, Rosita.

_____

8. Let the children enjoy themselves.

_____

9. Children, play over there and don't make noise.

_____

10. Jaime, don't let them bother the other guests.

_____

11. Don't be deceived, my friend, nothing is easy.

_____

12. Do it now.

_____

13. Don't wait any longer.

_____

14. Children, don't say such things.

_____

15. Let's leave now.

_____

16 Common Expressions with Verbs

Many Spanish verbs are used idiomatically in certain expressions. A list of common expressions follows.

1. Expressions with *acabar*

acabar de + infinitive *to have just*
acabar por + infinitive *to end by, to finally*

> **Acabo de volver de la escuela.**
> **Se enfermó gravemente y *acabó por morir*.**

> *I have just returned from school.*
> *He became seriously ill and finally died.*

2. Expressions with *dar*

dar a *to face, to look out upon*
dar un abrazo *to embrace*
dar con *to come upon, to run into, to find*
dar cuerda (a) *to wind*
dar de beber (comer) a *to give a drink to (to feed)*
dar en *to strike against, to hit*
dar las gracias (a) *to thank*
dar gritos (voces) *to shout*
dar la hora *to strike the hour*
dar un paseo *to take a walk; to go for a ride*
dar por + past participle *to consider*
dar recuerdos (a) *to give regards (to)*
dar una vuelta *to take a stroll*
darse cuenta de *to realize*
darse la mano *to shake hands*
darse prisa *to hurry*

> **Las ventanas *dan a* la avenida.**
> **Al llegar, le *dio un abrazo* a su madre.**
> ***Dimos con* Juan en el cine anoche.**

> *The windows face the avenue.*
> *On arriving, he embraced his mother.*
> *We ran into John at the movies last night.*

Cada mañana le *doy cuerda* a mi reloj.	Each morning I wind my watch.
Pedro le *dio de beber* a su perro.	Peter gave his dog a drink.
La pelota *dio en* el techo.	The ball hit the ceiling.
Le *di las gracias* por el regalo.	I thanked him for the gift.
Los niños *dieron gritos* de alegría.	The children shouted with joy.
Dio voces, pidiendo ayuda.	He shouted, asking for help.
El reloj *dio la una.*	The clock struck one.
Dimos un paseo en su carro.	We took a ride in his car.
El profesor *dio por terminada* la lección.	The teacher considered the lesson ended.
Dale mis recuerdos a tu padre.	Give my regards to your father.
Por la tarde, *doy una vuelta* por el parque.	In the afternoon I take a stroll in the park.
No se *dio cuenta* de su error.	He did not realize his mistake.
Al encontrarse, *se dieron la mano.*	Upon meeting, they shook hands.
¡*Dense prisa*! Ya son las ocho.	Hurry! It is already eight o'clock.

Ejercicio A

Julio cuenta lo que le pasó en el centro. Usando una expresión con dar(se) *o* acabar, *exprese lo mismo que dice Julio:*

EJEMPLO: Yo paseaba por la avenida Juárez.
Yo **daba un paseo** por la avenida Juárez.

1. Alfredo y yo andábamos por el centro.

_____

2. Nos encontramos con el papá de Gloria y nos saludamos.

_____

3. Él había dejado a Gloria en la biblioteca hacía un momento.

_____

4. Eran las doce en el reloj de la torre.

_____

5. El papá de Gloria no sabía que su reloj se había parado.

_____

6. Él arregló su reloj para que anduviera.

_____

7. Unos niños que gritaban en la esquina finalmente se callaron.

_____

8. Una pelota que tiraron cayó contra una ventana y quebró el vidrio.

_____

9. El papá de Gloria nos abrazó al despedirse.

_____

10. Mandé saludos a su familia y él me agradeció los saludos.

_____

Ejercicio B

Después de una fiesta en casa de Rogelio, su mamá le hace unas preguntas. Contéstelas, usando las sugerencias entre paréntesis:

1. ¿Dónde estabas cuando dieron las doce? (acabar de salir de la fiesta)

_____

2. ¿Cuántas veces le diste de comer al perro ayer? (dos)

_____

3. ¿Cómo saludaste a los señores Roldán? (darse la mano)

_____

4. ¿Por qué llegaste tan tarde a casa? (dar un paseo en carro)

_____

5. ¿Por qué se dieron prisa tus primos? (era tarde)

_____

6. ¿Cómo saludaste a tu tío? (dar un abrazo)

_____

7. ¿Por qué le diste las gracias a Miguel? (el regalo)

_____

8. ¿De qué te diste cuenta? (todos se divirtieron mucho)

_____

9. ¿Qué piensas hacer esta mañana? (dar una vuelta con mis amigos)

_____

10. ¿Le diste cuerda a tu despertador? (acabar de hacerlo)

_____

3. Expressions with *dejar*

dejar caer *to drop*
dejar de + infinitive *to fail to, to stop, to neglect to*

Juanito *dejó caer* el vaso de leche.	Johnny dropped the glass of milk.
Dejó de estudiar y cerró el libro.	He stopped studying and closed the book.

4. Expressions with *echar*

echar(se) a *to start to*
echar al correo *to mail*
echar la culpa *to blame*
echar de menos *to miss*

Al ver al policía, el ladrón *se echó a* correr.

On seeing the policeman, the thief started to run.

No te olvides de *echar* las cartas *al correo*.

Don't forget to mail the letters.

Le *echó la culpa* a su hermana.

He blamed his sister.

Los niños *echaron de menos* a su vecino.

The children missed their neighbor.

5. Expressions with *haber*

hay *there is, there are*
hubo ⎫
había ⎭ *there was, there were*

habrá *there will be*
habría *there would be*
ha habido *there has (have) been*

haber de + infinitive *to be (supposed) to, to have to*
haber que + infinitive *to be necessary*
haber (mucho) lodo *to be (very) muddy*
haber luna *to be moonlight*
haber neblina *to be foggy, misty*
haber (mucho) polvo *to be (very) dusty*
haber sol *to be sunny*

He de salir a las nueve.

I am to leave at nine o'clock.

Habrá que salir temprano.

It will be necessary to leave early.

Después de la lluvia *había lodo*.

After the rain it was muddy.

Anoche *hubo luna*.

There was moonlight last night.

Esta mañana *había neblina*.

This morning it was foggy.

Hay mucho polvo por el camino.

It is very dusty on the road.

No *hubo sol* ayer y llovió.

It wasn't sunny yesterday and it rained.

 **Ejercicio C**

Ofelia está de vacaciones y le escribe a su amiga Rosita. Complete la carta con las expresiones dadas:

Querida Rosita:

Por fin llegamos al hotel. El viaje fue terrible. _____ en el camino y

1 (it was very dusty)

_____ a lo largo del río. Por la mañana, cuando salimos,
    2 (it was muddy)

_____ . El portero _____ mi maleta y
    3 (it was foggy)   **4** (dropped)

_____ a un pobre perro que se le atravesó. Se enojó conmigo, porque
    5 (blamed)

_____ reír. _____ mucha gente buscando
    6 (I started to)   **7** (There were)

cuarto en el hotel. No sabían que _____ hacer reservaciones con tiempo.
    8 (it is necessary)

Voy a aprovechar que _____ ahora para nadar en la piscina. Pero antes
    9 (it is sunny)

quiero _____ esta carta. _____ escribirme. Ya te
    10 (mail)   **11** (Don't fail)

_____ .
    12 (miss)

Tu amiga

Ofelia

6. Expressions with _hacer_

hacer + time expression + **que** + preterite ⎫
preterite + **hace** + time expression   ⎬ _ago_
                            ⎭
hace poco _a little while ago_
hacer buen (mal) tiempo _to be good (bad) weather_
hacer (mucho) frío (calor) _to be (very) cold (warm)_
hacer (mucho) viento _to be (very) windy_
hacer caso _to pay attention, to heed, to notice_
hacer de _to work as, to act as_
hacer el papel de _to play the role of_
hacer pedazos (añicos) _to break to pieces, to tear to shreds, to smash_
hacer una pregunta _to ask a question_
hacer una visita _to pay a visit_
hacer un viaje _to take a trip_
hacerse + noun _to become_
hacerse tarde _to become (grow) late_
hacer(se) daño _to harm, to damage, to hurt (oneself)_

    Hace una semana que vino a verme. ⎫
    Vino a verme **hace una semana.** ⎬
                                  ⎭
He came to see me a week ago.

El tren salió _hace poco._
The train left a little while ago.

Ayer _hizo buen tiempo._
Yesterday the weather was good.

En el invierno _hace frío._
It is cold in the winter.

Ayer no salí porque _hacía viento._
Yesterday I didn't go out because it was windy.

Ese muchacho no _hizo caso_ **de mis consejos.**
That boy didn't heed my advice.

Diego _hizo de_ **capitán en el juego.**
In the game, James acted as captain.

La actriz se negó a *hacer el papel de* condesa.

El muchacho *hizo pedazos* el papel.

Me *hizo una pregunta*, pero no contesté.

Anoche le *hice una visita* a mi amigo.

Hice un viaje a México el año pasado.

Para *hacerse médico*, es necesario estudiar mucho.

Se *hicieron* muy buenos amigos.

Se *hizo tarde* y tuvimos que marcharnos.

El frío *hizo daño* a los árboles.

Se cayó y *se hizo daño*.

The actress refused to play the role of countess.

The boy tore the paper to shreds.

He asked me a question, but I didn't answer.

Last night I paid a visit to my friend.

I took a trip to Mexico last year.

In order to become a doctor, it is necessary to study a lot.

They became very good friends.

It became very late and we had to leave.

The cold damaged the trees.

He fell and hurt himself.

Ejercicio D

La emisora de su escuela transmite las noticias todos los días. Hoy Ud. va a dar las noticias sobre un huracán. Usando correctamente una de las expresiones dadas, complete el reporte siguiente:

En el noticiero de hoy yo _____ 1 _____ locutor del boletín meteorológico. _____ 2 _____ unos minutos me dieron este reporte sobre un huracán que está pasando por el sur de los Estados Unidos. Hoy por la mañana _____ 3 _____ en los pueblos de la costa. De repente, a eso de las dos de la tarde, empezó a

_____ 4 _____ . _____ 5 _____ y todo lo que no estaba amarrado voló. Estos objetos volantes

_____ 6 _____ las ventanas de tiendas y casas. Muchos habitantes no _____ 7 _____ los avisos que pasaron tanto por la radio como por la televisión. El huracán también

_____ 8 _____ en los pueblos del interior.

_____ 9 _____ un momento, el alcalde _____ 10 _____

a uno de los pueblos e _____ 11 _____ sobre los daños

1. hacer de
2. hacer
3. hacer buen tiempo
4. hacer mal tiempo
5. hacer mucho viento
6. hacer pedazos
7. hacer caso de
8. hacer mucho daño
9. hacer
10. hacer una visita
11. hacer preguntas
12. hacer

causados por el huracán. Un anciano dijo que _____
12

cincuenta años que no veía un huracán tan fuerte.

◇ **Ejercicio E**

✓ *Conteste las preguntas siguientes que le hace Pablo a un amigo:*

1. ¿Cuándo harás un viaje al exterior?

_____

2. ¿Cuánto tiempo hace que no viajas en avión?

_____

3. ¿Quién hará el viaje contigo?

_____

4. ¿Quién hará de guía?

_____

5. ¿Te hace daño a los oídos viajar en avión?

_____

6. ¿Qué tiempo hace ahora en la costa de España?

_____

7. ¿A quién quieres hacerle una visita?

_____

8. ¿Te gusta viajar cuando hace mal tiempo?

_____

7. Expressions with *perder*

echarse a perder *to be spoiled, to be ruined*
perder cuidado *not to worry*
perder de vista *to lose sight of*

La leche *se echó a perder.*	The milk *was spoiled.*
Pierda Ud. cuidado; **todo saldrá bien.**	Don't worry; everything will turn out right.
Lo siguieron, pero pronto *lo perdieron de vista.*	They followed him, but they soon lost sight of him.

8. Expressions with *ponerse*

ponerse + adjective *to become, to turn*
ponerse a + infinitive *to begin to, to set about*
ponerse de acuerdo *to come to an agreement*

Al oír la noticia, el niño *se puso pálido.*	On hearing the news, the child became pale.
El día *se puso gris.*	The day turned grey.
La alumna *se puso a llorar.*	The pupil began to cry.
Por fin *se pusieron de acuerdo.*	Finally, they came to an agreement.

9. Expressions with *tener*

tener (mucho) calor (frío) *to be (very) warm (cold)*
tener cuidado *to be careful*
tener dolor de cabeza (estómago, etc.) *to have a headache (stomach ache, etc.)*
tener éxito *to be successful*
tener ganas de *to feel like*
tener (mucha) hambre (sed) *to be (very) hungry (thirsty)*
tener la culpa (de) *to be to blame (for)*
tener lugar *to take place*
tener miedo de *to be afraid of*
tener por *to consider*
tener prisa *to be in a hurry*
tener que ver con *to have to do with*
tener razón (no tener razón) *to be right (to be wrong)*
tener (mucho) sueño *to be (very) sleepy*
tener (mucha) suerte *to be (very) lucky*
tener vergüenza (de + infinitive) *to be ashamed (of)*

Tenía calor **y se quitó el sobretodo.**	He was warm and took off his overcoat.
Tengan cuidado **al cruzar la calle.**	Be careful when crossing the street.
Ayer *tuve dolor de estómago.*	Yesterday I had a stomach ache.
Él *tiene éxito* **en todo lo que hace.**	He is successful in everything he does.
A veces *tengo ganas de* **bailar.**	At times I feel like dancing.
Cuando *tengo sed,* **tomo agua.**	When I am thirsty I drink water.
El muchacho *tiene la culpa* **de lo que pasó.**	The boy is to blame for what happened.
¿Cuándo *tendrá lugar* **la fiesta?**	When will the party take place?
El niño *tiene miedo de* **la oscuridad.**	The child is afraid of the dark.
Lo tengo por **persona honrada.**	I consider him an honest person.
Tenía prisa **y no pude detenerme a charlar.**	I was in a hurry and could not stop to chat.
No *tengo* **nada** *que ver* **con eso.**	I have nothing to do with that.
¿_Tengo razón_**?—No,** *no tienes razón.*	Am I right?—No, you are wrong.
María *tenía sueño* **y se acostó.**	Mary was sleepy and went to bed.
No *tuvo suerte* **y perdió el dinero.**	He wasn't lucky and lost the money.
¿No *tienes vergüenza?*	Aren't you ashamed?

Ejercicio F

Carolina lee una revista y se fija en las figuras que aparecen en los anuncios. Escriba lo que piensa Carolina al verlas:

EJEMPLO: Una señora lleva un abrigo grueso, una gorra, una bufanda y guantes.
Ella **tendrá mucho frío.**

1. Se ve la cabeza de un señor. Tiene las manos en las sienes y una mirada de dolor.

   El señor _____

2. Es una noche oscura. Un niño acaba de despertarse en su cama y tiene una mirada de pavor.

   El niño _____

3. Una pareja está sentada en el mostrador de un café. Miran el menú y hablan.

   Ellos _____

4. Una señora se ve muy contenta. Tiene un cheque de la lotería en la mano.

   Ella _____

5. Un joven está con sus padres delante de una universidad. Es el día en que el joven se gradúa.

   El joven _____

6. Hay un letrero en la carretera. El símbolo representa la forma de una «s».

   Los conductores _____

7. Un participante en un programa de la televisión acaba de acertar la respuesta correcta.

   El participante _____

8. Un señor corre para alcanzar un autobús. Mira su reloj.

   El señor _____

9. Un niño se estira y bosteza delante del televisor.

   El niño _____

10. En un restaurante elegante un niño volcó una copa de vino tinto y manchó el vestido de su mamá. La mamá está furiosa.

    El niño _____

Ejercicio G

*Enrique no se siente bien. Escriba lo que le dice a su mamá. Use una expresión con **tener**, **ponerse** o **perder** en cada frase:*

1. Mamá: ¿Qué tienes, hijo?

   Enrique: _____

2.   Mamá: ¿Por qué te pusiste el suéter?

Enrique: _____

3.   Mamá: ¿Quieres tomar una sopa caliente?

Enrique: _____

4.   Mamá: ¿Tomaste la leche que te dejé anoche?

Enrique: _____

5.   Mamá: ¿Por qué te acostaste tan temprano anoche?

Enrique: _____

6.   Mamá: ¿Qué hiciste en la cama?

Enrique: _____

7.   Mamá: Voy a medirte la fiebre.

Enrique: _____

8.   Mamá: Sin embargo, no debes bajarte de la cama.

Enrique: _____

10. Expressions with *volver*

volver a + infinitive *to . . . . again*
volver en sí *to regain consciousness, to come to*
volverse + adjective *to become*

> **El cantante *volvió a cantar*.**   *The singer sang again.*
> **El herido nunca *volvió en sí*.**   *The wounded man never regained*
>   *consciousness.*
>
> **Mi papá *se ha vuelto imposible*.**   *My father has become impossible.*

11. Other Common Verbal Expressions

encogerse de hombros *to shrug one's shoulders*
guardar cama *to stay in bed*
hacer saber *to inform, to let (someone) know*
llegar a ser *to become, to get to be*
llevar a cabo *to carry out, to carry through*
oír hablar de *to hear about*
oír decir que . . . *to hear that* . . .
pensar + infinitive *to intend to*

quedarse con *to keep, to hold on to*
quedar en que... (**quedar en** + infinitive) *to agree that, to agree to*
querer decir *to mean*
sacar una fotografía *to take a picture*
valer la pena *to be worthwhile*

Al oír la noticia, sólo *se encogió de hombros*.	On hearing the news, he only shrugged his shoulders.
Tenía fiebre y tuvo que *guardar cama* por dos días.	He had a fever and had to stay in bed for two days.
Me *hizo saber* que no volvía hoy.	He let me know that he wouldn't return today.
Después de muchos años de estudio, logró *llegar a ser* médico.	After many years of study, he managed to become a doctor.
El capitán *llevo a cabo* las órdenes del general.	The captain carried out the general's orders.
En la clase de historia *oímos hablar* de Simón Bolívar.	In history class, we heard about Simon Bolívar.
***Oí decir que* te vas a Venezuela.**	I heard that you are going to Venezuela.
***Pienso viajar* a España este verano.**	I intend to travel to Spain this summer.
***Se quedó con* mi pluma.**	He kept (walked off with) my pen.
¿*En qué quedaste* con Miguel?	What did you and Michael agree to?
***Quedamos en encontrarnos* aquí.**	We agreed to meet here.
¿Qué *quiere decir* esta palabra?	What does this word mean?
Me gusta *sacar fotografías*.	I like to take pictures.
A veces *vale la pena* escuchar las noticias.	Sometimes it's worthwhile to listen to the news.

Ejercicio H

Varios amigos hacen comentarios sobre diversos asuntos. Escoja la expresión necesaria y escríbala en la forma correcta:

guardar cama	pensar	querer decir
hacer saber	perder cuidado	valer la pena
llegar a ser	ponerse a	volver a
oír hablar de	quedarse con	volver en sí

1. «El tiempo es oro» es un proverbio que _____ que no debemos malgastar el tiempo.

2. Mi hermana se desmayó al ver al ratoncito, pero a poco ella _____.

3. María me parece una chica simpática. ¿Qué has _____ ella?

4. Yo voy a España durante las vacaciones. ¿Qué _____ hacer tú?

5. Cuando puedo, siempre asisto a conciertos de música clásica. Quiero _____ director de orquesta.

6. Mi tía no encontró el anillo la primera vez y _____ buscarlo.

7. Cuando fui a la feria con unos amigos, nos perdimos en el camino. Pero Jorge dijo:

   «_____, tengo un mapa».

8. Después de las vacaciones, Adolfo _____ estudiar seriamente.

9. Sarita me pidió mi vestido blanco para ir a una fiesta y _____ con él.

10. Es una película fabulosa. _____ que la veas pronto.

11. Después de dar a luz, Juanita tuvo que _____ por una semana.

12. Ojalá me _____ a tiempo si vienen o no.

Ejercicio I

Ud. acaba de volver de un viaje al extranjero. Conteste las preguntas que le hace un tío:

1. ¿Sacó Ud. muchas fotografías durante sus vacaciones?

   _____

2. ¿Quién se quedó con las fotos?

   _____

3. ¿Cree que vale la pena viajar al extranjero?

   _____

4. ¿Cuándo vuelve a hacer otro viaje?

   _____

5. ¿Se puso nervioso (nerviosa) al subir al avión?

   _____

6. ¿Qué piensa hacer el verano próximo?

   _____

7. ¿Vale la pena visitar los museos?

   _____

8. ¿Le gusta ver cuadros de los que ha oído hablar?

   _____

9. ¿En qué quedó con los amigos que conoció en el viaje?

   _____

10. ¿Pudo llevar a cabo todos sus planes para el viaje?

    _____

◆ MASTERY EXERCISES ◆

Ejercicio J

En la clase de composición, los alumnos aprenden a expresar sus ideas de otra forma.
Escriba estas frases, sustituyendo correctamente la expresión subrayada por una expre-
sión con **dar, haber, hacer** *o* **tener**:

EJEMPLO: Quiero un apartamento con vista a los árboles y los bancos.
Quiero un apartamento **que dé** al parque.

1. La mamá se apresura porque desea preparar una comida especial para su familia.

   _____

   _____

2. El padre le agradeció al salvavidas por ayudar a su hijita.

   _____

   _____

3. Cada tarde los ancianos solían andar por la calle principal del pueblo.

   _____

   _____

4. Mañana es necesario que los niños se despierten a las cinco.

   _____

   _____

5. Cuando le tocaba al hermano menor hacer algo en la casa, siempre decía que le dolía la cabeza.

   _____

   _____

6. Al ver al joven con quien rehusó ir al baile, Elsa se apenó de no haberlo aceptado.

   _____

   _____

7. El baile será el sábado por la noche en el gimnasio del colegio.

   _____

   _____

8. Cuando el profesor devolvió los exámenes, Martín temió mirar el suyo.

   _____

   _____

9. El mes pasado el frío dañó la cosecha de los campesinos.

   _____

   _____

10. Cuando mis hermanitos juegan, Ricardo es el médico y Gloria es la enfermera.

_____

_____

Ejercicio K

Complete la carta que Emilio les escribió a sus padres de la universidad, usando expresiones con **acabar, dar, dejar, echar, haber, hacer** _o_ **tener:**

Queridos padres:

Siempre me olvido de _____ mi reloj y nunca sé la hora ni la fecha en
                          1 (to wind)

que vivo. Anoche, al quitarme el reloj lo _____ y se rompió
                                               2 (to drop)

definitivamente. Esta mañana me desperté de repente y _____
                                                           3 (to realize)

que era tarde cuando el reloj de la iglesia _____ las nueve.
                                                 4 (to strike)

Me pareció que _____ dormirme. Había pasado una mala noche porque
                    5 (to have just)

algo que comí me _____ y _____ . Me
                      6 (to hurt)   **7** (to have a stomach ache)

levanté rápidamente y _____ porque las clases en la universidad
                           8 (to hurry)

habían comenzado _____ . Un amigo trató de
                      9 (an hour ago)

_____ , pero no pude detenerme. Cuando salí a la calle,
  10 (to ask me a question)

_____ . Yo _____ porque cuando iba a
  11 (to be windy)   **12** (to be lucky)

_____ correr, otro amigo pasó con su carro. Queríamos llegar a
  13 (to start to)

la universidad rápidamente, pero _____ _____
                                      14 (to be necessary)   **15** (to be careful)

con la policía. Cuando llegué al laboratorio, _____ la reacción del
                                                  16 (to be afraid)

profesor y también _____ haber llegado tan tarde. Al entrar yo en la
                        17 (to be ashamed of)

clase, el profesor _____ hablar y me miró tan fijamente que yo
                        18 (to stop)

_____ dar media vuelta y salir corriendo. Después de la clase, mis
  19 (to feel like)

compañeros _____ reír, _____ y fuimos a
                20 (to start to)   **21** (to shake hands with me)

tomar un café. Yo sé que tengo que ser más responsable si quiero _____

22 (to become)

un buen científico. ¡_____ toda la familia! Yo los

23 (Give my regards to)

_____ a todos.

24 (to miss)

Su hijo,

Emilio

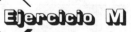

Ejercicio L

Complete el diálogo que oyó Pepe mientras esperaba en una oficina, usando correcta-mente una forma de las expresiones de la columna de la derecha:

1. Secretaria: ¿En qué puedo servirle, señor?

    Señor: Yo _____ verme con el Sr.
    Vargas aquí hoy.

2. Secretaria: Lo siento, pero él _____ salir
    de la oficina.

    Señor: _____ una semana que _____ él en
    la calle y _____ para encontrarnos hoy.

3. Secretaria: _____, señor. Yo le
    _____ que Ud. estuvo aquí.

    Señor: Gracias, señorita, porque no tengo tiempo de
    _____ a visitarlo hoy.
    _____ _____
    salir de viaje. ¿Es cierto?

4. Secretaria: Sí señor, _____. El va a una
    conferencia que _____ en
    Bogotá.

    Señor: ¡Qué _____!

quedar en
acabar de
hacer
dar con
ponerse de
acuerdo
perder cuidado
hacer saber
volver a
oír decir que
pensar
tener razón
tener lugar
tener suerte

Ejercicio M

A Ramoncito le fascina hacer muchas preguntas sobre cualquier tema. Conteste las pre-guntas que él hace:

1. ¿Sabes responder cuando el maestro te hace una pregunta?

    _____

2. ¿Qué tomas cuando tienes sed?

    _____

3. ¿Cuántas veces al día le das de comer a tu gato (perro)?

    _____

4. ¿Qué haces cuando tienes sueño?

    _____

5. Cuando hay mucho ruido en tu casa, ¿quién tiene la culpa generalmente?

    _____

6. Cuando tienes prisa, ¿te echas a correr?

    _____

7. ¿A quiénes les haces visita los domingos?

    _____

8. ¿Qué quieres llegar a ser?

    _____

9. ¿Crees que tus padres tienen razón en lo que te aconsejan?

    _____

10. ¿Les haces caso?

    _____

11. ¿Qué haces cuando tienes dolor de muelas?

    _____

12. ¿Te gusta salir cuando hace frío y hay neblina?

    _____

13. Cuando haces un viaje, ¿sacas fotos?

    _____

14. Cuando pides prestado un lápiz, ¿lo devuelves o te quedas con él?

    _____

15. ¿Sabes qué quiere decir «hacer cola»?

    _____

16. ¿Crees que vale la pena estudiar español?

    _____

17. ¿Qué piensas hacer cuando dejes de ir a la escuela?

    _____

18. ¿Te gusta volver a ver las buenas películas?

    _____

19. Cuando sacas malas notas, ¿te pones triste o te pones bravo?

_____

20. Cuando te enfermas y tienes que guardar cama, ¿cómo se lo haces saber a tu escuela?

_____

Ejercicio N

Exprese en español lo que Alicia le cuenta a una amiga de habla hispana:

1. In the play, Javier plays the part of a waiter.

_____

_____

2. It was warm, but it was also foggy, and he hurried to arrive early at the theater.

_____

_____

3. Although he was hungry, he was afraid to eat before the rehearsal.

_____

_____

4. He knew where the rehearsal was going to take place.

_____

_____

5. His girl friend plays the role of the princess in the play.

_____

_____

6. She was sleepy and cold and when she began to eat, she realized she was also hungry.

_____

_____

7. She strolled across the stage without paying attention to the script.

_____

_____

8. She dropped the tray of food and it smashed when it hit the floor.

_____

_____

9. She started to cry and the director became nervous.

_____

_____

10. Javier stopped eating and approached her to embrace her.

_____

_____

11. The director told them that to be successful it was necessary to work hard.

_____

_____

12. The director considered the rehearsal finished.

_____

_____

13. He told them: "Tomorrow it will be necessary to rehearse this scene again."

_____

_____

14. The actors had heard a long time ago that the director was good.

_____

_____

15. Javier and Gloria agreed to go to the theater together the next day.

_____

_____

PART

TWO

NOUNS
PRONOUNS
PREPOSITIONS

Nouns and Articles

1. Gender of Nouns

All nouns in Spanish are either masculine or feminine.

a. Nouns that refer to male beings are masculine. Nouns that refer to female beings are feminine:

MASCULINE	FEMININE
el hombre *man*	**la mujer** *woman*
el rey *king*	**la reina** *queen*
el príncipe *prince*	**la princesa** *princess*
el poeta *poet*	**la poetisa** *poet*

b. Nouns that end in **-o** are usually masculine. Nouns that end in **-a** are usually feminine:

MASCULINE	FEMININE
el hijo *son*	**la hija** *daughter*
el tipo *type*	**la distancia** *distance*
el zapato *shoe*	**la bota** *boot*

c. A few nouns that end in **-o** are feminine:

la mano *hand*	**la radio** *radio*
la foto* *photo*	**la moto*** *motorcycle*

d. Some nouns that end in **-a** are masculine:

el clima *climate*	**el planeta** *planet*
el día *day*	**el problema** *problem*
el drama *drama*	**el programa** *program*
el idioma *language*	**el telegrama** *telegram*
el mapa *map*	**el tranvía** *streetcar*

e. Nouns ending in **-dad**, **-tad**, **-tud**, **-umbre**, **-ie**, or **ión** are normally feminine:

la ciudad *city*	**la unión** *union*
la dificultad *difficulty*	
la juventud *youth*	Exceptions:
la certidumbre *certainty*	
la especie *species, kind*	**el avión** *airplane*
la excepción *exception*	**el camión** *truck*

---

*   **La foto** is an abbreviation of **la fotografía**. **La moto** is an abbreviation of **la motocicleta**.

f. Masculine nouns that refer to people and end in **-or**, **és**, or **-n** add **a** for the feminine equivalents:

MASCULINE	FEMININE
el **escultor** *sculptor*	la **escultora** *sculptress*
el **francés** *Frenchman*	la **francesa** *Frenchwoman*
el **alemán** *German*	la **alemana** *German*

Exceptions:

el **emperador** *emperor*	la **emperatriz** *empress*
el **actor** *actor*	la **actriz** *actress*

NOTE: If a masculine noun bears an accent mark on the last syllable, the accent is dropped in the equivalent feminine form:

el fran*cés*   la fran*cesa*   el alo*mán*   la ale*mana*

g. Some nouns are either masculine or feminine depending on their meaning:

MASCULINE	FEMININE
el **capital** *capital (money)*	la **capital** *capital (city)*
el **cura** *priest*	la **cura** *cure*
el **guía** *guide (male)*	la **guía** *guidebook, guide (female)*
el **policía** *policeman*	la **policía** *police force, policewoman*

h. Some nouns referring to people do not change their form but distinguish their gender only by the article:

el **(la) artista** *artist*	el **(la) joven** *youth*
el **(la) dentista** *dentist*	el **(la) mártir** *martyr*
el **(la) testigo** *witness*	el **(la) modelo** *model*

i. Days of the week, months of the year, and names of rivers and oceans are masculine:

el **lunes** *Monday*	**(el) septiembre** *September*
el **Amazonas** *the Amazon (river)*	el **Pacífico** *the Pacific (ocean)*

j. The gender of other nouns must be learned individually.

Ejercicio A

Ricardo cuida a su primo. Para entretenerlo, le hace identificar varias cosas. Escriba lo que responde el niño:

EJEMPLO:

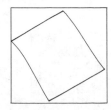

el papel

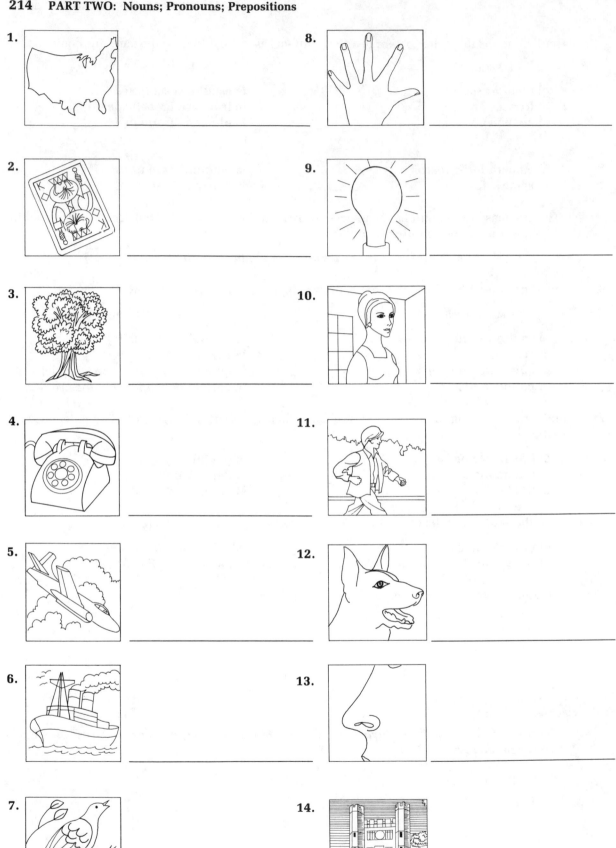

1. _____

2. _____

3. _____

4. _____

5. _____

6. _____

7. _____

8. _____

9. _____

10. _____

11. _____

12. _____

13. _____

14. _____

15. _____

16. _____

17. _____

18. _____

19. _____

20. _____

Ejercicio B

Dorotea ha hecho el árbol genealógico de su familia. Identifique a estas personas:

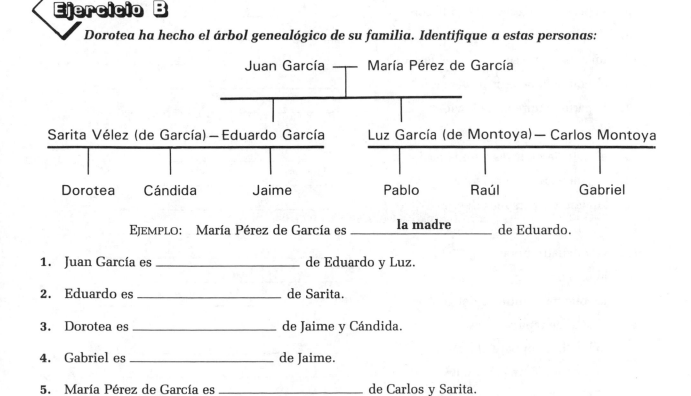

EJEMPLO: María Pérez de García es _____ **la madre** _____ de Eduardo.

1. Juan García es _____ de Eduardo y Luz.

2. Eduardo es _____ de Sarita.

3. Dorotea es _____ de Jaime y Cándida.

4. Gabriel es _____ de Jaime.

5. María Pérez de García es _____ de Carlos y Sarita.

6. Carlos es _____ de Eduardo.

7. Sarita es _____ de Juan García.

8. Carlos es _____ de María Pérez de García.

9. Luz es _____ de Dorotea, Cándida y Jaime.

10. Jaime es _____ de Sarita y Eduardo.

11. Raúl es _____ de Eduardo.

12. María Pérez de García es _____ de Dorotea, Cándida y Jaime.

Ejercicio C

Lolita va a participar en un concurso de vocabulario. Lea el significado y luego escriba la palabra apropiada:

EJEMPLO: un grupo de muchas personas   **la muchedumbre (la multitud)**

1. un representante de la iglesia   _____

2. un lugar como Chicago   _____

3. la persona que preside en la corte   _____

4. donde guardan a los prisioneros   _____

5. una obra representada en el teatro   _____

6. el hombre que escribe versos   _____

7. la parte temprana de la vida   _____

8. lo contrario de «la duda»   _____

9. el sistema de leyes de una nación   _____

10. lo que habla una persona   _____

11. cuando las personas duermen   _____

12. un sinónimo de «el gusto»   _____

13. veinticuatro horas   _____

14. el hijo de un rey   _____

15. las oficinas centrales del gobierno   _____

16. el acto de repartir cosas   _____

17. lo que buscan para el cáncer   _____

18. un hábito de una cultura   _____

19. el símbolo de los enamorados   _____

20. lo que tiene una persona sana y justa   _____

2. Plural of Nouns

a. Nouns ending in a vowel form the plural by adding **s**:

el líquido *liquid*	**los líquidos** *liquids*
la conquista *conquest*	**las conquistas** *conquests*
el hombre *man*	**los hombres** *men*

b. Nouns ending in a consonant (including **-y**) form the plural by adding **es**:

el papel *paper*	**los papeles** *papers*
el rey *king*	**los reyes** *kings, rulers*

NOTE:

1. Nouns ending in **-z** change the **-z** to **-c** before adding **es**: **el lápiz**, **los lápices**; **la actriz**, **las actrices**.

2. An accent mark is added or dropped to keep the original stress:

el joven	**los jóvenes**	**el francés**	**los franceses**
el examen	**los exámenes**	**la reunión**	**las reuniones**

3. Except for nouns ending in **-és**, nouns ending in **s** do not change in the plural:

el (los) lunes	**el (los) paréntesis**
la (las) dosis	**la (las) síntesis**

4. In a mixed plural (masculine and feminine), the masculine plural form of the noun is used:

los hijos = **el hijo y la hija** (los hijos y las hijas)
los amigos = **el amigo y la amiga** (los amigos y las amigas)
los abuelos = **el abuelo y la abuela**
los señores Gómez = **el señor y la señora Gómez**

 **Ejercicio D**

Rosita fue de compras. Escriba lo que cuenta, usando la forma plural de los sustantivos dados:

Al terminar la época de las _____ navideñas, los _____ ofrecen
                 1 (fiesta)   **2** (almacén)

muchas _____. En todos los _____ hay _____
       3 (ganga)   **4** (departamento)   **5** (cosa)

en rebaja. A mí me gusta ir de compras los _____. El sábado pasado todos los
                                 6 (sábado)

_____ estaban en rebaja; también los _____ de diversas
     7 (suéter)   **8** (traje)

_____ estaban a _____ reducidos. Vi que muchos
     9 (tela)   **10** (precio)

_____ compraron estas _____ de vestir.
11 (joven)   12 (prenda)

Entré en el departamento de los _____ de deporte porque necesito una raqueta de
                                13 (artículo)

tenis nueva. Había allí muchas _____, porque daban las pelotas gratis. Todos los
                               14 (persona)

_____ estaban ocupados y no pude esperar porque tenía que tomar dos
15 (vendedor)

_____ para llegar a casa. Sin embargo, mientras iba hacia la puerta de salida, no
16 (autobús)

pude resistir una ganga especial. Vendían _____ de _____ de
                                          17 (lápiz)   18 (labio)

unas _____ europeas a tres por el precio de uno. Tuve que comprar dos
     19 (marca)

_____ grandes para cargar todos mis _____. En la cola del
20 (bolsa)   21 (paquete)

autobús encontré a los _____ Pareda que habían comprado dos
                       22 (señor)

_____ a colores para unos _____ suyos. Al subir al autobús vi
23 (televisor)   24 (pariente)

que había solamente dos _____ para sentarse, y la señora Pareda y yo nos
                        25 (lugar)

sentamos.

3. Forms of the Articles

a. There are four definite articles in Spanish corresponding to English *the*:

	SINGULAR	PLURAL
MASCULINE	**el**	**los**
FEMININE	**la**	**las**

NOTE:
1. Feminine nouns that begin with the stressed sound of **a** (**a-** or **ha-**) take the article **el** in the singular. In the plural, the article is **las**:

    el agua *water*   **las aguas** *waters*
    el alma *soul*   **las almas** *souls*
    el hacha *ax*   **las hachas** *axes*

    But:

    la amiga } initial **a** is not stressed
    la alumna

2. The masculine article **el** combines with the prepositions **de** and **a** to form **del** and **al**.
3. The neuter article **lo**, used with adjectives, does not vary in form:

        lo bueno the good (*that which is good*)

b. There are four indefinite articles in Spanish corresponding to English *a (an)*, *some*, *several*, *a few*:

	SINGULAR	PLURAL
MASCULINE	**un**	**unos**
FEMININE	**una**	**unas**

El sobrino de Graciela va a cumplir un año. Escriba una lista de las cosas que ella debe comprar para su fiesta:

EJEMPLO: platos   **unos platos**

1. pastel   _____
2. servilletas   _____
3. juguete   _____
4. helados   _____
5. cucharas   _____
6. tenedores   _____
7. refrescos   _____
8. adornos   _____
9. premios   _____
10. invitaciones   _____
11. vela   _____
12. mantel de papel   _____
13. vasos   _____
14. globos   _____
15. litros de leche   _____

Ejercicio F

Mientras Leonardo camina por las calles de Salamanca, él identifica lo que ve:

EJEMPLO: farmacia   **una farmacia**

1. peluquería   _____

2. café _____

3. restaurante _____

4. lavandería _____

5. iglesia _____

6. perfumería _____

7. almacén _____

8. hospital _____

9. museo _____

10. universidad _____

11. cuartel de bomberos _____

12. carnicería _____

13. escuela _____

14. parque _____

15. asilo de ancianos _____

16. supermercado _____

17. río _____

18. terminal de autobuses _____

19. plaza _____

20. jardín _____

Ejercicio G

Escriba lo que Gregorio saca de su maleta al llegar a casa de sus abuelos:

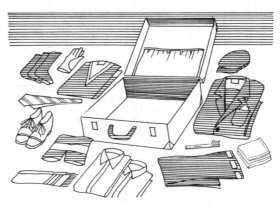

Gregorio saca de su maleta _____

_____

_____

_____

CHAPTER 17: Nouns and Articles **221**

_____

_____

_____

_____

4. Uses of the Articles in Spanish

a. The definite article is used in Spanish before the names of languages, except after **hablar**, **en**, or **de**:

El español **es importante hoy día.**	*Spanish is important nowadays.*

But:

Mi amigo *habla francés.*	*My friend speaks French.*
Todo el libro está escrito *en alemán.*	*The whole book is written in German.*
La clase *de español* **es interesante.**	*The Spanish class is interesting.*

NOTE:
1. If an adverb occurs between **hablar** and a name of a language, the article may be used with the language:

Habla bien el español.	*He speaks Spanish well.*

2. Current everyday usage tends to omit the definite article after the verbs **estudiar**, **aprender**, **leer**, **escribir**, **enseñar**, and **saber**:

Yo estudio portugués.	*I study Portuguese.*
¿Sabes francés?	*Do you know French?*

b. The definite article is used before titles, except when addressing the person:

El señor Gómez **salió ayer.**	*Mr. Gómez left yesterday.*
¿Cómo está Ud., Señora Álvarez?	*How are you, Mrs. Alvarez?*

NOTE: The article is omitted before **don** (**doña**), **Santo** (**San**, **Santa**).

c. The definite article is used instead of the possessive adjective with parts of the body or wearing apparel when the possessor is clear:

Ella se lava *el pelo.*	*She washes her hair.*
Se puso *el sombrero.*	*He put on his hat.*

d. The definite article is used with the time of day:

Es *la una.*	*It's one o'clock.*
Me acuesto a *las diez.*	*I go to bed at ten o'clock.*

e. The definite article is used before nouns used in a general or abstract sense:

El hombre **es mortal.**	*Man is mortal.*
La libertad **es preciosa.**	*Liberty is precious.*
Los diamantes **son caros.**	*Diamonds are expensive.*

f. The definite article is used before infinitives functioning as nouns. The article is often omitted, however, when the infinitive is the subject in a sentence. Infinitive nouns are always masculine:

> **(El) mentir es un vicio.**   Lying is a vice.

g. The definite article is used with the names of seasons:

> **Me gusta *la primavera* (*el verano, el***   I like spring (summer, autumn,
> ***otoño, el invierno*).**   winter).

> NOTE: The article may be omitted after the preposition **en**:

> **Voy a España *en (el) verano*.**   I am going to Spain in the summer.

h. The definite article is used with the days of the week, except after the verb **ser** when expressing dates:

> **Iré al teatro *el domingo*.**   I will go to the theater (on) Sunday.
> ***Los viernes* hay pruebas.**   (On) Fridays there are tests.
> **El examen fue *el lunes* pasado.**   The exam was last Monday.

> But:

> **Hoy *es jueves*.**   Today is Thursday.
> **Se acordó que el día siguiente *era***   He remembered that the following day
> ***sábado* y no había clases.**   was Saturday and there were no
>   classes.

i. The definite article is used before names of rivers, oceans, and mountains:

> **los Andes** the Andes   **el Amazonas** the Amazon (river)
> **los Alpes** the Alps   **el Orinoco** the Orinoco (river)
> **el Pacífico** the Pacific   **el Mediterráneo** the Mediterranean

j. The definite article is used before certain names of countries, states, and cities:

> **el Brasil** Brazil   **la Argentina** Argentina
> **los Estados Unidos** the United States   **el Perú** Peru
> **la Florida** Florida   **la Habana** Havana
> **el Japón** Japan   **el Uruguay** Uruguay
> **el Paraguay** Paraguay   **el Canadá** Canada
> **el Ecuador** Ecuador   **el Cairo** Cairo

NOTE:
1. Current everyday usage tends to omit the definite article before the names of countries:

> **Vivo en Estados Unidos desde hace dos años.**

2. The definite article is used with geographical names that are modified:

> **América tiene muchas riquezas.**   **España está en Europa.**
> **La América del Sur tiene muchas**   **Me interesa *la* España del siglo XV.**
> **riquezas.**

k. The definite article is used before nouns of weight or measure. English uses the indefinite article:

> **un dólar *la libra***   a dollar a pound
> **diez centavos *la docena***   ten cents a dozen

Ejercicio H

Escriba la forma apropiada del artículo definido, si es necesario, en este diálogo entre Javier y un alumno de intercambio de su escuela:

Javier: ¿De dónde eres?

Tomás: Soy de _____ Perú.
                              1

Javier: ¿Hay montañas cerca de tu país?

Tomás: Sí, _____ Andes.
                        2

Javier: ¿Vas allí a menudo?

Tomás: Sí, _____ esquiar es mi deporte favorito.
                        3

Javier: ¿Qué estación te gusta más?

Tomás: Me gusta más _____ invierno.
                                    4

Javier: ¿Quién es ese señor?

Tomás: Es _____ señor Lobos. Es _____ profesor de _____ inglés.
                    5   6   7

Javier: ¿Estudias _____ inglés?
                              8

Tomás: Sí, puesto que vivo en _____ Estados Unidos _____ inglés es un idioma
                                            9   10
          importante para mí.

Javier: ¿Hablas otro idioma también?

Tomás: Yo no, pero mi mamá habla _____ francés.
                                              11

Javier: ¿Ves muchas películas?

Tomás: Sí, suelo ir a _____ cine _____ viernes por _____ noche.
                              12   13   14

Javier: ¿Qué hora será?

Tomás: Son _____ doce y media. ¿Por qué?
                    15

Javier: Tengo una cita con _____ señora Bello. Ella es mi consejera.
                                      16

Tomás: Debes apresurarte. _____ llegar tarde no es una buena idea.
                                    17

Javier: Ella es muy simpática. ¿La conoces? Ella tiene _____ pelo largo.
                                                                  18

Tomás: No la conozco. Mi consejero es _____ doctor Muñoz y él tiene _____ nariz
$\quad\quad\quad\quad$ 19 $\quad\quad\quad\quad\quad\quad\quad\quad\quad\quad\quad\quad\quad\quad\quad$ 20

$\quad\quad\quad\quad$ larga. Hasta luego.

Javier: Sí, nos vemos después.

Ejercicio 1

Conteste las preguntas que hace una alumna en una encuesta:

1.   ¿Qué día es hoy? (miércoles)

_____

2.   ¿Qué hora es? (1:00)

_____

3.   ¿En qué estación estamos? (primavera)

_____

4.   ¿De qué color tiene tu mamá el pelo? (castaño)

_____

5.   ¿Y los ojos? (verdes)

_____

6.   ¿Cuándo vas al parque? (sábado)

_____

7.   ¿Cuándo sales a cenar con tus padres? (martes)

_____

8.   ¿Dónde viven tus abuelos? (Florida)

_____

9.   ¿Quién es tu profesor de matemáticas? (señorita Castillo)

_____

10.   ¿Qué lengua estudias? (alemán)

_____

11.   ¿Cuál es tu ciencia favorita? (química)

_____

12.   ¿A qué hora te acuestas? (11:00)

_____

13.   ¿Cuál es tu deporte favorito? (béisbol)

_____

14.   ¿Cuánto cuesta un refresco en la cafetería? (50 centavos)

_____

15.   ¿Qué país te gustaría visitar? (Brasil)

_____

5. Neuter Article _lo_

_a._ The neuter article **lo** precedes an adjective used as a noun to express a quality or an abstract idea:

Lo nuevo no es siempre mejor que _lo viejo._	_The new (That which is new) is not always better than the old (what is old)._
Pienso _lo mismo_ que Ud.	_I think the same as you._

_b._ **Lo** + adjective (or adverb) + **que** = _how_

Ya veo _lo simpático (simpática) que_ es.	_I do see how nice he (she) is._
Me sorprende _lo rápidamente que_ corre.	_I am surprised how quickly he runs._

NOTE: Since the article **lo** is neuter, it has no plural form. **Lo** is used whether the adjective is masculine or feminine, singular or plural.

Ejercicio J

Escriba sus impresiones sobre los conceptos siguientes, usando **lo:**

> EJEMPLO: romántico
> **Lo romántico me aburre.**

1.   cómico _____

2.   pintoresco _____

3.   diferente _____

4.   raro _____

5.   peligroso _____

6.   emocionante _____

7.   imposible _____

8.   bello _____

9.   curioso _____

10.   difícil _____

Ejercicio K

Ud. acaba de volver de pescar en el lago. Usando lo y las sugerencias, escriba sus impresiones de la excursión:

SUGERENCIAS: cómico, difícil, divertido, peligroso, interesante, peor, mejor, impresionante

EJEMPLO: **Lo aburrido fue esperar.**

1.   perder el pez _____

2.   tocar los peces _____

3.   no hablar _____

4.   limpiar los pescados _____

5.   sentarse a esperar _____

6.   vender los pescados _____

Ejercicio L

Escriba sus impresiones de una novela que Ud. acaba de leer, usando lo + uno de los siguientes adjetivos:

emocionante	divertido	triste
romántico	mejor	aburrido
interesante	curioso	impresionante
cómico	raro	

EJEMPLO: **Lo romántico fue la boda.**

1.   _____
2.   _____
3.   _____
4.   _____
5.   _____
6.   _____
7.   _____

6. Omission of the Article

a. The article is omitted:

(1) Before nouns in apposition:

Madrid, *capital* de España, está en el centro del país.   Madrid, *the capital of Spain, is in the center of the country.*

> **Lope de Vega, *dramaturgo* español, escribió muchas comedias.** · *Lope de Vega, a Spanish dramatist, wrote many plays.*

(2) Before numerals expressing the numerical order of rulers:

Carlos Quinto	*Charles the Fifth*
Isabel Segunda	*Isabel the Second*

b. The indefinite article is omitted:

(1) Before predicate nouns denoting a class or group (social class, occupation, nationality, religion, etc.):

Es peluquero.	*He is a barber.*
Soy americano.	*I am (an) American.*
Quiero hacerme médico.	*I want to become a doctor.*

NOTE: If the predicate noun is modified, the indefinite article is expressed:

Era *un peluquero hábil*.	*He was a skillful barber.*
Quiero ser *un médico bueno*.	*I want to be a good doctor.*

(2) Before or after certain words that ordinarily have the article in English: **otro** (*another*), **cierto** (*a certain*), **ciento** (*a hundred*), **mil** (*a thousand*), **tal** . . . (*such a* . . .), **¡qué** . . . ! (*what a* . . . !):

otra carta	*another letter*
cierto día	*a certain day*
cien dólares	*one (a) hundred dollars*
mil soldados	*one (a) thousand soldiers*
tal hombre	*such a man*
¡Qué memoria!	*What a memory!*

Ejercicio M

Escriba los recados que la secretaria le dejó a su jefe:

EJEMPLO: Pedro Cabal / presidente / Industrias Modernas / llamó
Pedro Cabal, presidente de Industrias Modernas, llamó.

1. Elvira Soto / dueña / Fábrica Equis / canceló su cita

_____

2. General Vidal / director / Banco Nacional / aprobó su préstamo

_____

3. Sra. Moreno / esposa / Gabriel Moreno / llamó

_____

4. Esteban Núñez / ayudante / Sra. Amador / telefoneó dos veces

_____

5.   Rodolfo Esteves / padre / su yerno / dejó otro número

_____

6.   David Rivera / agente / la policía / devolvió su llamada

_____

7.   Carlos / chofer / Sr. Asturias / dejó un paquete

_____

8.   Sr. Cuevas / gerente / la compañía / quiere verlo mañana

_____

Ejercicio N

Conteste estas preguntas que le hace un aduanero en el aeropuerto de Barajas:

1.   ¿Cuál es su nacionalidad?

_____

2.   ¿Cuál es su profesión? (estudiante)

_____

3.   ¿Qué clase de estudiante es Ud.?

_____

4.   ¿Qué quiere Ud. hacerse?

_____

5.   ¿En qué hotel se quedará Ud.? (Felipe II)

_____

6.   ¿Por qué escogió Ud. ese hotel? (bueno)

_____

7.   ¿Cuánto dinero piensa Ud. gastar en el viaje? ($1,000)

_____

Ejercicio O

*Complete este monólogo con el artículo apropiado, si es necesario, o con **otro, cien, cierto, mil, tal** o **¡qué!**:*

Buenos días. Soy Patricia Bulnes y soy _____ actriz. Los críticos dicen que soy
                                              1

_____ actriz buena y popular. El público me manda más de _____
        2   3

cartas al día. Ya he hecho _____ películas y mañana comienzo a trabajar en
                                    4

_____ película. ¡Y _____ película! Hago el papel de _____
        5   6   7

mujer rica y elegante. _____ mujer se aburre rápidamente y pasa el tiempo
                                 8

viajando. La película comienza en París, _____ capital de Francia. _____
                                                   9   10

día estamos en Londres, _____capital de Inglaterra, porque la acción también se
                                11

desarrolla allí. La protagonista es _____ mujer caprichosa que se mete en muchos
                                            12

líos. Hay _____ escena en que _____ hombres se visten de policía y la
              13   14

acompañan a _____ fiesta grandísima. ¡_____ segura me sentí cuando
                   15   16

filmaron esa escena! _____ película va a costar más de cien mil dólares porque cada
                            17

actor recibe _____ dólares al día. No me importa. Tengo _____ vida
                    18   19

interesante y emocionante. ¡_____ buena suerte tengo!
                                    20

◆ MASTERY EXERCISES ◆

Ejercicio P

Conteste estas preguntas, con las que Alicia practica para un examen:

1. ¿Cuál es el río más grande de la América del Sur?

   _____

2. ¿En qué país hispanoamericano vivían los incas?

   _____

3. ¿Qué idioma hablan en el Uruguay?

   _____

4. ¿Cuál es y dónde está la capital de España?

   _____

5. ¿Qué país está al norte de los Estados Unidos?

   _____

6. ¿Qué ciudad era popular para los turistas antes de Fidel Castro?

   _____

7. ¿Quién fue un dramaturgo español que escribió muchas comedias?

_____

8. ¿Cómo se llama el río que está entre México y los Estados Unidos?

_____

9. ¿Cómo se llama la capital del Perú que tiene mucha arquitectura colonial?

_____

10. ¿En qué país de Suramérica no se habla español?

_____

Ejercicio Q

Exprese en español lo que cuenta Alejandro de su abuelo:

1. My grandfather was a Spaniard; his wife was German.

_____

2. He married a pretty German girl.

_____

3. My grandfather wished for liberty and wealth.

_____

4. He was a businessman.

_____

5. He sold apples at twenty cents a pound.

_____

6. His store closed at three o'clock on Fridays.

_____

7. Smoking was prohibited in his store.

_____

8. Dr. Suárez was a good friend of my grandfather.

_____

9. His partner, Mr. Galán, accompanied him to the store every day.

_____

10. At four o'clock my grandfather used to go to the café.

_____

11. He used to go there twice a day.

_____

12. The funny thing is that he didn't like coffee.

_____

13. My father was surprised by how lively he was.

_____

14. What a memory he had! He remembered the names of all the customers.

_____

15. He was accustomed to comb his hair three times a day.

_____

16. During the war he met a prince.

_____

17. On Thursdays he went to his English class.

_____

18. The curious thing is that he never learned to speak English well.

_____

19. I was surprised at how quickly he talked.

_____

20. One day he sold everything in the store for one thousand dollars.

_____

21. Upon retiring, we were astonished at how relaxed he was.

_____

22. The good (part) of the matter is that he knew how to enjoy himself.

_____

Personal Pronouns

1. Subject Pronouns

SINGULAR	PLURAL
yo *I*	**nosotros, -as** *we*
tú *you* (familiar)	**vosotros, -as** *you* (familiar)
usted (Ud.) *you*	**ustedes (Uds.)** *you*
él *he*	**ellos** *they* (masculine)
ella *she*	**ellas** *they* (feminine)

Subject pronouns are not used in Spanish as often as in English. Normally the verb ending indicates the subject. Spanish subject pronouns are used for clarity, emphasis, and politeness:

Él leía mientras *yo* cantaba.	*He was reading while I was singing.*
No hagas eso: *yo* debo hacerlo.	*Don't do that: I must do it.*
¡Pase *Ud.*! Tome *Ud.* asiento.	*Enter! Take a seat.*

NOTE:

1. Even though subject pronouns are usually omitted, **usted** and **ustedes** are regularly used.

2. The **vosotros** form (familiar plural) is used in Spain but rarely in Latin America, where the form **ustedes** is preferred.

3. The English pronoun *it* is not expressed as a subject in Spanish:

| **¿Dónde está? Está en el cajón.** | *Where is it? It's in the drawer.* |
| **¿Qué es? Es un libro.** | *What is it? It's a book.* |

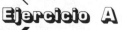 **Ejercicio A**

En una fiesta Víctor identifica a sus amigos y dice de dónde son. Escriba el pronombre apropiado en cada frase:

EJEMPLO: Elena y Rosa son hermanas. _____**Ellas**_____ nacieron en la Habana.

1. Jorge y Pedro son primos. _____ son de Bogotá.

2. Luz y Pilar son hermanas. _____ son de Cali.

3. Eduardo y yo somos amigos. _____ somos de Chicago.

4. Lola es la hermana de Carlos. _____ es de Caracas.

5. Esteban es el primo de Ricardo. _____ es de San José.

6. Rocío y María, ¿de dónde son _____? _____ soy de Panamá y
   _____ es de México.

7. Clara, ¿de dónde eres _____? _____ soy de San Juan.

8. Beto y Anita, ¿de dónde son _____? _____ somos de Buenos Aires.

9. Gustavo, ¿de dónde son tus padres? _____ son de Francia.

10. Beatriz y Sara, ¿dónde vivieron _____ antes de venir aquí?
    _____ vivimos cerca de la capital.

Ejercicio B

Conteste las preguntas que le hace un vecino nuevo. Use los pronombres apropiados:

1. ¿Cómo te llamas?

   _____

2. ¿Dónde están tus padres?

   _____

3. ¿Quién es esa chica?

   _____

4. ¿Cómo se llama la escuela a que vas?

   _____

5. ¿Quiénes son esos señores?

   _____

6. ¿Podemos tú y yo jugar tenis?

   _____

7. ¿Dónde juegan tú y tus amigos?

   _____

8. ¿Tienes otra raqueta?

   _____

9. ¿Es ese señor tu padre?

   _____

10. ¿Dónde podemos comprar leche?

   _____

2. Prepositional Pronouns

SINGULAR	PLURAL
mí me	**nosotros, -as** us
ti you (familiar)	**vosotros, -as** you (familiar)
usted (Ud.) you	**ustedes (Uds.)** you
él him, it	**ellos** them (masculine)
ella her, it	**ellas** them (feminine)
sí yourself, himself, herself, itself	**sí** yourselves, themselves

a. The prepositional pronoun is used as the object of a preposition and always follows the preposition:

> **No es para *mí*; es para *ellos.***   It's not for me; it's for them.

b. The pronouns **mí, ti,** and **sí** combine with the preposition **con** as follows:

conmigo	*with me*
contigo	*with you (fam.)*
consigo	*with you (yourself), with him(self), with her(self), with them(selves)*

NOTE:

1. The prepositional pronouns are identical with the subject pronouns, except for **mí, ti,** and **sí.**

2. The forms **conmigo, contigo,** and **consigo** do not change in gender and number.

3. The familiar plural form **vosotros, -as** is used in Spain but rarely in Spanish America, where the form **ustedes** is preferred.

c. Common prepositions

a to, at	**durante** during
acerca de about	**en** in, on
además de besides	**encima de** above, on top of
alrededor de around	**enfrente de** in front of, opposite
ante before, in the presence of	**entre** between, among
antes de before	**frente a** in front of
cerca de near	**fuera de** outside of; aside from
con with	**hacia** toward
contra against	**hasta** until
de of, from	**lejos de** far from
debajo de beneath, under	**para** for, in order to
delante de in front of	**por** for, by, through
dentro de within, inside	**según** according to
desde from, since	**sin** without
después de after	**sobre** over, above
detrás de behind	**tras** after

Ejercicio C

Su hermano le hace preguntas sobre sus compras. Escriba para quién(es) son estas cosas, usando el pronombre apropiado:

EJEMPLO: ¿Son los guantes para mi abuelita?
Sí, son para ella.

1. ¿Es la pelota para Jorge?

_____

2. ¿Son los discos para nosotros?

_____

3. La blusa es para mamá, ¿verdad?

_____

4. ¿Es el sombrero para papá?

_____

5. Los dulces son para los niños, ¿verdad?

_____

6. ¿Son los aretes para Luz y Alba?

_____

7. El abrigo es para ti, ¿verdad?

_____

8. El guante de béisbol es para mí, ¿verdad?

_____

9. ¿Es el rebozo para la tía Conchita?

_____

10. Los calcetines son para Luis y Paco, ¿verdad?

_____

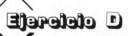

Ejercicio D

A Roberto no le gusta jugar con nadie. Escriba lo que dice cuando su mamá le hace sugerencias. Use los pronombres apropiados:

EJEMPLO: Enrique va a jugar baloncesto.
No quiero jugar con él.

1. Gloria va a jugar volibol.

_____

2.   Pedro y Arturo van a jugar fútbol.

_____

3.   Gladys y Beatriz van a jugar dominó.

_____

4.   Tu papá y yo vamos a jugar naipes.

_____

5.   Yo voy a jugar tenis.

_____

6.   Lupita va a jugar béisbol.

_____

Ejercicio E

Conteste las preguntas que le hace un compañero de campamento, usando el pronombre apropiado:

1.   ¿Vives cerca del estadio?

_____

2.   ¿Te gusta correr alrededor de la cancha de tenis?

_____

3.   ¿Juegas contra tus hermanos?

_____

4.   ¿Puedo ir contigo en el barco?

_____

5.   Según el consejero, ¿a qué hora debemos apagar la luz?

_____

6.   ¿Fuiste al cine sin tu tarjeta de identidad?

_____

7.   Camino hacia el bosque para llegar a la piscina, ¿verdad?

_____

8.   ¿Quién estaba delante de ti en la cola hoy?

_____

9.   ¿Qué pusiste debajo de la cama de Raúl?

_____

10.   ¿No te sentiste bien durante los ejercicios esta mañana?

_____

11. ¿Irás a la tienda por mí?

_____

12. ¿Plantaron flores detrás de la oficina?

_____

13. ¿Me vas a decir algo sobre la película?

_____

14. ¿Quiénes estaban allí además de Uds.?

_____

15. ¿Pusieron la bandera en la ventana?

_____

3. Object Pronouns

a. The object pronouns are as follows:

DIRECT	INDIRECT
SINGULAR	SINGULAR
me *me* **te** *you* (familiar) **le** *you* (masculine), *him* **lo** *you, him, it* (masculine) **la** *you* (feminine), *her, it* (feminine)	**me** *(to) me* **te** *(to) you* (familiar) **le** *(to) you, (to) him, (to) her, (to) it*
PLURAL	PLURAL
nos *us* **os** *you* (familiar) **los** *you, them* (masculine) **las** *you, them* (feminine)	**nos** *(to) us* **os** *(to) you* (familiar) **les** *(to) you, (to) them*

NOTE:
1. The forms **me, te, nos,** and **os** are both direct and indirect object pronouns. They are also reflexive pronouns (see page 119).

2. In Spanish America, **lo** is preferred to **le** as direct object.

3. Before an indirect object pronoun, the prepositions *to, for,* or *from* are not expressed in Spanish:

Me dio el dinero.	*He gave the money to me.*
Me compró el libro.	*He bought me the book.*
Me cobró el dinero.	*He collected the money from me.*

b. Position of object pronouns:

(1) Object pronouns, direct or indirect, normally precede the verb:

Juan *me* **ve.**	*John sees me.*
El maestro *les* **ha hablado.**	*The teacher has spoken to them.*

(2) When the direct or indirect object pronouns are used with an infinitive, a **gerundio,** or an affirmative command, they may be attached to the verb:

Deseo enviar*lo.*	
or	*I want to send it.*
Lo **deseo enviar.**	
Estoy cnviándo*lo.*	
or	*I am sending it.*
Lo **estoy enviando.**	
Enví*lo.* **Ud.**	*Send it.*
But:	
No *lo* **envíe Ud.**	*Don't send it.*

NOTE:

1. The object pronouns may either be attached to the infinitive or the **gerundio** or precede the conjugated form of the verb.

2. When an object pronoun is attached to the **gerundio** or the affirmative command, an accent mark is normally required on the stressed vowel of the verb in order to keep the original stress. If the affirmative command has only one syllable (**pon**), no accent mark is required (**ponlo**).

Ejercicio F

Conteste las preguntas que le hace un amigo en una llamada telefónica. Use un pronombre en cada frase:

1. ¿Buscaste la lista de los discos?

   _____

2. ¿Compraste el disco que querías?

   _____

3. ¿Viste a Carmen y a Gloria?

   _____

4. ¿Escuchaste las noticias hoy?

   _____

5. ¿Leíste el periódico de la mañana?

   _____

6. ¿Miraste las fotos en la página tres?

   _____

7. ¿Esperaste a tus padres en el centro?

_____

8. ¿Ayudaste a tu hermanito con la tarea?

_____

9. ¿Vas a ver la película a las ocho?

_____

10. ¿Invitaste a Tomás y a Luis a la fiesta?

_____

11. ¿Terminaste la tarea?

_____

12. ¿Aprendiste el poema de memoria?

_____

13. ¿Quién hizo el diseño?

_____

14. ¿Tienes los boletos para el teatro?

_____

15. ¿Pediste el carro prestado a tu papá?

_____

Ejercicio G

La abuela de Carmen es mexicana y va a preparar los platos favoritos de su familia. Escriba lo que ella le cuenta a su esposo y lo que él le responde:

EJEMPLO: a mi hijo / enchiladas suizas
A mi hijo le voy a preparar enchiladas suizas.
Bueno, ¡**Prepárale** enchiladas suizas!

1. a Carmen / chiles rellenos

_____

_____

2. a Roberto y a Paco / tacos de pollo

_____

_____

3. a ti / tamales

_____

_____

4. a nosotros / flan

_____

_____

5. a mí / sopa de fideos

_____

_____

Ejercicio H

La mamá de Joaquín le pregunta si ha empacado las cosas que necesita para ir a acampar. Escriba lo que le contesta Joaquín:

EJEMPLO: ¿Empacaste la manta? (Sí)
Sí, la empaqué.

1. ¿Y el suéter? (Sí) _____

2. ¿Y la mochila? (No) _____

3. ¿Y la tienda? (Sí) _____

4. ¿Y los platos de plástico? (Sí) _____

5. ¿Y los zapatos de tenis? (Sí) _____

6. ¿Y las botas? (No) _____

7. ¿Y el mapa? (Sí) _____

8. ¿Y las llaves? (Sí) _____

9. ¿Y el impermeable? (No) _____

10. ¿Y el cepillo de dientes? (Sí) _____

Ejercicio I

Según Lourdes, uno de sus profesores habla muchos idiomas. Escriba lo que ella cuenta:

EJEMPLO: a José / inglés
A José le habla en inglés.

1. a mí / español

_____

2. a Pierre y a Claude / francés

_____

3. a Sofía / italiano

_____

4. a María y a mí / inglés

_____

5. a Karl / alemán

_____

6. a Cristóbal y a Melina / griego

_____

7. a ti / ruso

_____

8. a Uds. / portugués

_____

Ejercicio J

Escriba cuándo visita Ud. a estas personas:

EJEMPLO: su abuela
La visito todos los domingos.

1. sus primos   _____

2. su mejor amigo/amiga   _____

3. sus compañeros de clase _____

4. su vecino   _____

5. su cura   _____

6. su tía   _____

7. su médico   _____

Ejercicio K

La tía de Alfredo está enferma y hay una enfermera en la casa. Escriba lo que Alfredo dice que hace la enfermera:

EJEMPLO: poner inyecciones a mi tía
Le pone inyecciones a mi tía.

1. dar la medicina a mi tía

_____

2.   bañar (a mi tía)

_____

3.   preparar la comida a mis tíos

_____

4.   arreglar el cuarto a ellos

_____

5.   peinar (a mi tía)

_____

6.   contestar el teléfono

_____

7.   vestir (a mi tía)

_____

Ejercicio L

Gloria hace una encuesta sobre los gustos de sus amigos. Escriba lo que ellos responden, usando **(no) gustar, (no) fascinar, (no) encantar:**

EJEMPLO: ¿Bailas mucho?
Sí, me encanta bailar.

1.   ¿Vas de compras a menudo?

_____

2.   ¿Reciben Uds. muchos regalos?

_____

3.   ¿Ven ellos muchas películas?

_____

4.   ¿Juega Antonio muchos deportes?

_____

5.   ¿Sabes conducir?

_____

6.   ¿Cocinan Uds. de vez en cuando?

_____

7.   ¿Leen ellas muchas novelas?

_____

8.   ¿Coso yo mi propia ropa?

_____

9. ¿Sabe Carlos esquiar?

_____

10. ¿Montan Uds. en bicicleta?

_____

Ejercicio M

En la clase de costura María está cosiendo un vestido. Escriba las instrucciones que le da la maestra y el comentario que hacen unas compañeras:

> EJEMPLO: cortar el patrón
> Maestra: **Córtalo.**
> Amiga: **Va a cortarlo.**
> Otra amiga: **Está cortándolo.**

1. medir la tela

Maestra: _____

Amiga: _____

Otra amiga: _____

2. poner los alfileres

Maestra: _____

Amiga: _____

Otra amiga: _____

3. coser las mangas

Maestra: _____

Amiga: _____

Otra amiga: _____

4. coser los botones

Maestra: _____

Amiga: _____

Otra amiga: _____

5. planchar el vestido

Maestra: _____

Amiga: _____

Otra amiga: _____

6. colgar el vestido

Maestra: _____

Amiga: _____

Otra amiga: _____

4. *Gustar* and Other Verbs Used with Indirect Object Pronouns

a. The verb **gustar** (*to please*) expresses English *to like*:

Me gusta **el vestido.**	*I like the dress.*
	(Literally: *The dress pleases me.*)
Te gustan **las flores.**	*You like the flowers.*
	(Literally: *The flowers please you.*)
Le gustaría **viajar a Europa.**	*He would like to travel to Europe.*
	(Literally: *To travel to Europe would please him.*)

b. **Gustar** is preceded by an indirect object pronoun. Note that the form of **gustar** agrees with the subject, which generally follows it:

Te gustará *el libro.*	*You will like the book.*
Te gustarán *los libros.*	*You will like the books.*
Nos gustó *la novela.*	*We liked the novel.*
Nos gustaron *las novelas.*	*We liked the novels.*
Les gusta *cantar.*	*They like to sing.*

NOTE: If the thing liked is not a noun but an ''action'' (expressed by a verb or clause), **gustar** is used in the third person singular:

Le gusta *cantar y bailar.*	*He likes to sing and dance.*
Me gustaría *que vinieras hoy.*	*I would like you to come today.*

c. The indirect object noun normally precedes the indirect object pronoun:

A María **no le gusta leer.**	*Mary doesn't like to read.*
A los niños **les gusta ir al cine.**	*The children like to go to the movies.*
A Roberto **le gustan los dulces.**	*Robert likes sweets.*

d. Other verbs used like **gustar:**

agradar *to be pleased with, to please*

Les agradó mi regalo.	*They were pleased with my gift.*
	(*My gift was pleasing to them.*)

bastar *to be enough, to suffice*

Me bastan tres dólares.	*Three dollars are enough for me.*

doler *to be painful, to cause sorrow*

Me duele el pie izquierdo.	*My left foot hurts (is painful to me).*

faltar
hacer falta } *to be lacking, to need*

Le faltan cincuenta centavos.	*He lacks fifty cents. (Fifty cents are lacking to him.)*
Le hace falta dinero.	*He needs money. (Money is lacking to him.)*

parecer *to seem*

Me parece imposible.	*It seems impossible to me.*

placer *to be pleasing, to be pleased*

    Me place poder ayudarlo.   *I am pleased to be able to help you.*

quedar (a uno) *to remain (to someone), to have left*

    Nos queda un solo día.   *We have only one day left.*

sobrar *to be left over, to have too much*

    Me sobran tres cartas.   *I have three cards too many.*

tocar (a uno) *to be one's turn*

    A mí **me toca** lavar los platos.   *It is my turn to wash the dishes.*

Ejercicio N

Algunos amigos hablan de sus gustos. Escriba lo que dicen:

    EJEMPLO: A mí / gustar / los deportes
                         A mí me gustan los deportes.

1. A nosotros / gustar / la música popular

_____

2. A Elena / gustar / cantar mientras trabaja

_____

3. A ti / gustar / las ferias

_____

4. A Pedro y a Carlos / no gustar / patinar en el hielo

_____

5. A ustedes / gustar / ir al teatro

_____

6. A mí / gustar / las películas románticas

_____

7. A ellas / gustar / los bailes

_____

8. A Ramón / no gustar / el helado de fresa

_____

9. A tí y a mí / gustar / pasar un buen rato

_____

10. A Celia / no gustar / las bromas

_____

Ejercicio O

Unos amigos piensan hacer una fiesta de disfraces. Escriba un comentario para cada frase, usando la información dada:

EJEMPLO: Jaime: Me invitaron a una fiesta de disfraces.
Lourdes: A mí / agradar / los disfraces
A mí me agradan los disfraces.

1. Eduardo: Tenemos que comprar los refrescos. Cuestan doce dólares.
Silvia: A mí / quedar / sólo cinco dólares

    _____

2. Rosa: No tengo tela para hacer el disfraz que quiero usar.
Gloria: A mi mamá / sobrar / tela

    _____

3. Gabriel y Luz: ¿Quién va a llevar la comida?
Esteban: A Alfonso / tocar / llevar la comida

    _____

4. Victoria: Vamos a dar un premio por el mejor disfraz.
Beto y Felipe: A nosotros / parecer / una buena idea

    _____

5. Lola: Voy a comprar las máscaras. ¿Cuántas necesitamos?
Manuel: A nosotros / bastar / veinte máscaras

    _____

6. Héctor: Voy a ir de compras al supermercado con Raúl.
Víctor: A Raúl / doler / las piernas

    _____

7. Sarita: Ya terminamos de decorar el salón.
Tomás: A tí / no faltar / imaginación

    _____

8. Pablo: Va a ser una fiesta fabulosa. ¡Todos muestran tanto entusiasmo!
Adela: A mí / placer / el entusiasmo de la gente

    _____

9. David y Javier: Vas a quedar muy impresionado con nuestro disfraz.
Fernando: Lo sé. A ustedes / gustar / lo absurdo

    _____

10. María: Hemos invitado a diecinueve personas.
Pilar: A nosotras / hacer falta / invitar a otro chico

    _____

Ejercicio P

Roberto y Pedro han pasado un mes en un programa de intercambio en México. Conteste las preguntas que les hicieron sus amigos:

1. ¿Les pareció buena la experiencia? (Sí, muy buena)

    _____

2. ¿A Uds. les agradó la familia con que vivieron? (mucho)

    _____

3. Roberto, ¿te sobró dinero del viaje? (50 dólares)

    _____

4. Pedro, ¿qué te hizo falta durante el viaje? (nada)

    _____

5. ¿A quién le dolió el estómago en México? (A Pedro)

    _____

6. ¿Les queda tiempo ahora para mostrar las fotografías que sacaron? (Sí)

    _____

7. ¿Cuánto tiempo les hace falta para terminar de mostrarlas? (15 minutos)

    _____

8. ¿Qué les parecieron las playas que visitaron? (muy bonitas)

    _____

9. ¿Qué les tocaba hacer en la casa? (arreglar las camas)

    _____

10. ¿Qué les gustó de esta experiencia? (hacer nuevos amigos)

    _____

5. Double Object Pronouns

a. When a verb has two object pronouns, the indirect object pronoun (usually a person) precedes the direct object pronoun (usually a thing):

Juan *me lo* da.	John gives it to me.
Juan *te la* da.	John gives it to you (fam.).
Juan *se los* da.	John gives them to you (him, her, them).
Juan *nos las* da.	John gives them to us.

NOTE:

1. **Le** and **les** change to **se** before **lo, la, los, las:**

Juan *le* da el libro.	John gives the book to you (him, her).
Juan *se lo* da.	John gives it to you (him, her).

2. The various meanings of **se** may be clarified by adding **a Ud. (Uds.), a él (ella), a ellos (ellas):**

> **Su madre** *se lo* **da** *a ella (a ellos).*   Her mother gives it to her (to them).

b. The position of double object pronouns is the same as for single object pronouns:

Me lo **da.**	He gives it to me.
Desea dár*melo.* or *Me lo* **desea dar.**	He wants to give it to me.
Está dándo*melo.* or *Me lo* **está dando.**	He is giving it to me.
¡Dém*elo* **Ud!**	Give it to me.
But:	
¡No *me lo* **dé Ud!**	Don't give it to me.

NOTE: When both object pronouns are attached to the verb, an accent mark is placed on the stressed syllable.

Ejercicio Q

Nicolás está muy contento porque su mamá le compró lo que necesita para su primer día de clases. Escriba lo que dice su mamá:

EJEMPLO: Voy a enseñarle el cuaderno a papá.
¡Enséñaselo!

1.   los lápices   _____
2.   la mochila   _____
3.   las gomas   _____
4.   la regla   _____
5.   la pluma   _____
6.   el diccionario _____

Ejercicio R

La madre le dice a su esposo lo que ella tiene que comprarles a los hijos. Escriba las dos formas en que el señor puede responder:

EJEMPLO: Tengo que comprarles suéteres a los niños.
Sí, debes comprárselos.
Sí, se los debes comprar.

1. Tengo que comprarle zapatos a Gregorio.

_____

_____

2. Tengo que comprarle una blusa a María.

_____

_____

3. Tengo que comprarle medias a Alicia.

_____

_____

4. Tengo que comprarles una corbata a los niños.

_____

_____

5. Tengo que comprarle un traje a Gregorio.

_____

_____

Ejercicio S

El jefe de Clara es muy indeciso. Un minuto quiere una cosa y luego no la quiere. Escriba las órdenes contradictorias que le da a Clara:

EJEMPLO: darme el calendario
¡Démelo Ud.!
¡No me lo dé Ud.!

1. llevar estos documentos a la señora Guzmán

_____

_____

2. pedir ayuda a otra secretaria

_____

_____

3. cancelar el pedido a los señores Ruiz

_____

_____

4. darme las cartas para firmar

_____

_____

5.   buscarme el otro archivo

_____

_____

6.   contestarnos el teléfono

_____

_____

7.   mandar un telegrama a mi socio

_____

_____

8.   entregar el sueldo a los empleados

_____

_____

Ejercicio T

Felipe estudia para un examen en que tiene que explicar varias profesiones. Escriba lo que dice su hermano cuando Felipe acierta las respuestas:

EJEMPLO: Un cajero da dinero a las personas.
            Sí, se lo da.

1. Un profesor enseña la lección a la clase.

_____

2. Un médico receta medicinas a los enfermos.

_____

3. Un juez dicta una sentencia al prisionero.

_____

4. Una criada limpia la casa a la señora.

_____

5. Un ladrón roba las joyas a las personas.

_____

6. Un locutor presenta a los artistas al público.

_____

7. Un ingeniero construye casas a la gente.

_____

8. Un mesero sirve el almuerzo a los clientes.

_____

9. Un dependiente vende cosas a los compradores.

   _____

10. Un gerente da órdenes a los empleados.

   _____

◆ **MASTERY EXERCISES** ◆

Ejercicio U

Complete, con los pronombres apropiados, esta carta que Rocío le escribe a una amiga:

Querida Dolores,

Fui de compras hoy con mi hermana. Es imposible ir de compras con _____ porque
1

_____ siempre da con algún conocido y se pone a charlar con _____ .
2   3

_____ fuimos a un nuevo centro comercial. La avenida era ancha y caminando por
4

_____ vimos que estaba llena de chicas y con _____ , sus novios.
5   6

¿Te acuerdas _____ de los hermanos Castro? Hoy _____ encontramos a
7   8

_____ en el centro comercial. _____ me acordaba de _____ , pero
9   10   11

_____ no se acordaban de _____ . Juan es muy alto y _____ estudia
12   13   14

en la universidad. Tiene su propio apartamento cerca de _____ . Manuel es mayor y
15

_____ trabaja. Graciela es su novia y va a casarse con _____ en junio.
16   17

Tengo muchas ganas de ver las fotos. Espero que _____ _____ mandes en
18   19

cuanto _____ tengas.
20

Otra noticia. A Estela _____ gusta montar en bicicleta. El sábado pasado _____
21   22

recorrió toda la ciudad, montada en _____ y llevando con _____ una guía.
23   24

Anoche visité la casa de Rogelio. _____ entré en la casa y dentro de _____
25   26

estaba la familia: los padres, y además de _____ , los tres hijos. _____
27   28

hicieron sentir tan nerviosa.

_____ he contado muchas nuevas a _____ en esta carta. Ahora tú _____
  29   30   31

debes una carta. ¡Escribe _____ pronto!
                              32

Saludos de

Rocío

Ejercicio V

Algunos amigos recuerdan escenas, que para ellos son inolvidables. Escriba cómo terminaron estas escenas:

EJEMPLO: Al ver a los ciegos, el bondadoso doctor sacó una limosna.
                Se apresuró a _____**dársela**_____ .

1. En la juguetería la niña insistía en que su padre comprara la muñeca.

   Por fin el padre _____ .

2. El matador no quería dedicar el toro, pero al recibir el aplauso del público

   él _____ .

3. Mi sobrino no se acuesta sin que alguien le lea un cuento. Tenía tanto sueño que se durmió

   antes de que yo _____ .

4. El primer día que Luz sacó su licencia de conducir, ella corrió un semáforo. Tuvo que enseñar

   la licencia al policía cuando él le dijo: ¡_____ !

5. Cuando el novio de mi hermana llegó a la casa, escondía unos claveles detrás de él. Yo le dije:

   Juan, _____ .

6. Un chofer compraba un periódico mientras esperaba un semáforo durante las horas de punta.
   Tenía sólo un billete de cinco dólares y mientras esperaba su cambio, el tráfico empezó a mo-

   verse. El vendedor se apresuró a _____ .

7. Una señora encontró una cartera cerca de la jefatura. Ella recogió la cartera del suelo y siguió

   caminando. Es seguro que ella _____ .

8. Cuando el equipo de Hugo ganó el campeonato, él les repitió la noticia a todos sus amigos. Su

   padre dijo: Otra vez está _____ .

9. Antes de la Navidad se publicó una foto del alcalde visitando a los niños en el hospital. Va allí

   para distribuir regalos. Otra vez el alcalde estaba _____ .

10. Victoria iba a una fiesta, pero la blusa que iba a ponerse tenía una mancha. Su hermana, Elena,

    dijo que tenía una blusa que Victoria podía usar. Elena dijo: _____ .

Ejercicio W

Exprese en español lo que cuenta este señor de su perro:

1. My dog always travels with me.

    _____

2. He doesn't like to be far away from me.

    _____

3. He always listens to me.

    _____

4. When I tell him "Sit down!", he obeys me.

    _____

5. He barks only to warn us.

    _____

6. When you throw the ball to him, he brings it back to you.

    _____

7. Your hat? Look at him; he's playing with it.

    _____

8. If he destroys it, I will pay you for it.

    _____

9. Don't tell him to do that.

    _____

10. He is afraid of you. You shouldn't be afraid of him.

    _____

11. I have three dogs but he is my favorite.

    _____

12. Children? He loves to play with them.

    _____

13. Bring him a bone. He buries them in the garden.

    _____

14. He eats ice cream. You can give it to him now.

    _____

15. Tell me, why don't you like them?

    _____

16. Don't show him a glove. Give it to him and watch what he does with it.

    _____

    _____

17. I never have any problems with him.

_____

18. I have a cage for him when we travel but he doesn't like to be in it.

_____

_____

19. If I put him in it he will try to destroy it.

_____

_____

20. You don't permit dogs? Please explain it to me again.

_____

_____

CHAPTER 19

Relative Pronouns

1. Que

Que is the most frequently used relative pronoun. **Que** refers to both persons and things. After a preposition, however, **que** refers only to things; **quien(es)** refers to persons.

	NO PREPOSITION	PREPOSITION
PERSONS	**el hombre *que* habló**	**la mujer *con quien* hablé**
THINGS	**el libro *que* leo**	**la pluma *con que* escribo**

El libro *que* estoy leyendo, es muy difícil.
The book (that) I am reading is very difficult.
Este libro, *que* es muy difícil, fue escrito en el siglo XV.
This book, which is very difficult, was written in the 15th century.
El hombre *que* fue elegido presidente, es muy popular.
The man who was elected president is very popular.
Plácido Domingo, *a quien* escuché cantar el sábado, nació en España.
Placido Domingo, whom I heard singing on Saturday, was born in Spain.
Las circunstancias *en que* me encuentro, son terribles.
The circumstances in which I find myself are terrible.

NOTE:

1. The relative pronoun is never omitted in Spanish, as it may be in English:

    Las señoras **que** esperábamos...   The ladies we expected...

2. In Spanish, a comma is used after a relative clause. If the relative clause is nonrestrictive, a comma is also used before the relative pronoun:

    El tema **que eligió**, es demasiado complicado.
    Este diccionario, **que es bastante malo**, me lo regalaron ayer.

3. In Spanish, the preposition always precedes the relative pronoun:

    Las leyes **a que** estamos sujetos... *The laws (which) we are subject to...*

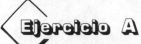

Ejercicio A

Escriba lo que dice el guía que acompaña a unos turistas en el Museo del Prado:

EJEMPLO: los colores / usar / el pintor
Fíjense en los colores que usó el pintor.

1.   las líneas / crear / los escultores

_____

2.   las figuras / crear / el pintor

_____

3.   el estilo / usar / el artista

_____

4.   las sombras / pintar / los artistas

_____

5.   los detalles / incluir / el pintor

_____

6.   la sonrisa / captar / el artista

_____

7.   el mensaje / expresar / el pintor

_____

Ejercicio B

Ud. le enseña una foto a un amigo e identifica a las personas que viajaron en su grupo a España. Escriba lo que Ud. dice de las personas en la foto:

EJEMPLO: el joven / perder su dinero
Éste es el joven que perdió su dinero.

1.   la chica / gastar 500 dólares

_____

2.   los chicos / hacernos bromas

_____

3.   el chico / visitar a unos primos

_____

4.   las chicas / alejarse del grupo

_____

5.   el chico / no comer nada

_____

6. la señorita / dirigir el grupo

_____

7. los chicos / mandar cien tarjetas postales

_____

8. la chica / no visitar los museos

_____

Ejercicio C

Ud. ayuda a su mamá a limpiar el desván. Escriba lo que ella dice al encontrar unas cosas viejas en un baúl:

EJEMPLO: el vestido / en. / casarme
Mira el vestido en que me casé.

1. las zapatillas / en / dar mi primer paso

_____

2. la pluma / con / escribir cartas a tu papá

_____

3. el cepillo / con / peinar a tu hermana

_____

4. el álbum / en / escribir versos

_____

5. el reloj / en / aprender a decir la hora

_____

6. el menú del restaurante / a / ir con los amigos

_____

7. la cámara / con / sacar muchas fotos

_____

Ejercicio D

Roberto ganó el premio en un concurso científico. Escriba lo que les dice a unas personas que lo visitan en el laboratorio:

EJEMPLO:

los condiscípulos / con / trabajar
Éstos son los condiscípulos con quienes trabajé.

1. el laboratorio / en / hacer el estudio

_____

2. el profesor / a / pedir consejos

_____

3. la computadora / con / resolver los problemas

_____

4. el científico / por / enterarme del tema

_____

5. el cuaderno / en / anotar mis observaciones

_____

6. la biblioteca / en / pasar muchas horas

_____

7. la persona / a / dedicar el trabajo

_____

8. el catre / en / dormir la siesta

_____

9. los jueces / a / deber mi gratitud

_____

10. mis amigos / con / trabajar por un mes

_____

Ejercicio E

Gabriel se despierta en el hospital y no recuerda lo que le pasó. Escriba lo que le dice la enfermera, combinando las dos frases:

EJEMPLO: Aquí está el médico. Lo llamé por la mañana.
Aquí está el médico **a quien llamé** por la mañana.

1. Éste es el jarabe. Se lo dimos ayer.

_____

2. Éstas son las píldoras. El médico se las recetó.

_____

3. Trajeron la medicina. El médico la recetó anoche.

_____

4. Ese señor es el boticario. Él preparó la medicina.

_____

5. Este hombre es el otro doctor. Ud. habló con él anoche.

_____

6. Soy la enfermera. Ud. se quejó de mí.

_____

7. Éste es el hospital Caridad. Lo trajeron aquí en una ambulancia.

_____

2. *Quien(es)* and Alternate Forms

Quien(es) is also used as subject to express *he (she, those, the one, the ones) who*. An alternate form is **el (la, los, las) que**:

Quien estudia, siempre aprende. He (She) who studies always learns.
Los que estudian, siempre aprenden. Those who study always learn.

Ejercicio F

La abuela de Estela usa muchos refranes cuando habla. Complete los refranes que Estela trata de recordar:

EJEMPLO: _____**El que**_____ no se atreve, no pasa el mar.

1. _____ busca, encuentra.

2. _____ va despacio y con tiento, hace dos cosas a un tiempo.

3. _____ mal anda, mal acaba.

4. _____ temprano se levanta tiene una hora más de vida y en su trabajo adelanta.

5. _____ a hierro matan, a hierro mueren.

6. _____ esperan, desesperan.

7. _____ la hace, la paga.

8. _____ mucho hablan, mucho yerran.

9. _____ mucho abarcan, poco aprietan.

10. _____ siembra amigos, cosecha amigos.

Ejercicio G

Escriba lo que la maestra dice el primer día de clases, usando quien, quienes, el que, la que, los que *o* las que:

EJEMPLO: _____**Quienes**_____ estudian reciben buenas notas.

1. _____ no falta a la clase, aprende más.

2. _____ se esfuerzan, tienen éxito.

3. _____ llega temprano, está listo para trabajar.

4. _____ preparan la tarea, están mejor preparados.

5. _____ prestan atención en la clase, comprenden más.

6. _____ participan en la lección, aprenden mejor.

3. Two Antecedents

If there are two antecedents, and there is need for clarification, **quien(es)** or **que** is used to indicate the nearer of the two. The more distant antecedent is indicated by a form of **el (la, los, las) cual(es)** or **el (la, los, las) que**:

<table>
<tr><td>El padre de **Felipe**, *quien (que)* está enfermo, le cuida con cariño. (Philip is ill.)</td><td>*The father of Philip, who is ill, cares for him lovingly.*</td></tr>
<tr><td>**El padre** de Felipe, *el cual (el que)* está enfermo, no saldrá hoy. (The father is ill.)</td><td>*Philip's father, who is ill, will not go out today.*</td></tr>
</table>

4. Relative Pronouns after Prepositions

The relative pronouns **el (la, los, las) cual(es)** and **el (la, los, las) que** are used after all prepositions, regardless of the location of the antecedent. **Que** and **quien(es)** may be used after the prepositions **a, de, en,** and **con**:

<table>
<tr><td>Subió a la cumbre, **desde la cual (la que)** vio el valle.</td><td>*He climbed to the mountain top, from which he saw the valley.*</td></tr>
<tr><td>La casa **delante de la cual (la que)** estamos, es la antigua residencia del gobernador.</td><td>*The house in front of which we are standing is the old residence of the governor.*</td></tr>
<tr><td>Es un hombre **del que (de quien)** poco se sabe.</td><td>*He is a man about whom little is known.*</td></tr>
<tr><td>El apartamento **en (el) que** vivía era muy pequeño.</td><td>*The apartment in which he lived was very small.*</td></tr>
</table>

Ejercicio H

Complete las frases con las que Jorge describió una visita a un pueblo en la Costa del Sol, usando el pronombre relativo apropiado en cada frase:

1. Fue un día glorioso en _____ llegamos.

2. Las nubles, detrás de _____ brillaba el sol, parecían ser de algodón.

3. El administrador del hotel abrió un cuaderno grande en _____ escribió nuestros nombres.

4. Nos acercamos a la iglesia, delante de _____ quedamos asombrados.

5. Los pescadores, entre _____ no se encontraba ninguna mujer, estaban en la playa.

6. El guía, con _____ yo hablé mucho, nos explicó las costumbres de los pescadores.

7. Las lanchas de los pescadores, delante de _____ había una red enorme, parecían de juguete.

8. Con aire misterioso los pescadores abrieron la red, dentro de _____ había más de doscientos pescados.

9. A la mañana siguiente salí al balcón del hotel, desde _____ podía ver la salida de los pescadores.

10. Tomamos el desayuno a las diez, después de _____ salimos del pueblo.

Ejercicio I

Combine las frases siguientes para expresar los datos que apuntó un policía en su libreta para seguirle la pista a un ladrón:

EJEMPLO: Conozco a varios policías. Siento verdadero afecto por ellos.
Conozco a varios policías **por los cuales** siento verdadero afecto.

1. En la sala vi una cortina. El criminal se escondió detrás de ella.

_____
_____

2. Quería ver los dormitorios. Había otra puerta cerca de ellos.

_____
_____

3. Me fijé en la mesa del comedor. Encontré una colilla debajo de ella.

_____
_____

4. Me asomé al garaje. Encontré un coche abandonado dentro de él.

_____
_____

5. Traté de usar el teléfono. Había pintura fresca sobre él.

_____
_____

5. Lo que

a. **Lo que** is equivalent to the English relative pronoun *what (that which)*:

Le di **lo que** me pidió.   *I gave him what he asked me for.*

b. **Lo que** and **lo cual** are equivalent to English *which (a fact; something)* if the antecedent is a clause or an idea:

<table>
<tr>
<td>Pepe llegó tarde, lo que (lo cual) no le gustó al maestro.</td>
<td>Joe arrived late, (something) which did not please the teacher.</td>
</tr>
</table>

 **Ejercicio J**

Exprese lo que piensan los pasajeros de un autobús al llegar a la primera parada de descanso. Use **lo que** *con las sugerencias:*

SUGERENCIAS: tomar un refresco   comer una hamburguesa
llamar a casa   comprar un helado
lavarme las manos   buscar un periódico

EJEMPLO: **Lo que yo necesito es lavarme las manos.**

1. _____

2. _____

3. _____

4. _____

5. _____

Ejercicio K

Escriba las preguntas que hace un guía turístico a los turistas:

EJEMPLO: encontrar / buscar
¿Encontró Ud. lo que buscaba?

1.   comprar / necesitar

_____

2.   hallar / esperar

_____

3.   hacer / querer

_____

4.   conocer / desear

_____

5.   ver / interesarle

_____

6.   experimentar / yo decirle

_____

Ejercicio L

Exprese en una sola frase lo que comentan estos amigos:

> EJEMPLO: El chico reparó en la señorita. Esto le molestó a ella.
> El chico reparó en la señorita, **lo cual** le molestó a ella.

1. El policía puso una multa en el carro. Esto enfureció al señor.

   _____

2. El mesero trajo el café en seguida. Esto no le agradó a la señora.

   _____

3. Mi papá limpió el sótano de la casa. Esto dio gusto a mi mamá.

   _____

4. El señor se cayó en el hielo. Esto causó risa a la niña.

   _____

5. Mi hermanito perdió diez dólares. Mi mamá se esperaba esto.

   _____

6. *Cuyo*

Cuyo (-a, -os, -as), meaning *whose*, refers to both persons and things. **Cuyo** is a relative adjective and agrees with the thing (or person) possessed, not with the possessor:

El muchacho **cuya corbata** llevo, es mi primo.	*The boy whose tie I am wearing is my cousin.*

Ejercicio M

Exprese cómo identifica José a varias personas en una fiesta:

Aquel señor		carro está delante de la casa		mi tío	
Esa señora		canción están tocando		mi jefe	
Ese hombre	cuyo (-a, -os, -as)	chistes son aburridos	es	mi abuela	
Aquella joven		flores están en la mesa		mi prima	
Esa muchacha		novio baila solo		mi padre	
		sombrero está en el piso		mi hermana	

> EJEMPLO: **Esa señora, cuyo carro está delante de la casa, es mi abuela.**

1. _____

   _____

2. _____
   _____

3. _____
   _____

4. _____
   _____

5. _____
   _____

◆ MASTERY EXERCISES ◆

Ejercicio N

Escriba lo que Roberto le aconseja a un amigo en una carta. Use el pronombre relativo apropiado:

Tú no estás al corriente. _____ debes hacer es mirar las noticias en la televisión.
1

Hay un programa de noticias _____ se llama «24 Horas». Es un programa
2

_____ se transmite desde México todos los días, por _____
3 4

te enterarás de las noticias del día. El locutor, _____ voz es conocida tanto en
5

el extranjero como en su país, presenta todos los acontecimientos con claridad. ¿Recuerdas

al hombre _____ te presenté en la fiesta de Marisol? Bueno, él es el sobrino
6

del locutor a _____ me refiero. Mi tía Aurora, _____
7 8

vive en México, es su vecina. Él tiene un rancho fuera de la ciudad en _____
9

tiene muchos caballos. Eran éstos los caballos de _____ te hablé después de mi
10

último viaje. También, fue en su casa _____ mis padres pasaron el año
11

nuevo. A ver si haces _____ te aconsejo para estar al día.
12

Tu amigo,

Roberto

 **Ejercicio O**

*Escriba lo que cuenta Rafael de un amigo suyo. Junte las dos frases usando un pronombre relativo. El símbolo * indica el comienzo de la cláusula relativa:*

> EJEMPLO: Voy a comprarme un carro modelo deportivo.* Tengo muchas ganas de un carro deportivo.
>
> Voy a comprarme un carro modelo deportivo, **del que (del cual) tengo muchas ganas.**

1. Voy a salir con unos amigos.* Me gusta mucho salir con ellos.

   _____

   _____

2. Mi mejor amigo* ha conseguido entradas para el partido de fútbol. Mi mejor amigo se llama Paco.

   _____

   _____

3. Paco tiene un tío.* Su tío trabaja en el estadio.

   _____

   _____

4. Él tiene cinco entradas.* Las entradas cuestan veinte y cinco dólares cada una.

   _____

   _____

5. Los primos de Paco* no van a los partidos a menudo. Su padre consigue las entradas.

   _____

   _____

Ejercicio P

Imagínese que Ud. trabaja en la oficina del alcalde durante una sequía. Ud. tiene que leerles a unos periodistas una declaración del alcalde sobre la escasez de agua. Escriba los pronombres relativos que faltan:

Experimentamos una escasez de agua _____ tiene dos causas principales.
                                          1

Primero, aunque ha llovido mucho, las lluvias _____ cayeron no llenaron las
                                                      2

represas de agua. Segundo, la falta de agua _____ existe, se debe también a la
                                                   3

falta de nieve durante el invierno pasado. Debido a esto, _____ yo les aconsejo
                                                                  4

a todos los ciudadanos es _____ 5 conserven el agua, _____ 6

ahora es tan valiosa como una joya. _____ 7 los ciudadanos pueden hacer es

no malgastar el agua, no regar los céspedes y no lavar los carros. Estas advertencias,

_____ 8 son de máxima importancia, pueden ayudar a conservar el agua

que nos queda. Los habitantes de nuestra ciudad, en _____ 9 tengo

mucha confianza y a _____ 10 estimo mucho, podrán disminuir el riesgo

_____ 11 existe. Todo _____ 12 digo es para nuestro bien y

_____ 13 no cooperen harán daño a los demás. Hay inspectores

_____ 14 vigilarán el consumo de agua por toda la ciudad. Ellos multarán a

los ciudadanos _____ 15 no obedezcan estas reglas.

Ejercicio Q

Exprese en español los comentarios que preparó Lupe para escribir un artículo para el periódico estudiantil:

1. Last Friday, the exchange students who attended our school returned home.

   _____

   _____

2. These fifteen students, who came from seven different cities in Spain, spent three weeks in our city.

   _____

   _____

3. The students with whom I spoke said that they had enjoyed themselves and that they learned a lot.

   _____

   _____

4. Their guide, whose name is Claudio Ramos, brought other students to our school last year.

   _____

   _____

5. The families in whose houses the students stayed were sad to see them leave.

   _____

   _____

6. During the first weekend, the students attended a dance given in their honor.

_____

_____

7. Although some of the Spanish students spoke English, the American students were the ones who tried to speak Spanish.

_____

_____

8. A few of the girls were shy, but they were the ones who tried to speak English all the time.

_____

_____

9. The students and their guide, who was very interesting, explained many Spanish customs to us.

_____

_____

10. Gloria, who was the oldest in the group, had visited the city before.

_____

_____

11. She has cousins who live here.

_____

12. She and her cousins, who also attend our school, gave a party.

_____

_____

13. Gloria was the one who helped to organize this exchange.

_____

_____

14. Our friends were able to make several trips which they enjoyed.

_____

_____

15. They saw three films, two of which they want to see again in Spain.

_____

_____

16. What they liked most was the trip to the amusement park, in which they spent an entire day.

_____

_____

17. They visited several department stores, in which they bought gifts for their families.

_____

_____

18. The families with whom the students lived planned many activities for them.

_____

_____

19. It rained on the day on which they hoped to go to the beach.

_____

_____

20. The principal to whom the students gave a trophy accompanied them to the airport.

_____

_____

Prepositions

Prepositions relate two elements of a sentence (noun to noun, verb to noun, verb to infinitive, verb to pronoun, and the like):

Entra *en* **él.**	*He enters it.*
Comienza *a* **leer.**	*He begins to read.*

NOTE: For a list of common prepositions, see page 234.

1. Prepositional Modifiers

a. A preposition + noun modifying another noun is equivalent to an adjective:

un anillo *de oro*	*a gold ring (a ring of gold)*
un vaso *de agua*	*a glass of water*
un vaso *para agua*	*a water glass (a glass for water)*

b. A preposition + noun modifying a verb is equivalent to an adverb:

Sale *con frecuencia.*	*He goes out frequently (with frequency).*

Ejercicio A

Identifique los objetos que Adela vio en un catálogo de regalos de Navidad:

EJEMPLO:

una taza para café

1.

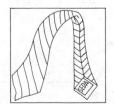

2.

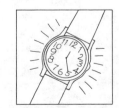

_____   _____

3.

_____

7.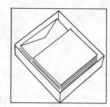

_____

4.

_____

8.

_____

5.

_____

9.

_____

6.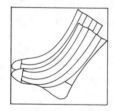

_____

10.

_____

Ejercicio B

Escriba lo que Elena y Carmen comentan de otra amiga, usando las sugerencias:

SUGERENCIAS: vestirse, peinarse, ir al cine, visitarme, hablar, no hacernos caso

con (sin) cuidado, con (sin) atención, con (sin) gusto, con (sin) frecuencia, de prisa, con (sin) intención

EJEMPLO: **Ella se viste sin gusto.**

1. _____

2. _____

3. _____

4. _____

5. _____

6. _____

2. Prepositions Used with Infinitives

In Spanish, the infinitive is the only verb form that may follow a preposition:

El avión tardó **en aterrizar.**	The plane was delayed in landing.
Acabo **de terminar de estudiar.**	I just finished studying.
Se negó **a ayudar**me.	He refused to help me.

a. Verbs requiring **a** before an infinitive

Verbs expressing beginning, motion, teaching, or learning, and a few other verbs, require the preposition **a** before an infinitive:

comenzar a ⎫	**acertar a** *to happen to (by chance)*
empezar a ⎬ *to begin to*	**acostumbrarse a** *to become*
ponerse a ⎪	*accustomed to*
principiar a ⎭	**aspirar a** *to aspire to*
acercarse a *to approach*	**atreverse a** *to dare to*
apresurarse a *to hasten (hurry) to*	**ayudar a** *to help to*
correr a *to run to*	**convidar a** *to invite to*
ir a *to go to*	**decidirse a** *to decide to*
regresar a *to return to (to . . . again)*	**dedicarse a** *to devote oneself to*
salir a *to go out to*	**disponerse a** *to get ready to*
venir a *to come to*	**invitar a** *to invite to*
volver a *to return to (to . . . again)*	**llegar a** *to succeed in*
enseñar a *to teach to*	**negarse a** *to refuse to*
aprender a *to learn to*	**obligar a** *to force, to compel to*
	resignarse a *to resign oneself to*

La niña *se puso a* **llorar.**	The girl started to cry.
Salió a **comprar** pan.	He went out to buy bread.
Estoy aprendiendo a **tocar** la guitarra.	I am learning to play the guitar.
Lo *convidé a* **almorzar** conmigo.	I invited him to have lunch with me.
¿Te *decidiste a* **venir** *a* **cenar?**	Did you decide to come for dinner?
Me *obligaron a* **quedar**me en casa.	They forced me to stay home.

b. Verbs requiring **de** before an infinitive:

acabar de *to have just*	**dejar de** *to fail to, to stop*
acordarse de *to remember to*	**encargarse de** *to take charge of*
alegrarse de *to be glad*	**olvidarse de** *to forget to*
cesar de *to stop*	**tratar de** *to try to*

Acuérdate de regresar temprano.   Remember to return early.
Roberto dejó de escribirme.   Robert stopped writing to me.
Trataré de llegar a tiempo.   I will try to arrive on time.
No te olvides de llamar a Pedro.   Don't forget to call Peter.

c. Verbs requiring en before an infinitive:

consentir en to consent to, to agree	empeñarse en to be determined to; to insist on
consistir en to consist of	insistir en to insist on
convenir en to agree to	tardar en to delay in, to be long in

Consintió en ir al baile conmigo.   She agreed to go to the dance with me.
Convenimos en estudiar juntos.   We agreed to study together.
Se empeña en comprar una bicicleta   He insists on buying an expensive
    cara.   bicycle.
No creo que tarde en llegar.   I don't believe he will be long in
        coming.

d. Verbs requiring con before an infinitive:

amenazar con to threaten to	soñar con to dream of
contar con to count on, to rely on	

Me amenazó con contárselo a mi   He threatened to tell my mother.
    madre.
Cuento con ganar el premio.   I count on winning the prize.
Soñaba con viajar por el mundo.   He dreamed of traveling around the
        world.

 Ejercicio C

Complete, con las preposiciones apropiadas, esta cartita que Jorge le escribió a un amigo:

Acabo _____ presenciar una escena chistosa en la calle. Un señor altísimo se disponía
        1

_____ casarse con una mujer muy baja. Los novios comenzaron _____ bajarse del carro
    2   3

delante de la iglesia, cuando un grupo de personas se acercó _____ saludarlos. La novia
                                                4

trató _____ bajarse del carro, pero estas personas la obligaron _____ volver _____
    5   6   7

sentarse. El novio se apresuró _____ ayudarle, porque no quería que la ceremonia tardara
                8

_____ comenzar. La novia se empeñaba _____ tratar _____ salir del carro. Con
    9   10   11

eso un policía acertó _____ pasar por allí e insistió _____ correr a las personas. Pero
                12   13

el novio las invitó _____ entrar en la iglesia. Ellas consintieron _____ hacerlo, y el
                       14   15

policía se encargó _____ ayudarle a la novia _____ salir del carro. Parecía como
                    16   17

si la pobre novia se hubiera resignado _____ quedarse en el carro. Los novios se decidieron
                                        18

_____ salir por otra puerta de la iglesia al concluir la ceremonia. Cuando terminó la cere–
  19

monia, empezó _____ llover.
               20

Ejercicio D

Ud. es periodista y acaba de entrevistar a un cantante famoso de España. Usando sus apuntes de la entrevista, escriba el artículo en frases completas. Tendrá que añadir las preposiciones:

EJEMPLO: empeñarse / dar gusto a su público
            Se empeña en dar gusto a su público.

1. el cantante / alegrarse / estar / los EE. UU.

   _____

2. él / empezar / cantar / tener diez años

   _____

3. su madre / enseñarle / tocar la guitarra

   _____

4. él / dedicarse / entretener a la gente

   _____

5. en sus conciertos / el público / obligarle / cantar más

   _____

6. él / siempre consentir / hacerlo

   _____

7. desde chico / él / aspirar / ser famoso

   _____

8. él / insistir / cantar canciones populares

   _____

9. él / acabar / dar conciertos / quince ciudades

   _____

10. él / volver / visitar / los EE. UU. pronto

    _____

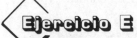

Ejercicio E

Margarita es una chica envidiosa. Escriba lo que les cuenta a sus padres, añadiendo las preposiciones necesarias:

EJEMPLO: El padre de Lourdes / enseñarle / conducir
El padre de Lourdes **le enseñó a** conducir.

1. Los padres de Marta / consentir / mandarla al campamento de tenis

_____

2. Los hermanos de Rocío / nunca / olvidarse / darle un regalo

_____

3. La madre de Luisa / ayudarle / escoger la ropa

_____

4. Los padres de Beatriz / no insistir / acompañarla a todas partes

_____

5. La abuela de Rosa / encargarse / organizar una fiesta

_____

6. Los padres de Susana / decidirse / comprarle un carro

_____

7. La mamá de Luz / acabar / hacerle un vestido nuevo

_____

3. Prepositions Used Before Infinitives

The following prepositions are commonly used before an infinitive. The equivalent English construction normally uses a present participle:

a *to, at*	**en** *in, on, of*
al + inf. *upon, on*	**en lugar de** ⎱ *instead of*
antes de *before*	**en vez de** ⎰
con *with* (sometimes *to* or *of*)	**hasta** *until*
de *of, to*	**sin** *without*
después de *after*	

Al entrar, vio a su hija.
Antes de salir, prepárese.
Después de descansar un rato, se levantó.
Se acostó **en vez de estudiar.**
Salió **sin decir** nada.

(On) Entering, he saw his daughter.
Before going out, prepare yourself.
After resting a while, he got up.

He went to bed instead of studying.
He left without saying anything.

NOTE: A verb + preposition + infinitive construction must have the same subject. If the subjects are different, **que** is required and a conjugated verb form is used instead of the infinitive. Compare:

Me alegro de estar aquí.	*I am glad to be here.*
Me alegro *de que Ud.* **esté** aquí.	*I am glad that you are here.*
Insiste en vender la casa.	*She insists on selling the house.*
Insiste *en que su marido venda* **la casa.**	*She insists that her husband sell the house.*
Se desayunó después de preparar el café.	*He ate breakfast after preparing the coffee.*
Se desayunó *después (de) que su madre preparó* el café.	*He ate breakfast after his mother prepared the coffee.*

Ejercicio F

Escriba lo que Ud. o sus parientes hacen en estas circunstancias. Combine, en cualquier orden, expresiones de las cuatro columnas para expresarlo:

al	desayunarse	mi padre	cepillarse los dientes
antes de	entrar en la casa	yo	dar las gracias
después de	comer	mi madre	saludar a mis padres
en vez de	estudiar	mis padres	mirar la televisión
en lugar de	ayudar a mis hermanos	mi hermano	escuchar discos
sin	tomar el café	mi hermana	no hablar con nadie
	decir adiós		salir de la casa

EJEMPLO: **Al entrar en la casa, yo saludo a mis padres.**

1. _____
2. _____
3. _____
4. _____
5. _____
6. _____
7. _____

Ejercicio G

Jaime cuenta lo que pasó durante una visita al despacho de su profesor de química. Añada las preposiciones que faltan en español:

 llegar a su despacho, vi que   Upon arriving at his office, I saw that he was

estaba leyendo un telegrama. Leía el telegrama

_____ creerlo. Estaba calificando
        2

unos exámenes _____ leer el
                    3

telegrama. _____ leerlo varias
               4

veces, empezó a sonreír._____
                            5

ayudarme, se puso el abrigo y _____
                                    6

decir una palabra, se marchó. _____
                                  7

perder un minuto, lo seguí al ascensor.

reading a telegram. He read the telegram without believing it. He was grading some tests before reading the telegram. After reading it several times, he began to smile. Instead of helping me, he put on his coat and, without saying a word, he left. Without wasting any time, I followed him to the elevator.

4. Verbs Used Without Preposition Before an Infinitive

deber *ought to, must*	**poder** *to be able, can*
dejar *to let, to allow*	**preferir** *to prefer*
desear *to wish, to desire*	**pretender** *to attempt*
esperar *to hope, to expect*	**prometer** *to promise*
hacer *to make, to have (something done)*	**querer** *to want, to wish*
lograr *to succeed in*	**saber** *to know how to*
necesitar *to need*	**soler** *to be accustomed to, usually*
oír *to hear*	**ver** *to see*
pensar *to intend*	

Debo ir a la escuela hoy.
No me **dejan salir.**
Hizo construir una casa.
Pienso comenzar mañana.
Suele volver a las doce.

I ought to go to school today.
They don't let me go out.
He had a house built.
I intend to begin tomorrow.
He usually returns at twelve o'clock.

Ejercicio H

Conteste las preguntas que le hace un(a) amigo(a) nuevo(a):

1. ¿Qué sueles hacer durante el fin de semana?

_____

2. ¿Qué piensas hacer este fin de semana?

_____

3. ¿Qué prefieres, ir al cine o visitar el museo?

_____

4. ¿Con quién prometiste salir el viernes por la noche?

_____

5. ¿A quién esperas ver en el parque?

_____

6. ¿Podrás acompañarme al centro el sábado por la mañana?

_____

7. ¿Sabes conducir un carro?

_____

8. ¿Qué quehaceres debes hacer en casa?

_____

9. ¿Necesitas pedirles permiso a tus padres para salir?

_____

10. ¿Prometes llamarme por teléfono esta noche?

_____

Ejercicio I

Ud. está trabajando de consejero en un campamento de verano. Escriba lo que les diría a los chicos de ocho años de edad de su grupo el primer día. Use las expresiones sugeridas en las tres columnas:

yo	deber	prestar atención
Uds.	dejar	ayudarse el uno al otro
nosotros	desear	aprender muchas cosas
tú	esperar	ir a acampar
	lograr	obedecer las reglas del campamento
	necesitar	ser amables
	pensar	acostarse a la hora indicada
	poder	levantarse en seguida
	preferir	mantener todo en orden
	prometer	jugar muchos deportes
	querer	no hacer bromas
	saber	dar premios cada semana
	soler	cooperar siempre
		respetarse el uno al otro
		divertirse mucho

EJEMPLOS: **Uds. deben prestarme atención.**
Pienso enseñarles muchas cosas este verano.

1. _____

2. _____

3. _____

4. _____

5. _____

6. _____

7. _____

8. _____

9. _____

10. _____

11. _____

12. _____

13. _____

14. _____

15. _____

5. Common Expressions with Prepositions

a causa de *because of*

No salió **a causa de** su resfrío.

He didn't go out because of his cold.

a eso de *about + time*

Nos reuniremos **a eso de** las cinco.

We'll get together at about five o'clock.

a fines de *at the end of*

La primavera comienza **a fines de** de marzo.

Spring begins at the end of March.

a fuerza de *by dint of (by persevering)*

A fuerza de estudiar, aprendió bien la historia.

By (persevering in) studying, he learned history well.

a la + adjective *in the style, in the manner*

Se viste **a la** antigua.

She dresses in an old-fashioned manner.

Sirvieron una comida **a la** mexicana.

They served a meal in the Mexican style.

a pie *on foot*

Fueron de Madrid a Toledo **a pie.**

They went from Madrid to Toledo on foot.

a principios de *at the beginning of, early in*

Pienso estar allí **a principios de** mayo.

I intend to be there early in May.

a tiempo on time

Si quieres comer, vuelve **a tiempo.**   *If you want to eat, return on time.*

a través de through, across

Supe la noticia **a través de** un amigo.   *I learned the news through a friend.*

al aire libre outdoors, in the open air

Le gusta nadar **al aire libre.**   *He likes to swim in the open air.*

de hoy en adelante henceforth, from now on

De hoy en adelante, estudiaré a diario.   *From now on I'll study every day.*

de otro modo otherwise

Pague Ud. ahora; **de otro modo** llamo   *Pay now; otherwise I'll call the police.*
a la policía.

de pie standing

El alumno se levantó y se quedó **de**   *The pupil stood up and remained*
pie.   *standing.*

de vez en cuando from time to time

De vez en cuando me gusta ir al cine.   *From time to time I like to go to the*
    movies.

desde luego (que no) of course (not), naturally (not)

Desde luego, el carro costó mucho.   *Of course the car cost a great deal.*

en cambio on the other hand

Juan es perezoso; **en cambio** su   *John is lazy; on the other hand, his*
hermano es diligente.   *brother is diligent.*

en cuanto a as for, in regard to

En cuanto a ti, ya sabes lo que te   *As for you, you know what awaits*
espera.   *you.*

en efecto in fact, really; yes, indeed (as a response)

En efecto, lo compré ayer.   *Yes, indeed, I bought it yesterday.*

(en) ocho días (in) a week

Se casan de hoy **en ocho días.**   *They are getting married a week from*
    today.

(en) quince días (in) two weeks, (in) a fortnight

Prometió regresar **en quince días.**   *He promised to return in two weeks.*

en vez de instead of

En vez de estudiar, se fue al cine.   *Instead of studying, he went to the*
    movies.

Ejercicio J

Conteste las preguntas que le hace un alumno de intercambio, usando los modismos indicados:

1.   ¿Cuándo comenzó a nevar anoche? (a eso de)

_____

2.   ¿Por qué no fueron Uds. al cine? (a causa de)

_____

3.   Si no hay autobús, ¿cómo podré ir a la escuela? (a pie)

_____

4.   ¿Cómo lograste comprar la bicicleta nueva? (a fuerza de)

_____

5.   ¿Cuándo terminan las clases aquí? (a fines de)

_____

6.   Y, ¿cuándo comienzan de nuevo? (a principios de)

_____

7.   Durante el invierno, ¿nieva aquí con frecuencia? (en efecto)

_____

8.   ¿Piensas trabajar durante el verano? (desde luego)

_____

Ejercicio K

Gabi pasa el verano en España. Escriba la expresión necesaria para completar su carta a una prima:

Saludos desde Madrid. El avión llegó _____ y _____ las ocho
                                       1 (on time)   **2** (at about)

de la mañana ya estaba en la casa de huéspedes. Mi cuarto es amplio, bonito y limpio.

_____ los árboles, puedo ver la plaza mayor.
   3 (through)

La universidad queda cerca y puedo ir allí _____ . Sin embargo, sé que
                                              4 (on foot)

_____ me despertaré tarde y tendré que tomar el metro. Cuando va muy lleno
5 (from time to time)

hay que viajar _____ .
                  6 (standing)

En la plaza hay un café _____ y _____ pienso sentarme allí
                              7 (outdoors)   **8** (from now on)

todas las tardes. Las clases comienzan _____ la semana próxima y terminan
                                          9 (at the beginning of)

_____ agosto. _____ la profesora, todavía no puedo contarte
  10 (at the end of)   **11** (As for)

nada. Sólo sé que tendré que estudiar mucho. _____, tendré que encerrarme en
                                                12 (In fact)

el cuarto por las noches _____ salir con mis amigos; _____ no
                           13 (instead of)   **14** (otherwise)

aprenderé nunca español. _____ encontraré la manera de divertirme también.
                           15 (Of course)

Hasta pronto.

6. Personal *a*

The preposition **a** is used before the direct object of a verb if the direct object is:

a. A definite person or persons:

> Visita *a* su amigo (*a* sus padres, *a*   He visits his friend (his parents,
>   Roberto, etc.).   Robert, etc.).

b. A domestic animal (pet, etc.):

> Quiere *a* su perrito (*a* Fido, *a* su gato,   She loves her little dog (Fido, her cat,
>   etc.).   etc.).

c. A geographic name (unless preceded by the definite article):

> Desea ver *a* España (*a* México, *a*   He wants to see Spain (Mexico, New
>   Nueva York, etc.).   York, etc.).
>
> But:
>
> Desea ver la Argentina (los Estados   He wants to see Argentina (the United
>   Unidos, el Perú, etc.).   States, Peru, etc.).

d. A pronoun referring to a person:

> Veo *a* alguien.   I see someone.
> No veo *a* nadie.   I see no one.

NOTE:

1. The personal **a** is not used with the verb **tener:**

> **Tengo un amigo.**   I have a friend.

2. In current usage, the personal **a** tends to be omitted with geographical names: **Quisiera visitar París.**

Ejercicio L

Raúl y su primo Carlos celebran el mismo cumpleaños. Escriba lo que la mamá de Raúl le dice que debe hacer:

EJEMPLO:　amar / tu primo
Debes amar a tu primo.

1.　visitar / Carlos _____

2.　llamar / tus abuelos _____

3.　comprar / un regalo para él _____

4.　invitar / sus amigos a la fiesta _____

5.　mandar / una tarjeta _____

6.　felicitar / tu primo _____

Ejercicio M

Gloria está estudiando en México durante el verano. Complete la carta que ella le va a mandar a su profesora de español. Use la a personal cuando sea necesario:

Por fin llegué a visitar _____ México. Vivo con una familia _____ quien quiero mucho. Tienen
　　　　　　　　　　　　　　1　　　　　　　　　　　　　　　　2

_____ un perro que me sigue por todas partes. Amo mucho _____ este perro porque es muy
3　　　　　　　　　　　　　　　　　　　　　　　　　　　　　4

cariñoso y juguetón. Extraño _____ los Estados Unidos, pero estoy aprendiendo mucho aquí.
　　　　　　　　　　　　　　5

Llamé _____ su tío la semana pasada y voy a verlos _____ ellos antes de volver a casa. Conocí
　　　　6　　　　　　　　　　　　　　　　　　　　7

_____ un joven que vive cerca de la casa de mi prima. Él ha visitado _____ la Argentina y
8　　　　　　　　　　　　　　　　　　　　　　　　　　　　　9

_____ España. Habla español y tiene _____ muchos amigos. Veo _____ Juan todos los
10　　　　　　　　　　　　　　　　11　　　　　　　　　　12

días en la escuela. Él conoce _____ la familia con quien vivo porque es amigo del hijo mayor.
　　　　　　　　　　　　　13

Llamo _____ mis padres una vez por semana. Al final del mes voy a visitar _____ Acapulco
　　　14　　　　　　　　　　　　　　　　　　　　　　　　　　　15

con los otros estudiantes. ¿Ha visto Ud. _____ algunos de mis amigos?
　　　　　　　　　　　　　　　16

7. *Para* and *por*

Both **para** and **por** have similar basic meanings in English. Whether to use **para** or **por** depends on the Spanish context. Their meanings in English may vary with the context.

a. Para

(1) **Para** expresses purpose or goal:

Estudia **para médico.**	*He studies to be a doctor.*
Trabajé *para* **comprar un coche.**	*I worked in order to buy a car.*
Estudió *para* **pasar el examen.**	*He studied to pass the exam.*

(2) **Para** expresses the special use of an object:

Necesito un **cepillo** *para* **el pelo.**	*I need a hairbrush.*
Es una **caja** *para* **dulces.**	*It is a candy box (a box for candy).*

But:

Es una **caja** *de* **dulces.**	*It is a box of candy.*

(3) **Para** expresses destination or direction:

Ayer salió *para* **México.**	*Yesterday he left for Mexico.*
Esta carta es *para* **ti.**	*This letter is for you.*

(4) **Para** indicates a time or date in the future:

Estará listo *para* **el viernes.**	*It will be ready for (by) Friday.*
Estaré de regreso *para* **la una.**	*I will be back by one o'clock.*

(5) **Para** means *for* or *considering that*, when comparing a person, object, or situation with others of its kind:

Para **un extranjero,** habla bien el inglés.	*For a foreigner, he speaks English well.*
Se ve joven *para* **su edad.**	*He looks young considering his age.*

(6) **Para** is used with the reflexive pronoun **sí** to mean *to* or *for himself (herself, themselves)*:

Abrió el libro y leyó **para sí.**	*He opened the book and read to himself.*
Lo quieren todo **para sí.**	*They want everything for themselves.*

b. Por

(1) **Por** introduces the agent (doer) in a passive construction:

México fue conquistado *por* **Pizarro.**	*Mexico was conquered by Pizarro.*

(2) **Por** expresses "in exchange for":

Pagó un dólar *por* **el cuchillo.**	*He paid a dollar for the knife.*
Quiero cambiar este coche *por* **uno más grande.**	*I want to exchange this car for a larger one.*

(3) **Por** means *along, through, by,* and *around* after a verb of motion:

Entraron *por* el jardín.	*They came in through the garden.*
Me pasearé *por* esa calle.	*I will stroll along that street.*
Pasó *por* aquí a las tres.	*He came by here at three o'clock.*

(4) **Por** expresses the duration of an action:

Fue a Europa *por* **dos meses.**	*He went to Europe for two months.*
Tendrá que guardar cama *por* **una semana.**	*He will have to stay in bed for a week.*

(5) **Por** expresses indefinite time:

Por **la tarde** juego tenis.	*In the afternoon I play tennis.*
¿Quieres venir mañana *por* **la mañana?**	*Do you want to come tomorrow morning?*

(6) **Por** means *for the sake of* and *on behalf of:*

Habló *por* **la clase.**	*He spoke on behalf of the class.*
Lo hago todo *por* **ti.**	*I do it all for your sake.*

(7) **Por** (meaning *for*) is used after the verbs **enviar, ir, luchar, mandar, preguntar, regresar, venir,** and **volver:**

Fue (Envió, Preguntó), *por* el médico.	*He went (sent, asked) for the doctor.*
Vino (Volvió, Regresó) *por* sus libros.	*He came (came back, returned) for his books.*

(8) **Por** expresses a reason or motive:

Trabaja *por* **necesidad.**	*He works out of necessity.*
Lo castigaron *por* **llegar tarde.**	*He was punished for arriving late.*

(9) **Por** expresses manner or means:

Lo pidieron *por* **escrito.**	*They asked for it in writing.*
Lo enviaron *por* **avión.**	*It was sent by plane.*

(10) **Por** is equivalent to English *per* or *by the:*

Gana cien dólares *por* **semana.**	*He earns a hundred dollars per (a) week.*
Es más barato *por* **docena.**	*It is cheaper by the dozen.*

(11) **Por** expresses opinion or estimation and is equivalent to English *for* or *as:*

Se le conocía *por Pepe Navaja.*	*He was known as Pepe Navaja.*
Se hace pasar *por médico.*	*He passes himself off as a doctor.*
Me tomaron *por natural* **del país.**	*They took me for a native.*

(12) **Por** is used in certain adverbial expressions:

> **por eso** *that's why, therefore, and so*
> **por lo común** ⎫
> **por lo general** ⎬ *generally*
> **por lo visto** *apparently*
> **por supuesto (que)** *of course, naturally*

Hace calor y humedad; **por eso** hay muchos insectos.	*It's hot and humid; that's why (and so) there are many insects.*
Por lo común llueve mucho en abril.	*Generally it rains a lot in April.*
Por lo visto todo está en orden.	*Apparently everything is in order.*
Por supuesto que vendrá hoy.	*Naturally he'll come today.*

NOTE:

1. **Por** or **para** are not used with the verbs **buscar** (*to look for, to seek*), **esperar** (*to wait for, to await*), and **pedir** (*to ask for, to request*). These verbs take a direct object in Spanish:

Buscaron un asiento.	*They looked for a seat.*
Esperó dos horas a su amiga.	*He waited two hours for his girlfriend.*
Quiero pedirle un favor.	*I want to ask a favor of you. (I want to ask you for a favor.)*

2. **En** is used instead of **por** to mean by a means of transportation for passengers:

Envió el paquete **por avión.**   He sent the package by plane.

But:

Viajé por Europa **en tren.**   I traveled through Europe by train.

Ejercicio N

Escriba los consejos que da la abuelita de Miguel:

EJEMPLO: Las naranjas son buenas __para__ la salud.

1. _____ iluminar la sala, hay que encender la luz.

2. Deben estudiar más _____ llegar a la universidad.

3. No dejen _____ mañana lo que puedan hacer hoy.

4. Deben tener una sonrisa _____ todo el mundo.

5. La leche es buena _____ los huesos.

6. Hay que poner los platos _____ sopa en la mesa primero.

7. Si hacen el trabajo ahora, _____ el fin de semana estarán libres.

8. _____ verme sólo tienen que llamarme.

9. _____ vieja, comprendo bien a los jóvenes.

10. En 1950 yo salí _____ España.

Ejercicio O

*Complete, con **por** o **para**, lo que el abuelo de Pepe le contó sobre sus viajes:*

En la época que fui a España _____ primera vez, se viajaba _____ barco.
                                       1   2

Estuvimos en el mar _____ seis días _____ una tempestad terrible. Recuerdo
                              3   4

que casi todos los pasajeros enviaron _____ el médico y éste, _____ ser tan
                                              5   6

dedicado a su trabajo, no durmió _____ tres días. _____ ser un viaje tan
                                         7   8

difícil, mis hermanos y yo nos divertimos mucho. Podíamos correr _____ todos los
                                                                          9

rincones del barco y parecía que teníamos el barco sólo _____ nosotros.
                                                                10

_____ comer, teníamos que ir al comedor. _____ mi mamá, esto no era fácil
        11   12

_____ tener que vestir a tres niños. _____ entrar en el comedor pasábamos
        13   14

_____ dos puertas grandísimas de vidrio. A mi hermanito Pablo le fascinaba poner las
15

manos _____ todo el vidrio. _____ más que tratara, mi mamá no podía
16   17

detenerlo.

Mi último viaje a España fue _____ avión. ¡Qué diferencia! Estuve en el avión sólo
18

_____ seis horas. Mi compañero de asiento era un joven español que estudiaba
19

_____ piloto. _____ ser español, hablaba bien el inglés. Caminé _____
20   21   22

el avión, pero no era tan largo ni tan interesante como cuando caminaba _____ el barco.
23

La comida fue servida _____ tres aeromozos agradables. Uno de ellos ha trabajado de
24

aeromozo _____ veinte años. Me dijo que sólo hace seis vuelos _____ mes y
25   26

_____ lo general descansa _____ unos cinco días entre los vuelos. El viajar
27   28

_____ avión es más rápido pero ¡cuánto daría yo _____ un viaje en barco!
29   30

Ejercicio P

Escriba las respuestas de Doris a estas preguntas que le hizo una amiga después de un viaje a España:

1.   ¿Cuántos días estuvieron Uds. en España?   (15)

   _____

2.   ¿Cuánto pagó Elena por la bolsa?   ($50)

   _____

3.   ¿Cómo mandaron Uds. las cartas desde España?   (avión)

   _____

4.   ¿Cuál es la mejor forma de viajar dentro del país?   (autobús)

   _____

5.   ¿Cuánto gastaste por día?   ($100)

   _____

6.   ¿Cuándo jugaban Uds. tenis?   (la tarde)

   _____

7.   ¿Cuántas horas remaron Uds. en el lago del Retiro?   (3)

   _____

8.   ¿Cómo entraron las moscas en el autobús?   (la ventana)

   _____

♦ MASTERY EXERCISES ♦

 **Q**

Ud. quiere trabajar de asistente social. Conteste las preguntas que le hacen en la entre-vista:

1. ¿Le gustaría a Ud. ayudar a las personas necesitadas?

_____

2. ¿Cómo podría Ud. ayudar a esas personas?

_____

3. ¿Ha hecho Ud. algo por los menos afortunados?

_____

4. ¿Suele Ud. burlarse de las personas que tienen menos que Ud.?

_____

5. ¿Tarda Ud. generalmente en hacer lo que le piden?

_____

6. Para ser justo, ¿qué haría Ud.?

_____

7. ¿Para qué profesión estudió Ud.?

_____

8. ¿Visitaría Ud. a las personas en sus casas?

_____

9. ¿Para qué?

_____

10. ¿Cuánto espera Ud. ganar por mes?

_____

Ejercicio R

Lea este cuento y subraye la preposición que debe usarse en cada caso:

El zapatero tropezó (con / en) el carnicero en la calle. Éste quería (a / —) saber cómo le iba en el
        1   **2**

negocio. El zapatero le dijo que (por / para) más que trataba, no podía (en / —) vender más de un
                                  3   **4**

par de zapatos (por / para) día. (A / Al) oír esto el carnicero se puso nervioso. Trató (de / en) darle
                 5   **6**   **7**

una respuesta pero (antes de / con) contestar, el zapatero le dijo: «(En vez de / después de)
                    8   **9**

comprar zapatos, la gente compra carne. Si nos hacemos socios, la gente no puede (a / —)
                                                                                      10

negarse (a / de) comprar zapatos también. (Por / Para) comenzar, vamos (a / en) regalar un par de
        11   12   13

zapatos (por / para) cada cincuenta dólares que compren de carne. Acabo (de / en) leer en una
        14   15

revista que un comerciante puede (— / de) manejar mejor sus fondos si tiene (a / —) un socio».
                                 16   17

El carnicero tardó mucho (en / a) contestar. Pensó: «¿Por qué insiste este señor (en / de) tratar
                        18   19

(de / a) arruinarme? Si le hago caso y convengo (en / con) juntarme con él, (por / para) la semana
20   21   22

que viene habré cesado (de / en) ganar dinero y vender carne». (Por / Para) no ser descortés le
                       23   24

preguntó al zapatero si él sabía (a / —) preparar la carne para los clientes. El zapatero, lleno de
                                 25

entusiasmo, le replicó (sin / de) vacilar: «No, pero tú puedes (a / —) enseñarme (a / de) ser un
                       26   27   28

carnicero próspero como tú». El carnicero suspiró y se dijo: « (Por / Para) ser un mal comer-
                                                              29

ciante, sabe (a / —) resolver sus problemas».
             30

Ejercicio S

Exprese en español lo que Pedro le contó al hijo de un socio hispanohablante:

1. My father agreed to meet with your father to discuss the matter at the end of the month.

   _____

   _____

2. We arrived at his office at about 8 o'clock.

   _____

3. We came on foot because your father had invited us to accompany him in his car.

   _____

   _____

4. We passed through many small towns at eighty kilometers per hour.

   _____

   _____

5. From time to time, I had dreamed of visiting your city.

   _____

   _____

6. My father forgot to bring some papers with him.

_____

7. He tried to call his secretary several times.

_____

8. As a matter of fact, we waited near a telephone booth for two hours.

_____

_____

9. His pride did not permit him to ask for a favor.

_____

_____

10. I looked at my father curiously.

_____

11. My father threatened to send me home.

_____

12. He refused to buy me ice cream.

_____

13. Your father drove without saying anything.

_____

14. When it stopped raining, we began to return home.

_____

_____

15. On passing through a town, my father remembered something.

_____

_____

16. Suddenly he began to whistle.

_____

17. He hurried to find another telephone.

_____

18. He said that he would teach me to be a good businessperson.

_____

_____

19. We happened to pass a telegraph office.

_____

20. He paid twenty dollars for the telegram.

_____

21. He succeeded in locating his secretary.

_____

22. She agreed to bring him the papers.

_____

23. While we waited, he insisted on buying us a wooden toy.

_____

_____

24. The secretary was able to meet us on time.

_____

25. After meeting with some people, we went to see the house your father had built.

_____

_____

PART

THREE

ADJECTIVES

ADVERBS

NUMBERS

Adjectives and Adverbs

1. Adjectives

a. Gender of adjectives

(1) Adjectives ending in **-o** form the feminine by changing **o** to **a**. Most adjectives ending in a consonant form the feminine by adding **a**:

pequeño, pequeña	*small, little*
feo, fea	*ugly*
seco, seca	*dry*
español, española	*Spanish*
francés, francesa	*French*
hablador, habladora	*talkative*
trabajador, trabajadora	*hard-working*

(2) Many adjectives have the same form for both the masculine and the feminine:

fácil, fácil	*easy*
popular, popular	*popular*
grande, grande	*large*
agradable, agradable	*pleasant*
agrícola, agrícola	*agricultural*

b. Plural of adjectives

The plural of adjectives is formed by:

(1) adding **s** when the singular form ends in a vowel:

secos, españolas, agradables

(2) adding **es** when the singular form ends in a consonant:

españoles, populares, fáciles.

NOTE:
1. Adjectives with singular forms ending in **-z** change **z** to **c** in the plural:

feliz, felices

2. Some adjectives add or drop an accent mark in order to keep the original stress:

joven, jóvenes	young
francés, francesa, franceses, francesas	French
inglés, inglesa, ingleses, inglesas	English
alemán, alemana, alemanes, alemanas	German
cortés, corteses	courteous, polite

Ejercicio A

La señorita Ruiz habla de sus alumnos. Escriba cómo los describe, usando estos adjetivos:

inteligente	cortés	bondadoso	cómico
perezoso	puntual	juguetón	popular
diligente	cumplido	bonito	joven
trabajador	amable	hablador	dedicado

1. Los alumnos son _____

2. Las alumnas son _____

3. Todos los alumnos son _____

Ejercicio B

Rogelio y Anita preparan una lista de los adjetivos que usarían para describirse a sí mismos. Escriba la lista que prepara cada uno:

	ROGELIO	ANITA
1. joven		
2. español		
3. trabajador		
4. diligente		
5. encantador		
6. amable		
7. guapo		
8. cortés		
9. leal		
10. interesante		

C. Position of adjectives

(1) Descriptive adjectives normally follow the nouns they modify:

un libro *interesante*	*an interesting book*
la casa *blanca*	*the white house*

(2) Descriptive adjectives may stand before the noun to emphasize the quality of the adjective or its inherent characteristic:

Admiré los árboles, con sus **verdes hojas.**	*I admired the trees, with their green leaves.*
El invierno me trae **malos recuerdos.**	*Winter brings me bad memories.*

NOTE: Some adjectives have different meanings, depending on their position:

Wáshington fue un **gran** hombre.	*Washington was a great man.*

But:

Mi tío es un **hombre** *grande,* casi un gigante.	*My uncle is a big man, almost a giant.*

Common adjectives that may change their meaning with a change in position are:

	AFTER THE NOUN	BEFORE THE NOUN
antiguo, -a	*old (ancient)*	*old (former), old-time*
cierto, -a	*sure; true*	*a certain*
grande	*large, big*	*great*
mismo, -a	*him (her, it)-self*	*same*
nuevo, -a	*new*	*another, different*
pobre	*poor*	*unfortunate*
simple	*silly, simpleminded*	*simple, mere*

(3) Limiting adjectives (numbers, possessive and demonstrative adjectives, adjectives of quantity) usually precede the noun:

dos **plumas** *two pens*	*aquel* **hombre** *that man*
algún **día** *some day*	*tal* **cosa** *such a thing*
mis **primos** *my cousins*	*menos* **dinero** *less money*

Common adjectives of quantity are:

algunos (-as) *some*	**poco (-a, -os, -as)** *little, few*
cada *each, every*	**tanto (-a, -os, -as)** *so much, so many*
cuanto (-a, -os, -as) *as much*	**todo (-a, -os, -as)** *all, every*
más *more*	**unos (-as)** *some*
menos *less*	**unos (-as) cuantos (-as)** *a few*
ningunos (-as) *no, not any*	**varios (-as)** *several*
numerosos (-as) *numerous*	

Ejercicio C

Arturo acaba de llegar a la ciudad de México y no habla bien el español. Ayúdele a decir lo siguiente:

1. I'm looking for the old Hotel Majestic.

    _____

2. I need a large room with many big windows.

    _____

3. I intend to spend a few days here.

    _____

4. I am going to take several interesting tours.

    _____

5. This is my new camera.

    _____

6. My friends want many good pictures of the pyramids.

    _____

7. Numerous people have told me that this is a great city.

    _____

8. I was going to travel with various friends but these poor friends had to work.

    _____

Ejercicio D

A la mamá de Pablo siempre le gusta usar muchos adjetivos. Usando los adjetivos entre paréntesis, conteste las preguntas que le hace Pablo sobre una boda a la que ella asistió:

> EJEMPLO: ¿Cuántas **personas** había en la boda? (tanto)
> ¡Había **tantas personas** en la boda!

1. ¿Usó la novia el **vestido** de su abuela? (antiguo, blanco)

    _____

2. ¿Qué clase de **cena** sirvieron? (uno, delicioso)

    _____

3. ¿Con qué **amigos** se sentaron en la mesa? (uno, viejo, simpático)

    _____

4. ¿Había **orquesta** en la fiesta? (dos, animado)

    _____

5. ¿Qué **recuerdo** les dieron a los invitados? (barato, simple)

    _____

6. ¿Viste a tus **primos**? (amable, algunos)

_____

7. ¿Con cuántas **parejas** bailaste? (varios, encantador)

_____

8. ¿Cómo es el **carro** del novio? (nuevo, amarillo)

_____

9. ¿Cómo eran los **regalos** que recibieron? (caro, numeroso)

_____

10. ¿Acompañó una **cantante** a la orquesta? (antipático, cierto)

_____

Ejercicio E

Escriba las palabras que faltan en español en este cuento sobre los gatos de Tomás. Use el cuento en inglés de referencia:

Tomás tiene _____ .
                              1

_____ se llama Gatito y
              2

_____ se llama Botitas.
              3

_____ los cuida. Aunque
              4

_____ tiene _____ ,
          5   6

prefieren comer del _____ .
                                    7

Gatito es _____ pero es
                        8

_____ . Ayer Tomás les
              9

compró _____ . Botitas es
                      10

muy indiferente. Para ella _____
                                          11

es solamente _____ .
                          12

_____ Gatito y Botitas se
              13

enojaron y empezaron a pelear. Aunque los

dos tienen _____ , prefieren
                      14

jugar con _____ .
                      15

Thomas has two cats. One cat is called Gatito and the other cat Botitas. Thomas himself takes care of them. Although each cat has its own plate, they prefer to eat from the same plate. Gatito is a big cat, but he is a pleasant animal. Yesterday Thomas bought them a new toy. Botitas is very indifferent. To her this toy is just another toy. One day (A certain day), Gatitos and Botitas got angry and they began to fight. Although the two have many new toys, they prefer to play with their old toys. Poor Botitas! She has few old toys because her master gave these toys to a friend. Nevertheless, her favorite toy is a big red ball.

¡———————————————! Ella tiene
            16

——————————————— porque su amo
          17

regaló ——————————————— a un amigo.
        18

Sin embargo, ———————————————
           19

es ———————————————.
       20

d. Agreement of adjectives

(1) Adjectives agree in gender and number with the nouns they modify:

Juana es **aplicada.**	*Jane is studious.*
Mis hijos son **perezosos.**	*My children are lazy.*

(2) An adjective modifying two or more nouns of different gender is masculine plural:

La pluma y el lápiz son **rojos.**	*The pen and pencil are red.*

Ejercicio F

La señora Abanico describe las diferencias que existen entre sus dos hijos, Roberto y Sara. Use los adjetivos dados para expresar lo que ella dice:

alegre	diligente	gordo	perezoso
ambicioso	divertido	independiente	quieto
cómico	encantador	melancólico	responsable
delgado	generoso	pensativo	serio

EJEMPLO: Roberto es cómico y Sara es seria.

1. _____
2. _____
3. _____
4. _____
5. _____
6. _____
7. _____
8. _____
9. _____
10. _____

Ejercicio G

David tiene que conseguir los muebles para el escenario de una obra que va a presentarse en su escuela. Escriba lo que él debe obtener:

EJEMPLO: un sofá / verde   **un sofá verde**

1. dos butacas / viejo   _____

2. una mesa / redondo   _____

3. un ramo de flores / fresco   _____

4. dos cortinas / azul   _____

5. unos libros / antiguo   _____

6. una alfombra / grueso   _____

7. una caja / fuerte   _____

8. tres lámparas / pequeño   _____

9. una almohada / blando   _____

10. una silla / cómodo   _____

Ejercicio H

Complete el cuento que escribió Ricardo, usando la forma apropiada de los adjetivos dados. Los adjetivos no están colocados en el orden que deben usarse:

Era una noche _____ y _____ de invierno.
                    1   2

En la casa todo el mundo se sentía _____ por el calor que
                                          3

salía de la chimenea _____ en la cual ardían
                             4

_____ leños _____ .
        5   6

El abuelo _____ estaba sentado en una silla
                 7

_____ . En sus manos _____ y
        8   9

_____ tenía un libro. Desde el piso, sus nietos miraban sus
        10

ojos _____ que reflejaban la luz _____ y
            11   12

_____ del fuego. Les leía un cuento de las hazañas
        13

_____ y _____ de un héroe
        14   15

_____ . Mientras afuera soplaba un viento
        16

_____ , los niños escuchaban con interés
        17

_____ las palabras _____ del anciano. Él
        18   19

1–6
largo
tranquilo
uno
grande
oscuro
antiguo

7–13
rojo
cómodo
fuerte
simpático
claro
arrugado
caliente

14–19
famoso
intenso
fabuloso
señorial
amenazador
emocionante

_____ se divertía leyendo _____ historias
     20   21

_____ a sus nietos _____ . Poco a poco
     22   23

los ojos _____ de los niños empezaban a cerrarse. Una
               24

sonrisa _____ llenaba la cara _____ del
         25   26

abuelo.

20–26
este
querido
arrugado
brillante
mismo
interesante
satisfecho

e. Shortened forms of adjectives

(1) The following adjectives drop the final **-o** when used before a masculine singular noun:

uno one, a, an	*un* **libro** one (a) book
bueno good	*un buen* **caballo** a good horse
malo bad	*un mal* **año** a bad year
primero first	**el** *primer* **día** the first day
tercero third	**el** *tercer* **piso** the third floor
alguno some	*algún* **día** some day
ninguno no, not any	*ningún* **objeto** no object

NOTE:

1. The adjectives **alguno** and **ninguno** require an accent mark when the **-o** is dropped: **algún, ningún.**

2. If a preposition comes between the adjective and the noun, the full form of the adjective is used:

uno de **los tres**	one of the three
el *tercero del* **grupo**	the third (one) of the group

(2) **Santo** becomes **San** before the masculine name of a saint, except with names beginning with **To-** or **Do-**:

San **Juan**	Saint John
San **Francisco**	Saint Francis

But:

Santo **Tomás**	Saint Thomas
Santo **Domingo**	Saint Dominic

(3) **Grande** becomes **gran** when used before a singular noun of either gender:

un *gran* **poeta** **una** *gran* **poetisa**	a great poet

But:

un edificio **grande**	a large building
una casa **grande**	a large house

(4) **Ciento** becomes **cien** before a noun of either gender and before the numbers **mil** and **millones.** This short form is not used with multiples of **ciento** (**doscientos, trescientos,** etc.) or in combination with any other number (**ciento diez**):

cien **libros (muchachas)**	one (a) hundred books (girls)
cien mil **años**	one (a) hundred thousand years
cien millones **de dólares**	one (a) hundred million dollars

But:

cuatrocientos coches	*four hundred cars*
cuatrocientas personas	*four hundred people*
ciento veinte y siete sillas	*one (a) hundred twenty-seven chairs*

 **Ejercicio I**

Gabriel y unos amigos hablan de las ciudades de los Estados Unidos que emplean la palabra Santo como parte de su nombre. Escriba los nombres de las ciudades que usan San, Santo o Santa:

EJEMPLO: **Santa Fe**

San	Santo	Santa
_____	_____	_____
_____	_____	_____
_____	_____	_____
_____	_____	_____

Ejercicio J

Complete, con la forma apropiada del adjetivo, esta carta que Gloria le escribió a una amiga:

Querida Rosita:

Saludos desde Puerto Rico, donde estoy pasando unas _____ vacaciones.
                                                    1 (bueno)

Estamos alojados en un hotel _____ cerca de la playa, que se llama el
                              2 (grande)

_____ Hotel. Ayer fue la _____ vez que no llovió por la tarde.
   3 (grande)   **4** (primero)

Tengo _____ noticias: el _____ día del viaje conocí a un chico
        5 (bueno)   **6** (tercero)

muy simpático. Lo conocí durante mi _____ excursión al Viejo
                                     7 (tercero)

_____ Juan. Entré en _____ tiendas porque buscaba
   8 (Santo)   **9** (alguno)

_____ regalo para mi hermano. Encontré _____ cinturón de
   10 (uno)   **11** (uno)

cuero, pero costaba _____ dólares. No pude comprarlo, pero
                     12 (ciento)

_____ día espero tener bastante dinero para hacerlo.
   13 (alguno)

Roberto es de la República Dominicana. Él vive en la capital, _____ Domingo.
14 (Santo)

_____ de sus amigos conoce nuestra _____ ciudad de
15 (Ninguno)   16 (grande)

_____ Francisco. A Roberto le gusta viajar. Él tiene parientes que viven en
17 (Santo)

_____ Fe, Nuevo México.
18 (Santo)

Roberto es de ascendencia española. Hace más de _____ años su familia llegó de
19 (ciento)

España. Su abuelo era el alcalde de una ciudad _____ y todos decían que era un
20 (grande)

_____ hombre.
21 (grande)

Nuestra habitación da al mar y estamos en el _____ piso. En el hotel hay
22 (tercero)

_____ cincuenta habitaciones. Tengo que levantarme temprano porque hay
23 (ciento)

menos de _____ sillas en la playa, y trato de ser la _____
24 (ciento)   25 (primero)

persona que llega a la playa para conseguir un _____ lugar cerca de las palmas.
26 (bueno)

Pasado mañana será un _____ día porque terminan estos _____
27 (malo)   28 (bueno)

días de descanso. Saldremos en el _____ avión de la mañana.
29 (primero)

Tu _____ amiga,
30 (bueno)

Gloria

2. Adverbs

a. Adverbs are formed regularly by adding **-mente** to the feminine singular form of an adjective:

un hombre **rico**	*a rich man*
un hombre **ric*amente*** vestido	*a richly dressed man*
Es un trabajador **hábil.**	*He is a skillful worker.*
Lo fabricó **hábil*mente*.**	*He made it skillfully.*

NOTE: In a series of two or more adverbs, the ending **-mente** is added only to the last one:

Pablo escribió **clara, rápida** y **fácil*mente*.**	*Frank wrote clearly, rapidly, and easily.*

b. Adverbial phrases may be formed by using **con** + noun:

La joven cantaba **con alegría** (*alegremente*).	*The girl sang with happiness (happily).*
Saludó a la dama **con cortesía** (*cortésmente*).	*He greeted the lady with courtesy (courteously).*

c. The words **más, menos, poco, mucho, mejor, peor**, and **demasiado** may be used either as adjectives or adverbs:

<table>
<tr><td align="center">ADJECTIVE</td><td align="center">ADVERB</td></tr>
<tr><td>

Pablo tiene ***menos* dinero** que yo.
Paul has less money than I do.
La Sra. Álvarez compra ***demasiadas* joyas.**
Mrs. Alvarez buys too many jewels.
Mi **voz es *peor*** que la tuya.
My voice is worse than yours.

</td><td>

Él es ***más* pobre.**
He is poorer.
Ella es ***demasiado* rica.**
She is too rich.
Tú **cantas *mejor*** que yo.
You sing better than I.

</td></tr>
</table>

NOTE: As adjectives, **mucho, poco**, and **demasiado** vary in gender and number; as adverbs, they do not change.

d. Some adverbs have forms distinct from the adjective forms:

bueno *good*   **bien** *well*
malo *bad*   **mal** *badly*

Arturo es un ***buen* músico** y **toca *bien***
  el piano.
Juan es un **muchacho *malo*; trata *mal***
  a su hermana.

Arthur is a good musician and plays
  the piano well.
John is a bad boy; he treats his sister
  badly.

Ejercicio K

Escriba el adverbio que describe lo que Jorge dice de sus amigos después de un viaje:

EJEMPLO: Eduardo condujo _____.   (cuidadoso)
            Eduardo condujo **cuidadosamente.**

1. Héctor volvió al carro _____. (rápido)

2. Lorenzo pidió instrucciones _____. (cortés)

3. Gabriel hizo todo _____. (lento)

4. Eduardo condujo _____. (hábil)

5. Los jóvenes hablaban _____. (alegre)

Ejercicio L

Conteste las preguntas que le hace un alumno nuevo de la escuela:

1. ¿Quién juega tenis mejor, tú o tu mejor amigo?

    _____

2. ¿Cuál de tus profesores enseña mejor?

    _____

3. ¿Estudias mucho antes de un examen?

    _____

4. ¿Es demasiado difícil el español?

    _____

5. ¿Por qué dices que este año es peor que el año pasado?

    _____

6. ¿Cómo te sientes hoy, bien o mal?

    _____

7. ¿Trabajas mucho o poco todos los días?

    _____

8. ¿Cuánto gastas cuando sales con tus amigos, mucho, poco o demasiado?

    _____

Ejercicio M

Lea este relato de Juan. Luego, hágalo más vivo, completando los espacios con adverbios. Forme los adverbios de los adjetivos dados. Use cada adjetivo solamente una vez:

claro	dulce	rápido
completo	fácil	repentino
cortés	inmediato	total
desafortunado	malo	violento
desgraciado	profundo	

Mi hermana mayor siempre trata _____ a las personas que le hablan por

                                                         1

teléfono. Ayer por la tarde ella dormía la siesta y estaba _____ dormida

                                                                2

cuando _____ sonó _____ el teléfono. Lo

              3   4

contestó _____, pero no reconoció _____ la

                  5   6

voz de la persona que llamaba. No contestó _____ porque no se había

                                      7

despertado _____. Era un extranjero que hablaba español

                    8

_____ y _____. Mi hermana no comprendió

         9   10

_____ lo que quería. _____, la persona llamaba

       11   12

de un teléfono público. Cuando mi hermana comenzó a comprenderlo, _____

                                                        13

se le acabó el dinero y se cortó la comunicación _____.

                                              14

Ejercicio N

Escriba lo que varios amigos dijeron después de salir de una ópera. Use la expresión adverbial con + sustantivo:

EJEMPLO: El público aplaudió _____**con energía**_____ .
(energetically)

1.   Los cantantes cantaron _____ .
(happily)

2.   Los músicos tocaron _____ .
(enthusiastically)

3.   El conductor dirigió la orquesta _____ .
(skillfully)

4.   Los bailarines bailaron _____ .
(gracefully)

5.   El cantante principal cantó _____ .
(clearly)

6.   Los aficionados aplaudieron _____ .
(frequently)

e. Some adverbial expressions are formed by combining prepositions with other words:

(1) preposition + noun:

a fondo *thoroughly*
a la derecha (izquierda) *to the right (left)*
a la vez *at the same time*
al cabo (de) *at the end of*
al fin *finally*
de día *by day*
de memoria *by heart*
de noche *at night*
de repente *suddenly*
de rodillas *kneeling*
de veras *really, truly*
en seguida *immediately, at once*
por desgracia *unfortunately*
sin duda *undoubtedly*
sin embargo *nevertheless*

Pablo estudió el capítulo *a fondo*.	Paul studied the chapter thoroughly.
Ahora tienes que doblar *a la derecha*.	Now you must turn to the right.
Puede escribir y hablar *a la vez*.	He can write and speak at the same time.
Regresó *al cabo de* dos meses.	He returned at the end of two months.
***Al fin* consintió en que su hijo saliera.**	Finally, he consented to his son's going out.
***De día* trabajo, *de noche* duermo.**	By day I work, at night I sleep.
Se sabe la poesía *de memoria*.	He knows the poem by heart.
***De repente* se oyó un gran ruido.**	Suddenly a loud noise was heard.
Pidió perdón *de rodillas*.	Kneeling, he asked for forgiveness.
¿La quieres *de veras*?	Do you really love her?
Se marchó *en seguida*.	He left immediately (at once).

Por desgracia, mi reloj está roto.   *Unfortunately my watch is broken.*
Sin duda el clima es mejor allá.   *Undoubtedly the climate is better there.*

Estaba enfermo y, *sin embargo*, se   *He was sick; nevertheless, he got up.*
levantó.

(2) preposition + adjective:

a menudo *often*
a solas *alone*
de nuevo *again*
de pronto *suddenly*
en general, por lo general *generally*
por consiguiente *consequently*
por supuesto *of course*

Se encuentran en la calle *a menudo*.   *They often meet in the street.*
Al día siguiente tuvieron *de nuevo* un   *On the following day, they had a test*
examen.   *again.*
De pronto decidió irse.   *Suddenly he decided to leave.*
En general las joyas son muy caras.   *Generally jewels are very expensive.*
Estaba hablando y, *por consiguiente*,   *He was speaking, and, consequently,*
no oyó la pregunta del profesor.   *he didn't hear the teacher's question.*

Por supuesto, es necesario trabajar.   *Of course, it's necessary to work.*

(3) preposition + adverb:

al (a lo) menos *at least*
en cuanto *as soon as*

Esa señora tendrá *a lo menos* ochenta   *That lady must be at least eighty years*
años.   *old.*
Llámame *en cuanto* llegues.   *Call me as soon as you arrive.*

(4) preposition + verb form:

al amanecer *at daybreak*
al anochecer *at nightfall*
al parecer *apparently, seemingly*
por lo visto *apparently, evidently*
por escrito *in writing*

Se puso en marcha *al amanecer* y   *He got started at daybreak and*
regresó *al anochecer*.   *returned at nightfall.*
Al parecer no piensa regresar.   *Apparently he doesn't intend to come back.*

Por lo visto ya se acostó.   *Evidently he already went to bed.*
Preparen los ejercicios *por escrito*.   *Prepare the exercises in writing.*

(5) preposition + adjective + noun:

de buena gana *willingly*
de mala gana *unwillingly*
en ninguna parte *not anywhere, nowhere*
en otra parte *elsewhere*
en todas partes *everywhere*

Me prestó el libro *de buena gana*, pero el dinero *de mala gana*.	He lent me the book willingly, but the money unwillingly.
No encontró la revista que quería *en ninguna parte*.	He didn't find the magazine he wanted anywhere.
La lluvia cayó *en otra parte*.	The rain fell elsewhere.
Había papeles regados *en todas partes*.	There were papers scattered everywhere.

Escriba una frase para describir cada dibujo, empleando una expresión adverbial con preposición:

EJEMPLO:

Arturo se puso **de rodillas** y le pidió a María que se casara con él.

1.

Gabriel _____

_____

2.

El Sr. Vargas _____

_____

3.

Julia _____

_____

4.

Ernesto y Carlos _____

_____

5.

6.

_____

_____

_____

_____

Ejercicio P

Eduardo y Edgardo son unos gemelos traviesos. Complete, con la expresión necesaria, lo que dice su madre de ellos:

¡No puedo creer lo que hacen mis hijos! Se despiertan _____ y

1 (at daybreak)

_____ comienzan a hacer travesuras. Siempre hablan

2 (at once)

_____ y discuten muy _____. Ayer salieron

3 (at the same time)   **4 (often)**

corriendo _____ y no pude encontrarlos _____.

5 (suddenly)   **6 (nowhere)**

Los busqué _____, pero no di con ellos. En la esquina, una vecina me

7 (everywhere)

dijo que los había visto doblar _____, pero otra dijo que los vio ir

8 (to the right)

_____. _____ regresaron a casa

9 (to the left)   **10 (Finally)**

_____ _____. _____

11 (again)   **12 (at nightfall)**   **13 (Apparently)**

habían estado jugando en la casa de un amigo a donde van _____.

14 (often)

f. The following are common adverbial expressions formed with two or more words:

ahora mismo *right now*
a pesar de *in spite of*
cada vez más *more and more*
cuanto antes *as soon as possible*
de cuando en cuando *from time to time*
(abrir) de par en par *(to open) wide*
dentro de poco *shortly*
fuera de sí *beside oneself*

hoy (en) día *nowadays*
hoy mismo *this very day*
junto a *beside*
mientras tanto *meanwhile*
rara vez *seldom*
sano y salvo *safe and sound*
tal vez *perhaps*
tan pronto como *as soon as*
ya no *no longer*

¡Acuéstate *ahora mismo*!	Go to bed right now!
A pesar de la tormenta, aterrizamos sanos y salvos.	In spite of the storm, we landed safe and sound.
El español se pone *cada vez más* difícil.	Spanish is becoming more and more difficult.
Escribe esa carta *cuanto antes*.	Write that letter as soon as possible.
Lo veo en la escuela *de cuando en cuando*.	I see him at school from time to time.
Las puertas estaban abiertas *de par en par*.	The doors were wide open.
Dentro de poco llegarán las vacaciones.	Vacation time will come shortly.
Al ver el error, se puso *fuera de sí*.	On seeing the mistake, he was beside himself.
Hoy día todo cuesta caro.	Nowadays everything is expensive.
Tienes que entregarme los documentos *hoy mismo*.	You have to hand me the documents this very day.
Estaba sentado *junto a* la ventana.	He was sitting beside the window.
Los niños jugaban; *mientras tanto*, su madre preparaba la cena.	The children were playing; meanwhile, their mother prepared supper.
Me escribe muy *rara vez*.	He writes to me very seldom.
Tal vez regrese mañana.	Perhaps he'll return tomorrow.
Tan pronto como recibió el dinero, se lo gastó.	As soon as he received the money, he spent it.
Ya no asiste a los conciertos de los domingos.	He no longer attends Sunday's concerts.

Ejercicio Q

Conteste en español y en frases completas, las preguntas que le hace un amigo sobre sus clases:

1. ¿Qué materias te parecen más útiles hoy en día?

   _____

2. Si pudieras cambiar tus clases ahora mismo, ¿cuáles cambiarías?

   _____

3. ¿Te gustan las matemáticas, a pesar de que son difíciles?

   _____

4. ¿Cuál de tus clases se pone cada vez más difícil?

   _____

5. Si fueras el (la) profesor(a), ¿cuándo darías exámenes, rara vez, de cuando en cuando o a menudo?

   _____

6. ¿Cómo prefieres contestar preguntas en clase, oralmente o por escrito?

   _____

7. ¿Prefieres estudiar de día o de noche?

   _____

8.   ¿Haces tus tareas de buena gana o de mala gana?

_____

Ejercicio R

La mamá de Sarita le dejó un recado por escrito antes de salir a trabajar. Complete ese recado con la expresión correcta:

¡_____ vas a limpiar tu cuarto! Se ve _____
      1 (This very day)   **2** (more and more)

desorganizado. Debes hacerlo _____ te levantes. Abres las ventanas
                                  3 (as soon as)

_____ para airearlo y _____ recoges la ropa que
      4 (wide)   **5** (meanwhile)

_____ esté limpia. _____ es necesario hacer
      6 (no longer)   **7** (From time to time)

ciertas cosas _____ que no te gusten. _____
               8 (in spite of)   **9** (Shortly)

comienzan las clases de nuevo y sería bueno que comenzaras a prepararte

_____ . Salgo _____ de la casa y cuando
    10 (as soon as possible)   **11** (right now)

regrese _____ salgamos de compras.
          12 (perhaps)

♦ MASTERY EXERCISES ♦

Ejercicio S

Conteste las preguntas que encontró Adolfo en un artículo del periódico sobre la personalidad:

1.   ¿Tiene Ud. pocos o muchos amigos?

_____

2.   ¿Toma Ud. baños fríos o calientes?

_____

3.   ¿Saluda Ud. cortésmente a sus conocidos?

_____

4.   ¿Es Ud. más o menos perezoso (-a) que sus hermanos?

_____

5.   ¿Le gusta a Ud. la compañía de gente culta?

_____

6. ¿Hace Ud. ejercicios físicos todos los días?

_____

7. ¿Prefiere Ud. una almohada dura o blanda?

_____

8. ¿Escucha Ud. atentamente a las otras personas?

_____

9. ¿Está Ud. orgulloso (-a) de todo lo que Ud. hace?

_____

10. ¿Hace Ud. las cosas lenta o rápidamente?

_____

11. ¿Se enoja Ud. fácil o difícilmente?

_____

12. ¿Trata Ud. a sus padres cariñosamente?

_____

13. ¿Trabaja Ud. bien o mal en compañía de sus amigos?

_____

14. ¿Tiene Ud. un gran sueño para el futuro?

_____

15. ¿Daría Ud. su último dólar a un pobre hombre?

_____

Ejercicio T

Complete el diálogo entre Rosa y Roberto, dos gemelos que hablan del futuro. Use el diálogo en inglés como guía:

Rosa: _____1_____ día quiero casarme con

_____2_____ señor _____3_____ .

Some day I want to marry a rich man.

Roberto: Yo pienso casarme con _____4_____

mujer _____5_____ pero hay

_____6_____ cosas que quiero hacer

_____7_____ .

I intend to marry a beautiful woman, but there are other things I want to do first.

Rosa: Tú sabes _____ que al
              8

graduarme de la universidad quiero tener

_____ carrera _____ .
       9   10

Voy a ser _____ diseñadora
                  11

_____ .
       12

You know well that after
graduating from college I want
to have a good career. I want
to be a famous designer.

Roberto: A mí me gusta la vida _____ .
                                      13

Quiero hacer _____ viaje
                    14

_____ al Amazonas y encontrar
       15

lo que _____ hombre haya
              16

descubierto todavía.

I like the adventurous life. I
want to make a long trip to the
Amazon and find what no man
has discovered yet.

Rosa: _____ sueños suenan
             17

_____ .
       18

Our dreams sound good.

Roberto: _____ personas nunca realizan
                19

sus sueños. Tenemos que trabajar

_____ para realizarlos.
       20

Some people never realize
their dreams. We have to work
a lot to realize them.

Rosa: _____ tú y yo nos ayudamos.
             21

Luckily you and I help each
other.

Roberto: Sí, tú y yo nos ayudamos el _____
                                            22

por _____ .
          23

Yes, we help each other one
hundred percent.

Rosa: Mi _____ hermano, te deseo
               24

_____ éxito en todo lo que
       25

hagas.

My dear brother, I wish you
great success in everything
you do.

Roberto: Gracias. Igualmente.

Thank you and the same to
you.

◆ **Ejercicio U**

*Está lloviendo. Carlos y un amigo juegan un juego que consiste en completar una
situación con un comentario apropiado. Escriba en español los comentarios para cada
situación, usando la expresión dada:*

1. Arturo y sus amigos fueron a la playa. En menos de una hora están en casa. Arturo le dice a su mamá:

   (por desgracia) _____

2. El niño tiene todos sus juguetes en el piso de la sala. Su mamá espera visita y le dice:

   (ahora mismo) _____

3. Hoy es el quince de abril. Mi cumpleaños es el veinte y nueve de abril. Anita dice para sí:

   (cuanto antes) _____

   _____

4. Rafael vio un accidente en la calle. Había sólo unos cuantos heridos:

   (sano y salvo) _____

   _____

5. Los actores trabajaron bien en la obra, pero la escenografía no era muy buena. Roberto comentó:

   (a pesar de) _____

   _____

6. El señor Cabral encontró una cartera en la calle con doscientos dólares. Quiere devolverla a su dueño:

   (por supuesto) _____

   _____

7. Ud. no está bien y tiene mucha calentura.

   (en seguida) _____

8. La señora Ramírez contesta el teléfono. Preguntan por alguien que no vive allí. Despés hay otra llamada y piden lo mismo. Ella dice para sí:

   (sin duda — de nuevo) _____

   _____

9. Jaime encontró un libro en el que pronostican que el hombre viajará al espacio. Piensa para sí:

   (hoy día) _____

10. María está muy cansada. Todavía tiene una lista larga de cosas para hacer. Piensa para sí:

    (cada vez más) _____

Ejercicio V

Exprese en español lo que Lola cuenta de su amiga Gloria:

1. Gloria is at the airport right now.

   _____

2. Finally, she won a round-trip ticket to San Juan.

   _____

3. She was informed about the trip in writing.

   _____

4. I was next to her when she opened the letter.

_____

5. Of course, she started to make plans immediately.

_____

_____

6. She had to leave without delay.

_____

7. There is no doubt that since she was born there she wanted to visit Puerto Rico again.

_____

_____

8. Nowadays it is a short trip, but apparently it is still expensive.

_____

_____

9. Gloria seldom pays attention to contests.

_____

10. Generally she asks for my advice.

_____

11. However, I didn't know about this contest. Unfortunately, I am not lucky.

_____

_____

12. She promised to write to me as soon as she arrives in San Juan.

_____

_____

13. Her plane will be taking off shortly. I hope she'll arrive safe and sound.

_____

_____

14. Meanwhile, I will be working here.

_____

15. At least one of us will be having fun.

_____

Ejercicio W

Ud. está en una ferretería hispana cuando entra un cliente que no habla español. Exprese en español lo que él quiere decirle al dependiente:

1. This electrical machine does not work in this dry climate.

_____

2. It is worse than the one you sold me last week.

_____

3. In our modern civilization, these new products should work perfectly.

_____

_____

4. The first time I tried to use it I was very frightened.

_____

_____

5. It made strange noises, and long flames came out of it.

_____

_____

6. I don't care if you have sold more than one hundred of them.

_____

_____

7. They charge a lot for these new inventions.

_____

8. A good worker should never blame his bad tools.

_____

_____

9. I don't want another machine.

_____

10. It's a good thing that I used it in the open air.

_____

11. My brother-in-law has the same machine and it works well for him.

_____

_____

12. I followed the instructions carefully.

_____

13. Certain companies manufacture tools of low quality.

_____

_____

14. The new machine costs one hundred and fifteen dollars!

_____

_____

15. Thanks a lot. Fortunately, my brother-in-law will lend me his old machine.

_____

_____

Comparison

1. Comparison of Inequality

a. Adjectives are compared as follows:

POSITIVE	**bello(-a, -os, -as)**	*beautiful*
COMPARATIVE	*más (menos)* **bello(-a, -os, -as)**	*more (less) beautiful*
SUPERLATIVE	**el (la, los, las)** ... *más (menos)* **bello(-a, -os, -as)**	*the most (least) beautiful*

Este monumento es *bello.*
Ése es *más (menos) bello que* **éste.**

Aquél es *el monumento más (menos) bello del* **país.**
Aquella flor es *la más (menos) bella del* **jardín.**
Es *la mejor (peor) actriz del* **mundo.**

This monument is beautiful.
That one is more (less) beautiful than this one.

That one is the most (least) beautiful monument in the country.
That flower is the most (least) beautiful (one) in the garden.
She is the best (worst) actress in the world.

NOTE:

1. In the superlative, the noun stands between the article (**el, la, los, las**) and the adjective:

   Sirven **la comida más rica** de la ciudad.

   They serve the most delicious meal in town.

2. After the superlative, **de** means *in.*

Ejercicio A

Durante una excursión por la ciudad de Madrid, Xavier hace muchas comparaciones. Escriba las comparaciones que hace, usando más *o* menos *por turnos en cada oración:*

EJEMPLO: Esta iglesia / alto / la otra
Esta iglesia **es más alta que** la otra.

1. esta estatua / antiguo / las otras

2. este edificio / alto / el otro

_____

3. aquel museo / tener / pinturas / éste

_____

4. ese barrio / interesante / éste

_____

5. estas tiendas / caro / las otras

_____

6. este puente / largo / aquél

_____

7. esta puerta / ancho / ésa

_____

_____

Ejercicio B

Imagínese que alguien le ha hecho preguntas sobre los miembros de su familia. Escriba quién es el (la) más (menos)...de su familia:

EJEMPLO: tranquilo
Mi mamá es la más tranquila de la familia.

1. paciente

_____

2. bondadoso

_____

3. nervioso

_____

4. alegre

_____

5. divertido

_____

6. triste

_____

7. generoso

_____

8. amable

_____

9. ambicioso

_____

10. indeciso

_____

Ejercicio C

La señora Espejuelas compara a sus alumnos. Escriba lo que dice de ellos. Use más *o* menos *por turnos en cada oración:*

EJEMPLO: Roberto es diligente. (Carmen)
Carmen es menos diligente que Roberto.

1. Luz es estudiosa. (Ramón)

_____

2. Carlos es hablador. (Héctor)

_____

3. Esteban es inteligente. (Ana)

_____

4. Beto es independiente. (Clara)

_____

5. Estela es nerviosa. (Beatriz)

_____

6. Jorge es atlético. (Víctor)

_____

7. María es seria. (Cristina)

_____

b. The comparative forms of **bueno, malo, grande,** and **pequeño** are irregular.

POSITIVE	COMPARATIVE	SUPERLATIVE
bueno(-a, -os, -as) *good*	**mejor(es)** *better*	**el (la) mejor** **los (las) mejores** *the best*
malo(-a, -os, -as) *bad*	**peor(es)** *worse*	**el (la) peor** **los (las) peores** *the worst*

POSITIVE	COMPARATIVE	SUPERLATIVE
grande(s) *great, big*	**mayor(es)** *greater; older*	**el (la) mayor** **los (las) mayores** *the greatest; the oldest*
	más grande(s) *larger*	**el (la) más grande** **los (las) más grandes** *the largest*
	menos grande(s) *less large*	**el (la) menos grande** **los (las) menos grandes** *the least large*
pequeño(-a, -os, -as) *small*	**menor(es)** *minor, lesser; younger*	**el (la) menor** **los (las) menores** *the least; the youngest*
	más pequeño(-a, -os, -as) *smaller*	**el (la) más pequeño(-a)** **los (las) más pequeños(-as)** *the smallest*
	menos pequeño(-a, -os, -as) *less small*	**el (la) menos pequeño(-a)** **los (las) menos pequeños(-as)** *the least small*

NOTE:

1. **Mejor** and **peor** generally precede the noun. **Mayor** and **menor** generally follow the noun:

mi *mejor* amigo	my best friend
la **hermana** *mayor*	the older (oldest) sister

2. The regular and irregular comparative forms of **grande** and **pequeño** have different meanings. **Más grande** and **más pequeño** compare differences in size or height (physical meaning); **mayor** and **menor** compare differences in age or status (figurative meaning):

mi hermano *más pequeño*	my smaller (smallest) brother
mi hermano *menor*	my younger (youngest) brother
de *menor* importancia	of lesser importance

Ejercicio D

Un amigo quiere saber su opinión sobre varias cosas. Escriba cuál, en su opinión, es la mejor y la peor de las cosas indicadas:

EJEMPLO: película
 «Star Wars» es la mejor película. «The Sound of Music» es la peor.

1. disco

   _____

   _____

2. programa de televisión

   _____

   _____

3. beisbolista profesional

_____

_____

4. jugadora de tenis profesional

_____

_____

5. obra de teatro

_____

_____

6. equipo de fútbol

_____

_____

7. novela

_____

_____

8. grupo musical

_____

_____

9. comida

_____

_____

10. cantante

_____

_____

Ejercicio E

Su mamá comenta cómo Ud. y sus hermanos hacen los quehaceres de la casa. Escriba lo que ella dice, usando los comparativos por turnos:

EJEMPLO: lavar los platos
Gloria lava los platos mejor (peor) que yo.

1. planchar

_____

2. usar la aspiradora

_____

3. limpiar el sótano

_____

4. lavar el carro

_____

5. regar el jardín

_____

6. cocinar

_____

7. cuidar al bebé

_____

8. pintar

_____

Ejercicio F

Describa a un pariente mayor y a otro menor que Ud. Use los adjetivos **bueno, malo, grande** *y* **pequeño** *para describirlos:*

EJEMPLO: Arturito es mi hermano menor. Él es el menor de la familia y es el más pequeño también. Mis otros hermanos, Pedro y Linda, son mayores que él también. Él grita mejor que yo.

1. El pariente mayor

_____

_____

_____

_____

_____

2. El pariente menor

_____

_____

_____

_____

_____

C. Adverbs are compared as follows:

POSITIVE	**rápidamente**	*rapidly*
COMPARATIVE	**más (menos) rápidamente**	*more (less) rapidly*
SUPERLATIVE	**más (menos) rápidamente**	*more (less) rapidly than*

Este tren corre *rápidamente.* — *This train runs rapidly.*
Este tren corre *más rápidamente.* — *This train runs more rapidly.*
Este tren corre *más rápidamente que* los otros. — *This train runs more rapidly than the others.*

NOTE:
1. The superlative of adverbs is not distinguished from the comparative.
2. The adverbial superlative formed with the neuter article **lo** is an absolute superlative and not a superlative of comparison. It is usually followed by a phrase expressing possibility:

Ese tren corre **lo menos rápidamente posible.**	*That train runs the least rapidly possible.*
Ella llegó **lo más temprano posible.**	*She arrived the earliest possible.*

Ejercicio G

*La señora Valdés compara a los chicos y las chicas de su clase. Escriba lo que ella dijo de ellos al hablar con otra profesora de un proyecto que la clase llevó a cabo. Use **más o menos** + adverbio por turnos en cada frase:*

EJEMPLO: Los chicos trabajaron _____. (cuidadoso)
Los chicos trabajaron **menos cuidadosamente.**
Las chicas trabajaron **más cuidadosamente.**

1.   Los chicos decoraron el salón de clase _____. (rápido)

_____

2.   Las chicas cortaron los diseños _____. (hábil)

_____

3.   Los chicos crearon diseños _____. (fácil)

_____

4.   Las chicas hicieron preguntas _____. (frecuente)

_____

5.   Las chicas aceptaron los comentarios _____. (alegre)

_____

Ejercicio H

*Los jueces de un concurso literario hablan de los participantes en el concurso. Escriba lo que dijeron, usando **más o menos** (por turnos) + adverbio + **que** en cada frase:*

EJEMPLO: Lourdes / expresarse claramente / los demás
Lourdes **se expresó más claramente que** los demás.

1.   Raúl / contestar rápidamente / Lourdes

_____

2.   Elena / escribir el ensayo fácilmente / Octavio

_____

3.   Gabriel / hablar fuertemente / Raúl

_____

4. Clarita / portarse respetuosamente / los demás

_____

5. Sara / recitar hábilmente / los otros

_____

6. Octavio / pensar cuidadosamente / Clarita

_____

d. **Que** (*than*) is used after a comparative:

Es **más alta** *que* yo.   *She is taller than I.*
Tienen **menos dinero** *que* yo.   *They have less money than I.*

De (*than*) replaces **que** before a number if the sentence is affirmative. If the sentence is negative, **que** is used:

Ganó **más (menos)** *de* ocho dólares.   *He earned more (less) than eight dollars.*

But:

No ganó **más** *que* ocho dólares.   *He earned only eight dollars. (He didn't earn more than eight dollars.)*

If the second part of the comparison is a clause with a different verb, **de** is used together with a form of **el (la, los, las) que:**

Gasta más dinero *del que* **gana** su padre.   *He spends more money than his father earns.*
Leyó menos libros *de los que* le **recomendó** el profesor.   *He read fewer books than the professor recommended.*

NOTE: In each of these sentences, the nouns **dinero** and **libros** are the objects of both verbs: **gasta — dinero, gana — dinero** (implied); **leyó — libros, recomendó — libros** (implied). If the noun is not the object of both verbs, or if an adjective or adverb is being compared, **de lo que** is used:

Gasta más dinero *de lo que* **crees.**   *He spends more money than you think.*

Habla más rápidamente *de lo que* **escribe.**   *He speaks more rapidly than he writes.*

The word **dinero** in the first example is not the object of both verbs (**gasta — dinero,** but **crees — que gasta**). In the second example, the adverb **rápidamente** is being compared.

Ejercicio I

María visita a unos primos y cada noche escribe en su diario. Complete las frases con de, que, del que, de la que, de los que, de las que, o de lo que:

El pueblo donde estoy tiene menos _____ mil habitantes. Es más pequeño

1

_____ el parque central de mi ciudad. En esta aldea hay más guardias
       2

_____ necesitan. Ayer mi tía me llevó a una tertulia en la que hubo más
       3

_____ treinta personas. Esta tía es mayor _____ mi mamá.
       4   **5**

No recuerdo cuántos años hace que ella vive aquí, pero lleva menos _____
                                                             6

cinco años en esta aldea. Durante la tertulia, mi tía tradujo lo que las personas decían, pero ellas

hablaban más rápidamente _____ ella podía traducir. Sirvieron café y unas
                                          7

galletitas, pero era menos _____ yo hubiera podido comer. Tenía más hambre
                                        8

_____ una persona que no hubiera comido en veinte y cuatro horas. Mi prima
       9

Adela come más _____ nadie pero no pesa más _____
                     10   **11**

cincuenta kilos.

Cuando fui a la tienda, compré más tarjetas _____ podré usar. ¡Ojalá tuviera más
                                                    12

dinero _____ encuentro en el bolsillo! Así podría comprar otros regalos. Todavía
                 13

tengo menos regalos _____ voy a necesitar.
                     14

Me alegro de haber venido aquí. Estoy divirtiéndome más _____ me imaginaba.
                                                      15

2. Comparison of Equality

a. **tan** + adjective or adverb + **como** (*as . . . as*)

> Ella no es **tan pobre como** él.
> Mi coche corre **tan rápidamente como** el suyo.

> *She is not as poor as he.*
> *My car runs as fast as hers.*

Ejercicio J

Doña Alicia es la abuela de los gemelos Carlos y Martín. Para ella, los dos son iguales. Escriba lo que dice de ellos:

> EJEMPLO: alto
> **Carlos es tan alto como Martín.**

1. bonito _____

2. serio _____

3. inteligente _____

4. vivo _____

5. alegre _____

6. risueño _____

7. cómico _____

Ejercicio K

Ahora escriba cómo los nietos de doña Alicia hacen varias cosas:

EJEMPLO: llorar fuertemente
Carlos llora tan fuertemente como Martín.

1. caminar rápidamente

_____

2. hablar cortésmente

_____

3. jugar hábilmente

_____

4. reírse alegremente

_____

5. comer lentamente

_____

b. (1) **tanto (-a, -os, -as)** + noun + **como** (*as much / as many…as*)

Esta vaca da **tanta leche como** ésa.	*This cow gives as much milk as that one.*
Recibió **tantos juguetes como** pidió.	*He received as many toys as he asked for.*

(2) **tanto (-a, -os, -as)** (pronoun) + **como** (*as much / as many…as*)

Leímos **tanto como** ellos.	*We read as much as they.*

Ejercicio L

Luisa cree que es necesario hacer tanto como sus amigas. Escriba lo que ella hizo:

EJEMPLO: gastar   **Ella gastó tanto como sus amigas.**

1. correr _____

2. comer _____

3. trabajar _____

4. dormir _____

5. estudiar _____

6. leer _____

7. comprar _____

8. hablar _____

9. jugar _____

10. descansar _____

Ejercicio M

Clara y Rocío viajan juntas, pero nunca están de acuerdo. Escriba lo que Rocío responde después de una excursión:

EJEMPLO: Clara: Había muchos americanos en la excursión. (alemanes)
Rocío: **No había tantos americanos como alemanes en la excursión.**

1. Clara: Había muchas rosas en el jardín del palacio. (claveles)

   Rocío: _____

2. Clara: Vendían unas banderas bonitas. (tarjetas)

   Rocío: _____

3. Clara: Visitamos muchos museos. (iglesias)

   Rocío: _____

4. Clara: Comimos muchas tapas. (galletas)

   Rocío: _____

5. Clara: Gastamos muchas pesetas. (dólares)

   Rocío: _____

6. Clara: Entramos en muchos almacenes. (librerías)

   Rocío: _____

7. Clara: Hizo mucho calor al mediodía. (a las dos)

   Rocío: _____

c. Expressions of comparison:

cuanto antes	
lo más pronto posible	*as soon as possible*
tan pronto como sea posible	

cuanto (-a, -os, -as) más (menos)..., tanto (-a, -os, -as) más (menos)...	*the more (less)...,*
cuanto (-a, -os, -as) más (menos)..., más (menos)...	*the more (less)...*

Venga a verme **lo más pronto posible.**   *Come to see me as soon as possible.*
Cuanto más habla, **(tanto) menos** escucho.   *The more he talks, the less I listen.*

NOTE: **Tanto** may be omitted in the expression **cuanto más (menos)..., tanto más (menos).**

Escriba lo que una maestra dice de sus estudiantes. Use **cuanto(-a, -os, -as) más (menos)...,**
tanto(-a, -os, -as) más (menos) *por turnos:*

EJEMPLO: estudiar / aprender
           Cuanto menos estudian, tanto menos aprenden.

1.   escuchar / saber

_____

2.   trabajar / ganar

_____

3.   dar / recibir

_____

4.   tratar / lograr

_____

5.   leer / aprender

_____

6.   viajar / conocer

_____

3. Absolute Superlative

a. To express an absolute superlative (when no comparison is involved), **-ísimo (-a, -os, -as)** is often added to the adjective. The meaning is the same as **muy** + adjective:

muy barato ⎫
baratísimo ⎬ *very cheap*

NOTE:
1. **Muchísimo** = *very much.*

2. Adjectives ending in a vowel drop that vowel before adding **-ísimo.**

3. Adjectives ending in **-co, -go,** or **-z** change **c** to **qu,** **g** to **gu,** and **z** to **c** before adding **-ísimo:**

fresco	**fresquísimo**
largo	**larguísimo**
feroz	**ferocísimo**

b. To form adverbs from adjectives in **-ísimo,** add **-mente** to the feminine form of the adjective: **riquísimamente, lentísimamente.**

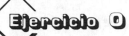

Ejercicio O

Alberto tiene la costumbre de exagerar mucho cuando habla de su vida. Usando -ísimo, escriba cómo describe las cosas:

EJEMPLO: Yo / vivir / casa / grande
Yo vivo en una casa grandísima.

1.   Yo / vivir / avenida / ancha

_____

2.   Yo / tener / perro / feroz

_____

3.   Mi coche / ser / lujoso

_____

4.   Mis primos / ser / ricos

_____

5.   Yo / dar / fiestas / elegantes

_____

6.   Mis padres / ser / generosos

_____

7.   La piscina de mi casa / ser / larga

_____

8.   Yo / viajar / mucho

_____

Ejercicio P

Conteste estas preguntas que le hace un amigo, usando la forma -ísimo:

1.   ¿Estudió Ud. mucho anoche?

_____

2.   ¿Es muy larga la distancia desde su casa a la escuela?

_____

3.   ¿Vuelve Ud. muy rápidamente a casa al salir de la escuela?

_____

4.   ¿Escucha Ud. muy atentamente en la clase?

_____

5. ¿Trabaja Ud. muy diligentemente todos los días?

_____

6. ¿Está Ud. muy cansado / cansada después de un día de trabajo?

_____

7. ¿Sabe Ud. cocinar muy ricamente?

_____

8. ¿Se divierte Ud. mucho con sus amigos?

_____

9. ¿Tiene Ud. un horario muy difícil?

_____

10. ¿Es Ud. muy animado / animada en una fiesta?

_____

♦ MASTERY EXERCISES ♦

Ejercicio Q

Lázaro es un joven colombiano que acaba de inscribirse en su escuela. Conteste las preguntas que él le hace sobre su pueblo:

1. ¿Cae tanta lluvia en agosto como en abril?

_____

2. ¿Hace tanto calor en la primavera como en el verano?

_____

3. ¿Hay tantos insectos en diciembre como en julio?

_____

4. ¿Es más bella la primavera que el invierno?

_____

5. ¿Hay tantas hojas en los árboles en enero como en julio?

_____

6. ¿Fue ayer un día más claro que hoy?

_____

7. ¿Es septiembre mejor que enero?

_____

8. ¿Son los jardines tan verdes en marzo como en agosto?

_____

9. ¿Es éste el árbol menos alto del jardín?

_____

10. ¿Cuándo hay menos nieve, en el otoño o en el invierno?

_____

Ejercicio R

Imagínese que Ud. trabaja en una agencia de publicidad donde preparan anuncios sobre ciertos productos para la televisión. Escriba un anuncio en el que Ud. describe las semejanzas y las diferencias entre un producto y otro y por qué su producto es mejor:

EJEMPLO: una radio portátil
Esta radio portátil es mejor que las otras. Ud. puede escuchar tantas emisoras como en las otras, pero el precio es más económico que el de las otras marcas.

_____

_____

_____

_____

_____

_____

_____

Ejercicio S

Elena acaba de encontrar trabajo y habla con una amiga que trabaja en la misma oficina. Exprese en español lo que la amiga le cuenta a Elena:

1. This businessman is very ambitious.

_____

2. You should work as diligently as possible.

_____

3. The more you work, the more you will earn.

_____

4. This office is as quiet as a library.

_____

5.   The manager permits you to make as many telephone calls as you wish.

   _____

   _____

6.   You are the youngest secretary in this office.

   _____

7.   The owner was the most respected man in the group.

   _____

   _____

8.   This manager is better than the previous one.

   _____

9.   I am usually very busy in the morning.

   _____

10.   There are as many letters on your desk as on mine.

   _____

11.   He gives you more work than you can finish in one day.

   _____

   _____

12.   In this office there are more than twenty-five employees.

   _____

   _____

13.   It is a very big company.

   _____

14.   The owner is crazier than you can imagine.

   _____

15.   This letter doesn't need more than one stamp.

   _____

   _____

16.   The owner is younger than his wife.

   _____

17.   You should answer this letter as soon as possible.

   _____

18.   The manager likes to write very long letters.

   _____

19.   Managers can be stricter than owners.

   _____

20.   Everyone here works as hard as everyone else.

   _____

Numbers; Times; Dates

1. Cardinal Numbers

0 **cero**	
1 **uno**	20 **veinte**
2 **dos**	21 **veintiuno, -a, veintiún**
3 **tres**	**(veinte y uno, -a, un)**
4 **cuatro**	22 **veintidós (veinte y dos)**
5 **cinco**	23 **veintitrés (veinte y tres)**
6 **seis**	24 **veinticuatro (veinte y cuatro)**
7 **siete**	25 **veinticinco (veinte y cinco)**
8 **ocho**	26 **veintiséis (veinte y seis)**
9 **nueve**	27 **veintisiete (veinte y siete)**
10 **diez**	28 **veintiocho (veinte y ocho)**
11 **once**	29 **veintinueve (veinte y nueve)**
12 **doce**	30 **treinta**
13 **trece**	31 **treinta y uno, -a, un**
14 **catorce**	40 **cuarenta**
15 **quince**	50 **cincuenta**
16 **dieciséis (diez y seis)**	60 **sesenta**
17 **diecisiete (diez y siete)**	70 **setenta'**
18 **dieciocho (diez y ocho)**	80 **ochenta**
19 **diecinueve (diez y nueve)**	90 **noventa**
100 **ciento (cien)**	400 **cuatrocientos, -as**
101 **ciento uno, -a, un**	500 *quinientos, -as*
115 **ciento quince**	600 **seiscientos, -as**
116 **ciento dieciséis**	700 *setecientos, -as*
200 **doscientos, -as**	800 **ochocientos, -as**
300 **trescientos, -as**	900 *novecientos, -as*
1.000 **mil**	1.000.000 **un millón (de)**
2.000 **dos mil**	2.000.000 **dos millones (de)**
100.000 **cien mil**	100.000.000 **cien millones (de)**

NOTE:

1. Spanish uses periods rather than commas to separate digits:

(Spanish) **1.376.426**   (English) *1,376,426*

2. In decimals, Spanish uses a comma where English uses a period:

(Spanish) $5,35   (English) $5.35
Cinco dólares (con) treinta y cinco   *Five dollars and thirty-five cents.*
(centavos).

3. The conjunction **y** is used only between tens and units, that is, in numbers 31 to 99:

43   **cuarenta y tres**   56   **cincuenta y seis**
74   **setenta y cuatro**   99   **noventa y nueve**

But:

109   **ciento nueve**   304   **trescientos cuatro**

4. The numbers 16 to 19 and 21 to 29 are usually written as one word. In such compounds, the numbers 16, 22, 23, and 26 have an accent on the last syllable:

17   **diecisiete**   16   **dieci*séis***
21   **veintiuno**   22   **veinti*dós***

5. The only numerals that vary with gender are **uno (una, un)** and the compounds of **ciento** (**doscientos, -as; trescientos, -as;** and so on):

un libro   *a (one) book*
una pluma   *a (one) pen*

trescien*tos* hombres   *three hundred men*
cuatrocien*tas* mujeres   *four hundred women*

veinte y *un* lápices   *twenty-one pencils*
cincuenta y *una* tarjetas   *fifty-one cards*

6. **Ciento** becomes **cien** before nouns and before the numbers **mil** and **millones.** In all other numbers, the full form **ciento** is used:

cien pesetas   *cien* mil soldados
cien buenos libros   *cien* millones de habitantes

But:

ciento veinte y cinco dólares

7. **Un** is not used before **ciento** or **mil. Un** is used before the noun **millón.** If another noun follows **millón, de** is placed between **millón** and the other noun:

ciento dos alumnos   *un* millón *de* dólares
mil doscientos años

Ejercicio A

Ud. está en un congreso que tiene lugar en un hotel de la ciudad de México. Ud. tiene la responsabilidad de contar el número de personas que hay en cada salón. Escriba los números que Ud. contó:

EJEMPLO: Salón Guanajuato   18 personas   **diez y ocho (dieciocho) personas**

1. Salón Acapulco   63 personas   _____

2. Salón Veracruz   71 personas   _____

3. Salón Guadalajara   15 personas   _____

   4. Salón Tampico   37 personas   _____

   5. Salón Oaxaca   126 personas   _____

   6. Salón Tijuana   54 personas   _____

   7. Salón Ixtapa   89 personas   _____

   8. Salón Querétaro   162 personas   _____

   9. Salón Torreón   41 personas   _____

  10. Salón Morelia   25 personas   _____

Ejercicio B

Ud. está trabajando en el departamento internacional de un banco y le toca escribir la cantidad de los giros en letras. Escriba estos números:

1. 568 pesetas _____

2. 1.381 pesetas _____

3. 2.010 dólares _____

4. 30.432 sucres _____

5. 891 bolívares _____

6. 5.755,86 dólares _____

7. 12.967 pesetas _____

8. 184 pesos _____

9. 1.989 pesos _____

10. 1.750.322 dólares _____

Ejercicio C

Ud. piensa hacer un viaje a España. Antes de ir, Ud. va a la biblioteca para averiguar el número de habitantes de las ciudades que piensa visitar. ¿Cuántos habitantes tiene cada ciudad? Exprese los números en letras en español:

1. Madrid   3.890.320 _____

_____

2. Barcelona   1.809.722 _____

_____

3. Sevilla   611.374 _____

_____

4. Valencia   745.022 _____

_____

5. Málaga   430.008 _____

_____

Ejercicio D

Ud. lee una lista que tiene el número de estudiantes que hay en sus clases. ¿Cuántos estudiantes hay en cada clase? ¿Cuántos son chicos? ¿Cuántas son chicas? Escriba los números en letras en español:

CLASE	NÚMERO DE ALUMNOS	NÚMERO DE CHICOS	NÚMERO DE CHICAS
Álgebra	28	16	12
Inglés	34	21	13
Español	25	11	14
Biología	30	19	11
Historia	27	6	21
Coro	76	31	45
Arte	18	8	10
Educación Física	82	41	41

Ejercicio E

Ud. ha conocido a muchas personas en un congreso. Antes de terminar el congreso, Ud. pide el número de teléfono de varias personas de los Estados Unidos. Escriba los números de teléfono en español:

EJEMPLO: Luz Armendáriz   212 – 375 – 2669

dos doce – tres setenta y cinco – veinte y seis sesenta y nueve

1.   Arturo López   609-832-5508

2.   Sarita Claveles   202-541-8297

3.   Gilberto Robles   305-422-1746

4.   Gabriela Coles   513-668-7033

5.   Javier Muñiz   815-342-4351

_____

6.   Blanca Flores   914-282-6625

_____

7.   Sergio Bulnes   717-951-1965

_____

Ejercicio F

Conteste estas preguntas en español. Escriba los números en letras:

1.   ¿Cuántos habitantes hay en la ciudad en que Ud. vive?

_____

2.   ¿Cuántos alumnos hay en su escuela? ¿Cuántos chicos? ¿Cuántas chicas?

_____

_____

3.   ¿Cuánto cuesta el automóvil que más le gusta a Ud.?

_____

4.   ¿Cuánto pagó Ud. por los zapatos que lleva ahora?

_____

5.   ¿Cuánto quiere Ud. ganar al año cuando empiece a trabajar?

_____

6.   ¿Cuál es su número de teléfono?

_____

2. Arithmetic Expressions

The following expressions are used in arithmetic problems in Spanish:

y _plus_ (+)
    Cuatro **y** nueve **son** trece.

menos _minus_ (−)
    Veinte **menos** once **son** nueve.

por (_multiplied_) _by,_ "_times_" (×)
    Ocho **por** siete **son** cincuenta y seis.

dividido por _divided by_ (÷)
    Ciento cuarenta y cuatro **dividido por** doce **son** doce.

son _equals_ (=)

Ejercicio G

Usted va a trabajar en una tienda durante el verano. Antes de darle el trabajo, el patrón quiere saber si Ud. puede expresar estos números en español. Escriba lo siguiente en letras en español:

1. $414 - 363 = 51$ _____

   _____

2. $336 \times 12 = 4032$ _____

   _____

3. $254 + 587 = 841$ _____

   _____

4. $911 - 276 = 635$ _____

   _____

5. $31,217 \div 31 = 1007$ _____

   _____

6. $419 + 716 = 1135$ _____

   _____

7. $1818 \div 18 = 101$ _____

   _____

8. $345 + 577 = 922$ _____

   _____

9. $864 \div 16 = 54$ _____

   _____

10. $990 \div 9 = 110$ _____

    _____

11. $93 \times 71 = 6603$ _____

    _____

12. $119 \times 17 = 2023$ _____

    _____

3. Ordinal Numbers

1st	primero, -a (primer)	6th	sexto, -a
2nd	segundo, -a	7th	séptimo, -a
3rd	tercero, -a (tercer)	8th	octavo, -a
4th	cuarto, -a	9th	noveno, -a
5th	quinto, -a	10th	décimo, -a

Ordinal numbers are used only through tenth; thereafter, cardinal numbers are used:

la **tercera** fila	*the third row*
la **Quinta** Avenida	*Fifth Avenue*
Carlos **Quinto**	*Charles V*

But:

el siglo **diez y nueve**	*the 19th century*
la página (número) **doce**	*page 12*

NOTE:

1. A cardinal number used in place of an ordinal is always masculine, since **número** is understood.

2. The ordinals **primero** and **tercero** drop the final **-o** before a masculine singular noun:

el *primer* **día**
el *tercer* **edificio**

But:

la **primera** visita
el siglo **tercero**

3. Ordinal numbers are often printed as 1°, 1er (**primero, primer**); 2° (**segundo**); 5^a (**quinta**); 10^a (**décima**), and so on.

Ejercicio H

Usted está hablando con unos amigos y discuten el número de veces que han hecho varias cosas. Indique el número de veces que Ud. ha hecho las actividades indicadas:

EJEMPLO: visitar el museo de arte / 2
Es la segunda vez que visito el museo de arte.

1. montar a caballo / 2

   _____

2. hacer un viaje en avión / 5

   _____

3. ver esta película / 3

   _____

4. ir a acampar / 6

   _____

5. regresar a esta tienda / 4

   _____

6. marcar su número de teléfono / 9

   _____

7. conocer a los padres de su amigo / 1

_____

8. comer en un restaurante español / 8

_____

9. repetir la respuesta / 10

_____

10. ir a esquiar / 7

_____

Ejercicio 1

Usted va de compras a un almacén y consulta el directorio de la tienda para saber en qué piso venden las cosas que quiere comprar. Escriba los pisos a que Ud. debe ir para comprar lo que tiene en su lista:

Artículos para Caballeros:	2	Juguetes	10
trajes, sombreros, abrigos		Libros	5
Artículos para Caballeros:	1	Loza — Cristalería — Plata	9
camisas, ropa interior, corbatas		Mantelería — Ropa de	6
		Cama	
Artículos para casa:	7	Películas	1
cortinas, lámparas, alfombras		Restaurantes — Café	1
		— Patio	8
Boletos de Teatro	1	Salón de Belleza	11
		Sombreros — Damas	3
Cámaras	5	Telas	7
Carteras para Damas	1	Maletas	5
Centro Musical — Discos,	3	Vestuario — Damas	2, 3, 4
Grabadoras,		Vestuario — Niños	4
Radio, Televisión			
Cosméticos	1	Zapatos — Caballeros	2
Cuarto para Caballeros	4-7	Zapatos — Damas	6
Cuarto para Damas	6, 8	Zapatos — Niños	4
Guantes — Damas	1		
Impermeables, Paraguas	1		

¿En qué piso venden . . . ?

EJEMPLO: un sombrero para hombre _____ **el segundo piso** _____

1. platos _____

2. zapatos para niño _____

3. una grabadora _____

4. una lámpara _____

5. una novela _____

6. un juguete _____

7. refrescos _____

8. guantes para mujer _____

9. toallas _____

10. maletas _____

4. Fractions

½	**medio(-a), la mitad de**	(the/one) half
⅓	**un tercio, la tercera parte de**	(the/one) third
¼	**un cuarto, la cuarta parte de**	(the/one) fourth, quarter
⅔	**dos tercios, las dos terceras partes de**	(the) two thirds
¾	**tres cuartos, las tres cuartas partes de**	(the) three fourths, quarters
⅘	**cuatro quintos, las cuatro quintas partes de**	(the) four fifths
¹⁄₁₀	**un décimo, la décima parte de**	(the/one) tenth

NOTE:

1. Except for **medio** and **tercio**, noun fractions are formed with ordinal numbers through tenth. Thereafter, the ending **-avo** is usually added to the cardinal number:

   ¹⁄₁₂ **un doceavo, la doceava parte de**   (the/one) twelfth

2. Fractions are masculine nouns:

   3⅓ **tres y un tercio**   three and one third

   When the fraction precedes the thing divided, it may be used with the feminine noun **parte,** unless a unit of measure is expressed:

   una tercera parte (un tercio) del libro   a third of the book

   But:

   un tercio de libra   a third of a pound

3. The adjective **medio(-a)** means *half*, while the noun **la mitad** means *half of*:

   media **docena de huevos**   half a dozen eggs
   la mitad **de la clase**   half of the class

5. Multiples

Multiple numerals are used in the same manner as their English equivalents:

una vez	once		**simple**	single, simple
dos veces	twice		**doble**	double
tres veces	three times		**triple**	triple

Lo llamé **dos veces**.	*I called him up twice.*
Vino a visitarme **una vez**.	*He came to visit me once.*
Comí **el doble** de lo que comiste tú.	*I ate twice as much as you.*

NOTE:

1. Numeral adverbs expressing the number of times of an occurrence are formed by a cardinal number and the feminine noun **vez** (*a time*):

He visto la película **cuatro veces**.	*I have seen the film four times.*

2. Multiples like **doble, triple** may be either adjectives or nouns:

Es una máquina de *doble* acción.	*It's a double action machine.*
Este cuadro vale hoy **el doble**.	*This painting is worth twice as much today.*

Ejercicio J

Exprese en letras los números indicados en español:

1. la 5ª columna _____

2. la Avenida 8ª _____

3. el 9º día _____

4. Alfonso XIII _____

5. el 4º párrafo _____

6. el siglo XX _____

7. la 3ª fila _____

8. la 7ª serie _____

9. ⅓ de kilo _____

10. el 10º aniversario _____

11. el 2º edificio _____

12. el 3ᵉʳ capítulo _____

13. ⅖ _____

14. el tranvía 43 _____

15. ½ mes _____

16. de 1ª calidad _____

17. Carlos V _____

18. el 1ᵉʳ Congreso Panamericano _____

19. el 6º renglón _____

20. el 3ᵉʳ grado _____

6. Time

¿Qué hora es?	What time is it?
Es la una.	It is one o'clock.
Son las dos (**tres, cuatro,** etc.).	It is two (three, four, etc.) o'clock.
Son las diez y veinte.	It is 10:20 (twenty after ten).
Son las ocho y cuarto (quince).	It is 8:15 (a quarter past eight).
Son las seis y media (treinta).	It is 6:30 (half past six).
Son las doce menos veinte (dos, cuarto, etc.).	It is 11:40 (11:58, 11:45, etc.).
¿A qué hora salió Ud.?	At what time did you leave?
a(l) mediodía	at noon
a (la) medianoche	at midnight
a eso de las siete	at about seven o'clock
Dio la una (Dieron las dos).	It struck one (It struck two).

NOTE:

1. **Es** is equivalent to *it is* for one o'clock, **son** for the other hours; **a** expresses *at*.

2. The article **la** (for **la hora**) is always used with one o'clock; **las** (for **las horas**) is used with the other hours.

3. *After* or *past* is expressed by **y**; *to* or *of* by **menos.** After "half past," time may be expressed by the following hour minus (**menos**) the minutes or by the expression **faltar** + minutes + **para** + following hour.

Son las tres *y* **veinte y cinco.**	It is 3:25.
Es la una *menos* **diez.** (*Faltan* **diez** *para* **la una)**	It is 12:50 (ten minutes to one).

It is not uncommon to hear 12:50 expressed numerically: **Son las doce y cincuenta.**

4. **Media,** an adjective, agrees with **hora; cuarto,** a noun, does not vary.

5. The expressions **de la madrugada** and **de la mañana** correspond to English A.M. (morning). The former refers to the hours before daylight, the latter to the daylight hours. **De la tarde** (*afternoon*) and **de la noche** (*evening*) correspond to P.M. **En punto** means *sharp*.

a las tres *de la madrugada*	at 3 A.M.
a las ocho y media *de la mañana*	at 8:30 A.M.
a las cuatro *de la tarde*	at 4 P.M.
Eran las nueve *en punto de la noche.*	It was 9 P.M. sharp.

Ejercicio K

Ud. le enseña a un primo a decir la hora en español. Exprese las horas indicadas en los relojes:

1.

_____

2.

_____

3.

_____

4.

_____

5.

_____

6.

_____

7.

_____

8.

_____

9.

_____

10.

_____

11.

_____

12.

_____

13.

_____

14.

_____

15.

_____

16.

_____

17.

_____

19.

_____

18.

_____

20.

_____

Ejercicio L

Ud. tiene la costumbre de hacer ciertas cosas a la misma hora todos los días. Escriba la hora a la que Ud. suele hacer las cosas indicadas:

EJEMPLO: comer el almuerzo
Yo **como** el almuerzo **a las doce (a mediodía).**

1. despertarse para ir a la escuela

_____

2. mirar su programa favorito de televisión

_____

3. cenar con su familia

_____

4. ir a la clase de español

_____

5. acostarse todos los días

_____

6. llegar a la escuela

_____

7. preparar las tareas

_____

8. hablar por teléfono con un amigo

_____

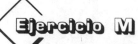

Ejercicio M

Lea estos problemas y conteste las preguntas:

1. Ud. tiene que estar en la escuela a las siete y media todos los días. El viaje a la escuela en bicicleta dura veinte y ocho minutos. ¿A qué hora debe Ud. salir de su casa?

   _____

2. Su clase de matemáticas dura cuarenta y dos minutos. Comienza a las nueve y doce. ¿A qué hora termina?

   _____

3. Ud. estudia durante una hora y media para un examen. Cuando cierra los libros, son las once menos quince. ¿A qué hora comenzó Ud. a estudiar?

   _____

4. A Ud. le gusta hablar por teléfono. Ud. llama a su amigo a las ocho menos cinco y cuelga el teléfono cuarenta minutos después. ¿Qué hora es?

   _____

5. El viaje de su casa a la playa dura ochenta y nueve minutos. Ud. sale a las siete y media de la mañana. ¿Qué hora es cuando Ud. llega a la playa?

   _____

Ejercicio N

Ud. lleva un diario donde escribe por las noches. Describa a qué hora hizo hoy diez actividades durante el día:

EJEMPLO: **Hoy me bañé a las siete de la mañana.**

1. _____
2. _____
3. _____
4. _____
5. _____
6. _____
7. _____
8. _____
9. _____
10. _____

7. Dates

¿Cuál es la fecha de hoy? }
¿A cuántos estamos hoy? }   *What is today's date?*

Es el primero de enero. }
Estamos a primero de enero. }   *It is January 1.*

Es el dos (tres, cuatro) de marzo.   *It is March 2 (3, 4).*
Es el diez de febrero de mil   *It is February 10, 1984.*
    novecientos ochenta y cuatro.
Salió **el tres de agosto.**   *He left on August 3.*

NOTE:

1. Cardinal numbers are used for all dates except **primero** (*first*).

2. The names of months are written with small letters in Spanish.

3. The years are expressed in thousands and hundreds, not in hundreds alone, as in English:
    1400 = **mil cuatrocientos.**

4. With dates, **el** corresponds to *on.*

    Te veré *el* lunes.   *I will see you on Monday.*

Ud. habla con un amigo de Venezuela sobre las fechas culturales importantes de los Estados Unidos. Escriba las fechas indicadas:

1. February 14 _____

2. July 4 _____

3. October 12 _____

4. December 25 _____

5. February 12 _____

6. January 1 _____

7. February 22 _____

8. November 11 _____

9. April 1 _____

10. October 31 _____

Ejercicio P

Escriba en español, expresando los números en letras:

1. May 2, 1808 _____

2. December 20, 1910 _____

3. October 12, 1492 _____

4. December 7, 1941 _____

5. March 31, 1519 _____

6. February 22, 1732 _____

7. April 1, 1649 _____

8. September 16, 1810 _____

9. November 1, 1396 _____

10. April 12, 1823 _____

Ejercicio Q

Ud. está preparando su «árbol genealógico». Escriba la fecha en que nacieron estas personas de su familia:

1. Su abuelo paterno _____

2. Su abuela paterna _____

3. Su abuelo materno _____

4. Su abuela materna _____

5. Su padre _____

6. Su madre _____

7. Un hermano (-a) mayor _____

8. Un hermano (-a) menor _____

9. Su fecha de nacimiento _____

10. Un tío o una tía _____

Ejercicio R

Ud. acaba de entablar amistad con un amigo por correspondencia de Chile. Escriba una carta en la que le cuenta lo siguiente en español:

1. el país en que Ud. vive

2. el número de estados que hay en su país

3. la fecha en que su país ganó la independencia

4. el nombre del primer presidente de su país

5. la población de su ciudad o estado (aproximadamente)

6. el número de la escuela de su barrio

7. el año de estudios en que Ud. está

8. su fecha de nacimiento

9. el horario de su escuela

10. la fecha de su último día de clases este año

_____

_____

_____

_____

_____

_____

_____

_____

_____

_____

_____

_____

Ejercicio S

Ud. habla con un estudiante de Colombia que visita su clase de español y hace muchas preguntas sobre su escuela y la vida de los jóvenes norteamericanos. Contéstele las preguntas que hace:

1. El colombiano: ¿Cuántos días a la semana vas a la escuela?

    Ud.:   _____

2. El colombiano: ¿Cuántos alumnos hay en tu año escolar?

    Ud.:   _____

3. El colombiano: ¿Cuántos minutos dura cada clase?

    Ud.:   _____

4. El colombiano: ¿A qué hora es tu primera clase?

    Ud.:   _____

5. El colombiano: ¿A qué distancia vives de la escuela?

    Ud.:   _____

6. El colombiano: ¿Cuánto tiempo necesitas para llegar a la escuela a tiempo?

    Ud.:   _____

7. El colombiano: ¿Por qué no hay clases el primer martes de noviembre?
    Ud.:   _____

8. El colombiano: ¿Cuántos años debes tener para poder votar?
    Ud.:   _____

9. El colombiano: ¿Cuánto vale un buen diccionario de inglés?
    Ud.:   _____

10. El colombiano: ¿En qué año piensas graduarte?
    Ud.:   _____

♦ MASTERY EXERCISES ♦

Ejercicio T

Ud. trabaja en la oficina de servicios sociales de su ciudad, y tiene que preparar las preguntas que hacen los trabajadores sociales a la gente de habla hispana. Pregunte lo siguiente en español:

1. The person's name and date of birth.

    _____

2. His/her social security number (número de seguro social)

    _____

3. The amount of money he/she earned last year.

    _____

4. The amount of money he/she has in the bank.

    _____

5. The amount of money he/she owes and to whom.

    _____

6. The amount of money he/she pays in rent each month/each year.

    _____

7. The year of the car he/she has.

    _____

8. The number of people that live in his/her home.

    _____

9. The number of times this person has come to this office.

    _____

10. The date he/she wants to receive the first check.

    _____

Ejercicio U

Ahora imagínese que Ud. es la persona que busca ayuda en la oficina de servicios sociales y conteste las preguntas que formuló en el Ejercicio T:

1. _____
_____

2. _____
_____

3. _____
_____

4. _____
_____

5. _____
_____

6. _____
_____

7. _____
_____

8. _____
_____

9. _____
_____

10. _____
_____

Ejercicio V

Imagínese que usted es locutor de una emisora y le toca dar las noticias en español. Exprese estas noticias en español:

1. There was a flood in Rosario, Argentina.

_____
_____

2. Twenty-one inches of rain fell in a period of thirty-one hours.

_____
_____

3.   The storm began at five o'clock in the morning of April 23rd and ended at noon on April 24th.

_____

_____

4.   Of the population of 750,455, more than 50,000 people find themselves without homes.

_____

_____

5.   Over thirty million tons of wheat and vegetables were lost.

_____

_____

6.   More than 30,000 heads of cattle (**ganado**) drowned.

_____

_____

7.   The government estimates the losses at more than fifty billion Argentine australes.

_____

_____

8.   More than 2,000 people from Buenos Aires have gone to Rosario to help.

_____

_____

9.   This is the first time Rosario has suffered a flood.

_____

10.   The audience can call 1-800-365-7803 to offer help to the people of Rosario.

_____

_____

PART

FOUR

OTHER STRUCTURES

Interrogatives; Exclamations

1. Interrogatives

a. Common interrogative expressions

PRONOUNS	ADVERBS
¿quién(es)? *who?* **¿prep. + quién(es)?** *...whom?* **¿qué?** *what?* **¿cuál(-es)?** *what, which (one [s])?* **¿cuánto(-a)?** *how much?* **¿cuántos(-as)?** *how many?*	**¿cómo?** *how?* **¿para qué?** *why? (for what purpose?)* **¿por qué?** *why? (for what reason?)* **¿dónde?** *where?* **¿cuándo?** *when?*

ADJECTIVES
¿qué? *what?, which?* **¿cuánto(-a)?** *how much?* **¿cuántos(-as)?** *how many?*

NOTE: In Spanish, questions have an inverted question mark (¿) at the beginning and a normal one (?) at the end.

b. ¿Qué? and ¿cuál?

The pronoun **¿qué?** asks about a description, definition, or explanation; **¿cuál?** asks about a choice or selection:

¿Qué es esto?	*What is this?*
¿Cuál de los dos desea Ud.?	*Which (one) of the two do you want?*
¿Cuáles son los meses del año?	*What are the months of the year?*

As an adjective **¿qué?** is generally used instead of **¿cuál(es)?**:

¿Qué libro desea Ud.?	*Which book do you want?*

c. ¿Por qué? and ¿para qué?

Both expressions are equivalent to English *why?* **¿Por qué?** asks about a reason. **¿Para qué?** asks about a purpose:

¿Por qué no viene Ud. con nosotros?
   —Porque no quiero.
	Why don't you come with us?
	   —Because I don't want to.

¿Para qué desea Ud. consultar ese libro? — Para ver las fotos.	*Why do you want to consult that book?* — To see the photos.

NOTE:

1. **¿Por qué?** is logically used in a question calling for a reply with **porque** (*because*); **¿para qué?** calls for a reply with **para**.

2. Interrogative words, whether in direct or indirect questions, have written accents. Indirect questions, however, do not have question marks.

  ¿Quién es? — No sé **quién** es.   *Who is he? — I don't know who he is.*

 **Ejercicio A**

Orlando no presta mucha atención cuando sus amigos hablan y no oye quién(es) hará(n) ciertas cosas. Escriba las preguntas que él hace para saber quién(es) hará(n) lo siguiente:

  EJEMPLO: Roberto va a acampar.
          ¿Quién va a acampar?

1. Mis hermanas van de compras.

   _____

2. Heriberto trabaja en el almacén.

   _____

3. Mi abuelo piensa viajar a México.

   _____

4. Nosotros compramos un televisor más grande.

   _____

5. Ustedes escribirán la carta esta noche.

   _____

6. Clara venderá su bicicleta.

   _____

Ejercicio B

Ricardo y su hermanito estudian en el mismo cuarto. El hermanito encuentra muchas palabras que no comprende. Según las respuestas de Ricardo, escriba las preguntas que hizo el hermanito:

  EJEMPLO: **¿Qué es la vida?**   La vida es un misterio.

1. _____   El acero es un metal.

2. _____   El béisbol es un deporte.

3. _____   La cabra es un animal.

4. _____   Un discípulo es un alumno.

5. _____   Un novelista es un escritor.

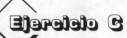

Ejercicio C

Estela lleva a su hermanita a la juguetería para ver qué juguete ella prefiere recibir de regalo de cumpleaños. Escriba las preguntas que hace Estela:

EJEMPLO: **¿Qué muñeca deseas?**
Deseo esta muñeca.

1. _____
Me gusta más la muñeca gorda.

2. _____
Prefiero el vestido amarillo.

3. _____
La segunda muñeca es la más bonita.

4. _____
Voy a buscar un sombrero de paja.

5. _____
También quiero una cuna para la muñeca.

Ejercicio D

Usted trabaja en una tienda de ropa, y atiende a una señora que quiere comprar un suéter. Escriba las preguntas que Ud. le hace para saber (1) lo que ella busca; (2) el color; (3) la talla; (4) el estilo; (5) el dinero que piensa gastar; y (6) el modo de pagar la cuenta:

1. _____
2. _____
3. _____
4. _____
5. _____
6. _____

Ejercicio E

Cuando Beto visitó a México, él quiso aprender lo máximo posible sobre el país. Según las respuestas dadas, escriba las preguntas que hizo Beto:

EJEMPLO: **¿Cuál es la comida de mediodía?**
La comida de mediodía es el almuerzo.

1. _____
El jarabe tapatío es un baile regional.

2. _____

Los mariachis son los músicos típicos.

3. _____

El Distrito Federal es la ciudad más grande del país.

4. _____

Acapulco es un puerto muy bonito.

5. _____

El peso es la moneda nacional.

6. _____

Los colores de la bandera son verde, blanco y colorado.

7. _____

El metro es un medio de transporte dentro de la capital.

Ejercicio F

Ud. tiene una entrevista con un escritor famoso que acaba de recibir un premio impor-tante e ilustre. Escriba las preguntas que Ud. le hará, usando ¿Qué?, ¿Quién(es)?, ¿Cuál?, ¿Dónde?, ¿Cuándo?, ¿Cuánto?, ¿Por qué?, ¿Para qué? y ¿Cómo?:

1. _____

2. _____

3. _____

4. _____

5. _____

6. _____

7. _____

8. _____

9. _____

Ejercicio G

La primera vez que Alberto sacó el carro de su papá, un policía lo detuvo. Escriba las preguntas que hizo el policía, según las respuestas de Alberto:

1. Policía: _____

Alberto: El carro es de mi papá.

2. Policía: _____

Alberto: Mi nombre es Alberto Zuloaga.

3. Policía: _____

    Alberto: Tengo diez y ocho años.

4. Policía: _____

    Alberto: Mi dirección es Avenida Reforma, 27.

5. Policía: _____

    Alberto: Estos jóvenes son mis amigos.

6. Policía: _____

    Alberto: Vamos al cine.

7. Policía: _____

    Alberto: Estacioné el carro aquí porque tenemos prisa.

8. Policía: _____

    Alberto: Recibí la licencia de conducir el mes pasado.

9. Policía: _____

    Alberto: Es la primera vez que me detiene un policía.

10. Policía: _____

    Alberto: Le diré a mi papá que aprendí una lección cara.

2. Exclamations

Exclamatory words, like interrogative words, have written accents. The most common exclamatory words are:

¡Qué...! *What...! What a...! How...!*
¡Cuánto(-a)...! *How much...!*
¡Cuántos(-as)...! *How many...!*
¡Cuán...! *How...!*

¡Qué día!	*What a day!*
¡Qué grande es!	*How large it is!*
¡Cuánto dinero tiene!	*How much money he has!*

NOTE:

1. Exclamatory sentences have an inverted exclamation mark (¡) at the beginning and a normal one (!) at the end.

2. If the noun is modified, the exclamation is made more intense by placing **tan** or **más** before the adjective:

    ¡Qué día *tan (más)* hermoso!   *What a beautiful day!*

3. Before an adjective or adverb, **¡qué...!** (*how...!*) may be replaced by **¡cuán...!** Cuán occurs mainly in literary style:

    ¡Qué fácilmente lo hace! }
    ¡Cuán fácilmente lo hace! }   *How easily he does it!*

Ejercicio H

Después de ver un ballet, unos amigos hablan de las bailarinas y de la producción. Escriba lo que dicen, usando ¡qué...!, ¡cuánto...! o ¡cuántos...!:

EJEMPLO: gracia / tener / ellas
¡Cuánta gracia tienen ellas!

1. bonitas / ser / ellas

   _____

2. energía / tener / ellas

   _____

3. fácilmente / saltar / ellas

   _____

4. vestuario / bonito

   _____

5. ligeramente / moverse / ellas

   _____

6. música / dulce

   _____

7. músicos / tener / la orquesta

   _____

8. estilo / clásico

   _____

Ejercicio I

David y un amigo acaban de ver una película. Su amigo está de acuerdo con los comentarios que David hace sobre la película. Escriba lo que el amigo exclama al oír los comentarios de David:

EJEMPLO: Era una película ridícula.
¡Qué película más (tan) ridícula!

1. Los actores trabajaron mal.

   _____

2. La acción era muy lenta.

   _____

3. El paisaje era muy bello.

   _____

4.   Mostraron muchas playas.

_____

5.   El lenguaje era muy infantil.

_____

Ejercicio J

Escriba lo que Ud. exclamaría al ver lo siguiente:

EJEMPLO:

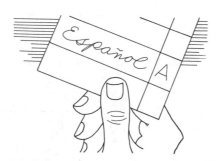

nota / buena
¡Qué nota más buena!

1.

bicicleta / nueva

_____

3.

cola / larga

_____

2.

león / feroz

_____

4.

autobús / lleno

_____

5.

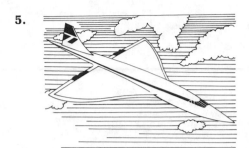

avión / veloz

_____

_____

8.

gente / en una caseta

_____

_____

0.

pájaros / en el cielo

_____

_____

9.

partido / emocionante

_____

_____

7.

tráfico / en el centro

_____

_____

10.

casas / misteriosas

_____

_____

♦ MASTERY EXERCISES ♦

Ejercicio K

Al salir de un examen, varios estudiantes hacen los comentarios siguientes. Subraye la forma admirativa correcta:

1. ¡(Qué, Cuánta) desgracia! Salí mal en esta prueba.
2. ¡(Cuál, Qué) examen más difícil!
3. ¡(Cuán, Qué) memoria! Tú supiste todas las fechas históricas.

4. ¡(Qué, Lo que) prueba más larga!
5. ¡(Qué, Cuán) maestro tan estricto!
6. ¡(Cuántas, Cuán) preguntas más complejas había!
7. ¡(Cómo, Qué) aplicados debemos ser!
8. ¡(Qué, Cómo) lentamente trabajé!
9. ¡(Cuántos, Cómo) detalles pidió!
10. ¡(Cuán, Qué) mala suerte tengo!

Ejercicio L

Beto llama por teléfono a su amigo Luis, pero no lo encuentra en casa. Complete esta llamada telefónica, formulando las preguntas que Beto le hizo a la persona que contestó el teléfono. Las palabras subrayadas son las respuestas a las preguntas.

1. Beto: _____

   José: Habla José.

2. Beto: _____

   José: Creo que Luis fue al teatro.

3. Beto: _____

   José: Salió a eso de las siete.

4. Beto: _____

   José: Creo que volverá tarde.

5. Beto: _____

   José: La función dura dos horas y media.

6. Beto: _____

   José: Yo le diré que lo llame mañana.

7. Beto: _____

   José: El número es el 525-67-85.

8. Beto: _____

   José: Le llamará antes de las nueve. Adiós.

Ejercicio M

Pilar va a hacer un viaje a España y quiere saber cómo decir varias cosas. Exprese en español lo que ella quiere saber:

1. What is the exchange rate?

   _____

2. How much does this belt cost?

   _____

3. Where can I buy soap?

   _____

4. Which bus do I take to the Prado Museum?

   _____

5. When do the stores open?

   _____

6. At what time is dinner served?

   _____

7. Who can help me with my suitcases?

   _____

8. Why do you want to see my passport? (for what purpose?)

   _____

9. How many cents are there in one peseta?

   _____

10. How much do the taxis charge?

    _____

11. Which are the best restaurants?

    _____

12. Where is there an inexpensive hotel?

    _____

13. What a delicious meal!

    _____

14. What a bargain!

    _____

15. What a beautiful house you have!

    _____

16. What a day! How much rain has fallen?

    _____

17. I don't know where the bus stop is.

    _____

18. Do you know who those people are?

    _____

19. How quickly the days pass!

    _____

20. It is so hot! When does the sun set?

    _____

21. How happy I am to be with you!

    _____

22. Who left this message for me?

_____

23. I don't know how to say "you're welcome" in Spanish.

_____

24. Which of these trains stops at the Plaza España?

_____

Ejercicio N

_Ud. tiene un amigo por correspondencia y los dos intercambian cintas. En la última cinta que Ud. recibió, no se grabó todo el mensaje de su amigo. Formule preguntas para hacerle a su amigo sobre lo que faltó en la cinta. El símbolo _____ indica que algo no se grabó._

EJEMPLO: No recibí tu última _____.
           ¿Qué no recibiste?

Hola amigo,

Recibí tu cinta y tenía toda intención de contestarla en seguida, pero debido a _____ no lo hice.
$\qquad$1

La semana pasada _____ me visitó. Nos divertimos mucho aunque no pudimos _____.
$\qquad$2 $\qquad$ 3

Pensamos ir allí cuando _____ otra vez.
4

El sábado fui al estadio para ver _____. El equipo _____ ganó el partido. Fue un partido muy
5 6

_____. Tuve suerte porque mi _____ me regaló el boleto.
7 8

Debes mandarme _____ cintas de las canciones más populares de tu país. _____ te mandan
9 10

muchos saludos.

Tu amigo,
Carlos

1. _____

2. _____

3. _____

4. _____

5. _____

6. _____

7. _____

8. _____

9. _____

10. _____

C•H•A•P•T•E•R

25

Possession

1. Expressing Possession

a. Possession is normally expressed in Spanish by **de** + the possessor:

el suéter *de* **Alberto**	*Albert's sweater*
el coche *de* **los señores Molina**	*the Molina's car*
los cuadernos *de* **los estudiantes**	*the students' notebooks*
los guantes *de* **mi hermana**	*my sister's gloves*

> NOTE: To avoid repetition in a sentence, the noun representing the thing possessed is replaced by its definite article + **de:**
>
> | | |
> |---|---|
> | Este sombrero y **el de** Pedro son nuevos. | *This hat and Peter's (that of Peter) are new.* |
> | Su opinión es diferente de **la de** su tío. | *His opinion differs from his uncle's (that of his uncle).* |

b. **¿De quién(es)?,** when followed by a form of **ser,** is equivalent to the English interrogative *whose?*:

¿De quién es el suéter verde?	*Whose green sweater is it?*
¿De quiénes es el coche nuevo?	*Whose new car is it?*
¿De quiénes son estos cuadernos?	*Whose notebooks are these?*
¿De quién son estos guantes?	*Whose gloves are these?*

c. The possessive relative **cuyo (-a, -os, -as)** is equivalent to the English relative *whose*. **Cuyo** agrees in gender and number with the person or thing possessed and not with the possessor. (See Chapter 19, page 263.)

El hombre *cuya* **casa** compré, vive ahora en Toledo.	*The man whose house I bought now lives in Toledo.*

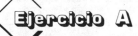

Ejercicio A

A Marta siempre le gusta prestar mucha atención a las acciones de sus amigos y hacerles preguntas. Según las respuestas, escriba las preguntas que Marta les hace a sus amigos:

> EJEMPLO: Llevo la chaqueta de Rosa.
> **¿De quién es la chaqueta que llevas?**

1. Estoy leyendo la revista de Susana.

2. La profesora de Alberto está ausente hoy.

_____

3. Eché al correo las cartas del señor Gómez.

_____

4. Lavamos el coche de los señores Laredo ayer.

_____

5. Celebramos el aniversario de los padres de Arturo anoche.

_____

6. Volvimos a la casa de Roberto y Juan después del partido.

_____

7. Voy a la fiesta de Lourdes esta noche.

_____

8. Estoy copiando la tarea de Pablo.

_____

Ejercicio B

Juanito y Carmen han encontrado una caja que contiene muchas cosas. Juanito quiere saber de quién son las cosas. Carmen adivina de quién son. Escriba (1) las preguntas que hace Juanito y (2) las respuestas que da Carmen, según los ejemplos:

EJEMPLOS: estos lápices / Alejandro
¿De quién son estos lápices?
Estos lápices son de Alejandro.

esta bandera verde, blanca y colorada / los mexicanos
¿De quiénes es esta bandera verde, blanca y colorada?
Esta bandera verde, blanca y colorada es de los mexicanos.

1. los guantes negros / la señora Álvarez

_____

_____

2. la mochila roja / un estudiante distraído

_____

_____

3. esta pluma de oro / el profesor

_____

_____

4. estos zapatos viejos / el presidente

_____

_____

5. las carteras nuevas / Alicia y Rocío

_____

_____

6. este cinturón grande / una persona gorda

_____

_____

7. las botas de vaquero / el chico guapo

_____

_____

8. esta regla rota / la maestra de geometría

_____

_____

9. estas camisas sucias / los jugadores

_____

_____

10. esta cámara cara / Enrique

_____

_____

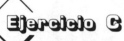

Ejercicio C

Imagínese que Ud. y un amigo están en una feria en la que todos los países hispano-americanos están representados. Conteste las preguntas que le hace su amigo:

EJEMPLO: ¿Prefieres la comida de Cuba o la de Puerto Rico?
            Prefiero la de Puerto Rico.

1. ¿Te gusta más el arte de Venezuela o el de Guatemala?

_____

2. ¿Prefieres las costumbres de Bolivia o las de Costa Rica?

_____

3. ¿Cuál te interesa más, la poesía de la Argentina o la de Chile?

_____

4. ¿Te gustaría visitar las playas de la República Dominicana o las de México?

_____

5. ¿Cuál te parece más fácil de comprender, el dinero del Perú o el de Panamá?

_____

6.   ¿Te interesa más la música de Puerto Rico o la de México?

_____

7.   ¿Quiénes te parecen mejores futbolistas, los jugadores de la Argentina o los de Chile?

_____

2. Possessive Adjectives

SHORT FORM	LONG FORM	MEANINGS
mi, mis	mío, -a, -os, -as	my
tu, tus	tuyo, -a, -os, -as	your (familiar singular)
su, sus	suyo, -a, -os, -as	your, his, her, its, their
	nuestro, -a, -os, -as	our
	vuestro, -a, -os, -as	your (familiar plural)

a. The short forms of possessive adjectives precede the noun:

mi abrigo	my overcoat
su reloj	his (your, her, its, their) watch
nuestra casa	our house
tus corbatas	your ties
nuestros sacos	our jackets

NOTE: Possessive adjectives agree in gender and number with the person or thing possessed, not with the possessor.

b. The long forms of possessive adjectives follow the noun:

¡Dios *mío*!	My God!
una camisa *mía*	a shirt of mine
un primo *tuyo*	a cousin of yours
unos amigos *nuestros*	some friends of ours

NOTE: To avoid ambiguity, **su (sus)** and **suyo (suya, suyos, suyas)** may be replaced by the article plus **de Ud. (Uds.), de él (ella),** or **de ellos (ellas):**

Estaba esperando a **su** tía.	He was waiting for his (her, your, their) aunt.
Estaba esperando a **la** tía **de ella.**	He was waiting for her aunt.

c. The definite article is used instead of the possessive adjective with parts of the body or wearing apparel when the possessor is clear:

Pablo abrió *el* paraguas.	Paul opened his umbrella.
El alumno levantó *la* mano.	The pupil raised his hand.
Juan se puso *los* zapatos.	John put on his shoes.

But:

Juan se puso *mis* zapatos.	John put on my shoes.

Ejercicio D

Ud. y un amigo preparan una lista de las cosas que Uds. y otros amigos van a llevar a una fiesta. Su amigo quiere saber de quién(es) son las cosas. Escriba las respuestas a sus preguntas:

EJEMPLO: ¿De quién es el tocadiscos que Raúl va a llevar a la fiesta?
Es su tocadiscos.

1.   ¿De quién es la grabadora que Gilberto va a llevar a la fiesta?

_____

2.   ¿De quiénes son los discos que tú y Rafael van a llevar a la fiesta?

_____

3.   ¿De quién son los adornos que María va a llevar a la fiesta?

_____

4.   ¿De quién son las cintas que Adela va a llevar a la fiesta?

_____

5.   ¿De quiénes es el juego electrónico que Pedro y Luis van a llevar a la fiesta?

_____

6.   ¿De quién es el juego nuevo que tú vas a llevar a la fiesta?

_____

7.   ¿Sabes de quién es la guitarra que yo voy a llevar a la fiesta?

_____

Ejercicio E

A Guillermo le gusta usar la ropa de otras personas. Habla con un amigo que le espera mientras se viste para salir juntos. Escriba los adjetivos posesivos necesarios en cada frase:

Roberto: Hoy llevas un suéter muy bonito. ¿Es _____ suéter nuevo?
1

Guillermo: No, no es _____ suéter nuevo. Es de _____ hermano Pablo.
2   3

Roberto: ¿Siempre usas _____ cosas?
4

Guillermo: Casi siempre. Me gustan _____ suéteres y _____ sombreros.
5   6

Roberto: Esta corbata es bonita. ¿Dónde la compraste?

Guillermo: No la compré. No es _____ corbata. Es de _____ hermano
7   8

Eduardo. Me gusta usar _____ corbatas.
9

Roberto: ¿Qué más usas de _____ hermanos?
                                      10

Guillermo: A veces me pongo _____ calcetines y _____ abrigo.
                                      11   12

Roberto: ¿No tienes _____ propio abrigo?
                              13

Guillermo: Sí, pero _____ abrigo no es tan caliente como los de _____
                            14   15

             hermanos.

Roberto: Bueno, vámonos. Ya es tarde.

Guillermo: Espera un momento. Tengo que buscar _____ cinturón negro.
                                                        16

Roberto: Creo que está allí en la mesa pero me parece que es de _____ papá.
                                                                          17

Guillermo: Sí, es de él, pero como él y yo lo usamos, decimos que es _____ cinturón.
                                                                              18

Roberto: Tienes suerte. _____ hermanos no me dejan usar nada.
                                  19

Guillermo: Estoy listo. Vamos, porque _____ amigas nos esperan.
                                              20

Ejercicio F

Esteban es un joven distraído. Lea la descripción de lo que pasa en su casa todas las mañanas. Luego escriba debajo de cada oración la forma larga del adjetivo posesivo subrayado:

EJEMPLO: Esto pasa en su casa cada mañana.
           la casa suya

1. Esteban nunca oye su reloj despertador.

    _____

2. Por eso su mamá tiene que despertarlo cada mañana.

    _____

3. Mientras Esteban se levanta y se viste, ella le dice: «Puse tu camisa y tus pantalones en la silla».

    _____

4. Debes usar tu suéter nuevo hoy porque hace mucho frío.

    _____

5. Debes darte prisa porque nuestra vecina va a llevarte a la escuela hoy en su coche.

    _____

6. Recuerda que vas a su dentista hoy. Tu cita es a las tres y media.

    _____

7. <u>Mi</u> horario es muy pesado hoy.

_____

8. Tengo que preparar una cena especial porque vienen <u>nuestros</u> amigos.

_____

9. ¿Dónde está <u>tu</u> gorra? ¿Y <u>tus</u> libros?

_____

10. ¡Ay, <u>mi</u> Dios! ¿Por qué será tan distraído <u>mi</u> hijo?

_____

Ejercicio G

Sarita, una niña de cuatro años, le cuenta a su mamá lo que pasó en su clase hoy. Complete las frases con la palabra necesaria:

1. Roberto se quitó _____ zapatos.

2. Clara se lastimó _____ dedo.

3. Eduardo levantó _____ cabeza para ver mejor.

4. La maestra abrió _____ paraguas cuando bajamos del autobús.

5. Luz se cortó _____ pelo con las tijeras.

6. Yo me lavé _____ manos después de pintar.

7. La enfermera se puso _____ guantes de goma cuando curó a Juan.

8. Pablo se rompió _____ nariz cuando se cayó.

9. Perdí _____ pañuelo en la escuela.

10. Después de jugar fútbol, a Humberto le dolieron _____ piernas.

Ejercicio H

Cuando los jóvenes están juntando sus cosas al terminar la fiesta, de repente se va la luz. Cuando la luz vuelve, se dan cuenta de que tienen cosas que no son de ellos. Usted y Héctor tratan de corregirlo. Escriba lo que usted dice:

EJEMPLO: Héctor: Jorge tiene el abrigo de Pedro.
          Usted: **Tienes razón, no es el abrigo suyo; es el de Pedro.**

1. Héctor: María tiene las botas de Adela.

   Usted: _____

2. Héctor: Pablo tiene el sombrero de Enrique.

   Usted: _____

3.   Héctor: Anita se puso el suéter de Clara.

Usted: _____

4.   Héctor: José tiene mis guantes.

Usted: _____

5.   Héctor: Pilar y Ema tienen las revistas de Lourdes y Marisol.

Usted: _____

6.   Héctor: Ricardo tiene el paraguas de Alejandro.

Usted: _____

7.   Héctor: Juan y yo tenemos los discos dc Carlos.

Usted: _____

8.   Héctor: Tú tienes la cinta de Rosa.

Usted: _____

Antes de salir de la casa por la mañana, la señora Ramos hace una serie de preguntas.
Conteste las preguntas con la forma larga del adjetivo posesivo:

EJEMPLO: ¿Tienes tus llaves?
            Sí, tengo las llaves mías.

1.   ¿Apagaste tu máquina de escribir?

_____

2.   ¿Preparasteis vuestras tareas?

_____

3.   ¿Llevó Rocío su almuerzo?

_____

4.   ¿Dejé mi cartera en la mesa del comedor?

_____

5.   ¿Diste tú de comer a tu perro?

_____

6.   ¿Encendió Roberto la lámpara de su alcoba?

_____

7.   ¿Cerramos bien la puerta de nuestra casa?

_____

8.   ¿Tienes tú tus anteojos?

_____

3. Possessive Pronouns

el mío, la mía, los míos, las mías	*mine*
el tuyo, la tuya, los tuyos, las tuyas	*yours (fam. sing.)*
el suyo, la suya, los suyos, las suyas	*yours, his, hers, its, theirs*
el nuestro, la nuestra, los nuestros, las nuestras	*ours*
el vuestro, la vuestra, los vuestros, las vuestras	*yours (fam. pl.)*

a. Possessive pronouns consist of the definite article + the long form of the possessive adjective.

b. The possessive pronoun agrees in number and gender with the noun it replaces, not with the possessor:

> **Mi automóvil es más hermoso que el** | *My automobile is more beautiful than*
> (= el automóvil) ***suyo.*** | *yours.*
> **Esos libros y** *los* (= los libros) ***míos*** | *Those books and mine are novels.*
> **son novelas.** |

NOTE:

1. The specific meaning of **el suyo (la suya, los suyos, las suyas)** may be made clear by replacing the possessive with the expressions **de Ud. (Uds.), de él (ella),** or **de ellos (ellas)** after the article:

> **sus plumas y** *las de Ud.* | *his pens and yours*
> **mis billetes y** *los de ella* | *my tickets and hers*

2. After forms of **ser,** the article preceding the possessive pronoun is usually omitted:

> Estas corbatas **son mías.** | *These ties are mine.*
> Aquella corbata **es suya.** | *That tie is his.*

 **Ejercicio J**

Jorge es un niño de seis años. A Jorge le gusta decir que todo lo que él tiene es mejor que lo que tienen otras personas. Cambie las frases según el ejemplo:

> EJEMPLO: Mi bicicleta es más nueva que la bicicleta de Raimundo.
> Mi bicicleta es más nueva **que la suya.**

1. Mi hermano es más alto que el hermano de Elena.

_____

2. Mi uniforme es más lindo que tu uniforme.

_____

3. Su gato no es más grande que nuestro gato.

_____

4. Mis amigos son más fuertes que tus amigos.

_____

5. Sus abuelos son más pobres que nuestros abuelos.

_____

6. Las amigas de mi hermano son más bonitas que las amigas de Pablo.

_____

7. Tu casa es menos moderna que mi casa.

_____

8. Tu juego electrónico es menos interesante que el juego electrónico de mis hermanos.

_____

9. Mi mamá cocina mejor que tu mamá.

_____

10. El hermano de Alfredo es más cobarde que mi hermano.

_____

Ejercicio K

Usted reflexiona sobre varias cosas. Escriba las frases según el ejemplo:

EJEMPLO: Mis impresiones del viaje y las impresiones de José son buenas.
Mis impresiones del viaje y **las suyas** son buenas.
Mis impresiones del viaje y **las de él** son buenas.

1. Mi coche y el coche de Alicia son del mismo color.

_____

_____

2. Mis gustos y los gustos de Jorge son parecidos.

_____

_____

3. Mi cumpleaños y el cumpleaños de los gemelos caen el primero de marzo.

_____

_____

4. Los consejos de mis padres y los consejos de los padres de Raquel no son parecidos.

_____

_____

5. Mis joyas y las joyas de ustedes son lindas.

_____

_____

6. Nuestra idea y la idea de Jaime y Beto son interesantes.

_____

_____

7. Tu fiesta y las fiestas de tus amigas son alegres.

_____

_____

8. Las calificaciones de Ana y las calificaciones de Elena son altas.

_____

_____

Ejercicio L

Elsa y Beatriz son gemelas. Elsa siempre sabe dónde está todo. Beatriz, al contrario, nunca encuentra nada. Elsa siempre tiene que decirle dónde están las cosas que busca. Escriba las respuestas a las preguntas de Beatriz:

EJEMPLO: Beatriz: Busco la cámara de Alfredo. (en la mesa del comedor)
Elsa: **La suya está en la mesa del comedor.**

1. Beatriz: ¿Dónde está mi blusa verde? (en el armario)

Elsa: _____

2. Beatriz: Aquí está el reloj de mamá. No encuentro el reloj de papá. (en la cocina)

Elsa: _____

3. Beatriz: ¿Dónde dejé nuestros boletos para el teatro? (en tu mochila)

Elsa: _____

4. Beatriz: ¿Viste mi cepillo de pelo? (en el baño)

Elsa: _____

5. Beatriz: No encuentro mi cinturón rojo. ¿Puedo usar tu cinturón rojo? (en el cajón)

Elsa: _____

6. Beatriz: Busco las cartas de Alfredo. (en el escritorio)

Elsa: _____

7. Beatriz: Tengo que buscar tu cinta de Julio Iglesias. (en la grabadora)

Elsa: _____

♦ MASTERY EXERCISES ♦

Ejercicio M

Bárbara tiene la costumbre de comparar sus cosas con las de sus amigas. Exprese en español los posesivos dados en inglés:

1. (yours, ours) Mi abrigo es verde. ¿De qué color es _____ ? _____
es negro.

2.   (her, Clara's, ours) _____ joyas cuestan mucho. _____ son

más caras. _____ no valen nada.

3.   (Pablo's, Ernesto's, mine) El sombrero _____ es de paja. _____

es de felpa. _____ es de lana.

4.   (my, yours, mine) He gastado todo _____ capital. ¿Qué has hecho con

_____? _____ está en el banco.

5.   (his, whose, Anna's) La pluma verde es _____. ¿_____ es

la pluma azul? Es _____.

6.   (my, whose, theirs) He perdido _____ paraguas. ¿_____ es

ése? Es _____.

Ejercicio N

Sofía vive con una familia venezolana durante su visita a Caracas. Conteste las preguntas que ella le hace al hijo menor de la familia:

1.   ¿Cuándo celebras tu cumpleaños?

_____

2.   ¿Cuándo celebran tus padres el aniversario de su boda?

_____

3.   ¿Te quitas o te pones los zapatos al salir de casa?

_____

4.   ¿De quién son los juguetes que están en el cuarto de tu hermana?

_____

5.   ¿Prefieres cenar en tu propia casa o en la de tus abuelos?

_____

6.   ¿Eres más inteligente que tus hermanos?

_____

7.   ¿Te lavas las manos antes de comer?

_____

8.   ¿Cuál de estas muñecas es la tuya, la grande o la gorda?

_____

9.   ¿Te gusta sacar fotos de tus amigos?

_____

10. La escuela de tus hermanos es la escuela Simón Bolívar, ¿cuál es la tuya?

_____

11. ¿Cómo saludas a tu maestro?

   _____

12. ¿Es Arturito uno de tus amigos?

   _____

13. ¿Acompañan Uds. a sus padres cuando van al cine?

   _____

14. ¿Hasta qué hora te permiten tus padres mirar la televisión?

   _____

15. ¿Oyes y comprendes bien mis palabras?

   _____

16. ¿Son mejores las notas de los otros estudiantes que las tuyas?

   _____

17. ¿Cuál es tu clase favorita?

   _____

18. ¿Juegas con los amigos de tus hermanos?

   _____

19. ¿Quién es el mayor de tus hermanos?

   _____

20. ¿Te prestan tus hermanos sus juguetes?

   _____

Ejercicio O

Exprese en español lo que Paula le cuenta a una argentina que hace el mismo viaje en barco que ella:

1. The ship's captain said that we could sit at his table tonight.

   _____

   _____

2. He explained the city's strange customs.

   _____

3. My family and my uncle's live near the port.

   _____

4. Their daughter and that of their friend danced almost all night.

   _____

   _____

5. In whose chair are you seated? In Mr. Zuleta's?

   _____

   _____

6. Whose suntan oil is that? Is it Elizabeth's?

   _____

7. Whose hat is this? It is more beautiful than mine.

   _____

   _____

8. That boy had to carry his father's and his brother's suitcases.

   _____

   _____

9. Whose guide book did you consult? Was it your father's?

   _____

   _____

10. Today's newspaper relates the news of our trip.

    _____

    _____

11. None of the crew knows today's date.

    _____

12. Our guide has more problems than the other group's guide.

    _____

    _____

13. This ship's itinerary is longer than the other ship's.

    _____

    _____

14. Your (fam. sing.) plans and mine are good.

    _____

    _____

15. My brother's vacation will take place in the same month as your sister's.

    _____

    _____

16. Her travel plans are similar to your brother's.

    _____

    _____

17. That book's author is also on this ship.

    _____

    _____

18. My copy of the book is newer than yours.

_____

_____

19. This evening's meal should be very enjoyable.

_____

_____

20. If you loan me your earrings, I'll loan you mine.

_____

_____

C·H·A·P·T·E·R 26

Demonstratives

1. Demonstrative Adjectives

MASCULINE	FEMININE	
este estos	esta estas	*this* *these*
ese esos	esa esas	*that* *those*
aquel aquellos	aquella aquellas	*that* *those*

Demonstrative adjectives precede the nouns they modify and agree with them in number and gender:

este libro   *this book*
esas plumas   *those pens*

NOTE:

1. **Este** (**estos,** etc.) (*this* [*these*]) refers to what is near or directly concerns the speaker. **Ese** (**esos,** etc.) (*that* [*those*]) refers to what is not so near or directly concerns the person addressed. **Aquel** (**aquellos,** etc.) (*that* [*those*]) refers to what is remote from both the speaker and the person addressed or does not directly concern either:

   Este **lápiz es rojo.**   *This pencil is red.*
   Juan, déme Ud. *ese* **libro que tiene en**   *John, give me that book you have in*
      la mano.   *your hand.*
   Juan, déme Ud. *aquel* **libro.**   *John, give me that book over there.*

2. The adverbs **aquí** (*here*), **ahí** (*there*), and **allí** ([*over*] *there*) correspond to the demonstratives **este, ese,** and **aquel:**

   Deja { *esta* **mesa** *aquí.*   **Leave** { *this table here.*
            { *ese* **asiento** *ahí.*   { *that chair there.*
            { *aquel* **sofá** *allí.*   { *that sofa over there.*

378

 **Ejercicio A**

Alicia acaba de comprar la ropa que va a llevar en un viaje que va a hacer. Su amiga quiere saber cuánto costó cada cosa. Escriba las preguntas que le hace la amiga:

EJEMPLOS: blusa
¿Cuánto costó esta blusa?

guantes
¿Cuánto costaron estos guantes?

1. zapatos

_____

2. traje do baño

_____

3. impermeable

_____

4. falda

_____

5. bolso

_____

6. pantalones

_____

7. gafas de sol

_____

8. pijamas

_____

Ejercicio B

Cuando Ramón fue a la corrida de toros, llevó sus binoculares para ver mejor desde su asiento. Escriba lo que dice al ver la corrida por los binoculares:

EJEMPLO: filosa / espada
¡Qué filosa es aquella espada!

1. valiente / torero

_____

2. fuertes / toros

_____

3. bonitas / capas

_____

4. larga / espada

_____

5. veloces / banderilleros

_____

6. impresionante / desfile

_____

7. elegante / traje de luces

_____

Ejercicio C

En un mercado de frutas, Gloria desea comprar toda la fruta que ve. Escriba lo que va a comprar:

EJEMPLOS: melón / aquí
Va a comprar este melón.

uvas / ahí
Va a comprar esas uvas.

plátanos / allí
Va a comprar aquellos plátanos.

1. naranjas / aquí

_____

2. toronjas / allí

_____

3. piña / ahí

_____

4. melocotones / allí

_____

5. manzanas / aquí

_____

6. pera / ahí

_____

7. sandía / allí

_____

8. cerezas / ahí

_____

 **Ejercicio D**

Gilberto y sus amigos presencian un desfile. Escriba lo que dicen mientras se les acerca el desfile:

EJEMPLO: globos
Miren Uds. esos globos.

1. payaso

    _____

2. caballo

    _____

3. flores

    _____

4. banderas

    _____

5. luces

    _____

6. cartel

    _____

7. coches

    _____

8. cohetes

    _____

Ejercicio E

Alfonso hace preguntas sobre el pueblo que visita. Contéstelas, usando un adjetivo demostrativo:

1. ¿Está abierta todo el día la librería de allí?

    _____

2. ¿Son caros los restaurantes de ahí?

    _____

3. ¿Venden sangría en los cafés de aquí?

    _____

4. ¿Son viejos los árboles de allí?

    _____

5.   ¿Hay un lago en el parque de ahí?

_____

6.   ¿Dan una buena obra en el teatro de aquí?

_____

_____

7.   ¿Venden tarjetas postales en la papelería de ahí?

_____

_____

8.   ¿Es posible nadar en el río de allí?

_____

_____

2. Demonstrative Pronouns

MASCULINE	FEMININE	NEUTER	
éste **éstos**	**ésta** **éstas**	**esto**	*this (one)* *these*
ése **ésos**	**ésa** **ésas**	**eso**	*that (one)* *those*
aquél **aquéllos**	**aquélla** **aquéllas**	**aquello**	*that (one)* *those*

a. Demonstrative pronouns agree in number and gender with the nouns they replace:

   este libro y **aquél** (= aquel libro)   *this book and that (one)*

b. (1) The neuter forms **esto, eso, aquello** do not refer to specific nouns but to statements, ideas, understood nouns, and the like. These forms do not vary in number and gender:

   Pablo siempre llega tarde, y **eso** no le   *Paul always comes late, and the*
      gusta al maestro.   *teacher doesn't like that.*
   Su padre está enfermo, y **esto** lo pone   *His father is ill, and this makes him*
      triste.   *sad.*

   (2) The question ¿**Qué es esto (eso, aquello)**? uses the neuter form because the noun is not known. After the noun has been mentioned, the form of the demonstrative adjective or pronoun must correspond to the noun:

   ¿Qué es **esto**?—Es una flor.   *What is this?—It is a flower.*
   ¿Es bonita **esta flor**?—Sí.   *Is this flower pretty?—Yes.*

   NOTE: Demonstrative pronouns are distinguished from demonstrative adjectives by an accent mark. The neuter pronouns have no accent mark, since there are no corresponding neuter adjectives.

 **Ejercicio F**

Cuando Esteban llegó al campamento de verano, encontró muchos anuncios pegados por dondequiera. Subraye la forma demostrativa correcta:

1. Coloque Ud. la maleta en este armario, no en _____ .

   (a) éste   (b) aquél   (c) ese   (d) esos

2. No se permite entrar por esa puerta, sino por _____ .

   (a) esto   (b) éste   (c) ésta   (d) aquél

3. Este horario marca las actividades, _____ no.

   (a) ese   (b) ése   (c) aquello   (d) aquélla

4. Ponga Ud. los juguetes en este estante, no en _____ .

   (a) éste   (b) ése   (c) aquel   (d) esto

5. No apague Ud. esa luz, sino _____ .

   (a) aquella   (b) estas   (c) ésta   (d) ésa

 **Ejercicio G**

Pablo y Jorge comparan cosas que su madre siempre les decía. Complete las oraciones con el pronombre demostrativo apropiado:

> EJEMPLO: ***Esto*** es bueno para la salud. Debes comerlo todo.

1. No debes hacer _____ porque tu papá se enojará.

2. _____ es importante para nosotros.

3. _____ no es bueno para ti.

4. Los niños no deben decir _____ .

5. _____ es algo bonito.

6. Un niño decente no haría _____ .

7. _____ me alegra mucho.

8. Si haces _____ , tendré que castigarte.

 **Ejercicio H**

Conteste las preguntas que la mamá de Julia le hace cuando van de compras al almacén. Use el pronombre demostrativo apropiado:

1. Mamá: ¿Te gusta este suéter o aquella blusa?   (la blusa)

   Julia: _____

2. Mamá: ¿Prefieres esa falda o este vestido?   (el vestido)

   Julia: _____

3. Mamá: ¿Deseas estas botas o aquellos zapatos?   (las botas)

   Julia: _____

4. Mamá: ¿Quieres esa gorra o este sombrero?   (el sombrero)

   Julia: _____

5. Mamá: ¿Debo comprar aquel abrigo o este impermeable?   (el abrigo)

   Julia: _____

6. Mamá: ¿Prefieres estos guantes de lana o esos guantes de piel?   (los guantes de piel)

   Julia: _____

C. The pronoun **éste (-a, -os, -as)** also means *the latter* (the latest, the most recently mentioned);
aquél (-la, -los, -las) also means *the former* (the most remotely mentioned):

> Juan es mayor que Pablo; **éste** tiene
> seis años, **aquél** tiene nueve.

> *John is older than Paul; the former is*
> *nine years old, the latter is six.*

NOTE: In English, we usually say "the former and the latter." In Spanish, the order is reversed; **éste** (*the latter*) comes first.

Ejercicio I

Después de su primer día de clases, Pepe hace varios comentarios. Complete cada oración con la forma apropiada de éste *y* aquél:

1. Eduardo y Rocío: _____ es alta, _____ es bajo.

2. Los juguetes y los rompecabezas: _____ son difíciles, _____ son viejos.

3. Gregorio y Beatriz: _____ es chistosa, _____ es serio.

4. Los niños y las niñas: _____ son habladoras, _____ son juguetones.

5. Las pinturas y los lápices:_____ son largos, _____ son brillantes.

Ejercicio J

Carlos siempre repite lo que su hermana mayor dice. Escriba lo que Carlos dice, usando la forma correcta de éste *y* aquél:

> EJEMPLO: Ana: Alicia es bonita pero Luz es más bonita.
> Carlos: **Sí, ésta es más bonita que aquélla.**

1. Ana: El señor Rivas es más estricto que la señorita Ramos.

    Carlos: _____

2. Ana: Gerardo es menos alto que sus hermanos Arturo y Beto.

    Carlos: _____

3. Ana: Clara es más aplicada que sus condiscípulos.

    Carlos: _____

4. Ana: Juan es gordo. Su amiga María es delgada.

    Carlos: _____

5. Ana: Mi bicicleta es nueva. La tuya es vieja.

    Carlos: _____

d. The definite article (**el, la, los, las**) followed by **de** (*that of, the one of*) or **que** (*the one that*) functions like a demonstrative pronoun:

el (la) de María	*that of (the one of) Mary*
los (las) de María	*those of (the ones of) Mary*
el (la) que está aquí	*the one that is here*
los (las) que están aquí	*the ones that are here*

El vestido de María es distinto **del de** Juana; es muy parecido **al que** lleva Isabel.

Mary's dress is different from Joan's; it is very similar to the one Elizabeth is wearing.

Ejercicio K

Nicolás le escribió a Ud. una tarjeta postal de México. Escriba el pronombre demostrativo, empleando la forma correcta del artículo (el, la, los, las):

Pude planear mi propio itinerario pero no _____ de Roberto. Mi viaje es más interesante que
                                            1

_____ de mi primo. El clima mexicano es semejante a _____ de otras partes de Latinoamérica.
   2   3

La gente de México y _____ de Guatemala hablan español. Los precios de este año son más altos
                        4

que _____ del año anterior. Las montañas del norte son enormes, _____ del sur son más
       5   6

pequeñas. El nuevo guía es menos interesante que _____ que se marchó. Será posible llevar
                                                    7

a cabo mis planes y _____ de mis amigos.
                       8

♦ MASTERY EXERCISES ♦

Ejercicio L

Imagínese que Ud. está en un museo y hay pinturas, esculturas, tapices y otros objetos de arte a su alrededor. Describa cinco de los objetos de arte que Ud. ve, usando un adjetivo demostrativo:

SUGERENCIAS: pintura   cruz
                tapiz   figura
                escultura   cajita
                joya   modelo

EJEMPLOS: Miren Uds. esos cofres antiguos.
             Este cuadro de un ángel es hermoso.
             Me gusta aquel paisaje.

1. _____

2. _____

3. _____

4. _____

5. _____

Ejercicio M

Mientras Sergio se baña y se viste, reflexiona sobre el viaje que está haciendo y lo que todavía quiere hacer. Complete el párrafo, usando un demostrativo apropiado:

_____ tarde voy a ir a _____ tienda que vi ayer cuando pasamos por
        1   2

_____ calle angosta. Allí se venden _____ instrumentos musicales típicos de
        3   4

_____ país. _____ señora elegante del grupo dijo que _____
        5   6   7

instrumentos cuestan mucho en los Estados Unidos. Voy a comprar _____ que sean
                                                                         8

fáciles de meter en _____ maleta de mano que tengo. Necesito buscar el regalo de mi
                            9

papá y _____ de mi abuelo también. Si no encuentro nada en _____ almacén,
              10   11

iré a _____ de la esquina. _____ viaje me va a costar mucho porque los
            12   13

precios de los regalos y _____ de la comida son altos. Sin embargo, me he divertido
                                14

mucho en _____ vacaciones; son más divertidas que _____ del año pasado
                15   16

cuando pasé todo el tiempo en _____ hotel aislado en las montañas. _____
                                        17   18

vez hay personas interesantes y simpáticas. Voy a recomendar _____ excursión
                                                                      19

a Rafael y a Alberto. A _____ le gusta ir de compras y a _____ le encanta
                                20   21

conocer lugares nuevos. No debo olvidar _____ parque que está cerca del centro, donde
                                                22

saqué _____ fotos de la gente remando en _____ lago tranquilo. Todo
              23   24

_____ me da mucha alegría.
        25

Ejercicio N

Rosa visita a su amiga Laura en el dormitorio de la universidad y le hace preguntas sobre lo que ve en el cuarto. Conteste las preguntas de Rosa:

1. ¿Sacaste ese libro de la biblioteca?

   _____

2. ¿Cuándo compraste aquella cinta?

   _____

3. ¿Cuál de estos álbumes te gusta más, éste o aquél?

   _____

4. ¿Es tuyo este vestido?

   _____

5. De las dos estaciones que pasaste aquí, el otoño y el invierno, ¿te gustó más éste o aquél?

   _____

6. ¿Cambiarías esta compañera de cuarto por la de Lourdes?

   _____

7. ¿Es esa señora el ama de llaves del dormitorio?

   _____

8. ¿Quién te regaló aquellos guantes?

   _____

9. ¿Quieres prestarme esta falda o aquélla?

   _____

10. ¿Es más fácil este semestre o el del otoño?

    _____

Ejercicio O

Oscar y Rafael tratan de ganar algún dinero, haciendo varios trabajos para sus vecinos. Exprese en español lo que ellos quieren decirle al señor Muñoz:

1. These curtains are clean, those are very dirty.

   _____

   _____

2. This is our problem; that stain doesn't disappear.

   _____

   _____

3. This is impossible; I cannot move this table.

   _____

4. Mr. Muñoz, put that vase here and this one there.

   _____

5. This soap is too strong; I prefer that one.

   _____

6. This room is larger than that one.

   _____

7. We removed that broken chair.

   _____

8. I put the dishes in this cupboard.

   _____

9. This job is not inexpensive.

   _____

10. Mr. Muñoz, what is that?

    _____

11. The kitchen and the basement are dirty; I will clean the former and Rafael will clean the latter.

    _____

    _____

12. This house is larger than that of Mr. Adobe.

    _____

13. Can you repair this lamp?

    _____

14. That seems strange to me.

    _____

15. Can we finish that tomorrow?

    _____

16. Those chairs over there are too close to that table.

    _____

    _____

17. Do you want us to paint that fence this month?

    _____

    _____

18. That's a good idea; we'll try to do that this week.

    _____

19. These windows also need to be washed.

    _____

    _____

20. Whose car is that? The one in front of the house.

    _____

    _____

Negation

1. Negatives

a. Principal negatives and their opposite affirmatives:

NEGATIVE	AFFIRMATIVE
no *no, not*	**sí** *yes*
nadie *no one, nobody, (not) anyone*	**alguien** *someone, somebody, anyone*
nada *nothing, (not) anything*	**algo** *something, anything*
nunca *never, (not) ever* **jamás**	**siempre** *always*
tampoco *neither, not either*	**también** *also*
ninguno (-a) *no, none, (not) any*	**alguno (-a)** *some, any*
ni . . . ni *neither . . . nor; not . . . nor*	**o . . . o** *either . . . or*
sin *without*	**con** *with*

b. The most common negative is **no,** which always precedes the conjugated verb:

Ud. *no* **sabe** la lección. You don't know the lesson.
¿*No* **ha estudiado** Ud.? Haven't you studied?

c. If an object pronoun precedes the verb, the negative precedes the object pronoun:

Ud. *no* **la sabe.** You don't know it.

d. Spanish sentences may have two or more negatives. If one of the negatives is **no,** it precedes the verb. If **no** is omitted, another negative precedes the verb:

No veo a nadie nunca. ⎫
Nunca veo a nadie.   ⎬ I never see anyone.
No lo leyó tampoco. ⎫ He didn't read it either. (Neither did
Tampoco lo leyó.   ⎬   he read it.)
No usó ni papel ni lápiz. ⎫ He used neither paper nor pencil. (He
Ni papel ni lápiz usó.   ⎬   didn't use either paper or pencil.)

NOTE:

1. A negative preceded by a preposition retains that preposition when placed before the verb:
   A nadie veo.

2. The negatives **nadie, nada, ninguno, nunca,** and **jamás** are used after comparatives:

<table>
<tr><td>Toca el piano **mejor que** *nadie.*</td><td>*He plays the piano better than anyone.*</td></tr>
<tr><td>Ahora lo creo **más que** *nunca.*</td><td>*Now I believe it more than ever.*</td></tr>
<tr><td>La niña desea una muñeca **más que** *nada.*</td><td>*The child wants a doll more than anything.*</td></tr>
</table>

3. The negatives **nadie, nada, ninguno, nunca,** and **jamás** are used in questions expecting negative answers:

<table>
<tr><td>¿Has visto **jamás** una película más aburrida?</td><td>*Have you ever seen a more boring film?*</td></tr>
</table>

4. The negatives **nadie, nada, ninguno, nunca,** and **jamás** are used in phrases beginning with **sin** and **antes** (**de** or **que**):

<table>
<tr><td>Salió *sin* decir *nada.*</td><td>*He left without saying anything.*</td></tr>
<tr><td>*Antes de* hacer *nada,* tienes que limpiar tu cuarto.</td><td>*Before doing anything, you must clean your room.*</td></tr>
<tr><td>Llegó **antes que** *nadie.*</td><td>*He arrived before anyone else.*</td></tr>
</table>

5. **Ninguno** as an adjective may be replaced by **alguno.** When so used, **alguno** follows the noun, and the negative is more emphatic:

<table>
<tr><td>No tengo *ninguna* amiga. ⎱
No tengo **amiga** *alguna.* ⎰</td><td>*I have no friend. (I don't have any friend.)*</td></tr>
</table>

Ejercicio A

Javier es un joven de Acapulco y quiere conocerlo a Ud. mejor. Conteste las preguntas que él le hace, usando expresiones negativas:

1. ¿Juega Ud. fútbol los sábados?

_____

2. ¿Mira Ud. su programa favorito con alguien?

_____

3. ¿Cuándo va Ud. al museo?

_____

4. ¿Le gustan los tacos y los tamales?

_____

5. ¿Conoce Ud. a algunos mexicanos?

_____

6. A mí no me gusta la nieve. ¿Y a Ud.?

_____

7. ¿Preparó Ud. algo para la fiesta?

_____

8. ¿Dice Ud. algo cuando sale de la casa?

_____

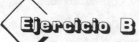

Ejercicio B

La mamá de Carmen siempre la contradice. Escriba lo que ella niega:

EJEMPLO: Mi hermana es fea.
            Tu hermana no es fea.

1. Jorge es aburrido.

    _____

2. Luis y Daniel son futbolistas famosos.

    _____

3. Mi papá es médico.

    _____

4. Sarita tiene las muñecas de Elena.

    _____

5. Rafael y Ernesto trabajan en la librería.

    _____

Ejercicio C

La señora Cabado tiene un problema porque sus hijos no le ayudan con los quehaceres de la casa. Escriba lo que le cuenta a su hermana:

EJEMPLO: sacar la basura
            Nadie saca la basura.

1. usar la aspiradora

    _____

2. arreglar su cuarto

    _____

3. lavar el carro

    _____

4. sacar al perro

    _____

5. planchar la ropa

    _____

6. regar el jardín

    _____

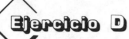 **Ejercicio D**

A Héctor le gusta presumir de lo atlético que es, pero su hermanito dice la verdad. Escriba lo que dice su hermanito:

EJEMPLO: Yo corro dos millas todos los días.
Tú nunca corres dos millas.

1.   Yo levanto pesas cada mañana.

_____

2.   Yo nado en la piscina todos los días.

_____

3.   Yo siempre hago muchos ejercicios.

_____

4.   Yo juego tenis por la tarde.

_____

5.   Yo juego boliche cada semana.

_____

 **Ejercicio E**

El señor Soto tiene antojo de postre, pero no hay nada en la casa. Escriba lo que le dice su esposa:

EJEMPLO: ¿Tenemos fruta?
No tenemos ninguna fruta.

1.   ¿Tenemos helado?

_____

2.   ¿Tenemos dulces?

_____

3.   ¿Tenemos chocolate?

_____

4.   ¿Tenemos galletas?

_____

5.   ¿Tenemos bizcochos?

_____

6.   ¿Tenemos torta de manzana?

_____

Ejercicio F

Ricardito es un niño problemático porque no le gusta hacer nada. Escriba lo que contesta:

EJEMPLO: ¿Te gusta correr o patinar?
No me gusta ni correr ni patinar.

1.   ¿Te gusta hablar o callarte?

_____

2.   ¿Te gusta bailar o cantar?

_____

3.   ¿Te gusta pintar o dibujar?

_____

4.   ¿Te gusta jugar o descansar?

_____

5.   ¿Te gusta salir o quedarte en casa?

_____

6.   ¿Te gusta escuchar discos o mirar la televisión?

_____

Ejercicio G

A César no le gusta contestar las preguntas que le hacen. Escriba las respuestas de César, según el ejemplo:

EJEMPLO: ¿Viste a alguien en la calle?
Yo no vi a nadie en la calle.

1.   ¿Bailaste con María en la fiesta?

_____

2.   ¿Hablaste con tus primos?

_____

3.   ¿Escribiste una carta a Gloria?

_____

4.   ¿Te acuerdas de los hermanos Silva?

_____

5.   ¿Viste a la novia de Roberto?

_____

Ejercicio H

La hermanita de Clarisa repite lo que dice su hermana. Escriba lo que dice:

EJEMPLO: Yo no voy al cine.
Yo no voy al cine **tampoco.**

1. Yo no preparé la tarea anoche.

_____

2. Mis amigas y yo no hablamos por teléfono.

_____

3. Juanito no pidió holado de fresa.

_____

4. Mi prima no compró el regalo.

_____

5. Yo no visité a mis abuelos.

_____

2. Negative Expressions

Él no lo ve. **Ni** yo **tampoco.**	He doesn't see it. Neither do I.
Ya no tengo dinero.	I no longer have money.
No me quedan **más que** diez centavos.	I have no more than ten cents left.
No me quedan **sino** diez centavos.	(I have only ten cents left.)
¿Estás listo? **Todavía no.**	Are you ready? Not yet.
¿Puede Ud. pagarme? **Ahora no.**	Can you pay me? Not now.
Ni siquiera visita a su madre.	He doesn't even visit his mother.
¿Cómo van las cosas? **Sin novedad.**	How are things going? Nothing new. (The same as usual.)
¿Me prestas tu auto? **¡De ninguna manera!**	Will you lend me your car? Certainly not! (By no means.)
Tenemos que esperar dos horas; **no hay remedio.**	We have to wait two hours; it can't be helped.
No cabe duda; la libertad es preciosa.	There's no doubt; liberty is precious.
No importa.	It doesn't matter.
No obstante mis esfuerzos, no pude llegar a tiempo.	In spite of my efforts, I couldn't arrive on time.

Ejercicio I

Complete estas situaciones, usando una de las expresiones siguientes:

ya no	ahora no	ni . . . tampoco
no . . . más que	ni siquiera	todavía no
sin novedad	de ninguna manera	no importa

1. Hay mucha neblina. Su amigo oye el ruido de un avión y dice: —No puedo ver el avión.

   Ud. responde: _____

2. Un amigo le dice: —Vamos a visitar a Carlos. Vive en esa casa verde.

   Ud. responde: _____

3. Ud. va de compras con su mamá. Ella le pregunta si está listo(a).

   Ud. responde: _____

4. Su hermanito pide que Ud. le ayude con su tarea de matemáticas. Ud. está ocupado(a).

   Ud. responde: _____

5. Después de una cena enorme, Ud. y un amigo van al cine. Al pasar la dulcería en la entrada del cine, su amigo le dice: —Yo no puedo comer nada más.

   Ud. responde: _____

6. Por casualidad, Ud. da con un amigo en la calle. El amigo le pregunta: —¿Cómo van las cosas?

   Ud. responde: _____

7. Su papá le cuenta que el hijo de un amigo suyo ha ganado el campeonato de tenis. Ud. sabe que el chico no sabe jugar bien.

   Ud. responde: _____

8. Después de un día en el parque de diversiones, Ud. y sus amigos tienen hambre. Buscan el dinero que les queda y no tienen suficiente. A Ud. le quedan veinte y cinco centavos.

   Ud. responde: _____

9. Una amiga suya quiere pedirle prestada una falda morada. Ud. no la tiene.

   Ud. responde: _____

10. Al salir de un concierto al aire libre, al que acudieron más de un millón de personas, su hermano dice que no volverá a esa clase de espectáculo.

    Ud. responde: _____

3. *Pero* and *sino*

Both **pero** and **sino** mean *but*. **Pero** is more general and may also mean *however;* **sino** is used only after a negative statement to express a contrast with a sense of "on the contrary," "but rather." Compare:

No llueve ahora, *pero* va a llover más tarde.	*It's not raining now but it's going to rain later.*
Tiene dinero, *pero* no es feliz.	*He has money but (however) he is not happy.*
No habla portugués, *sino* español.	*He doesn't speak Portuguese but (rather) Spanish.*
No llevaba camisa blanca, *sino* azul.	*He wasn't wearing a white shirt but (rather) a blue one.*

NOTE:

1. The comparison is always between two equivalent parts of speech (noun — noun, adjective — adjective, infinitive — infinitive):

No me gusta **estudiar,** *sino* **ir** al cine.

I don't like to study but (on the contrary) to go to the movies.

No compré zapatos **blancos** *sino* **rojos.**

I didn't buy white shoes but red ones.

2. If the contrasting verbs are not infinitives, **sino que** is used:

No cerró la puerta, *sino que* la **dejó abierta.**

He didn't close the door but (on the contrary) left it open.

Ejercicio J

Manuel está enojado con su amiga, Rosalinda. Conteste las preguntas de su mamá usando **pero:**

1. Mamá: Rosalinda te invitó a su fiesta, ¿verdad? (No fui.)

    Manuel: _____

2. Mamá: ¿Le compraste un regalo? (No se lo di.)

    Manuel: _____

3. Mamá: ¿Te llamó ella por teléfono? (No contesté el teléfono.)

    Manuel: _____

4. Mamá: Ella es una chica inteligente. (antipática)

    Manuel: _____

5. Mamá: ¿Vas a llamar para disculparte? (No hablaré con ella.)

    Manuel: _____

Ejercicio K

Alfredo ayuda a su hermanito a estudiar unas palabras nuevas. El hermanito no acierta ninguna de las palabras. Escriba lo que Alfredo dice:

EJEMPLO: Un hogar es una fábrica. (una casa)
Un hogar no es una fábrica sino una casa.

1. Un cirujano es un abogado. (un médico)

    _____

2. Una guitarra es un deporte. (un instrumento musical)

    _____

3. Un colegio es una universidad. (una escuela)

   _____

4. Una butaca es un cuarto. (un mueble)

   _____

5. La horchata es un pan. (una bebida)

   _____

Ejercicio L

Es la primera vez que Analuz cuida a los hijos de un vecino. Escriba lo que le cuenta a su mamá al volver a casa:

EJEMPLO: preparar la tarea / mirar la televisión
Los niños no prepararon la tarea sino que miraron la televisión.

1. lavar los platos / dejarlos en la mesa

   _____

2. beber leche / tomar refresco

   _____

3. comer en la cocina / cenar en la sala

   _____

4. quedarse en casa / salir al patio

   _____

5. estudiar la lección / hacer gimnasia

   _____

Ejercicio M

*Gloria está de vacaciones en Madrid y escribe una carta a su hermana, después de un día de muchas frustraciones. Use **pero**, **sino**, o **sino que** para expresar lo que Gloria quiere decir:*

Querida Anita,

Estoy cansada, _____ quiero escribirte esta cartita. Hoy no hizo frío _____
                    1   2

llovió por la tarde, cuando íbamos a visitar el Parque del Buen Retiro. Por eso no fuimos al

parque _____ al museo del Prado. Creí que conocía el arte español _____ me
              3   4

equivoqué muchas veces. El cuadro «Las Meninas» no fue pintado por Goya _____ por
                                                                                   5

Velázquez. Es muy bonito _____ no pude pasar mucho tiempo estudiándolo porque
                                   6

había mucha gente en el museo. Después de la visita al museo no fuimos a un café _____
                                                                                          7

regresamos al hotel, porque no paraba de llover. A la hora de la cena no fui a un restaurante,

_____ pedí la comida en mi cuarto. No aproveché el tiempo para descansar
        8

_____ para escribir muchas tarjetas postales. Mañana no visitaré otros lugares famosos
        9

_____ las tiendas.
       10

Hasta pronto,

Gloria

◆ MASTERY EXERCISES ◆

Ejercicio N

Conteste las preguntas que un(a) amigo(a) nuevo(a) le hace, expresando en sentido negativo todo lo posible:

1. ¿Le ha dado el maestro mucho trabajo?

   _____

2. ¿Sabe Ud. hablar otras lenguas?

   _____

3. ¿Duerme Ud. la siesta algunas tardes?

   _____

4. ¿Tiene Ud. necesidad de algo?

   _____

5. ¿Compró Ud. algo en el almacén ayer?

   _____

6. ¿Cuál prefiere Ud., la música clásica o la música flamenca?

   _____

7. ¿Prestó Ud. a alguien su cámara?

   _____

8. ¿Hay algo que le molesta a Ud.?

   _____

9.   ¿Conoce Ud. a alguien que repare bicicletas?

_____

10. ¿Siempre trata Ud. a sus amigos igualmente?

_____

11. ¿Ha ido Ud. jamás a otra ciudad solo(a)?

_____

12. ¿Piensa Ud. ir al teatro esta noche también?

_____

13. Cuando hace mucho frío, ¿sale Ud. con gorra?

_____

14. ¿Alguien le ha engañado alguna vez?

_____

15. ¿Qué prefiere Ud. beber, jugo o refresco?

_____

Ejercicio O

Pilar hace comentarios de su viaje a España. Complete las oraciones con **pero, sino,** *o* **sino que:**

1.   España no es un país industrial, _____ agrícola.

2.   El clima de la Mancha no es húmedo, _____ seco.

3.   Visitamos a Toledo, _____ nos alojamos en Madrid.

4.   No quería gastar mucho dinero, _____ tenía que comprar muchos regalos.

5.   Conocí a muchos jóvenes, _____ ninguno me dio su dirección.

6.   Quería pasar más tiempo en Segovia, _____ nos marchábamos al día siguiente.

7.   No había perdido mi boleto de avión, _____ lo había guardado en otro bolsillo.

Ejercicio P

Emilio le cuenta a un amigo peruano la historia de una prima suya que se escapó con su novio. Exprese en español:

1.   They didn't want to get married in either June or August.

_____

_____

2. No one knew what they were planning.

_____

3. They never discussed their plans with anyone.

_____

4. I didn't believe the news either.

_____

5. They didn't have a big wedding, but they eloped.

_____

6. He wanted to tell his brother but he decided not to say anything.

_____

_____

7. When their parents found out, you never heard such screams.

_____

_____

8. Their parents don't even speak to them.

_____

9. When I speak to them they tell me that it doesn't matter to them.

_____

_____

10. They didn't even receive any presents.

_____

11. My aunt wanted to buy them something, but finally she bought nothing.

_____

_____

12. We'll never hear the end of this!

_____

13. They spent a month in the south without writing to anyone.

_____

_____

14. In spite of my efforts, I no longer see them.

_____

15. I want to see them, but my parents forbid it.

_____

_____

16. They took nothing with them, neither their television set nor their stereo.

_____

_____

17. My uncle never speaks to them.

_____

18. They had nothing when they eloped.

_____

19. They are happy but they miss their families. It can't be helped.

_____

_____

20. I hope that the situation changes; there is no doubt that it will.

_____

_____

PART
FIVE

CIVILIZATION:
SPAIN

El Idioma Español

El idioma conocido como español es realmente el castellano, la lengua del reino de Castilla, que se convirtió en el idioma nacional de
España y llegó al Nuevo Mundo con los conquistadores. La pronunciación del español de
América se parece a la de Andalucía y las Islas
Canarias, donde no hay diferencias entre la **c**
(en **ce** o **ci**), la **z** y la **s**.

El español es una lengua romance, o sea
que es derivada del latín vulgar que hablaban
los romanos cuando llegaron a la península
ibérica. Otras dos lenguas que aún se hablan
en ciertas regiones de España, el catalán y el
gallego, son también lenguas romances; en catalán sobre todo hay hasta hoy en día una rica tradición literaria.

En el castellano se notan, además del latín,
influencias de los otros pueblos que vivieron en
la península. La menor es la de los visigodos,
porque éstos aprendieron el latín vulgar. No hay
más de sesenta palabras en español de origen
visigodo, y la mayoría son nombres propios
como **Fernando, Rodrigo** y **Álvaro.** Los griegos
contribuyeron más vocabulario, aunque muchas de las palabras de origen griego llegaron al
español a través del latín. Éstas se pueden reconocer fácilmente porque tienen las mismas
raíces en inglés. Algunos ejemplos son **la filosofía, la geometría, la química, la lógica, el al-
fabeto, la aritmética, la democracia, el teatro,
el dragón, el poema, el problema** y **el programa.**

De todos los pueblos invasores los árabes,
que estuvieron en España por ocho siglos,
fueron los que más palabras contribuyeron al
español. Más de 4.000 palabras del español de
hoy fueron adaptadas del árabe. Entre ellas están
**el arroz, el azúcar, azul, el ajedrez, el alcohol,
el algodón, el alcalde, el álgebra, ojalá** y **el
marfil.**

En América, palabras indígenas enrique-
cieron el español. El vocabulario adoptado depende de las culturas y dialectos indígenas de
cada región. De esos dialectos hay todavía dos
que se hablan hoy en día extensamente: el guaraní en el Paraguay y en el nordeste de la Argentina y el quechua en el Perú, Bolivia y zonas
del Ecuador y de Chile. Estos dos dialectos han
influido sobre todo en el español de las regiones
donde se hablan, pero hay palabras que han
trascendido fronteras y se usan universalmente
como **la papa, la pampa** y **el cóndor,** de origen
quechua, y **el ananás, el jaguar** (o **yaguar**), **el
tapir** y **la tapioca,** del guaraní. Además, aún
idiomas indígenas que ya no se hablan, como el
de los aztecas, contribuyeron muchas palabras
al español. Algunas de éstas han pasado al inglés, como **el tomate, el cacao, el chocolate, el
chicle, el chile, el aguacate** y **el coyote.**

En este siglo, al surgir los Estados Unidos
como potencia económica mundial, y debido
también a la proximidad geográfica, muchas
palabras del inglés han pasado a formar parte
del español familiar. Tenemos, por ejemplo, **el
béisbol, el sandwich, el match, el picnic, el
test, la interviú** (o **interview**), **los jeans, el
report, el rock, el rocket, el job, el lonche, el
mitin** (o **meeting**) y, en los últimos años, **el
jogging** (o **footing**).

Aunque nos referimos en general al
«idioma español», existen diferencias de uso y
vocabulario en los varios países en que lo hablan. La situación es semejante a la del inglés
de los Estados Unidos y el de Inglaterra, con la
diferencia que el español se habla en diez y
nueve países autónomos, en Puerto Rico y en
las grandes comunidades hispanas de los Estados Unidos.

---

3   **convertirse en** to become
26 **a través de** through
51 **trascender fronteras** to spread beyond bor-
    ders

60 **al surgir los Estados Unidos** when the U.S.
    emerged

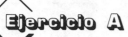

Ejercicio A

¿Cierto o falso? Indique si cada frase es cierta o falsa. Si es falsa, cámbiela para que sea cierta:

1. El catalán es otro nombre que se le da a la lengua española.

_____

2. La pronunciación del español de América se parece a la del sur de España.

_____

3. El español es una lengua germánica.

_____

4. En ciertas regiones de España la gente habla catalán y gallego.

_____

5. Los visigodos tuvieron mucha influencia en el castellano.

_____

6. Las palabras en español derivadas del griego no aparecen en otras lenguas del mundo.

_____

7. Los árabes contribuyeron muchas palabras al español.

_____

8. Las civilizaciones indígenas de América no influyeron en la lengua española.

_____

9. El uso y el vocabulario de la lengua española son iguales dondequiera que ésta se hable.

_____

10. El español es un idioma que se habla en unos veinte países del mundo.

_____

Ejercicio B

Complete cada frase correctamente:

1. El idioma español se conoce también como el _____ .
2. La pronunciación del español de América se parece a la de _____ .
3. El español se deriva del _____ .
4. Otras lenguas que todavía se hablan en España son el _____

   y el _____ .
5. De los pueblos que vivieron en la península, _____
   tuvieron la menor influencia en la lengua española.
6. Geometría, lógica y democracia son palabras españolas de origen _____ .

7. El pueblo invasor que más palabras contribuyó al español fue el _____ .

8. En América, la lengua española fue enriquecida por palabras _____ .

9. Dos dialectos indígenas que todavía se hablan en ciertas partes de América son el

    _____ y el _____ .

10. Hoy en día se nota mucha influencia del _____
    en el idioma español.

La Geografía de España

EXTENSIÓN, CLIMA Y POBLACIÓN

España está situada al sudoeste del continente europeo, ocupando las cuatro quintas partes de la Península Ibérica. Limita con Portugal al oeste y con Francia al nordeste. El resto del país está rodeado por las aguas del Mar Mediterráneo al este y las del Océano Atlántico al oeste. Al sur, el Estrecho de Gibraltar separa a España del continente africano. Políticamente, el territorio español también abarca las Islas Baleares en el Mediterráneo, las Islas Canarias en el Atlántico y los puertos de Melilla y Ceuta sobre la costa mediterránea de Marruecos.

En total, unos 39 millones de habitantes viven en un área algo menor que la del estado de Tejas, pero cuatro veces más grande que la del estado de Nueva York.

España se halla en la zona templada, pero las diferencias físicas que se notan en su territorio hacen que el clima sea muy variado. A lo largo de la costa norte y en las montañas del noroeste, el clima es templado; ésta es la region más fría y lluviosa del país. En cambio en las tierras del sur y del este el clima es cálido. En la meseta central y en parte de la costa sudeste predomina un clima de extremos: altísimas temperaturas y gran sequedad en el verano e intenso frío en el invierno. Por eso se ha dicho que Castilla tiene «seis meses de invierno y seis de infierno».

CORDILLERAS Y RÍOS PRINCIPALES

España es el país más montañoso de Europa después de Suiza. Casi la mitad del interior del país está cubierta por una extensa altiplanicie llamada la meseta. Varias cadenas de montañas rodean esta meseta. Las sierras de Guadarrama (al norte de Madrid) y Gredos la dividen en dos: al norte Castilla y León y al sur Castilla-La Mancha, donde queda la extensa llanura do La Mancha, famosa en el mundo por la novela de Miguel de Cervantes, «El ingenioso hidalgo Don Quijote de la Mancha». Al sur del país están la Sierra Morena, que separa la Mancha del valle del Guadalquivir, y la Sierra Nevada, donde se encuentra el pico más alto de la península, el Mulhacén (3.478 metros), cerca de Granada.

Al noroeste están los Montes Cantábricos, con picos hasta de 2.600 metros, y al norte se extienden los Pirineos, que marcan la frontera con Francia y tienen cumbres de más de 3.300 metros.

Entre las cordilleras mencionadas se encuentran los ricos valles formados por los cinco ríos más grandes de España. En el norte el Ebro, llamado antiguamente Iberus, le dio su nombre a la península. Este río pasa por la ciudad de Zaragoza y desemboca en el Mediterráneo. Los otros cuatro desembocan todos en el Atlántico. El río más largo es el Tajo, que pasa por la ciudad de Toledo y atraviesa Portugal para desembocar cerca de Lisboa. El Duero, que nace cerca de Burgos en Castilla y León, pasa por Valladolid y entra en Portugal en su camino al Atlántico. El Guadiana, al sur del país, pasa por Mérida y Badajoz, dos antiguos centros romanos. El Guadalquivir, en cuyas orillas se hallan las ciudades de Córdoba y Sevilla, es el río más navegable de España. Su nombre viene del árabe y quiere decir «rio grande».

MINERALES Y PRODUCTOS PRINCIPALES

España es un país básicamente agrícola. En el norte abundan la madera y la pesca. En la parte central se cultivan el trigo y otros cereales;

---

3 **las cuatro quintas partes** four fifths

21 **a lo largo de** along

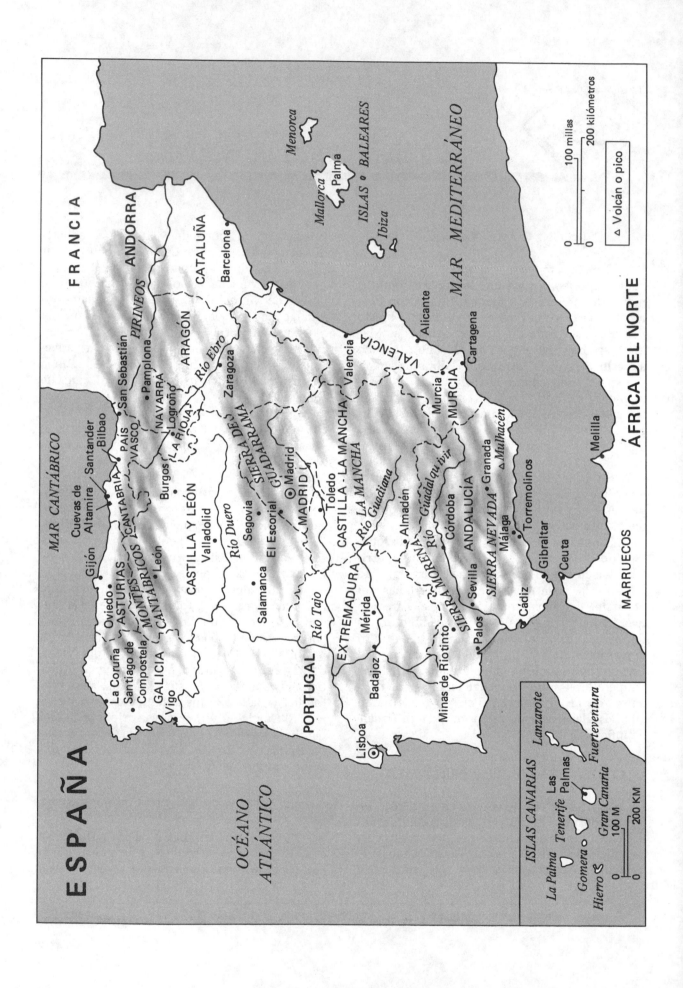

E S P A Ñ A

OCÉANO ATLÁNTICO

MAR CANTÁBRICO

FRANCIA

ANDORRA

PIRINEOS

CATALUÑA

Barcelona

Menorca

ISLAS · BALEARES

Mallorca
Palma

Ibiza

MAR MEDITERRÁNEO

ÁFRICA DEL NORTE

MARRUECOS

Cuevas de Altamira
Santander
Gijón
Oviedo
La Coruña
Santiago de Compostela
Vigo
GALICIA
ASTURIAS
MONTES CANTÁBRICOS
CANTABRIA
León
PAÍS VASCO
Bilbao
San Sebastián
Pamplona
NAVARRA
Logroño
LA RIOJA
Burgos
Zaragoza
ARAGÓN
Río Ebro

CASTILLA Y LEÓN
Valladolid
Río Duero
Segovia
SIERRA DE GUADARRAMA
Salamanca
El Escorial
Madrid
MADRID
Toledo
Río Tajo
PORTUGAL
Lisboa
EXTREMADURA
Mérida
Badajoz
CASTILLA · LA MANCHA
Río Guadiana
Almadén
Minas de Riotinto
Palos
SIERRA MORENA
Río Guadalquivir
Córdoba
Sevilla
Cádiz
ANDALUCÍA
SIERRA NEVADA
△Mulhacén
Granada
Málaga
Torremolinos
Gibraltar
Ceuta
Melilla

Valencia
VALENCIA
Alicante
MURCIA
Murcia
Cartagena

ISLAS CANARIAS
Lanzarote
Fuerteventura
La Palma
Tenerife
Gomera
Hierro
Las Palmas
Gran Canaria

100 millas
200 kilómetros
△ Volcán o pico

100 M
200 KM

en el sur la vid, de donde vienen los célebres
vinos de Jerez y de Málaga, y las aceitunas de
las que se produce el aceite de oliva. España es
el país con más olivares en el mundo y el tercer
5 productor mundial de vino. En el sudeste del
país se cultivan el arroz, las famosas naranjas de
Valencia, los limones, los dátiles y otras frutas
tropicales.

España es además muy rica en minerales.
10 El más importante es el hierro, que se extrae en
la provincia de Vizcaya, en el norte. En el sur
del país están las minas de plomo de Linares y
en el sudeste, las minas de cobre de Río Tinto.
En la parte central del sur están las minas de
15 mercurio de Almadén, las **más** grandes del
mundo.

En los últimos treinta años se han desarrollado la industria siderúrgica y la meta-
lúrgica, particularmente la fabricación de
20 automóviles. La industria textil se concentra en
Cataluña y es también importante para el país.

DIVISIÓN TERRITORIAL DEL PAÍS

Administrativamente, España, incluyendo
sus posesiones, tiene cincuenta provincias. His-
25 tóricamente, está dividida en quince regiones,
cada una de las cuales tiene sus propias tradiciones, cultura y en muchos casos su propia
lengua.

EL NORTE

30 Las regiones del norte del país incluyen a
Galicia, Asturias, Cantabria, el País Vasco, Navarra y La Rioja.

1. Galicia está al norte de Portugal, rodeada
por el Atlántico. Sus habitantes, los galle-
35 gos, son descendientes de los celtas que
llegaron del centro de Europa. Además
del español hablan gallego, una lengua re-
lacionada con el portugués. Los puertos
principales de esta región son Vigo y La
40 Coruña.
2. Asturias está entre Galicia y Cantabria y es
famosa por su industria minera. Allí se
halla Covadonga, donde el héroe Pelayo
venció a los moros en el año 718, iniciando
45 así el período conocido como la Reconquista. Las ciudades principales de esta región son Oviedo y Gijón.

3. Cantabria está al este de Asturias. Allí se
halla la cueva de Altamira, famosa por sus
pinturas prehistóricas.   50
4. El País Vasco está cerca de los Pirineos, en
la parte norte central del país. Es montañoso, bien irrigado y hermoso. Sus habitantes, los vascos, son descendientes de un
pueblo de origen desconocido y hablan el   55
vascuence. Este idioma es también de
origen muy antiguo y desconocido y no se
ha podido relacionar con ningún otro
idioma europeo. Los vascos tienen un carácter independiente y un profundo senti-   60
miento religioso. San Ignacio de Loyola,
fundador de la Compañía de Jesús (los jesuitas) [1], nació allí. En esta región se halla
la célebre playa de San Sebastián, conocida
como el «Biarritz» [2] o el «Lido» [3] de Es- 65
paña.
5. Navarra es una región montañosa al este del
País Vasco. Pamplona, su capital, es famosa por sus ferias anuales. Allí se celebra
en julio la fiesta de San Fermín, que atrae a   70
muchos turistas de todo el mundo.
6. La Rioja es famosa por sus vinos de buena
calidad, los vinos de Rioja. Su capital es
Logroño.

EL CENTRO   75

En el centro del país están las regiones de
Castilla, Madrid y Extremadura.

7. Castilla, que ocupa la mayor parte de la
Meseta Central, está dividida en Castilla y
León al norte y Castilla-La Mancha al sur.   80
Tomó su nombre por los muchos castillos
que se construyeron allí durante las guerras
entre moros y cristianos. Su idioma, el castellano, es el idioma oficial de España. Ninguna otra región ha influido tanto en la vida 85
nacional como Castilla, cuyos reyes jugaron un papel decisivo en la unificación de
las varias regiones en una nación. La región
de Castilla y León tiene además ricas minas
de hierro y carbón.   90
8. Madrid es el centro económico de España.
Es también la residencia del Gobierno y de
las Cortes. Allí se halla la capital del país,
Madrid.

---

2 **el vino de Jerez** sherry (wine)

18 **la industria siderúrgica** iron and steel
works

9. Extremadura, al sur de Castilla y León, está llena de montes. El río Guadiana corre por estas tierras, donde se hallan muchos monumentos de la época romana. Allí nacieron tres de los grandes conquistadores, Francisco Pizarro, Hernán Cortés y Vasco Núñez de Balboa.

EL SUR

10. Andalucía, la región del sur del país, recibió la influencia más profunda de la cultura árabe. Sus ciudades principales representan los distintos períodos de su historia. Cádiz, por ejemplo, fue el centro del comercio fenicio. Más tarde, durante la época musulmana, florecieron centros como Córdoba, Granada y Sevilla. En Andalucía se hallan las típicas casas españolas, pintadas de vivos colores, con patio en el centro y con rejas y balcones que dan a la calle.

EL ESTE

En la parte este del país están las regiones de Cataluña, Valencia, Murcia y Aragón.

11. Cataluña está situada al nordeste del país, en la costa mediterránea, y es la región más industrial de España. Su ciudad principal, Barcelona, es el puerto más grande del país. Los catalanes son bilingües, pues además del castellano hablan su propio idioma, el catalán, derivado también del latín. Fuertes sentimientos separatistas por parte de los catalanes los han hecho buscar su independencia del gobierno central de España en varias ocasiones.

12. Valencia, conocida por la fertilidad de su tierra y su excelente sistema de riego, está al sur de Cataluña. Es llamada «la huerta de España» a causa de sus numerosos productos agrícolas, entre los cuales son bien conocidas las deliciosas naranjas valencianas. El sistema de canales de irrigación que se usa allí fue introducido en España por los moros. Las costumbres de los valencianos, así como sus tradiciones, están bien representadas en algunas de las novelas del escritor Vicente Blasco Ibáñez (1867–1928).

13. Murcia, al sur de Valencia, es típicamente mediterránea. Es rica en minerales como el hierro y el cobre. Los productos principales de esta región son los dátiles, los limones y las naranjas.

14. Aragón está al nordeste del país. La cría de ovejas es una industria importante de esta región. Zaragoza, su ciudad principal, deriva su nombre del emperador romano Julio César (Caesaraugusta) y fue de gran importancia militar durante la ocupación romana de España.

POSESIONES EXTRATERRITORIALES

España tiene todavía algunas posesiones extraterritoriales, residuos del gran imperio español.

1. Las Islas Baleares forman un archipiélago en el Mediterráneo. Las más conocidas son Mallorca, Menorca e Ibiza, y su capital es Palma de Mallorca. Su industria principal es el turismo.

2. Las Islas Canarias forman un archipiélago de siete islas grandes en el Atlántico, frente a la parte sur de Marruecos. Las islas están divididas en dos provincias, Santa Cruz de Tenerife y Las Palmas. Desde 1982 las Canarias se constituyeron en Comunidad Autónoma.

3. Melilla y Ceuta son dos puertos en la costa de Marruecos que le pertenecen a España desde los siglos XV y XVII, respectivamente.

CIUDADES PRINCIPALES

1. Madrid es la capital y la ciudad más grande de España, con casi cuatro millones de habitantes. Situada en el centro del país, tiene muchos lugares históricos de interés. Entre ellos están el Museo del Prado, donde se encuentra una colección impresionante de las obras de los grandes pintores españoles como Velázquez, El Greco y Goya; el Palacio Real, uno de los palacios más grandes y lujosos del mundo: el Parque del Buen Retiro, el parque principal del la capital y antiguo campo de recreo de los nobles españoles; y la Puerta del Sol, la plaza principal de donde se dice que salen todas las carreteras de España.

Cerca de la capital está El Escorial, un enorme monasterio fundado por el rey Felipe II en 1563, cuya construcción duró 22 años. Es de estilo severo, clásico y majes-

---

59   **extraterritorial** outside territorial limits

63   **el archipiélago** archipelago (a group of islands)

73   **Comunidad Autónoma** self-governing community

tuoso. El edificio contiene el Panteón de los Reyes, donde están enterrados muchos de los reyes de España. También hay una valiosa biblioteca, una iglesia y una rica colección de cuadros y tapices.

Otro monumento enorme cerca de la capital es el Valle de los Caídos, construido en memoria de los soldados que murieron en la Guerra Civil española (1936–39) y dedicado en 1959. Encima de la ancha bóveda hay una cruz que tiene más de 125 metros de altura. Allí fue enterrado en 1975 el general Francisco Franco, dictador de España desde 1939 hasta su muerte.

2. Barcelona es la capital de Cataluña y el puerto principal de España. La ciudad está dividida en dos partes por Las Ramblas, una de las avenidas más hermosas de toda Europa. La Plaza de Cataluña es el centro comercial y social de la ciudad. Barcelona ha sido tradicionalmente un gran centro artístico y cultural, donde han vivido muchos pintores y escritores de fama mundial. En las afueras de la ciudad se halla el famoso monasterio de Montserrat, visitado todos los años por miles de turistas y peregrinos.

3. Sevilla, a orillas del Guadalquivir, es la ciudad principal de Andalucía. Durante la época colonial era el único puerto de donde salían los buques para el Nuevo Mundo. La Catedral de Sevilla es la catedral gótica más grande del mundo y allí se encuentra la tumba de Cristóbal Colón. La Giralda, construida en el siglo XII, es la torre de la catedral y un admirable ejemplo de arquitectura árabe. En lo alto de la torre hay una estatua que hace de veleta y gira con el viento. Sevilla es una típica ciudad andaluza, cuya parte antigua posee calles estrechas y hermosos patios que adornan el interior de las casas.

4. Valencia es un puerto a orillas del Mediterráneo y un gran centro agrícola, industrial y comercial.

5. Granada está situada al pie de la Sierra Nevada. Fue la última fortaleza de los moros en España, conquistada por los Reyes Católicos en 1492. Entre los lugares de interés están el Albaicín, un pintoresco barrio donde viven los gitanos desde principios del siglo XVI; la Alhambra, antiguo palacio de los reyes moros, inmortalizado por el escritor norteamericano Washington Irving (1783–1859) en su libro «The Alhambra», y donde están el famoso Patio de los Leones y otros ejemplos del arte musulmán; y el Generalife, otro palacio moro que tiene fama por sus jardines encantadores y por haber sido la residencia de verano de los reyes moros.

6. Toledo está situada a orillas del río Tajo, a poca distancia de Madrid. Fue capital de la España visigoda y residencia de los reyes de España hasta 1560. La ciudad ha quedado inmortalizada en los cuadros del gran pintor El Greco. El famoso Alcázar de Toledo, un castillo moro que fue destruido durante la Guerra Civil en 1936, ha sido totalmente reconstruido.

7. Cádiz es un puerto sobre el Atlántico. En tiempos primitivos fue una colonia de los fenicios.

8. Bilbao, capital de la provincia de Vizcaya, es el centro de la industria minera del norte. Hizo un papel muy importante durante las Guerras Carlistas a la muerte de Fernando VII en 1833.

9. Burgos es la antigua capital de Castilla y León. Tiene una famosa catedral del mismo nombre que es una de las maravillas de la arquitectura gótica en España. Allí se halla la tumba del Cid Campeador, el héroe nacional de España.

10. Santiago de Compostela es una ciudad de Galicia visitada todos los años por miles de peregrinos religiosos. Según la tradición, allí se encuentra la tumba del apóstol Santiago, santo patrón de España.

11. Salamanca es el sitio de una de las universidades más viejas de Europa, la Universidad de Salamanca, fundada en el siglo XIII. La ciudad conserva una catedral románica del siglo XII y otra gótica del siglo XVI, además de numerosos edificios de los siglos XVI a XVIII.

12. Córdoba, a orillas del Guadalquivir, fue en los siglos X y XI la capital del gobierno musulmán en España y el centro cultural más importante de toda Europa. Es una de las

---

1 **Panteón de los Reyes** burial place for kings

38 **hacer de** to act as

76 **hacer un papel** to play a role

ciudades más pintorescas de España. Su famosa mezquita, hoy en día catedral, es un monumento árabe cuya construcción fue iniciada en el año 786.

NOTES:

[1] **Compañía de Jesús o los jesuitas:** Catholic religious order founded by San Ignacio de Loyola in 1534. Almost from the beginning, education, scholarship, and missionary work became its principal activities. The society grew rapidly and quickly assumed a prominent role in the defense of Catholicism, emphasizing obedience to the Pope. The Jesuits are today the largest order of male religious. The order has continued work on all levels of education and has played an important role not only in Spain but also in Spanish America.

[2] **Biarritz:** famous French seaside resort on the Atlantic Ocean.

[3] **Lido:** island close to Venice, Italy, famous for its fashionable beaches.

Ejercicio A

Escriba la letra que indique la relación correcta con cada expresión de la columna de la izquierda:

1. montañas cerca de Madrid _____
2. río más navegable de España _____
3. pico más alto de España _____
4. vinos famosos _____
5. antiguo centro romano _____
6. montañas del sur de España _____
7. río más largo de España _____
8. frontera occidental _____
9. montañas del noroeste de España _____
10. montañas entre Francia y España _____
11. el mercurio _____
12. frontera oriental _____
13. el plomo _____
14. río que dio su nombre a la península _____
15. río que nace en Castilla _____

a. la Sierra de Guadarrama
b. Badajoz
c. el Ebro
d. el Guadiana
e. Linares
f. el Duero
g. Jerez y Málaga
h. Almadén
i. Portugal
j. la Sierra Morena
k. el Guadalquivir
l. el Tajo
m. los Pirineos
n. los Montes Cantábricos
o. el Mulhacén
p. el Mediterráneo

Ejercicio B

¿Cierto o falso? Indique si cada frase es cierta o falsa. Si es falsa, cámbiela para hacerla cierta:

1. Todos los ríos de España desembocan en el Mar Mediterráneo.

_____

2. Los Pirineos forman la frontera entre España y Portugal.

_____

3. España y Portugal forman la Península Ibérica.

_____

4. El río más navegable de España es el Guadiana.

_____

5. El Ebro es el único río que desemboca en el Océano Atlántico.

_____

6. El clima de España es muy variado.

_____

7. La cordillera que está en el norte de España es la Sierra de Guadarrama.

_____

8. El río Tajo pasa por Toledo y Lisboa.

_____

9. La extensión de España es mayor que la del estado de Tejas.

_____

10. Las naranjas y otras frutas tropicales abundan en el norte de España.

_____

Ejercicio C

Escriba la letra que indique la relación correcta con cada expresión de la columna de la izquierda:

1. Montserrat _____		**a.** plaza principal de Madrid
2. Museo del Prado _____		**b.** santo patrón de España
3. Puerta del Sol _____		**c.** el río Tajo
4. El Retiro _____		**d.** última fortaleza de los moros en España
5. Bilbao _____		**e.** monumento de la Guerra Civil
6. Santiago _____		**f.** el Cid Campeador
7. Burgos _____		**g.** parque público de Madrid
8. Granada _____		**h.** paseo moderno
9. Toledo _____		**i.** grandes pintores españoles
10. Valle de los Caídos _____		**j.** catedral gótica más grande del mundo
11. la Catedral de Sevilla _____		**k.** mezquita iniciada en 786
12. Salamanca _____		**l.** centro comercial y social de Barcelona
13. Córdoba _____		**m.** tumba de Cristóbal Colón
14. la Plaza de Cataluña _____		**n.** una universidad antigua
15. Sevilla _____		**o.** monasterio famoso
		p. centro de la industria minera del norte

Ejercicio D

Escriba la letra que indique la relación correcta con cada expresión de la columna de la izquierda:

1. Ibiza _____
2. Valencia _____
3. San Sebastián _____
4. el vascuence _____
5. Santa Cruz de Tenerife _____
6. Pamplona _____
7. Covadonga _____
8. Andalucía _____
9. Barcelona _____
10. Galicia _____

a. región del centro del país
b. idioma de origen desconocido
c. una de las Islas Baleares
d. Pelayo
e. La Coruña
f. «la huerta de España»
g. gran influencia árabe
h. ciudad principal de Cataluña
i. playa famosa
j. las Islas Canarias
k. monumentos romanos
l. capital de Navarra

Ejercicio E

Complete las frases siguientes en español:

1. La Universidad de Salamanca fue fundada en el siglo _____.
2. El Albaicín se halla en la ciudad de _____.
3. El famoso Patio de los Leones está en _____, un palacio construido por los moros.
4. El puerto principal de España es _____.
5. La ciudad más grande de España es _____.
6. El santo patrón de España es _____.
7. Felipe II hizo construir _____.
8. _____, el hermoso castillo moro en Toledo, fue destruido durante la Guerra Civil española.
9. La tumba del Cid está en la catedral de _____.
10. _____ pintó muchas escenas de la ciudad de Toledo.

Ejercicio F

¿Cierto o falso? Indique si cada frase es cierta o falsa. Si es falsa, cámbiela para hacerla cierta:

1. Palma es la capital de las Islas Canarias.

_____

2. Los vascos son descendientes de la raza céltica.

_____

3. La Reconquista empezó con una batalla que tuvo lugar en Asturias.

_____

4. Las Islas Canarias se hallan en el continente de África.

_____

5. San Ignacio de Loyola fundó la Compañía de Jesús.

_____

6. Los puertos de La Coruña y Barcelona están en la provincia de Galicia.

_____

7. La capital de España está en Castilla-La Mancha.

_____

8. Málaga es el puerto más grande de España.

_____

9. Los sistemas de irrigación usados en Valencia fueron introducidos por los moros.

_____

10. Murcia está al norte de Valencia.

_____

11. Asturias recibió la influencia más profunda de la cultura árabe.

_____

12. Muchos extranjeros van a Pamplona en el mes de julio.

_____

13. El gallego es un idioma relacionado con el francés.

_____

14. La ciudad principal de Cataluña es Barcelona.

_____

15. Cádiz fue un gran centro comercial establecido por los romanos.

_____

Ejercicio G

Complete cada frase escribiendo el nombre de la región:

1. _____ está directamente al norte de Portugal.

2. _____ es la región más industrial de España.

3. _____ es la «huerta de España».

4. _____ ha tenido la mayor influencia en la vida nacional.

5. _____ tiene una ciudad que fue nombrada por un emperador romano.

6. En _____ se inició la Reconquista.

7. Los habitantes de _____ hablan español y un idioma de origen desconocido.

8. _____ dio al mundo muchos conquistadores.

9. _____ todavía conserva mucho de la gran cultura árabe.

10. _____ es una región típicamente mediterránea.

11. _____ se constituyeron en Comunidad Autónoma.

12. En _____ se encuentran ricas minas de carbón y de hierro.

13. La famosa playa de San Sebastián se halla en _____ .

14. _____ son la única posesión española en el Mediterráneo.

15. En la capital de _____ se celebra la fiesta de San Fermín.

ÉPOCA PRIMITIVA

La España de hoy es el producto de los diversos pueblos que la invadieron, trayendo consigo sus propias lenguas, costumbres y ca-
5 racterísticas.

Los iberos son el primer pueblo sobre el cual hay informes, aunque no se sabe mucho de su historia. Eran de origen mediterráneo y se extendieron por toda la región sudoriental de
10 España.

Los celtas, de origen centroeuropeo, entra-ron en la península por el norte a eso del año 1.000 a. de J.C. Los iberos eran hombres bajos y morenos; en cambio los celtas eran rubios y más
15 altos. De la unión de las dos razas se formó la raza celtíbera.

Mientras tanto los fenicios, grandes nave-gantes y comerciantes del norte de África, es-tablecieron colonias en el sur de la península.
20 Eran un pueblo de una cultura avanzada, que introdujeron en España el arte de escribir, el uso de la moneda y el arte de trabajar los metales. Los fenicios fundaron muchos centros comer-ciales, entre ellos Cádiz y Málaga.

25 En el siglo VII a. de J.C. los griegos, otro pueblo de comerciantes, establecieron algunas colonias en la costa oriental e introdujeron el cultivo de la uva y el olivo.

Los cartagineses entraron en la península
30 en el siglo VI a. de J.C. para ayudar a los feni-cios en sus guerras contra los celtíberos. Pronto, sin embargo, los cartagineses emplearon sus ar-mas contra los fenicios, los vencieron, y se apoderaron de gran parte de la península. Luego
35 había de venir lógicamente el enfrentamiento con la otra potencia marítima del Mediterráneo, Roma.

Los celtíberos lucharon tanto contra los cartagineses como contra los romanos. Celosos de su independencia, preferían morir antes que
40 rendirse. Un ejemplo de su heroísmo fue el sitio de Sagunto (219 a. de J.C.) que duró nueve meses. Cuando los cartagineses, bajo el mando de Aníbal, su famoso general, entraron por fin en la ciudad, no hallaron más que muerte y
45 ruinas.

Las legiones romanas finalmente vencie-ron a los cartagineses en el año 202 a. de J.C. en las llamadas Guerras Púnicas. Entonces Roma pudo dedicarse a la conquista de la pe-
50 nínsula, cuyos habitantes, sin embargo, ofrecie-ron dura resistencia a los romanos. El sitio de Numancia (133 a. de J.C.), que duró más de quince meses, fue otro ejemplo del heroísmo es-
55 pañol.

Los romanos permanecieron en España unos seis siglos, y esa época es sin duda una de las más significativas en la formación de la cul-tura hispana. Los romanos dieron la base del idioma actual, un magnífico sistema de leyes,
60 su estructura económica y social y muchas obras públicas, grandes carreteras, puentes y acueductos. Fundaron ciudades, levantaron es-cuelas y construyeron teatros y anfiteatros al aire libre. El cristianismo, que había nacido dentro
65 de los confines del imperio romano, se convir-tió en una de las fuerzas permanentes de la so-ciedad hispanoromana.

Hacia el siglo V d. de J.C., sin embargo, Roma se hallaba ya en decadencia. Los visigo-
70 dos, una de las tribus germánicas del norte, in-vadieron a España, terminaron la dominación romana y establecieron su gobierno en Toledo. Pero a pesar de la dominación visigoda, que duró casi cuatro siglos, la gran influencia ro-
75 mana continuó en la península. Los godos adoptaron la lengua hispanoromana, las leyes y

---

3 **traer consigo** to bring with them
13 **a. de J.C. (antes de Jesucristo)** B.C.

36 **potencia marítima** sea power
69 **d. de J.C. (después de Jesucristo)** A.D.

las costumbres. El catolicismo triunfó definitivamente en España, y la iglesia llegó a tener un
enorme poder al lado de los reyes feudales.

LOS MOROS Y LA RECONQUISTA

5   Los musulmanes (árabes, moros y beré-
beres) comenzaron a entrar por el sur en el año
711. En la batalla de Guadalete vencieron a los
soldados del rey Rodrigo, el último rey visigodo. Los moros lograron dominar toda la pe-
10 nínsula, con excepción de algunas regiones del
norte. En el año 718 Pelayo, con un pequeño
ejército de visigodos, venció a los moros en
Covadonga (Asturias). Así comenzó la llamada
Reconquista, una lucha constante entre moros y
15 cristianos que duró casi ocho siglos, hasta 1492.

Gracias en parte a la influencia árabe, España llegó a ser el país más avanzado y más
culto de toda Europa. Los moros trajeron su arquitectura, su arte y sus sistemas de irrigación,
20 que aún hoy se usan. De todas partes llegaban
estudiantes a Córdoba (la capital de los moros)
para estudiar matemáticas, ciencias y medicina.
El rey cristiano de León, Alfonso X, llamado el
Sabio, reunió en su corte a muchos sabios, entre
25 los cuales había árabes, cristianos y judíos. Allí
estudiaron y enseñaron, y a ellos se debe mucho
de lo que hoy sabemos de la España medieval.

Durante los tres primeros siglos de la dominación mora, se vivió mayormente en paz. Pero
30 más tarde llegaron otros invasores del norte de
África, y los reinos cristianos empezaron a
unirse para reconquistar sus tierras. El Cid
Campeador, Rodrigo Díaz de Vivar, vivió en el
siglo XI y se distinguió en las luchas entre mo-
35 ros y cristianos. Era muy temido de los moros,
quienes le dieron el título de El Cid, que significa «señor» en árabe. En el año 1094 venció a
los moros de la ciudad de Valencia y gobernó
esta ciudad hasta su muerte en 1099. Sobre sus
40 hazañas se escribió un poema épico, el Poema
del Cid, una de las obras maestras de la literatura española.

La Reconquista no fue rápida porque los
habitantes de la península no estaban unidos y
45 pensaban en términos regionales, no como una
sola nación. En 1469 Isabel, princesa de Cas-

tilla, se casó con Fernando, príncipe de Aragón.
Más tarde, cuando ella llegó a ser reina de Castilla y él rey de Aragón, dos de los reinos más
poderosos, la España cristiana quedó unificada   50
por primera vez. Del gran imperio árabe sólo
quedaba el reino de Granada, gobernado por
Boabdil, el último rey moro. Fernando e Isabel,
llamados los Reyes Católicos, conquistaron a
Granada en 1492, terminando así la Recon-   55
quista.

Los Reyes Católicos entonces trataron de
reunir bajo su corona las otras regiones independientes. Crearon la Santa Hermandad, una
institución encargada de proteger a la población   60
rural, y reorganizaron la Inquisición [1], cuya
misión era mantener la unidad religiosa. En
1492 expulsaron a todos los judíos de España.

GRANDEZA DE ESPAÑA

Bajo el reinado de los Reyes Católicos, Es-   65
paña llegó a ser la primera nación de Europa.
Fue la reina Isabel quien recibió a Cristóbal Colón, un navegante genovés, y resolvió ayudarle
en su empresa, dándole tres barcos, la Pinta, la
Niña y la Santa María. El día 3 de agosto de   70
1492, estos tres barcos partieron de Palos, en el
sur de España. El día 12 de octubre del mismo
año, Colón y sus marineros pisaron tierra en una
isla que llamaron San Salvador (hoy en día conocida por el nombre de Watling Island).   75

Con el descubrimiento del Nuevo Mundo
empezó el gran imperio español. Gonzalo Fernández de Córdoba, el «Gran Capitán», que había adquirido fama durante las guerras contra
los moros, conquistó gran parte de Italia para   80
los Reyes Católicos.

Durante el reinado de Carlos V (1517–
1556), nieto de los Reyes Católicos, la nación
española llegó a tener posesiones en Alemania,
Austria, Italia, los Países Bajos, América, el   85
norte de África y el sur del Pacífico. Ésta fue la
época de los grandes descubrimientos y conquistas.

En 1556 Carlos V se retiró a un monasterio
y entregó el poder a su hijo, Felipe II, quien   90
reinó hasta 1598. Era un hombre inteligente,
pero austero y fanático. Desde el Escorial, soñaba con poner fin al protestantismo y hacer

---

35 **ser temido de** to be feared by
48 **llegar a ser** to become

84 **llegar a tener** to succeed in having, to manage to have
85 **los Países Bajos** the Netherlands (Holland)

eterna la gloria de España. Durante su reinado tuvo lugar la famosa batalla de Lepanto contra los turcos, que acabó con el poder otomano en el Mediterráneo. También ocurrió el mayor de-
5 sastre naval sufrido por España, la destrucción de la Armada Invencible en 1558 a manos de Inglaterra, su rival religioso y político. Esta derrota inició la decadencia del imperio español.

DECADENCIA

10 Felipe II murió en 1598 y sus sucesores, Felipe III y luego Felipe IV, no fueron capaces de gobernar territorios tan grandes. España empezó a sufrir derrotas y a perder tierras. Además, el dominio del mar ya no le pertenecía a
15 España, sino a Inglaterra. Aunque la literatura y el arte seguían floreciendo, había mucha corrupción en los asuntos del gobierno, y el pueblo sufría mucha miseria. España experimentaba la ruina económica a causa de las fre-
20 cuentes guerras, la emigración al Nuevo Mundo y la expulsión de los judíos y los moros.

Durante el reinado de Carlos II la decadencia de la nación española llegó a ser casi completa. La muerte del rey en 1700 marca el fin de
25 la dinastía de los Habsburgos [2] en España y el comienzo de la dinastía de los Borbones [3], que dura hasta tiempos modernos.

En 1759 subió al poder Carlos III, bajo cuyo reinado se nacionalizó la enseñanza, se estable-
30 ció el servicio de correos, se hicieron muchas reformas urbanas y se fomentaron la agricultura, la industria y el comercio.

SIGLOS XVIII A XX

Desgraciadamente Carlos IV era tan débil
35 que deshizo toda la obra de su padre, Carlos III. Durante su reinado, Napoleón invadió a España en 1808 y nombró rey a su hermano José. El dos de mayo del mismo año, los ciudadanos madrileños se rebelaron contra los soldados
40 franceses, y así comenzó la Guerra de Independencia que duró hasta 1813. Esta guerra ha quedado inmortalizada en las obras del gran pintor español Francisco Goya.

Con la ayuda de Inglaterra, España logró finalmente expulsar a las tropas francesas de su 45 territorio. Desde entonces, el dos de mayo se ha considerado como la fiesta nacional del país.

Después de la derrota de los franceses, subió Fernando VII al poder, un monarca reaccionario que suprimió el espíritu liberal del país 50 y gobernó como rey absoluto. Durante su reinado, España perdió casi todas sus colonias en el Nuevo Mundo.

Después de la muerte de Fernando VII en 1833, estalló una guerra civil entre los carlistas 55 tradicionalistas (partidarios del príncipe Don Carlos, hermano de Fernando) y los liberales (partidarios de Isabel II, hija del rey y todavía menor de edad). Esta guerra es conocida como las Guerras Carlistas que ocasionaron batallas e 60 incidentes de 1833 a 1839, de 1855 a 1860 y de 1872 a 1876. La tercera guerra carlista fue ganada por los ejércitos liberales en 1876.

La primera república, que había sido establecida en 1873, duró sólo once meses du- 65 rante los cuales pasaron por el poder cuatro presidentes. Alfonso XII, hijo de Isabel II, volvió como rey en 1874, pero murió en 1885. Durante la regencia de su esposa, María Cristina, se acabó el resto del imperio español. Por el Tra- 70 tado de París (1898), que terminó la guerra entre España y los Estados Unidos, España perdió a Cuba, Puerto Rico, las Filipinas y Guam.

En 1902 Alfonso XIII subió al trono, pero fue expulsado en 1931 por haber permitido que 75 el dictador Primo de Rivera gobernase a España de 1923 a 1930, y por haber actuado mal en la guerra de Marruecos.

La segunda república española fue declarada en 1931 pero duró solamente cinco años, a 80 causa de las muchas luchas políticas. Bajo la república, España recibió una nueva constitución y muchas leyes liberales. Por desgracia, el gobierno no pudo mantenerse fuerte, y en 1936 estalló la Guerra Civil. Después de muchas luchas 85 sangrientas, el general Francisco Franco logró vencer las fuerzas de la República y estableció una dictadura en 1939, que duró hasta su muerte en 1975.

El gobierno actual de España es una mo- 90 narquía constitucional. En 1969, Franco y las Cortes (el parlamento) nombraron como futuro

---

2 **tener lugar** to take place, to occur

19 **a causa de** on account of, because of

38 **los ciudadanos madrileños** the citizens of Madrid

55 **estallar** to break out

rey y jefe del estado al príncipe Juan Carlos, nieto de Alfonso XIII, quien subió al trono en 1975. Desde 1982 el primer ministro del país es Felipe González Márquez, secretario general del partido socialista español. En 1985 se aprobó la admisión de España a la Comunidad Económica Europea [4].

NOTES:

[1] **la Inquisición:** Tribunal established during the Middle Ages to try heretics and those suspected of converting only nominally to Christianity. This institution was particularly powerful in Spain in the late fifteenth century. It influenced and affected the religious policies of the Catholic monarchs, Ferdinand and Isabella, who expelled first all Jews who refused to be baptized and later on all Moors. The Inquisition became synonymous with horror, religious bigotry, and cruel fanaticism.

[2] **los Habsburgos:** Royal family from Germany, one of the principal sovereign dynasties of Europe from the fifteenth to the twentieth century. The dynasty started in Spain with Charles V, who became the most powerful of the Habsburgs.

[3] **los Borbones:** Royal family from France. With the exception of a few years, from 1868–1874, the House of Bourbon ruled in Spain from 1700 to 1931. It returned to the throne of Spain in 1975 with Juan Carlos I.

[4] **la Comunidad Económica Europea:** European Common Market. Comprised of Belgium, Denmark, France, Germany, Greece, Ireland, Italy, Luxembourg, the Netherlands, Portugal, Spain, and the United Kingdom. These nations aim to integrate their economies, coordinate social development, and bring about the political union of the democratic states of Europe.

Ejercicio A

Escriba la letra que indique la relación correcta con cada expresión de la columna de la izquierda:

1. las Guerras Púnicas   _____
2. el uso de monedas   _____
3. Palos   _____
4. Numancia   _____
5. Boabdil   _____
6. Rodrigo Díaz de Vivar   _____
7. Pelayo   _____
8. derrota de la Armada Invencible   _____
9. Francisco Franco   _____
10. Isabel II   _____

a. Guerra Carlista
b. último rey de los moros
c. la segunda república española
d. la primera gramática española
e. Cristóbal Colón
f. los fenicios
g. invasión romana
h. Covadonga
i. derrota de los cartagineses
j. dictador
k. el héroe nacional de España
l. Felipe II

Ejercicio B

¿Cierto o falso? Indique si cada frase es cierta o falsa. Si es falsa la frase, cambie el elemento necesario para hacerla cierta:

1. Los habitantes primitivos del país fueron los celtíberos.

2. Los fenicios fundaron muchos centros comerciales.

_____

3. El sitio de Sagunto es un ejemplo del heroísmo de los cartagineses.

_____

4. Los visigodos dieron la base del idioma actual de España.

_____

5. Bajo la influencia romana, España llegó a ser el país más avanzado y más culto de Europa.

_____

6. Pelayo es el héroe nacional de España.

_____

7. La España cristiana se unificó con la boda de Fernando e Isabel.

_____

8. La destrucción de la Gran Armada terminó el período de la decadencia de España.

_____

9. La Guerra de Independencia comenzó el dos de mayo.

_____

10. Al terminar la Guerra Civil española en 1939, el gobierno de España era una monarquía constitucional.

_____

Ejercicio C
Identifique el personaje:

1. El rey de España que perdió el trono en 1931.

_____

2. Tomó el poder en 1939 y fue dictador hasta su muerte.

_____

3. Conquistó gran parte de Italia para los Reyes Católicos.

_____

4. Durante su reinado se estableció el servicio de correos.

_____

5. Durante su reinado, la decadencia de España llegó a ser casi completa.

_____

6. Se disputó el trono de España con Isabel II.

_____

7. Se casó con la princesa Isabel de Castilla.

_____

8. Los grandes descubrimientos y conquistas sucedieron durante su reinado.

_____

9. El rey actual de España.

_____

10. Durante su reinado, España perdió la mayor parte de sus colonias en América.

_____

Ejercicio D

Complete las frases siguientes en español:

1. España tuvo el mayor número de posesiones durante el reinado de _____.
2. _____ gobernó en España durante el reinado de Alfonso XIII.
3. Los _____ introdujeron el cultivo de la uva y el olivo en España.
4. Bajo Felipe II, España venció a los turcos en la batalla de _____.
5. Un rey español muy progresista de la Casa de Borbón fue _____.
6. El gobierno actual de España es _____.
7. Napoleón invadió a España en el año _____.
8. Los primeros habitantes de España fueron los _____.
9. España logró expulsar a los franceses con la ayuda de _____.
10. La dominación romana terminó en el siglo _____.

Ejercicio E

Indique el orden cronológico de las personas siguientes, escribiendo en orden ascendente los números 1–10 en los espacios correspondientes:

1. _____ Pelayo
2. _____ Carlos V
3. _____ Juan Carlos
4. _____ Alfonso XII
5. _____ el rey Rodrigo
6. _____ Felipe II
7. _____ Fernando e Isabel
8. _____ Rodrigo Díaz de Vivar
9. _____ Isabel II
10. _____ Fernando VII

CHAPTER 31
La Literatura de España

ORÍGENES Y EDAD MEDIA

Desde los tiempos antiguos, España ha estado bien representada en la literatura mundial.
Los orígenes de la literatura española pueden
5 encontrarse en pequeñas canciones líricas de
tipo popular que datan del siglo XI. Estas canciones, llamadas jarchas, fueron escritas en
dialecto español mozárabe y representan la primera manifestación de lo que será más tarde el
10 tipo de lírica tradicional española, el villancico.

El «Poema (o Cantar) de Mio Cid» es el más
antiguo y mejor ejemplo de la poesía épica española. Cuenta las hazañas del héroe nacional
de España, Rodrigo Díaz de Vivar, y está divi-
15 dido en tres partes o cantares que tratan de tres
épocas distintas de su vida. El poema, de autor
anónimo, fue compuesto hacia el año 1140.

Alfonso X, el Sabio (1221–1284) es la figura más prominente de la literatura española
20 de la Edad Media. Bajo su reinado la literatura
llegó a tener prestigio oficial. Además de escribir varias obras en prosa y en verso, reunió en
su corte a los hombres más cultos de la época
para estudiar, traducir y escribir textos en dis-
25 tintas áreas, desde historia hasta astronomía. A
Alfonso se deben «Las siete partidas», una vasta
colección de leyes y costumbres que reflejan la
sociedad de la época.

En el siglo XIV empezaron a aparecer los
30 libros de caballería, que fueron populares hasta
finales del siglo XVI. Se caracterizaban por su
idealismo sentimental, su atmósfera lírica y las
aventuras sobrenaturales de sus héroes.

En el siglo XV comenzó una renovación de
35 la poesía. Los romances, poemas narrativos épi-
co-líricos que se cantan, tuvieron su origen en
ese siglo y han sobrevivido hasta hoy día. Tratan de temas heroicos, históricos o líricos, y se

considera que reflejan el alma y la tradición del
pueblo español. 40

Jorge Manrique (1440–1479) es famoso
por sus «Coplas», un poema escrito para honrar
la muerte de su padre. Se considera tal vez como
la mejor obra de poesía lírica escrita durante la
Edad Media. Fue traducida al inglés, en verso, 45
por el poeta norteamericano Henry Wadsworth
Longfellow (1807–1882).

Antonio de Nebrija (1441–1522) es conocido por haber escrito la primera gramática
castellana, publicada en 1492. Fue la primera 50
gramática escrita sobre una lengua moderna.

SIGLO DE ORO

El llamado Siglo de Oro es la época más
gloriosa de la literatura española. En este período de casi dos siglos, vivieron los autores 55
considerados como clásicos por excelencia.
Comienza durante la primera mitad del siglo
XVI y termina hacia fines del siglo XVII, con la
muerte de Pedro Calderón de la Barca.

Garcilaso de la Vega (1501–1536), sol- 60
dado y poeta, fue un verdadero representante
del Renacimiento. Introdujo en España nuevas
formas de poesía lírica y popularizó la forma
poética llamada soneto. Con Garcilaso comienza la literatura española moderna. 65

En el siglo XVI surge un género de narración literaria de tipo realista y satírico que se
llama la novela picaresca. Ésta describe las
aventuras de un pícaro, una persona sin raíces,
que sirve de criada, cambia con frecuencia de 70
amo y ciudad y engaña para poder vivir. Sus
comentarios son una verdadera sátira de la vida
y la sociedad de la época. La primera y más
típica de las novelas de este género es el

---

1 **la Edad Media** the Middle Ages
3 **la literatura mundial** world literature

30 **el libro de caballería** romance of chivalry
43 **tal vez** perhaps

423

«Lazarillo de Tormes», de autor anónimo, que apareció en 1554.

Miguel de Cervantes Saavedra (1547–1616) es conocido en todo el mundo como el autor de «Don Quijote de la Mancha», uno de los libros más leídos en todos los idiomas. Siendo joven, Cervantes se distinguió como soldado en la batalla de Lepanto [1], donde perdió el uso del brazo izquierdo. De allí su sobrenombre de «el manco de Lepanto». Su vida personal fue una serie de fracasos. Pasó cinco años cautivo de los piratas turcos. Luego tuvo mala suerte en los negocios y pasó algún tiempo en la cárcel. Tampoco tuvo éxito en su matrimonio. Como escritor dejó poesías, novelas, obras de teatro y una colección de doce novelas cortas, las «Novelas ejemplares».

En 1605 se publicó la primera parte de su obra maestra, «El ingenioso hidalgo don Quijote de la Mancha». En 1615 se publicó la segunda parte. El libro trata de un hombre de edad avanzada que se imagina caballero y sale en su caballo, Rocinante, para buscar aventuras y combatir las injusticias del mundo, pero sin éxito. Lleva como escudero a Sancho Panza, un labrador ignorante pero de mucho sentido común. Este libro, que Cervantes escribió para burlarse de los libros de caballería, está lleno de episodios ridículos. Pero, además del humorismo de las aventuras, hay una base filosófica, el conflicto entre el idealismo y el materialismo. Desde el día de su publicación, el libro logró un éxito tremendo que todavía no ha disminuido.

Francisco de Quevedo (1580–1645) fue el escritor satírico por excelencia en la literatura española. «Los sueños», una serie de relatos, es su obra maestra en prosa. Escribió también una gran novela picaresca, «La vida del buscón», y dejó un tesoro de poesía lírica.

Lope de Vega (1562–1635) fue un verdadero «monstruo de la naturaleza», como lo llamó Cervantes a causa de su gran producción literaria. Escribió toda clase de obras, pero su fama se debe más a sus obras dramáticas, entre las que se cuentan más de mil comedias, todas en verso.

Se ha dicho que Lope de Vega es el padre de la comedia moderna y el creador del teatro nacional español. Expuso su teoría y técnica de escribir comedias, afirmando que el teatro es una representación de la vida y que el escritor debe tener libertad total. Sus obras más famosas son las que tratan de la historia de España y de la dignidad humana. Se pueden mencionar entre éstas «Fuenteovejuna» y «Peribáñez y el Comendador de Ocaña». En estas dos obras, la gente del pueblo lucha contra las injusticias de los nobles.

Juan Ruiz de Alarcón (1581–1639) nació en México de padres españoles. Escribió más de veinte obras teatrales en las cuales castigaba el vicio y alababa la virtud. Entre las principales deben mencionarse «Las paredes oyen», contra la calumnia, y «La verdad sospechosa», contra la mentira.

Tirso de Molina (1584–1648) fue uno de los más grandes dramaturgos españoles. Su verdadero nombre era Fray Gabriel Téllez. Es famoso por haber creado el personaje de don Juan en su drama «El burlador de Sevilla». Desde la época de Tirso, la figura de don Juan ha inspirado la obra de muchos autores en diversos países. En la música, por ejemplo, el gran compositor Mozart usó el tema de don Juan en su ópera «Don Giovanni».

Pedro Calderón de la Barca (1600–1681) fue el último de los grandes dramaturgos del Siglo de Oro. El tema principal de sus obras es el honor. Sus dos obras principales son «El alcalde de Zalamea» y «La vida es sueño». En la primera, un hombre del pueblo, elegido alcalde, manda matar a un noble para vengar el honor de su hija. La segunda contiene ideas filosóficas profundas sobre la realidad y los sueños.

SIGLOS XVIII Y XIX

En el siglo XVIII hubo poca producción literaria de valor en España. La mayor parte de las obras publicadas fueron imitaciones en español de escritores franceses. En 1713 se estableció la Real Academia de la Lengua Española, cuya tarea era la de mantener la pureza del idioma español.

En 1833, a la muerte de Fernando VII, regresaron al país muchos españoles que habían salido durante su reinado. Éstos trajeron consigo las ideas liberales que habían aprendido en otros países. Así comenzó en España el roman-

---

14　**tener éxito** to be successful
28　**burlarse de** to make fun of

37　**la obra maestra** the masterpiece

ticismo, movimiento literario que exaltaba al individuo, sus ideas y sus sentimientos, sin preocuparse por las reglas literarias clásicas del siglo XVIII.

5   Ángel Saavedra, **Duque de Rivas** (1791–1865) escribió «Don Álvaro o la fuerza del sino», un drama romántico que más tarde inspiró al compositor italiano Giuseppe Verdi para su ópera «La fuerza del destino».

10   **José de Espronceda** (1808–1842) fue un poeta romántico, cuyas obras principales son «El estudiante de Salamanca» y «Canto a Teresa». Se le ha comparado, en su vida y en su obra, con el poeta inglés Lord Byron (1788–15 1824).

    Mariano José de Larra (1809–1837) fue un ensayista y crítico importante. Escribió bajo varios seudónimos, uno de ellos «Fígaro», una colección de «Artículos de costumbres» que son 20 una sátira al modo de vivir de su tiempo.

    José Zorrilla (1817–1893) escribió «Don Juan Tenorio», un drama basado en el tema de don Juan, pero desde el punto de vista romántico. Tan popular es este drama, que se repre-25 senta hasta hoy día anualmente el Día de los Difuntos, es decir, el dos de noviembre.

    Gustavo Adolfo Bécquer (1836–1870) escribió «Rimas», una colección de unas setenta poesías líricas, algunas de las cuales son po-30 pularísimas.

    El romanticismo fue seguido por un movimiento literario llamado realismo, que pretendía representar la «realidad» sin idealizarla. La novela del siglo XIX se caracteriza por su rea-35 lismo y su regionalismo. Muchos autores escribieron acerca de la región donde habían nacido, su «patria chica».

    Fernán Caballero es el seudónimo de Cecilia Böhl de Faber (1796–1877). Esta autora 40 inició la novela costumbrista [2] en España. Describió las costumbres de su época y de su región, Andalucía, en un estilo sencillo y natural. Su obra principal es «La Gaviota».

    Las novelas de **Juan Valera** (1824–1905) 45 son una visión poética de la vida en Andalucía. Le interesaba la psicología de sus personajes, y su obra más famosa, «Pepita Jiménez», es un estudio psicológico sobre la vocación religiosa.

    Benito Pérez Galdós (1843–1920), el no-50 velista español más importante del siglo XIX,

dejó una vasta producción literaria. Fue liberal y crítico violento de la intolerancia religiosa y de la injusticia social. Entre sus obras deben mencionarse la novela «Doña Perfecta», contra la intolerancia religiosa, y los «Episodios Na-55 cionales», una serie de más de sesenta narraciones históricas sobre la España del siglo XIX.

    Emilia Pardo Bazán (1852–1921) introdujo el naturalismo [3] en España y estableció contacto entre la vida literaria europea y la es-60 pañola. Escribió acerca de su región, Galicia. Sus novelas principales son «Los pazos de Ulloa» y «La madre naturaleza».

    Armando Palacio Valdés (1853–1938) fue un novelista muy popular. Escribió «La her-65 mana San Sulpicio», sobre la región de Andalucía, y «José», acerca de los pescadores de Asturias.

    Vicente Blasco Ibáñez (1867–1928) fue muy popular, no sólo en España sino también 70 en el extranjero. Su obra principal es «La barraca», que describe la vida de los campesinos valencianos. También escribió «Sangre y arena», sobre la corrida de toros, y «Los cuatro jinetes del Apocalipsis», que trata de la Primera 75 Guerra mundial. Fue un gran defensor de las ideas republicanas y de la libertad del individuo frente al Estado y estuvo muchas veces en la cárcel por sus ideas políticas.

LA «GENERACIÓN DEL '98» HASTA   80
NUESTROS DÍAS

    Como resultado de la guerra de 1898 contra los Estados Unidos, España perdió lo poco que le quedaba de su imperio colonial. A raíz de este desastre, un grupo de intelectuales jó-85 venes españoles comenzó a examinar el estado cultural y espiritual de su país dentro del mundo moderno. Estos escritores se conocen hoy como la «Generación del '98» e incluyen ensayistas, novelistas, poetas y dramaturgos. 90

    Francisco Giner de los Ríos (1839–1915) fue filósofo, profesor y el gran educador de los intelectuales. Su influencia se nota en los escritores de la «Generación del '98». Fundó la Escuela Libre de Enseñanza, centro de ideas 95 liberales.

---

25 **el Día de los Difuntos** All Soul's Day

71 **en el extranjero** abroad
84 **a raíz de** as a result of

Miguel de Unamuno (1864–1936) es la figura dominante de la «Generación del '98», y su influencia sigue siendo importante. Fue filósofo, crítico, poeta y novelista. Su atractivo es la pasión y la violencia con que se muestra al lector. Su ensayo más conocido es «Del sentimiento trágico de la vida», que explora uno de sus temas favoritos, el abismo que existe entre la fe y la razón, entre la falta de fe y el deseo de inmortalidad.

Ramón del Valle-Inclán (1866–1936) fue famoso por la riqueza de su lenguaje. Su prosa puede casi llamarse poesía. Entre sus obras deben mencionarse las cuatro «Sonatas», de primavera, de estío, de otoño y de invierno, y la novela «Tirano Banderas».

En el teatro **Jacinto Benavente** (1866–1954) es un nombre bien conocido. Este dramaturgo ganó el Premio Nobel de Literatura en 1922. Sus obras más importantes son «La malquerida» y «Los intereses creados».

Ramón Menéndez Pidal (1869–1968) fue un erudito muy importante de la España del siglo XX. Hizo estudios profundos sobre la lengua y la literatura medievales de España, entre ellos «Los orígenes del español», «El romancero español» y «La España del Cid».

Pío Baroja (1872–1956) fue tal vez el novelista principal de la «Generación del '98». En sus novelas hay mucha fuerza y acción. Dos de las más importantes son «El árbol de la ciencia» y «Camino de perfección». La primera se considera una novela autobiográfica, en la que el autor expone sus ideas incomformistas y los problemas sociales de su época.

José Martínez Ruiz, llamado **«Azorín»**, (1873–1967) escribió ensayos y novelas. En sus obras relacionó la España antigua con la moderna, en un lenguaje muy sencillo y natural. Entre sus obras principales deben mencionarse «La voluntad», «Castilla» y «Los valores literarios». Se le considera el crítico literario más importante de la «Generación del '98».

Antonio Machado (1875–1939) fue uno de los mejores poetas de este siglo y uno de los más amados y respetados. Sus poemas son breves, pero tratan de temas fundamentales. Introdujo el modernismo de Rubén Darío en la poesía española, pero sin dejarse influir totalmente por este estilo. Su obra «Campos de Castilla» tiene por tema el paisaje austero de su país.

Gregorio Martínez Sierra (1881–1947) logró crear notables personajes femeninos en sus obras dramáticas. La más conocida es «Canción de cuna». Fue también autor del texto sobre el que de Falla compuso su ballet «El amor brujo».

José Ortega y Gasset (1883–1955) fue un filósofo y ensayista que buscó los valores espirituales de España en su tradición. Se le considera el maestro de toda una generación de escritores españoles e hispanoamericanos. Dos de sus obras principales son «La rebelión de las masas» y «Meditaciones del Quijote».

La época de la Guerra Civil en España (1936–39) afectó tanto la literatura como la vida diaria de los españoles. Muchos escritores se opusieron a la dictadura que estableció Franco al terminar la guerra y salieron del país para vivir en el extranjero. Otros fueron encarcelados o condenados a muerte.

Juan Ramón Jiménez (1881–1958), maestro del modernismo, radicaba en Puerto Rico cuando ganó el Premio Nobel de Literatura en 1956. Además de varias colecciones de poesías, escribió también libros en prosa. De éstos el más conocido es «Platero y yo», que describe los recuerdos de su juventud.

Federico García Lorca (1898–1936) fue un notable poeta y dramaturgo andaluz que escribió en forma dramática sobre temas folklóricos y tradicionales. Su teatro trata en gran parte de las pasiones humanas. Entre sus obras deben mencionarse los dramas «Bodas de sangre» y «La casa de Bernarda Alba» y los poemas de su «Romancero gitano». García Lorca murió en circunstancias trágicas durante la Guerra Civil.

Jorge Guillén (1893–1984) es el poeta de la llamada «poesía pura»; es decir, poesía que carece de anécdota y está hecha de conceptos y abstracciones. Hasta 1957 fue autor de un solo libro, «Cántico», que se publicó por primera vez en 1928 y llegó a incluir 500 poemas en su quinta edición. Su última colección de poemas, publicada en 1981, se titula «Final». Enseñó en muchas universidades del mundo, entre ellas Harvard y Wellesley College en los Estados Unidos.

Vicente Aleixandre (1898–1984) fue un ensayista y poeta que recibió el Premio Nobel de Literatura en 1977. En su ensayo «Los encuentros», el autor pinta con palabras, retratos de los grandes escritores españoles a quienes conoció. Su obra poética es surrealista y neorromántica a la vez; el tema central es el amor en su doble aspecto de fuerza destructora e ilusión de la vida. Entre esta obra poética se distinguen «La destrucción o el amor» y «Sombras del paraíso».

Alejandro Casona (1900–1965) fue un dramaturgo que vivió muchos años en la Argentina después de la Guerra Civil. Escribió con mucha fuerza dramática. Dos de sus obras principales son «La dama del alba» y «Los árboles mueren de pie».

Ramón J. Sender (1902–1982) abandonó España después de la Guerra Civil. Vivió en Guatemala y México y luego se radicó en los Estados Unidos. Es conocido por sus novelas «Requiem por un campesino español», sobre sus experiencias en la Guerra Civil, «Mr. Witt en el Cantón», «Crónica del alba» y «En la vida de Ignacio Morel». Por estas obras recibió varios premios literarios.

Después de la Guerra Civil, aparece en España una nueva generación de escritores. Muchos de ellos habían vivido sus años de juventud cara a cara con los horrores de esa guerra. Influidos por ella, estos escritores se han preocupado por los problemas sociales y económicos que España ha afrontado desde la posguerra hasta hoy.

Julián Marías (1914–   ) es un filósofo y ensayista contemporáneo, discípulo fiel de Ortega y Gasset. Ha hecho un examen sincero y veraz sobre los problemas del inmediato futuro de España en su contexto real. Ha enseñado en la Universidad de Madrid, en Harvard, Yale y la Universidad de California en Los Angeles. Entre sus obras más conocidas están «Historia de la Filosofía», «Introducción a la Filosofía», «Los Estados Unidos en escorzo» y «Los españoles».

Camilo José Cela (1916–   ) es tal vez el más famoso de los novelistas de la España contemporánea. Es un maestro del lenguaje y posee un humor de tono burlón. Su novela «La familia de Pascual Duarte» lamenta la falta de dignidad personal que se notaba en la España de la posguerra. Con esta obra, cruel y dura, se inicia un movimiento en la novela llamado «tremendista». Cela escribió también, entre otras, «La colmena» y «Camilo, 1936».

Antonio Buero Vallejo (1916–   ) escribió obras dramáticas que dieron dignidad al teatro español y lo modernizaron. Trata de invadir la realidad humana y social de nuestro tiempo, tanto de España como del resto del mundo. Sus obras más famosas incluyen «Las meninas», «En la ardiente oscuridad» e «Historia de una escalera».

Miguel Delibes (1920–   ) es un novelista de estilo sobrio y sencillo que ha retratado la realidad de la sociedad española de la posguerra, en especial al hombre humilde. Entre sus novelas más conocidas están «El camino», «Diario de un cazador» y «Las ratas».

Carmen Laforet (1920–   ) causó una gran conmoción con la publicación de su novela «Nada» en 1946. Ésta trata del vacío espiritual de la España de la posguerra y le valió un premio literario. Desde entonces ha ganado otros premios y ha publicado, entre otras, las novelas «La isla y los demonios» y «La mujer nueva».

José Hierro (1922–   ) es uno de los poetas más destacados de la posguerra, por haber logrado una poesía honda, humana y apasionada con un mínimo de imágenes. Su obra poética incluye «Alegría», «Cuanto sé de mí» y «Poesía del momento».

Ana María Matute (1926–   ) es una escritora que ha dado al mundo una producción literaria de primera calidad. Trae a sus cuentos y novelas la nota distintiva de una delicada sensibilidad que no ciega su visión clara y perceptiva de la realidad. «Fiesta al noroeste», «Pequeño teatro», «Los hijos muertos» y «Primera memoria» son novelas que le valieron premios nacionales de literatura.

Alfonso Sastre (1926–   ) es un dramaturgo que escribe sobre la sociedad con el fin de dar un mensaje social a su público. «La mordaza» y «Escuadra hacia la muerte» son dos de sus obras conocidas.

Juan Goytisolo (1931–   ) es otro novelista importante de la España contemporánea. Presenta los problemas e inquietudes de la época en sus obras «Juegos de manos», «El circo», «Duelo en el paraíso» y «Fiestas».

Antonio Gala (1937–   ) es un poeta y dramaturgo que discute temas actuales, a veces a través de los ojos de personajes históricos. Entre sus obras más conocidas están «Anillos para una dama», «Noviembre y un poco de yerba» y «Petra Regalada».

NOTES:

[1] **la batalla de Lepanto:** Battle of Lepanto

---

19   **cara a cara** face to face
22   **la posguerra** postwar (refers to the years after the Civil War)

62   **le valió** it earned her

(1571, Lepanto, Greece). Naval battle between allied Christian forces, led by the king of Spain's brother, and the Ottoman Turks. The victory of the Christian forces had great impact in Europe.

[2] **la novela costumbrista:** A literary genre referring to novels with strong regional flavor that describe local customs and manners.

[3] **el naturalismo:** Naturalism, a theory in literature emphasizing the role of heredity and environment upon human life and character development. It states that literature should conform to describing nature without idealization or avoidance of the ugly.

Ejercicio A

¿Cierto o falso? Indique si cada frase es cierta o falsa. Si es falsa, cámbiela para que sea cierta:

1. Una de las óperas de Mozart está basada en un tema popular de una obra de Tirso de Molina.

   _____

2. «Don Quijote de la Mancha» fue escrito para burlarse de los libros de caballería.

   _____

3. Los siglos XVI y XVII se llaman también el Siglo de Oro.

   _____

4. La vida de Espronceda fue semejante a la del poeta inglés Byron.

   _____

5. Emilia Pardo Bazán introdujo el realismo en España.

   _____

6. En su novela «Los cuatro jinetes del Apocalipsis», Blasco Ibáñez describe los desastres de la Primera Guerra mundial.

   _____

7. La primera guerra carlista causó la formación de un grupo de intelectuales llamado la «Generación del '98».

   _____

8. Azorín fue el crítico más conocido de la «Generación del '98».

   _____

9. Camilo José Cela es un autor del siglo XIX.

   _____

10. En su obra «Platero y yo», Juan Ramón Jiménez describe su juventud.

    _____

11. Vicente Aleixandre fue un poeta que recibió el Premio Nobel de Literatura en 1977.

    _____

12. Antonio Gala es el dramaturgo cuyas obras dramáticas dieron dignidad al teatro español.

    _____

13. El modernismo de Rubén Darío fue introducido en la poesía española por Jorge Guillén.

_____

14. Los autores de la posguerra han escrito sobre los problemas sociales y económicos de la España de esa época.

_____

15. Julián Marías se distinguió en la literatura española como dramaturgo.

_____

Ejercicio B

Escriba la letra que indique la relación correcta con cada expresión de la columna de la izquierda:

1. El Cid   _____

2. Larra   _____

3. «Novelas ejemplares»   _____

4. «Episodios nacionales» _____

5. Gustavo Adolfo Bécquer _____

6. Blasco Ibáñez   _____

7. «Los intereses creados» _____

8. «La vida es sueño»   _____

9. «Sonatas»   _____

10. Fernán Caballero   _____

a. Benavente

b. Calderón de la Barca

c. «La barraca»

d. «La Gaviota»

e. Rodrigo Díaz de Vivar

f. Valle-Inclán

g. «Fígaro»

h. Cervantes

i. «Rimas»

j. «Don Álvaro o la fuerza del sino»

k. Pérez Galdós

Ejercicio C

Subraye el nombre correcto:

1. Dramaturgo del Siglo de Oro: Quevedo, Palacio Valdés, Tirso de Molina

2. Poeta romántico: Espronceda, Jorge Manrique, Fernán Caballero

3. Daba importancia al individuo: realismo, regionalismo, romanticismo

4. Ganó el Premio Nobel: Pérez Galdós, Juan Ramón Jiménez, Juan Valera

5. Escudero de don Quijote: Sancho Panza, Rocinante, Fígaro

6. Escribió acerca de la España de la posguerra: Laforet, Palacio Valdés, Unamuno

7. Dramaturgo español que vivió en la Argentina: Pío Baroja, Alejandro Casona, José Martínez Ruiz

8. El gran maestro de los intelectuales de la Generación del '98: Ortega y Gasset, Valle-Inclán, Giner de los Ríos

9. Erudito importante del siglo XX: Alfonso el Sabio, Menéndez Pidal, el Duque de Rivas

10. Escribió sobre el tema de «don Juan»: Duque de Rivas, Larra, Zorrilla

Ejercicio D

Identifique estos autores u obras de la literatura española:

1. Soy el autor de «Las siete partidas».

   _____

2. Soy una serie de relatos que representan la obra maestra en prosa de Quevedo.

   _____

3. Fui el último gran dramaturgo del Siglo de Oro.

   _____

4. Escribí la primera gramática de la lengua española.

   _____

5. Escribí más de mil comedias y expuse mis ideas sobre este género.

   _____

6. Soy el más antiguo y mejor ejemplo de la poesía épica española.

   _____

7. Fui soldado y poeta en el Siglo de Oro; popularicé el soneto en España.

   _____

8. Soy una obra poética importantísima de Jorge Manrique.

   _____

9. Fui llamado «el manco de Lepanto».

   _____

10. Me consideran el héroe nacional de España.

    _____

Ejercicio E

Identifique las obras siguientes, escribiendo para cada una (a) el género de la obra (drama, poesía, novela, ensayo), (b) el autor y (c) la época (Siglo de Oro, romanticismo, realismo, Generación del '98, posguerra):

   EJEMPLO: Don Quijote   **novela   Cervantes   Siglo de Oro**

1. Lazarillo de Tormes

   _____

2. Nada

   _____

3. Doña Perfecta

   _____

4. Fiesta al noroeste

_____

5. Historia de la filosofía

_____

6. Los intereses creados

_____

7. La Gaviota

_____

8. En la ardiente oscuridad

_____

9. Don Juan Tenorio

_____

10. Del sentimiento trágico de la vida

_____

11. El árbol de la ciencia

_____

12. La familia de Pascual Duarte

_____

13. Fuenteovejuna

_____

14. El alcalde de Zalamea

_____

15. La rebelión de las masas

_____

16. Bodas de sangre

_____

17. El burlador de Sevilla

_____

18. Cántico

_____

19. Requiem por un campesino español

_____

20. La vida del buscón

_____

Las Bellas Artes y la Ciencia

LA MÚSICA

España es un país muy rico en música folklórica. Un buen ejemplo de este género de música es el flamenco de la región de Andalucía. Sus orígenes se encuentran en la música árabe, gitana, andaluza y judía del siglo XIV. El flamenco es un cante acompañado de música de guitarra y un baile improvisado. El llamado «cante jondo» (hondo o profundo) es muy triste y trata de temas como la muerte y la angustia. El cante chico trata sobre temas alegres.

El instrumento típico y tradicional de España es la guitarra, en la que se toca tanto música clásica como popular. Para acompañamiento se tocan la pandereta y las castañuelas. En la región de Galicia el instrumento típico es la gaita.

España ha dado al mundo un género de música llamado zarzuela. La zarzuela es una combinación de música, canto, diálogo hablado, coros y bailes. Es un género entre la comedia musical de los Estados Unidos y la ópera. Uno de los mejores compositores de zarzuela fue **Francisco Asenjo Barbieri** (1823–1894). Sus obras más conocidas son «Pan y Toros» y «El barberillo de Lavapiés». «La verbena de la paloma», del compositor **Tomás Bretón** (1850–1923), es quizá la zarzuela más famosa.

COMPOSITORES, INSTRUMENTISTAS, CANTANTES

Los tres compositores españoles más conocidos son Isaac Albéniz, Enrique Granados y Manuel de Falla. **Isaac Albéniz** (1860–1909) compuso una ópera y música para piano. Entre sus composiciones principales están «Iberia» y «El Albaicín». **Enrique Granados** (1867–1916) también compuso música para piano. Su obra maestra, «Goyescas», está inspirada en la obra del pintor Francisco Goya. **Manuel de Falla** (1876–1946) fue el más célebre de los compositores españoles del siglo XX. Como Granados y Albéniz, también de Falla se inspiró en temas folklóricos. Pero de Falla compuso principalmente música para orquesta. Fue autor de varios ballets, entre ellos «El amor brujo», que tiene la popularísima «Danza ritual del fuego», y «El sombrero de tres picos». Éste fue basado en la famosa novela del mismo nombre del escritor andaluz Pedro Antonio de Alarcón (1833–1891). En 1939, después de la Guerra Civil, de Falla se radicó en Argentina.

Entre los instrumentistas se distinguen Pablo Casals, José Iturbi, Andrés Segovia y Alicia de Larrocha. **Pablo Casals** (1876–1973) fue uno de los mejores violonchelistas del mundo. Salió de España en 1939, después de la Guerra Civil, porque se oponía a la dictadura de Franco. En 1956 se estableció en Puerto Rico, donde organizó un festival internacional de música que se sigue celebrando anualmente en su memoria. **José Iturbi** (1895–1980) fue pianista y director de orquesta sinfónica. También actuó en varias películas de Hollywood en los años cuarenta. **Andrés Segovia** (1894–1987) fue uno de los maestros de la guitarra y se presentó en todas las salas de concierto del mundo. Su fama se debe no sólo a su maestría, sino a que rehabilitó la guitarra como instrumento de música clásica en el siglo XX. **Alicia de Larrocha** (1923–   ) es una pianista contemporánea que ha ganado fama mundial, tanto por su interpretación de los grandes compositores españoles, como por su interpretación de otros compositores clásicos mundiales.

Otros españoles se han destacado en el género operático. Son famosos, y han cantado en los grandes teatros de ópera del mundo, las sopranos **Victoria de los Ángeles** y **Monserrat Ca-**

---

las bellas artes fine arts

7 **un cante** song, singing (used mostly in expressions related to flamenco music)

66 **la sala de concierto** concert hall

ballé y los tenores **Alfredo Krauss, Plácido Domingo** y **Juan Carreras.**

En el área de la música popular hay cantantes que han logrado fama mundial por su interpretación de canciones de la última onda. Entre ellos se hallan **Sarita Montiel, Julio Iglesias, Raphael, Camilo Sesto, Rocío Jurado** y **Lolita. Joan Manuel Serrat** es famoso por haber popularizado con su música la poesía de Antonio Machado.

EL BAILE

Casi todas las regiones de España tienen sus propios bailes, y hay grandes diferencias entre ellos. La región que tiene mayor variedad es Andalucía. De allí vienen el bolero, el fandango, la seguidilla, el jaleo, la malagueña, la sevillana y el flamenco. Muchas veces el baile se acompaña con una pandereta y castañuelas. De Aragón viene la jota, un baile muy alegre que se baila en parejas, acompañado de castañuelas y coplas cantadas. La sardana es el baile regional de Cataluña; se baila en grupo, en un gran círculo. El baile regional de Galicia es la muñeira, que se baila en parejas con música de gaita.

A través de los años han habido varios intérpretes famosos del baile flamenco, que lo han llevado a todos los rincones del mundo. Estos bailarines incluyen a **Vicente Escudero, Carmen Amaya, Antonio** y su compañera **Rosario** y **Antonio Gades.**

LA ARQUITECTURA

Romanos, moros y españoles, todos dejaron en España ejemplos magníficos de su arquitectura. De los romanos existen todavía puentes y acueductos, como el acueducto de Segovia. De los moros quedan mezquitas, alcázares y el exquisito palacio de la Alhambra, en Granada.

De la Edad Media se conservan muchas catedrales de estilo románico, como la de Santiago de Compostela, y de estilo gótico, como las catedrales de Burgos, Sevilla y Toledo.

De los tiempos posteriores debe mencionarse El Escorial, cuyo arquitecto principal fue **Juan de Herrera** (1530–1597). El estilo barroco

fue introducido en España por **José de Churriguera,** un arquitecto famoso del siglo XVIII. El llamado «estilo churrigueresco» mezcla elementos góticos y barrocos.

LA PINTURA

España ha tenido una tradición muy rica en la pintura. No hay prácticamente museo de importancia en el mundo que no tenga cuadros de los maestros españoles. El Prado, en Madrid, es el museo principal de España. Entre los pintores españoles de renombre internacional están los siguientes:

Doménico Theotocopulos (1541–1614), llamado **el Greco,** nació en Creta. Estudió varios años en Italia y pasó luego a España, estableciéndose en Toledo. Allí vivió hasta su muerte. Su obra se caracteriza por lo religioso y por la originalidad de su dibujo, que alarga y estiliza las figuras. Entre sus cuadros más famosos están «El entierro del Conde de Orgaz» y «Vista de Toledo».

José de Ribera (1588–1652) nació en España, pero pasó la mayor parte de su vida en Italia. Su obra se caracteriza por su gran realismo y los efectos de luz y color. Su cuadro más famoso es «El martirio de San Bartolomé».

Francisco de Zurbarán (1598–1664) pintó cuadros religiosos en un estilo realista y sobrio. Su «Monje en meditación» es representativo de su obra artística.

Diego Velázquez (1599–1660) fue el pintor más original y perfecto de la escuela española. Fue pintor de cámara del rey Felipe IV y pintó muchos cuadros de la familia real. Entre sus obras maestras están «Las Meninas», «La rendición de Breda», conocida también por «Las lanzas», «Los borrachos», «Las hilanderas» y muchos retratos de nobles de la época.

Bartolomé Esteban Murillo (1617–1682) fue principalmente un pintor religioso y es famoso por sus cuadros de «La Inmaculada Concepción». Es conocido también como dibujante y pintó tipos populares de gran realismo.

Francisco de Goya y Lucientes (1746–1828) fue el pintor más famoso de su época y uno de los grandes precursores de la pintura moderna. Fue pintor de los reyes Carlos III y

---

5 **canciones de la última onda** the latest popular songs

78 **el pintor de cámara** court painter
79 **la familia real** the royal family

Carlos IV y autor de varios retratos satíricos de la familia real. Son famosos la colección de aguafuertes llamadas «Caprichos», la serie de grabados sobre la Guerra de Independencia contra Napoleón «Los desastres de la guerra», y el cuadro «Los fusilamientos del tres de mayo». Entre sus obras más conocidas están también «La maja vestida» y «La maja desnuda».

Joaquín Sorolla (1863–1923) es el pintor de «sol y color». Muchos de sus cuadros se encuentran en la ciudad de Nueva York, en el Museo de la Sociedad Hispánica.

Ignacio Zuloaga (1870–1945) pintó muchos tipos españoles con gran realismo: toreros, pordioseros y gitanos, entre otros.

José María Sert (1876–1945) es famoso por sus murales y por una serie de cuadros que representan episodios del Quijote. Estos cuadros se hallan en el salón Sert del hotel Waldorf-Astoria en la ciudad de Nueva York.

Pablo Picasso (1881–1973) nació y fue educado en Málaga, pero pasó la mayor parte de su vida en Francia. Es famoso como iniciador del cubismo, un estilo de pintura que rechaza la perspectiva tradicional, presentando objetos fragmentados cuyas partes se ven simultáneamente. Pero la obra total de Picasso muestra su genio en diversos medios y estilos. Su famoso cuadro «Guernica» representa la destrucción de ese pueblo vasco durante la Guerra Civil española.

Joan Miró (1893–1983) es uno de los más grandes representantes del arte abstracto unido a la fantasía surrealista. Su obra se caracteriza por su sencillez y la riqueza de su imaginación. En 1950 pintó un mural para la Universidad de Harvard.

Salvador Dalí (1904–1989) pertenece a la escuela surrealista. Sus obras representan los pensamientos fantásticos de su subconsciente, con gran atención al detalle. Dalí mismo dijo que sus cuadros eran «fotografías de sueños pintadas a mano».

HOMBRES DE CIENCIA

España ha producido varios científicos de renombre. Entre ellos están **Santiago Ramón y Cajal** (1852–1934), quien ganó el Premio Nobel de Medicina en 1906 por sus muchos descubrimientos acerca de las funciones del sistema nervioso; **Juan de La Cierva** (1895–1936), quien inventó el autogiro, precursor del helicóptero; y **Severo Ochoa** (1905–   ), quien ganó el Premio Nobel de Medicina en 1959 por sus estudios sobre las enzimas.

---

43   **pintadas a mano** hand painted

Ejercicio A

¿Cierto o falso? Indique si cada frase es cierta o falsa. Si es falsa, cámbiela para que sea cierta:

1. El cante jondo es un ejemplo de la música popular de España.

   _____

2. El instrumento típico de España es el piano.

   _____

3. La zarzuela es un género musical que combina la música, el canto, la danza y el diálogo hablado.

   _____

4. Manuel de Falla compuso principalmente música para piano.

   _____

5. Andrés Segovia fue el mejor violonchelista del mundo.

   _____

6. Raphael y Julio Iglesias son conocidos por sus pinturas.

    _____

7. Los bailes tradicionales de España incluyen distintos bailes regionales.

    _____

8. Monserrat Caballé y Plácido Domingo son dos cantantes de ópera muy famosos.

    _____

9. Miró pintó el famoso cuadro «Guernica».

    _____

10. La jota es un baile regional muy alegre que se baila en parejas.

    _____

11. El museo más importante de España se llama el Museo del Prado.

    _____

12. Murillo es un pintor conocido por la originalidad de su dibujo, que alarga y estiliza las figuras.

    _____

13. El pintor más perfecto y original de la escuela española fue Sorolla.

    _____

14. Zuloaga fue el pintor que captó escenas de la Guerra de Independencia contra Napoleón.

    _____

15. Salvador Dalí es el pintor español que inició el cubismo.

    _____

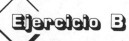 Ejercicio B

Subraye la palabra o expresión que complete correctamente cada frase:

1. El compositor que escribió la música del ballet «El sombrero de tres picos» es
    (a) Albéniz   (b) Granados   (c) Iturbi   (d) de Falla

2. Un baile regional de Aragón es
    (a) la malagueña   (b) la sardana   (c) la jota   (d) el fandango

3. Un tipo de obra teatral que puede corresponder a la comedia musical de los Estados Unidos es
    (a) la zarzuela   (b) la seguidilla   (c) la pandereta   (d) el ballet

4. De los siguientes, el que no se emplea como instrumento de música es
    (a) la gaita   (b) la guitarra   (c) el flamenco   (d) la pandereta

5. Un bailarín español muy conocido fue
    (a) Granados   (b) Victoria de los Ángeles   (c) Casals   (d) Escudero

6. Uno de los mejores violonchelistas del mundo fue
    (a) Iturbi   (b) Casals   (c) Segovia   (d) Albéniz

7. Un baile regional de Cataluña es
    (a) el flamenco   (b) la sardana   (c) la muñeira   (d) la sevillana

8. Un ejemplo de música folklórica es
    (a) el cante jondo   (b) la zarzuela   (c) el ballet   (d) Goyescas

9. El gran maestro de la guitarra fue
    (a) Segovia   (b) Escudero   (c) Granados   (d) Asenjo Barbieri

10. La música que acompaña la muñeira se toca con
    (a) la guitarra   (b) el piano   (c) la gaita   (d) las castañuelas

Ejercicio C

Complete correctamente estas frases.

1. Un pintor español famoso por sus cuadros surrealistas fue _____.

2. Un acueducto construido por los romanos está en la ciudad de _____.

3. «El entierro del Conde de Orgaz» es una obra maestra del pintor _____.

4. La construcción más famosa de los moros es _____ en Granada.

5. «Las Meninas» es una obra maestra del pintor _____.

6. El fundador del cubismo fue _____.

7. El museo principal de España es el Museo _____.

8. «Los fusilamientos del tres de mayo» es una obra de _____.

9. El pintor español cuyas obras se hallan en un gran hotel de Nueva York es

    _____.

10. El arquitecto principal del Escorial fue _____.

Ejercicio D

Identifique qué o quién es (fue)

1. el artista que creó «Los caprichos».

    _____

2. una bailarina conocida por sus interpretaciones del baile flamenco.

    _____

3. el músico que compuso el ballet «El amor brujo».

    _____

4. una cantante de ópera española conocida internacionalmente.

    _____

5. un pintor extranjero que fue a España y se estableció en Toledo.

_____

6. un pintor surrealista contemporáneo.

_____

7. el músico que compuso «Iberia» y «El Albaicín».

_____

8. el pintor español del siglo XVII que pasó la mayor parte de su vida en Italia.

_____

9. el científico conocido por sus estudios sobre las enzimas.

_____

10. el compositor de música que se inspiró en las obras de Goya.

_____

11. una obra teatral con música, diálogo hablado, coros y bailes.

_____

12. el inventor del autogiro.

_____

13. el pintor de «sol y color».

_____

14. el gran científico español que hizo estudios sobre el sistema nervioso.

_____

15. el arquitecto que introdujo en España el estilo barroco.

_____

16. un baile regional que se baila en un gran círculo.

_____

17. la música gitana con influencia de música árabe.

_____

18. el estilo de pintura que presenta objetos fragmentados y rechaza la perspectiva tradicional.

_____

19. el pintor español, muchas de cuyas obras están en el Museo de la Sociedad Hispánica.

_____

20. el pintor del siglo XVII que pintó «La rendición de Breda».

_____

La Vida y las Costumbres

La vida diaria contemporánea en España se parece a la vida diaria contemporánea en los Estados Unidos. Sin embargo, cada país del mundo tiene algo de particular. En España hay muchas tradiciones y costumbres interesantes y a la vez diferentes de las que tenemos en nuestro país.

LA CASA Y LA FAMILIA

La casa

Las casas de las ciudades grandes son semejantes a las de las otras ciudades del mundo. Hay casas particulares y casas de apartamentos. Muchos españoles tienen su condominio, que forma parte de un edificio alto.

En los pueblos de España y en las ciudades antiguas, las casas suelen estar situadas en calles estrechas. Por lo general, suelen ser de un solo piso, con balcones, ventanas con rejas y patios pintorescos. En muchas casas las paredes están cubiertas de azulejos.

Nombres y apellidos

Los nombres españoles son diferentes a los de los Estados Unidos. Además del nombre de pila, cada niño español lleva dos apellidos, el de su padre seguido del de su madre. A veces se pone «y» entre los dos apellidos. Por ejemplo, el Sr. Carlos Pérez (y) Gómez se casa con doña María Vega (y) González. Tienen un hijo que se llama Juan Pérez (y) Vega. La hermana de Juan se llama Adela Pérez (y) Vega. Si Adela se casa con Leandro Fernández (y) Álvarez, ella se llamará doña Adela Pérez de Fernández. Esta manera de llamar a las personas se extiende a todos los países hispanos.

El día del santo

Los españoles generalmente llevan el nombre de un santo y, además de su propio cumpleaños, celebran el día de ese santo.

TIPOS PINTORESCOS

El sereno es un tipo pintoresco español que data de los tiempos antiguos, cuando las llaves de las casas eran muy grandes y pesadas. El sereno se pasa la noche cuidando las calles de su barrio. Lleva consigo las llaves de todas las casas. Su deber principal es el de ayudar a los que vuelven a casa sin llave, por lo cual se le da una propina. También anuncia la hora: «¡las tres y sereno!» Hoy en día los serenos han casi desaparecido de las calles de las grandes ciudades.

Los gitanos viven en el sur de España. Son llenos de vida y tienen fama de ser muy listos. Muchos de ellos se ganan la vida diciendo la buenaventura. Mantienen muchas de sus tradiciones, dentro de las que la música y el baile son muy importantes.

El aguador es un tipo muy común en las regiones áridas. Lleva el agua por las calles y la vende en las varias casas.

La tuna es un grupo de veinte a veinte y cinco músicos callejeros que ha sido parte de la vida estudiantil universitaria de España desde antes del siglo XVI. Los tunos usan un traje tradicional de color negro y llevan una capa. Los instrumentos que tocan incluyen el laúd, la bandurria, el requinto, la guitarra y la pandereta.

ACTIVIDADES SOCIALES Y COSTUMBRES

La vida social es muy importante para los

---

16 **soler** + infinitive to usually...
24 **nombre de pila** first name
25 **seguido de** followed by
53 **decir la buenaventura** to tell someone's fortune

61 **los músicos callejeros** street musicians
66 **la bandurria** Spanish string instrument of the lute type
66 **el requinto** Spanish string instrument, similar to a small guitar with only four strings

españoles. Acostumbran pasar mucho tiempo en los cafés y los bares, charlando con sus amigos. Cenan mucho más tarde que en nuestro país y, por consiguiente, se acuestan más tarde.

5   En muchas ciudades existe el ateneo, un club intelectual donde se reúnen grupos literarios y científicos. La tertulia es una reunión informal en casa, con el propósito de charlar y divertirse.

10   Cuando un novio sigue la costumbre de hablar con su novia a través de una reja de la casa, se dice que está «pelando la pava». Él se queda afuera, de pie, y ella está dentro de su casa, sentada. Hoy en día muchas de las cos-

15   tumbres tradicionales para cortejar a las muchachas están desapareciendo, sobre todo en las grandes ciudades.

La lotería está dirigida por el gobierno y es muy popular. El sorteo tiene lugar tres veces al

20   mes. Hay muchos premios, y el premio mayor se llama «el gordo».

La siesta es la costumbre de acostarse por la tarde durante las horas de mayor calor. Se cierran las tiendas y las oficinas, y los trabaja-

25   dores regresan a sus casas a comer y descansar o dormir la siesta. Después de la siesta, las oficinas y tiendas se abren de nuevo y quedan abiertas hasta muy tarde. Ésta es una costumbre que también ha ido desapareciendo en las ciu-

30   dades grandes.

COMIDAS Y BEBIDAS

En España, como en los Estados Unidos, por lo general se comen tres comidas principales. La diferencia está en el horario, pues allá

35   comen más tarde. El desayuno se toma alrededor de las ocho de la mañana y puede consistir en café con leche o chocolate y pan con mantequilla y mermelada o bollos. Tanto la comida, que se toma cerca de las dos de la tarde, como

40   la cena, que se toma después de las ocho o nueve de la noche, son comidas completas. Un menú normal puede consistir en sopa, ensalada, carne con arroz o verduras y postre. Entre la comida y la cena, alrededor de las seis de la

45   tarde, se toma la merienda, algo ligero como un sandwich. Con el aperitivo antes de la cena, o para acompañar bebidas alcohólicas, se acostumbra comer bocados que se llaman «tapas».

La comida española es variada, interesante y deliciosa. No es picante, como cree la gente.   50
Entre los platos tradicionales está el puchero, que se puede considerar el plato nacional de España. Es un guisado que se sirve casi a diario, sobre todo entre los campesinos. Se llama también olla o cocido.   55

El arroz con pollo es, quizás, el plato más conocido de España. Se prepara de esos dos ingredientes, bien sazonados con sal, ajo, pimientos y azafrán. En Valencia añaden mariscos y otros ingredientes al arroz con pollo y lo llaman   60
paella.

Las bebidas que toman los españoles incluyen el café, el té, la leche y los refrescos. Una bebida tradicional es la horchata, hecha de almendras, agua y azúcar. Se toma fría en el ve-   65
rano como refresco.

A los españoles también les gusta tomar chocolate al desayuno y a la merienda. Lo preparan muy espeso y lo toman muy caliente, con panecillos, bizcochos o churros. Éstos se pare-   70
cen a nuestros «donuts», pero son como palos largos y son más ricos cuando están calientes.

LA ROPA

En general, la ropa de los españoles es semejante a la del resto de Europa. Pero también   75
tienen algunas prendas tradicionales.

La mantilla es un gran pañuelo de seda y encajes, que lleva la mujer para cubrirse la cabeza. Debajo de la mantilla se usa un peine alto, ricamente adornado, que se llama peineta.   80

El mantón es un chal grande, ricamente bordado, que sirve de adorno o de abrigo.

La boina es una gorra de lana redonda semejante al «beret» francés.

Las alpargatas son sandalias de lona con   85
suela de soga. Son comunes entre los trabajadores en muchas partes de España.

DÍAS DE FIESTA

Religiosos

Puesto que la mayoría de los españoles   90
practican la religión católica, las fiestas religiosas son muy importantes en el país.

La Navidad cae el 25 de diciembre. En No-

---

4   **por consiguiente** therefore
19   **el sorteo** drawing of numbers in a lottery

27   **de nuevo** again
90   **puesto que** since

chebuena, la gente va a las iglesias para oír la misa de gallo. Grupos de personas andan por las calles cantando villancicos. Cada casa tiene su nacimiento, o sea un conjunto de pequeñas figuras que representan el nacimiento de Jesucristo. También se acostumbra dar regalos, llamados aguinaldos, a las personas que han servido a la familia durante el año (el cartero, los criados y otros). Los niños reciben sus regalos el día de los Reyes Magos, el 6 de enero. Los Reyes Magos son para los niños españoles lo que Santa Claus es para los niños de los Estados Unidos.

El Carnaval es un período de tres días de diversión y alegría antes del Miércoles de Ceniza, que comienza la Cuaresma. La Cuaresma son los cuarenta días que siguen, un período de ayuno y penitencia. Termina el domingo de Resurrección, la Pascua Florida. Este domingo es de nuevo un día de alegría y diversión, de comer y beber bien, de ir al teatro. La Semana Santa, que precede a la Pascua Florida, se celebra con mucha solemnidad y devoción, sobre todo en Sevilla. El Viernes Santo hay procesiones religiosas en muchos pueblos y ciudades.

Cada pueblo tiene su santo patrón, cuyo día se celebra con una fiesta. La víspera hay una verbena, o sea una fiesta nocturna. El día mismo del santo hay romerías a la tumba del santo. La gente se pasa el día comiendo, bebiendo, jugando y bailando. Dos santos muy populares en España son Santiago, patrón del país, y San Isidro, patrón de Madrid. Fuera de España es muy conocida la fiesta de San Fermín, santo patrón de Pamplona, que dura ocho días. Cada día de la fiesta, los toros que van a participar en las corridas se sueltan a correr por las calles, desde los corrales hasta la plaza de toros. Mucha gente trata de torearlos por las calles.

El Día de los Difuntos, el 2 de noviembre, está dedicado a la memoria de los que han muerto. La gente visita los cementerios para adornar con flores las tumbas de parientes y amigos.

Nacionales

Hay dos días de fiesta importantes. El 2 de mayo es el día de la fiesta nacional de España. Conmemora un suceso patriótico, el comienzo de la resistencia contra los franceses en 1808.

El Día de la Raza, el 12 de octubre, corresponde a nuestro «Columbus Day» y se celebra en todo el mundo hispano.

DIVERSIONES Y DEPORTES

La corrida de toros es un espectáculo de mucho colorido, muy típico de España. En las ciudades grandes, generalmente hay corridas los domingos por la tarde y los días de fiesta importantes. Esas tardes las plazas se llenan de gente, sobre todo si los toreros son famosos. Antes de comenzar la corrida, todos los participantes desfilan por la arena, mientras se escucha la música de pasodobles.

La corrida tiene tres partes, que se llaman suertes. En la primera suerte los picadores entran, montados a caballo. Llevan picas largas, con las cuales castigan al toro en la cerviz. En la segunda suerte entran los banderilleros, a pie, llevando las banderillas. Esperan la embestida del toro y, al pasar éste, le ponen las banderillas en la cerviz. En la tercera suerte el matador, armado de una espada de acero muy fino, y llevando una pequeña muleta roja, exhibe su arte y su valor. Ejecuta varios pases con la muleta, hasta que llega el momento ideal para matar al toro. Entonces, cara a cara con el adversario, le entierra la espada y lo mata. Lo que el público estima y aplaude más es la valentía y el arte del torero.

El jai-alai, también llamado pelota, es un juego vasco. Es muy popular en toda España, en algunos países hispanoamericanos y en la Florida. Se juega con una pelota dura en un gran frontón de tres paredes. Es semejante al «handball», pero en vez de tirar y coger la pelota con la mano, se emplea una cesta larga y estrecha, atada a la muñeca.

El fútbol es muy popular no sólo en España, sino también en el resto de Europa y en Latinoamérica. Se puede decir que es el deporte nacional de la mayoría de esos países.

---

1 **la misa de gallo** Midnight Mass
9 **los Reyes Magos** the Three Wise Men
14 **Miércoles de Ceniza** Ash Wednesday
18 **la Pascua Florida** Easter

37 **se sueltan a correr** are let loose to run
63 **el pasodoble** a typical Spanish march
73 **la muleta** matador's stick with attached red cloth hanging

Ejercicio A

En cada grupo subraye las dos palabras o expresiones relacionadas:

1. santo, mantilla, peineta, banderilla

2. nacimientos, alpargatas, horchata, villancicos

3. siesta, premio gordo, lotería, tertulia

4. ateneo, reja, tertulia, olla

5. boina, arroz con pollo, mendigo, puchero

6. santo, matador, muleta, aguador

7. Dos de Mayo, franceses, mantón, pelar la pava

8. aguinaldo, siesta, romería, verbena

9. Semana Santa, Día de la Raza, Pascua Florida, San Fermín

10. frontón, misa de gallo, picador, jai-alai

Ejercicio B

Complete las frases siguientes:

1. Los niños españoles reciben sus regalos de Navidad el Día de _____.

2. El apellido paterno (del padre) de Juan Díaz y Pérez es _____.

3. En el mundo hispano el doce de octubre se celebra el Día de _____.

4. En la corrida de toros, el torero que va montado se llama _____.

5. El santo patrón de Madrid es _____.

6. El plato de arroz, pollo y mariscos se llama _____.

7. La fiesta nacional de España se celebra el _____.

8. En la tercera suerte de la corrida de toros, el torero importante es _____.

9. Una bebida espesa y caliente que se toma en el desayuno es _____.

10. El premio más grande de la lotería es _____.

Ejercicio C

Escoja la respuesta correcta y escríbala en el espacio correspondiente:

1. En la corrida de toros, el picador _____.
    (mata al toro, emplea una muleta, va montado a caballo, usa las banderillas)

2. La fiesta de San Fermín se celebra _____.
    (en toda España, en Madrid, en Pamplona, en Barcelona)

3. La tuna es _____ .
    (un grupo de músicos, un baile, una canción, un instrumento musical)

4. El santo patrón de España es _____ .
    (San Juan, Santiago, Santo Tomás, San Isidro)

5. En el jai-alai, para tirar la pelota se emplea _____ .
    (una muleta, una espada, una peineta, una cesta)

6. Una boina se lleva en _____ .
    (la cabeza, los pies, las manos, el cuello)

7. La Semana Santa es un período _____ .
    (de diversión y alegría, que dura tres días, que precede a la Pascua Florida, que se llama también
    el Día de los Difuntos)

8. En la Navidad, los españoles ponen _____ .
    (un nacimiento, una mantilla, una verbena, una romería)

9. La bebida fría, hecha de almendras, es _____ .
    (el chocolate, la sangría, la horchata, el té)

10. Las tres partes de una corrida de toros se llaman _____ .
    (escenas, actos, jornadas, suertes)

Ejercicio D

*Escriba la letra que indique la relación correcta con cada expresión de la columna de la
izquierda:*

1. tertulia _____
2. tapas _____
3. gitano _____
4. ateneo _____
5. reja _____
6. Nochebuena _____
7. merienda _____
8. puchero _____
9. siesta _____
10. alpargata _____

a. aguador
b. pelar la pava
c. comida ligera
d. descanso
e. reunión
f. sandalia
g. la buenaventura
h. villancicos
i. club literario
j. bocados
k. cocido

PART

SIX

CIVILIZATION:
SPANISH
AMERICA

Al sur de los Estados Unidos, y ocupando una extensión mucho más grande que la de nuestro país, viven unos doscientos cuarenta millones de personas que constituyen la llamada América española, o sea lugares donde el idioma oficial es el español. La América española comprende diez y nueve países, situados en tres regiones distintas: (1) México y la América Central, (2) las Antillas y (3) la América del Sur.

MÉXICO Y LA AMÉRICA CENTRAL

1. **México** se halla al sur de Norteamérica, limitado al norte por los Estados Unidos, al oeste por el Pacífico, al sur por Guatemala y Belice y al este por el Golfo de México. El Río Bravo del Norte (que nosotros llamamos el Río Grande) lo separa de Tejas.

México es un país de contrastes. Dos cadenas de montañas, la Sierra Madre Oriental y la Sierra Madre Occidental, lo atraviesan de norte a sur, y desde el centro del país hasta el interior de los Estados Unidos se extiende una inmensa altiplanicie llamada la Mesa Mexicana. Por el contrario, en el este, la Península de Yucatán es un área baja, plana y selvática. En las montañas se hallan varios grandes volcanes, el más famoso de los cuales es el Popocatépetl. El país tiene además muchos ríos, lagos y lagunas.

La principal riqueza del país es la agricultura (maíz, frijol, algodón y papa entre otros) y la minería. México es el primer productor de plata del mundo y uno de los mayores productores de gas natural y petróleo. La capital del país, Ciudad de México, está situada en la meseta central a una altura de más de 2.200 metros. Fue fundada por Hernán Cortés sobre las ruinas de Tenochtitlán, la antigua capital azteca conquistada por los españoles en 1521. Como muchas de las ciudades de la América española, la Ciudad de México representa una mezcla impresionante de lo colonial y lo moderno. Allí se encuentra el Castillo de Chapultepec, un museo histórico que antes servía de residencia a los presidentes del país. Hay además muchos puntos de interés: (1) el Paseo de la Reforma, la avenida más elegante de la capital; (2) el Zócalo, la plaza mayor; (3) el Palacio de Bellas Artes, el teatro más grande de todo el país, que contiene también una magnífica colección de pinturas mexicanas; (4) el Museo de Antropología, donde se puede aprender la historia y admirar la cultura y el arte de las tribus indias de la región; (5) la Ciudad Universitaria; (6) la Basílica de Guadalupe, la iglesia más famosa del país, construida en honor de la Virgen de Guadalupe, patrona de México; (7) la Catedral; y (8) importantes ruinas arqueológicas como el Templo Mayor. Los famosos jardines flotantes de Xochimilco y los templos y pirámides de Teotihuacán se hallan a poca distancia de la capital.

Otras ciudades importantes de México son: Guadalajara, segunda ciudad del país y el centro principal de la agricultura y la ganadería; Veracruz y Tampico, puertos importantes sobre el Golfo de México; Acapulco y Puerto Vallarta, puertos sobre el Pacífico, famosos por sus playas; Taxco, monumento nacional a la arquitectura colonial y centro de la industria de la plata; Mérida, en la península de Yucatán, centro de la producción de henequén; y Chichén-Itzá, antigua ciudad maya en el norte de Yucatán, donde hay notables ruinas mayas y toltecas.

2. **Guatemala,** al sur de México, es un país de montañas y de lagos. Gracias a sus niveles diferentes, tiene un clima variado que le ha

permitido desarrollar una agricultura también muy variada. Sus productos principales son el café, las bananas, el chicle (del cual se hace la goma de mascar) y las maderas finas. Guatemala es el país de mayor población de Centroamérica y el que tiene un porcentaje más alto de indígenas puros (54% de la población). Fue la sede de una de las civilizaciones más avanzadas, los mayas. La capital del país es la Ciudad de Guatemala.

3. **Honduras** es el país más montañoso de Centroamérica. Como los otros países de la región, tiene un clima muy variado. Es un país básicamente agrícola, cuyos productos principales son las bananas, el café, el tabaco, la caña de azúcar y las maderas finas. Los Estados Unidos compran el 90% de los productos de exportación que son el plátano, el oro y la plata. La capital es Tegucigalpa.

4. **El Salvador** es la nación más pequeña de Centroamérica y además la única que no está bañada por el Atlántico. El país tiene más de 350 ríos y muchos lagos y lagunas muy hermosos. El café es su producto más importante, seguido por el algodón y la caña de azúcar. La capital es San Salvador.

5. **Nicaragua** es el país más grande de la América Central. Es también agrícola y produce maíz, algodón, café, plátano, caucho y maderas preciosas. Es además el país más ganadero de Centroamérica. La capital es Managua.

6. **Costa Rica** es el único país centroamericano donde la mayoría de la población es de raza blanca. Es, también, el único país de América que no tiene ejército; una Guardia Civil mantiene el orden. Costa Rica ha sido tradicionalmente democrático y ha fomentado la educación pública. Sus principales productos de exportación son el café y los plátanos, aunque produce también cacao, caña de azúcar, papas y una gran variedad de frutas. La capital es San José.

7. **Panamá** está en el istmo del mismo nombre, que une las dos Américas. El famoso Canal de Panamá, que atraviesa el país, fue comenzado por un francés, Fernando de Lesseps, en 1881 y terminado por los Estados Unidos en 1914. Una gran parte de la

población del país vive directa o indirectamente de las operaciones del Canal. La agricultura apenas comenzó a desarrollarse en los últimos veinte y cinco años, y su producto principal es el plátano. La capital del país es la Ciudad de Panamá y el puerto principal sobre la Zona del Canal es Balboa.

LAS ANTILLAS

Las Antillas son un grupo de islas en el Mar Caribe que incluyen a Cuba, Santo Domingo (o La Española, nombre dado por Cristóbal Colón a la isla) y Puerto Rico. Santo Domingo está compartida por Haití y la República Dominicana.

1. **Cuba,** la isla más grande de las Antillas, fue descubierta por Colón en su primer viaje. Debido a la fertilidad de su tierra y la belleza de su paisaje, se ha llamado «la perla de las Antillas». El país es el primer productor mundial de azúcar, una industria que fue establecida a fines del siglo XVI. Produce además tabaco, conocido universalmente por su calidad, café, arroz y una gran variedad de frutas. La ganadería y la pesca son industrias importantes y el país es también rico en minerales. La capital es La Habana.

De gran interés histórico es el Castillo del Morro, situado en el puerto de La Habana, que sirvió de fortaleza para proteger la isla contra los piratas ingleses en el siglo XVI. En Guantánamo hay una base naval que pertenece a los Estados Unidos.

2. **La República Dominicana** ocupa las dos terceras partes de la isla de La Española, llamada Quisqueya antes del Descubrimiento y bautizada La Española por Colón. Durante el período colonial, casi todas las expediciones conquistadoras del Nuevo Mundo partieron de esta isla.

La base de la economía es la agricultura, principalmente el cultivo de la caña de azúcar, el cacao, el café, el plátano y el maíz. La pesca está en pleno desarrollo.

La capital del país, Santo Domingo, es la ciudad más antigua de América, fundada en 1496. Allí se encuentra la universidad

---

85 **las dos terceras partes** two thirds   95 **en pleno desarrollo** developed at full scale

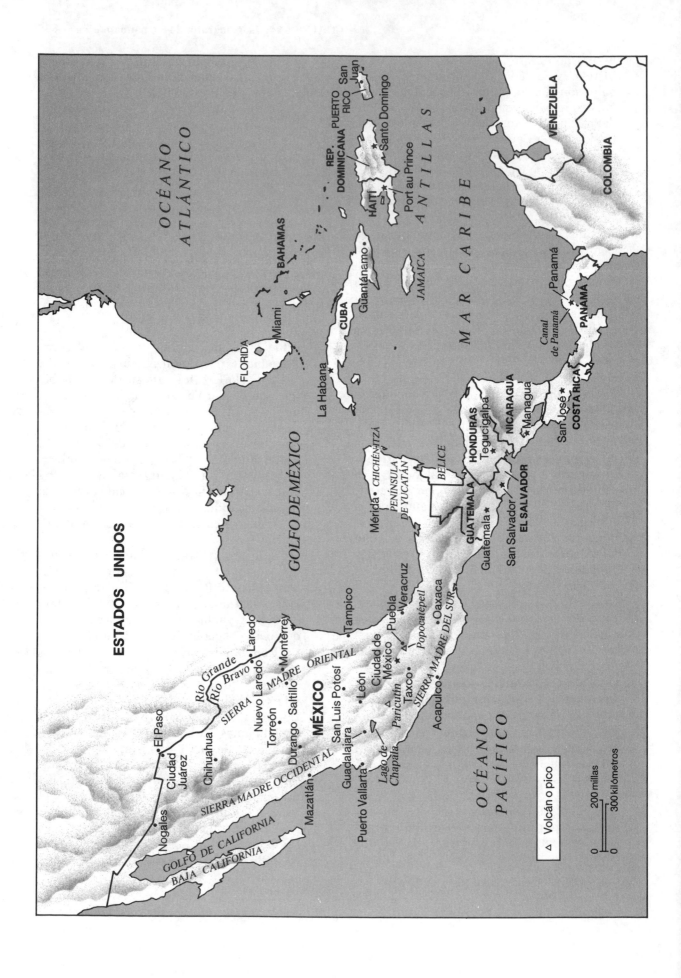

más antigua del Nuevo Mundo, la Universidad de Santo Tomás de Aquino, fundada en 1538 y llamada hoy la Universidad de Santo Domingo.

5 3. **Puerto Rico** pasó a manos de los Estados Unidos en 1898 y es hoy en día un Estado Libre Asociado. Sus habitantes han tenido la nacionalidad estadounidense desde 1917. Los productos principales de la isla son el café, la caña de azúcar y el tabaco.

10 La isla, llamada Borinquén por los indígenas, fue descubierta por Colón en 1493. Su capital, San Juan, fue fundada en 1508 por Ponce de León, el primer gobernador de la isla. Es un puerto comercial muy activo
15 y además aún conserva fortificaciones y hermosos edificios de la época colonial española.

LA AMÉRICA DEL SUR

20 La mayor parte de Sudamérica está al sur del ecuador, y las estaciones del año caen en orden opuesto a las nuestras. Cuando nosotros estamos en invierno, allí tienen verano.

Volando en avión sobre la América del
25 Sur, se ve que casi todos los países son montañosos. En el este están las tierras altas de las Guayanas y del Brasil. Al oeste la larga cordillera de los Andes, la mayor cadena del mundo, se extiende desde el Caribe hasta Antártica por
30 más de 7.500 kilómetros. Estas montañas, con sus vastas mesetas, sus valles y sus picos majestuosos, han tenido gran influencia en el lento desarrollo del continente. Han hecho muy difícil y costosa la construcción de ferrocarriles y
35 carreteras, impidiendo así el transporte y el comercio. Hasta cierto punto, el transporte aéreo ha mejorado las comunicaciones.

Las montañas tienen separados, no solamente a los diferentes países, sino también a
40 veces a las regiones de un mismo país, como sucede en el Perú, el Ecuador y Colombia. Los Andes son ricos en minerales como el oro, la plata, el aluminio, el cobre, el platino, el hierro y el estaño. Las mesetas son muy saludables y
45 allí se ha establecido la mayor parte de la población.

Tres vastas llanuras ocupan el interior del continente, extendiéndose hasta la costa del Atlántico. Éstas son las del Amazonas, el Chaco
50 y la Pampa, donde están los valles de los ríos Orinoco, Amazonas, Paraná y Paraguay. Allí se encuentran selvas, bosques y pantanos.

PAÍSES DEL ESTE

1. **La Argentina** recibió su nombre, que quiere decir «de plata», porque los primeros con-
55 quistadores pensaron que la región era rica en minas de plata. Los indios que encontraron a lo largo del Río de la Plata, llevaban hermosos ornamentos de plata, pero ésta provenía del Perú. La Argentina es el país
60 más grande de habla hispana. Se extiende desde la región del Chaco en el norte, hasta la Tierra del Fuego y el Estrecho de Magallanes en el sur; y desde el Atlántico en el este, hasta los Andes. Por lo general, el país
65 tiene un clima templado, aunque hay extremos de frío en el sur (Tierra del Fuego) y de calor y humedad en las selvas del Chaco. En el extremo nordeste, entre la Argentina y el Brasil, están las famosas cataratas del
70 Iguazú, de 70 metros de altura. En la región andina se halla el Aconcagua, un pico que alcanza una altura de 6.959 metros y es el pico más alto de todo el hemisferio occidental. La mayor parte del país es una lla-
75 nura extensa, llamada la Pampa, la tierra del gaucho y el centro de la agricultura y la ganadería. La Argentina es uno de los primeros productores de trigo del mundo y su riqueza ganadera es también una de las pri-
80 meras del mundo.

La población es de raza blanca en su totalidad, mayormente descendientes de españoles e italianos. Buenos Aires, la capital, es la ciudad más grande de Sudamérica
85 y su puerto figura entre los más activos del mundo. Es una ciudad moderna y cosmopolita, con grandes y elegantes avenidas, plazas, tiendas y teatros. Los habitantes de la ciudad se llaman porteños. La segunda
90 ciudad en importancia es Rosario, puerto a orillas del río Paraná y centro industrial.

2. **El Uruguay,** llamado antes la Banda Oriental, es la nación hispana más pequeña de la América del Sur. Limita al norte con el Bra-
95 sil, al oeste y al sur con la Argentina y

6 **Estado Libre Asociado** Commonwealth

MAR CARIBE

OCÉANO
ATLÁNTICO

Barranquilla
Cartagena
La Guaira
★ Caracas
Río Orinoco

LLANOS

Medellín
★ Bogotá
COLOMBIA

VENEZUELA
GUYANA
SURINAM
GUAYANA
FRANCESA

Río Magdalena

Ecuador

Quito ★
Cotopaxi
Chimborazo
Guayaquil
ECUADOR

Río Amazonas

LOS ANDES

PERÚ
Callao
Lima

Cuzco

BRASIL

★ Brasilia

Lago
Titicaca
★ La Paz
BOLIVIA

GRAN CHACO

Río Paraguay

Río de Janeiro

OCÉANO
PACÍFICO

PARAGUAY
Asunción ★
Tucumán

Iguazú

Río Paraná

Desierto de Atacama

LOS ANDES

CHILE
Aconcagua
Viña del Mar
Valparaíso
Santiago

Córdoba
Rosario
Buenos Aires ★

URUGUAY
★ Montevideo
Río de la Plata

OCÉANO
ATLÁNTICO

Islas Juan
Fernández
(Ch.)

PAMPAS

ARGENTINA

PATAGONIA

0   300 millas
0   500 kilómetros

△ Volcán o pico

Estrecho
De
Magallanes
Tierra del Fuego
Cabo de
Hornos

Islas Malvinas
(Falkland Islands)
(Ing.)

al este con el Océano Atlántico. El clima del país es templado, sin calores ni fríos extremos. Por sus costas se extienden muchas playas elegantes, de gran interés turístico. Entre ellas está la de Punta del Este, donde tuvo lugar en 1961 la Conferencia Interamericana que ratificó el programa de la Alianza para el Progreso.

La población del Uruguay es en su mayoría de origen europeo, principalmente español e italiano. El Uruguay ha sido un país progresista, donde hay muy poco analfabetismo. Las industrias principales se derivan de la ganadería, como la industria de la carne congelada y en conserva y la industria del cuero. Montevideo, capital y puerto principal de la nación, está al este de Buenos Aires, en la orilla opuesta del Río de la Plata.

3. **El Paraguay** es uno de los dos países de la América del Sur que no tienen puerto de mar, pero el río Paraná le permite comunicarse con el Atlántico. El país se halla entre Bolivia, el Brasil y la Argentina. Al oeste, la región del Gran Chaco ocupa las dos terceras partes del país. Es una vasta llanura semiárida, cubierta por selvas espesas en el norte, por la cual lucharon Bolivia y el Paraguay desde 1932 hasta 1935. El resultado de la guerra fue que el Paraguay recibió las dos terceras partes del territorio, y Bolivia consiguió una salida al mar por medio del río Paraguay. La famosa yerba mate, una especie de té, es un producto importante del Paraguay, así como también la madera de un árbol llamado quebracho, que se emplea para curtir el cuero. La capital del país, Asunción, es un puerto fluvial de considerable importancia.

PAÍSES ANDINOS

Los países andinos se encuentran en el oeste del continente y comprenden a Chile, Bolivia, el Perú, el Ecuador, Colombia y Venezuela. La cordillera de los Andes atraviesa casi todos estos países de norte a sur.

1. **Chile** se encuentra al extremo sudoeste, entre la Argentina y el Océano Pacífico. El país se extiende 4.270 kilómetros, desde la frontera con el Perú en el norte, hasta Tierra del Fuego en el sur, parte de la cual le pertenece a Chile. El país tiene una anchura media de 180 kilómetros y en algunas partes se vuelve mucho más estrecho. Es un país de mucha actividad sísmica y numerosos terremotos han destruido en el pasado regiones enteras. El desierto de Atacama, en el norte, es uno de los desiertos más secos del mundo; a veces pasan años y no cae ni una gota de agua. Allí se encuentra la región minera más importante; Chile es el segundo productor mundial de cobre.

En el extremo sur el clima es polar. El valle central, en cambio, tiene un clima excelente y es el centro agrícola del país. Los productos principales son la vid (de la cual se ha desarrollado una importante industria de vinos) y los cereales. En esta región se encuentran las ciudades más importantes del país: Santiago, la capital, y Valparaíso, el puerto principal. Viña del Mar, una playa muy famosa, queda cerca de Valparaíso. En el sur del país hay una región de grandes lagos que se llama la «Suiza chilena» por su extrema belleza e interés turístico para los deportes de invierno.

2. **Bolivia,** llamada así en honor de Simón Bolívar, se conocía en tiempos coloniales por Alto Perú. Aunque está en la zona tórrida, el país tiene un clima muy variado. En algunas partes es el país más frío del continente sudamericano, debido a su gran altura. Tiene fronteras con el Brasil al norte y al este, con el Paraguay al sudeste, con la Argentina al sur, con Chile al sudoeste y con el Perú al noroeste. Como se ve, Bolivia no tiene salida al mar y depende de los países vecinos para exportar sus productos. La población de Bolivia es india en más de un cincuenta por ciento, y los grupos más numerosos son los aimaraes, los quechuas y los guaraníes. El país es muy rico en minerales. Potosí era conocido en tiempos coloniales como el centro más importante de la producción de plata del mundo. Hoy en día Bolivia es uno de los primeros productores de estaño. Tiene además cobre, cinc, plomo, azufre y oro.

---

32 **por medio de** through, by (means of)

37 **curtir el cuero** to tan leather (hides)

38 **un puerto fluvial** river port

La capital del país, La Paz, es la capital más alta del mundo, situada a más de 3.600 metros sobre el nivel del mar. El lago Titicaca, entre Bolivia y Perú, es el lago navegable más alto del mundo; se encuentra a una altura de 3.800 metros.

3. **El Perú** es tres veces más grande que el estado de California. Está limitado al norte por el Ecuador y Colombia, al este por el Brasil y Bolivia, al sur por Chile y al oeste por el Pacífico. Los Andes dividen al país en tres regiones naturales: la costa pacífica, que es estrecha y desértica; la sierra, constituida por una altiplanicie y dominada por los Andes, donde vive más de la mitad de la población; y la selva hacia el Amazonas, un inmenso llano que cubre más de la mitad del país.

La agricultura es la actividad fundamental del país, pero la minería también ocupa un lugar importante en la economía. Casi toda la industria minera se concentra en Lima, la capital, y sus alrededores. La pesca ha tomado importancia debido a su abundancia y su variedad en las aguas peruanas. Las ovejas y, en las zonas más elevadas, animales como la alpaca, la llama y la vicuña producen lana para el consumo interno y también para la exportación.

Antes de la llegada de los españoles, florecieron grandes civilizaciones en el Perú. La más avanzada y mejor conocida fue la de los incas, destruida por Francisco Pizarro en 1533. Su capital era Cuzco, que hoy es el centro arqueológico del país. Cerca de Cuzco se hallan las ruinas de Machu-Picchu, restos de una ciudad sagrada inca, que atrae muchos turistas. Lima, capital del país, es también el centro comercial y cultural. Pizarro la llamó «Ciudad de los Reyes», porque la fundó el 6 de enero, Día de los Reyes Magos. Allí se halla la Universidad de San Marcos, fundada en 1551. El Callao, a trece kilómetros de Lima, le sirve de puerto y es el primer puerto exportador de harina de pescado.

4. **El Ecuador** se llama así por la línea geográfica del mismo nombre que lo atraviesa. En este país se hallan dos volcanes que fi-

guran entre los picos más altos del continente, el Chimborazo (de 6.300 metros) y el Cotopaxi (de 5.940 metros).

El Ecuador es un país agrícola, cuyo producto más importante hoy en día es el plátano, aunque hasta hace unos años el cacao constituía su riqueza principal. Produce también café, arroz, maderas finas, caucho, tagua (o marfil vegetal, que sirve para fabricar botones) y paja toquilla, con la cual se hacen los sombreros de jipijapa que nosotros llamamos «Panama hats».

Quito, la capital, está a una altura de 2.827 metros, al pie de un volcán. Por su altura tiene un clima bastante frío, a pesar de estar en el centro de la Zona Tórrida. La ciudad ha conservado mucho de su carácter colonial. Guayaquil es el puerto principal y el centro comercial del país.

5. **Colombia** está limitada al norte por el Mar Caribe, al sur por el Ecuador y el Perú, al oeste por el Pacífico y Panamá, y al este por Venezuela y el Brasil. Esta república, nombrada en honor de Colón, es el único país de la América del Sur que tiene puertos en dos mares, en el Caribe (Cartagena y Barranquilla) y en el Pacífico (Buenaventura). El territorio puede dividirse en tres regiones: la andina al oeste, donde vive la mayoría de la población y donde se encuentran nevados y volcanes de más de 5.400 metros; los llanos orientales y la selva del Amazonas. El país tiene grandes y caudalosos ríos, siendo el más importante el Magdalena, que atraviesa el país de sur a norte y es un importante medio de comunicación. Gracias a la diversidad de climas, hay toda clase de cultivos. Los productos principales de exportación son el café, los plátanos y el petróleo. El país es además rico en carbón, oro, plata, platino y esmeraldas.

Bogotá, la capital, está en el interior y ha sido, desde su fundación en 1538, el centro principal del país. En sus alrededores se encuentra el salto de Tequendama, de 157 metros de alto, mucho más alto que el Niágara, pero menos ancho. Medellín es la segunda ciudad del país y el centro de la producción de café.

---

3 **sobre el nivel del mar** above sea level

80 **el nevado** permanently snow-capped mountain

82 **caudaloso** having great volume of water

6. **Venezuela,** patria de Bolívar, el Libertador, está situada en el extremo norte de Suda-mérica. El país está bañado por las aguas del Mar Caribe al norte y tiene fronteras con Colombia al oeste, con el Brasil al sur y con Guyana al este. La población está concen-trada en las zonas montañosas del oeste y en las costas. El Orinoco, río principal de Venezuela, tiene más de 2.400 kilómetros de largo y sus llanos son un centro gana-dero importante. El país también produce café y cacao de primera calidad, pero la base de su economía es el petróleo. Venezuela es uno de los mayores productores mundiales.

Caracas es la capital política y comer-cial de la nación. Es una ciudad moderní-sima, con grandes avenidas y hermosos y elegantes edificios públicos y residenciales. La Guaira, a veinte y cinco kilómetros, le sirve de puerto en el Caribe.

Ejercicio A

Escriba la letra que indique la relación correcta con cada expresión de la columna de la izquierda:

1. Puerto Rico _____
2. Honduras _____
3. Xochimilco _____
4. Costa Rica _____
5. Río Bravo del Norte _____
6. Veracruz _____
7. Nicaragua _____
8. El Morro _____
9. El Salvador _____
10. La Española _____
11. Santo Domingo _____
12. Palacio de Bellas Artes _____
13. Castillo de Chapultepec _____
14. Cuba _____
15. Guantánamo _____

a. gran teatro mexicano
b. plaza mayor de la Ciudad de México
c. museo histórico
d. Estado Libre Asociado
e. país sin ejército
f. base naval
g. «Perla de las Antillas»
h. jardines flotantes
i. frontera con los Estados Unidos
j. país más grande de Centroamérica
k. puerto del Golfo de México
l. país más montañoso de Centroamérica
m. Haití y la República Dominicana
n. fortaleza del siglo XVI
o. ciudad más antigua de América
p. país más pequeño de Centroamérica

Ejercicio B

¿Cierto o falso? Indique si cada frase es cierta o falsa. Si es falsa, cámbiela para hacerla cierta:

1. México forma parte de la América Central.

_____

2. El Río Bravo del Norte separa a México de Guatemala.

_____

3. Guatemala produce chicle, del cual se hace la goma de mascar.

_____

4. Cuba era llamada Borinquén por los indígenas.

_____

5. La universidad más antigua del Nuevo Mundo está en La Habana.

_____

6. El Zócalo es la plaza mayor de la Ciudad de México.

_____

7. Tampico y Veracruz son puertos mexicanos en el Océano Pacífico.

_____

8. Costa Rica es un país industrial.

_____

9. Guadalajara es la tercera ciudad de México.

_____

10. El Salvador importa mucho café.

_____

Ejercicio C

¿Cierto o falso? Indique si cada frase es cierta o falsa. Si es falsa, cámbiela para que sea cierta:

1. En la mayor parte de Sudamérica las estaciones caen en orden semejante a las de los Estados Unidos.

_____

2. Casi todos los países de la América del Sur son montañosos.

_____

3. La cordillera de los Andes está en la parte este del continente.

_____

4. Bolivia y el Paraguay son los dos únicos países hispanoamericanos sin puertos de mar.

_____

5. Las cataratas del Iguazú están entre la Argentina y el Uruguay.

_____

6. Venezuela es el segundo productor mundial de cobre.

_____

7. El Aconcagua es el pico más alto del hemisferio oriental.

_____

8. El Paraguay es la nación hispana más pequeña de la América del Sur.

_____

9. Punta del Este es una famosa playa de Colombia.

_____

10. El Paraguay se comunica con el Océano Atlántico por medio del Río de la Plata.

_____

Ejercicio D

Escriba la letra que corresponde a la capital de cada país:

1. Honduras	_____	**a.** San José
2. Guatemala	_____	**b.** Tampico
3. Nicaragua	_____	**c.** Ciudad de México
4. Puerto Rico	_____	**d.** Tegucigalpa
		e. Ciudad de Panamá
5. México	_____	**f.** Guantánamo
6. la República Dominicana	_____	**g.** La Habana
7. Costa Rica	_____	**h.** Managua
8. El Salvador	_____	**i.** San José
		j. San Juan
9. Cuba	_____	**k.** Santo Domingo
10. Panamá	_____	**l.** Ciudad de Guatemala
		m. San Salvador

Ejercicio E

Escriba la letra que indique la relación correcta con cada expresión de la columna de la izquierda:

1. el Uruguay	_____	**a.** guerra entre Bolivia y el Paraguay
2. Quito	_____	**b.** industria ganadera
3. gaucho	_____	**c.** minerales
4. Bogotá	_____	**d.** grandes productores de petróleo
5. México y Venezuela	_____	**e.** capital del Ecuador
6. porteños	_____	**f.** Buenos Aires
7. río de La Plata	_____	**g.** capital del Paraguay
8. Gran Chaco	_____	**h.** la Banda Oriental
9. la Argentina y el Uruguay	_____	**i.** la pampa
10. Asunción	_____	**j.** Buenos Aires y Montevideo
		k. capital de Colombia

454 PART SIX: Civilization: Spanish America

Ejercicio F

Escriba la letra que indique la relación correcta con cada expresión de la columna de la izquierda:

1. Cartagena _____
2. Viña del Mar _____
3. Titicaca _____
4. Machu-Picchu _____
5. Bolivia _____
6. jipijapa _____
7. Atacama _____
8. La Guaira _____
9. Lima _____
10. Simón Bolívar _____

a. puerto de Caracas
b. desierto chileno
c. sombreros
d. Venezuela
e. puerto colombiano
f. Chimborazo
g. El Callao
h. lago navegable más alto del mundo
i. estaño
j. ruinas incaicas
k. famosa playa chilena

Ejercicio G

Escriba la palabra o expresión que complete correctamente cada frase:

1. La antigua capital de los incas fue _____.
   (Cuzco, Lima, Arequipa, La Paz)

2. Valparaíso es el puerto principal de _____.
   (Bolivia, el Ecuador, Chile, el Perú)

3. El país nombrado en honor del Libertador es _____.
   (Chile, el Perú, Venezuela, Bolivia)

4. La capital que Pizarro nombró en honor de un día de fiesta es _____.
   (Quito, Caracas, Bogotá, Lima)

5. La capital de Chile es _____.
   (Viña del Mar, Santiago, El Callao, Barranquilla)

6. El país andino que tiene costas en dos mares es _____.
   (Venezuela, Chile, Colombia, el Ecuador)

7. El río Orinoco se halla en _____.
   (el Perú, Venezuela, el Ecuador, Bolivia)

8. El país con la capital más alta del mundo es _____.
   (Chile, Bolivia, Colombia, el Ecuador)

9. La yerba mate es un producto importante de _____.
   (Chile, Bolivia, el Perú, el Paraguay)

10. El puerto principal del Ecuador es _____.
    (Guayaquil, Cartagena, La Guaira, Valparaíso)

La Historia de Hispanoamérica

CIVILIZACIONES INDIAS

Antes de la llegada de los españoles, florecieron varias civilizaciones en el Nuevo Mundo. La más avanzada fue la de **los mayas**,
5 que floreció del siglo tercero al diez y seis. Los mayas estaban establecidos en el territorio que hoy comprende la península de Yucatán, Belice, Guatemala y partes de Honduras y El Salvador. La civilización maya logró un desarrollo
10 increíble en la arquitectura, la astronomía y las matemáticas. Hoy en día, en lugares como Chichén-Itzá y Uxmal, podemos admirar las ruinas de sus templos, tumbas, esculturas y murales. Los mayas tenían su calendario y habían
15 logrado calcular con mucha precisión la duración del año solar. Fueron, además, los únicos indios de América que desarrollaron una forma avanzada de escritura. Después de la conquista española, indios educados tradujeron al es-
20 pañol muchos de los mitos, historias y leyendas mayas. Esos libros se consideran las primeras manifestaciones de literatura latinoamericana.

Los aztecas desarrollaron su imperio en México durante el siglo XV. Su capital, Tenoch-
25 titlán, se encontraba en el lugar que hoy ocupa la Ciudad de México. Los aztecas construyeron ciudades tan grandes como las de Europa de la época. La religión dominaba todos los aspectos de su vida diaria. Construyeron enormes tem-
30 plos en forma de pirámides, donde celebraban ceremonias religiosas que incluían sacrificios humanos. Muchas veces iban a la guerra sólo con el propósito de tomar prisioneros para sus sacrificios. Las esculturas aztecas son muy de-
35 talladas, y la más famosa es la gran piedra calendario circular, que representa la superficie del sol.

Los incas desarrollaron un imperio en los Andes, que se extendió desde lo que es hoy el
40 Ecuador hasta el centro de Chile, incluyendo partes de Bolivia y la Argentina. El centro de la civilización estaba en el Perú. Su éxito se debió a su fuerte y estructurado sistema político y social. Además, tenían un ejército muy bien organizado y un sistema de caminos magnífico 45 que comunicaba todos los puntos del imperio con la capital, Cuzco. Allí construyeron grandes palacios, templos y edificios del gobierno. Tenían un emperador que, según la leyenda, descendía de los dioses. Todas las tierras le 50 pertenecían al estado. Nunca desarrollaron la escritura, pero tenían un sistema especial de escribir y contar: hacían nudos en cuerdas de varios colores y tamaños, formando un «quipu». Indios especializados sabían de memoria el sig- 55 nificado de cada quipu. Usaban la llama y la alpaca, que les servían para el transporte y los proveían de carne para la alimentación y lana para la vestimenta. La lengua de los incas, el quechua, se habla todavía en el Perú y zonas de 60 Bolivia, el Ecuador y el norte de Chile.

Hubo también otras civilizaciones menores: **los caribes,** en las Antillas, eran una tribu guerrera que fue prácticamente exterminada por los primeros conquistadores. **Los chibchas** vi- 65 vían en la región andina de Colombia y eran expertos artesanos; trabajaban muy bien el oro, y muchos de sus productos pueden admirarse hoy día en el Museo del Oro en Bogotá. **Los guaraníes** eran de la región del Paraguay, y su len- 70 gua, el guaraní, se habla todavía en ese país casi tanto como el español. **Los araucanos** vivían originalmente en la costa de Chile, pero se fueron hacia la Argentina cuando llegaron los españoles. Son famosos porque lucharon fuerte- 75 mente contra los españoles y sólo fueron finalmente derrotados en el siglo pasado.

DESCUBRIMIENTO, EXPLORACIÓN Y CONQUISTA

Cristóbal Colón fue el primero de los 80

---

53 **hacer un nudo** to tie a knot

grandes descubridores y es conocido hoy como «el descubridor de América». Hizo cuatro viajes al Nuevo Mundo, pero nunca llegó a tocar el continente norteamericano. Descubrió varias islas de las Antillas, las costas de América del Sur (cerca del Orinoco) y parte de la América Central. La fecha de su primer descubrimiento (el 12 de octubre) se celebra en todo el mundo hispano como el «Día de la Raza».

Colón fundó en 1492 la primera colonia europea en el Nuevo Mundo, el Fuerte de Navidad, en lo que hoy es la isla de Santo Domingo. El siglo siguiente fue una época de conquista, colonización y expansión. Entre los conquistadores más famosos, figuran los siguientes:

Juan Ponce de León, quien estableció una colonia española en Puerto Rico en 1508. En 1513, buscando la Fuente de la Juventud, descubrió la Florida.

Vasco Núñez de Balboa, quien atravesó el istmo de Panamá y descubrió el océano Pacífico en 1513, dándole el nombre de Mar del Sur.

Fernando de Magallanes, un navegante portugués que emprendió el primer viaje alrededor del mundo. Fue una empresa heroica, completada por **Juan Sebastián Elcano,** español, al morir Magallanes en las Islas Filipinas.

Hernán Cortés, quien fue, tal vez, el más famoso de los conquistadores. Partió de Cuba hacia el continente en 1518 y llegó en 1519 a la capital del imperio azteca, poniendo fin a la autoridad del emperador Moctezuma. En 1521 logró derrotar definitivamente a los aztecas y fue nombrado gobernador de la Nueva España por Carlos V. Desde México organizó varias expediciones hacia Honduras y California.

Francisco Pizarro, quien acompañó a Balboa en su descubrimiento del Pacífico. En 1531 salió de Panamá hacia el sur y llegó hasta las tierras del imperio inca en 1532. Allí derrotó al último emperador inca, Atahualpa. Fundó la ciudad de Lima en 1535, llamándola «Ciudad de los Reyes».

Francisco Vásquez de Coronado, quien salió de México en busca de las fabulosas «siete ciudades de Cíbola», exploró gran parte de lo que es hoy el sudoeste de los Estados Unidos y descubrió el Gran Cañón.

Álvar Núñez Cabeza de Vaca, quien exploró gran parte de la Florida, Misisipi y el norte de México. Años más tarde fue nombrado gobernador de la provincia de la Plata y exploró la región del Chaco.

Pedro de Valdivia, quien estuvo en el Perú con Pizarro y luego conquistó Chile, luchando contra los araucanos. Fundó la ciudad de Santiago de Chile en 1541 y fue nombrado gobernador de la nueva provincia.

Junto con los conquistadores, llegaron también muchos misioneros al Nuevo Mundo. El más conocido de todos es **Bartolomé de Las Casas.** Fue llamado el «apóstol de las Indias» o el «protector de los indios» porque, desde su llegada a América en 1502, se dedicó a luchar en favor de los indios. Éstos estaban siendo destruidos por los duros trabajos a que eran sometidos y por la crueldad de los conquistadores. Escribió dos obras muy famosas, en las que cuenta la historia y pormenores de la conquista.

En nuestro país es muy conocido **Fray Junípero Serra,** un evangelizador y colonizador del siglo XVIII. Fundó una serie de misiones en California, entre ellas las de San Diego, Los Ángeles y San Francisco.

ADMINISTRACIÓN DE LAS COLONIAS

Todas las colonias se consideraban posesiones del rey. En 1509 se creó en España el Consejo de Indias, una organización encargada de dirigir la administración y economía del Nuevo Mundo. Las colonias estaban divididas en cuatro territorios administrativos, llamados virreinatos: (1) el de Nueva España, que incluía México, Centroamérica, parte de lo que es hoy los Estados Unidos y las Antillas; (2) el del Perú, que incluía el Perú y Chile; (3) el de Nueva Granada, que incluía el Ecuador, Colombia, Panamá y Venezuela; y (4) el del Río de la Plata, que incluía la Argentina, Bolivia, el Paraguay, el Uruguay y parte del Brasil. Estos virreinatos estaban gobernados por virreyes, nombrados directamente por el rey español.

La intención de la corona española era doble: (1) civilizar a los indios, convirtiéndolos a la religión católica; y (2) explotar las riquezas de las colonias para beneficio único de España.

El período colonial duró más o menos tres siglos. La población de las colonias estaba di-

---

47 **en busca de** in search of

vidida en cuatro clases: (1) los españoles, que gobernaban y gozaban de todos los privilegios; (2) los criollos (de origen español, pero nacidos en las colonias), que estaban muy bien eco-
5 nómicamente pero no podían gobernar; (3) los mestizos (mezcla de español e indio o negro), que no tenían ni categoría social ni derechos políticos; y (4) los indios y los esclavos negros.

LA INDEPENDENCIA

10 A principios del siglo XIX, las ideas revolucionarias de la época fueron propagadas por los criollos ricos en las colonias. Además de la injusticia social y política y de las restricciones económicas impuestas por España, tres sucesos
15 históricos influenciaron la rebelión de las colonias: (1) la independencia de los Estados Unidos; (2) el espíritu de la Revolución Francesa; y (3) la invasión de España por las fuerzas de Napoleón.
20 El más importante de los precursores de la independencia fue el venezolano **Francisco Miranda.** Luchó en la guerra de independencia de los Estados Unidos y en la Revolución Francesa. En 1806 organizó, desde Nueva York, una
25 expedición contra Venezuela que fracasó. Cuatro años más tarde, se unió a Simón Bolívar, a cuyo lado luchó hasta 1812. Fue tomado prisionero por los españoles y murió en una cárcel de Cádiz en 1816.
30 Tres de las revoluciones en las colonias estallaron en distintas partes en el mismo año, 1810. Los movimientos revolucionarios se pueden dividir en cuatro:

MÉXICO

35 El padre **Miguel Hidalgo,** cura del pueblo de Dolores (Guanajuato), inició la revolución mexicana el 16 de septiembre de 1810, con el famoso «Grito de Dolores». Al frente de un improvisado ejército de indios, logró varias
40 victorias. Unos meses más tarde, en 1811, fue capturado y fusilado.

José María Morelos, también sacerdote, se unió al movimiento de liberación de Hidalgo. Después de varias batallas, reunió el primer
45 Congreso Nacional mexicano en 1813. En 1815 cayó prisionero y fue fusilado.

Agustín de Iturbide luchó en un principio al lado de los españoles, pero después se unió a los revolucionarios. En 1821 formuló el fa-
50 moso Plan de Iguala, que reconocía a México como una monarquía constitucional, indepen-

diente de España. En 1822, un movimiento popular lo proclamó emperador, con el nombre de Agustín I. Pero una revolución republicana, encabezada por el general **Santa Anna,** le 55 obligó a abdicar. Iturbide murió fusilado en 1824, después de haber regresado al país y haber tratado de apoderarse del gobierno. Por la Constitución de 1824, México se constituyó en República Federal. 60

NUEVA GRANADA (Norte de Sudamérica)

El venezolano **Simón Bolívar,** llamado el Libertador, es la figura dominante de la independencia de casi toda Sudamérica. Fue a la vez militar brillante, gran estadista, escritor y ora- 65 dor. Comenzó su larga lucha en 1810 y con las victorias de Boyacá (Colombia, 1819), Carabobo (Venezuela, 1821) y Pichincha (Ecuador, 1822), aseguró la independencia de toda esa región. En 1822 se formó de esos territorios la República 70 de la Gran Colombia, que duró hasta 1829. Bolívar fue su primer presidente. Pero sus sueños de una América unida no se realizaron. Murió enfermo y decepcionado en Santa Marta, Colombia, en 1830. 75

Antonio José de Sucre, también venezolano, combatió al lado de Miranda. Luego fue el principal lugarteniente de Bolívar. Bajo su mando se ganaron las batallas de Pichincha y Ayacucho, lo que le ganó el título de Gran Ma- 80 riscal. Fue presidente de la nueva república de Bolivia de 1826 a 1828.

EL PERÚ Y EL RÍO DE LA PLATA (Sur de Sudamérica)

El argentino **José de San Martín,** el «santo 85 de la espada», hizo para el sur lo que Bolívar hizo para el norte. Declarada la independencia de la Argentina en 1816, San Martín organizó el Ejército de los Andes, con la ayuda del chileno **Bernardo O'Higgins,** para luchar por la in- 90 dependencia de Chile. Derrotaron a los españoles en las batallas de Chacabuco (1817) y Maipú (1818). Ésta última aseguró la independencia del norte y centro del país. En el sur, la lucha continuó hasta 1824. O'Higgins fue el 95 primer presidente de la nueva república de Chile.

En 1820, San Martín emprendió la liberación del Perú. En julio de 1821 entró en Lima. Desde allí envió ayuda a Sucre para la batalla 100 de Pichincha. En 1822, San Martín y Bolívar se entrevistaron en Guayaquil. A raíz de esta conferencia, San Martín entregó el mando militar a Bolívar, y se retiró de la lucha y del gobierno. La libertad del Perú fue asegurada finalmente por Sucre en la batalla de Ayacucho (1824).

5   *CUBA*

Durante la época de las grandes revoluciones, Cuba se mantuvo más o menos leal a España. Pero hacia el año 1845, comenzaron varios movimientos de independencia. En 1868, **Carlos Manuel de Céspedes** dio el «Grito de Cuba Libre», que inició una guerra de diez años. Desde entonces hasta 1895, Cuba se preparó para la independencia. **José Martí,** poeta, escritor y patriota cubano, fue el espíritu de ese movimiento. En Nueva York, en 1892, fundó el Partido Revolucionario Cubano, que trató de unificar todas las tendencias revolucionarias, y ordenó el levantamiento contra los españoles. Martí murió en 1895, en una invasión a la isla.

Más adelante, en 1898, a raíz de la guerra entre España y los Estados Unidos, éstos ocuparon Cuba, Puerto Rico y las Filipinas. Cuba se constituyó en república en 1901, pero la Enmienda Platt dio derecho a los Estados Unidos a intervenir en la isla hasta 1934.

DESDE LA INDEPENDENCIA HASTA NUESTROS DÍAS

La independencia trajo consigo graves problemas políticos, económicos y sociales, algunos de los cuales todavía existen hoy. Cada país hispanoamericano siguió su curso, y existen grandes diferencias entre ellos. Pero el sistema administrativo, económico y social heredado de los españoles afectó su desarrollo y les dio rasgos comunes.

La historia del siglo que siguió a la Independencia está llena de crisis económicas, rebeliones políticas e injusticia social. Los países no se industrializaron, y muchos dependían de economías basadas en la exportación de un solo producto. Además, la mayoría de los recursos naturales eran explotados por compañías extranjeras, que sólo estaban interesadas en sacar la materia prima. Las tierras estaban en manos de unos pocos terratenientes ricos, y una gran parte del resto de la población vivía en la miseria. La Iglesia Católica y los militares tenían mucho poder político y económico.

El primer cambio notable lo trajo la Revolución Mexicana, a partir de 1911. En 1917 se escribió una nueva constitución, que todavía está en vigor. Ésta reconocía los derechos de los trabajadores, reducía la influencia de la Iglesia y se mantenía fiel a los principios democráticos. Los gobiernos que siguieron organizaron una reforma agraria para darles tierra a los campesinos y nacionalizaron la industria del petróleo. Hacia 1950, México comenzó un programa de desarrollo industrial.

En los otros países hispanoamericanos no hubo ese tipo de revolución, y muchos de ellos fueron gobernados por dictadores durante muchos años. Los cambios económicos y sociales se han sucedido lentamente.

En Cuba y Nicaragua hubo revoluciones que trajeron cambios radicales. En ambos países se luchó contra dictaduras corruptas, pero el resultado ha sido otro tipo de gobierno absoluto y otro tipo de problemas. Cuba es el único país del hemisferio occidental que se ha declarado comunista.

Después de la Segunda Guerra mundial, Hispanoamérica comenzó a ganar importancia en el mundo. Su población creció rápidamente, se encontraron vastos depósitos de petróleo y gas natural, y los países comenzaron a industrializarse. Internamente, las ciudades crecieron y comenzaron a atraer aún más población. Surgieron nuevos problemas administrativos y sociales. Se tuvo que invertir mucho dinero en transporte, construcción, salud pública y educación. Surgieron también nuevas fuerzas políticas: la mujer ganó el voto, creció la clase obrera, los sindicatos tomaron fuerza y muchos sacerdotes jóvenes comenzaron a criticar abiertamente la injusticia económica y social. Aumentó el comercio con los nuevos países independientes de Asia y África, y los países hispanoamericanos comenzaron a tratar de cooperar entre sí.

Hoy en día, la mayoría de los países hispanoamericanos tienen gobiernos más o menos democráticos. Pero a pesar de esto, y del desarrollo económico de los últimos años, todavía existen muchos problemas económicos y sociales que tendrán que resolverse en este siglo.

---

41   **los recursos naturales** natural resources
44   **la materia prima** raw material

52   **estar en vigor** to be in effect
83   **la clase obrera** working class

RELACIONES INTERAMERICANAS

En 1826 Simón Bolívar dio el primer paso hacia la unidad del hemisferio occidental. Invitó a representantes de todos los países del
5 Nuevo Mundo a reunirse en Panamá. Aunque sólo cuatro naciones enviaron delegados, puede decirse que la Conferencia de Panamá no fue un fracaso. El ideal de Bolívar, de unir las Américas, tuvo sus comienzos allí.

10 En los años siguientes, el movimiento cobró fuerzas y creció. La Primera Conferencia Internacional de los Estados Americanos tuvo lugar en Washington, D.C. en 1889–1890. El propósito era el de mantener la paz en el he-
15 misferio y mejorar las relaciones comerciales entre los países. En la conferencia de Buenos Aires de 1910, se creó la Unión Panamericana. El propósito de esta organización era el de establecer estrechas relaciones económicas y cul-
20 turales entre las 21 naciones americanas.

En 1948 tuvo lugar, en Bogotá, la novena Conferencia Panamericana. La alianza fue reorganizada y recibió el nombre de Organización de los Estados Americanos (O.E.A.). La Unión
25 Panamericana sería su secretaría permanente hasta 1970, año en que fue reorganizada bajo el nombre de Secretaría General. La O.E.A. es un organismo regional dentro del cuadro de las Naciones Unidas. Sus objetivos son varios:
30 mantener la paz entre sus miembros, ayudarse mutuamente en caso de agresión y trabajar

por el desarrollo cultural, social y económico de los estados miembros.

A principios de este siglo, la política de los Estados Unidos con respecto a Latinoamé- 35 rica había creado malos sentimientos en esas naciones. Durante la presidencia de Franklin D. Roosevelt, el país trató de mejorar sus relaciones con Latinoamérica, iniciando un nuevo programa económico y político llamado «la Po- 40 lítica del Buen Vecino».

En la segunda guerra mundial, muchos países hispanoamericanos mostraron su fe en la democracia y su amistad con los Estados Unidos, declarando la guerra a nuestros enemigos, 45 enviando tropas al frente y proveyendo de materias primas a los Aliados.

En 1961, el presidente John F. Kennedy inició el programa de la Alianza para el Progreso, a raíz de la Revolución Cubana y su in- 50 fluencia en Hispanoamérica. El propósito de la Alianza para el Progreso era el de ofrecer ayuda financiera y técnica para mejorar la vivienda, educación y servicios públicos en los países latinoamericanos. Para recibir ayuda, esos países 55 debían iniciar reformas agrarias y cambios en sus sistemas tributarios. El programa no tuvo el éxito esperado y ha sido reemplazado por otros métodos de ayuda económica.

Durante este siglo las relaciones intera- 60 mericanas se han estrechado, y se espera que los países continuarán unidos en sus propósitos de mantener la paz en el hemisferio y de ayudarse mutuamente.

---

11 **cobrar fuerzas** to gather strength

57 **el sistema tributario** tax system

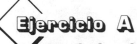

Ejercicio A

Escriba la palabra o expresión que complete correctamente cada frase:

1. El primer navegante que dio la vuelta al mundo fue _____.
   (Cabeza de Vaca, Elcano, Colón, Balboa)

2. Los indios que no fueron derrotados hasta el siglo XIX fueron los _____.
   (incas, caribes, aztecas, araucanos)

3. El rey azteca derrotado por Cortés se llamaba _____.
   (Tenochtitlán, Moctezuma, Cabeza de Vaca, Atahualpa)

4. Todas las colonias se consideraban posesiones _____.
   (de los indios, del descubridor, del rey, de los dioses)

5. La ciudad de Santiago fue fundada por _____.
   (Valdivia, Cabeza de Vaca, Cortés, Colón)

6. El imperio incaico fue destruido por _____.
    (Pizarro, Cortés, Valdivia, Colón)

7. Las colonias españolas eran gobernadas por _____.
    (piratas, misioneros, virreyes, reyes indios)

8. Los indios de Centroamérica de cultura más avanzada eran los _____.
    (toltecas, aztecas, guaraníes, mayas)

9. La Ciudad de México está hoy donde antes estaba situada la ciudad de _____.
    (Tenochtitlán, Chichén-Itzá, Cíbola, Santiago)

10. La Florida fue descubierta por _____.
    (Coronado, Ponce de León, Cabeza de Vaca, Balboa)

Ejercicio B

Escriba la letra que indique la relación correcta con cada expresión de la columna de la izquierda:

1. Ponce de León   _____
2. Fuerte de Navidad   _____
3. Coronado   _____
4. Tenochtitlán   _____
5. Balboa   _____
6. Chichén-Itzá   _____
7. Junípero Serra   _____
8. Bartolomé de las Casas _____
9. Cuzco   _____
10. Valdivia   _____

a. capital azteca
b. araucanos
c. apóstol de las Indias
d. siete ciudades de Cíbola
e. misiones en California
f. la Florida
g. Mar del Sur
h. ciudad maya
i. Santo Domingo
j. capital incaica
k. rey azteca

Ejercicio C

Complete correctamente las frases siguientes:

1. En 1910, en Buenos Aires, se creó _____.

2. Después de una entrevista entre San Martín y Bolívar, el mando militar fue entregado a _____.

3. El Plan de Iguala estableció en México una _____.

4. El famoso «Grito de Dolores» fue dado por _____.

5. La libertad del Perú fue asegurada en la batalla de _____.

6. El único país del hemisferio que se ha declarado comunista es _____.

7. El primer paso hacia la unidad del hemisferio fue dado por _____.

8. El precursor más importante de la lucha por la independencia fue _____ .

9. Hoy en día la mayoría de los países hispanoamericanos tienen gobiernos más o menos

   _____ .

10. El patriota cubano que fue el espíritu del movimiento de la independencia fue

    _____ .

Ejercicio D

Escriba la letra que indique la relación correcta con cada expresión de la columna de la izquierda:

1. Bolívar	_____	a. Chile
2. Martí	_____	b. Ayacucho
3. Unión Panamericana	_____	c. Grito de Dolores
4. San Martín	_____	d. el Libertador
5. Kennedy	_____	e. Cuba
6. Hidalgo	_____	f. santo de la espada
7. Roosevelt	_____	g. O.E.A.
8. O'Higgins	_____	h. Política del Buen Vecino
9. Agustín I	_____	i. Iturbide
10. Sucre	_____	j. la Alianza para el Progreso
		k. Boyacá

Ejercicio E

Complete correctamente las frases siguientes:

1. Cortés fue gobernador de México, cuyo nombre entonces era _____ .

2. Los _____ son personas de origen español nacidas en la América Hispana.

3. La gran piedra calendario circular que representa la superficie del sol fue hecha por los

   _____ .

4. Los incas habían establecido su capital en _____ .

5. Fray Junípero Serra estableció _____ en California.

6. Los dos héroes principales de la guerra sudamericana de independencia fueron Bolívar en el

   norte y _____ en el sur.

7. En tiempos de Cortés, los _____ dominaron la mayor parte de México.

8. La región de Bolivia, la Argentina, el Uruguay y el Paraguay se llamaba el virreinato de _____.

9. Ponce de León, buscando la Fuente de la Juventud, descubrió _____.

10. La gran época de la colonización española fue el siglo _____.

11. Santiago, capital de Chile, fue fundada por _____.

12. En vez de escribir, los incas usaban _____.

13. El primer conquistador que atravesó el istmo de Panamá fue _____.

14. Colón estableció la primera colonia del Nuevo Mundo en la isla de _____.

15. Los indios guerreros de las Antillas se llamaban los _____.

16. Los araucanos vivieron en el _____ de Sudamérica.

17. Chichén-Itzá fue la ciudad principal de los _____.

18. Las colonias fueron administradas por el Consejo de _____.

19. El misionero que luchó más que ningún otro en favor de los indios se llamaba _____.

20. Uno de los sucesos históricos que influyó en la rebelión de las colonias fue _____.

21. El Gran Cañón fue descubierto por _____.

22. En la guerra contra los Estados Unidos, España perdió las Islas Filipinas, Cuba y _____.

23. El rey inca ejecutado por Pizarro fue _____.

24. Tres de las revoluciones contra España estallaron en el año de _____.

25. O'Higgins fue el primer presidente de _____.

La Literatura de Hispanoamérica

DE LOS ORÍGENES A LA INDEPENDENCIA

Hispanoamérica tiene una literatura rica y abundante, cuyos orígenes se encuentran en los llamados cronistas de Indias. Éstos fueron his-
5 toriadores españoles que vinieron al Nuevo Mundo y registraron los sucesos de la conquista. Uno de los grandes soldados y cronistas de la época fue **Bernal Díaz del Castillo** (1492–1581). Fue compañero de Hernán Cortés y des-
10 cribió la conquista de México en su célebre «Historia verdadera de los sucesos de la conquista de la Nueva España».

Alonso de Ercilla (1533–1594) escribió uno de los mejores ejemplos de poesía épica del
15 Renacimiento. Su famoso poema épico «La araucana» trata de las guerras entre los conquistadores españoles y los indios araucanos de Chile. A pesar del carácter autobiográfico de la obra y de que Ercilla era un soldado español, los
20 héroes del poema son dos caciques araucanos, Caupolicán y Lautaro. El poeta muestra su admiración y simpatía por el valor y el heroísmo de los indígenas. «La araucana» sirvió de modelo para otros poemas épicos de la época y se con-
25 sidera el primer gran poema nacional chileno.

La cumbre de la poesía lírica americana de la época colonial está representada por la poetisa **Sor Juana Inés de la Cruz** (1651–1695). A esta monja mexicana se le llamó «la décima
30 musa» o «el fénix de México». Los temas de sus versos son el pesimismo, la angustia y la vanidad de la vida. En ellos se nota su temperamento apasionado y su gusto por los contrastes y los juegos de conceptos.

35 **José Joaquín Fernández de Lisardi** (1776–1827) se distingue como el primer novelista de Hispanoamérica y el escritor más influyente de México en el siglo XIX. Fue conocido con el seudónimo «el Pensador Mexicano», nombre de

40 uno de los siete periódicos que fundó. Su obra maestra, «El periquillo sarniento», es una novela picaresca que describe de manera realista la sociedad mexicana en vísperas de la independencia.

45 El venezolano **Andrés Bello** (1781–1865) se distinguió como abogado, educador, crítico literario, poeta, ensayista, periodista y filólogo. Pasó muchos años en Inglaterra, donde fundó tres revistas para dar a conocer la cultura de
50 América. Después fue a Chile, donde escribió el «Código Civil» del nuevo país y fundó la Universidad de Chile. Es el autor de una gramática que todavía se considera una de las mejores y más completas de la lengua castellana.

55 **Simón Bolívar** (1783–1830) representa la cumbre del pensamiento político de la época. Reveló una visión extraordinaria en sus documentos, como en la llamada «Carta de Jamaica», en la que revisa la situación política y social de
60 Hispanoamérica y defiende la formación de una América unificada en una gran federación.

EL SIGLO XIX

El siglo XIX se caracterizó en Hispanoamérica como el siglo de las revoluciones y de la independencia. Estos movimientos políticos se
65 reflejan en la literatura que se produjo.

El argentino **Domingo Faustino Sarmiento** (1811–1888) fue embajador de su país en los Estados Unidos y presidente de la república de 1868 a 1874. Su obra maestra, «Fa-
70 cundo o Civilización y barbarie», es un ensayo político y sociológico sobre las causas de la dictadura, el caudillismo y la barbarie de la pampa.

La época trágica de la dictadura de Juan Manuel de Rosas en la Argentina, fue descrita
75 en la novela «Amalia» del escritor y poeta ro-

---

33 **tener gusto por** to have a liking (an eye) for
43 **en vísperas de** on the eve of

49 **dar a conocer** to introduce
73 **el caudillismo** system of government by a political boss

mántico **José Mármol** (1817–1871). Esta obra describe el terror que reinaba en Buenos Aires en la época y pinta vívidamente al tirano y su familia. Se considera la primera novela política de Hispanoamérica.

El mejor representante del costumbrismo hispanoamericano es el peruano **Ricardo Palma** (1833–1919). Creó un género llamado «tradiciones», narraciones con base histórica que mezclan lo real y lo imaginario con humorismo e ironía. Escribió miles de «Tradiciones peruanas» que cubren toda la historia del Perú, desde los incas hasta los primeros años del siglo XX. Tiene mérito también porque incorporó a su español las expresiones y palabras nuevas surgidas en Hispanoamérica.

José Hernández (1834–1886) representa la llamada poesía gauchesca, un género de poesía que describe tipos y costumbres regionales. Su obra «Martín Fierro» se considera el poema más famoso de Hispanoamérica. El héroe de esta obra argentina es un gaucho que canta su propia historia, describiendo al mismo tiempo todos los personajes que habitan la pampa.

La novela más popular del siglo pasado fue escrita por el colombiano **Jorge Isaacs** (1837–1895). «María» es una obra sumamente sentimental, con descripciones exquisitas del paisaje del valle donde nació su autor.

Florencio Sánchez (1875–1910) se considera el mejor dramaturgo del siglo XIX. Este uruguayo estableció las bases para el renacimiento del teatro realista hispanoamericano del siglo XX. Sus obras presentan la realidad de los problemas humanos dentro de una sociedad a la que critica fuertemente. Entre ellas está «La gringa», un drama que trata de los conflictos entre los criollos y los inmigrantes.

El siglo XIX dio también muchos poetas románticos de fama internacional, entre los que se distinguen dos cubanos y un colombiano. **José María Heredia** (1803–1839) está considerado como el primer romántico de la lengua española. Su vida fue también un retrato del héroe romántico: tuvo que vivir en el exilio por sus ideas liberales, fue rebelde, sufrió y murió joven, pobre y tuberculoso. Su poema «Niágara», inspirado en las cataratas, es su obra más famosa.

La cubana **Gertrudis Gómez de Avellaneda** (1814–1873) está considerada hoy día como una de las mejores poetisas de la lengua española. Su poesía está llena de confesiones, y sus temas constantes son el amor, el arte y Dios. Escribió además seis novelas y una docena de tragedias al gusto de la época.

Rafael Pombo (1833–1912) es el poeta más completo que ha dado Colombia. Escribió poesía reflexiva y filosófica y tenía además un talento especial para la poesía popular y la humorística. Es importante porque enriqueció la literatura infantil y tradujo al español muchos de los poetas ingleses y norteamericanos, antiguos y contemporáneos.

Hacia fines del siglo XIX apareció un nuevo movimiento literario, el modernismo, en reacción a la falta de originalidad del realismo y al sentimentalismo excesivo del romanticismo. El modernismo ponía énfasis en los sentimientos de todos los hombres, expresados elegantemente a través de nuevas imágenes. Este movimiento fue más importante en la poesía que en la prosa y duró hasta bien entrado el siglo XX. Una multitud de poetas, españoles e hispanoamericanos, que lograron renombre internacional, fueron modernistas.

El cubano **José Martí** (1853–1895), además de ser uno de los precursores del modernismo, fue un hombre de grandes inquietudes morales, metafísicas y políticas, que luchó y murió por la independencia de su país. Vivió en la ciudad de Nueva York desde 1881 hasta el año de su muerte. Durante esa época escribió sus poemas más famosos, los «Versos sencillos», de los cuales se tomó la letra para la canción popular «Guantanamera».

Manuel Gutiérrez Nájera (1859–1895), de México, es uno de los mejores representantes de la transición del romanticismo al modernismo. Escribió poesías y prosa llenas de dulzura y gracia, cuyos temas son la tristeza, el dolor, la búsqueda de Dios y el misterio de la vida. Publicó dos colecciones importantes de cuentos, «Cuentos de color de humo» y «Cuentos frágiles».

Rubén Darío (1867–1916), poeta nicaragüense, fue el padre indiscutible del modernismo y tuvo gran influencia no sólo en Hispanoamérica, sino también en España. Viajó muchísimo durante toda su vida, llegando a casi todos los países de América y de Europa. Sus obras más importantes son «Cantos de vida y esperanza» y «Prosas profanas».

---

65   **hacia fines de** toward the end of   85   **la letra** lyrics

El ensayista más célebre de Hispanoamérica y el que más influyó sobre la juventud a principios de este siglo, fue el uruguayo **José Enrique Rodó** (1872–1917). En su obra más conocida, «Ariel», un maestro habla con sus estudiantes sobre la necesidad de tener ideales desinteresados, de desarrollar el sentimiento de lo bello y lo moral y sobre los peligros de las civilizaciones avanzadas y del espíritu de utilitarismo reflejado por los Estados Unidos.

EL SIGLO XX

LA POESÍA

El auge de la poesía hispanoamericana continuó en el siglo XX, en el que se encuentran poetas y poetisas de fama mundial.

Luis Palés Matos (1893–1959), de Puerto Rico, cultivó la poesía llamada «negra o afroantillana», de profunda raíz popular. En su obra poética ofrece una visión del mundo y el folklore negros, usando metáforas, ritmos y sonidos de gran sensualismo. Su poema más conocido es «Danza negra», en el que centra su atención en la expresión musical negra que tanta influencia ha tenido en el mundo.

El poeta cubano **Nicolás Guillén** (1902–) es otro gran representante de la poesía afro-antillana. Escribió poemas siguiendo el ritmo sensual del «són», uno de los bailes típicos de Cuba. Pero además su poesía es una protesta de tipo económico-social, presentada como un lamento de las clases oprimidas. Entre sus poemas más famosos están «Sóngoro cosongo», «Tú no sabe inglé», «Velorio de Papá Montero» y «No sé por qué piensas tú».

La obra del poeta peruano **César Vallejo** (1892–1938) no es muy extensa, pero le ganó fama internacional. Tiene como tema básico el sufrimiento del Hombre, tanto en su sentido individual como colectivo, por el solo hecho de haber nacido. Es uno de los poetas más hondos y humanos de la literatura en lengua española. «Poemas humanos» figura entre sus obras más conocidas.

El chileno **Pablo Neruda** (1904–1973) es sin duda el poeta hispanoamericano de más fama en el mundo entero, y no sólo por haber recibido el Premio Nobel de Literatura en 1971. Comenzó a escribir bajo la influencia del modernismo, pero luego encontró su forma y materia propias. Neruda, seudónimo de Ricardo Neftalí Reyes, recorrió el mundo entero como diplomático de su país. Sus colecciones de poesías más importantes han sido traducidas a más de treinta idiomas. Éstas incluyen «Odas elementales», «Veinte poemas de amor y una canción desesperada», «Residencia en la tierra» y «El canto general».

El poeta y ensayista mexicano **Octavio Paz** (1914–) fue diplomático de su país en la India, estudió un tiempo en los Estados Unidos y ha vivido en Suiza y Francia. Su poesía muestra esa combinación de filosofía oriental, cultura occidental y mexicanidad que la hace universal. Sus temas constantes son la soledad, la falta de comunicación entre los hombres y la búsqueda del ser. Sus ensayos principales son «El laberinto de la soledad» y «El arco y la lira», y entre sus colecciones de poesías se encuentran «Libertad bajo palabra» y «Viento entero». Ganó el Premio Nobel de Literatura de 1990.

La mujer se ha destacado como escritora en la obra poética hispanoamericana. Quizás la más conocida de las poetisas es la chilena **Gabriela Mistral** (1889–1957), quien ganó el Premio Nobel de Literatura en 1945. Fue maestra durante casi veinte años y luego siguió trabajando por la educación como representante diplomática de su país. Los últimos años de su vida los pasó de consulesa en Nueva York. Su obra más importante es una colección de poesías que se titula «Desolación», que refleja su humanismo, su sensibilidad y su ternura.

La argentina **Alfonsina Storni** (1892–1938) fue lo que hoy llamaríamos una feminista. Era una mujer de ideas liberales, que luchó contra los prejuicios sociales por más libertad para la mujer. Su obra poética trata de la condición de la mujer y de lo que significa ser mujer en un mundo masculino. Ésta incluye «La inquietud del rosal», «El dulce daño», «Ocre» y «Mundo de siete pozos».

Julia de Burgos (1916–1953), de Puerto Rico, escribió una poesía amorosa muy intensa y llena de dolor, como «Canción de la verdad sencilla». Pero también escribió una poesía nacionalista en la que recuerda momentos

---

3 **a principios de** at the beginning of
13 **el auge** period of prosperity
39 **por el solo hecho de** for the only reason that, just because

51 **recorrer el mundo** to travel around the world

dramáticos para América, como «23 de septiembre» e «Himno de sangre a Trujillo».

El amor romántico, representado en un tono menos exaltado, más coqueto e íntimo, se
5 presenta en la obra poética de la uruguaya **Juana de Ibarbourou** (1895–1979). Esta poetisa ha sido llamada «Juana de América» desde 1929, a raíz de un homenaje ofrecido por su país, en el que participaron escritores y poetas hispanoameri-
10 canos famosos. Sus poemas más conocidos incluyen «Las lenguas de diamante», «Raíz salvaje», «La rosa de los vientos» y «Perdida».

EL TEATRO

El teatro hispanoamericano comenzó a
15 surgir realmente después de la Segunda Guerra mundial. Anteriormente era un teatro regional, interesado en los problemas políticos, económicos y sociales de un lugar determinado. La nueva generación ha tratado de crear un teatro
20 de intereses más universales.

Uno de los más distinguidos dramaturgos fue el mexicano **Rodolfo Usigli** (1905–1979). Su teatro hace un análisis crítico de la idiosincrasia nacional mexicana. Sus obras más famosas son
25 «El gesticulador» y «Corona de sombra».

Carlos Solórzano (1922–   ), guatemalteco-mexicano, es uno de los autores y críticos que más han contribuido a la renovación del teatro hispanoamericano. Entre sus obras fi-
30 guran «La muerte hizo la luz», «Doña Beatriz», «Las manos de Dios», «El hechicero» y «Los fantoches».

Sebastián Salazar Bondy (1924–1965) fue un dramaturgo peruano en cuyas obras se ma-
35 nifiestan sus dotes de observador, su facilidad para manejar complejidades psicológicas y su dominio del lenguaje popular. Entre sus obras principales están «Algo quiere morir», «El fabricante de deudas», «Todo queda en casa» y
40 «No hay isla feliz».

Emilio Carballido (1925–   ), el dramaturgo mexicano más conocido de su generación, es autor de más de setenta y cinco obras dramáticas. Dos tendencias fundamentales en su
45 obra dramática son la realista y la fantástica. Sus dramas incluyen «El día en que se soltaron los leones», «La zona intermedia», «La danza que sueña la tortuga» y «Te juro Juana, que tengo ganas».
50 El chileno **Egon Wolff** (1926–   ) es un dramaturgo que muestra su conocimiento del teatro por la construcción y desenvolvimiento de sus temas. «Los invasores» es, quizás, su obra más importante.

Osvaldo Dragún (1929–   ) ha logrado 55 crear obras de sabor muy argentino, combinando temas trascendentales con un ambiente cotidiano. Entre sus dramas más importantes figuran «Historias para ser contadas», «Jardín del infierno» y «Y nos dijeron que éramos inmor- 60 tales».

Jorge Díaz (1930–   ) nació en la Argentina, pero es ciudadano chileno. Es el dramaturgo hispanoamericano que más se ha relacionado con el teatro del absurdo. En sus 65 últimas obras, sin embargo, se nota una tendencia hacia un teatro más comprometido política y socialmente. «El cepillo de dientes» se considera una de las mejores obras humorísticas del repertorio hispanoamericano. Sus otras obras 70 incluyen «Requiem para un girasol» y «Topografía de un desnudo».

LA NARRATIVA

La literatura narrativa hispanoamericana del siglo XX tiene representantes con renombre 75 internacional. Los autores contemporáneos van más allá de la preocupación por problemas políticos y sociales regionales y han logrado una dimensión universal. La novela, en especial, tuvo un gran resurgimiento a partir de los años 80 cincuenta.

Mariano Azuela (1873–1952) es un novelista mexicano que describe las luchas sangrientas de la Revolución Mexicana. Su obra más famosa, «Los de abajo», fue escrita mientras 85 el autor le servía de médico al ejército de Pancho Villa en 1915.

Horacio Quiroga (1878–1937), del Uruguay, debe su puesto en la literatura a sus excelentes cuentos cortos, los mejores de los 90 cuales tratan de temas de horror, crueldad y muerte. Sus colecciones más conocidas son «Los desterrados», «Más allá» y «Cuentos de amor, de locura y de muerte».

Hugo Wast (1883–1962) es el seudónimo 95 de Gustavo Martínez Zuviría, uno de los novelistas argentinos más populares y más traducidos. Escribió sobre los problemas sociales y económicos de la gente de las ciudades y los pueblos de la Argentina de su época. Entre sus 100

---

76   **ir más allá de** to go beyond   80   **a partir de** from (some specified time)

novelas más conocidas están «Flor de durazno», «La casa de los cuervos» y «Desierto de piedra».

Rómulo Gallegos (1884–1969) vivió muchos años en el exilio por sus ideas políticas y fue, por muy corto tiempo, presidente de su patria, Venezuela. Se le considera el mejor novelista de su país. Su obra más célebre, «Doña Bárbara», describe la vida de los llaneros venezolanos, llevando a la vez el mensaje que la tiranía no es indestructible.

El mejor novelista de la literatura gauchesca fue el argentino **Ricardo Güiraldes** (1886–1927). En su novela «Don Segundo Sombra», describió con gran realismo la vida y las costumbres de los gauchos.

Martín Luis Guzmán (1887–1976) fue coronel del ejército de Pancho Villa y describió sus memorias de la Revolución Mexicana en su obra «El águila y la serpiente»; estos animales forman el símbolo que aparece en la bandera mexicana. Vivió muchos años exilado en la ciudad de Nueva York.

El colombiano **José Eustasio Rivera** (1889–1928) escribió «La vorágine», considerada la novela por excelencia sobre la selva tropical. Es una novela de aventuras y de crítica social, que describe muy vívidamente la vida trágica de los caucheros en la selva del Amazonas.

El escritor argentino **Jorge Luis Borges** (1899–1986) es conocido mundialmente como poeta, cuentista y ensayista. Sus obras reflejan su conocimiento profundo de la expresión verbal, su habilidad analítica, su gran cultura universal, su maravillosa imaginación creadora y su experiencia de lo regional argentino. Entre sus colecciones de cuentos figuran «Ficciones», «El aleph» e «Historia universal de la infamia». Su ensayo más conocido es «Historia de la eternidad», en el que trata del tema del paso del tiempo que angustia a los hombres. En 1955 se quedó ciego y desde entonces tuvo que dictar sus escritos.

Las obras del guatemalteco **Miguel Ángel Asturias** (1899–1974) mezclan el misticismo de la cultura maya con la crítica político-social. Los diálogos de sus novelas reflejan la lengua popular hablada por el pueblo centroamericano. Su trilogía de novelas «Viento fuerte», «El Papa verde» y «Los ojos de los enterrados», describe la explotación de los indios por las grandes compañías yanquis en las zonas bananeras. Re-

cibió el Premio Nobel de Literatura de 1967 por novelas como «El señor presidente» y «Hombres de maíz».

El ecuatoriano **Jorge Icaza** (1906–1978) expuso la explotación del indio en su novela «Huasipungo». Ésta logró fama universal y ha sido traducida a catorce idiomas. Su obra literaria incluye otras novelas, comedias y libros de cuentos. En lenguaje muy directo y realista, presenta tipos básicos de su país y la lucha entre los pobres y sus opresores.

El peruano **Ciro Alegría** (1909–1967), como Icaza, se considera representante de la llamada novela indigenista. Describió los problemas de la vida de los indios de su país en su novela «El mundo es ancho y ajeno», considerada como su obra maestra.

Pocos narradores hispanoamericanos han gozado de tanto prestigio internacional como el cubano **Alejo Carpentier** (1904–1980). Fue autor de la primera historia de la música afro-cubana y de la primera novela afro-cubana, «Ecue-Yamba-O». Pero además escribió otras novelas llenas de encanto y de magia, en las que muestra sus grandes conocimientos de la música, el folklore, la historia y la antropología, ampliando su concepto de «lo maravilloso americano». Entre sus novelas más conocidas y traducidas están «El acoso», «El reino de este mundo» y «El siglo de las luces».

Ernesto Sábato (1911–   ), ensayista y novelista argentino, debe su éxito internacional a dos novelas de tipo metafísico, «El túnel» y «Sobre héroes y tumbas». Ambas tocan cuestiones fundamentales que angustian al hombre contemporáneo.

Las novelas y cuentos del argentino **Julio Cortázar** (1914–1984) revelan una intensa preocupación por la relación entre la realidad y la fantasía y por la condición absurda del hombre moderno. Entre sus obras más conocidas está «Rayuela», una novela cuya estructura fragmentada refleja la incoherencia de la vida y de la cultura contemporáneas.

La obra literaria del mexicano **Juan Rulfo** (1918–1986) presenta una voz y una visión tan profundas de su país, que ya forma parte de la herencia de la literatura hispanoamericana. Es conocido por una colección de sus cuentos más célebres, «El llano en llamas», y por su novela «Pedro Páramo», en la que todos los personajes

---

25 **por excelencia** preeminently, par excellence

28 **el cauchero** worker in a rubber plantation, person who searches for rubber trees

son fantasmas de un pasado cercano pero olvidado. Jugando con el espacio y el tiempo, utilizando imágenes muy intensas y un lenguaje muy directo, Rulfo logra comunicar la aterradora experiencia del sufrimiento, el dolor, el hambre, la muerte y la lucha del hombre contra un medio estéril.

El chileno **José Donoso** (1924–   ) es otro escritor que ha contribuido a la renovación de la novela hispanoamericana con sus obras «Este domingo», «El lugar sin límites» y «El obsceno pájaro de la noche». En ellas presenta una visión intensa y crítica de la burguesía de su país.

El escritor colombiano **Gabriel García Márquez** (1928–   ) recibió el Premio Nobel de Literatura de 1982. Entre sus obras más conocidas se hallan «Los funerales de la mama grande», que es una colección de cuentos, «La hojarasca» y «El coronel no tiene quien le escriba». Su novela más célebre es «Cien años de soledad», en la que conviven lo real con lo imaginario. Esta obra se sitúa en un pueblo imaginario llamado Macondo, que representa la realidad de muchos pueblos hispanoamericanos. Sus personajes centrales aparecen en otras obras del autor y llegan a cobrar vida propia.

Un autor mexicano de mucho renombre internacional es **Carlos Fuentes** (1929–   ). Sus obras utilizan técnicas del cine y del realismo mágico: alegorías, mitos, monólogos interiores y fragmentación del tiempo lógico. Entre las más conocidas están «La muerte de Artemio Cruz», «Cambio de piel» y «La cabeza de la hidra».

Guillermo Cabrera Infante (1929–   ) es un escritor cubano que vive en el exilio en Inglaterra desde 1966, y está considerado como uno de los grandes innovadores de la novela. Una de sus obras más conocidas, «Tres tristes tigres», se ha llevado varios premios literarios internacionales.

El novelista argentino **Manuel Puig** (1932–   ) es otro escritor conocido internacionalmente, cuyos libros han sido traducidos a la mayoría de los idiomas modernos. Sus novelas más importantes son «Boquitas pintadas», «La traición de Rita Hayworth» y «El beso de la mujer araña». Esta última estuvo prohibida por muchos años en la Argentina; de ella se filmó una película, co-producción internacional, que tuvo mucho éxito.

El novelista peruano que ha logrado mayor fama internacional es **Mario Vargas Llosa** (1936–   ). Muestra preocupación social y humana en todas sus obras, tratando de representar la violencia y la lucha por la vida en distintos niveles sociales de su país. Entre sus novelas más famosas están «La ciudad y los perros», «La casa verde», «Conversación en la catedral» y «La guerra del fin del mundo».

---

26 **cobrar vida propia** to acquire a life of its own

Escriba la letra que indique la relación correcta con cada expresión de la columna de la izquierda:

1. Sor Juana Inés de la Cruz _____
2. Bernal Díaz del Castillo _____
3. «Carta de Jamaica» _____
4. Ricardo Güiraldes _____
5. «El cepillo de dientes» _____
6. Ciro Alegría _____
7. «Cuentos de color de humo» _____
8. «Tradiciones peruanas» _____
9. Gabriel García Márquez _____
10. «El Aleph» _____

a. Ricardo Palma
b. la «décima musa»
c. la conquista de México
d. Manuel Gutiérrez Nájera
e. Jorge Luis Borges
f. «La vorágine»
g. «Cien años de soledad»
h. «Don Segundo Sombra»
i. «El mundo es ancho y ajeno»
j. Jorge Díaz
k. «Los de abajo»
l. Bolívar

Ejercicio B

Complete cada una de las frases siguientes, escribiendo el título de la obra o el nombre del autor:

1. El gran poema épico de los gauchos es _____.
2. «El beso de la mujer araña» fue escrita por _____.
3. «Doña Bárbara» fue escrita por _____.
4. El erudito venezolano que escribió una gramática famosa fue _____.
5. «Facundo», un estudio sobre los gauchos, fue escrito por _____.
6. La novela que describe la vida de los caucheros en la selva es _____.
7. Rodó escribió un libro de ensayos llamado _____.
8. «Ficciones» es una colección de cuentos de _____.
9. «Cantos de vida y esperanza» es una importante colección de poesías de _____.
10. Juan Rulfo es conocido por dos obras tituladas _____.
11. «Tres tristes tigres» es una novela de _____.
12. Macondo es el pueblo donde se sitúa la acción de _____.
13. Dos de las novelas famosas de Vargas Llosa son _____.
14. La novela cuya estructura fragmentada refleja la incoherencia de la vida, se titula

    _____.

15. «Cambio de piel» fue escrita por _____.

Ejercicio C

¿Cierto o falso? Indique si cada frase es cierta o falsa. Si es falsa, cámbiela para que sea cierta:

1. «El Pensador Mexicano» es el seudónimo de Bernal Díaz del Castillo.

    _____

2. «La araucana» es un poema lírico.

    _____

3. Andrés Bello es el autor de una gramática de la lengua castellana.

    _____

4. La obra «Facundo» trata de los gauchos y la barbarie de la pampa.

    _____

5. «Amalia» es una novela que se sitúa durante la dictadura de Trujillo en Santo Domingo.

    _____

6. Una novela que describe la vida de los caucheros en la selva del Amazonas es «Martín Fierro».

    _____

7. El modernismo fue un movimiento literario de reacción contra el clasicismo.

    _____

8. José Martí se distinguió por ser el padre del modernismo.

    _____

9. La canción «Guantanamera» se basa en la obra poética «Cantos de vida y esperanza» de Rubén Darío.

    _____

10. Dos novelistas mexicanos que describen las luchas sangrientas de la Revolución de 1910 son Mariano Azuela y Martín Luis Guzmán.

    _____

11. Uno de los mejores cuentistas de Hispanoamérica fue César Vallejo.

    _____

12. La vida de los llaneros venezolanos fue descrita en una novela de Ricardo Güiraldes.

    _____

13. «El mundo es ancho y ajeno» es una novela en la que se describen los problemas de los indios de México.

    _____

14. El escritor que expuso la explotación de los indios en las zonas bananeras fue Jorge Luis Borges.

    _____

15. García Márquez, Asturias, Neruda y Gabriela Mistral ganaron el Premio Nobel de Literatura.

    _____

16. «Pedro Páramo» es una novela que critica la burguesía de Chile.

    _____

17. Dos poetas que tratan temas afro-antillanos en su poesía son Luis Palés Matos y Octavio Paz.

    _____

18. La poetisa hispanoamericana ganadora de un premio prestigioso fue Alfonsina Storni.

    _____

19. El primer romántico de la lengua española fue Rafael Pombo.

    _____

20. Egon Wolff es el dramaturgo que más se ha relacionado con el teatro del absurdo.

    _____

 **Ejercicio D**

✔ *Subraye la expresión que mejor complete cada una de las frases siguientes:*

1. El padre del modernismo fue   (a) Hugo Wast   (b) Martín Luis Guzmán   (c) Alonso de Ercilla   (d) Rubén Darío

2. El primer novelista de Hispanoamérica fue   (a) José Mármol   (b) Jorge Isaacs
   (c) Fernández de Lisardi   (d) Florencio Sánchez

3. Una obra que trata de la conquista de Chile es   (a) «El periquillo sarniento»   (b) «Cantos de vida y esperanza»   (c) «La araucana»   (d) «Cuentos de color de humo»

4. Bernal Díaz del Castillo escribió acerca de la conquista de   (a) Cuba   (b) México   (c) la Argentina   (d) el Perú

5. La «décima musa» fue   (a) Sor Juana Inés de la Cruz   (b) Gertrudis Gómez de Avellaneda   (c) Gabriela Mistral   (d) Juana de Ibarbourou

6. Un dramaturgo importante de la América del Sur fue   (a) Rafael Pombo   (b) José Enrique Rodó   (c) Florencio Sánchez   (d) Manuel Gutiérrez Nájera

7. Las «Tradiciones peruanas» fueron escritas por   (a) Ricardo Palma   (b) José Eustasio Rivera   (c) Ciro Alegría   (d) Horacio Quiroga

8. Domingo Faustino Sarmiento   (a) fue presidente de la Argentina   (b) murió por la independencia de Cuba   (c) escribió novelas sobre la revolución mexicana   (d) nació en Nicaragua

9. Uno de los mejores cuentistas de Hispanoamérica fue   (a) Pablo Neruda   (b) Gutiérrez Nájera   (c) Alonso de Ercilla   (d) Horacio Quiroga

10. Rómulo Gallegos, además de ser novelista, fue presidente de   (a) México   (b) Colombia   (c) Venezuela   (d) la Argentina

11. La poetisa que recibió el honor de ser llamada «de América» fue   (a) Gabriela Mistral   (b) Alfonsina Storni   (c) Juana de Ibarbourou   (d) Julia de Burgos

12. El poeta chileno que recibió el Premio Nobel de Literatura fue   (a) Pablo Neruda   (b) Gabriel García Márquez   (c) Miguel Ángel Asturias   (d) Juan Ramón Jiménez

13. En las novelas de José Donoso el lector ve   (a) la explotación de los indios   (b) a la burguesía chilena   (c) los horrores de una guerra   (d) una caricatura del gran capitalista yanqui

14. La poetisa que luchó contra prejuicios sociales por la libertad de la mujer fue   (a) Gabriela Mistral   (b) Julia de Burgos   (c) Juana de Ibarbourou   (d) Alfonsina Storni

15. El dramaturgo mexicano más conocido de su generación fue   (a) Carlos Solórzano   (b) Rodolfo Usigli   (c) Emilio Carballido   (d) Osvaldo Dragún

El Arte y la Música de Hispanoamérica

EL ARTE

Cuando llegaron los conquistadores a Hispanoamérica, a principios del siglo XV, encontraron un arte muy rico desarrollado por los indios. El arte precolombino, es decir, el arte de antes de la llegada de Cristóbal Colón, representa el desarrollo increíble de las culturas indígenas en la arquitectura, la escultura, los murales y la joyería. Hicieron esculturas para sus pirámides y construyeron palacios, templos y edificios de gobierno, decorados con figuras de sus dioses. Elaboraron los metales preciosos como el oro y la plata y usaron piedras preciosas para adornar su joyería. Produjeron objetos de barro y de cerámica, que servían tanto de adorno y decoración como para el uso diario.

Hoy en día se pueden ver las ruinas de las pirámides, los templos y demás estructuras al visitar lugares como Chichén-Itzá y Uxmal (México, los mayas), la ciudad de México (los aztecas) y Cuzco y Machu Picchu (el Perú, los incas). También se exhibe el arte precolombino en los museos de muchos países, entre ellos el Museo de Antropología de la Ciudad de México, el Museo Arqueológico y el Museo del Oro de Lima y el Museo del Oro de Bogotá. Éste último tiene la colección más grande del mundo de objetos de oro precolombinos.

Los españoles trajeron al Nuevo Mundo el estilo de arte que estaba de moda en el siglo XVI. Éste era de tipo religioso, por lo general, y sirvió para la conversión de los indios al catolicismo. Tanto la pintura como la arquitectura que se desarrollaron en Hispanoamérica se parecían mucho a las de España. Por eso se ven ejemplos de la arquitectura románica, gótica, neoclásica y barroca o churrigueresca en las catedrales, las iglesias y los edificios que se construyeron en los países hispanoamericanos. Hoy día a este estilo se le llama «estilo colonial»; es decir, del estilo de la época en que el país era colonia de España. Las ciudades de Taxco y Guanajuato en México, Lima en el Perú y Cartagena en Colombia, entre otras, son ricos ejemplos del arte que floreció en Hispanoamérica durante la época colonial.

No fue sino hasta el siglo XX que Hispanoamérica produjo pintores de renombre internacional. Muchos de ellos representaron en su obra sus raíces indígenas y lo histórico, político y social de su país. Los más importantes son los pintores y muralistas mexicanos, que rechazaron la dominación cultural europea, cultivaron sus rasgos característicos y utilizaron la pintura como instrumento de protesta social.

El más conocido de los pintores mexicanos es **Diego Rivera** (1886–1957). En la primera parte de su vida pintó bajo la influencia del cubismo y postimpresionismo europeos. Hacia los años veinte comenzó a desarrollar su estilo vigoroso y se dedicó a la pintura mural, en la cual representó temas políticos y sociales. Sus murales adornan muchos edificios públicos por toda la república de México; el más gigantesco de todos es una historia épica del país que adorna el Palacio Nacional de la Ciudad de México.

El muralista mexicano **José Clemente Orozco** (1883–1949) defendió la causa de la Revolución Mexicana y muchos de sus cuadros representan escenas de esa revolución. Pintó además los frescos del Palacio de Bellas Artes de la Ciudad de México. Durante los varios años que vivió en los Estados Unidos, pintó una serie de frescos importantes en Dartmouth College.

El mexicano **David Alfaro Siqueiros** (1896–1974) ha sido el defensor más prominente del arte como expresión de ideología política en la segunda mitad del siglo XX. Estuvo preso muchas veces por sus ideas políticas. En sus cuadros y murales llenos de colores vivos,

---

17 **hoy (en) día** nowadays
30 **estar de moda** to be in fashion

79 **la segunda mitad** the second half
80 **estar preso** to be imprisoned

el realismo está mezclado con lo fantástico, y las figuras muestran sus emociones con gran fuerza. En 1932 Siqueiros organizó el Taller Experimental de la ciudad de Nueva York, en el que estudiaron pintores como Jackson Pollock.

Rufino Tamayo (1899–1991) fue un pintor mexicano de gran renombre. Sus cuadros, algunos de ellos semi-abstractos, han captado en colores vivos las alegrías y tragedias de su país. Ha ganado varios premios internacionales de pintura, y sus murales adornan lugares como el Palacio Nacional de Bellas Artes y el Museo de Antropología de la Ciudad de México y el edificio de la UNESCO en París.

Miguel Covarrubias (1904–1957), también de México, fue famoso tanto en su país como en los Estados Unidos como pintor de caricaturas de personas célebres. Ilustró muchos libros y revistas que muestran su interés por el estudio de diversos tipos raciales.

Lo pintoresco de la vida de los gauchos ha sido representado en los cuadros del pintor impresionista argentino **Cesáreo Bernaldo de Quirós** (1879–1969). Sus numerosos cuadros constituyen un recuerdo importante de la vida de la pampa.

El pintor peruano **José Sabogal** (1888–1956) representó en sus cuadros la cultura indígena de su país. Vio el porvenir de su patria en la civilización de los mestizos.

Wifredo Lam (1902–1982) fue un pintor cubano influido por el surrealismo. En su obra se ven elementos imaginarios y fantasmagóricos de los sueños junto con elementos afro-cubanos. Uno de sus cuadros más famosos, «La jungla», está en la entrada del Museo de Arte Moderno de la ciudad de Nueva York.

En las últimas décadas han surgido varios pintores hispanoamericanos que poco a poco han logrado renombre, cuyos cuadros han sido exhibidos y adquiridos por galerías y museos en los Estados Unidos y en Europa. Entre ellos pueden mencionarse el argentino **Emilio Pettoruti** (1892–1971), pintor cubista; el chileno **Roberto Matta** (1912–   ), de tendencia abstracta y surrealista; el ecuatoriano **Oswaldo Guayasamín** (1919–   ), de tendencia cubista; el colombiano **Alejandro Obregón** (1920–   ), de tendencia abstracta; **Rómulo Macció** (1931–   ), pintor vanguardista argentino; el colombiano **Fernando Botero** (1932–   ) de

tendencia expresionista figurativa; y el surrealista peruano **Gerardo Chávez** (1937–   ).

LA MÚSICA

Gran parte de la música hispanoamericana está basada en temas folklóricos e indígenas, y hay mucha variedad en la música tradicional y popular de los diversos países y de las diferentes regiones dentro de un país. En la región del Caribe (Puerto Rico, Cuba, la República Dominicana y las costas de Colombia y Venezuela), la música es por lo general alegre, con influencia de ritmos africanos. Por el contrario, las canciones indígenas de los Andes, como el yaraví, son casi siempre lentas y tristes. Entre estos dos extremos hay una enorme variedad de ritmos, por ejemplo el corrido mexicano, descendiente directo de los romances españoles; el candombe uruguayo, ritmo de sus carnavales; el joropo venezolano, música de los llaneros; los valses peruanos, ecuatorianos y argentinos, de descendencia europea; las canciones guaraníes del Paraguay y el tango argentino. En este siglo además ha surgido una nueva versión del jazz norteamericano, llamada jazz afro-cubano, donde se han incorporado ritmos e instrumentos de la música afro-cubana.

INSTRUMENTOS MUSICALES

La guitarra española es también muy popular en Hispanoamérica, pero además hay otros instrumentos musicales importantes que han sido heredados de las culturas indígenas o adaptados de otros traídos por los españoles o por los negros de África. Ejemplos de estos instrumentos son el **cuatro** (una especie de guitarra con sólo cuatro cuerdas), la **marimba** (un instrumento parecido al xilófono), el **bongó** (un tambor de origen africano), el **güiro** (hecho de un fruto seco parecido a la calabaza y que se toca con un palito), la **quena** (una flauta heredada de los incas), las **maracas** (calabazas secas con piedrecitas o granos de maíz adentro) y las **claves** (dos palitos de madera dura que se usan para marcar el ritmo). Músicas folklóricas tan diversas como la del Estado de Veracruz en México, y la de los guaraníes del Paraguay, usan

---

63 **por el contrario** on the contrary

versiones del arpa europea moderna del siglo
XVI.

EL BAILE

Los bailes tradicionales de Hispanoamé-
5 rica son tan ricos y variados como su música y
en muchos casos forman una unidad íntima con
ella. Así, muchos de los ritmos mencionados
más arriba como el corrido, el tango y el joropo,
son también bailes. Están además, entre mu-
10 chos otros, el bambuco colombiano, la zamacueca (o cueca) chilena, la milonga argentina y
uruguaya, la plena puertorriqueña y el jarabe tapatío mexicano. Hoy en día, gracias a los esfuerzos de varios grupos folklóricos que se han
15 formado en muchos países, como el Ballet Fol-
klórico de México, estas tradiciones se han
estudiado más a fondo para conservarlas. El
repertorio de estas compañías artísticas, que incluye danzas nacionales y regionales de di-
20 versos orígenes, ha sobrepasado las fronteras
hispanoamericanas y es conocido en otros
países del mundo.

Dentro del área de la música bailable popular, ritmos como la conga, la rumba, el
25 mambo y el chachachá cubanos, la guaracha
puertorriqueña y cubana, el merengue domini-
cano y la cumbia colombiana son conocidos en
casi todo el mundo. Éstos dos últimos tienen su
origen en bailes folklóricos.

30 ## COMPOSITORES, CANTANTES E
INSTRUMENTISTAS

En el área de la música clásica hay dos
compositores hispanoamericanos conocidos internacionalmente. **Carlos Chávez** (1899–1978),
35 mexicano, fue también un famoso director de
orquesta y fundó las orquestas Sinfónica de
México y la Sinfónica Nacional. Su música
mezcla elementos de ritmos indígenas con las
técnicas de la música moderna. Un ciclo de
40 conferencias que dictó en la Universidad de
Harvard, fue publicado bajo el título «Pensamiento musical». Entre sus obras más famosas
están el ballet «El fuego nuevo» y la «Sinfonía
india».

Alberto Ginastera (1916–1983), argen- 45
tino, fue compositor moderno de óperas, ballets, sinfonías y conciertos, en los que utilizó
elementos musicales regionales y nacionales.
Dos de sus obras más conocidas son la ópera
«Bomarzo» y la «Cantata para América mágica». 50
En el área de la música más popular hay
por lo menos cuatro nombres importantes. El
mexicano **Manuel Ponce** (1882–1948) inició el
movimiento nacionalista de la música de su
país, cultivando temas nativos. Compuso nu- 55
merosas obras para orquesta como «Balada mexicana» y «Chapultepec», pero su fama se debe
a canciones de inmensa popularidad como «Estrellita». El compositor y director de orquesta
cubano **Gonzalo Roig** (1890–1972) fue autor de 60
muchas zarzuelas, la más conocida de las cuales
es «Cecilia Valdés», y de popularísimas
canciones como «Quiéreme mucho». **Ernesto
Lecuona** (1896–1963), cubano, compuso la
«Rapsodia negra» para piano y orquesta, y can- 65
ciones muy famosas como «Siboney» y «Malagueña». El mexicano **Agustín Lara** (1897–1970)
debe su fama a canciones tan conocidas como
«María Bonita» y «Granada»; ésta última ha sido
favorita en el repertorio de tenores de habla his- 70
pana.

De Hispanoamérica también han salido
varios cantantes e instrumentistas que han
ganado fama en el extranjero. Entre ellos están
el tenor de ópera chileno **Ramón Vinay**, el 75
barítono puertorriqueño **Justino Díaz**, la gran
cantante peruana **Yma Sumac**, el cantante y
compositor argentino **Atahualpa Yupanqui**, y
el famoso pianista chileno **Claudio Arrau**,
intérprete de música clásica. 80

Hay cantantes de música popular que son
conocidos internacionalmente por su interpretación de canciones de la última onda. Entre
ellos se hallan el venezolano **José Luis Rodrí-
guez**, conocido como El Puma, los cantantes 85
mexicanos **José José, Emmanuel, Marco Antonio Muñiz** y **Rocío Banquels**, el argentino **José
Luis Perales** y las puertorriqueñas **Ednita Na-
zario, Nidia Caro** e **Iris Chacón**.

Tres actores mexicanos que lograron gran 90
éxito en películas norteamericanas y dentro de
su propio país fueron **Pedro Armendáriz, Dolores del Río** y el cómico **Cantinflas**, seudónimo de Mario Moreno.

---

17   **más a fondo** more thoroughly   74   **en el extranjero** abroad

Ejercicio A

Escriba la letra que indique la relación correcta con cada expresión de la columna de la izquierda:

1. Rufino Tamayo _____
2. Bernaldo de Quirós _____
3. marimba _____
4. Manuel Ponce _____
5. Covarrubias _____
6. Pedro Armendáriz _____
7. Agustín Lara _____
8. Siqueiros _____
9. Carlos Chávez _____
10. Sabogal _____

a. «Estrellita»
b. «Sinfonía india»
c. películas norteamericanas
d. Granada
e. pintor peruano
f. pintor mexicano semi-abstracto
g. caricaturas
h. xilofón
i. gauchos
j. canción mexicana
k. pintura mural de ideología política

Ejercicio B

¿Cierto o falso? Indique si cada frase es cierta o falsa. Si es falsa, cámbiela para que sea cierta:

1. Los indígenas de Hispanoamérica no dejaron ninguna huella de su civilización.

_____

2. El arte precolombino se refiere al arte después de la llegada de Cristóbal Colón.

_____

3. Las pirámides y los templos de los indígenas muestran su increíble desarrollo en la arquitectura.

_____

4. El arte de Hispanoamérica en la época colonial se parecía al arte de España.

_____

5. Acapulco es un rico ejemplo del arte colonial.

_____

6. En el siglo XIX, Hispanoamérica produjo pintores de fama mundial.

_____

7. Diego Rivera se dedicó a la pintura mural.

_____

8. Rivera, Orozco y Siqueiros representan problemas políticos y sociales en su obra artística.

_____

9. Covarrubias vio el porvenir de su patria en la civilización de los mestizos.

_____

10. Cesáreo Bernaldo de Quirós pintó escenas de la lucha por la independencia de Venezuela.

_____

11. Mucha de la música hispanoamericana se basa en temas modernos.

_____

12. El iniciador del movimiento nacionalista de la música mexicana fue Agustín Lara.

_____

13. Las composiciones musicales «Siboney» y «Malagueña» se deben a Carlos Chávez.

_____

14. Claudio Arrau fue un famoso tenor chileno.

_____

15. José José y Nidia Caro son cantantes hispanoamericanos de la última onda.

_____

16. Dolores del Río era conocida en Norteamérica por sus bellas pinturas.

_____

17. El güiro y las maracas son instrumentos musicales hechos de madera.

_____

18. Un instrumento que produce sonidos melancólicos es la marimba.

_____

19. El jarabe tapatío es un baile regional de México.

_____

20. La cueca es un baile típico cubano.

_____

 **Ejercicio C**

Subraye la palabra o expresión que complete correctamente cada frase:

1. El tango es un baile   (a) argentino   (b) venezolano   (c) chileno   (d) mexicano

2. Un célebre actor mexicano fue   (a) Lecuona   (b) Vinay   (c) Orozco   (d) Cantinflas

3. Claudio Arrau fue un   (a) compositor cubano   (b) pianista chileno   (c) actor mexicano (d) pintor cubano

4. (a) La guitarra   (b) La quena   (c) El güiro   (d) El yaraví   es una flauta incaica.

5. Un famoso muralista mexicano fue   (a) Ernesto Lecuona   (b) José Sabogal   (c) Pedro Armendáriz   (d) Diego Rivera

6. «Siboney» es una obra musical de   (a) Agustín Lara   (b) Carlos Chávez   (c) Manuel Ponce   (d) Ernesto Lecuona

7. Cartagena es   (a) un mural famoso   (b) una ciudad colonial   (c) una canción mexicana (d) una cantante de ópera

8. La zamacueca y el joropo son   (a) composiciones musicales clásicas   (b) canciones revolucionarias   (c) danzas indígenas   (d) bailes típicos

9. Un famoso compositor argentino fue   (a) Alberto Ginastera   (b) Claudio Arrau
(c) Miguel Covarrubias   (d) José Sabogal

10. Un famoso pintor mexicano fue   (a) Bernaldo de Quirós   (b) José Clemente Orozco
(c) Ramón Vinay   (d) Wifredo Lam

Ejercicio D

Complete correctamente cada frase:

1. Un baile típico de Puerto Rico es _____.

2. _____ fue un famoso cantante chileno de ópera.

3. El _____ es una canción triste de los Andes.

4. El _____ es un baile típico de México.

5. _____ pintó los murales del Palacio Nacional de México.

6. _____ es un instrumento muy popular en todo el mundo hispano.

7. _____, músico cubano, compuso «Malagueña».

8. _____ son dos palitos que se emplean para marcar el ritmo.

9. _____, del Perú, fue una de las mejores cantantes del mundo.

10. _____, pintor peruano, describió en sus cuadros
la cultura indígena de su país.

11. _____, cantante puertorriqueña, interpreta canciones de la última onda.

12. _____ se parece mucho al xilófono.

13. _____ son calabazas secas con granos de maíz adentro.

14. _____ se usa en la música folklórica de Veracruz
y el Paraguay.

15. _____ fue una actriz mexicana de fama internacional.

Costumbres Hispanoamericanas

Las costumbres y tradiciones hispano-americanas reflejan la influencia española e indígena sobre todo, y en ciertos lugares también la influencia negra (especialmente en la música y los bailes).

DÍAS DE FIESTA

La religión católica ha tenido un papel muy importante en la historia y en la vida diaria. Por eso muchas fiestas religiosas se han convertido en fiestas nacionales. Hay unas que son celebradas en todos los países y otras que son típicas de cada región. Las Navidades, por ejemplo, se celebran de una forma u otra en todas partes. En México empiezan con las «posadas», que consisten en visitas a los vecinos durante los nueve días anteriores a la Nochebuena. En la fiesta que sigue a las posadas, la gente baila alrededor de una piñata (una olla de barro vivamente decorada, que contiene dulces y regalos). Después rompen la piñata y cogen los dulces. En otros países se celebra más al estilo español, con misas (especialmente la misa de gallo), aguinaldos y una gran cena.

Otras fiestas religiosas católicas como la Semana Santa y el Día de Todos los Santos (el primero de noviembre) se celebran en casi todos los países.

Por supuesto que el primero de enero es un día de fiesta. La noche anterior en muchos pueblos la gente sale a bailar por las calles. Hay grupos que llevan muñecos con figuras de viejos para enterrarlos, enterrando así el año viejo.

En todos los países hay ferias o carnavales que son más o menos famosos. Durante varios días hay música, bailes y desfiles de comparsas, ya sea en las calles o en salones de fiesta. En países donde aún existe la tradición (por ejem-

plo, México y Colombia), hay también corridas de toros.

Cada país tiene su fiesta nacional, que conmemora la fecha en que comenzó la lucha por su independencia de España. Por ejemplo, en México es el 16 de septiembre, en Colombia el 20 de julio y en la Argentina el 9 de julio. Otros días de fiesta celebran sucesos históricos importantes, como el 5 de mayo en México, que conmemora la lucha de los mexicanos contra la dominación de Francia y el emperador Maximiliano.

Luego hay dos días que se celebran en toda Hispanoamérica: el primero de mayo, que es el Día del Trabajo, y el 12 de octubre, llamado el Día de la Raza, que conmemora el descubrimiento de América.

BEBIDAS Y COMIDAS

En general, las comidas representan una mezcla de lo español y lo indígena, y sus ingredientes principales son el maíz, el frijol, el plátano, la carne y la papa (hay lugares en los Andes donde existen más de 30 variedades de papas).

Casi todos los países tienen su versión del tamal, y en muchos ésta cambia según la región. Básicamente es una masa de maíz fresco molido o de harina de maíz que se cuece al vapor dentro de una hoja de maíz o de plátano. Puede rellenarse con pollo, puerco, carne de res, legumbres, garbanzos, etc.

Los frijoles (llamados habichuelas en Puerto Rico) se comen en diversos platos típicos. Los frijoles negros son muy populares en el Caribe y en Venezuela. Preparados con arroz, se llaman en Cuba «moros y cristianos». Los frijoles pintos o colorados se preparan refritos en

---

3   **sobre todo** above all, especially
16   **anteriores a** preceding
25   **Semana Santa** Holy Week (week preceding Easter Sunday)

35   **el desfile de comparsas** masquerade parade
65   **cocer al vapor** to steam

México, y en potajes con jamón o carne y papas en otros países.

De las harinas del maíz y de la yuca se hacen diversas tortas y pasteles que reemplazan al pan en muchas comidas: tortillas en México, arepas en Colombia y Venezuela, cazabe en Cuba.

La empanada (una especie de pastel relleno con carne o pescado y otros ingredientes) es de origen gallego, pero se transformó en el Nuevo Mundo y tomó aspecto diferente en cada país. No es lo mismo la empanada argentina que la chilena, o la cubana que la panameña o la colombiana, aunque todas tienen el mismo nombre.

En la Argentina y en el Uruguay un churrasco es una combinación de carnes y órganos de la vaca que se adoban y se asan a las brasas.

En nuestro país son más conocidas las comidas del norte de México, como las enchiladas (tortillas enrolladas, rellenas de carne, pollo o queso y cubiertas de salsa), los tacos y el chile con carne. La forma de preparar estas comidas también varía de Tejas a California o Nuevo México.

Las bebidas alcohólicas más populares de Hispanoamérica son el ron, que se produce en los países del Caribe y el norte de Sudamérica; el tequila, que se destila del maguey en México; y el aguardiente obtenido de la destilación de la caña de azúcar.

En ciertos países como la Argentina, el Paraguay y Bolivia, se toma mate, una especie de té que se prepara de la yerba mate. Típicamente se toma en una calabaza por medio de un tubito llamado bombilla.

En Hispanoamérica se preparan también muchos jugos de frutas tropicales y se toma café (solo o mezclado con leche hervida) y chocolate (mucho más espeso que en nuestro país).

TIPOS TRADICIONALES

En varias regiones de Hispanoamérica se ven aún tipos tradicionales. En los grandes llanos donde se cría ganado y el medio de transporte principal es el caballo, se encuentran los vaqueros. Se llaman llaneros en Venezuela y Colombia, gauchos en la Argentina y el Uruguay.

El charro, vestido con su traje tradicional, es el jinete típico mexicano. La muchacha que lo acompaña se llama china poblana. Su vestido típico consiste en una falda ancha y larga de color rojo o verde y una blusa blanca (los colores de la bandera mexicana).

Los mariachis son grupos de músicos y cantantes callejeros que tocan la música mariachi de Jalisco, estado del oeste de México.

TRAJES TÍPICOS

Uno de los artículos de vestido más típicos de Hispanoamérica es una especie de capa con abertura en el centro (para meter la cabeza), de la cual existen muchas variedades regionales. Se llama poncho en el centro y sur de Sudamérica, ruana en el norte.

El sarape es una especie de manta de colores vivos, hecha de lana o de algodón, que lleva el mexicano en los hombros.

La mayoría de los trajes femeninos consisten en blusas blancas y faldas largas y anchas de diversos colores, con franjas o cintas alrededor. De calzado usan alpargatas (especie de sandalia de tela gruesa y suela de soga que trajeron los españoles) y, en México, huaraches (también una especie de sandalia).

El sombrero más típico es una versión del sombrero de jipijapa, hecho a mano.

UNIDAD MONETARIA

La unidad monetaria de Argentina, Colombia, Cuba, Chile, la República Dominicana, México y el Uruguay se llama el peso. Sin embargo, los pesos de esos países no tienen el mismo valor. En los otros países circulan las monedas siguientes: en Bolivia, el boliviano; en Costa Rica y en el Salvador, el colón; en el Ecuador, el sucre; en Guatemala, el quetzal; en Honduras, el lempira; en Nicaragua el córdoba; en Panamá, el balboa; en el Paraguay, el guaraní; en el Perú, el sol; y en Venezuela, el bolívar.

---

78 **hecho a mano** hand made

78 **sombrero de jipijapa** straw hat (Panama hat)

Ejercicio A

Escriba la letra que indique la relación correcta con cada expresión de la columna de la izquierda:

1. lempira	_____	**a.** sombrero
2. las posadas	_____	**b.** tortilla
3. 5 de mayo	_____	**c.** Día de la Raza
4. yerba mate	_____	**d.** fiesta nacional mexicana
5. china poblana	_____	**e.** unidad monetaria
6. 12 de octubre	_____	**f.** sarape
7. enchilada	_____	**g.** olla llena de dulces
8. piñata	_____	**h.** té
9. jipijapa	_____	**i.** charro
10. mariachi	_____	**j.** Navidad
		k. cantante

Ejercicio B

¿Cierto o falso? Indique si cada frase es cierta o falsa. Si es falsa, cámbiela para que sea cierta:

1. En México se celebran las posadas durante los ocho días anteriores a la Navidad.

    _____

2. Los gauchos son de los llanos de Venezuela y Colombia.

    _____

3. El tequila es una bebida intoxicante.

    _____

4. El Día del Trabajo se celebra el primero de abril.

    _____

5. Los mariachis son músicos mexicanos.

    _____

6. Los huaraches se llevan en las manos.

    _____

7. El aguardiente es una especie de té hecho de yerba.

    _____

8. La china poblana es la compañera del llanero.

    _____

9. Los gauchos viven en la pampa argentina.

    _____

10. El peso es la unidad monetaria de la Argentina.

_____

11. El 16 de septiembre es el Día de la Independencia de Venezuela.

_____

12. La unidad monetaria de Colombia es el bolívar.

_____

13. El Día de la Raza se celebra el dos de octubre.

_____

14. El maíz es un ingrediente básico de la comida hispanoamericana.

_____

15. El sarape es una manta usada por los bolivianos.

_____

Ejercicio C

En cada grupo, subraye la palabra que se relacione más directamente con el país:

1. Venezuela: charro, bolívar, gaucho
2. el Perú: sucre, peso, sol
3. México: tacos, yerba mate, gaucho
4. Guatemala: mariachi, balboa, quetzal
5. la Argentina: gaucho, jipijapa, sarape
6. Honduras: guaraní, taco, lempira
7. México: china poblana, sucre, colón
8. el Paraguay: tamal, yerba mate, tequila
9. Bolivia: bolívar, córdoba, boliviano
10. Costa Rica: mariachi, llanero, colón

Ejercicio D

Identifique cada palabra, clasificándola como bebida, comida, moneda, tipo o traje:

1. churrasco _____

2. empanada _____

3. mate _____

4. llanero _____

5. poncho _____

6. tequila _____

7. gaucho _____

8. sol _____

9. enchilada _____

10. charro _____

11. guaraní _____

12. tamal _____

13. balboa _____

14. sucre _____

15. huarache _____

PART SEVEN

COMPREHENSIVE TESTING:

SPEAKING
LISTENING
READING
WRITING

1. Speaking

Read the information provided for each situation and prepare a spoken response of at least ten utterances to accomplish the specific task required. Assume that in each situation you are speaking with persons who speak Spanish.

An utterance is any spoken statement that leads to accomplishing the stated task. For example:

A mi hermana le gusta el helado. (one utterance)
A mí también. (one utterance)

1.   Task: To provide information

You are an exchange student in Colombia, and you are living with a family. Introduce yourself to them and tell them about yourself. Include the following: your name, where you are from, your age, the number of people in your family, a description of your family, your interests, details about the city/town in which you live, the purpose of your visit.

2.   Task: To provide information

Upon returning from a trip by plane, one of your suitcases has been lost. Tell the airline employee about your problem. Include the following: the nature of your problem, a description of the lost suitcase, its contents (including their value), the flight number and the city from which you departed, pertinent information about yourself (name, address, telephone number, and the like).

3.   Task: To provide information

You and some friends are planning to go to a Spanish restaurant for dinner. Call the restaurant to make a reservation. Include the following: the purpose of your call, the day, date, and time of the reservation, the number of people. Ask if there is a dress code and which credit cards are accepted.

4.   Task: To obtain information

You want to obtain information about a concert. Ask the following: When it will take place, where it will be held, who will perform, how long it will last, the cost and availability of the tickets.

5.   Task: To introduce

You take a guest to a party. Introduce your guest to the other people. Include the following: his/her name, where he/she is from, why he/she is with you, something about him/her.

6.   Task: To express gratitude

You have just spent a weekend at the home of a friend in another city/town. Call to thank him/her. Include the following: the reason for your call, why you enjoyed your visit, what you enjoyed most, how you hope to reciprocate.

7.   Task: To give information

You are playing a board game (Monopoly, Scrabble, Trivial Pursuit, and the like) with a friend. Explain the rules of the game to him/her.

8. Task: To offer an apology

   You have been punished by your parents for not observing your curfew. Apologize to them for your mistake. Include the following: why you were punished, why you didn't observe the curfew, what you have learned from this lesson.

9. Task: To give an opinion

   You have just returned from the movies and are talking to a friend on the telephone. Tell your opinion of the film. Include the following: the title of the film, the actors, the theme of the movie, where it takes place, why you liked it or didn't like it, where the film is playing.

10. Task: To persuade someone

    You want to go with your friends to an amusement park but need your parents' permission. Persuade them to permit you to go. Include the following: where you want to go, with whom, when, how you will get there, the amount of time you will spend there, what you will do there, when you will return, how much it will cost, why they should allow you to go.

2. Listening Comprehension

a. Multiple Choice English — Reactions

Listen to your teacher read twice in succession a situation in English and a short statement in Spanish. Then your teacher will pause while you circle the number of the best suggested reaction. Base your choice of answer on the situation and the statement only.

1 a. This show must be sold out.
   b. It's more expensive in the evening.
   c. There are too many people in line.
   d. The show begins in seven minutes.

2 a. I should take an umbrella with me.
   b. It's a perfect day to play tennis.
   c. A picnic is a great idea.
   d. I love the fog.

3 a. My parents finally decided where to spend their vacation.
   b. Maybe now I'll get a new bicycle.
   c. They didn't deliver the newspaper today.
   d. European cities are in the news again.

4 a. I have to study a lot tonight.
   b. That makes three tests in a row.
   c. I'm not eager to see the grade.
   d. Tomorrow's test will be very easy.

5 a. For once the airline didn't lose my baggage.
   b. I still have to check in at the counter.
   c. Will they serve a meal on the flight?
   d. I would have made the flight if there had been less traffic.

b.   Short Passage — English Response

Listen to your teacher read twice in succession a short passage in Spanish and a question in English based on the passage. Then your teacher will pause while you circle the number of the best suggested answer to the question. Base your choice of answer on the content of the passage only.

1   What is being sold in the flea market?

    a.   Well-known paintings by Picasso.
    b.   Soap that is artfully wrapped.
    c.   Items that make expensive gifts.
    d.   Special detergents for colored clothing.

2   What does this advertisement suggest?

    a.   The importance of consolidating one's debt.
    b.   The need for lower interest rates on loans.
    c.   Buying stocks while the market is solid.
    d.   Saving money with certificates of deposit.

3   How did this young man learn his trade?

    a.   He went to a special school.
    b.   He bought a mechanic's shop.
    c.   The Army Reserves trained him.
    d.   His friends taught him in one day.

4   What is the cause of this problem?

    a.   Excessive traffic on this highway.
    b.   Repairs being made to the bridges.
    c.   Malfunctioning of the traffic signals.
    d.   A strike by the bridge workers.

5   What will take place at the Unihotel?

    a.   A school reunion.
    b.   A fashion show.
    c.   A children's show.
    d.   A pep rally.

c.   Short Passage — Spanish Response

Listen to your teacher read twice in succession a question and a short passage in Spanish. Then your teacher will pause while you circle the number of the best suggested answer to the question. Base your answer on the content of the passage only.

1   ¿Quiénes deben aprovecharse de este anuncio?

    a.   Los que coleccionan pintura europea.
    b.   Los que pintan al estilo español.
    c.   Los que quieren vender arte de siglos pasados.
    d.   Los que conocen el arte de siglos pasados.

2   ¿Para quiénes es esta fiesta?

    a.   Para los deportistas.
    b.   Para los estudiantes del colegio.
    c.   Para los maestros del colegio.
    d.   Para los niños de los profesores del colegio.

3   ¿Qué ha causado esta preocupación?

    a.   La escasez de pollo en los mercados.
    b.   El precio elevado del pollo.
    c.   Un informe erróneo del Ministerio de Economía.
    d.   La falta de interés en el pollo como alimento.

4   ¿De qué se queja esta persona?

    a.   De las promesas no cumplidas de los candidatos.
    b.   De las aspiraciones de los candidatos.
    c.   De los candidatos hispanos que no se expresan bien.
    d.   De los candidatos que no representan al público hispano.

5   ¿Qué explica este anuncio?

    a.   Los servicios públicos han sufrido.
    b.   La policía interrumpió las llamadas telefónicas.
    c.   Lima tiene líneas de teléfono.
    d.   Hay ciertas partes del país sin servicio de teléfonos.

d. Longer Passage — Two Questions in Spanish

Listen to your teacher read twice in succession a passage in Spanish. Then your teacher will pause while you circle the number of the best suggested answer for each of the two questions. Base your answers on the content of the passage only.

1   **(a)**   ¿Cuál es el propósito de esta exhibición?

      1.   Enseñar maneras de conservar energía y ahorrar dinero.
      2.   Vender nuevos aparatos eléctricos.
      3.   Aumentar el consumo de la electricidad.
      4.   Ahorrar trabajo en el Centro de Conservación.

    (b)   ¿Cuánto vale la entrada a la exhibición?

      1.   Vale diez dólares.
      2.   Es gratis.
      3.   Cuesta cinco dólares.
      4.   No cuesta nada los lunes.

2   **(a)**   ¿Qué desea hacer el Banco Nacional?

      1.   Limitar los préstamos que pueden pedir los clientes.
      2.   Ofrecer servicios más amplios a sus clientes.
      3.   Disminuir los intereses que deben pagar los clientes.
      4.   Vender carros de último modelo a los clientes.

(b) ¿Cuál es la ventaja del financiamiento de 60 meses?

1. Los intereses son más bajos.
2. Los carros de último modelo son menos asequibles.
3. Los clientes pagan menos al banco cada mes.
4. Los préstamos son más fáciles de conseguir.

3 (a) ¿Qué pasa durante el recorrido de este tren?

1. Ponen una película en el tren.
2. Los viajeros pueden dejarse llevar por su imaginación.
3. Se descubren sucesos misteriosos.
4. Se viaja por el oriente.

(b) ¿Con qué frecuencia sale este tren?

1. Todas las noches.
2. Una vez por semana.
3. Todos los sábados.
4. Cada dos días.

4 (a) ¿Cuándo empiezan a salir los sellos dedicados a la Navidad?

1. Durante julio y agosto.
2. En el otoño.
3. Un mes antes de la Navidad.
4. Durante la época navideña.

(b) ¿Cómo son estos sellos?

1. Todos tienen una escena navideña tradicional.
2. Sacan el mismo sello año tras año.
3. Captan las figuras navideñas más populares.
4. Hay una gran variedad de dibujos y de temas.

5 (a) ¿Por qué llamó la madre al número indicado en el folleto?

1. A su hijo le era difícil completar el rompecabezas.
2. Faltaban piezas del rompecabezas.
3. Quería oír una voz electrónica.
4. Su hijo se sentía muy frustrado.

(b) ¿Por qué no le ayudó el mensaje?

1. La voz electrónica no sabía la respuesta.
2. La señora no pudo explicar el problema.
3. La madre no marcó el número correcto.
4. La voz electrónica no tenía ganas de ayudarle.

3. Reading Comprehension

a. Long Passages

Below each of the following two passages there are five questions or incomplete statements. For each, choose the expression that best answers the question or best completes the statement according to the meaning of the passage and circle its number.

1 Hay una nueva ley muy importante que afecta a todas las personas que viajan en automóvil. En julio la legislatura del estado de Nueva York aprobó una ley, según la cual todos los choferes de automóviles y sus acompañantes del asiento delantero deben usar el cinturón de seguridad mientras el coche esté en movimiento. Aunque la ley fue aprobada en julio y ha estado en vigor desde entonces, la patrulla de carreteras no ha comenzado a multar a los choferes que no cumplen aún con esta nueva ley. A partir del Año Nuevo, sin embargo, los que no usen el cinturón de seguridad serán multados. La pena establecida por la ley es una multa de 50 dólares por cada infracción.

Durante los seis meses de gracia, la patrulla de carreteras tratará de instruir al público sobre la necesidad de abrocharse el cinturón de seguridad. Lo hará por medio de folletos que se distribuirán en las carreteras, carteles grandes en las calles y anuncios en todas las emisoras de radio y de televisión. La ley establece que todos los choferes y personas que viajen en el asiento delantero de un coche deben usar obligatoriamente el cinturón. Pero además el chofer será responsable por cualquier daño sufrido por un pasajero menor de 16 años que viaje en el coche sin llevar puesto el cinturón. Existen muchas razones para usar el cinturón de seguridad, y ahora hay una más: la de cumplir con la ley.

1 **(a)**   ¿Desde cuándo está en vigor la nueva ley?
  1.   Desde hace una semana.
  2.   Desde mediados del año.
  3.   Desde el año pasado.
  4.   Desde hace tres meses.

(b)   ¿En qué fecha empezarán a multar a los choferes?

  1.   El primero de julio.
  2.   El primero de enero.
  3.   El treinta y uno de diciembre.
  4.   El treinta y uno de agosto.

(c)   ¿Por qué se ha tardado en multar a los choferes?

  1.   La ley no fue aprobada por toda la legislatura.
  2.   No estaban seguros de la validez de la ley.
  3.   Buscaban el apoyo del gobernador.
  4.   Había que educar al público poco a poco.

(d)   ¿Para qué sirven los folletos que se distribuirán?

  1.   Para conseguir la aprobación del público.
  2.   Para informar a los automovilistas.
  3.   Para prevenir a los familiares de los choferes.
  4.   Para averiguar la opinión del público.

(e)   Ahora los choferes deben usar el cinturón de seguridad porque

  1.   es su deber legal.
  2.   lo aconsejan los fabricantes de automóviles.
  3.   es una manera eficaz de evitar accidentes.
  4.   contradice la ley.

2 Siempre se ha dicho que las corridas de toros debían tener lugar al aire libre por dos razones importantes: la primera, porque el sol y el calor excitan más al toro y la segunda, porque al aire libre los olores de los animales se sienten menos. Pero los tiempos cambian. El aire acondicionado y las potentes luces indirectas pueden darle una nueva perspectiva a este espectáculo. En Madrid están estudiando la posibilidad de construir la primera plaza taurina subterránea y

totalmente cubierta. Esto evitaría el problema de las lluvias que con tanta frecuencia echan a perder una corrida, con la mala suerte además de que en caso de lluvia e interrupción de la corrida no se devuelve al público el importe de la localidad. Y además no habría problemas de calor ... o de olor, gracias al aire acondicionado.

El proyecto es de un arquitecto cubano que ha vivido en Madrid por más de 25 años. El sitio que quiere usar es una antigua plaza de toros que fue construida en 1908 y ha estado cerrada desde hace ocho años. Los dueños de esta plaza, entre los cuales se encuentra el famoso torero Luis Miguel Dominguín, iban a construir allí un centro comercial. Si los dueños renuncian a sus planes, el ayuntamiento les ayudará a realizar el proyecto de la plaza cubierta, que estaría a veinte metros bajo tierra.

2 (a) ¿Por qué las corridas de toros tienen lugar al aire libre?

  1. El sol anima más al público.
  2. Es difícil meter a los toros adentro.
  3. El tiempo caluroso agita más a los toros.
  4. Se conserva una tradición antigua.

(b) ¿Qué hace posible la idea de una plaza cubierta?

  1. La tecnología moderna.
  2. Una nueva raza de toros.
  3. Una perspectiva diferente de esta época.
  4. La falta de público.

(c) Cuando llueve durante una corrida,

  1. el espectáculo continúa.
  2. los toros se ponen más peligrosos.
  3. los espectadores pierden su dinero.
  4. los toreros se niegan a lidiar.

(d) ¿Quién propuso la idea de una plaza taurina cubierta?

  1. Un matador célebre.
  2. Un hispanoamericano que reside en España.
  3. Un ingeniero español.
  4. Los dueños de una antigua plaza.

(e) Si los dueños de la plaza aceptan el nuevo proyecto,

  1. recibirán apoyo del gobierno.
  2. podrán construir el centro comercial.
  3. el torero Dominguín inaugurará la plaza.
  4. tendrán que derrumbar la plaza antigua.

b. Short Passages

Below each of the following selections there is a question in English based on it. For each, choose the expression that best answers the question according to the meaning of the selection and circle its letter.

1 La nueva colección «Cuéntame un cuento», reúne en cada volumen tres o cuatro cuentos populares con ilustraciones a todo color. En el libro dedicado a los cuentos de brujas hay una variedad de cuentos muy famosos. Éstos, junto con las divertidas y coloridas ilustraciones, constituyen un buen libro para una biblioteca infantil.

1 What type of books does this collection contain?

   a. Science fiction.
   b. Mysteries.
   c. Children's stories.
   d. Famous cartoons.

2 ADVERTENCIA. Se hace saber que la libreta de cheques del BANCO BOSTON, Suc. ONCE, impresa y numerada para la cuenta corriente de RADIO VICTORIA INFORMÁTICA S.A., cheques Nros. 1.501.981 al 1.502.030, por haber sido extraviada en blanco, NO TIENE NINGÚN VALOR.

2 What is the purpose of this notice?

   a. To offer a reward for a lost checkbook.
   b. To cancel a book of blank checks.
   c. To close a checking account.
   d. To claim a checkbook that was found.

3 Si Ud. piensa irse de vacaciones y dejar la casa sola, es necesario que tome ciertas precauciones para que los ladrones crean que la casa está ocupada. Por ejemplo, cancele la entrega del periódico; baje el tono del timbre del teléfono; use un aparato para encender y apagar las luces automáticamente a diario y pídale a un vecino de confianza que le cuide la casa.

3 When should these suggestions be followed?

   a. When you will be away for an extended period of time.
   b. When you meet with your neighbors.
   c. When you expect guests at your home.
   d. After giving a big party at your home.

4 El número 76.250 ganó el premio mayor de 30 millones de sucres de la Lotería de Guayaquil jugada ayer. Publicamos el boletín con todas las suertes en la página 12.

4 What does 76.250 represent?

   a. The number of tickets sold for the lottery.
   b. The winning number in the lottery.
   c. The value of each winning ticket.
   d. The number of people who played the lottery.

5 Como todos los domingos, en la última página encontrará el lector nuestra sección de anuncios, destinada especialmente a aquellas personas que buscan trabajo. Junto a informaciones y comentarios a cargo de nuestro equipo especializado en asuntos económicos, publicamos anuncios específicos de «Ofertas de empleo», además de los que aparecen en sus secciones correspondientes en las páginas de Anuncios Clasificados.

5 To which section of the paper does this notice refer the reader?

   a. The comics.
   b. The stock market.
   c. The theater and the movies.
   d. The want ads.

C. Slot Completion

In each of the following passages, there are five blank spaces numbered 1 through 5. Each blank space represents a missing word. For each blank space, four possible completions are provided. Only one of them makes sense in the context of the passage.

First, read the passage in its entirety to determine its general meaning. Then read it a second time. For each blank space, choose the completion that makes the best sense and circle its letter.

1 Nunca ha sido fácil financiar la educación universitaria. En la actualidad hasta los estudiantes más capacitados tienen ___(1)___ serios para pagar la universidad, porque hay menos oportunidades para conseguir ayuda ___(2)___.

El Fondo Nacional de Becas (FNB) está haciendo todo lo posible para ___(3)___ esta dificultad. Gracias a las ___(4)___ de las compañías grandes, el FNB ha logrado que cientos de los mejores estudiantes cursen estudios superiores. Pero para poder ayudar a más estudiantes, el FNB necesita su apoyo también. El dinero no debe ser un ___(5)___ entre la juventud y una educación universitaria.

(1) a. programas
  b. problemas
  c. deseos
  d. vehículos

(2) a. económica
  b. social
  c. médica
  d. política

(3) a. crear
  b. deshacer
  c. meter
  d. solucionar

(4) a. facilidades
  b. contribuciones
  c. mentiras
  d. oportunidades

(5) a. puente
  b. enlace
  c. obstáculo
  d. medio

2 Cada año durante el mes de septiembre se celebra en los Estados Unidos la Semana de la Herencia Hispánica. Durante este período de ___(1)___ días, hay ceremonias y eventos oficiales, semi oficiales y populares en muchas ___(2)___ de la nación.

La Semana Nacional de la Herencia Hispánica fue establecida el 17 de septiembre de 1968, gracias a una resolución del Congreso que autorizaba y requería del Presidente de los Estados Unidos, que ___(3)___ se firmara una proclamación designando una semana que incluyera los días 14 y 15 de septiembre como la Semana Nacional de la Herencia Hispánica. Desde que fue aprobada esa resolución, cada presidente de la nación ha ___(4)___, año tras año, la proclamación.

Este ___(5)___ público a todos los hispanos, refrendado oficialmente por el presidente y el gobierno, implícitamente admite y acepta la importancia de la población hispana de los Estados Unidos.

(1) a. nueve
  b. siete
  c. quince
  d. ocho

(2) a. viviendas
  b. puertas
  c. fincas
  d. ciudades

(3) a. semanalmente
  b. mensualmente
  c. anualmente
  d. diariamente

(4) a. firmado
  b. otorgado
  c. buscado
  d. señalado

(5) a. descubrimiento
  b. reconocimiento
  c. nombramiento
  d. aislamiento

3 Los expertos dicen que esquiar es el mejor de los deportes aeróbicos. Produce los mismos ___(1)___ que correr, sin los efectos dañinos. Debido a que las ___(2)___ se deslizan en un movimiento fluido, los músculos del esquiador trabajan sin presionar las articulaciones. El único problema hasta ahora era que para esquiar hacía falta nieve. Este problema se ha resuelto con la máquina para esquiar . . . sin nieve. Practicando un mínimo de 15 minutos tres veces a la semana en una de estas máquinas, mejora la eficiencia cardiovascular y ___(3)___ muchas calorías. La máquina de esquiar desafía a las otras máquinas para hacer ejercicio como la bicicleta estacionaria, que ha sido la más popular, y las máquinas de remo. Para manejar la máquina de esquiar uno tiene que estar ___(4)___ en vez de sentado y por esa razón todo el cuerpo trabaja. Y, a diferencia de la bicicleta, en la máquina de esquiar se ejercita la parte ___(5)___ del cuerpo tanto como la de abajo. Hay varios modelos de esta máquina, aún uno que se puede guardar debajo de la cama. Se consiguen en todos los almacenes.

(1) a. beneficios
     b. daños
     c. problemas
     d. apoyos

(2) a. manos
     b. piernas
     c. muñecas
     d. orejas

(3) a. produce
     b. añade
     c. mezcla
     d. quema

(4) a. acostado
     b. de pie
     c. en cuclillas
     d. torcido

(5) a. delantera
     b. inferior
     c. superior
     d. posterior

4. Writing

a. Notes

Write an informal note in Spanish of at least five clauses based on the directions given to you in English. A clause must contain a verb, a stated or implied subject, and additional words necessary to convey meaning. The five clauses may be contained in fewer than five sentences if some of the sentences have more than one clause.

Examples:

One clause: Ayer salí de compras.

Two clauses: Ayer salí de compras y me encontré en la calle con Juana.

Three clauses: Ayer salí de compras y me encontré en la calle con Juana, quien me invitó a una fiesta en su casa.

1. Write a note to your parents in which you tell them that you will not be home on time and explain the reason.
2. You need a book from the library. Write a note to your brother/sister asking him/her to get it for you.
3. You have just celebrated a birthday and received many beautiful gifts. Write a thank you note to a friend/relative for the gift.
4. You are giving a party in your home on Saturday. Write a note to a friend inviting him/her to the party.
5. A friend (pen pal) is going to visit your home for the first time. Write a note in which you give him/her directions to your house.

_____

_____

_____

_____

_____

_____

b. Formal Letters

Write a formal letter in Spanish of at least ten clauses based on the directions given to you in English.

1. During a shopping trip you were helped by a very (in)efficient and (dis)courteous salesperson. Write a formal letter to the store in which you bring this to their attention. Include in your letter the date, salutation, and closing. You may wish to include the purpose of the letter; the name of the salesperson; when this took place; what the person did; why you wish to commend (report) this salesperson; how you feel about what happened.

_____

_____

_____

_____

_____

_____

_____

_____

_____

_____

_____

2. You have placed an order with a mail order company and have not yet received the merchandise. Write a letter to the company in which you bring this to their attention. Include the date, salutation, and closing. You may wish to include the nature of the problem; the date you placed the order; what you ordered; how you placed the order; the means of payment; what you would like them to do about the matter.

_____

_____

_____

_____

_____

_____

_____

_____

_____

_____

_____

_____

3. You have just returned from a visit to San Juan and realize that you forgot one of your possessions in your hotel room. Write a letter to the management in which you request their assistance in locating the item. Include the date, salutation, and closing. You may wish to include the nature of the problem; the article you left behind; a description of the item; the room you occupied; where you may have left it; how it can be returned to you.

_____

_____

_____

_____

_____

_____

_____

_____

_____

_____

_____

_____

4. Your local school is sponsoring a summer program in foreign languages in which the students speak only Spanish. They are looking for students to assist the teachers in the program. Write a letter to the director of the program in which you may wish to include your interest in the program; the reason for you interest; your qualifications; your special skills; your proficiency in Spanish; your desire for an interview. Be sure to include the date, salutation, and closing.

_____

_____

_____

_____

_____

_____

_____

_____

_____

_____

_____

_____

5. You wish to give a friend a duplicate of the watch that your parents gave you last year but you have not been able to locate it in any of the local stores. Write a letter to the manufacturer of the watch in which you request their assistance in helping you to obtain a similar watch. Include in your letter the date, salutation, and closing. You may wish to include the nature of the problem; a description of the watch; where your watch was purchased; how long you have had it; its cost; your request for information concerning where you can obtain it.

_____

_____

_____

_____

_____

_____

_____

_____

_____

6. You are planning a trip to Lima during the coming summer. Write a letter to the tourist office requesting information. Be sure to include the date, salutation, and closing. You may wish to include the purpose of the letter; your plans; the dates of your trip; your special interests; your request for pertinent information, including the availability of hotel rooms and special trips for students.

_____

_____

_____

_____

_____

_____

_____

_____

_____

C. Visual Stimulus

Write a story in Spanish about the situation suggested in the pictures. Write a well-organized composition of at least ten clauses for each picture.

1.   *Key words:*   **el mono**   monkey
                       el letrero   sign
                       la jaula   cage
                       el cacahuete (el maní)   peanut

_____

_____

_____

_____

_____

_____

_____

_____

_____

_____

_____

_____

_____

_____

_____

_____

2.   *Key words:*   **la limonada**   lemonade
                      el letrero   sign
                      el puesto   stand
                      el abanico   fan

_____

_____

_____

_____

_____

_____

_____

_____

_____

_____

_____

_____

_____

_____

_____

_____

_____

_____

_____

_____

_____

3.   *Key words:*   **el horno**   oven
                       la estufa   stove
                       el humo   smoke

_____
_____
_____
_____
_____
_____
_____
_____
_____
_____
_____
_____
_____
_____
_____
_____
_____
_____
_____
_____
_____
_____

4.   *Key words:*   **la comida al aire libre**   picnic
                             la manta   blanket
                             la hormiga   ant
                             la nube   cloud

5.   *Key words:*   **la oficina de correos**   post office
                             la estampilla   stamp
                             la tarjeta   card
                             la balanza   scale
                             el bolsillo   pocket

_____

_____

_____

_____

_____

_____

_____

_____

_____

_____

_____

_____

_____

_____

_____

_____

_____

_____

_____

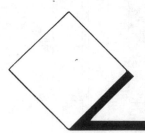

1. Regular Verbs

a. Simple Tenses

INFINITIVE	us**ar**		beb**er**		sub**ir**
GERUNDIO	us**ando**		beb**iendo**		sub**iendo**
PAST PARTICIPLE	us**ado**		beb**ido**		sub**ido**

INDICATIVE

PRESENT	us**o**	us**amos**	beb**o**	beb**emos**	sub**o**	sub**imos**
	us**as**	us**áis**	beb**es**	beb**éis**	sub**es**	sub**ís**
	us**a**	us**an**	beb**e**	beb**en**	sub**e**	sub**en**
IMPERFECT	us**aba**	us**ábamos**	beb**ía**	beb**íamos**	sub**ía**	sub**íamos**
	us**abas**	us**ábais**	beb**ías**	beb**íais**	sub**ías**	sub**íais**
	us**aba**	us**aban**	beb**ía**	beb**ían**	sub**ía**	sub**ían**
PRETERITE	us**é**	us**amos**	beb**í**	beb**imos**	sub**í**	sub**imos**
	us**aste**	us**asteis**	beb**iste**	beb**isteis**	sub**iste**	sub**isteis**
	us**ó**	us**aron**	beb**ió**	beb**ieron**	sub**ió**	sub**ieron**
FUTURE	usar**é**	usar**emos**	beber**é**	beber**emos**	subir**é**	subir**emos**
	usar**ás**	usar**éis**	beber**ás**	beber**éis**	subir**ás**	subir**éis**
	usar**á**	usar**án**	beber**á**	beber**án**	subir**á**	subir**án**
CONDITIONAL	usar**ía**	usar**íamos**	beber**ía**	beber**íamos**	subir**ía**	subir**íamos**
	usar**ías**	usar**íais**	beber**ías**	beber**íais**	subir**ías**	subir**íais**
	usar**ía**	usar**ían**	beber**ía**	beber**ían**	subir**ía**	subir**ían**

COMMANDS

us**a** (tú)	beb**e** (tú)	sub**e** (tú)
no us**es** (tú)	no beb**as** (tú)	no sub**as** (tú)
us**ad** (vosotros)	beb**ed** (vosotros)	sub**id** (vosotros)
no us**éis** (vosotros)	no beb**áis** (vosotros)	no sub**áis** (vosotros)
us**e** (Ud.)	beb**a** (Ud.)	sub**a** (Ud.)
us**en** (Uds.)	beb**an** (Uds.)	sub**an** (Uds.)
us**emos** (nosotros)	beb**amos** (nosotros)	sub**amos** (nosotros)

SUBJUNCTIVE

PRESENT	us**e**	us**emos**	beb**a**	beb**amos**	sub**a**	sub**amos**
	us**es**	us**éis**	beb**as**	beb**áis**	sub**as**	sub**áis**
	us**e**	us**en**	beb**a**	beb**an**	sub**a**	sub**an**

IMPERFECT	usara	usáramos	bebiera	bebiéramos	subiera	subiéramos
(-ra form)	usaras	usarais	bebieras	bebierais	subieras	subierais
	usara	usaran	bebiera	bebieran	subiera	subieran
IMPERFECT	usase	usásemos	bebiese	bebiésemos	subiese	subiésemos
(-se form)	usases	usaseis	bebieses	bebieseis	subieses	subieseis
	usase	usasen	bebiese	bebiesen	subiese	subiesen

b. Compound Tenses

INDICATIVE

PRESENT PERFECT

he	hemos				
has	habéis	}	usado	bebido	subido
ha	han				

PLUPERFECT

había	habíamos				
habías	habíais	}	usado	bebido	subido
había	habían				

PRETERITE PERFECT

hube	hubimos				
hubiste	hubisteis	}	usado	bebido	subido
hubo	hubieron				

FUTURE PERFECT

habré	habremos				
habrás	habréis	}	usado	bebido	subido
habrá	habrán				

CONDITIONAL PERFECT

habría	habríamos				
habrías	habríais	}	usado	bebido	subido
habría	habrían				

PERFECT INFINITIVE

haber	usado	bebido	subido

PERFECT PARTICIPLE

habiendo	usado	bebido	subido

SUBJUNCTIVE

PRESENT PERFECT

haya	hayamos				
hayas	hayáis	}	usado	bebido	subido
haya	hayan				

PLUPERFECT (-ra form)

hubiera	hubiéramos				
hubieras	hubierais	}	usado	bebido	subido
hubiera	hubieran				

PLUPERFECT (**-se** form)

hubiese	hubiésemos	⎫			
hubieses	hubieseis	⎬	usado	bebido	subido
hubiese	hubiesen	⎭			

2. Stem-Changing Verbs

a. Infinitive in **-ar**

pensar (**e** to **ie**)		**mostrar** (**o** to **ue**)		**jugar** (**u** to **ue**)	

INDICATIVE

PRESENT	pienso	pensamos	muestro	mostramos	juego	jugamos
	piensas	pensáis	muestras	mostráis	juegas	jugáis
	piensa	piensan	muestra	muestran	juega	juegan

SUBJUNCTIVE

PRESENT	piense	pensemos	muestre	mostremos	juegue	juguemos
	pienses	penséis	muestres	mostréis	juegues	juguéis
	piense	piensen	muestre	muestren	juegue	jueguen

b. Infinitive in **-er**

perder (**e** to **ie**)		**volver** (**o** to **ue**)	

INDICATIVE

PRESENT	pierdo	perdemos	vuelvo	volvemos
	pierdes	perdéis	vuelves	volvéis
	pierde	pierden	vuelve	vuelven

SUBJUNCTIVE

PRESENT	pierda	perdamos	vuelva	volvamos
	pierdas	perdáis	vuelvas	volváis
	pierda	pierdan	vuelva	vuelvan

c. Infinitive in **-ir**

pedir (**e** to **i, i**)		**sentir** (**e** to **ie, i**)		**dormir** (**o** to **ue, u**)	

INDICATIVE

PRESENT	pido	pedimos	siento	sentimos	duermo	dormimos
	pides	pedís	sientes	sentís	duermes	dormís
	pide	piden	siente	sienten	duerme	duermen
PRETERITE	pedí	pedimos	sentí	sentimos	dormí	dormimos
	pediste	pedisteis	sentiste	sentisteis	dormiste	dormisteis
	pidió	pidieron	sintió	sintieron	durmió	durmieron

SUBJUNCTIVE

PRESENT	pida	pidamos	sienta	sintamos	duerma	durmamos
	pidas	pidáis	sientas	sintáis	duermas	durmáis
	pida	pidan	sienta	sientan	duerma	duerman

IMPERFECT	pidiera	pidiéramos	sintiera	sintiéramos	durmiera	durmiéramos
	pidieras	pidierais	sintieras	sintierais	durmieras	durmierais
	pidiera	pidiera	sintiera	sintieran	durmiera	durmieran
GERUNDIO	pidiendo		sintiendo		durmiendo	

d. Infinitives in -uir (except -guir)

huir (y)

INDICATIVE

PRESENT	huyo, huyes, huye, huimos, huís, huyen
PRETERITE	huí, huiste, huyó, huimos, huisteis, huyeron

SUBJUNCTIVE

PRESENT	huya, huyas, huya, huyamos, huyáis, huyan
IMPERFECT	huyera, huyeras, huyera, huyéramos, huyerais, huyeran
GERUNDIO	huyendo

e. Infinitives in -iar and -uar

enviar (i to í)   **actuar (u to ú)**

INDICATIVE

PRESENT	envío	enviamos	actúo	actuamos
	envías	enviáis	actúas	actuáis
	envía	envían	actúa	actúan

SUBJUNCTIVE

PRESENT	envíe	enviemos	actúe	actuemos
	envíes	enviéis	actúes	actuéis
	envíe	envíen	actúe	actúen

3. Spelling-Changing Verbs

a. Infinitives in -cer or -cir

convencer (c to z)   **conocer** (c to zc)

INDICATIVE

PRESENT	convenzo	convencemos	conozco	conocemos
	convences	convencéis	conoces	conocéis
	convence	convencen	conoce	conocen

SUBJUNCTIVE

PRESENT	convenza	convenzamos	conozca	conozcamos
	convenzas	convenzáis	conozcas	conozcáis
	convenza	convenzan	conozca	conozcan

b. Infinitives in **-ger** or **-gir**

dirigir (**g** to **j**)

INDICATIVE

PRESENT   dirijo, diriges, dirige, dirigimos, dirigís, dirigen

SUBJUNCTIVE

PRESENT   dirija, dirijas, dirija, dirijamos, dirijáis, dirijan

c. Infinitives in **-guir**

distinguir (**gu** to **g**)

INDICATIVE

PRESENT   distingo, distingues, distingue, distinguimos, distinguís, distinguen

SUBJUNCTIVE

PRESENT   distinga, distingas, distinga, distingamos, distingáis, distingan

d. Infinitives in **-eer**

leer (**i** to **y**)

INDICATIVE

PRETERITE   leí, leíste, leyó, leímos, leísteis, leyeron

SUBJUNCTIVE

IMPERFECT   leyera, leyeras, leyera, leyéramos, leyerais, leyeran
                leyese, leyeses, leyese, leyésemos, leyeseis, leyesen
GERUNDIO   leyendo
PAST PARTICIPLE leído

e. Infinitives in **-car, -gar,** and **-zar**

sacar (**c** to **qu**)		**pagar** (**g** to **gu**)		**gozar** (**z** to **c**)	

INDICATIVE

PRETERITE					
saqué	sacamos	pagué	pagamos	gocé	gozamos
sacaste	sacasteis	pagaste	pagasteis	gozaste	gozasteis
sacó	sacaron	pagó	pagaron	gozó	gozaron

SUBJUNCTIVE

PRESENT					
saque	saquemos	pague	paguemos	goce	gocemos
saques	saquéis	pagues	paguéis	goces	gocéis
saque	saquen	pague	paguen	goce	gocen

4. Irregular Verbs

NOTE: Only the tenses containing irregular forms are given.

andar

PRETERITE: **anduve, anduviste, anduvo, anduvimos, anduvisteis, anduvieron**
IMPERFECT SUBJUNCTIVE: **anduviera, anduvieras, anduviera, anduviéramos, anduvierais, anduvieran**
  anduviese, anduvieses, anduviese, anduviésemos, anduvieseis, anduviesen

caber

PRESENT INDICATIVE: **quepo,** cabes, cabe, cabemos, cabéis, caben
PRETERITE: **cupe, cupiste, cupo, cupimos, cupisteis, cupieron**
FUTURE: **cabré, cabrás, cabrá, cabremos, cabréis, cabrán**
CONDITIONAL: **cabría, cabrías, cabría, cabríamos, cabríais, cabrían**
PRESENT SUBJUNCTIVE: **quepa, quepas, quepa, quepamos, quepáis, quepan**
IMPERFECT SUBJUNCTIVE: **cupiera, cupieras, cupiera, cupiéramos, cupierais, cupieran**
  cupiese, cupieses, cupiese, cupiésemos, cupieseis, cupiesen

caer

PRESENT INDICATIVE: **caigo,** caes, cae, caemos, caéis, caen
PRETERITE: caí, **caíste, cayó, caímos, caísteis, cayeron**
PRESENT SUBJUNCTIVE: **caiga, caigas, caiga, caigamos, caigáis, caigan**
IMPERFECT SUBJUNCTIVE: **cayera, cayeras, cayera, cayéramos, cayerais, cayeran**
  cayese, cayeses, cayese, cayésemos, cayeseis, cayesen
GERUNDIO: **cayendo**
PAST PARTICIPLE: **caído**

conducir (and verbs ending in -ducir)

PRESENT INDICATIVE: **conduzco,** conduces, conduce, conducimos, conducís, conducen
PRETERITE: **conduje, condujiste, condujo, condujimos, condujisteis, condujeron**
PRESENT SUBJUNCTIVE: **conduzca, conduzcas, conduzca, conduzcamos, conduzcáis, conduzcan**
IMPERFECT SUBJUNCTIVE: **condujera, condujeras, condujera, condujéramos, condujerais, condujeran**
  condujese, condujeses, condujese, condujésemos, condujeseis, condujesen

dar

PRESENT INDICATIVE: **doy,** das, da, damos, dais, dan
PRETERITE: **di, diste, dio, dimos, disteis, dieron**
PRESENT SUBJUNCTIVE: **dé,** des, **dé,** demos, deis, den
IMPERFECT SUBJUNCTIVE: **diera, dieras, diera, diéramos, dierais, dieran**
  diese, dieses, diese, diésemos, dieseis, diesen

decir

PRESENT INDICATIVE: **digo, dices, dice,** decimos, decís, **dicen**
PRETERITE: **dije, dijiste, dijo, dijimos, dijisteis, dijeron**
FUTURE: **diré, dirás, dirá, diremos, diréis, dirán**
CONDITIONAL: **diría, dirías, diría, diríamos, diríais, dirían**
PRESENT SUBJUNCTIVE: **diga, digas, diga, digamos, digáis, digan**
IMPERFECT SUBJUNCTIVE: **dijera, dijeras, dijera, dijéramos, dijerais, dijeran**
  dijese, dijeses, dijese, dijésemos, dijeseis, dijesen

GERUNDIO: **diciendo**
PAST PARTICIPLE: **dicho**
COMMAND: **di** (tú)

estar

PRESENT INDICATIVE: **estoy, estás, está,** estamos, estáis, **están**
PRETERITE: **estuve, estuviste, estuvo, estuvimos, estuvisteis, estuvieron**
PRESENT SUBJUNCTIVE: **esté, estés, esté,** estemos, estéis, **estén**
IMPERFECT SUBJUNCTIVE: **estuviera, estuvieras, estuviera, estuviéramos, estuvierais, estuvieran**
estuviese, estuvieses, estuviese, estuviésemos, estuvieseis, estuviesen

haber

PRESENT INDICATIVE: **he, has, ha, hemos,** habéis, **han**
PRETERITE: **hube, hubiste, hubo, hubimos, hubisteis, hubieron**
FUTURE: **habré, habrás, habrá, habremos, habréis, habrán**
CONDITIONAL: **habría, habrías, habría, habríamos, habríais, habrían**
PRESENT SUBJUNCTIVE: **hubiera, hubieras, hubiera, hubiéramos, hubierais, hubieran**
hubiese, hubieses, hubiese, hubiésemos, hubieseis, hubiesen

hacer

PRESENT INDICATIVE: **hago,** haces, hace, hacemos, hacéis, hacen
PRETERITE: **hice, hiciste, hizo, hicimos, hicisteis, hicieron**
FUTURE: **haré, harás, hará, haremos, haréis, harán**
CONDITIONAL: **haría, harías, haría, haríamos, haríais, harían**
PRESENT SUBJUNCTIVE: **haga, hagas, haga, hagamos, hagáis, hagan**
IMPERFECT SUBJUNCTIVE: **hiciera, hicieras, hiciera, hiciéramos, hicierais, hicieran**
hiciese, hicieses, hiciese, hiciésemos, hicieseis, hiciesen
PAST PARTICIPLE: **hecho**
COMMAND: **haz** (tú)

ir

PRESENT INDICATIVE: **voy, vas, va, vamos, vais, van**
IMPERFECT INDICATIVE: **iba, ibas, iba, íbamos, ibais, iban**
PRETERITE: **fui, fuiste, fue, fuimos, fuisteis, fueron**
PRESENT SUBJUNCTIVE: **vaya, vayas, vaya, vayamos, vayáis, vayan**
IMPERFECT SUBJUNCTIVE: **fuera, fueras, fuera, fuéramos, fuerais, fueran**
fuese, fueses, fuese, fuésemos, fueseis, fuesen
GERUNDIO: **yendo**
COMMAND: **ve** (tú)

oír

PRESENT INDICATIVE: **oigo, oyes, oye,** oímos, oís, **oyen**
PRETERITE: oí, oíste, **oyó,** oímos, oísteis, **oyeron**
PRESENT SUBJUNCTIVE: **oiga, oigas, oiga, oigamos, oigáis, oigan**
IMPERFECT SUBJUNCTIVE: **oyera, oyeras, oyera, oyéramos, oyerais, oyeran**
oyese, oyeses, oyese, oyésemos, oyeseis, oyesen
GERUNDIO: **oyendo**

poder

PRESENT INDICATIVE: **puedo, puedes, puede,** podemos, podéis, **pueden**
PRETERITE: **pude, pudiste, pudo, pudimos, pudisteis, pudieron**
FUTURE: **podré, podrás, podrá, podremos, podréis, podrán**
CONDITIONAL: **podría, podrías, podría, podríamos, podríais, podrían**
PRESENT SUBJUNCTIVE: **pueda, puedas, pueda,** podamos, podáis, **puedan**
IMPERFECT SUBJUNCTIVE: **pudiera, pudieras, pudiera, pudiéramos, pudierais, pudieran
    pudiese, pudieses, pudiese, pudiésemos, pudieseis, pudiesen**
GERUNDIO: **pudiendo**

poner

PRESENT INDICATIVE: **pongo,** pones, pone, ponemos, ponéis, ponen
PRETERITE: **puse, pusiste, puso, pusimos, pusisteis, pusieron**
FUTURE: **pondré, pondrás, pondrá, pondremos, pondréis, pondrán**
CONDITIONAL: **pondría, pondrías, pondría, pondríamos, pondríais, pondrían**
PRESENT SUBJUNCTIVE: **ponga, pongas, ponga, pongamos, pongáis, pongan**
IMPERFECT SUBJUNCTIVE: **pusiera, pusieras, pusiera, pusiéramos, pusierais, pusieran
    pusiese, pusieses, pusiese, pusiésemos, pusieseis, pusiesen**
PAST PARTICIPLE: **puesto**
COMMAND: **pon** (tú)

querer

PRESENT INDICATIVE: **quiero, quieres, quiere,** queremos, queréis, **quieren**
PRETERITE: **quise, quisiste, quiso, quisimos, quisisteis, quisieron**
FUTURE: **querré, querrás, querrá, querremos, querréis, querrán**
CONDITIONAL: **querría, querrías, querría, querríamos, querríais, querrían**
PRESENT SUBJUNCTIVE: **quiera, quieras, quiera,** queramos, queráis, **quieran**
IMPERFECT SUBJUNCTIVE: **quisiera, quisieras, quisiera, quisiéramos, quisierais, quisieran
    quisiese, quisieses, quisiese, quisiésemos, quisieseis, quisiesen**

saber

PRESENT INDICATIVE: **sé,** sabes, sabe, sabemos, sabéis, saben
PRETERITE: **supe, supiste, supo, supimos, supisteis, supieron**
FUTURE: **sabré, sabrás, sabrá, sabremos, sabréis, sabrán**
CONDITIONAL: **sabría, sabrías, sabría, sabríamos, sabríais, sabrían**
PRESENT SUBJUNCTIVE: **sepa, sepas, sepa, sepamos, sepáis, sepan**
IMPERFECT SUBJUNCTIVE: **supiera, supieras, supiera, supiéramos, supierais, supieran
    supiese, supieses, supiese, supiésemos, supieseis, supiesen**

salir

PRESENT INDICATIVE: **salgo,** sales, sale, salimos, salís, salen
FUTURE: **saldré, saldrás, saldrá, saldremos, saldréis, saldrán**
CONDITIONAL: **saldría, saldrías, saldría, saldríamos, saldríais, saldrían**
PRESENT SUBJUNCTIVE: **salga, salgas, salga, salgamos, salgáis, salgan**
COMMAND: **sal** (tú)

ser

PRESENT INDICATIVE: **soy, eres, es, somos, sois, son**
IMPERFECT INDICATIVE: **era, eras, era, éramos, erais, eran**

PRETERITE: **fui, fuiste, fue, fuimos, fuisteis, fueron**
PRESENT SUBJUNCTIVE: **sea, seas, sea, seamos, seáis, sean**
IMPERFECT SUBJUNCTIVE: **fuera, fueras, fuera, fuéramos, fuerais, fueran**
fuese, fueses, fuese, fuésemos, fueseis, fuesen
COMMAND: **sé** (tú)

tener

PRESENT INDICATIVE: **tengo, tienes, tiene,** tenemos, tenéis, **tienen**
PRETERITE: **tuve, tuviste, tuvo, tuvimos, tuvisteis, tuvieron**
FUTURE: **tendré, tendrás, tendrá, tendremos, tendréis, tendrán**
CONDITIONAL: **tendría, tendrías, tendría, tendríamos, tendríais, tendrían**
PRESENT SUBJUNCTIVE: **tenga, tengas, tenga, tengamos, tengáis, tengan**
IMPERFECT SUBJUNCTIVE: **tuviera, tuvieras, tuviera, tuviéramos, tuvierais, tuvieran**
tuviese, tuvieses, tuviese, tuviésemos, tuvieseis, tuviesen
COMMAND: **ten** (tú)

traer

PRESENT INDICATIVE: **traigo,** traes, trae, traemos, traéis, traen
PRETERITE: **traje, trajiste, trajo, trajimos, trajisteis, trajeron**
PRESENT SUBJUNCTIVE: **traiga, traigas, traiga, traigamos, traigáis, traigan**
IMPERFECT SUBJUNCTIVE: **trajera, trajeras, trajera, trajéramos, trajerais, trajeran**
trajese, trajeses, trajese, trajésemos, trajeseis, trajesen
GERUNDIO: **trayendo**
PAST PARTICIPLE: **traído**

valer

PRESENT INDICATIVE: **valgo,** vales, vale, valemos, valéis, valen
FUTURE: **valdré, valdrás, valdrá, valdremos, valdréis, valdrán**
CONDITIONAL: **valdría, valdrías, valdría, valdríamos, valdríais, valdrían**
PRESENT SUBJUNCTIVE: **valga, valgas, valga, valgamos, valgáis, valgan**

venir

PRESENT INDICATIVE: **vengo, vienes, viene,** venimos, venís, **vienen**
PRETERITE: **vine, viniste, vino, vinimos, vinisteis, vinieron**
FUTURE: **vendré, vendrás, vendrá, vendremos, vendréis, vendrán**
CONDITIONAL: **vendría, vendrías, vendría, vendríamos, vendríais, vendrían**
PRESENT SUBJUNCTIVE: **venga, vengas, venga, vengamos, vengáis, vengan**
IMPERFECT SUBJUNCTIVE: **viniera, vinieras, viniera, viniéramos, vinierais, vinieran**
viniese, vinieses, viniese, viniésemos, vinieseis, viniesen
GERUNDIO: **viniendo**
COMMAND: **ven** (tú)

ver

PRESENT INDICATIVE: **veo,** ves, ve, vemos, veis, ven
IMPERFECT INDICATIVE: **veía, veías, veía, veíamos, veíais, veían**
PRETERITE: **vi,** viste, **vio,** vimos, visteis, vieron
PRESENT SUBJUNCTIVE: **vea, veas, vea, veamos, veáis, vean**
PAST PARTICIPLE: **visto**

5. Punctuation

Spanish punctuation, though similar to English, has the following major differences:

(a) The comma is used at the end of restrictive relative phrases:

El tema **que eligió,** es muy aburrido.   *The subject he chose is very boring.*

(b) The comma is not used before **y, e, o, u,** and **ni** in a series:

El viento, la lluvia y el frío causaron   *The wind, the rain, and the cold*
daños al techo.   *damaged the roof.*

(c) In Spanish, questions have an inverted question mark (**¿**) at the beginning and a normal one at the end:

¿Qué estás haciendo?   *What are you doing?*

(d) In Spanish, exclamatory sentences have an inverted exclamation mark (**¡**) at the beginning and a normal one at the end:

¡Qué calor hace!   *How hot it is!*

(e) In decimals, Spanish uses a comma where English uses a period:

7,5 (siete coma cinco)   *7.5 (seven point five)*

(f) Spanish final quotation marks, contrary to English, precede the comma or period:

Cervantes es el autor de **«Don**   *Cervantes is the author of "Don*
Quijote».   *Quixote."*

6. Syllabication

Spanish words are generally divided at the end of a line according to units of sound:

(a) A syllable normally begins with a consonant. The division is made before the consonant:

de/**c**ir   pre/**c**i/**s**o   a/**m**e/**r**i/**c**a/**n**o   re/**p**e/**t**ir

(b) **ch, ll,** and **rr** are never divided:

ca/**rr**o   ca/**ll**a/do   he/**ch**o

(c) If two or more consonants are combined, the division is made before the last consonant, except in the combinations **bl, br, cl, cr, pl, pr,** and **tr:**

t**r**ans/**p**or/te   des/**c**u/**b**ier/to   con/**t**i/nuar   al/**h**a/ja

But:

ha/**bl**ar   a/**br**ir   des/**cr**i/bir   a/**pr**en/der   des/**tr**o/zar

(d) Compound words, including words with prefixes and suffixes, may be divided by components or by syllables:

sur/a/me/ri/ca/no   *or*   **su/ra**/me/ri/ca/no
mal/es/tar   *or*   **ma/les**/tar

Spanish-English Vocabulary

The Spanish-English Vocabulary is intended to be complete for the contexts of this book. Basic terms usually taught in first-level courses and some obvious cognates are not included.

Nouns are listed in the singular. The gender of nouns is indicated as follows:

        m.   = masculine
        f.   = feminine
        m.&f. = masculine and feminine

Irregular plurals are given in full:

tapiz *m.* (*pl.* **tapices**)

Adjectives are listed in the masculine form.

Verbs with spelling changes, stem-changing verbs, and irregular verbs are identified by the type of change in parentheses after the verb: **conocer (zc)**; **tener** (irr.). Refer to the Appendix for sample conjugations.

abarcar (qu) to take in, include, encompass; to comprise
abertura *f.* opening; hole
abismo *m.* abyss, gulf
abogado *m.*, **abogada** *f.* lawyer
aborrecer (zc) to hate, loathe
abrazar (c) to embrace, hug
abrochar to fasten
aburrido bored; boring
aburrir to bore; **aburrirse** to get bored, be bored
acabar to finish; **acabar de** to have just
acampar to camp
aceite *m.* oil; **aceite de oliva** olive oil
aceituna *f.* olive
acerca de about
acercarse (qu) (a) to approach
acero *m.* steel
acertar (ie) to hit the mark, guess right
acompañar to accompany
aconsejar to advise
acontecimiento *m.* happening, event
acordarse (ue) (de) to remember
acostar (ue) to put to bed; **acostarse** to go to bed, lie down
acostumbrarse (a) to accustom oneself, get used to
actual current; present

actuar (ú) to act
acuático aquatic; **el esquí acuático** water skiing
acudir (a) to go or come to
acuerdo *m.* agreement; **estar de acuerdo (con)** to agree (with), be in agreement (with); **ponerse de acuerdo** to come to an agreement
adelantar to move forward, advance
adivinar to guess
adobar to prepare, dress; to season
adorno *m.* decoration
adquirir (ie) to acquire
aduana *f.* customs
advertencia *f.* warning
advertir (ie) to notify, warn
aeromozo *m.*, **aeromoza** *f.* flight attendant
afecto attached to, fond of; *m.* affection
afeitarse to shave
aficionado *m.*, **aficionada** *f.* fan, devotee; **teatro de aficionados** *m.* amateur theater
afligirse (j) to grieve
afrontar to confront; to face up to
afuera outside; **afueras** *f. pl.* outskirts
agitado agitated; upset; excited

agitar to stir up, rouse, excite
agradar to be pleased with; to please
agradecer (zc) to thank
agregar to add
aguafuerte *m.* etching
aguantar to bear, endure
aguardiente *m.* alcoholic beverage
aguinaldo *m.* bonus; Christmas gift
ahogarse (gu) to drown
ahorrar to save
aire *m.* air; **al aire libre** in the open air, outdoors
aislado isolated
ajedrez *m.* chess
ajeno somebody else's; alien, foreign
ajo *m.* garlic
alabar to praise
alargar (gu) to lengthen, elongate
alcalde *m.* mayor
alcanzar (c) to reach, catch up with
alcázar *m.* fortress; royal palace
alcoba *f.* bedroom
aldea *f.* village
alegrarse (de) to be glad, rejoice
alegría *f.* happiness
alemán German
alfiler *m.* pin
alfombra *f.* carpet

algodón m. (pl. **algodones**) cotton
alguien someone
alguno some
alma f. (**el alma**) soul
almacén m. (pl. **almacenes**) department store
almendra f. almond
almohada f. pillow
almorzar (ue, c) to eat (have) lunch
almuerzo m. lunch
alojamiento m. lodgings
alojar(se) to lodge; to be lodged, stay
alquilar to rent
alquiler m. rent
alrededor de around
altiplanicie f. high plateau
altura f. height
alzar (c) to raise (up), lift
ama f. (**el ama**) mistress, lady of the house; **ama de llaves** housekeeper
amanecer (zc) to dawn; m. dawn; **al amanecer** at dawn
amargura f. bitterness
amarrar to tie, fasten
ambos both
amenazador threatening
amenazar (c) to threaten
amistad f. friendship; pl. friends
amo m. master
analfabetismo m. illiteracy
anciano old; m. old man
ancho wide
anchura f. width; breath
andar (irr.) to walk, go
andén m. (pl. **andenes**) platform
angosto narrow
angustia f. anguish, distress
anillo m. ring
animado lively
animar to cheer up; to stimulate
anoche last night
anochecer m. nightfall, dusk; **al anochecer** at nightfall
anónimo anonymous
ante before, in the presence of
anteojos m. pl. eyeglasses
anterior previous, preceding
antes (de) before
antiguo old, ancient; former; old-time
antipático disagreeable, unpleasant
anuncio m. announcement; advertisement
añadir to add
aparecer (zc) to appear

apatía f. apathy
apenarse to grieve, distress oneself
apenas hardly, scarcely
aplicado studious, industrious
apoyo m. support
apresurarse to hurry
apretar (ie) to tighten; to be tight; to clasp
aprovecharse (de) to take advantage (of)
apuntar to note down, take a note of
apunte m. note, memorandum
archivar to file
archivo m. file
arder to burn
arena f. sand
arete m. earring
armario m. closet, wardrobe
arquitectura f. architecture
arrancar (qu) to root out, pull out; to snatch
arreglar to arrange; **arreglar la cama** to make the bed
arrepentirse (ie) (de) to repent, regret
arroz m. (pl. **arroces**) rice
arrugado wrinkled
arruinar to ruin
artesano m. craftsman
ascendencia f. ancestry, descent, origin
ascender (ie) to ascend; to promote
ascensor m. elevator
asegurar to assure
asequible within reach; available
así so, thus, in this way; **así que** as soon as
asilo m. asylum; **asilo de ancianos** old age home
asistir (a) to attend
asombrarse to be astonished, amazed
aspiradora f. vacuum cleaner; **pasar la aspiradora** to vacuum
aspirar (a) to aspire (to)
asunto m. matter, subject
asustado frightened
asustarse to be frightened, get scared; to get alarmed
atacar (qu) to attack
atención f. (pl. **atenciones**) attention; **prestar atención** to pay attention, to listen to
atender (ie) to wait on; to look after
atentamente attentively; thought-

fully; **le saluda atentamente** yours faithfully
aterrador frightening, terrifying
aterrizar (c) to land
atraer (irr.) to attract
atrapar to trap; to catch
atravesar (ie) to cross, pass through
atreverse (a) to dare
atrevido daring, bold; disrespectful, insolent
auge m. acme, period of prosperity
aumentar to increase
aún still, even
aunque although, even though, even if
auricular m. receiver, earpiece
avanzar (c) to advance
ave f. (**el ave**) bird
averiguar (ü) to find out, ascertain
aviso m. notice, warning
ayuda f. help, assistance
ayudante m.&f. assistant, helper
ayuno m. fasting
azafrán m. (pl. **azafranes**) saffron
azúcar m. sugar
azufre m. sulphur
azulejo m. tile

bajar (de) to lower; to take down; to reduce; to turn down; to get off; to go down
bajo short
baloncesto m. basketball
bandera f. flag
banquero m. banker
bañar to bathe; **bañarse** to take a bath
barato cheap, inexpensive
barco m. boat; ship
barrer to sweep
barro m. clay; mud
bastante enough, sufficient
bastar to be enough, suffice
basura f. garbage
bata f. robe
baúl m. trunk
belleza f. beauty
beréber Berber
billete m. ticket; banknote, bill
bizcocho m. biscuit; sponge cake
blando soft

boda *f.* wedding
boleto *m.* ticket
boliche *m.* bowling; bowling alley
bolsa *f.* bag; sack
bolso *m.* bag, purse
bollo *m.* roll, bun
bombero *m.* fireman; **cuartel de bomberos** *m.* firehouse (station)
bombilla *f.* light bulb; small tube for drinking mate
bondadoso kind
bosque *m.* woods, forest
bostezar (c) to yawn
bota *f.* boot
boticario *m.* pharmacist, druggist
botones *m.* (*pl.* **botones**) bellman
bóveda *f.* dome
bravo angry
breve brief
brillar to shine
broma *f.* joke; prank
bruja *f.* witch
burguesía *f.* bourgeoisie
burlarse (de) to make fun of
burlón mocking
busca *f.* search; **en busca de** in search of
buscar (qu) to look for
búsqueda *f.* search
butaca *f.* armchair
buzón *m.* (*pl.* **buzones**) mailbox

caber (irr.) to fit; to be room for
cabo *m.* end; **llevar a cabo** to carry out, carry through
cabra *f.* goat
cacique *m.* Indian chief
cadena *f.* chain
caer (irr.) to fall; **caerse** to fall down
caja *f.* box
cajero *m.*, **cajera** *f.* cashier
calabaza *f.* gourd, pumpkin
calcetín *m.* (*pl.* **calcetines**) sock
calentura *f.* fever
calidad *f.* quality
calificación *f.* (*pl.* **calificaciones**) grade, mark
calificar (qu) to grade
calumnia *f.* slander
calzar (c) (footwear) to put on, to wear; to take or wear a certain shoe size

callarse to become silent, stop talking
cámara *f.* camera; chamber; **pintor de cámara** *m.* court painter
camarera *f.* chambermaid; waitress
cambiar to change
cambio *m.* change; exchange; exchange rate; **en cambio** on the other hand
campamento *m.* camp
campana *f.* bell
campaña *f.* campaign
campeonato *m.* championship
campesino *m.*, **campesina** *f.* peasant
campo *m.* country, countryside
canasta *f.* basket
cancha *f.* court; **cancha de tenis** tennis court
cansado tired; **estar cansado** to be tired
cantante *m.&f.* singer
cantidad *f.* quantity
capítulo *m.* chapter
caprichoso whimsical; wilful
cara *f.* face; **cara a cara** face to face
carbón *m.* (*pl.* **carbones**) coal
carcajada *f.* loud laugh; **reír a carcajadas** to laugh heartily, roar with laughter
cárcel *f.* jail
carecer (zc) de to lack, be in need of
cargado laden
cargar (gu) to load; to carry
caridad *f.* charity
carnicería *f.* butcher shop
caro expensive; dear
carpintero *m.* carpenter
carrera *f.* race; career
carretera *f.* road
carril *m.* lane
cartaginés Carthaginian
cartel *m.* poster
cartera *f.* wallet, pocketbook; handbag, purse
casarse (con) to marry
caseta *f.* booth
casi almost
caso *m.* case, event; **hacer caso a** to heed, mind; **hacer caso de** to pay attention to
castañuelas *f. pl.* castanets
castigar (gu) to punish
castigo *m.* punishment
castillo *m.* castle

casualidad *f.* chance; coincidence; **por casualidad** by chance
cataratas *f. pl.* waterfall, falls
catre *m.* cot
caucho *m.* rubber
causa *f.* cause, motive; **a causa de** because of, on account of
cautivo captive
cebolla *f.* onion
cegar (gu) to blind
célebre famous
celoso jealous
celta Celt
cena *f.* supper, dinner
centro *m.* center; downtown
ceñir (i) to encircle, surround; to fasten around one's waist
cepillar(se) to brush (oneself)
cepillo *m.* brush
cercano near, close; nearby
cereza *f.* cherry
certidumbre *f.* certainty
cerviz *f.* nape of the neck
cesar to cease, stop
césped *m.* lawn, grass
cesta *f.* basket
ciego blind; *m.* blind man
cielo *m.* sky
ciencia *f.* science
científico *m.*, **científica** *f.* scientist
cine *m.* movie theater, movies
cinta *f.* tape; ribbon
cinturón *m.* (*pl.* **cinturones**) belt
circo *m.* circus
cirujano *m.*, **cirujana** *f.* surgeon
cita *f.* appointment; date
ciudadano *m.*, **ciudadana** *f.* citizen
clima *m.* climate
cobrar to charge; to collect; to acquire; **cobrar fuerzas** to gather strength
cobre *m.* copper
cocer (ue, z) to cook
cocinar to cook, do the cooking
cochero *m.* driver, coachman
cofre *m.* chest; case (for jewels)
coger (j) to seize, grasp, catch, take
cohete *m.* rocket
cola *f.* line; tail
coleccionar to collect
colgar (ue, gu) to hang (up)
colilla *f.* (cigarette) butt
colocar (qu) to place, put; to arrange; to place (in a job)
colorado red; **ponerse colorado** to blush

comedia f. play, comedy
comedor m. dining room
comentar to comment on; to discuss, gossip about
comenzar (ie) to begin, start
comestible m. foodstuff; **comestibles** m. pl. foods; groceries
como as; **¡cómo no!** certainly! of course!
cómodo comfortable
compañía f. company
compartir to share
competencia f. competition
complejo complex
componer (irr.) to compose; to repair
compra f. purchase; **ir de compras** to go shopping
comprador m. buyer
comprender to include; to understand
comprometido engaged; committed
compromiso m. commitment; engagement; obligation
común common
concluir (y) to conclude, finish
concurso m. contest
condenar to sentence, condemn
condesa f. countess
condiscípulo m., **condiscípula** f. classmate
conducir (irr.) to conduct, lead; to drive
conductor m. driver
confesar (ie) to confess
confianza f. trust; **de confianza** reliable, trustworthy
confiar (í) en to rely on; to confide in
confín m. (pl. **confines**) boundary
conforme a consistent with; in accordance with; **estar conforme** to agree
congelar to freeze
congreso m. convention; conference
conmover (ue) to stir, move, affect
conocer (zc) to know, be acquainted with; **dar a conocer** to introduce, to present
conocido known; m. acquaintance; **conocido como** known as
conseguir (i, g) to get, obtain; to succeed in
consejero m. counselor
consejo m. advice
consentir (ie) to consent; to allow; to pamper, spoil

consiguiente resulting; **por consiguiente** therefore, and so
consistir en to consist of; to be made of
constituir (y) to constitute, make up
construir (y) to construct; to build
consultorio m. doctor's office
consumo m. consumption
contado: al contado for cash
contar (ue) to count; to tell
contener (irr.) to contain
contra against
contradecir (irr.) to contradict
contrario m. contrary; **por el contrario** on the contrary
contribuir (y) to contribute
convencer (z) to convince
convenir (irr.) en to agree about (to, that); **convenir con** to agree with
convertir (ie) to convert; **convertirse** to be converted; to turn (into), to become
convidar to invite
convivir to live together, coexist
copa f. glass
cordillera f. mountain range
coro m. chorus
corona f. crown
corregir (i, j) to correct
correo m. mail; post office; **echar al correo** to mail
corrida f. run, dash; **corrida de toros** bullfight
corrido running; fluent, continuous
corriente current; **estar al corriente** to be informed, be aware
cortar to cut
corte f. court; pl. Spanish parliament
cortejar to court, woo
cortés courteous, polite
cortesía f. courtesy
cortina f. curtain
cosecha f. harvest
coser to sew
costar (ue) to cost
costumbre f. custom, habit
creador creative
crecer (zc) to grow
creer (y) to believe; to think
cría f. breeding
criado m., **criada** f. servant
criollo m., **criolla** f. Creole
cruz f. (pl. **cruces**) cross
cruzar (c) to cross

cuadra f. (street) block
cuadro m. painting, picture; frame
cualquier any
cuando when; **cuando quiera** whenever
cuanto all that, whatever; **¿cuánto?** how much?; **¡cuánto!** how!; **en cuanto** as soon as
cuaresma f. Lent
cuartel m. barracks
cuarto fourth; quarter; m. room
cubrir to cover
cuclillas: en cuclillas squatting
cuchillo m. knife
cuenta f. bill, check
cuentista m. & f. storywriter
cuenta f. account; bill; **cuenta corriente** current account
cuento m. story
cuerda f. rope, cord; string; **dar cuerda a un reloj** to wind a clock/watch
cuero m. leather
cueva f. cave
cuidado m. care; **tener cuidado** to be careful; **perder cuidado** not to worry
cuidadoso careful
cuidar to take care of, look after
culpa f. blame; fault; **echar la culpa** to blame; **tener la culpa de** to be to blame for; **Ud. tiene la culpa** it's your fault
cumbre f. top; mountain top; pinnacle
cumplir to fulfill; to do one's duty; **cumplir con la palabra** to keep one's word
cuna f. cradle
cura f. cure; m. priest
curiosidad f. curiosity
curioso curious; odd
cuyo whose

chal m. shawl
chaqueta f. jacket
charlar to chat
chico small; m. boy, **chica** f. girl
chimenea f. fireplace
chiste m. joke
chistoso funny
chocar(se) (qu) con to crash into, collide with

dado given

dama f. lady; **damas** f. pl. checkers

dañar to damage, hurt; **dañarse** to get damaged; to spoil, go bad

daño m. hurt; **hacer (se) daño** to hurt (oneself)

dar (irr.) to give; **dar a** to face

debajo de under

deber ought to, must; to owe

debido a due to

débil weak

decadencia f. decline

décimo tenth

decir (irr.) to say; **querer decir** to mean

declamar to recite

declaración f. (pl. **declaraciones**) statement; explanation

decorado m. scenery, set

dedicar (qu) to dedicate; to devote

defectuoso defective

defender (ie) to defend

delgado thin

dejar to leave out; to leave; to allow

demás: lo demás the rest; **los (las) demás** the others

demasiado too much; excessively; too

dentro de within

dependiente m.&f. clerk, salesperson

deportivo sports; sporting

derecha f. right hand; right side; **a la derecha** to the right

derecho straight

derrotado defeated

derrotar to defeat

derrumbar to knock down

desaparecer (zc) to disappear

desarrollar to develop

desarrollo m. development

desayunarse to have (eat) breakfast

descansar to rest

descanso m. rest, break

descolgar (ue, gu) to take down

desconocer (zc) not to know, be ignorant of

descortés discourteous, impolite

descubierto discovered

descubrir to discover

desde from; since; **desde hace** for + length of time

desembocar (qu) en to flow into, empty into

desenvolvimiento m. unfolding, development

desesperar to despair, lose hope

desfilar to parade, march past

desfile m. parade

desgraciadamente unfortunately

deshacer (irr.) to undo; to destroy

deslizarse (c) to slip, slide; glide

desmayarse to faint

despacio slowly

despacho m. office; study

despedirse (i) (de) to say goodbye (to), take leave (of)

despertador m. alarm clock

despertar(se) (ie) to awaken, wake up

después afterwards, later; **después de** after

destacado outstanding, distinguished

destacarse (qu) to distinguish oneself; to stand out

destruir (y) to destroy

desván m. (pl. **desvanes**) attic

detalle m. detail

detener (irr.) to detain; to hold up, delay; to stop

detrás (de) behind

devolver (ue) to return, give back

día m. day; **todos los días** every day, daily; **hoy (en) día** nowadays

dibujante m.&f. sketcher

dibujo m. drawing, sketch

dictadura f. dictatorship

dictar (una sentencia) to pass, pronounce (judgement)

dieta f. diet

dios m. god; idol

dirigir (j) to direct

disculparse to excuse oneself; to apologize

diseñador m., **diseñadora** f. designer

diseño m. design

disfraz m. (pl. **disfraces**) disguise; mask

disfrutar to enjoy

disparo m. shot

disponer (irr.) to dispose; **disponer de** to have at one's disposal; **disponerse a** to get ready to

distinguir (g) to distinguish

distraído distracted; absentminded

distribuir (y) to distribute

diversión f. (pl. **diversiones**) amusement, entertainment

divertirse (ie) to enjoy oneself, have a good time

doblar to fold (up, over); to turn, go round

docena f. dozen

doler (ue) to hurt, ache, pain

dolor m. pain, ache

domicilio m. home; **servicio a domicilio** home delivery service

dominio m. control; supremacy

dondequiera wherever

dormitorio m. bedroom

dramaturgo m. playwright

dudar to doubt

dueño m., **dueña** f. owner

dulce m. sweet, candy

dulcería f. candy store

dulzura f. sweetness; gentleness

durar to last, go on for

echar to throw; to throw out, dismiss, expel; to put in, add; **echar(se) a** to start to + inf.

edad f. age; period

educar (qu) to educate; to train

eficaz effective; efficient

ejemplar exemplary, model

ejercer (z) to exert; (power) to exercise, wield; (profession) to practice

ejército m. army

elaborar to work on

elegir (i, j) to elect; to choose

embajador m., **embajadora** f. ambassador

embarcarse (qu) to embark, go on board

embargo: sin embargo still, however, nonetheless

embestida f. charge

emisora f. radio station

emocionante exciting, thrilling; moving, touching

empeñarse en to insist on; to persist in; to be determined to

emperador m. emperor

emperatriz f. (pl. **emperatrices**) empress

empezar (ie) to begin, start

empleado m., **empleada** f. employee

emplear to employ; to use

emprender to undertake; to embark on

empresa f. undertaking; enterprise

enamorado m., **enamorada** f. lover, beloved; **estar enamorado** to be in love

encaje m. lace
encantador charming, enchanting, delightful
encarcelado imprisoned, jailed
encargar (gu) to entrust; to put in charge; (*goods*) to order; **encargarse de** to take charge of; to see about, attend to
encender (ie) to light; to ignite
encerrar (ie) to lock in; to contain; **encerrarse** to shut (lock) oneself
encima de above, on top of
encogerse (j) to shrink; **encogerse de hombros** to shrug
encontrar (ue) to find; to meet, run into
encuesta f. survey; inquiry
energía f. energy; power; vigor, drive
enfadarse to get angry, get annoyed
enfermedad f. sickness, illness
enfermera f., **enfermero** m. nurse
enfermo sick, ill; m., **enferma** f. sick person; patient
enfrente de opposite, in front of
engañar(se) to deceive (oneself)
enlace m. link
enojar to anger; to upset; **enojarse** to get angry, lose one's temper
enojo m. anger; annoyance
enriquecer (zc) to enrich; **enriquecerse** to get rich; to prosper
entablar (*conversation*) to start, strike up
enterarse de to find out about, to learn
enterrar (ie) to bury
entonces then; **en aquel entonces** at that time
entrada f. entrance; admission; (*theater, etc.*) ticket
entregar (gu) to deliver; to hand over; to give up, surrender; **entregarse a** to devote onself to
entretener (irr.) to entertain, amuse
entrevista f. interview
entrevistar to interview
enviar (í) to send; **enviar por** to send for, fetch
envidiar to envy
envidioso envious, jealous
envolver (ue) to wrap (up)
época f. epoch, age; time, period
equipo m. team; outfit, gear
equivocarse (qu) to be mistaken, make a mistake

erudito learned, scholarly
escalera f. staircase, stairs; ladder
escaparse to escape; to elope
escasez f. (pl. **escaseces**) scarcity, shortage
escenario m. stage
escenografía f. scenery
escoger (j) to choose, select
escolar school; scholastic
esconder to hide
escrito m. writing; **por escrito** in writing
escritor m., **escritora** f. writer
escritorio m. desk
escritura f. writing
escuchar to listen to; to pay attention to
escudero m. squire
escultor m., **escultora** f. sculptor
esfuerzo m. effort
esmeralda f. emerald
eso that; **a eso de** at about; **por eso** therefore, and so
espada f. sword
especie f. species; kind
esperar to wait for; to hope; to expect
espeso thick
espiar (í) to spy
esquí m. (pl. **esquís**) ski; skiing
esquiar (í) to ski
esquina f. corner
establecer(se) (zc) to establish (oneself); to settle
estación f. (pl. **estaciones**) season; station
estacionar(se) to park
estadio m. stadium
estado m. state, condition
estallar to break out; to burst, explode
estante m. shelf
estaño m. tin
estatua f. statue
estilizar (c) to stylize
estilo m. style; manner, fashion
estío m. summer
estirarse to stretch
estrecharse to become closer
estrecho m. strait
estremecerse (zc) to shudder
estreno m. first use; first performance
excelencia f. excellence; **por excelencia** preeminently, par excellence
exigir (j) to demand, require
éxito m. success; **tener éxito** to be successful

experimentar to experience, go through; to suffer
exponer (irr.) to expose, exhibit; to expand, set forth
expulsar to expel
extensión f. (pl. **extensiones**) area
extinguir (g) to extinguish, put out
extranjero foreign; **al extranjero, en el extranjero** abroad
extrañar to miss; to feel the lack of
extraño strange, odd

fábrica f. factory
fabricar (qu) to make, manufacture
facultad f. faculty; school (of a university)
falda f. skirt
falta f. fault, mistake
faltar to be lacking, be wanting; to be missing, be absent from
fama f. fame; reputation
fantasma m. ghost
fantasmagórico phantasmagoric
fascinar to fascinate; to captivate
fe f. faith
felicitar to congratulate
feliz happy
felpa f. plush
fenicio Phoenician
feria f. fair; weekly market
feroz fierce
ferretería f. hardware store
ferrocarril m. railroad
fiarse (í) de to trust
fideo m. noodle
fiebre f. fever
fiel faithful
figurarse to figure, imagine; to suppose
fijarse (en) to stare (at); to notice, pay attention
filólogo m. philologist
filoso sharp
fin m. end; **fin de semana** m. weekend; **hacia fines de** toward the end of
fingir (j) to pretend, feign
firmar to sign
flan m. custard
florecer (zc) to flourish
florero m. vase; florist
folleto m. pamphlet; brochure
fomentar to promote, encourage, foster

fondo m. bottom; **a fondo** thoroughly; **fondos** m. pl. funds
foro m. upstage area
fortaleza f. fortress, stronghold
foto f. picture, photo; **sacar fotos** to take pictures
fracasar to fail; to fall through
fracaso m. failure
francés French
frecuencia f. frequency; **con frecuencia** frequently, often
frente f. forehead; **frente a** opposite, facing, in front of; **de frente** forward
fresa f. strawberry
fresco fresh; cool
fríjol, frijol m. bean
frontera f. border, frontier; boundary
frontón m. (pl. **frontones**) ball court
fuego m. fire
fuera outside; **fuera de** outside of; in addition to, besides; **estar fuera de sí** to be beside onself
fuerte strong
fuerza f. strength, force; **a fuerza de** by dint of; **cobrar fuerzas** to gather strength
fumar to smoke
función f. (pl. **funciones**) performance, show
fundar to found; to establish
fusilar to shoot, execute

gafas f. pl. eyeglasses
gaita f. bagpipe
galletita f. cookie
gana f. desire, will; **de buena gana** willingly, gladly; **de mala gana** reluctantly, grudgingly
ganadería f. cattle raising
ganado m. cattle
ganar to win; to earn; **ganarse la vida** to earn (make) a living
ganga f. bargain
garbanzo m. chickpea
garganta f. throat
gastar to spend
gemelo m. twin
gemir (i) to groan, moan
género m. genre; kind, sort
gente f. people
gerente m.&f. manager, director
gigante giant
gigantesco gigantic
gimnasio m. gym

girar to turn, revolve
gitano m., **gitana** f. gypsy
globo m. balloon
gobernador m., **gobernadora** f. governor
gobernar (ie) to govern
gobierno m. government
goma f. rubber; gum; **goma de borrar** eraser
gorra f. cap
gota f. drop
gozar (c) to enjoy
grabado m. engraving, print
grabadora f. recorder
grabar to record; to engrave
graduarse (ú) to graduate
granja f. farm
grano m. seed; grain
griego Greek
grito m. cry, scream; shout
grueso thick; bulky
gruñir to growl, grunt
guapo good-looking; (man) handsome; (girl) pretty, attractive
guardar to keep, hold on to; to put away; to keep safe; to preserve; **guardar cama** to stay in bed
guardia f. guard
guerra f. war
guerrero warlike
guía m.&f. guide; f. guidebook
guiar (i) to guide
guisado m. stew
guisante m. pea
gusto m. pleasure; taste; **dar gusto a** to please; **tener gusto por** to have a liking (an eye) for

haba f. (**el haba**) bean
hábil skillful; able, capable
hablador talkative
hacer (irr.) to do; to make; **hacer de** to act as, play the part of; **hacerse + noun** to become; **hacer saber** to inform
hacia towards
hacha f. (**el hacha**) ax
hamaca f. hammock
harina f. flour
hasta until; as far as; up to
hazaña f. deed, feat, exploit
hecho m. act; fact; **por el solo hecho de** just because
helar (ie) to freeze
heredado inherited
herido wounded
hermoso beautiful

hervir (ie, i) to boil
hielo m. ice
hierba f. grass
hierro m. iron
historia f. history; story
historiador m. historian
hoja f. leaf
hombro m. shoulder; **encogerse de hombros** to shrug
hondo deep
horario m. schedule; timetable
huelga f. strike
huerta f. orchard
huésped m., **huéspeda** f. guest
huir (y) to flee
humedad f. humidity
humilde humble

ibero Iberian
identidad f. identity
iglesia f. church
igual equal; the same; **igualmente** the same to you; likewise
ilustre illustrious, famous
impedir (i) to prevent; to obstruct, hinder
impermeable m. raincoat
imponer (irr.) to impose
importar to matter, be important
importe m. amount; cost
impreso printed
imprimir to print
impuesto m. tax
incluir (y) to include; to enclose
inconformista nonconformist
indeciso indecisive; hesitant
indicar (qu) to indicate; to suggest
indígena indigenous, native; m.&f. Indian, native
indio m., **india** f. Indian
influir (y) to influence, have influence
informes m. pl. references
ingeniero m., **ingeniera** f. engineer
iniciar to initiate
inmigración f. (pl. **inmigraciones**) immigration
inolvidable unforgettable
inscribir(se) to register, enroll
intercambio m. exchange
inundar(se) to flood
inútil useless
invitado m., **invitada** f. guest
inyección f. (pl. **inyecciones**) injection, shot; **poner(se) una inyección** to give (oneself) an injection

ir (irr.) to go; **ir más allá de** to go beyond
ira *f.* anger, rage
isla *f.* island
izquierdo left; **a la izquierda** to the left

jamás never, not ever
jamón *m.* (*pl.* **jamones**) ham
jarabe *m.* cough syrup
jardín *m.* (*pl.* **jardines**) garden
jardinero *m.*, **jardinera** *f.* gardener
jarro *m.* jug, pitcher
jefatura *f.* headquarters
jefe *m.*, **jefa** *f.* chief, boss
jinete *m.* horseman
joyería *f.* jewelry
judío *m.*, **judía** *f.* Jew
juez *m.* (*pl.* **jueces**) judge
jugador *m.*, **jugadora** *f.* player
jugar (ue, gu) to play
juguetería *f.* toy store
juguetón playful
juicio *m.* judgement
juntar to join, unite
junto together; **junto a** next to, close to
jurado *m.* jury; panel
juventud *f.* youth

lado *m.* side; **al lado de** beside
ladrillo *m.* brick
ladrón *m.* (*pl.* **ladrones**), **ladrona** *f.* thief
lago *m.* lake
lamentar to be sorry about, regret
lana *f.* wool
lanzar (c) to throw
largo long; **a lo largo de** along, alongside; throughout
lástima *f.* pity, shame
lastimar(se) to hurt (oneself)
laúd *m.* lute
lavandería *f.* laundry
lavaplatos *m.* (*pl.* **lavaplatos**) dishwasher
leal loyal
lectura *f.* reading
lechería *f.* dairy store
lechuga *f.* lettuce
legumbre *f.* vegetable
lejano distant

lejos (de) far (from)
lenguaje *m.* language; speech
lento slow
leña *f.* firewood
leño *m.* log
letra *f.* lyrics
letrero *m.* sign; poster
ley *f.* law
leyenda *f.* legend
libertad *f.* freedom, liberty
libra *f.* pound
libre free
librería *f.* bookstore
libreta *f.* notebook
lidiar (bull) to fight
ligero quick, rapid; light
limitar (con) to border on, be adjacent to
limosna *f.* alms, charity; **pedir limosna** to beg
limpiar to clean
limpio clean, neat
linterna *f.* lantern; flashlight
lío *m.* mess; fuss
listo ready; **estar listo** to be ready; **ser listo** to be clever, smart
localidad *f.* ticket
locutor *m.*, **locutora** *f.* announcer; newscaster
lodo *m.* mud
lograr to achieve, attain; **lograr + inf.** to succeed in, manage to
lona *f.* canvas
lotería *f.* lottery
loza *f.* dishes, china
lucha *f.* fight, struggle; conflict
luchar to fight, struggle
luego then, next; afterwards; presently
lugar *m.* place; **tener lugar** to take place
lugarteniente *m.* lieutenant, deputy
lujoso luxurious
luna *f.* moon
luz *f.* (*pl.* **luces**) light

llamada *f.* call
llanero *m.* plainsman
llano flat, level
llanura *f.* plain
llave *f.* key; faucet
llegada *f.* arrival
llegar (gu) to arrive; **llegar a ser** to become; **llegar a + inf.** to manage to, to succeed in

llenar to fill
lleno (de) full; filled with
llevar to carry, take; to wear

madera *f.* wood
madrileño of Madrid
madrugada *f.* dawn, daybreak
madrugar (gu) to get up early, be an early riser
maestría *f.* mastery; skill, expertise
maíz *m.* (*pl.* **maíces**) corn
maleta *f.* suitcase
malgastar to waste
manco one-armed, one-handed
mancha *f.* stain, spot
manchar to stain, dirty, soil
mandar to send; to order
mando *m.* command
manejar to drive; to manage; to handle
manera *f.* way, manner; **de manera que** so that
manga *f.* sleeve
manta *f.* blanket
mantel *m.* tablecloth
mantener (irr.) to maintain, support
mantequilla *f.* butter
manto *m.* cloak, mantle
manzana *f.* apple
manzano *m.* apple tree
Mañanitas *f. pl.* Mexican birthday song
máquina *f.* machine; **escribir a máquina** to type
marca *f.* brand, make
marcar (qu) to mark; (*telephone*) to dial; **el tono de marcar** dial tone
marcharse to leave, go away
marido *m.* husband
marisco *m.* shellfish
marrón brown; maroon
Marruecos Morocco
mascar (qu) to chew
máscara *f.* mask
masticar (qu) to chew
materia *f.* subject; matter
materno maternal
matricularse to enroll, register
mayor older; greater, larger
mayoría *f.* majority
media *f.* stocking; sock
médico *m.*, **médica** *f.* doctor
medio half; means; **por medio de** by means of, through

mediodía *m.* noon; **al mediodía** at noon
medir (i) to measure
mejorar to improve
melocotón *m.* (*pl.* **melocotones**) peach
menester *m.* need; **es menester** it is necessary
menor younger; minor
menos less; **echar de menos** to miss
mentir (ie) to lie
mentira *f.* lie
menudo tiny, minute; **a menudo** often, frequently
merecer (zc) to deserve, be worthy of
merienda *f.* afternoon snack
mermelada *f.* jam, jelly
mesero *m.* waiter
meter to put in; to fit in
metro *m.* meter; subway
mezcla *f.* mixture
mezclar to mix
mezquita *f.* mosque
mientras while; **mientras tanto** meanwhile
milagro *m.* miracle
milla *f.* mile
miseria *f.* poverty, destitution; **una miseria** a tiny amount, a mere pittance
mismo same; himself
misterio *m.* mystery
mitad *f.* half; middle
mito *m.* myth
mochila *f.* knapsack
moda *f.* style, fashion; **de moda** fashionable, in fashion
modismo *m.* idiom
modo mean, way; **de modo que** so that
mojarse to get wet
molido ground, crushed
moneda *f.* coin; currency
monja *f.* nun
montaña *f.* mountain; **montaña rusa** *f.* roller coaster
montañoso mountainous
montar to mount; **montar a caballo** to go horseback riding
monte *m.* mountain
morado purple, violet
morder (ue) to bite
morir(se) (ue) to die, pass away
mostrador *m.* counter
mostrar (ue) to show; **mostrarse** to appear
mover (ue) to move

mozo *m.* waiter
muchedumbre *f.* crowd
mudarse to move (house)
mudo mute
mueble *m.* piece of furniture; **muebles** *m. pl.* furniture
muela *f.* tooth, molar
muerte *f.* death
muerto dead
multa *f.* fine, penalty
multar to fine
multitud *f.* multitude, crowd
mundial world; worldwide
mundo *m.* world; **todo el mundo** everybody
muñeca *f.* doll; wrist
musulmán Moslem

nacer (zc) to be born
nacimiento *m.* birth
nada nothing; **de nada** you're welcome
nadador *m.*, **nadadora** *f.* swimmer
nadar to swim
nadie no one, nobody
naipe *m.* playing card
naranja *m.* orange
natación *f.* swimming
naturaleza *f.* nature
nave *f.* vessel, ship
navegante *m.* navigator, sailor
Navidad *f.* Christmas
neblina *f.* fog
necesitado needy
necesitar to need
negar (ie, gu) to deny; **negarse a** to refuse to
negocio *m.* business
nieta *f.* granddaughter
nieto *m.* grandson
ninguno none, not any
niñera *f.* nursemaid
nivel *m.* level
noche *f.* night; **esta noche** tonight; **por la noche** at night
nombrar to name; to appoint
nombre *m.* name; **nombre de pila** first name; **nombre y apellido** full name
nota *f.* grade; note
noticia *f.* news item; **noticias** *f. pl.* news; information
noticiero *m.* newscast
novedad *f.* novelty; **sin novedad** as usual

noveno ninth
novia *f.* girlfriend, fiancée, bride
novio *m.* boyfriend, fiancé, bridegroom
nube *f.* cloud
nublado cloudy
nudo *m.* knot; **hacer un nudo** to tie a knot
nuevo new; **de nuevo** again
nunca never

obedecer (zc) to obey
obligar (gu) to force, compel
obra *f.* work
obrero working; *m.*, **obrera** *f.* worker
obstante: no obstante notwithstanding, nevertheless
obtener (irr.) to obtain, get
occidental western
octavo eighth
ocupado busy; occupied, taken; **estar ocupado** to be busy
ocurrir to happen, take place, occur
odiado hated
oeste *m.* west
ofrecer (zc) to offer
oír to hear; **oír decir que** to hear that; **oír hablar de** to hear about, of
¡ojalá que...! I wish (hope) that..., If only...!
oler (hue) to smell
oliva *f.* olive; **aceite de oliva** *m.* olive oil
olivar *m.* olive grove
olvidar to forget
olla *f.* pot; **olla de barro** earthenware pot
onda *f.* wave; **de última onda** currently most popular
oponerse (a) (irr.) to be opposed to; to object to
oprimido oppressed
oprimir to press; to oppress
opuesto opposite
oración *f.* (*pl.* **oraciones**) sentence
orgulloso proud
oriental eastern
orilla *f.* shore; **a orillas de** on the banks of
oro *m.* gold
oscuridad *f.* darkness
oscuro dark
otomano Ottoman

otorgar to grant; to award
oveja *f.* sheep

paisaje *m.* landscape
paja *f.* straw
pájaro *m.* bird
pajita *f.* drinking straw
pálido pale
palito *m.* small stick
palma *f.* palm tree
panadería *f.* bakery
pandereta *f.* tambourine
pantano *m.* swamp
pañuelo *m.* handkerchief
papa *f.* potato
papel *m.* paper; role, part; **hacer el papel de** to play the role of
papelería *f.* stationery store
paquete *m.* package
par *m.* pair
parada *f.* stop
parado: estar parado to be stopped, be standing (up)
paraguas *m.* (*pl.* **paraguas**) umbrella
parecer (zc) to seem; **parecerse (a)** to resemble
parecido similar
pareja *f.* couple
pariente *m.* relative
párrafo *m.* paragraph
partidario *m.*, **partidaria** *f.* supporter, follower
partido *m.* game, match; (*politics*) party
partir to start; to depart; **a partir de** from (some specified time)
pasado past; **el sábado pasado** last Saturday
pasajero *m.*, **pasajera** *f.* passenger
pasar to pass; to pass on; to cross; (*time*) to spend
pasatiempo *m.* hobby
pasearse to stroll, take a walk
paseo *m.* stroll; outing
pasillo *m.* aisle
paso *m.* step
pastel *m.* cake
paterno paternal
patinar to skate
patria *f.* native land, fatherland, mother country
patrón *m.* (*pl.* **patrones**), **patrona** *f.* boss, master
patrulla *f.* patrol
pavor *m.* dread, terror

payaso *m.* clown
pedazo *m.* piece; **hacer pedazos** to break (tear) to pieces
pedir (i) to ask for, request; **pedir prestado** to borrow
pegar (gu) to stick (on, up); to glue; to hit, strike, beat
peinar(se) to comb (one's hair)
pelear to fight; to come to blows
película *f.* film, movie
peligroso dangerous
peluquería *f.* hairdresser's, barber shop
peluquero *m.*, **peluquera** *f.* hairdresser
pena *f.* grief, sorrow; penalty; **valer la pena** to be worthwhile
pensamiento *m.* thought
pensar (ie) to think; **pensar + inf.** to intend to; **pensar de** to have an opinion of; **pensar en** to think about, of
pensativo thoughtful, pensive
peor worse
pera *f.* pear
perder (ie) to lose; **echarse a perder** to be spoiled; **perder cuidado** not to worry; **perder de vista** to lose sight of
peregrino *m.*, **peregrina** *f.* pilgrim
perezoso lazy
periodista *m.&f.* journalist
permanecer (zc) to remain, stay
permiso *m.* permission; **con permiso** excuse me; **pedir permiso** to ask for permission
perseguir (i, g) to pursue; to persecute
personaje *m.* (*literature*) character
personalidad *f.* personality
pertenecer (zc) to belong
pesa *f.* weight; dumbbell
pesado heavy
pesar to weigh; *m.* regret; sorrow; **a pesar de** in spite of
pesca *f.* fishing
pescado *m.* fish
pescador *m.* fisherman
pescar (qu) to fish
petróleo *m.* oil, petroleum
pez *m.* (*pl.* **peces**) fish
picante spicy, hot
pícaro mischievous; sly; *m.* rogue, rascal
pico *m.* peak, summit
pie *m.* foot; **estar de pie** to be standing; **a pie** on foot
piedra *f.* stone
piel *f.* skin; leather; fur

pierna *f.* leg
píldora *f.* pill
pintar to paint
pinto spotted
pintor *m.*, **pintora** *f.* painter
pintoresco picturesque
piña *f.* pineapple
pisar to step on
piscina *f.* swimming pool
piso *m.* floor
pista *f.* clue
placer (zc) to be pleased; *m.* pleasure, joy
planchar to iron, press
plano flat, level
plata *f.* silver
plátano *m.* banana
platino *m.* platinum
playa *f.* beach
plaza *f.* plaza, square; **la plaza mayor** the main square
plomo *m.* lead
población *f.* (*pl.* **poblaciones**) population
pobre poor
poco little; **hace poco** a short time ago
poder (irr.) to be able to, can, may; *m.* power
poesía *f.* poetry; short poem
poeta *m.*, **poetisa** *f.* poet
policía *f.* police force; *m.* policeman
policíaco police; **novela policíaca** *f.* detective story
polvo *m.* dust
poner (irr.) to put; to place; **poner la mesa** to set the table; **ponerse** to put oneself; to put on; **ponerse + adj.** to become, turn; **ponerse a + inf.** to begin to, set about
pordiosero *m.*, **pordiosera** *f.* beggar
pormenor *m.* detail, particular
portarse to behave; **portarse mal** to misbehave
portero *m.* doorman; porter
porvenir *m.* future
poseer (y) to possess, own
potable drinkable
potaje *m.* stew
potencia *f.* power
precio *m.* price
precioso precious; lovely
preciso necessary, essential; **es preciso** it is necessary
precursor *m.*, **precursora** *f.* forerunner

preferir (ie, i) to prefer
prejuicio m. prejudice
premio m. prize
prenda f. garment, article of clothing
preocupado worried
preocuparse to worry
preparar to prepare, get ready
preparativo m. preparation
preparatoria f. preparatory school
presenciar to be present at; to witness
presidir to preside at (over)
preso imprisoned; m. prisoner
préstamo m. loan
prestar to lend, loan
presumir to show off; to be conceited
pretender to try to, attempt
prevenir a to warn, forewarn
primaria f. elementary school
primo m., **prima** f. cousin
principio m. beginning; **a principios de** at the beginning of
prisa f. hurry, haste; **de prisa** quickly; **estar de prisa** to be in a hurry
probar (ue) to prove; to try; **probarse** to try on
producir (irr.) to produce; to bring about
prometer to promise
pronosticar (qu) to predict, forecast
pronóstico m. forecast
pronto soon; **tan pronto como** as soon as
propietario m., **propietaria** f. owner
propina f. tip
propio own, of one's own
proponer (irr.) to propose
propósito m. purpose
proseguir (i, g) to proceed with, continue
protagonista m. & f. main character
proteger (j) to protect
próximo next
prueba f. test
publicar (qu) to publish
publicidad f. publicity
público m. public; audience
pueblo m. town
puente m. bridge
puerco m. pig, pork
puerto m. port
puesto m. place; position; job; **puesto que** since, as
pulga f. flea; **mercado de las pulgas** m. flea market

punto m. point; **en punto** sharp
pureza f. purity

quebrar (ie) to break, smash
quedar(se) to remain; to have (be) left; (place) to be; **quedarse con** to keep, hold on to; **quedar en que** to agree that
quehacer m. chore
quejarse (de) to complain (about)
quemar to burn (up)
querer (irr.) to want, wish, love; **querer decir** to mean
querido dear
queso m. cheese
quienquiera whoever
química f. chemistry
quinto fifth
quitar(se) to remove, take off
quizás perhaps

rábano m. radish
radicar (qu) to be situated (in a place); **radicarse en** to settle
raíz f. (pl. **raíces**) root; **a raíz de** as a result of
ramo m. (of flowers) bunch
rana f. frog
rápido fast
raqueta f. racquet
rasgo m. characteristic, trait
rato m. while, (short) time; **pasar un buen rato** to have a good time
raza f. race
razón f. (pl. **razones**) reason; right; **tener razón** to be right; **no tener razón** to be wrong
reaccionar to react
real real; royal
realizar (c) to achieve; to fulfill
rebajado reduced
rebozo m. wrap, shawl
recado m. message; errand
receta f. recipe; prescription
recetar to prescribe
recibir to receive
recoger (j) to gather; to pick up
reconocer (zc) to recognize
recordar (ue) to remember
recorrer to travel, tour; **recorrer el mundo** to travel around the world
recorrido m. journey, run
recuerdo m. remembrance, souvenir; memory; **recuerdos** m. pl. regards, best wishes
recursos m. pl. resources

rechazar (c) to reject
red f. net
redondo round
reducir (irr.) to reduce
referir (ie) to recount; to refer
refrendar to endorse
refresco m. cool drink, soft drink
refrito refried
regado irrigated
regalar to give (away), present
regalo m. gift, present
regar (ie, gu) to water; to strew (in all directions)
regencia f. regency
regla f. rule; ruler
regresar to return
rehusar to refuse
reina f. queen
reinado m. reign
reino m. kingdom
reírse (i) de to laugh at
reja f. grating, grille
relámpago m. lightning
relato m. story, tale
rellenar to stuff, fill
relleno filled, stuffed
remar to row
remendar (ie) to patch, mend
Renacimiento m. Renaissance
rendir (i) to produce, yield; **rendirse** to surrender
renglón m. (pl. **renglones**) line (of writing)
renombre m. renown, fame
renovación f. (pl. **renovaciones**) renovation; renewal
renovar (ue) to renew; to restore, redecorate
reñir (i) to quarrel; to scold
reparar to repair; **reparar en** to observe, notice
repartir to distribute; to divide up
repente m. sudden movement; **de repente** suddenly; unexpectedly
repentino sudden; unexpected
replicar (qu) to answer back, argue
represa f. dam
res f. animal, beast; **carne de res** f. beef
resfriarse (i) to catch (a) cold
resfrío m. cold
resolver (ue) to resolve; to solve
respirar to breathe
restos m. pl. remains
retratar to portray
retrato m. portrait
reunión f. (pl. **reuniones**) meeting, gathering; social gathering

reunirse to reunite; to join together, gather

rezar (c) to pray

riego m. irrigation

rincón m. (pl. **rincones**) (inside) corner

riqueza f. wealth, riches

risa f. laugh; **causar risa a** to make (someone) laugh

risueño smiling; cheerful

robo m. theft, robbery

rodear to surround; **estar rodeado de** to be surrounded by

rodilla f. knee; **de rodillas** kneeling

rogar (ue, gu) to beg, plead for

rompecabezas m. (pl. **rompecabezas**) puzzle

romper to break; to tear up

roto broken

ruido m. noise

rumor m. murmur; buzz; confused noise

ruso Russian

saber (irr.) to know; **saber de** to know about, be aware of; **hacer saber** to inform

sabio m., **sabia** f. learned person; scholar

sabor m. taste, flavor

sabroso delicious, tasty

sacar (qu) to take out

sacerdote m. priest

saco m. jacket

sacrificar (qu) to sacrifice

sacudir to shake; **sacudir el polvo** to dust

sagrado sacred

sala f. living room; (concerts, etc.) hall, house

salchicha m. frankfurter; sausage

salida f. exit; departure

salir (irr.) to come out; to go out, leave; (sun) to rise

saltar to jump

salto m. jump, leap; waterfall

salud f. health

saludable healthy; beneficial

saludar to greet

saludo m. greeting; m. pl. (in letter) greetings, regards

salvavidas m. (pl. **salvavidas**) life guard

salvo safe; **sano y salvo** safe and sound

sandía f. watermelon

sangriento bloody

sano healthy, fit

santo saint

satisfacer (irr.) to satisfy

secadora f. dryer

seco dry

secundaria f. high school

seda f. silk

sede f. headquarters; seat

seguido continuous; **seguidos** consecutive; **en seguida** at once, right away

seguir (i, g) to continue; to follow

según according to

seguridad f. security; safety

seguro safe; secure; certain; sure; m. insurance

selva f. forest; jungle

sello m. stamp

semáforo m. traffic light; **correr un semáforo** to run through a traffic light

sembrar (ie) to seed, sow

semejante similar

semejanza f. similarity, resemblance

sencillez f. simplicity

sentido m. sense; meaning

sentir (ie, i) to feel; to regret, feel sorry; **sentirse** to feel

señal f. sign

señorial lordly, majestic, stately

séptimo seventh

serpentina f. paper streamer

servilleta f. napkin

servir (i) to serve

sexto sixth

sien f. temple

siglo m. century

significado m. meaning

significar (qu) to mean

siguiente following; next

sillón m. (pl. **sillones**) chair

simpático likeable, pleasant, nice

sindicato m. union

sino m. fate, destiny

siquiera at least; even if; **ni siquiera** not even

sirena f. siren

sitio m. place; site; siege

sobrar to be left over, be more than enough

sobre m. envelope

sobre on; over, above; about

sobrenatural supernatural

sobrenombre m. nickname

sobrepasar to surpass, exceed

sobretodo m. overcoat

sobrevivir to survive

sobrio sober; moderate, restrained

socio m., **socia** f. partner; member

soga f. rope

soldado m. soldier

soledad f. loneliness; solitude

soler (ue) + inf. to be in the habit of, to usually

solicitud f. application

solo alone

soltar (ue) to let go of; to turn loose

sombra f. shade

sombrero m. hat; **sombrero de jipijapa** straw (Panama) hat

sometido subjected

sonar (ue) to sound

sonreír(se) (í) to smile

soñar (ue) con to dream of

sopa f. soup

soplar to blow

sordo deaf

sorprenderse de to be surprised (amazed) at

sorpresa f. surprise

sostener (irr.) to sustain; to support

sótano m. basement, cellar

subir to raise; to go up; to climb

subrayado underlined

suceder to happen; to succeed, follow

suceso m. event, happening

sucio dirty

sueldo m. salary

suelo m. ground; floor

sueño m. dream; sleep

sufrimiento m. suffering; misery

sugerencia f. suggestion

superficie f. surface

suplicar (qu) to beg for, implore

suprimir to suppress

supuesto supposed; assumed; **¡por supuesto!** of course!, naturally!

sur m. south

surgir (j) to arise, emerge

suspirar to sigh

suspiro m. sigh

sustituir (y) to substitute, replace

tabaco m. tobacco; cigar

tabla f. plank, board; shelf

talla f. (of clothes) size

taller m. workshop

tamaño m. size

tambor m. drum

tampoco neither, not either

tapa *f.* lid; cover; snack (*taken with drinks*)

tapiz *m.* (*pl.* **tapices**) tapestry

taquilla *f.* box office

tardanza *f.* delay

tardar to be long; to be late; to delay; to be slow to

tarde late; *f.* afternoon, evening; **por la tarde** in the afternoon (evening); **hacerse tarde** to be getting late

tarea *f.* assignment; chore

tarjeta *f.* card; **tarjeta postal** postcard

techo *m.* roof

tela *f.* cloth, fabric

telefonear to telephone

telefonista *m.&f.* (telephone) operator

teléfono *m.* telephone; **por teléfono** by phone

televisor *m.* television set

tema *m.* theme; topic

temblar (ie) to tremble, shake; to shiver

temer to fear, be afraid of

templado temperate

tenedor *m.* fork

tener (irr.) to have; **tener que** + inf. to have to; **tener por** + adj. to consider (someone) to be

terminar to end, finish

ternura *f.* tenderness

terrateniente *m.&f.* landowner

terraza *f.* terrace; balcony

terremoto *m.* earthquake

terreno *m.* terrain; land

tertulia *f.* regular informal gathering; group, circle

tesoro *m.* treasure

testigo *m.&f.* witness

tiempo *m.* time; weather; **a tiempo** on time

tienda *f.* store

tiento *m.* feeling, touch

tigre *m.* tiger

tijera *f.* scissors

tinto dyed; **vino tinto** *m.* red wine

tipo *m.* type, kind

título *m.* title

toalla *f.* towel

tocadiscos *m.* (*pl.* **tocadiscos**) record player

tocar (qu) to touch; (*music*) to play; **tocarle a uno** to be one's turn

todavía still, yet

todo all; **todos** everyone; **sobre todo** especially, above all

tontería *f.* foolishness; *f. pl.* nonsense

torcer (ue, z) to twist; to bend; to turn

torero *m.* bullfighter

tormenta *f.* storm

toronja *f.* grapefruit

torre *f.* tower

torta *f.* cake

tos *f.* cough

trabajador *m.*, **trabajadora** *f.* worker

traducir (irr.) to translate

traer (irr.) to bring; to carry; to take

traje *m.* suit; **traje de luces** bullfighter's costume

tranquilo tranquil; peaceful; calm

tranvía *m.* streetcar

tras after

tratar to treat; **tratar de** + inf. to try to; **tratarse de** to concern, be a question of

través: a través de through; across

travesura *f.* prank

trigo *m.* wheat

tristeza *f.* sadness

tronar (ue) to thunder

tropezar (ie, c) to stumble, trip; **tropezarse con** to run into

trozo *m.* fragment; passage, section; **trozos escogidos** selections

trueno *m.* thunder

tumba *f.* tomb, grave

tuna *f.* student music group

único only; unique

unidad *f.* unit; unity

unido close; united

útil useful

uva *f.* grape

vaca *f.* cow

vacilar to hesitate

vacío *m.* emptiness; void

valer (irr.) to be worth; to cost; **valer la pena** to be worthwhile

valioso valuable

valor *m.* value, worth; courage

vanguardia *f.* vanguard; **pintor de vanguardia** *m.* ultramodern painter

vapor *m.* steam

vaquero *m.* cowboy

variar (í) to vary, alter

variedad *f.* variety

varios several

vaso *m.* glass

vecino *m.*, **vecina** *f.* neighbor

vela *f.* candle

veleta *f.* weather vane

veloz swift, quick, fast

vencer (z) to conquer; to defeat; to overcome

vendedor *m.*, **vendedora** *f.* salesperson

vengar (gu) to avenge

veraz truthful

verdad *f.* truth

verdura *f.* green vegetable

vestimenta *f.* clothing

vestuario *m.* wardrobe, costumes; dressing room

vez *f.* (*pl.* **veces**) time; **a veces** sometimes; **a la vez** at the same time; **tal vez** perhaps

vicio *m.* vice

vid *f.* vine

vidrio *m.* glass

viento *m.* wind

vigilar to watch (over); to guard

vigor *m.* vigor; **en vigor** in force, applicable

villancico *m.* (Christmas) carol

vino *m.* wine

virreinato *m.* viceroyship

virrey *m.* viceroy

visigodo Visigoth

víspera *f.* eve, day before; **en vísperas de** on the eve of

vista *f.* sight; **perder de vista** to lose sight of

viuda *f.* widow

viudo *m.* widower

vivo alive; lively

volante flying

volar (ue) to fly

volcar (ue, qu) to overturn

volver (ue) to return, come (go) back; **volver a** + inf. to...again; **volver en sí** to regain consciousness; **volverse** + adj. to become

voz *f.* (*pl.* **voces**) voice

vuelo *m.* flight

vuelta *f.* turn; **dar vuelta** to turn; **estar de vuelta** to be back

zapatería *f.* shoe store

zarzuela *f.* Spanish musical comedy

English-Spanish Vocabulary

The English-Spanish Vocabulary includes only those words that occur in the English-to-Spanish exercises.

able hábil, capaz; **to be able to** poder + inf.

about acerca de, **at about** a eso de; **to be about to** estar para + inf., estar a punto de + inf.

absent ausente

accompany acompañar

according to según

accustom acostumbrar; **to be accustomed to** acostumbrar + inf., tener la costumbre de

ache dolor m.

across a través (de); por

act actuar (ú)

advice consejo m.

afraid: to be afraid temer, tener miedo

after después de, después (de) que, tras

afternoon tarde f.; **in the afternoon** por la tarde

again de nuevo; otra vez; volver (ue) a + inf.

agree to convenir (irr.) en; **to agree with** estar conforme (con); estar de acuerdo (con)

agreement acuerdo m.; **to come to (reach) an agreement** ponerse de acuerdo

air aire m.; **in the open air** al aire libre

allow dejar, permitir

almost casi

alone solo; a solas

already ya

although aunque

always siempre

ambitious ambicioso

among entre

amount cantidad f.

amusement diversión f. (pl. diversiones); **amusement park** parque de diversiones m., parque de atracciones m.

angry enojado; **to become (get) angry** enojarse, enfadarse

anniversary aniversario m.

announcement anuncio m.

annoy molestar

anxiously con ansiedad, ansiosamente

apparently al parecer, por lo visto

appear aparecer (zc)

apple manzana f.

application solicitud f.

approach acercarse (qu) a

around alrededor de

ashamed avergonzado; **to be ashamed of** avergonzarse (üe, c)

ask preguntar; **to ask for** pedir (i)

asleep: to fall asleep dormirse (ue), quedarse dormido

assignment tarea f., deberes m. pl.

astonish asombrar; **to be astonished** asombrarse de

attack atacar (qu)

attend (be present at) asistir a; **to attend school** ir a la escuela (al colegio, a la universidad), seguir estudios en

attention atención f. (pl. atenciones); **to pay attention** poner (prestar) atención

audience público m.

aunt tía f.

away: to go away irse (irr.), marcharse

back atrás; **to be back** estar de vuelta

ball pelota f.

bargain ganga f.

bank banco m.

banker banquero m.

bark ladrar

baseball béisbol m.

basement sótano m.

bath baño m.; **to take a bath** bañarse

bathe bañar(se)

bathing suit traje de baño m.

beach playa f.

beauty belleza f., hermosura f.

because porque; **because of** a causa de

become hacerse (irr.); llegar (gu) a ser; ponerse (irr.) + adj.

bed cama f.; **to go to bed** acostarse (ue); **to stay in bed** (sick) guardar cama

bedroom alcoba f., dormitorio m.

before antes de, antes (de) que; (in the presence of) ante

beg rogar (ue, gu), suplicar

begin comenzar (ie), empezar (ie), principiar; ponerse a + inf.; echarse a + inf.

beginning principio m.; **at the beginning of** a principios de

behave (oneself) portarse bien

believe creer (y)

belt cinturón m. (pl. cinturones)

beside junto a, al lado de; **beside oneself** fuera de sí

better mejor; **it is better** es mejor, más vale

between entre

bird pájaro m.

birth nacimiento m.

birthday cumpleaños m. (pl. cumpleaños)

blame culpar, echar la culpa

bone hueso m.

booth caseta f., cabina f.; **telephone booth** caseta de teléfono f., cabina telefónica f.

bored aburrido; **to get (become) bored** aburrirse

born: to be born nacer (zc)

boss jefe m., jefa f., patrón m. (pl. patrones), patrona f.

bother molestar

break romper, quebrar (ie); **to break in pieces** hacer pedazos

breakfast desayuno m.; **to eat (have) breakfast** desayunarse

bright claro, luciente
bring traer (irr.); **to bring back**
(*return*) devolver (ue)
broken roto
brother-in-law cuñado *m.*
build construir (y)
bury enterrar (ie)
bus autobús *m.* (*pl.* autobuses),
bus *m.*; **bus stop** parada de
autobuses (de buses) *f.*
businessman negociante *m.&f.*,
comerciante *m.&f.*
busy ocupado

cage jaula *f.*
call llamada *f.*; **to call** llamar;
telephone call llamada telefónica *f.*
camp campamento *m.*
candidate candidato *m.*, candi-
data *f.*
capable capaz
captain capitán *m.* (*pl.* capitanes)
care cuidado *m.*; **I don't care** me
es igual, no me importa; **to take**
care of cuidar (a, de)
careful cuidadoso; **carefully** con
cuidado, con cautela, cuidadosamente
carry llevar; traer (irr.); acarrear;
cargar (gu)
catalogue catálogo *m.*
catastrophe catástrofe *f.*
cent centavo *m.*
century siglo *m.*
certain cierto
chair silla *f.*
change cambio *m.*; **to change**
cambiar
charge cobrar; **to take charge of**
encargarse (gu) de
check cheque *m.*; **traveler's**
checks cheques de viajero
choose escoger (j), elegir (i, g)
classmate condiscípulo *m.*,
condiscípula *f.*, compañero de
clase *m.*, compañera de clase *f.*
clean limpiar; limpio
climate clima *m.*
close (*nearby*) cerca, cercano (a)
closet armario *m.*
clothes (clothing) ropa *f.*
comb peine *m.*; peinar; **to comb**
one's hair peinarse
come venir (irr.); **to come out** salir
(irr.) de; **to come to** volver (ue)
en sí; **to come upon** dar con,
tropezar (ie, c) con

company compañía *f.*, empresa *f.*
complain (of) quejarse (de)
complaint queja *f.*
complete terminar, acabar,
completar; completo
composer compositor *m.*,
compositora *f.*
consent (to) consentir (ie) en
consider dar (irr.) por; tener (irr.)
por; considerar
contest concurso *m.*
cool fresco; **to be cool** hacer fresco
copy copia *f.*
cost costar (ue)
count contar (ue)
courageous valiente
course: of course por supuesto,
desde luego
cousin primo *m.*, prima *f.*
crazy loco
credit crédito *m.*
crew tripulación *f.* (*pl.* tripula-
ciones)
criminal delincuente *m.&f.*
cross cruzar (c), atravesar (ie)
cry llorar
cup taza *f.*
curiously con curiosidad
curtain cortina *f.*
custom costumbre *f.*
customer cliente *m.&f.*

danger peligro *m.*
dangerous peligroso
dare (to) atreverse (a)
date fecha *f.*; compromiso *m.*
day día *m.*; **the day after**
tomorrow pasado mañana; **by**
day de día; **every day** todos los
días; **some day** algún día; **the**
next day el (al) día siguiente;
this very day hoy mismo
daybreak amanecer *m.*; **at**
daybreak al amanecer
dear querido
deceive engañar; **to be deceived**
engañarse
delay (in) tardar (en); **without**
delay cuanto antes
delicious delicioso, rico
demand exigir (j)
deny negar (ie, gu)
depart partir, salir (irr.)
department departamento *m.*;
department store almacén *m.*
(*pl.* almacenes)
descend bajar, descender (ie)

deserve merecer (zc)
desk escritorio *m.*
destination destino *m.*
destroy destruir (y); acabar con
different distinto, diferente
diligently diligentemente
dining room comedor *m.*
dinner cena *f.*; **to have dinner**
cenar
dirty sucio
disappear desaparecer (zc)
dish plato *m.*
distance distancia *f.*; **in the**
distance a lo lejos
distinguish distinguir (g); **to**
distinguish oneself destacarse
(gu)
do hacer (irr.); **to have nothing to**
do with no tener nada que ver
con
doubt duda *f.*; **there is no doubt**
no cabe duda, sin duda
doubtful dudoso
draw dibujar
dream sueño *m.*; **to dream of**
soñar (ue) con
drink bebida *f.*; **to drink** beber,
tomar
drive conducir (irr.), manejar
drop dejar caer (irr.)
drown (oneself) ahogar(se) (gu)
drugstore botica *f.*, farmacia *f.*
dry seco
during durante
dust polvo *m.*; **to dust** sacudir el
polvo, limpiar; **to be dusty**
haber (irr.) polvo

early temprano; con tiempo, con
anticipación
earn ganar
earring arete *m.*, zarcillo *m.*
effort esfuerzo *m.*
elect elegir (i, j)
electrical eléctrico
elevator ascensor *m.*
elope fugarse (gu), escaparse
embrace abrazar (c), dar un abrazo
employ emplear
employee empleado *m.*, empleada
f.
empty vacío
end fin *m.*; **to end** terminar; **at the**
end of a fines de; al cabo de; **to**
end by acabar por; **not hear the**
end of no olvidarse fácilmente
(pronto) de

enjoy gozar (c) (de), disfrutar (de);
　to enjoy oneself divertirse (ie),
　pasarlo bien
enjoyable agradable
enough bastante; **to be enough**
　bastar
enroll inscribirse; matricularse
enthusiasm entusiasmo m.;
　enthusiastically con entusiasmo
entire todo; entero
equal igual
escape escaparse
estimate calcular
even: even though aunque; **not
　even** ni siquiera
evening noche f.; **in the evening**
　por la noche; **every evening**
　todas las noches
every todos los, todas las; **every-
　body, everyone** todos, todo el
　mundo; **everyone else** todos los
　demás; **everything** todo; **every-
　where** en (por) todas partes
except excepto, con excepción de
exchange cambio m.; intercambio
　m.; **to exchange** cambiar (por);
　exchange student estudiante de
　intercambio m.&f.; **exchange
　rate** (tipo de) cambio m.
expensive caro
explain explicar (qu)
eyeglasses anteojos m. pl., gafas f.
　pl.

face cara f., rostro m.; **to face** dar
　(irr.) a
fact hecho m.; **as a matter of fact**
　de hecho, en realidad
fail fracasar; **to fail to** dejar de +
　inf.
failure fracaso m.
faint desmayarse
fall caída f.; **to fall** caer (irr.); **to
　fall down** caerse
far, far away lejos (de)
fear miedo m.; **to fear** temer,
　tener miedo
feel sentir(se) (ie, i); **to feel like**
　tener ganas de
fence cerca f., valla f.
few pocos; **a few** algunos, unos
　cuantos, varios
film película f.
finally al fin, por fin, finalmente
find encontrar (ue), hallar; **to find
　out** enterarse (de)
finish terminar, acabar
fire fuego m.

fireman bombero m.
fireplace chimenea f.
firm firme; **to be firm** mostrarse
　(ue) decidido
fit caber (irr.)
fix arreglar, componer (irr.)
flame llama f.
flee huir (y)
flood inundar; inundación f. (pl.
　inundaciones)
floor piso m.
fog neblina f.; **to be foggy** haber
　neblina
follow seguir (i, g)
following siguiente
foot pie m.; **on foot** a pie
for para, por; **as for** en cuanto a
forbid prohibir
foreign extranjero
forget olvidar, olvidarse de
former (the) aquél, aquélla,
　aquéllos, aquéllas
fortunately afortunadamente
freeze helar (ie); **to freeze over**
　helarse
frequently con frecuencia, a
　menudo, frecuentemente
frighten asustar; **to be frightened**
　asustarse, tener miedo
front de frente; **in front of**
　enfrente de, delante de, ante
full lleno
funny chistoso; **the funny thing** lo
　curioso
furious furioso
furniture muebles m. pl.

garbage basura f.; **garbage
　collector** basurero m.
garden jardín m. (pl. jardines)
gather recoger (j)
generally por lo general, por lo
　común, generalmente
German alemán
get obtener (irr.); conseguir (i, g);
　recibir
gift regalo m.
glove guante m.
go ir (irr.), andar (irr.); **to go out**
　salir (irr.)
grade nota f., calificación f.; (pl.
　calificaciones); clase f.; grado
　m.
graduate graduarse (ú) (de)
granddaughter nieta f.
grandparents abuelos m. pl.
grandson nieto m.
greet saludar

guest invitado m., invitada f.;
　huésped m.
guide guía m.&f.; **travel guide**
　guía turístico (de turismo) m.&f.
guidebook guía f.
guy chico m.

hair pelo m., cabello m.; **to comb
　one's hair** peinarse
hand mano f.; **to hand over**
　entregar (gu); **on the other hand**
　en cambio; **to shake hands**
　darse la mano
hang (up) colgar (ue, gu)
happen pasar, ocurrir, suceder; **to
　happen to** por casualidad,
　acertar (ie) a + inf.
have tener (irr.); haber (irr.); **to
　have just** acabar de + inf.; **to
　have to** tener que + inf.
hear oír (irr.); **to hear from** tener
　noticias, recibir carta
　(respuesta) de; **to hear of
　(about)** oír hablar de
help ayuda f.; **to help** ayudar; **it
　cannot be helped** no hay
　remedio, no tiene remedio
hit golpear; (target) dar en
hope esperar
however sin embargo, no obstante
hunger hambre f. (el hambre); **to
　be hungry** tener hambre
hurry darse prisa, apresurarse
hurt doler (ue); hacer (irr.) daño
　(a); **to hurt oneself** hacerse daño

ice hielo m.
ice cream helado m.
if si; **as if** como si
ill enfermo
illness enfermedad f.
imagine imaginarse
immediately en seguida, de inme-
　diato, inmediatamente
inch pulgada f.
increase aumentar
inexpensive barato
influence influencia f.; **to have
　influence on** influir (y), afectar
inn posada f.
instead of en vez de, en lugar de
intend to pensar (ie) + inf.
interest interés m. (pl. intereses);
　to interest interesar; **to be inter-
　ested in** interesarse en (por)
invention invento m.
itinerary itinerario m.

job empleo *m.*, trabajo *m.*, puesto *m.*

joy alegría *f.*

jump saltar, brincar (qu), dar saltos

just solamente; precisamente; **to have just** acabar de + inf.

keep guardar; quedarse con; **to keep on** seguir (i, g)

kitchen cocina *f.*

know saber (irr.); conocer (zc); **to know about** saber de, estar enterado de, tener conocimiento de; **to know how** saber; **to get to know** (llegar a) conocer

lack carecer (zc) de; **to be lacking** faltar, hacer falta

lady dama *f.*, señora *f.*, señorita *f.*; **young lady** señorita *f.*

lake lago *m.*

last último; **to last** durar; **last** (*month, year*) (el mes, el año) pasado

late tarde; **to be getting late** hacerse tarde; **later** más tarde, después

latter (the) éste, ésta, éstos, éstas

least menos; menor, más pequeño; **at least** a lo (al) menos, por lo menos

leave salir (irr.) (de), irse (irr.); dejar; **to take leave of** despedirse (i) de

left izquierdo; **to the left** a la izquierda

left: to have left (*remaining*) quedarle a uno

lend prestar

less menos

let dejar

liberty libertad f.

library biblioteca *f.*

light luz *f.* (*pl.* luces); **to light** encender (ie)

lightning (bolt) relámpago *m.*

like gustarle (a uno); **to feel like** tener ganas de

line línea *f.*; cola *f.*

listen (to) escuchar; prestar atención

liveliness animación *f.*; energía *f.*

loan préstamo *m.*; **to loan** prestar

locate encontrar (ue), localizar (c)

lock encerrar (ie)

long largo; **a long time** mucho tiempo; **how long** ¿cuánto tiempo?; **longer** más (tiempo); **no longer** ya no

look (at) mirar; **to look for** buscar (qu)

lose perder (ie); **to get lost** perderse

loss pérdida *f.*

lot: a lot mucho

lottery lotería *f.*

love encantarle; amar, querer (irr.); **to be in love (with)** estar enamorado (de); **to fall in love (with)** enamorarse (de)

lucky afortunado; **to be lucky** tener suerte

luggage equipaje *m.*

lunch almuerzo *m.*; **to have (eat) lunch** almorzar (ue, c)

luxurious lujoso

magazine revista *f.*

mail echar al correo

maintain mantener (irr.)

man hombre *m.*; **old man** viejo *m.*

manager gerente *m.&f.*

manufacture fabricar (qu)

marry casarse (con); **to get married** casarse (con)

matter asunto *m.*; **to matter** importar; **as a matter of fact** de hecho, en realidad; en efecto; **no matter how** por + adj. + que + subj.

meanwhile mientras tanto

measure medir (i)

meat carne *f.*

meet encontrarse (ue) con; reunirse; conocer (zc)

memory recuerdo *m.*; memoria *f.*

message recado *m.*, mensaje *m.*

milk leche *f.*

minute minuto *m.*

miss echar de menos

mistake error *m.*, falta *f.*; **to be mistaken** equivocarse (qu); **to make a mistake** cometer un error

more más; **more and more** cada vez más

morning mañana *f.*; **in the morning** por la mañana

movies cine *m.*

much mucho; **how much** ¿cuánto?; **so much** tanto; **too much** demasiado; **to be too much** sobrar

mud lodo *m.*; **to be muddy** haber lodo

multiplied by por

must deber de, tener (irr.) que; **one must** hay que + inf.

near cerca de; **nearby** cercano

necessary necesario, preciso

need necesidad *f.*; **to need** necesitar, hacerle falta (a uno), faltarle (a uno)

nephew sobrino *m.*

nervous nervioso

never nunca, jamás

nevertheless sin embargo, no obstante

new nuevo; **nothing new** sin novedad

news noticia *f.*; noticias *f. pl.*

newspaper periódico *m.*, diario *m.*

next próximo, entrante; siguiente; junto a, al lado de; **the next day** el (al) día siguiente

niece sobrina *f.*

night noche *f.*; **at night** de noche; **last night** anoche; **tonight** esta noche

nightfall anochecer *m.*; **at nightfall** al anochecer

noise ruido *m.*

none ninguno

now ahora; **from now on** de hoy en adelante; **not now** ahora no; **right now** ahora mismo; **nowadays** hoy día, actualmente

nowhere en ninguna parte

numerous numeroso; muchos

obey obedecer (zc)

occur ocurrir, suceder, acontecer (zc), pasar

offer ofrecer (zc)

office oficina *f.*, despacho *m.*

often a menudo; muchas veces

oil aceite *m.*; **suntan oil** aceite bronceador *m.*

old viejo; **oldest** el (la) mayor, los (las) mayores

only solamente; **if only!** ¡ojalá!

orchestra orquesta *f.*
order (*command*) orden *f.* (*pl.* órdenes); **to order** ordenar, mandar; pedir (i)
other otro; **otherwise** de otro modo
owe deber
owner dueño *m.*, dueña *f.*

paint pintar
pair par *m.*
paper ensayo *m.*; papel *m.*, documento *m.*
park parque *m.*; **to park** estacionar; **amusement park** parque de diversiones
participate participar, tomar parte (en)
partner socio *m.*, socia *f.*
passenger pasajero *m.*, pasajera *f.*
passport pasaporte *m.*
pay (for) pagar (gu) (por)
perhaps tal vez, quizás
permit permitir, dejar; admitir
pick escoger (j), elegir (i, j); **to pick up** recoger (j)
picture fotografía *f.*; cuadro *m.*; (*movie*) película *f.*; **to take a picture** sacar (qu) una foto
piece pedazo *m.*; **piece of furniture** mueble *m.*; **to break in pieces** hacer pedazos
pity lástima *f.*; **it is a pity** es lástima
place lugar *m.*, sitio *m.*; **to place** colocar (qu), poner (irr.); **to take place** tener lugar
plan plan *m.*; **to plan** planear
plate plato *m.*
play comedia *f.*; obra dramática *f.*; **to play** (*music*) tocar (qu); (*game*) jugar (ue, gu); (*a role*) hacer el papel de
pleasant agradable
please por favor; **to please** gustar, agradar
poem poesía *f.*, poema *m.*
politician político *m.*, política *f.*
population población *f.* (*pl.* poblaciones)
port puerto *m.*
poster cartel *m.*
pound libra *f.*
prefer preferir (ie)
prepare preparar
pretend fingir (j); pretender
previous anterior

price precio *m.*
pride orgullo *m.*
prince príncipe *m.*
princess princesa *f.*
principal director *m.*, directora *f.*
prize premio *m.*; **first prize** (*lottery*) premio gordo *m.*
prohibit prohibir
project proyecto *m.*
promise promesa *f.*; **to promise** prometer
protect proteger (j)
provided that con tal que, siempre que
pursue perseguir (i, g)
put poner (irr.); **to put on** ponerse; **to put in** meter; **to put out** apagar (gu)
pyramid pirámide *f.*

quality calidad *f.*
question pregunta *f.*; **to be a question of** tratarse de
quickly rápidamente; pronto
quiet tranquilo; **to become quiet** callarse
quite bastante

race carrera *f.*; raza *f.*
railroad ferrocarril *m.*
rain lluvia *f.*; **to rain** llover (ue)
raise aumentar; levantar; alzar (c)
rate tipo *m.*; **exchange rate** (tipo de) cambio *m.*
ray rayo *m.*
reach llegar (gu) a, alcanzar (c)
ready listo; disponible; **to get ready to** disponerse (irr.) a
reality realidad *f.*
realize darse cuenta de
really de veras
receive recibir; admitir; aprobar (ue)
recommend recomendar (ie)
record disco *m.*
refuse negarse (ie, gu) a, rehusar
regard respecto *m.*; **in regard to** en cuanto a, con respecto a; **regards** (*greeting*) recuerdos *m. pl.*
rehearsal ensayo *m.*
rehearse ensayar
relate contar (ue), relatar
relative pariente *m.*
relax descansar; **relaxed** descansado, relajado

remember recordar (ue), acordarse (ue) de
remove quitar
rent alquiler *m.*; **to rent** alquilar
repair reparar, componer (irr.)
request pedir (i)
respect respetar; **respected** respetado, estimado
responsibility responsabilidad *f.*
rest descanso *m.*; **to rest** descansar
retire jubilarse
return volver (ue), regresar; (*give back*) devolver (ue)
right derecho *m.*; **at (to) the right** a la derecha; **to be right** tener razón; **it will be all right** saldrá bien, se arreglará
river río *m.*
role papel *m.*; **to play a role** hacer un papel
room cuarto *m.*, habitación *f.* (*pl.* habitaciones); sitio *m.*, espacio *m.*; **to be room for** caber
routine rutina *f.*
rule regla *f.*; **to rule** gobernar (ie)
run correr
rush apresurarse

sacrifice sacrificio *m.*; **to sacrifice** sacrificar(se) (qu)
sad triste
sadness tristeza *f.*
safe seguro; **safe and sound** sano y salvo
same mismo; **at the same time** a la vez
scene escena *f.*
schedule horario *m.*
scream grito *m.*; **to scream** gritar, dar voces
script guión *m.* (*pl.* guiones)
seat asiento *m.*; **seated** sentado
seem parecer (zc)
seldom rara vez
sell vender
send mandar, enviar (í)
serve servir (i); **to serve as** servir de
set juego *m.*; **to set** (*the sun*) ponerse (irr.); **to set the table** poner la mesa
several varios
shame vergüenza *f.*
share compartir
shelf estante *m.*
shine brillar
ship barco *m.*, buque *m.*
shopkeeper tendero *m.*, tendera *f.*

short corto; **shortly** dentro de poco

show mostrar (ue), enseñar

shy tímido

side lado *m.*

sidewalk acera *f.*

similar parecido, semejante

since desde; puesto que, ya que

sit sentar (ie); **to sit down** sentarse

skillfully con habilidad, hábilmente

skit sátira *f.*, parodia *f.*

sleepy soñoliento; **to be sleepy** tener sueño

sleigh trineo *m.*

smart inteligente

smash hacer pedazos

smile sonrisa *f.*; **to smile** sonreír (í)

smoke humo *m.*; **to smoke** fumar

snow nieve *f.*; **to snow** nevar (ie)

so tan; **so that** de modo (manera) que

soap jabón *m.* (*pl.* jabones)

some alguno, algún; **someone** alguien; **something** algo; **sometimes** a veces

soon pronto; **as soon as** así que, tan pronto como, en cuanto

sorry ¡perdón!; **to be sorry** sentirlo (ie)

south sur *m.*

souvenir recuerdo *m.*

spend (*time*) pasar; (*money*) gastar

spite despecho *m.*; **in spite of** a pesar de

stage escenario *m.*, tablas *f. pl.*

stain mancha *f.*; **to stain** manchar

stamp estampilla *f.*, sello *m.*

stand (up) levantarse; **standing** de pie, parado

start empezar (ie), comenzar (ie); echarse a

stay quedar(se), permanecer (zc); **to stay in bed** (*ill*) guardar cama

stereo estéreo *m.*

still todavía, aún

stomach estómago *m.*; **stomach ache** dolor de estómago *m.*

stop parar(se); dejar de + inf.; **bus stop** parada *f.*

store tienda *f.*

storm tormenta *f.*

strange extraño, raro

strict estricto

stroll dar una vuelta, dar un paseo, pasearse

strong fuerte

student alumno *m.*, alumna *f.*, estudiante *m.&f.*; **exchange student** estudiante de intercambio *m.&f.*

studies estudios *m. pl.*

succeed (in) lograr + inf.

success éxito *m.*; **to be successful** tener éxito

such tal

suddenly de repente, de pronto

sugar azúcar *m.*

suit traje *m.*; **bathing suit** traje de baño *m.*

suitcase maleta *f.*

sunrise salida del sol *f.*

support apoyo *m.*; **to support** apoyar, mantener (irr.)

surprise sorpresa *f.*; **to surprise** sorprender; **to be surprised** asombrarse (de)

swim nadar

table mesa *f.*; **to set the table** poner la mesa

tablecloth mantel *m.*

take tomar; llevar; **to take off** quitarse; (*plane*) despegar (gu); salir (irr.); **to take out** sacar (qu)

telegraph telégrafo *m.*

telephone teléfono *m.*; **on the telephone** por teléfono

tell decir (irr.)

tent tienda *f.*

textbook libro de texto *m.*

thank dar las gracias, agradecer (zc)

theater teatro *m.*

then luego; entonces

therefore por consiguiente, por eso

thing cosa *f.*; **it's a good thing that** menos mal que

think pensar (ie); **to think of** pensar en; **to think about** (*consider*) considerar, pensar en

thirst sed *f.*; **to be thirsty** tener sed

threaten (to) amenazar (c) (con)

through por; a través de

throw echar, tirar, arrojar

ticket billete *m.*, boleto *m*; **round-trip ticket** billete de ida y vuelta

tight apretado; **to be tight** apretar (ie)

time tiempo *m.*; (*hour*) hora *f.*; (*in a series*) vez *f.* (*pl.* veces); **on time** a tiempo; **from time to time** de vez en cuando; **to have**

a good time divertirse (ie), pasar un buen rato; **for a long time** durante mucho tiempo, por largo rato

tired cansado; **to become tired** cansarse

together junto

tomorrow mañana; **the day after tomorrow** pasado mañana

ton tonelada *f.*

tonight esta noche

too demasiado, muy; (*also*) también

tool herramienta *f.*

tour excursión *f.* (*pl.* excursiones)

town pueblo *m.*

toy juguete *m.*

travel viajar

tray bandeja *f.*

trip viaje *m.*; **to take a trip** hacer un viaje; **round trip** viaje de ida y vuelta

trophy trofeo *m.*

try (to) tratar (de + inf.), intentar; **to try on** probar(se) (ue)

twice dos veces

twist torcer (ue, z)

umbrella paraguas *m.* (*pl.* paraguas)

uncle tío *m.*

unfortunately por desgracia, desgraciadamente, desafortunadamente

university universidad *f.*

unless a menos que

until hasta

up arriba; **up and down** de un lado para otro

use usar; **I used to go** iba, solía ir, acostumbraba ir

usually por lo común, por lo general, generalmente

vase florero *m.*, jarrón *m.* (*pl.* jarrones)

vegetable legumbre *f.*, verdura *f.*

visit visitar

wait (for) esperar

waiter mesero *m.*, mozo *m.*; camarero *m.*

want desear, querer (irr.)

war guerra f.

warm caliente; **to warm oneself** calentarse (ie); **to be warm** (*weather*) hacer calor; (*person*) tener calor

warn avisar, advertir (ie), prevenir (irr.)

wash lavar(se)

waste (*time*) perder (ie)

watch reloj m.; **to watch** mirar, reparar en

way camino m.; manera f.; **to get one's way** salirse con la suya

wealth riqueza f.

wedding boda f.

weekend fin de semana m.

welcome bienvenido; **you're welcome** de nada, no hay de qué

wet mojado; **to get wet** mojarse

wheat trigo m.

whenever cuando quiera (que)

wherever dondequiera (que)

while mientras (que); **a little while ago** hace poco; **in a little while** dentro de poco

whistle silbar

whoever quien(es) quiera

wide ancho

wife esposa f., mujer f., señora f.

win ganar; **winning** (*number*) premiado

wind viento m.; **to be windy** hacer viento

wind (*a watch*) dar cuerda (a un reloj)

wish (for) desear, anhelar

with con; **with me** conmigo; **with you** contigo, con Ud., con Uds.; **with him(self)** consigo

within dentro de

without sin, sin que

wood madera f.; **wooden** de madera

word palabra f.; **to keep one's word** cumplir con la palabra

work trabajar; funcionar

worry preocupación f. (*pl.* preocupaciones); **to be worried** estar preocupado; **not to worry** perder (ie) cuidado, no preocuparse

worse peor; **worst** el (la) peor, los (las) peores

write escribir; **written** escrito; **in writing** por escrito

yet todavía; **not yet** todavía no

young joven; **younger** menor; **youngest** el (la) menor, los (las) menores

Index